Anthropology and International Health

Anthropology and International Health

Asian Case Studies

Mark Nichter

and

Mimi Nichter

University of Arizona, Tucson

Gordon and Breach Publishers

Australia Canada China France Germany India Japan
Luxembourg Malaysia The Netherlands Russia Singapore
Switzerland Thailand United Kingdom

Emmaplein 5
1075 AW Amsterdam
The Netherlands

First edition by Mark Nichter published in 1989 as *Anthropology and International Health: South Asian Case Studies* by Kluwer Academic Publishers, Dordrecht, The Netherlands.
Copyright © 1989 by Kluwer Academic Publishers, Dordrecht, The Netherlands.

Versions of some chapters were published previously in the journal *Social Science and Medicine*. Chapter 7 appeared under a different title in vol. 14B (1980); chapter 8 is from vol. 17(14) (1983); chapter 10 appeared in vol. 41(5) (1995); chapter 11 is from vol. 23(4) (1986); and chapter 12 is from vol. 21(6) (1985). These are reprinted with permission of Elsevier Science Ltd., UK.
  Chapters 1, 2, and 5 originally appeared in *Human Organization* in vols. 46(1) (1987), 42(3) (1983), and 52(1) (1993), respectively.
  Chapter 4 was first published in *Reviews of Infectious Diseases*, vol. 13 (Suppl. 4) (1991), under a different title. Chapter 6 previously appeared in *Medical Anthropology*, vol. 15(4) (1994). Chapter 13 is an updated version of an article originally published in *Convergence: Journal of Adult Education*, vol. XIX(1) (1986).

British Library Cataloguing in Publication Data

Nichter, Mark
  Anthropology and international health : Asian case studies.
  – 2nd ed. – (Theory and practice in medical anthropology and international health ; v. 3)
  1.Medicine – South Asia   2.Medical anthropology – South Asia
  3.Public health – South Asia
  I.Title   II.Nichter, Mimi
  610.9'54

  ISBN 2-88449-171-6   (hardcover)
         2-88449-172-4   (softcover)

CONTENTS

Section Three Pharmaceutical Practice

Section Four Health Service Research and Health Communication

INTRODUCTION TO THE SERIES

Theory and Practice in Medical Anthropology and International Health seeks to promote works of direct relevance to anthropologically informed international health issues, practice, and policy. It aims to bridge medical anthropology — both biological and cultural — with international public health, social medicine, and sociomedical sciences. The series' theoretical scope is intentionally flexible, incorporating the most current advances in social science theory, while its topical breadth ranges from specific issues to contemporary debates to practical applications informed by current anthropological theory. The distinguishing characteristic of this new series is its emphasis on cultural aspects of medicine and their links to larger social contexts and concrete applicability of the anthropological endeavor.

FOREWORD

Mark Nichter and Mimi Nichter bring many years of field experience to this book. Their observations and interpretations reflect the best that social science has to offer international health. Working with them in the field gave me an opportunity to observe firsthand the way in which they engage in problem solving and the respect and affection they hold for the people with whom they work. What is unique about their book is that the case studies are at once rich in anthropological detail and sophisticated in terms of an understanding of the public health issues they address — be this the prevention or timely treatment of illness. It is for this reason that it seems appropriate for me to write a foreword to their book as a public health clinician who has worked for decades in developing countries on the very issues presented.

There is much talk about cultural sensitivity in public health these days, and considerable confusion about intracultural variability and such taken-for-granted concepts as "community participation." Implicit in much of the discussion is a concern about cultural imperialism captured by the question: "What entitles *us* to think that *our* way of problem solving is any better than other ways?" In some cases, our own arrogance precludes us from learning from the empirical observations of others, observations inspired by different ways of looking at the world. In other cases, existing patterns of reasoning about health and illness place the lives of people at great risk.

Two of the public health problems the Nichters focus upon in this book are acute respiratory infection and diarrheal diseases — the chief causes of death in children. These two diseases are a source of great confusion, both to practitioners of all types of medicine and child caretakers. The case fatality rate (CFR) for diarrheal disease is especially low. According to the best estimates — and estimates are all we have to work with — the CFR for diarrheal disease is roughly 1:1000. What this means is that everyday around the world, thousands and thousands of children survive their episode of diarrhea, regardless of how it is treated or who provides the treatment. The same is true of respiratory complaints, which seem to trouble young children six to eight times a year regardless of where they live. Mothers and practitioners, whether modern or traditional, assume on the basis of high rates of recovery to these diseases that whatever they offered as treatment was efficacious; it was the "right thing to do."

It is important to recognize when "treatment as usual" or the "best that traditional medicine has to offer" is not the right thing to do. Inexpensive, simple treatment measures exist that can prevent needless deaths in children from diarrhea and respiratory infection. Simple and effective as these measures may be, their effectiveness depends on timely recognition of illness severity, the need for treatment, and prompt and correct administration of appropriate treatment regimes.

In order to be successful in encouraging the proper use of effective treatments, the challenge is to understand why parents do what they do and the assumptions and beliefs upon which existing actions are based. It is necessary to make remedies and recommendations understandable and acceptable to local populations. Simple as this prescription may sound, anyone who has tried to administer it knows how complex and difficult the task at hand is to implement. The Nichters make the difficulties and complications abundantly clear. They do not, however, leave us with the impression that the practice of culturally sensitive population-based medicine is hopeless. Rather, they invite us to engage local health cultures (and problem solvers) instead of viewing them as intractable barriers to progress — an impression which leads many in public health to devalue, if not dismiss, "culture."

This book spells out in detail a range of issues which need to be considered when attempting to introduce or evaluate public health interventions. The Nichters provide many useful suggestions on how to collect appropriate baseline data before planning an intervention and how to communicate complex ideas to local populations using conceptual frameworks which are familiar. Illustrated are methodological approaches to working within local cultures which are described as dynamic, not "traditional" in the sense of being rigid or closed. The book makes a convincing case for putting in the time and effort to understand local problems and existing solutions before attempting to offer new answers, and for studying the way local populations have responded to "new solutions" and their reasons for doing so. Among other things, they invite us to take a hard look at the way in which medicines are currently being used by lay people in developing countries and to critically examine "rational drug use" from the vantage point of the practitioner trying to survive in a competitive marketplace. Given alarming rises of drug resistance which threaten to undermine the success of public health programs, their investigations could not be more timely.

The type of medical anthropology which the Nichters practice seems to me to be essential for effective health education. Why *essential*? One salient reason is that improvement in family-level treatment requires real and sustained behavior change on the part of mothers or other caretakers. Immunizations, for example, seemingly demand minimal behavior change; the mother takes the child to receive an injection and that's it. But the perceived efficacy of these injections and how many of them a mother feels her children need depend upon what she thinks the injections are for in the first place. Improving the management of infants or children with diarrhea or pneumonia requires the mother to change her understanding of the disease and to learn new ways of evaluating her child's condition prior to as well as during treatments. Educational campaigns designed to elicit changes in thinking about illness as well as treatment must address local notions of causation as well as expectations from treatment. With respect to the evaluation of public health messages, the Nichters invite us to monitor the local understanding of interventions over time as opposed to being content with short-term measures of message familiarity or medicine use.

In their preface to this volume, the Nichters note the sensitivity that medical anthropologists feel when working with those in public health or medicine. After all, their role is to study all aspects of health culture: from the conditions which foster ill health and the treatment of illness by different types of practitioners, to health programs and the factors which influence how they are carried out and who gets the lion's share of the resources. When anthropologists do get involved in public health problem solving, it seems that they run the risk of being accused of complicity in propagating the influence of the biomedical system.

During my career, I have seen my fair share of social scientists "manipulated" by doctors. I can recall several occasions when clinicians called on anthropologists to "evaluate programs" when all they really wanted was someone to tell them how to get their target population to "comply" with their orders — in other words, to blindly do what they were told. Some anthropologists have been willing to do just that. The Nichters are examples of a very different type of health social scientist–medical anthropologist who critically examines the appropriateness of solutions put forward by public health colleagues in particular contexts. To do so in a constructive manner requires a firm understanding of both the problem being addressed and the solutions being offered.

Other medical anthropologists I have had occasion to meet have been satisfied with describing health problems as interesting cultural artifacts. This has often resulted in the accumulation of information which is often not read by practitioners or health planners because they are not quite sure what relevance it has for them. What makes this book so valuable to public health practitioners is that it highlights why information on health culture, illness behavior, medicine-taking practice, and styles of cultural communication are relevant and indeed crucial to public health success. Practitioners are also asked to take a sobering look at relationships among staff at primary health centers who are affected by changes in health policy which threaten their professional identity. Readers are asked to examine not just the lay person, but the health care system and how it is managed.

This book is thought provoking. It will cause the most experienced practitioner to reflect and the practitioner preparing to enter the field of international health to pay heed to more than just what is found in their books on tropical medicine. Other medical anthropologists, I trust, will find the book inspiring.

Joe Wray, MD
Professor Emeritus
Center for Population
and Family Health
Columbia University
School of Public Health

PREFACE

The second edition of this volume has been revised substantially yet its goal remains the same: to provide a series of case studies illustrating how medical anthropology has contributed to the study of international health problems and initiatives. The cases chosen for the volume have been drawn from two decades of field research conducted in South and Southeast Asia. They focus on issues related to women's reproductive health, child survival, infectious disease control, pharmaceutical use, health service research, and health education.

Eight of the original eleven chapters from the first edition have been retained and five new chapters have been added. Section One on women's reproductive health has been revised but its content is largely unaltered. Three chapters are presented which examine lay perceptions of fertility, popular interpretations of how modern family planning methods work, and folk dietetic practices during pregnancy which affect maternal nutrient stores and infant birth weight. Section Two is entirely new and focuses on two of the major threats to child survival in less developed countries: diarrheal disease and acute respiratory infection. A chapter on anthropological contributions to the epidemiological study of diarrhea and dysentery highlights and expands upon points raised in the three chapters originally included in this section.[1] This is followed by two chapters which focus on acute respiratory infection (ARI). The first provides an overview of lessons learned from research on diarrheal disease and their relevance for the study of ARI, while the second presents a detailed ethnographic study of ARI in the Philippines. The utility of employing a mix of research methods when conducting focused ethnographic studies of illness is emphasized.[2]

Section Three focuses on different aspects of pharmaceutical-related practice ranging from the lay perception of medicines to patterns of paying for practitioner consultations through medicine costs, and from prescription practice to medicine production and the commodification of health. This section has been retained from the first edition, but has been revised significantly.[3] Emphasis is shifted from the theme of rational drug use prominent in international health discourse to rationales underscoring how and why medicines are used, prescribed, and combined in particular ways.

Section Four explores the role of anthropology in health service research and health education. Two of the four chapters in this section are new. The first examines consumer demand for preventive health services. Expanding upon an earlier article (Nichter 1990), lay notions about immunizations are considered in relation to perceptions of need and issues related to program sustainability as well as the politics of immunization. A second chapter considers teamwork among different cadres of primary health workers. It draws attention to the primary health care system as a social system requiring ethnographic research which attends to issues of social organization, power, and status. Factors which inhibit teamwork within primary health centers are identified.

The remaining two chapters in Section Four appeared in the first edition and focus on health education. The first chapter is concerned with the critical evaluation of a health education message concerning the boiling of drinking water. This case illustrates why even "simple" messages require formative research and cultural assessment. In a final chapter, an approach to health communication is explored. This approach to "teaching by analogy" is modeled after an indigenous process of knowledge transfer common in Asia. A procedure for framing teaching analogies is presented which advocates participatory research and a privileging of local funds of knowledge.

Several of the issues raised by new and expanded essays invite consideration of: a) how determinations are made about whether an illness is deemed serious enough to warrant health care activity which is out of the ordinary; and b) how health fixes (both curative and preventive) are assessed in terms of perceived vulnerability, need, and impact over time. A sampling of issues raised includes: Are temporary methods of family planning (such as pills) viewed as benign or thought to compromise one's long-term fertility? Do trends in self-medication mirror prescription practice in countries where medicines are readily available over-the-counter? Do changing patterns of self-medication affect prescription practice? How serious does a child's illness have to be before a drugstore attendant suggests that a caretaker consult a doctor instead of engaging in self-medication? On what basis is such advice made and does it differ by age of the child?

Questions raised in relation to specific categories of illness include: Are cases of watery and bloody diarrhea responded to in the same way by populations exposed to health education messages recommending oral rehydration in cases of "diarrhea"? Are children promptly brought to a doctor by concerned parents when they develop bloody stools or noisy, labored breathing? Or is it deemed prudent to consult a traditional practitioner first to rule out the possibility of factors which might obstruct expensive treatment prescribed by doctors? Is educating parents about ARI enough or is setting up patterns of triage with traditional practitioners called for in such circumstances? Is health-care seeking substantially different for a child having labored breathing with/without manifest fever? How is fever perceived culturally; are different types of fever recognized? If "measles" (or an indigenous illness category encompassing measles) is rumored to be in the area, does this affect the health-care-seeking behavior of mothers? Are individual immunizations perceived to protect against different diseases or are all immunizations thought to protect against the same diseases? Are all children thought to require the same number of immunizations or does a child's health status and relative strength affect parental decisions? To what extent does a concern about decreasing parental trust lead primary health care workers to miss opportunities to immunize children who have mild illnesses?

Issues highlighted in this volume emerge from studies inspired by both ethnomedical agenda and applied medical anthropology directives attentive to international health priorities.[4] In our experience one type of study often leads into the other. Let us illustrate such cross-fertilization with the case presented in chapter 1.

The case study presented in the first chapter focuses on indigenous perceptions of fertility: when in the monthly cycle do South Asian women think they are most/least likely to become pregnant? The case study has clear applied relevance for family planning, but its genesis was ethnomedical. Our initial interest was gender ideology as it is articulated at the site of the body through ideas and practices related to reproduction.[5] In an area of South India populated by both matrilineal and patrilineal castes, we wondered whether marked differences in ideas about reproduction might coexist. We searched for distinct ideas favoring women's or men's roles in reproduction which might serve as a charter for ideologies of descent and inheritance.

We did not find such marked differences, but rather an eclectic and loosely formulated set of ideas about fertility. Many of the ideas informants expressed took the form of extended analogies which indexed common conceptual frameworks such as agriculture and the lunar cycle. Data from this ethnomedical study led us to consider popular perceptions of contraceptive need at various times during a woman's monthly cycle and following delivery. One might suspect that this would have been a well-researched topic, given the amount of funds invested in family planning in Asia in the 1970s. Surprisingly, we found little data on popular perceptions of fertility in the applied social science or family-planning literature.

Follow-up "applied" research on lay response to family planning and other biomedical technology in India (such as immunizations and medicines) led us to reconsider ethnomedical data we had previously collected on notions of ethnophysiology. We came to recognize that notions of ethnophysiology were not static, but are constantly being revised partly in response to interpretations of how new technical fixes worked. Interpretations often indexed established conceptual frameworks (such as hot/cold), while extending analogies which drew upon new funds of knowledge, empirical observations, and imagery. An "applied study" of when and why family planning fixes (immunization, medicine fixes, and so on) were/were not used, deepened our understanding of South Indian perceptions of the physical body as well as the social body and body politic. We were led to revisit concepts such as "strength" which index issues ranging from social to physiological control, collective anxieties associated with purity, to sources of anxiety related to gender and generational identity. We offer this example to illustrate how applied medical anthropology and ethnomedicine can inspire one another and render important insights for international health.

In addition to ethnomedical studies and focused illness ethnographies responsive to international health program needs, issues highlighted in this volume emerge from research explicitly conducted to study life contingencies which affect health care decision making. Case studies draw upon investigations of the household production of health (Berman et al. 1994, Nichter and Kendall 1991) and the microeconomics and social relations of health care seeking, as well as the practice of medicine in a world marked by changing expectations and resource bases.

Who is the intended audience(s) for this volume? Our primary audience(s) are anthropologists and practitioners (broadly defined) working in the field of health and development who wish to examine practical examples of how medical anthropology can contribute to international health.[6] This includes the critical examination of international health initiatives and medical practices to the extent that new lines of inquiry facilitate problem solving.[7] Does this endeavor have an inherent management bias? We feel that it places us in the type of creative double bind that Hazel Weidman described some years ago (Weidman 1976) when speaking of the necessity for anthropologists working in applied settings to maintain reflexivity. To keep from "going native" or being blindsided, Weidman noted how important it was for anthropologists to examine problems and "solutions" through the multiple lenses of social science theory(s) offering the researcher myriad perspectives from which to view the terrain.[8]

This brings us to the remarks of one reviewer of the first edition of this book (van der Geest 1993). In a largely positive review, he questioned whether we had privileged health education as a means of solving public health problems. He then proceeded to caution anthropologists about becoming "middlemen" brokering local funds of knowledge to the public health world. His caution is noteworthy.

We are acutely aware of the issues highlighted in Taussig's (1980) straw-man critique of Kleinman's work on a negotiated approach to patient care in the United States.[9] Taussig speaks to anthropology's complicity in furthering the agenda of medicine, noting that increases in patient manipulation may result from providing practitioners with greater knowledge about patients and their culture. At the population level, the same critique may be extended to anthropologists who contribute to international health education efforts.

As argued in an article on anthropology and therapy facilitation (Nichter, Trockman, and Grippen 1985), we believe that it is important for anthropologists operating in applied contexts to engage in two-way brokering of information. Just as information about local worlds needs to be brought to the attention of health practitioners to facilitate culturally sensitive care management, so information about the agenda, resources, constraints, and procedures of practitioners (ministries of health, donor agencies, and so on) needs to be brought to the attention of the patient, "community," local action groups, and so on. Through such an endeavor, alternative approaches to the solving of problems may be explored in relation to contingencies influencing all stakeholders.

Is such an exchange possible given vast differences in knowledge and power? If being a middleman means looking for middle ground in which rapport may be established and agency enhanced, we are so motivated. Only when such rapport is established will "participation" have meaning beyond compliance such that partnerships may be established. Will new knowledge translate into behavior change? Clearly, this is too simplistic. It is not just knowledge which needs to be assessed, but power relations and resource distribution, stakes in knowledge production/reproduction, perceptions of entitlement and responsibility, factors favoring alternative approaches to problem solving, and the socialization of practitioners as well as health care consumers. In need of consideration are reasons why particular health ideologies and practices are privileged, neglected, or resisted by different actors at different times in specific contexts. This requires the longitudinal monitoring of health perceptions and health care practices in environments sensitive to social, political–economic, and ecological transformation. It further requires the monitoring of national as well as international health policy and its implementation.[10]

Our aim in this volume is to broaden the scope of inquiry in international health by illustrating the contribution anthropology can make in grounding international health initiatives in the shifting realities of local worlds. In a field dominated by body counts and rational man calculation, there are important lessons to be learned from ethnographic investigation. If nothing else, such studies invite practitioners to pause and reflect on how health problems are conceived and "solutions" responded to by different segments of given populations.

Such reflection is surely needed at a time when funding crises and mounting debt threaten the implementation of international health initiatives and the long-term effects of development programs are being questioned (e.g., Sardar 1988). In such a climate, renewed emphasis is being placed on "community participation" as a means to achieving program sustainability through cost-sharing. Given such an emphasis and increased recognition of the private sector as a source of health care, there is mounting interest in popular perceptions of health need, demand for services, and health care provision. At a time of health transition marked not only by changes in demographic and epidemiological patterns but changes in lifestyle, health practice, and health care consumption, new challenges await medical anthropologists.

NOTES

1. The three case studies which originally appeared in Section Two have been replaced: case studies of children's malnutrition and the language of illness in India, and lay response to diarrheal disease in Sri Lanka.
2. Readers interested in additional studies on anthropology and ARI are referred to a special edition of the journal *Medical Anthropology* focusing on this topic (Nichter, Pelto, and Steinhoff 1994).
3. Readers are invited to study this chapter in conjunction with a paper Mark recently co-authored with Nancy Vuckovic (Nichter and Vuckovic 1994). The paper builds upon lessons highlighted in the chapter and suggests agenda for future anthropological research on pharmaceutical practice.
4. In the introduction to an edited volume on anthropology and ethnomedicine (Nichter 1992b:x–xi), a distinction is drawn between ethnomedicine, applied medical anthropology, and health and development. Ethnomedicine broadly contextualizes and encompasses the anthropology of the body (Scheper-Hughes and Lock 1987), health ideology and practice, and approaches to healing inclusive of, but not limited to, medical "systems." Among other things, ethnomedicine examines relationships between political, religious, and medical systems; at once documents the embodiment of ideology and contests of meaning at the site of the body; and directs attention to the relationship between knowledge, power, and practice.

   Applied medical anthropology is more problem-based and focuses attention on biological, social, and cultural factors having a bearing on the distribution of health problems and resources as well as the forms they assume. It is biocultural in the sense that it is concerned with ecological dynamics fostering illness and favoring health. Applied medical anthropology is political in the sense that class, gender, and ethnic patterns of illness distribution and health care support are investigated in relation to resource allocation and conditions which place some groups at greater risk to illness than others. Beyond the study of illness, applied medical anthropology is concerned with the efficacy and efficiency of health care provision, access to and use of pluralistic health resources, and the organization of health care institutions. Cultural response to alternative solutions to health problems is investigated as are modes of educating local populations about health-related issues. Health and development entail a broad-based approach to the study of health transition wherein health is seen as both an outcome and a contributor to processes of development–underdevelopment.

5. For example, see McLaren (1984) on the differential contribution of male and female bodily substance and emotional predisposition to the creation of life as an expression of gender ideology in Greece and eighteenth-century England.

6. Trying to address both anthropology and public health audiences presents a special set of challenges. While we try and assume a transdisciplinary perspective in much of this volume, readers will find that some chapters are more anthropological and others more public health in orientation. For example, arguments made about how health ideology affects health care seeking (chapter 8) and the commodification of health (chapter 9) require greater discussion of anthropological theory. Discussions of nutritional needs during pregnancy (chapter 2), ARI (chapters 5 and 6), and dysentery (chapter 4) require an overview of epidemiological and nutritional data. In some cases, we have taken the liberty to use endnotes quite extensively to explain in greater detail theoretical and technical issues which some readers might want to consider further.

7. It is beyond the scope of the present volume to present the full range of our research on health and development. Readers interested in our more political–economic-inspired research are referred to articles on the international tobacco trade and changing patterns of tobacco consumption (Nichter and Cartwright 1991), and political ecological analysis of Kyasanur Forest Disease (Nichter 1992a), a disease associated with deforestation. Much of our present research focuses on the interface between environmental health, lifestyle, consumer behavior, and the politics of responsibility. These issues are highlighted, albeit in passing, in the essay on the commodification of health which appears in Section Three.

8. For additional comments on the relevance of Weidman's argument for applied medical anthropology in light of recent developments in the field, see Nichter (1991).

9. For an example of Kleinman's approach to a negotiated approach to patient care, see Katon and Kleinman (1981).

10. In the best of all worlds this would entail some element of participatory research initiated not only at the grassroots (Nichter 1984), but also within the medical and public health community. Also required are ethnographies of ministries of health, international health agencies, and NGOs (Foster 1987a and 1987b, Justice 1987, Mburu 1989, Peabody 1995). Studies presented in chapters 2 and

13 were generated during fledgling attempts to train community diagnosis teams in rural India in 1979–1980. Data presented in chapter 11 were collected while training members of Sri Lanka's Health Education Bureau in the organizational assessment of primary health care delivery in 1983–1984.

REFERENCES

Berman, P., C. Kendall, and K. Bhattacharya. 1994. The Household Production of Health: Integrating Social Science Perspectives on Micro-Level Health Determinants. Social Science and Medicine 38(2):205–215.

Foster, G. 1987a. Bureaucratic Aspects of International Health Agencies. Social Science and Medicine 25(9):1039–1048.

Foster, G. 1987b. World Health Organization Behavioral Science Research: Problems and Prospects. Social Science and Medicine 24(9):709–717.

Justice, J. 1987. The Bureaucratic Context of International Health: A Social Scientist's View. Social Science and Medicine 25(12):1301–1306.

Katon, W. and A. Kleinman. 1981. Doctor–Patient Negotiation and Other Social Science Strategies in Patient Care. In The Relevance of Social Science for Medicine. L. Eisenberg and A. Kleinman, eds. Pp. 253–282. Boston: Reidel Press.

Mburu, F. 1989. Non-Government Organizations in the Health Field: Collaboration, Integration and Contrasting Aims in Africa. Social Science and Medicine 24(5):591–597.

McLaren, A. 1984. Reproductive Rituals: The Perception of Fertility in England from the Sixteenth Century to the Nineteenth Century. London: Methuen.

Nichter, Mark. 1984. Project Community Diagnosis: Participatory Research as a First Step Toward Community Involvement in Primary Health Care. Social Science and Medicine 19(3):237–252.

Nichter, Mark. 1989. Anthropology and International Health: South Asian Case Studies. 1st ed. Dordrecht, The Netherlands: Kluwer Press.

Nichter, Mark. 1990. Vaccinations in South Asia: False Expectations and Commanding Metaphors. In Anthropology and Primary Health Care. J. Coreil and D. Mull, eds. Pp. 196–221. Connecticut: Westview Press.

Nichter, Mark. 1991. Preface. In Training Manual in Applied Medical Anthropology. C. Hill, ed. Pp. 1–13. Washington, DC: American Anthropology Association.

Nichter, Mark. 1992a. Of Ticks, Kings, Spirits, and the Promise of Vaccines. In Paths to Asian Medical Knowledge. C. Leslie and A. Young, eds. Pp. 224–256. Berkeley: University of California Press.

Nichter, Mark, ed. 1992b. Anthropological Approaches to the Study of Ethnomedicine. The Netherlands: Gordon and Breach.

Nichter, M. and E. Cartwright. 1991. Saving the Children for the Tobacco Industry. Medical Anthropology Quarterly 5(3):236–256.

Nichter, M. and C. Kendall. 1991. Beyond Child Survival: Anthropology and International Health in the 1990s. Medical Anthropology Quarterly 5(3):195–203.

Nichter, M., G. Pelto, and M. Steinhoff. 1994. Acute Respiratory Infection. Medical Anthropology 15(4) (Special Issue):319–450.

Nichter, M., G. Trockman, and J. Grippen. 1985. Clinical Anthropologist as Therapy Facilitator: Role Development and Clinician Evaluation in a Psychiatric Training Program. Human Organization 44(1):72–79.

Nichter, M. and N. Vuckovic. 1994. Agenda for an Anthropology of Pharmaceutical Practice. Social Science and Medicine 39(11):1509–1525.

Peabody, J. 1995. An Organizational Analysis of the World Health Organization: Narrowing the Gap Between Promise and Performance. Social Science and Medicine 40(6):731–742.

Sardar, Z., ed. 1988. The Revenge of Athena: Science, Exploitation and the Third World. London: Mansell.

Scheper-Hughes, N. and M. Lock. 1987. The Mindful Body: A Prolegomenon to Future Work in Medical Anthropology. Medical Anthropology Quarterly 1(1):6–41.

Taussig, M. 1980. Reification and the Consciousness of the Patient. Social Science and Medicine 14b:3–13.

van der Geest, S. 1993. *Review of* Anthropology and International Health: South Asian Case Studies (by Mark Nichter). Social Science and Medicine 37(7):953–955.

Weidman, H. 1976. In Praise of the Double Bind Inherent in Anthropological Applications. *In* Do Anthropologists Apply Anthropology? M. Angrosino, ed. Pp. 105–117. Athens: University of Georgia Press.

ACKNOWLEDGMENTS

We would like to acknowledge the support of several individuals who assisted us in our research in South India, Sri Lanka, and the Philippines. In India, we owe many of our insights on popular health culture and communication dynamics to Srinivas Devadigas, a long-term research assistant. H. K. Bhat assisted us in the collection of survey data introduced in chapter 2. Amrith Someshvar has served as our resident expert on Tuḷuva folk culture. Poet, folklorist, and participant in South Kanara's rich cultural life, Amrith generously shared his knowledge with us, never tired of our questions, and accompanied us on many field excursions in search of missing pieces to emergent puzzles.

Vaidya P. S. Ishwara Bhat (deceased) served as our local expert on *āyurvedic* theory for more than fifteen years, and *Vaidya* P. S. Ganapathy Bhat (deceased) and Kangila Krishna Bhat served as advisors on practitioner–patient communication and medicinal plants. Pharmacists Shah and Shenoy (deceased) from Mangalore provided us invaluable insights into the business of medicine and the social relations of pharmaceutical practice. Advocate A. K. Rao assisted us in understanding the politics of divination as well as the art of negotiation in both the profane world of law and the sacred realm of spirit cult activity. We would also like to acknowledge the many Primary Health Center staff and medical practitioners who afforded us the opportunity to observe and interview them on the job. Confidentiality prohibits our mentioning these people by name.

The Poogavana, Daithota, Kalpana, and Bhide households literally adopted our family and allowed us to carefully observe village life from their porches and family life from their kitchens. Our gratitude to members of these households and especially P. S. Venkataramana and Jaya, Shampa Daithota, P. S. Shankarnarayan Bhat, Sumathi, and Amma is beyond words.

We owe thanks to many people in Bantval, Puttur, and Beltangadi Taluks of South Kanara, and Ankola Taluk in North Kanara for sharing with us their life experiences in good times and bad over the past two decades. At first tolerated as participant-observers (scholars) and eventually welcomed as friends having established social networks, it has been our good fortune to maintain long-term relationships with households from a variety of castes and social classes. It is through such relationships, above all else, that we have gained insights into therapy management, the politics and art of everyday living, gender and generation, and social change at a time of rapid economic transition.

In Sri Lanka, we would like to acknowledge the assistance of Shantha Veragowda who periodically served as our research assistant and the eleven health education masters degree candidates with whom we lived and worked for over a year. Virtually all of our research findings were discussed with this group of seasoned field staff assigned to the Health Education Bureau. The researchers with whom we worked broadened our understanding of Sinhalese health culture and assisted us in conducting research on many of the issues discussed in chapters 1, 3, 11, and 13. We would especially like to thank B. A. Ranaveera.

In the Philippines, we would like to acknowledge the assistance of our research assistants from San Tedoro, Belma and Cora, and Christina from Pinnamalyan. Support and advice from colleagues at the Regional Institute of Tropical Medicine, and the University of the Philippines Clinical Epidemiology Unit (CERT) are very much appreciated. Mark would especially like to thank CERT members for making him feel at home during his sabbatical visit in 1990–1991.

Research in India was supported by a Radcliffe Brown award (U.K.) to Mark in 1974–1976 and an Indo-U.S. Subcommission on Education and Culture Award in 1979–1980. During this time, our research was sponsored by the National Institute of Mental Health and Neurosciences, Bangalore.

A Fulbright Fellowship supported research in Sri Lanka in 1984 and a WHO assignment facilitated research conducted in 1985. In Sri Lanka, Mark was affiliated with the Postgraduate Institute of Medicine, University of Colombo, and the Bureau of Health Education, and Mimi coordinated a family planning research project sponsored by the Bureau of Census and Statistics. Subsequent short field trips to South Asia have been indirectly funded by our consultant activities and small grants from the University of Arizona. Research conducted in the Philippines was funded by the WHO and the Rockefeller Foundation. Work on acute respiratory infection conducted in 1989 was sponsored by the Regional Institute of Tropical Medicine (Alabang) and research conducted in 1991 was sponsored by the University of the Philippines (Manila). Thanks also go to Charles Leslie and Joe Wray for their continued support and encouragement over the years.

Finally, we would like to acknowledge our children, Simeon and Brandon, who have spent much of their formative years on the road and in far off places. They have contributed in innumerable ways to our field experiences. Their flexibility, openness, and capacity to make friends have enriched our lives immensely and have helped us gain the trust of those whom we have had the fortune to meet along the path.

Section One

Women's Reproductive Health

This section focuses on lay perceptions of reproductive physiology. A range of issues including how perceptions of bodily processes influence women's health practices during pregnancy, fertility related practices, and interpretations of and demand for fertility control methods are discussed. Attention is drawn to both patterns of thought about the body which have broad inter-regional relevance as well as coexisting notions of ethnophysiology which reflect intracultural variability. The importance of ethnophysiology is also noted in several other chapters in this volume where explanatory models of illness and medicine are examined. Much popular knowledge of how the body functions is tacit, embodied, and practice based as distinct from being objectified and abstract. When practice-based knowledged is discussed, analogical reasoning is often employed as a means of facilitating health communication. Popular health concerns and practices reveal ways in which the physical body is perceived to function. They also index notions of vulnerability which have socio-moral significance and metamedical meaning.

The public health ramifications of lay health practices influenced by notions of reproductive ethnophysiology are profound. Ironically, while images of ethnophysiology and popular health concerns are appealed to by marketers of pharmaceutical products, they are paid less credence by those engaged in health education and the development of biotechnological resources.

1

CHAPTER 1

Cultural Notions of Fertility in South Asia and Their Impact on Sri Lankan Family Planning Practices

Mark Nichter and Mimi Nichter

INTRODUCTION

In this chapter we address a topic crucial to the field of family planning, yet rarely identified as a subject for research: cultural perceptions of fertility. Data from two ethnographic contexts are presented: South Kanara District, Karnataka State, India, and Low Country, Southwest Sri Lanka.[1] A case study which sparked our curiosity in the cultural perception of fertility is introduced, followed by a general discussion of the anthropological literature on fertility and conception in India. Most of this literature has addressed conception in relation to systems of descent. Moving beyond textual sources, we will present field data on folk notions of fertility collected in both South India and Sri Lanka. In the Sri Lankan context, attention is additionally paid to how health ideology affects family planning behavior and how "safe period" is utilized as a popular mode of fertility control.[2] Turning to family planning programs in Sri Lanka, we suggest that the provision of fertility cycle education for those 25–35 years of age could result in a more effective usage of "safe period" with condoms as a means of birth control. While most members of this age group have expressed a marked desire for birth postponement and spacing, they presently underutilize modern family planning methods (CPS 1983).

3

THE INDIAN STUDY

In 1974, while conducting ethnographic research on health culture in South Kanara, we became intrigued by the numerous references in local folklore to a woman's heightened fertility after her purification bath taken on the fourth day of menses. Some of these references described a woman as being so fertile at this time that the mere sight of a man was enough to influence the features of a child conceived during that month. In as much as the region was predominately matrilineal, we initially interpreted such references within the context of matrilineal kinship and descent. Later, however, while studying popular notions of physiology, we found members of both matrilineal and patrilineal castes who considered the first week following menstruation to be particularly fertile.[3]

A case which highlighted to us the importance of cultural notions of fertility involved a middle-aged Brahman couple who frequented a traditional *āyurvedic* practitioner for fertility medicines. The husband and wife both had college educations and resided in a rural village. They had been married for seven years and family members described their marital relationship as close. Not having conceived a child in the first three years of marriage, they had initially consulted a relative who was a qualified doctor. They were both tested thoroughly and found biologically capable of having children. The doctor did not, however, discuss with the couple their sexual behavior. After consultations with three other doctors, the couple visited numerous temples where vows were made. Additionally, the woman underwent two dilation and curettage procedures because she felt that perhaps her womb was "unclean or blocked." Dilation and curettage procedures are popular among the middle class in India since they are perceived to increase fertility (Nichter 1981a).[4] Finally, the couple sought the advice of a renowned *āyurvedic* practitioner who prescribed special dietary practices and herbal preparations. In addition to the balancing of body humors, these regimens were taken to increase, strengthen, and thicken the husband's *dhātu* (the vital part of semen) and to cool the wife's overly hot body, purify her blood, and stop female *dhātu* loss manifest as leucorrhea (Nichter 1981b). Despite these efforts, the woman had not conceived.

We came to know this couple quite well and on one occasion we questioned them individually about their sexual behavior — a matter of utmost intimacy. To our astonishment, we found that for seven years the couple had been having sexual relations only for the first three days following the menstruation purification bath. Having a child was of such importance to this couple that they had abstained from sexual activity during most of the month in an effort to save enough *dhātu* to afford them "the best chance of having a strong child at the easiest time for conception." When we discussed this case with three middle-aged local *āyurvedic* practitioners, we found that two out of the three considered this time period to be particularly fertile. Two of the practitioners noted additionally that they had learned from books that mid-cycle was "also" a fertile time. Traditional and modern knowledge had been incorporated into an eclectic knowledge base.

Returning to the region's oral tradition, we found references associating the fourth day after menstruation with both purity and fertility.[5] We questioned whether it was just purity in itself which was associated with the power of fertility or perhaps some set of contingent factors.[6] With respect to contingent factors influencing states of fertility, we noted that menstrual blood is not only deemed impure, but also heating. When discussing menstruation as a state of non-fertility during interviews, informants placed emphasis on the heating nature of menstrual blood, rather than on its impurity. An image commonly offered was that contact with menstrual blood was so "heating" as to dry a man's semen, just as the touch of a menstruating woman was heating enough to "cause a vine of cooling betel leaves to wilt."

Following up on the idea that menstrual blood was heating, we questioned a local *āyurvedic* scholar (*pundit*) about conception among animals which are fertile ("in heat") during menstruation. Conception among humans and animals was contrasted by the *pundit*. He described animals, creatures of the wild, as conceived from a state of heat. Heat constituted a state of uncontrol, "unbound desire ruled by hunger." Humans, as higher, more controlled, and "purer" beings were conceived through the containment of heat during coitus.[7] This image was elaborated upon in relation to metamedical dimensions of Brahmanic Hinduism, an analysis of which lies outside the scope of this chapter.[8]

Closer to popular Brahmanic Hindu thought were analogical descriptions of conception made by the *pundit* which employed agriculture as a referential framework. Agricultural analogies for conception are widely reported throughout India (Das 1976, Dube 1978, Fruzzetti and Ostor 1976, Inden and Nicholas 1977, Mayer 1960).[9] They are found in the Ramayana and Dharmasastra (Trautmann 1981), as well as in such *āyurvedic* texts as the Charaka Samhita (Inden and Nicholas 1977). Moreover, they play an important part in the marriage rituals of several patrilineal castes (Dube 1978). The most prevalent analogy describes conception in terms of the "male seed" and "female field." Reference to this image of conception has most often been cited by social scientists in the course of examining patrilineal descent. The following quote is illustrative:

> The quality of the field can affect the quality of the grain, but it cannot determine the kind.... The seed determines the kind. The offspring belongs

to one to whom the seed belongs. In fact he also owns the field.... By equating the woman's body with the field or earth, and the semen with the seed, the process of reproduction is equated with the process of production and rights over the children with the rights over the crop.... The language of the seed and the field is used for stressing the woman's lack of rights over her children in the event of separation or divorce. (Dube 1978:8–9)

The importance of the seed–field analogy extends beyond its use as a charter for patrilineal descent in particular caste cultures. Data from South Kanara District, which is largely matrilineal, are illustrative. A common way to note that a woman is pregnant in the Tuḷu language is to say *alena bangida onji bittu koddyondundu*, literally "in her stomach a seed sprouts." An analogical model linking descent to notions of conception, however, is notably absent in this region's rich oral tradition. Agricultural imagery is used only loosely in reference to conception.

Living in a region of intensive rice cultivation, people widely employ agricultural imagery as a referential framework in discussing a wide range of topics (see Chapters 7, 9, and 13). *Āyurvedic* practitioners commonly use such imagery in their efforts to explain health topics to their clients, including those related to fertility and infertility.[10] Once introduced, agricultural analogies are often extended, with patients drawing their own inferences. For example, we documented one instance where a villager extended an analogy about conception in a way not envisioned by the *āyurvedic* practitioner he had visited. In passing, the practitioner had compared the informant's wife to a dry rice bed when explaining the action of a fertility medicine prescribed for the woman during the first 16 days of her cycle. When we later asked the informant about times of fertility during a woman's monthly cycle, the informant noted that after a rice field is plowed and manured, it is left standing for three days before seed is sown. On the third day "the soil is soft, moist, and easily able to sprout fertile seed. Then, day by day, the soil becomes more and more difficult to penetrate." The informant stated that this was also the case with women who "after three days of menstruation are wet, soft, and most capable of conceiving." According to the informant, a woman's condition was less and less favorable for conception as her cycle progressed. After 15 or 16 days (from the onset of menstruation), conception became unlikely as the woman, like the field, became dry. The informant was quick to note, however, that when reckoning the likelihood of conception, one also had to consider the strength of the man's seed to "take root." A strong seed might root even under less opportune conditions. This idea was echoed in the advice offered by another *āyurvedic* practitioners to couples desiring progeny. The practitioner's notion was that stronger, healthier seed would sprout seven to 12 days after the onset of menstruation whereas any seed might sprout four to six days after onset. The practitioner therefore advised couples to engage in sexual exchange for strong progeny only during the later fertile days of a woman's cycle.

An analysis of this practitioner's prescription patterns revealed an implicit assumption about a woman's cycle being divided into two 15 day sectors. For women who wanted to conceive, he prescribed two kinds of herbal decoctions (*kaśāya*), the first to be taken the day after the onset of menses to day 15 and the second from day 16 to menses onset. The first of these "family" medicines functioned to prepare the womb (*garbha kōsha*) to accept seed and reduce the possibility of *sutaka vāyu* (literally, "pollution wind"), an ailment linked to seed rejection. The second medicine was taken to make the womb strong enough to hold the seed. A local proprietor of a commercial *āyurvedic* medicine shop with whom we discussed this idea noted that the same pattern was reflected in the prescription practices of practitioners who used commercial *āyurvedic* medicines.[11]

While analogies linking conception to agriculture emerged during our interviews, it would be misrepresentative to describe the seed–field analogy as a pervasive cultural model for conception in South Kanara. Conception is not a widely thought about or elaborately worked out cultural concept among the non-Brahman, largely matrilineal castes of South Kanara. The most common idea expressed was that in order for conception to occur the mingling of both male and female semen (*dhātu*) was required at the proper time of the month. More emphasis was placed on the time of the month when a woman is fertile than on details about why this time is physiologically fertile. A notion of the mixing of *dhātu* would seemingly endorse a more cognatic theory of descent.[12] We found, however, that an eclectic mix of ideas linked blood as life force to descent. Some informants spoke of all children conceived by a couple as sharing a mixture of both parents' blood. Others spoke of girls sharing their mother's blood and boys their father's blood.[13] Many informants found the subject of conception troublesome to think about abstractly. They shifted between references to blood which incorporated ideas about descent and ideas about health and illness. Ideas were diffuse and not well integrated. It might be argued that such an eclectic body of ideas about conception better serves the prevailing pattern of discerning descent. The latter is more determined by pedigree (family fame, property, etc.) than strict interpretations of descent by blood line.

LAY NOTIONS OF FERTILITY: CROSS-CULTURAL REFERENCES

Upon returning to the West we conducted a literature search on cultural ideas pertaining to fertility. Despite the existence of voluminous literature on cultural aspects of family planning attitudes and practices, very little data were available on the subject of cultural notions of fertility.[14] In India, Nag (1968:83) reported that some West Bengali women consider the fourth to twelfth days following the onset of menstruation to be favorable for conception. A related reference to lay perceptions of "safe period" was found in Mandelbaum's (1970) book on social and cultural dimensions of human fertility in India. Mandelbaum devoted one paragraph to this subject while making note of the implications of postmenstruation taboos:

> There is one kind of abstinence that paradoxically may result in higher rather than lower fertility. It is popularly believed that a woman's most fertile period comes in the days immediately following the cessation of menstruation and that the rest of the menstrual cycle is "safer." Sexual relations are forbidden during menstruation and almost all couples rigorously observe this taboo. But in a number of groups a postmenstrual taboo period is also favored. In a sample of women from a Mysore village, 66% reported abstinence for at least 8 days after onset, as did 40% of the women in a sample from a middle-class part of Delhi. Some women reported up to 15 days of abstinence after onset. As C. Chandrasekaran points out, with such abstinence periods, "the timing of coitus appears to coincide with the days of the woman's ovulation." (1970:64)

No indication is given by either Nag or Mandelbaum as to why the time period immediately following menstruation should be considered fertile, or what ramifications such a conceptualization might have on family planning practices. Indeed, it is not clear from the data presented by Mandelbaum as to why a formal prohibition on sexual relations exists during the most fertile time of the month. Is it related to ritual impurity, health concerns (for the woman or man), or perhaps to a deliberate, but unstated, practice of birth control? Gould (1975) goes a step further in speculating about the ramifications of existing ideas about fertility and suggests that fertility education might have a positive impact on the practice of family planning.

> Villagers are interested in and do practice a folk based rhythm method. The problem is that their conception of the fertility cycle is inaccurate. They believe that the safe period embraces the middle 15 days of the menstrual cycle. Rhythm practiced in accordance with this idea must increase rather than decrease fertility. But if family planning workers concentrated on teaching the villagers the correct safe period, plus coitus interruptus, I feel these

methods would prove to be more acceptable at this stage than more sophisticated approaches. In the West, after all, the birth rate began to drop through
the adoption of methods like this. (Gould 1975:549)

Our literature search revealed that the Indian subcontinent is not the only
ethnographic region where the period of time immediately following menstruation is thought to be particularly fertile. Historically, references to this
perception of fertility are abundantly found in the writings of classical Greek
physicians (Finch and Green 1963) as well as English physicians during the
19th century (McLaren 1984).[15]

Rubel et al. (1975) note that in Cebu, Philippines, it is believed that
conception is facilitated if coitus takes place on the fourth day after the onset
of the menstrual cycle. Laing (1984), in a survey in Bicol in the Philippines,
asked women when they thought was the best time to avoid sex in order to
avoid pregnancy. Among current users of the rhythm method, almost 40%
said right after the period, 24% said immediately before the period, and 3%
said during the period. Only one third of the respondents noted that it was
best to avoid sex midway between periods. Notably, almost 50% of the
respondents believed that a woman is fertile during the first seven days after
the start of the menstrual period.

Maynard-Tucker (1989) reports that in Peru a significant percentage of
her sample believed that a woman was most fertile during her menstruation.
In one of the few studies to investigate both women's and men's views, she
found that between 44% and 49% of her informants shared this perception.
Of a sample of users of "natural methods," 88% of couples practiced sexual
abstinence during menses which they described as the rhythm method (*el
ritmo, la regla*). Their practice of the rhythm method was backward by
biomedical standards, for they resumed what they considered safe sex one
week after menstruation as a means of family planning.

In Afghanistan, Hunte (1985) has noted that the practice of a folk rhythm
method involves abstinence from intercourse directly before and after the
menstrual period. These are times in a woman's cycle perceived as fertile.
Similarly, among the Ngwa Igbo of Nigeria, the effectiveness of rhythm is
reduced by the fact that it is incorrectly practiced because women believe that
their most fertile period is soon after menstruation (Ukaegbu 1975). Likewise, Hansen (1975), in his book on the Polynesian island of Rapa, notes:

> Most Rapans would like to limit their families to two or three children. To
> this end, they practice a rhythm method of birth control, but they find it most
> ineffective. "I don't understand it," remarked one woman, then expecting her
> eighth child. "We abstain from intercourse for three or four days right after
> my period every month, but I keep getting pregnant...." Further checking

revealed it to be the general opinion on Rapa that conception occurs during the few days immediately following menstruation. (Hansen 1975:52)

Hansen is one of only a few researchers who has investigated why an indigenous population perceived the days following menstruation to be fertile.[16] His research led him to consider the "mechanics of the uterus," what we prefer to call the "ethnophysiology of fertility."

> The uterus is conceived to be a mechanical organ which opens and closes. Remaining tightly closed most of the time, it opens for several days each month to allow the stale blood to run out. Rapans support their concept of a mechanical uterus with their belief that blood is harbored in the uterus in liquid form, like water in a bottle. If the uterus did not open and close but remained perennially open, they argue, then instead of regular menstrual periods there would be a constant seepage of blood. Just as blood cannot escape a closed uterus, semen cannot enter it, so there is no possibility of conception during the greater part of the cycle. [Hence one can understand their incredulity at our assertion that conception is most likely to occur about midway between menses]. Conception could occur during menstruation but ideas that menstrual flow is contaminating lead them to avoid intercourse at this time. However the uterus remains open for a few days after menstruation, and this is the time when, in Rapan eyes, conception occurs. (Hansen 1975:53)

We will see shortly that Rapan ideas about conception are not far removed from lay ideas expressed by some Sri Lankans.

Before turning to the Sri Lankan context, however, it is insightful to briefly present some data collected by Johnson et al. (1978) about knowledge of reproduction in a central Michigan prenatal clinic for multi-ethnic, low income clientele in the United States. These data may serve to illustrate that lay knowledge of fertility is an issue in need of study in developed as well as developing countries.

> The majority of women interviewed in the prenatal clinic did not understand reproductive physiology. Sixty one percent could not correctly answer questions as to why their menstrual periods occurred, the source of menstrual blood, or why the menstrual flow stopped.... One of the most prominent misconceptions about menstruation involved uterine anatomy. Many of the women seemed to perceive it as an organ which was closed between menstrual periods and which had to open up to allow the blood to get out. They were greatly concerned that nothing impede this process.... Sixteen percent believed that pregnancy was most likely to occur during menses because the uterus was open, allowing the sperm to enter. Conversely, it is logically closed at mid-cycle and therefore thought safe for intercourse without risk of pregnancy. (Johnson et al. 1978:860–861)

In a follow-up study of 200 undereducated black inner-city women, Johnson and Snow (1982) found that 64% of their informants were unable to answer when in their cycle they could become pregnant, 79% did not know of a safe period for intercourse, and 60% did not know they could become pregnant while breastfeeding infants. We have collected similar data among both middle class high school students in Arizona and university students hailing from communities around the United States.

THE SRI LANKAN STUDY

What difference, if any, do ethnophysiological notions of fertility have on the layperson's family planning behavior? We had the opportunity to look into this issue in 1984 while conducting anthropological fieldwork in southwest Sri Lanka. With respect to existing data on lay notions of fertility in Sri Lanka, Nag (1968:43) has summarized the observations made by Ryan in the early 1950s in a low-country Sinhalese village. "According to folk physiology, conception is not likely to occur during the period of 14 days preceding menstruation. People, however, have little faith nowadays in this theory, probably because they have noticed many exceptions." The implication of this statement is that folk ideas about fertility have little impact on family planning related behavior. McGilvray (1982:52), in a later study, notes that among Tamils in the Batticaloa region of eastern Sri Lanka, the 12–14 day post menstruation fertility idea continues to be prevalent. McGilvray did not comment on Ryan's statements regarding the degree of faith the lay population places in traditional ideas of fertility nor how ideas about fertility influence their family planning behavior. His more general impressions of folk health behavior are, however, suggestive of possible family planning related behavior:

> There is quite a bit of skepticism about many aspects of traditional ethnomedical doctrine, just as there is skepticism about the gods and penicillin. You can be skeptical but still want to cover your bets. The entire pluralistic domain of healing strategies reflects this sort of pragmatism and lack of concern with adherence to one specific doctrine. (McGilvray, Personal communication)

Among the rural low country Buddhist informants whom we interviewed, a wide range of ideas coexist about when a woman is *most* fertile during her monthly cycle. The inventory of ideas generated from interviews with 100 rural literate Sinhalese mothers under the age of 45 are summarized in Figure 1.1. Two overlapping time frames were noted by more than 80% of this sample of mothers:[17]

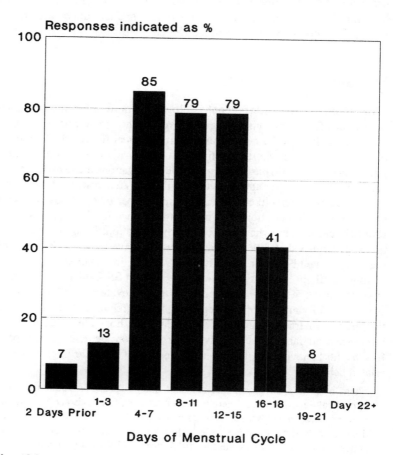

N ▪ 100

Figure 1.1. Ideas of when a woman is *most* fertile during her monthly cycle among rural literate Sinhalese mothers under the age of 45.

1. From the fourth day following the menstruation purification bath until the 11–12th day of a woman's cycle.

2. From the fourth day following the menstruation purification bath until the 14–15th day of a woman's cycle.

Evoking responses to the question of when one is most/least fertile required tact and innovative interviewing techniques. In Sri Lanka, fertility is not a subject easily spoken about through direct questioning. When we talked with interviewers who had worked on the World Fertility Survey (WFS 1978) and the Contraceptive Prevalence Survey (CPS 1983), we asked how survey respondents had discussed "safe period" as a method. Interviewers remarked that when probed about traditional methods, women respondents spoke of "being careful" (*api paressam venava*). This was ticked on the survey form as indicative of "safe period."

In our own interviews, we spent considerable time engaging in cultural free association with informants about a wide range of subjects spanning the dynamics of how they met their partners to issues involving health and the economics of family life. When introducing the topic of fertility, we did not present ourselves to informants as authorities on the subject, but rather as trying to learn from folk wisdom and their individual experiences. Moreover, we worked with Sri Lankan co-interviewers to develop a metaphorical interview style to be used with informants who responded poorly to direct questioning. Although the metaphorical interview was only used with approximately one quarter of our informants, it generated some of the most insightful data pertaining to why specific time periods were considered particularly fertile.

In order to engage in metaphorical interviewing, the interviewer needed to identify a familiar referential framework within which a sensitive topic could be addressed while maintaining an acceptable degree of social distance. Interviews within the metaphor (Buck et al. 1983, Mimi Nichter 1982) move back and forth from reference to specificity in an accordion like fashion. An example of a metaphor developed for interviews on fertility follows and introduces the discussion of lay ideas which underscore the notions of fertility noted above.

When we first began our interviews about fertility, we found that most informants initially had a far more difficult time replying to a direct question about "safe period" as a family planning practice, than to the question "when in the month is it easiest to become pregnant?" Direct questions focusing on fertility evoked the responses noted earlier, but there was little information as to why these times of the month were considered fertile. Informants commonly stated that this was what others had told them or what they had heard. At this point, we engaged a select group of key informants in metaphorical interviews.

One of the most effective *referential frameworks* that was utilized evoked the image of the womb as like a flower. This image was suggested by our senior co-interviewer, a retired rural development research officer, who was also a popular local poet. Poetic expression is commonplace in Sinhala culture and the image of a flower is pervasive in Sinhala poetry as a symbol of fertility, a symbol utilized in the ritual marking of a girl's first menstruation.[18] After the image of the flower was introduced, informants were given a chance to free associate, eventually being asked a question such as "When in the month is the bud most ready for the bloom of conception?"

One image which emerged from this question frame was quite similar to the ideas expressed by the Rapan Islanders. The flower was most "open" to conception during and following menstruation. Ideas varied as to how long the flower stayed open following menstruation, indicative of the variety of ideas reported about fertility duration. Ideas also varied as to whether one could become pregnant during menstruation. While no Sri Lankan informant spoke of a woman being too hot to conceive during menstruation, as informants had noted in South India, most informants pointed out that the flow of blood outward would prevent conception.[19] Reference would inevitably be made to a woman being impure (*killi*) at this time, but this state was not explicitly linked to infertility. Fifteen of our 100 informants noted that having intercourse during menstruation could lead to conception, and two informants specifically mentioned that newlyweds anxious for a child engage in intercourse during menstruation because the chances of conceiving at that time were high. Six informants believed that the uterus opened a few days prior to menstruation and that conception was possible at this time.

Two other ideas associated with fertility behavior emerged from cultural free association about the image of a uterus opening and closing. The first was that following delivery a woman is at high risk of becoming pregnant while she is still bleeding — a period of time ranging from two weeks to three months. During this time her womb is spoken of as an "open" healing wound. The first 14 days following childbirth are considered to be high risk days when a woman may easily become pregnant. Several women expressed the idea that abstention from intercourse is necessary until a woman's periods become regular for reasons relating to both her general health as well as the prevention of pregnancy.[20]

With respect to the relationship between postpartum amenorrhea and fecundity, many women expressed the opinion that the months following delivery were a "safe period" as long as a woman had not menstruated and was breastfeeding. Empirical observations and two possible logics may underlie this impression. Although not expressed directly, one logic may that the uterus remains closed "after the wound has healed" and until menstruation reoccurs. A second logic was expressed through a series of associations interlinking a series of contiguous events. A widespread perception was that menstrual blood is utilized in the formation of breastmilk and that indulgence in sex resulted in both a reduction of breastmilk and a resumption of menstruation. Some Sinhalese informants perceived the birth rate of Muslims to be higher than among the Sinhalese because sexual relations resumed soon after childbirth, babies were bottlefed early and therefore menstruation returned early.[21] Ethnophysiological notions incorporated from *āyurvedic* humoral ideology could well be underscoring such a chain complex. According to the *āyurvedic* humoral ideology, food is progressively transformed into a series of body substances from blood, flesh and bone to breastmilk and semen (*dhātu*). The interpretation of one popular *āyurvedic* practitioner was that as *dhātu* reserves in the form of semen become depleted through sexual experience, the body attempts to replenish these reserves. This leads to a reduction of the amount of *dhātu* availablIe for breastmilk production.

There was a range of opinions regarding how long postpartum amenorrhea reduced fecundity even among those who believed that it did. Far more older women (over 45) than younger women tended to believe that postpartum amenorrhea protected one against pregnancy. Several younger women spoke of knowing at least one other woman who had become pregnant in the three to six months following their delivery. An observation made by some of the older women was that the safe period afforded by amenorrhea had either decreased in duration or become less reliable as a means of birth control. Curiously, their explanations for this trend tended to focus more on the diet and lower activity levels of younger mothers than upon changes in breastfeeding and the feeding of infants with liquid supplements and solid foods. Such changes were, however, noted when these women were asked to reflect on child feeding behavior and how it had altered over the last 10 to 20 years, especially among town dwellers.[22]

Biomedically speaking, ovulation may either precede or follow the onset of the first postpartum menstrual period. In the absence of menses and food supplementation in infants, somewhere around 90% of women remain anovular up to six months following birth (Grey et al. 1990, Israngkura et al. 1989, Kennedy et al. 1989, Ross and Frankenberg 1993). Food supplementation to breastfed children results in shorter postpartum infecundity associated with changes in the frequency and intensity of breastfeeding (Grey et al. 1990, Huffman et al. 1987).[23] The effect of supplementation has also been found to differ by age. Younger women are more fecund than older women and resume menstruation after delivery earlier for any given pattern of full or partial breastfeeding (Huffman et al. 1987, Jain and Sun 1972, Jones 1990). Government midwives spoke to us about the popularity of the belief that a woman could not become pregnant after childbirth before the resumption of menstruation. This belief, compounded by a fear of reduced breastmilk if one used "heaty" birth control pills, made it all but impossible for them to encourage the use of family planning methods during postpartum amenorrhea, even when menstruation was delayed as long as one year.[24] Female informants noted that if a woman became pregnant while breastfeeding she must stop breastfeeding for both the health of her fetus and her breastfed child. *Mandama dosa*, a folk illness often manifest as acute protein calorie malnutrition, was directly linked to breastfeeding while pregnant. In as much as most mothers considered one and a half years as an optimum amount of time to breastfeed children, there was considerable concern about not becoming pregnant before this time had passed.

Analogical associations comparing a woman to an agricultural field were less prominent in Sri Lanka than in India. However, two agricultural analogies evoked during interviews were noteworthy. The first was elicited while interviewing women about how modern family planning methods were perceived to work. Oral contraceptives are considered by Sri Lankan women to have heating and drying properties. These properties are not perceived as "side effects" of the oral contraceptives but rather the very properties which constitute the means by which the pill effectively prevents fertility. In the context of articulating this, one female informant noted that the uterus is dried by the heating effect of the pill so the seed cannot take root.[25] She went on to note that a woman taking oral contraceptives was as dry as she would be in the latter days of her cycle before menstruation. She then warned that being in this hot, dry state for a long period of time led to the uterus "crumbling" like a piece of wood disintegrating when left out in the sun. This rendered a woman incapable of conception. The image of a crumbling uterus reemerged in subsequent interviews with other women about the properties and dangers of using oral contraceptives (see Chapter 3). These interviews led us to question whether a wetness–dryness folk model of conception might not be more prevalent than our interviews had revealed.

Cultural free association led to a second analogy generated between the fertility of women and the land. During a conversation with a male agriculturist, a woman's menstrual cycle was compared to the moon's cycle. Follow-up research on qualitative aspects of moon phases led to a string of associations being made between subjects as ranging from crop sowing to hair cutting and signs of a good and bad death. A brief consideration of these data are insightful. In Sri Lanka, all crops with the exception of tubers are sown prior to the full moon. Plants are sown as the moon is waxing, a time known in Sinhala as *puru paksha*, and in Tamil as *valar pirai*.[26] Concordantly, during this time of development, weddings are planned as are house warming ceremonies and the laying of foundations. Hair is cut during this time in the belief that a longer, healthier quantity will grow back. Birth and death during this time are deemed auspicious. To the contrary, occurrence of death during the waning of the moon is deemed inauspicious. Only yams are planted while the moon is waning, in as much as tubers grow downward.

Accordingly, our informant associated the waxing of the moon with the first 16 days of a woman's cycle, a time of fertility and growth. The waning of the moon was associated with the latter half of a woman's cycle, a time of decreasing fertility. This conceptualization evoked through a set of images during cultural free association may well constitute a metadimension to lay ideas about the first 15–16 days of a woman's cycle being her fertile period. It is also feasible that the second most common fertility duration range cited by informants, 14–15 days from the menstruation purification bath, constitutes a variation on this theme. There was considerable confusion among many informants as to whether one calculated fertile days from the first day of the cycle or the day of the menstruation purification bath.

IMPLICATIONS FOR FAMILY PLANNING

Two broad family planning issues arise in light of the data presented from Sri Lanka. The first involves research on the prevalence and effectiveness of traditional fertility regulation practices in Sri Lanka, while the second involves family planning education. Sri Lanka is a rapidly developing country which boasts a high literacy rate for both men (90%) and women (82%), a low infant mortality rate (37/1000), good access to medical services, and an island wide transportation and mass media network (Pollack 1983). With respect to family planning, data from both the World Fertility Survey (WFS 1978) and the Contraceptive Prevalence Survey (CPS 1983) reveal that a large number of Sri Lankans are in favor of population control. Indeed, almost all our informants were interested in limiting their family size in response to economic pressures and changes of "wealth flow" within the family (Caldwell 1980). Despite family planning as a documented felt need, the CPS showed that less than one quarter of the women who did not want more children were using a modern method, 40% were using a traditional practice and about one third were using no method at all.[27] According to the results of the WFS and CPS surveys, low utilization of modern methods could not be attributed to lack of familiarity with these methods. Knowledge, or what may more accurately be termed familiarity with methods, was noted by 91% of the WFS and 99% of the CPS survey populations. Quantitative data collected on the practice of safe period (when people are "careful") may, at best, be considered impressionistic because surveys to date have neglected to follow up on "when people are careful and how."[28] This limitation aside, it is evident that in Sri Lanka traditional practices are clearly popular and that barriers to the adoption of modern methods exist for reasons which go beyond literacy and familiarity with modern methods.

It is beyond the scope of this chapter to consider why modern methods are not more popular. This issue is the focus of Chapter 3, which highlights lay perceptions of how modern fertility regulation works and related ideas about side effects in the context of popular health culture. What may be noted here is that ideas about how modern methods work impact on when couples adopt methods and what couples choose to use as birth control. Let us consider this point in relation to CPS data. According to CPS data (1983:67–71), the rhythm method is clearly the temporary birth control practice of choice for women aged 15–49. With respect to all methods of birth control, rhythm is the most popular mode until age 24. In the 25–34 year old age groups, sterilization takes a slight lead in popularity, with this lead becoming prominent after age 35.[29] These data suggest that women who want to space their children or postpone childbirth prefer traditional practices of fertility control to modern methods, while those women who no longer desire conception opt for sterilization.

How common are the use of traditional practices of birth control? According to the CPS (1983:67) of ever married women aged 30–34 who had ever used contraception, 47% had used traditional methods (safe period and withdrawal). This is significantly higher than the findings of the WFS which estimated that 21% of this cohort had at some time used traditional practices. Our impression is that the practices of "safe period" and withdrawal are far more pervasive than indicated by either of these two surveys. In defense of this impression, let us cite data from both our own research and that of a health educator graduate student (Chullawathi 1985) who conducted a village study in an effort to validate and expand upon our findings. During our 10 months of research, we felt close enough to 35 of our married female informants aged 25–35 to interview them about their traditional birth control practices. Each of these women was literate, had one to two children, and was considering the possibility of having another child. Of this group, two thirds were using or had used safe period and/or withdrawal as a birth control method in the past two years. Only five of these women had tried the pill and two had tried the IUD. Six reported that their husbands sometimes used condoms at times they considered unsafe. Two of these women took oral contraceptives "only" during the perceived unsafe period.

Chullawathi followed up on the impressions cast by these interviews and conducted a more rigorous cluster survey in three villages of Galle District. With the assistance of two local field assistants, she interviewed all mothers under 35 years of age. Of the 95 women interviewed, 97% were literate with 52% educated to the 10th standard. Chullawathi found that 65% of these women had used safe period as a primary means of birth control with 44% of the women currently using this practice. Fifty six percent of her sample reported that they had experienced an unexpected pregnancy. Of those in her sample who had specifically used safe period, 31% reported conceiving while using this practice. Of the 42 women currently using safe period, only seven stated that their husbands used condoms in conjunction with this practice. Chullawathi further noted that 87% of her informants said that they had a regular menstrual cycle. With respect to the probable effectiveness of their practice, 13% of her sample had sexual relations only between the 20–28th days of the cycle, yielding a high probable efficacy. Another 18% engaged in coitus after the 15th day of the cycle. The remaining women reported a wide range of ideas about safe period which indicated that the 14th–18th days of the cycle were considered safe.

The question may be asked how is it that the lay people have not realized that their ideas about fertility do not accord with their experience of conception? In the first instance, folk ideas of fertility do in some cases cover peak fertility periods.[30] Further, it need be recognized that interpretation is a hermeneutic process and common sense has a cultural dimension. Three points may be made in this regard. First, communication between husband and wife about perceived fertility is often minimal in as much as it entails discussion of a personal practice as opposed to a publicly sanctioned method.[31] Moreover, many women feel that they must succumb to their husband's sexual demands. This is not to say, however, that women do not have available to them means by which to distance themselves from sexuality, for cultural institutions such as religion do provide such means.[32] What we would emphasize is that there are slips in the practice of safe period regardless of the scientific validity of this practice. Humans are as much rule breakers as rule makers and obeyers. Pregnancy is often attributed to slip-ups during the first 16 days of a woman's cycle during which time she is culturally perceived to be fertile.

A second point involves menstrual irregularity and the range of factors from diet to physical activity and stress which impact on the frequency and duration of a woman's cycle (Harrel 1981). Menstrual irregularity, particularly amenorrhea, contributes to confusion about a woman's fertility and raises doubt as to whether a woman is pregnant or not. The latter point has important ramifications. Periodic amenorrhea is not uncommonly suspected to be pregnancy in both rural southwest India and Sri Lanka. Many women, experiencing amenorrhea, engage in activities to "bring back menstruation" as soon as they feel that their cycle is past due and that they might be "becoming pregnant." Their use of dietary manipulation, herbal decoctions, and hard work to bring back their menses is not viewed as causing an abortion. It is rather a form of menstrual regulation.[33] Menstrual regulation is particularly common among lactating women wishing to continue breast-feeding, but who think they may be "becoming" pregnant. As previously noted, there are cultural sanctions against breastfeeding a baby while a woman is pregnant.

Lay interpretation of a delayed menstrual cycle followed by its return after dietary manipulation leads some women to interpret that they were indeed in the process of becoming pregnant. Retrospective thinking is often more influenced by ideas about fertility than it is by notions of safe period. While many women entertain some measure of doubt as to the validity of their ideas about a nonfertile period, they still maintain traditional ideas about when they are most fertile. These women tend to associate their perceived state of pregnancy, prior to bringing back their menses, with an act of coitus during the first 16 days of their cycle. For others who have not experienced coitus within this time frame, or for whom pregnancy continues despite alterations of diet and the taking of herbal decoctions, there is always a fatalistic theme to fall back on. Among Sinhalese Buddhists, a common expression noted at this time is "the child that is meant to be born, will be born."

EDUCATION ABOUT FERTILITY

In the Yucatan, as in many parts of the world, women believe that the most fertile time is immediately before and after menstruation, because at that time "the uterus is open." Women who want to avoid pregnancy will have intercourse in mid-cycle when they believe the uterus to be closed — exactly at the most fertile time. The medical staff, however, were not aware of this belief. So the family course failed to impart the single piece of information which could be expected to have a real impact on contraceptive behavior. (Jordan 1987:6)

Fertility is not a subject discussed with lay people by family health workers, public health midwives, or hospital staff in Sri Lanka. Reasons why this subject is not introduced involve both the sensitivity of the topic and the attitude that "to talk to lay people about such things will only reduce their interest in accepting scientific family planning methods." The latter argument was commonplace in our discussions with health staff. The argument complements the strong position which Sri Lankan politicians take against sex education which they feel will lead to premarital sex among youth.[34] Proponents of both arguments underestimate the potential for miseducation when appropriate education is not provided, and fail to appreciate existing family planning and sexual behavior. In regard to family planning knowledge and behavior, the following points may be emphasized:

1. The belief that literacy in itself will "correct false, and superstitious beliefs about the body" is naive. Most of our literate informants continued to entertain traditional ideas about fertility, at times incorporating these with modern ideas. Less than 15% of our 100 literate informants had adopted a biomedical idea of safe period.

2. Literacy in itself provides one with an equal opportunity to both education and miseducation, in accord with the range of information available to read. In the Sri Lankan context, more information of dubious scientific merit is available on sexuality than information on fertility which addresses lay concerns in a manner which is culturally responsive and understandable. According to one Sri Lankan sociologist, some 153 sex magazines are available in the streets of Sri Lanka spreading inaccurate information about human sexuality.[35]

3. By not addressing lay ideas about the ethnophysiology of fertility, current family planning education is less effective than it could be. This is illustrated by women failing to heed advice from government midwives about adopting family planning methods after delivery before menstruation resumes. As noted, many women feel it is unnecessary to adopt contraceptive behavior until 12–18 months after delivery.

4. There is a marked reluctance to adopt temporary modern family planning methods among many recently married couples having no children or only one child. This reluctance is related to an expressed concern that the use of modern methods may interfere with their ability to have healthy children in the future. Based on our interviews, we suspect that many such couples practice a combination of safe period–withdrawal, or safe period–condom use. Indigenous and eclectic notions of fertility affect practice as well as efficacy of practice.

This point needs to be considered in light of international interest in identifying potential user groups for natural family planning methods and a combination of natural and modern methods.[36] From the interview data gathered, it would appear that literate, young Sri Lankan couples having no or only one child, who wish to postpone or space childbirth would constitute ideal candidates for such programs. Many of these couples are not current users of modern methods and many of those who use condoms do so in combination with an idea of fertility which is unscientific. A culturally sensitive program which educates about fertility, both in respect to the planning and prevention of conception, would constitute a visible example of family planning, not just a program to lower population growth. In order for such a program to be successful it will be necessary to generalize the recommendations made by Johnson et al. (1978) on the basis of research in the U.S. clinical context:[37]

> Most educational schemes in clinical settings are based on the premise that the presentation of proper information is what is required to improve patient knowledge and behavior. This is the case only where patients lack information. A very different sort of problem is the replacement of incorrect information. A patient who is presented with a fact which conflicts with what she believes to be true culturally is not necessarily going to reject the old and take on the new because the correctness of the new is scientific fact. To deal with this problem, health care personnel must learn to ask other sorts of questions, to elicit information which may seem to them ridiculous and to do so in a non-judgmental and non-condescending manner. They will then have to develop educational programs in an individualized manner to allow for the variety of beliefs among their patients. (Johnson et al. 1978:853)

Broadening these recommendations in the development context will entail the coordination of interpersonal and mass media health communication approaches responsive to formative ethnographic research incorporated within the health education process.[38]

NOTES

1. The population studied in South Kanara was a multicaste mix of Tuḷu and Kannaḍa speakers residing in Bantval, Puttur, and Beltangadi Taluks. In Sri Lanka, the population studied were multicaste Sinhalese Buddhists. Field work was conducted in Ratnapura, Horana, Galle, and Matara Districts of Sri Lanka.

2. "Safe period" is a term designating a time during a woman's monthly cycle which she perceives as a time of low fertility. By the "practice of safe period"

we mean either that a woman engages in sexual activity only during the time associated with low fertility, or that she avoids times she associates with high fertility.

3. We also found similar references to times of peak fertility in the folklore of patrilineal caste groups inhabiting the nearby Deccan Plains.

4. Dilation and curettage procedures are generally undertaken in private "nursing homes" and are also a popular means of abortion. As one of the biggest money makers at nursing homes, the procedures are encouraged for women having problems in becoming pregnant or sustaining pregnancy.

5. The fourth day following the onset of menstruation is marked by a bath which denotes that a woman is ritually pure whether or not she is still bleeding. In keeping with anthropological theory involving purity and danger (Douglas 1966), it could be argued that a woman is open to forces of transformation at a transitional time of *rite de passage*. This might explain legends linking the time of the fourth day bath to immaculate conception from the gods (children being "born in truth") and children taking on the characteristics of those whom a woman's eyes first befall. What it does not explain is why the first half of a woman's cycle (following menses) is deemed more fertile than the second half of her cycle. Reference to a child looking like a man other than a woman's husband as being related to who she cast her eyes upon after her purification bath may also be a slur upon the woman's moral character.

6. As Neff (1994) notes fertility among South Indian women is also associated with properly attending to ritual duties to gods and the ancestors such that feminine powers may be released in the form of fertility which serves the family's social interests.

7. The *āyurvedic* concept that heat is contained during coitus leading to conception is underscored by an epistemology regarding the creation of the universe. With regard to human conception, the idea is that "*dhātu ojus,*" the potent factor within semen, is a "cooling-light substance" capable of containing heat. Contained heat is a creative force, while uncontained heat is a power of the "wild" (Personal communication, *Vaidya* P. S. Ishvara Bhat). According to *āyurvedic* texts, a women's fertility extends to the 16th night of her cycle, or the 12th night after cessation of her menstrual flow (Dash 1975:11). Sexual relations during menstruation can lead to conception but results in fetus malformation. The idea that copulation during menstruation can lead to conception but results in ill health is not limited to the Indian subcontinent. According to Talmudic Judaism, sexual taboo at menstruation is due to a belief that children conceived at this time would be lepers (Spivak 1891, noted in Snowden and Christian 1983:233).

8. For example, the informant described the Havik Brahman ritual of *oupasana* as symbolizing the union of man and woman through the bonding of heat, a metaphor for conception and creativity. During Havika and other Brahman caste marriage rituals, the couple attends to a ritual fire. Following this act the couple is given a bamboo tube. Placed in this tube by the priest with his left

hand are 68 pieces of *durbe* grass. This grass is a symbol of purity which is used as a sacred perimeter to contain the ritual fire. With his right hand the priest places into the tube a branch of *Ficus glomerata* (*āti*), a symbol of fire, wrapped in a sacred thread symbolizing a twice born Brahman male. At the death of either partner the *oupasana* tube must be burned in the funeral pyre signifying the nonbound nature of heat on the part of the remaining partner. If the remaining partner is a male under the age of 50, he is immediately advised to become remarried "for the sake of controlling his heat." If female, the partner is subject to a series of biosocial restrictions to control her state of heat manifest as sexuality.

9. The field–seed image of conception is noted elsewhere in South Asia. For example, Maloney et al. (1981:119) note that in rural Bangladesh a woman is compared to the land if a couple does not have offspring. "The land is blamed if it gives not a good harvest.... If a crop is not forthcoming it is because of the conditions of the land and its moisture rather than the seed." Similarly, Delaney (1991) notes that women in Turkey provide the soil while men provide the seed. Notably, men's and women's contribution to procreation are differentially valued, with the male seed viewed as the sole source that creates a child and its identity.

10. Also employed by *āyurvedic* practitioners are analogies associating a woman's menstrual cycle to the movement of the sun and moon. Elsewhere in India, Marglin (1992) has found that a woman's menstrual cycle is perceived to be analogous to the movement of the earth through the seasons. Marglin notes that a woman's *ritu*, her embodied eternal cosmic rhythm, is poorly characterized by the English term "nature" (given its popular juxtaposition to "culture") in as much as Hindu perceptions of propriety are based on the interplay of cosmic principles. What is notable about Marglin's analysis is the questions she raises about descriptions of women as dangerous purveyors of pollution. Closely examining the use of pollution terminology to describe menstruation, she calls for a more complete understanding of term use responsive to conceptualizations of menstruation as a time of cosmic regeneration. During this time, an *āyurvedic* practitioner told us, a woman is to be "left fallow and undisturbed." The metaphors he used shifted from seasonal to agricultural referential frameworks.

11. The medicine *Ayapan* would be prescribed during the first 15 days of a woman's cycle followed by "Loes Compound" during the next 15 days.

12. In an examination of Tuluva matrilineal kinship, Claus (1978) provides additional details about Tuluva ideas of procreation collected from regions of the district less influenced by Brahmanic culture. Claus documented the notions that a) semen from both partners is required for conception, and b) that the relative quantity of male or female semen determines the sex of the child.

   We encountered a variant on this theme that it was the strength of the semen and not the quantity which determined the gender of a child. Other informants stated that the stars also influence the gender of the fetus. These notions support a bilateral notion of descent mediated by the powers of the cosmos.

13. The idea expressed by some informants that a boy is descended from his father and a girl from her mother supports the notion of double unilineal descent and was used by one informant to explain to us the reason why cross-cousins could marry and the children of like gender siblings could not. Claus (1978) emphasizes that the brother–sister bond is too closely integrated to support a strong case for double unilineal descent.

14. It is noteworthy that a collaborative World Health Organization study on Patterns and Perceptions of Menstruation (Snowden and Christian 1983) in 10 countries (including India) does not address the issue of fertility in relation to popular perceptions of the menstrual cycle. This is particularly striking because the study was largely oriented toward examining perceptions of menstruation in relation to family planning methods and issues.

15. Humoral theories of procreation based on wet–dry, hot–cold, and open–closed states underscore a wide range of fertility enhancing practices concordant with notions of proper timing and positioning during intercourse. Notions of ethnophysiology are often inspired by analogical reasoning which indexes multiple experiential domains. For example, McLaren (1984) notes that in 18th century England, the warm, moist months of spring were seen as most conducive for fertility as opposed to the hot, dry months of late summer. The days following a woman's period were most fertile for reasons linking her internal milieu with seasonal reasoning. McLaren further notes in these historical texts, a woman's cycle is discussed in relation to her most fertile period, not her least fertile period, as a means of birth control. A woman's least fertile period was perceived in relation to blood flow. Copulation just prior to or during menses was not thought to result in conception as the seed would not be able to "root" before being washed away. Indeed, whores were believed to reproduce less than other women because their wombs were rendered "slippery due to overuse" (p. 45).

16. Two other ethnographic studies describe folk models of fertility similar to those presented in this chapter: the open uterus model and the wet–dry uterus model. Kay (1977) notes that among Mexican-Americans in Tucson, an idea exists that the week before menstruation is a time when a woman is fertile because her uterus is open. Likewise, a woman must be careful not to engage in coitus after a baby is born as her uterus is open at this time as well (the duration is not specified). Niehof (1985) describes the ideas of women living on the island of Madura in Indonesia:

> Most women do not regard their menstrual cycle as consisting of fertile and infertile days and those who do, unfortunately misunderstand it. They think that they have a greater chance to conceive on the days just before and just after menstruation, and consider the mid-period of the cycle to be sterile. The reversal of the actual pattern of fecundity is caused by the association of dry with sterile and moist with fertile. The

womb is thought to be dried in the middle of the cycle. Just before menstruation it is thought to be moist and swollen with blood, providing an ideal host environment for the seed. After menstruation the womb is thought to be like an open wound, facilitating penetration and settling of the seed. (Niehof 1985:223–24)

17. Sixty five key informant interviews with married women aged 25–38 having at least one child were initially carried out over a period of seven months in rural villages of Horana, Ratnapura, and Matara Districts of low country Sri Lanka. All informants were literate and lower/middle class. Twenty to 22 informants in each district were interviewed. An additional 35 interviews of women with similar socioeconomic/age backgrounds were carried out by masters degree students, all seasoned health workers from the Sri Lankan Bureau of Health Education. Data were collected from known informants in Galle, Colombo, Kalutara, and Kurenagala Districts. The range of ideas noted in this chapter was further substantiated by focus group interviews carried out by research staff of the Family Planning Association of Sri Lanka (personal communication, Victor de Silva, June 1985).

18. McGilvray (1982: 52) notes that among Batticaloa Tamils the uterus is commonly referred to as a flower and fecundity a time when it is in bloom. In a subsequent (1986) field trip to South Kanara we encountered the image of a woman's uterus opening and closing like a flower during an interview with an *āyurvedic vaidya* concerning his prescription practices for women having problems conceiving.

19. This is not to suggest that in Sri Lanka menstruation is not associated with overheat, for it clearly is. For example, restrictions against bathing involve the idea that the coolness of a bath may interfere with the process of menstruation.

20. There is a popular belief among middle class, quasi-educated women that the need for a hysterectomy after menopause is related to engaging in sex too soon after delivery. This act is described as causing the intestines and uterus to "come down." We documented three separate cases where women feared pregnancy to the point of attempting to bring on their menses after engaging in intercourse within the third month following delivery.

21. This perception has scientific validity. Muslim women in southwestern Sri Lanka do tend to wean their children early or to place them on formula soon after birth. Research has found that the frequency and intensity of infant suckling induces prolactin activity which inhibits ovulation (Delgado et al. 1978; Huffman et al. 1978).

22. Data presented in Ross et al. (1992) suggest that exclusive breastfeeding in Sri Lanka, even during the first four months, is not common.

23. In developing countries, where lactating mothers are undernourished and have more limited milk production, the introduction of supplementary foods to infants after each breastfeed may not diminish the number of suckling epi-

sodes. Vis (1985) has suggested that in such cases, supplementation may not influence milk production and prolactin levels. He argues that the relationship between supplementation and postpartum fecundity may differ in developing as distinct from developed countries. On this issue see also Jones (1990).

24. The economic ramifications of breasts drying up was a concern expressed by several women. An inability to breastfeed would require the purchase of milk or formula, which constituted a significant investment for the poor. For studies which discuss South Asian mothers' concerns about the quality and quantity of breastmilk in general, see Mull (1992) as well as Reissland and Burghart (1988).

25. Laderman (1987), writing about Malaysia, also notes the association of overheat with an inability to conceive. Women who experienced an "inconvenient" pregnancy would try to expel the embryo by making their womb uncomfortably hot. This was done by a hot massage which brought hot blood to the area.

26. In South Kanara, the waxing and waning of the moon are likewise linked to fertility and infertility. For example, a central fertility ritual known as *kedvāsa* is begun on a no moon (*amavāse*) day when the earth is said to be menstruating. During the three day ritual, fields may not be plowed nor wild plants gathered. As in Sri Lanka, most crops are sown while the moon is waxing (*shukla pakśa*). During the waning period (*krisna pakśa*), trees are cut for timber as it is said they will be "hard." Trees cut in *shukla pakśa* are thought to be "soft" and can rot more easily.

27. Traditional methods of birth control on the CPS survey included rhythm and withdrawal. On the WFS survey, traditional methods included abstinence in addition to rhythm and withdrawal. We choose to use the term "safe period" instead of rhythm method so as to present the practice as perceived by villagers (see note 2 as well as Chapter 3).

28. On a methodological note, we would emphasize that the collection of accurate quantitative data about traditional practices of birth control is problematic. Our experience, corroborated by that of CPS and WFS survey interviewers, is that data collection on traditional practices is far more difficult than data collection on modern methods. Some degree of social distance is afforded by the technological status of modern methods. Indeed, the community has become somewhat desensitized to discussions of "methods" through the media if not through interactions with health/medical staff. Discussion of traditional fertility control entails the discussion of "practices" (as opposed to methods). One's practices are highly personal and individualistic and are rarely, if ever discussed in Sinhala culture, even among friends.

29. Shedlin and Hollerbach (1981) propose a model for fertility decision making and stress that it changes with each successive birth. The Sri Lanka data concord with this model.

30. Efficacy would depend on the duration and regularity of a woman's cycle as well as ideas about fertility and safe days. There may be a notable difference in the efficacy of birth control practices among those believing in the 15 day range beginning on the first day of menses and the range beginning on the fourth day of menses. According to biomedicine, ovulation occurs 14 days before the onset of menses. Depending on the length of a woman's cycle, ovulation could occur on day 14 (in a 28 day cycle), day 7 (in a 21 day cycle), or even on day 28 (in a 42 day cycle). Little research has been conducted on how menstrual cycle duration varies from cycle to cycle for a woman as she ages, or on environmental determinants of hormonal patterns (Koblinsky et al. 1993).

31. We might note that among couples where communication between husband and wife about safe period did exist, it was far more common for men to initiate discussions of the topic than women.

32. Other means of reducing sexual contact during perceived peak fertility periods include sleeping with children and complaining about physical ailments, especially leucorrhea, which is linked to impurity and loss of strength. In some regions of India as well as Sri Lanka, contact with a woman who has leucorrhea is deemed dangerous to the health of men. See Bang and Bang (1994) and Nichter (1981b).

33. A similar idea of "bringing down the period" through the use of traditional medicines has been noted by Shedlin (1982:82) in Mexico. Shedlin makes the point that these women do not see this practice as an abortion and speak of it comparatively freely. This idea has also been reported in Afghanistan (Hunte 1985:53), Colombia (Browner 1979, 1980), Jamaica (Brody 1985:168), and Malaysia (Ngin 1985:35). Scrimshaw (1985) has also discussed the idea of "bringing the period down" among women in Ecuador through the use of home remedies (herbal teas) and self-prescribed calcium injections. Similar to Shedlin, Scrimshaw points out that as long as the problem is one of a delayed period, a woman is able to distance the pain of admitting that she is trying to induce an abortion.

34. With regard to the topic of sex education, Kodagoda (1986) has noted that:

    Many parents freely admit the ignorance of their children in matters of sex and accept the need to rectify the situation. Yet they are not ready to concede the need for instruction and the sharing of experience towards that end. This probably stems from a mistaken notion that sex education inevitably leads to permissiveness and moral degradation and perhaps from a fear of exposure of their own ignorance. Family life education, with its content of human sexuality, is an explosive subject in the field of politics. However, a survey of experienced teachers showed "a virtually unanimous view that the male and female reproductive system and the process of maturation associated with pregnancy should be covered in family life education."

35. Dr. Nanda Ratnapala, personal communication, 1984.

36. Interest in natural family planning has been expressed by the Family Planning Association of Sri Lanka and international donor agencies. There is some evidence that natural family planning programs elsewhere in South Asia have reached some degree of success. Rao and Mathur (1970) documented some success of an All-India Institute of Hygiene and Public Health program in teaching rural Indian women to recognize times of fertility by the use of a wall calendar which calculated "baby days" from the time of a woman's menstrual bath. Baby days were denoted as the eight days between the 11th–18th day after the onset of menstruation. According to a more recent study, the Billings ovulation method of natural family planning was successfully introduced on a trial basis in South India (Mascarenhas et al. 1979). This method is based on self-recognition by women of their fertile and infertile periods by the subjective sensation of wetness in the genital area. Given an idea as to when their fertile period occurred, illiterate women were able to calculate and mark on a color coded chart (available to their husbands) dry and wet, safe and at risk to pregnancy days. Limitations of the Billings method include the existence of widespread leucorrhea and cervitis among the rural population as well as a lack of privacy for the practice of sympto-thermal techniques. Moreover, the cost effectiveness of the method is questionable (Betts 1984). We are not suggesting that this technique is suitable for all segments of Sri Lanka's population. We have rather identified young married couples (age 25–35) as a focal group for fertility education efforts which focus on combined safe period/condom use as well as the need for contraceptive behavior during postpartum amenorrhea.

37. Another example of this same issue can be found in Jordan (1989).

38. With respect to the probable response of the Sinhalese population to the kind of education advocated, we may note the experience of Chullawathi (1985). As part of her study, this health educator found that 98% of the mothers whom she interviewed wanted information about the safe period. Indeed, she noted that many women visited her at her quarters in an effort to obtain additional information. With respect to the form of information desired, almost three quarters of her sample wanted to receive information interpersonally from health workers. About half of the respondents preferred getting written materials along with or in lieu of interpersonal communication.

REFERENCES

Bang, R. and A. Bang. 1994. Women's Perceptions of White Vaginal Discharge: Ethnographic Data from Rural Makarastra. *In* Listening to Women Talk About Their Health: Issues and Evidence from India. Joel Gittelsohn, Margaret Bentley, Pertti Pelto, Moni Nag, Abigail Harrison, and Laura Landman, eds. New Delhi: Har Anand.

Betts, K. 1984. The Billings Method of Family Planning. An Assessment of Studies in Family Planning 15(6/1):235–266.

Brody, E. 1985. Everyday Knowledge of Jamaican Women. *In* Women's Medicine: A Cross Cultural Study of Indigenous Fertility Regulation. L. Newman, ed. Pp. 162–178. New Jersey: Rutgers Press.

Browner, C. 1979. Abortion Decision Making: Some Findings from Colombia. Studies in Family Planning 10(3):96–106.

Browner, C. 1980. The Management of Early Pregnancy: Folk Concepts of Fertility Control. Social Science and Medicine 14b(1):25–32.

Buck, B., L. Kincaid, M. Nichter, and M. Nichter. 1983. Development Communication in the Cultural Context: Convergence Theory and Community Participation. *In* Communication Research and Cultural Values. W. Dissanayake and A. R. M. Said, eds. Pp. 106–126. Singapore: Amic Press.

Caldwell, C. 1980. The Theory of Wealth Flow. *In* Determinants of Fertility Trends: Theories Re-Examined. C. Hohn and R. Macksen, eds. Pp. 75–98. Belgium: Ordina.

Chullawathi, M. K. 1985. Lay Ideas on Fecundity During a Woman's Monthly Cycle and Post-Partum till Twelve Months. Unpublished M.Sc. Project Report, Post Graduate Institute of Medicine, University of Colombo, Sri Lanka.

Claus, P. 1978. Terminological Aspects of Tuḷu Kinship. *In* American Studies in the Anthropology of India. Sylvia Vatuk, ed. Pp. 211–241. New Delhi: Manohar Press.

Contraceptive Prevalence Survey. 1983. Sri Lanka Contraceptive Prevalence Survey Report 1982. Department of Census and Statistics of the Ministry of Plan Implementation and Westinghouse Health Systems, Colombo, Sri Lanka.

Das, V. 1976. Masks and Faces: An Essay on Punjabi Kinship. Contributions to Indian Sociology NS 10(1):1–30.

Dash, Vd. B. 1975. Embryology and Maternity in Ayurveda. New Delhi: Delhi Deary.

Delaney, C. 1991. The Seed and the Soil: Gender and Cosmology in Turkish Village Society. Berkeley: University of California Press.

Delgado, H., R. Martorell, E. Brineman, and R. Klein. 1978. Nutrition, Lactation, and Post Partum Amenorrhea. American Journal of Clinical Nutrition 31:322–327.

Douglas, M. 1966. Purity and Danger. London: Routledge and Kegan Paul.

Dube, L. 1978. The Seed and the Earth: Symbolism of Human Reproduction in India. Unpublished paper presented at the Tenth International Congress of Anthropological and Ethnological Sciences, New Delhi, India.

Finch, B. E. and H. Green. 1963. Contraception Through the Ages. London: Peter Owen.

Fruzzetti, L. and A. Ostor. 1976. Seed and Earth: A Cultural Analysis of Kinship in a Bengali Town. Contributions to Indian Sociology (N.S.) 10(1):97–132.

Gould, K. 1975. Sexual Practices and Reproductive Decisions. Journal of the Christian Medical Association of India 4:547–550.

Grey, R., O. Campbell, R. Apelo, et al. 1990. Risk of Ovulation During Lactation. Lancet 335:25–29.

Hansen, F. A. 1975. Meaning in Culture. London: Routledge and Kegan Paul.

Harrel, B. 1981. Lactation and Menstruation in Cultural Perspective. American Anthropologist 83: 796–823.

Huffman, S. L., A. K. M. Chowdhury, and W. H. Mosley. 1978. Postpartum Amenorrhea: How is it Affected by Maternal Nutritional Stores? Science 200: 1155–1157.

Huffman, S. L., K. Ford, H. Allen, and P. Streble 1987. Nutrition and Fertility in Bangladesh: Breastfeeding and Post Partum Amenorrhea. Population Studies 41:447.

Hunte, P. 1985. Indigenous Methods of Fertility Regulation in Afghanistan. *In* Women's Medicine: A Cross-Cultural Study of Indigenous Fertility Regulation. L. Newman, ed. Pp. 43–75. New Brunswick, NJ: Rutgers University Press.

Inden, R. and R. Nicholas. 1977. Kinship in Bengali Culture. Chicago: Chicago University Press.

Isrongkuro, B., K. Kennedy, B. Leelapatana, and H. Cohen. 1989. Breastfeeding and Return of Ovulation in Bangkok. International Journal of Gynecology and Obstetrics 30:335–342.

Jain, A. and T. Sun. 1972. Interrelationships Between Sociodemographic Factors, Lactation, and Postpartum Amenorrhea. Demography India 1:78.

Johnson, S. and L. Snow. 1982. Assessment of Reproductive Knowledge in an Inner-City Clinic. Social Science and Medicine 16(19):1657–1662.

Johnson, S., L. Snow, and H. Mayhew. 1978. Limited Patient Knowledge as a Reproductive Risk Factor. Journal of Family Practice 6(4):855–862.

Jones, R. 1990. The Effect of Initiation of Child Supplementation on Resumption of Postpartum Menstruation. Journal of Biosocial Science 22(2):173–189.

Jordan, B. 1989. Cosmopolitical Obstetrics: Some Insights from the Training of Traditional Midwives. Social Science and Medicine 28(9):925–944.

Jordan, B. 1993. Birth in Four Cultures: A Crosscultural Investigation of Childbirth in Yucatan, Holland, Sweden, and the United States. Prospect Heights, IL: Waveland.

Kay, M. 1977. Mexican American Fertility Regulation. *In* Communicating Nursing Research. M. V. Batey, ed. Pp. 279–295. Boulder: Witche Press.

Kennedy, K. I., R. Rivera, and A. S. McNeilly. 1989. Consensus Statement on the Use of Breastfeeding as a Family Planning Method. Contraception 39(5):447–496.

Koblinsky, M., M. Campbell, and S. Harlow. 1993. Mother and More: A Broader Perspective on Women's Health. *In* The Health of Women: A Global Perspective. Marge Koblinsky, Judith Timyan, and Jill Gay, eds. Pp. 33–62. Boulder: Westview Press.

Kodagoda, N. 1986. Guidelines in Family Life Education from Sri Lanka. World Health Forum 7:281–285.

Laderman, C. 1987. Destructive Heat and Cooling Prayer: Malay Humoralism in Pregnancy, Childbirth and Postpartum Period. Social Science and Medicine 25(4):357–367.

Laing, J. 1984. Natural Family Planning in the Philippines. Studies in Family Planning 15(2):49–61.

Maloney, C., K. M. A. Aziz, and P. Sarker. 1981. Beliefs and Fertility in Bangladesh. International Center for Diarrhoeal Disease Research, Dacca, Bangladesh.

Mandelbaum, D. 1970. Human Fertility in India. Berkeley: University of California Press.

Marglin, F. 1992. Women's Blood: Challenging the Discourse of Development. The Ecologist 22(1):22–32.

Mascarenhas, M., A. Lobo, and A. Ramesh. 1979. Contraception and the Effectiveness of the Ovulation Method in India. Tropical Doctor 9: 209–211.

Mayer, A. C. 1960. Caste Kinship in Central India. Berkeley: University of California Press.

Maynard-Tucker, G. 1989. Knowledge of Reproductive Physiology and Modern Contraceptives in Rural Peru. Studies in Family Planning 20(4): 215–224.

McGilvray, D. 1982. Sexual Power and Fertility in Sri Lanka: Batticaloa Tamils and Moors. *In* Ethnography of Fertility and Birth. Carol MacCormack, ed. Pp. 25–74. London: Academic Press.

McLaren, A. 1984. Reproductive Rituals: The Perception of Fertility in England from the Sixteenth Century to the Nineteenth Century. London: Methuen Press.

Mull, D. 1992. Mother's Milk and Pseudoscientific Breastmilk Testing in Pakistan. Social Science and Medicine 34(11):1277–1290.

Nag, M. 1968. Factors Affecting Human Fertility in Non Industrial Societies: A Cross Cultural Study. Yale University Publications in Anthropology No. 66. Reprinted by the Human Relations Area Files Press.

Neff, D. 1994. The Social Construction of Infertility: The Case of Matrilineal Nayars in South India. Social Science and Medicine 39(4):475–485.

Ngin, C. S. 1985. Indigenous Fertility Regulating Methods Among Two Chinese Communities in Malaysia. *In* Women's Medicine: A Cross-Cultural Study of Indigenous Fertility Regulation. L. Newman, ed. Pp. 26–41. New Brunswick, NJ: Rutgers University Press.

Nichter, Mark. 1981a. Negotiation of the Illness Experience: The Influence of Ayurvedic Therapy on the Psychosocial Dimensions of Illness. Culture, Medicine and Psychiatry 5:5–24.

Nichter, Mark. 1981b. Idioms of Distress: Alternatives in the Expression of Psychosocial Distress. Culture, Medicine and Psychiatry 5:379–408.

Nichter, Mimi. 1982. The Use of Metaphor as a Communication Strategy. Unpublished M.A. thesis, University of Hawaii, Department of Communication.

Niehof, A. 1985. Women and Fertility in Madura. Ph.D. Dissertation, University of Leiden, Department of Social Anthropology.

Pollack, M. 1983. Health Problems in Sri Lanka: An Analysis of Morbidity and Mortality Data. American Public Health Association, Washington, DC.

Rao, M. N. and K. K. Mathur. 1970. Rural Field Study of Population Control (1957–1969). All India Institute of Hygiene and Public Health, Calcutta, India.

Reissland, N. and R. Burghart. 1988. The Quality of a Mother's Milk and the Health of Her Child: Beliefs and Practices of the Women of Mithila. Social Science and Medicine 27(5):461–469.

Ross, J. A. and E. Frankenberg. 1993. Findings From Two Decades of Family Planning Research. New York: Population Council.

Ross, J. A., W. P. Mauldwin, S. R. Green, and E. R. Cooke. 1992. Family Planning and Child Survival Programs as Assessed in 1991. New York: Population Council.

Rubel, A., K. Weller-Fahy, and M. Trosdal. 1975. Conception, Gestation and Delivery According to Some Mananabang of Cebu. Phillipine Quarterly of Culture and Society 3:131–145.

Scrimshaw, S. C. M. 1985. Bringing the Period Down: Government and Squatter Settlement Confront Induced Abortion in Ecuador. *In* Micro and Macro Levels of Analysis in Anthropology: Issues in Theory and Research. B. R. DeWalt and P. J. Pelto, eds. Pp. 121–146. Boulder: Westview Press.

Shedlin, M. 1982. Anthropology and Family Planning: Culturally Appropriate Intervention in a Mexican Community. Unpublished Ph.D. dissertation, Columbia University.

Shedlin, M., and P. Hollerbach. 1981. Modern and Traditional Fertility Regulation in a Mexican Community: The Process of Decision Making. Studies in Family Planning 12(67):278–296.

Snowden, R., and B. Christian. 1983. Patterns and Perceptions of Menstruation. A World Health Organization International Collaborative Study. London: Croom Helm.

Trautmann, T. 1981. Dravidian Kinship. Cambridge: Cambridge University Press.

Ukaegbu, A. O. 1975. Marriage and Fertility in East Central Nigeria: A Case Study of Ngwa Igbo Women. Ph.D. Thesis, University of London.

Vis, H. 1985. Commentary. *In* Maternal Nutrition and Lactational Infertility. J. Dobbing, ed. New York: Raven Press.

World Fertility Survey. 1978. First Report of the World Fertility Survey (1975). Department of Census and Statistics. Colombo, Sri Lanka.

CHAPTER 2

The Ethnophysiology and Folk Dietetics of Pregnancy: A Case Study from South India

Mark Nichter and Mimi Nichter

INTRODUCTION

A series of successive pregnancies subject most rural South Indian women to dietary restrictions for a significant part of their lives (Gopalan and Naidu 1972). While folk dietary restrictions have frequently been cited in Indian health sector reports (United States Department of Health, Education and Welfare 1979; Voluntary Health Association 1975b) as negatively affecting the health status of pregnant women among the rural poor, little attempt has been made to understand how and to what extent.[1] Even fewer studies have examined folk dietetics during pregnancy in relation to popular notions of ethnophysiology, lay health concerns, and preventive and promotive health behavior.[2] In this chapter, we investigate these issues in a coastal region of Karnataka. The first topic discussed is the relationship between a layperson's ideas about appropriate baby size and her food consumption behavior. Both the quantity and quality of food considered appropriate to eat during pregnancy are considered and alternative patterns of food preference are discussed in relation to folk health ideology. Concepts of reproductive ethnophysiology are highlighted with regard to specific dietary practices and folk medical behavior. Public health ramifications of the study are discussed and suggestions are made for the incorporation of greater anthropological perspective into nutrition education efforts.

Our interest in nutrition education should not be taken to mean that we consider malnutrition in rural India to be primarily a problem rectified by education, for this is clearly not the case. Economic considerations far outweigh the conceptual. However, simply relying on economic explanations for the food habits of rural poor pregnant women are insufficient.[3] Within the "continuum of poverty," resources are maximized to varying extent by those with similar economic capacities. Moreover, income increments among the low and lower middle classes have not been strongly associated with substantial alterations in dietary behavior (Anderson 1989, Baroda Operations Research Group 1972, Thimmayamma et al. 1976). Issues affecting dietary behavior, in addition to purchasing capacity, are health ideology, competing felt needs, and the relative importance of investing limited funds in food once a perceived minimal requirement of staple food has been reached. Our conceptual analysis of the folk dietetics followed during pregnancy is meant to complement socioeconomic analyses of income investment and nutritional analysis of nutrient intake and absorption, as well as activity levels.

STUDY AREA AND METHODOLOGY

This discussion of the folk dietetics and ethnophysiology of pregnancy draws upon ethnographic fieldwork and survey research collected during a community diagnosis of health project (Nichter 1984). The project was conducted in two districts of Karnataka: South Kanara District (*Puttur Taluk*) and North Kanara District (*Ankola Taluk*). These two field sites are approximately 300 km apart and differ significantly in respect to regional language, folk traditions, patterns of settlement and residence, levels of overall economic development, and relative health status. South Kanara is more densely populated and relatively "developed" in comparison to North Kanara. The overall health status of South Kanara District is the highest in the state, while North Kanara is ranked 11th out of 19 districts in Karnataka (Population Centre 1978). Despite their differences, both regions share many of the same features of folk health culture.

Initial fieldwork was carried out in South Kanara. Participant observation was used as a method for collecting data on general dietary patterns and special dietary practices followed during pregnancy. The dietary behavior of 10 pregnant women was periodically observed. Data on the ethnophysiology of pregnancy was obtained from both laypersons and indigenous medical specialists.

The layperson in any society rarely turns attention to the body or its processes until one of these processes malfunctions or seems to have done so by cultural criteria (Manning and Fabrega 1973, Fisher 1974). When first interviewing villagers about notions of physiology, we found that they had difficulty in speaking about body processes abstractly, although they could provide names for most major body organs. We were best able to gather data about lay notions of general physiology and the physiology of pregnancy in the context of illness by being present when the ill described their symptoms to family members or to indigenous medical specialists. Descriptions were noted down and later discussed with a variety of other informants — laypersons as well as indigenous specialists, including midwives. The accounts presented here are descriptions of *lay* informants recorded during field interviews. In some cases, notions about physiological processes are discussed in relation to physical disorders. In other cases, analogies, a common means of description used by informants to explain body processes, are highlighted.

Following the collection of ethnographic data, a data profile on the ethnophysiology and folk dietetics of pregnancy was constructed. Key ideas identified on this profile concerning levels of activity during pregnancy, appropriate dietary behavior, and preferred baby size, were developed into survey questions to ascertain their pervasiveness in the general population. The survey was conducted by local investigators who had been trained in participatory research methods as part of the community diagnosis of health project. Survey data in turn generated additional issues for follow-up ethnographic investigation.

Survey data on the perceived relationship between baby size and food consumption are presented from both North and South Kanara Districts. The data are introduced to document a general preference by rural South Indian women for small babies as well as to raise questions about the nature of folk beliefs and dietary behavior associated with this preference. The cultural reasoning behind the folk dietetics of pregnancy is discussed in the remainder of this chapter, which focuses on in-depth analysis of data from South Kanara.

BABY SIZE AND FOOD CONSUMPTION: THE BIG BABY/SMALL BABY DILEMMA

The diets of pregnant and lactating women of the low income groups are deficient in several respects. The major reason for the low intakes has been found to be the poor purchasing capacity. But an important additional reason is the practice of food taboos and food fads which prevented the intake of certain nutrient foods both during pregnancy and lactation. The fear of difficult delivery as a consequence of a large infant also prevented some pregnant women from consuming adequate amounts of food. (Voluntary Health Association 1975b)

A preference among rural Indian women for smaller babies and a tendency for pregnant women to consume less as opposed to more food has been noted in passing in anthropological, nutrition, and public health reports (Anderson 1989, Brems and Berg 1988, Katona-Apte 1973, Jeffrey et al. 1989, Mathews and Benjamin 1979, Rao 1985, Sewa Rural Research Team 1994, U.S. Department of Health, Education and Welfare 1979).[4] Common explanations as to why a small baby is desired and less food is eaten during pregnancy have been ease in delivery and fear of pain associated with difficult delivery.[5] These explanations, while relevant, tend to underestimate pregnant women's concern for the health of their babies. In reality, there are a range of factors involved with baby size preference and food consumption habits during pregnancy. Single answer or one-sided explanations tend to gloss over a complex of ideas associated with notions of ethnophysiology and preventive health.

A review of survey data on three interrelated questions serves to facilitate discussion on this complex of issues:

1. For the health of the baby, is it better for the baby to be relatively large or small at birth?

2. During pregnancy, is it better for a woman to eat a greater amount of food, the same amount of food, or less food?

3. If less food is consumed during pregnancy will the baby be large or small?

The Community Diagnosis Survey

A stratified sample of 200 rural poor households in North Kanara and 82 households in South Kanara was selected for the survey. Women who had young children were interviewed.[6] Sample selection reflected the social and demographic characteristics of the two field areas as well as assumptions maintained by health planners as to factors influencing the health behavior of the "rural poor." Informal discussions with health planners at the national, state, and regional levels revealed implicit assumptions that health behavior (not just status) would be positively influenced by any or all of the following:

increased access to government health facilities and trained medical practitioners, increased health education efforts by Primary Health Center (PHC) staff, and rises in general education and economic status.

The terms "rural" and "poor" were defined contextually. A mapping of the social landscape revealed that a trajectory of rural settlements with varying access to transportation facilities and the services of medical practitioners existed in both field areas. Three types of settlements were chosen for study: interior villages with poor access to transportation and cosmopolitan medical practitioners, roadside villages with good access to transport and a resident medical practitioner, and small crossroads towns (population 5,000 to 12,000) in which government medical facilities coexisted with the clinics of private medical practitioners. Including these three types of locales within a sampling frame provided a means of evaluating behavioral and attitudinal changes associated with increased access to a broad range of practitioners, government health facilities, and government health workers as well as greater varieties of food, medical resources, and communications media. In order to select representative settlements for sampling, the general distribution of health resources was ascertained by making a crude spot map of all available practitioners (traditional, eclectic, and allopathic). This endeavor was undertaken with the assistance of PHC field workers, local chemists, herbal merchants, and local practitioners.

Relative levels of poverty on the poverty continuum were defined by community advisors selected from the local population. For the purposes of this chapter, economic status is discussed in relation to a higher and lower strata among the rural poor. Both samples were also stratified by educational status and caste culture. The educational status of women informants is discussed in relation to two levels: illiterate women and literate women who had attended school beyond third standard but not beyond ninth standard. In North Kanara, specific castes were the primary unit of study. Residence in North Kanara was primarily in single-caste nucleated settlement, making for caste-centered social networks. In South Kanara where multicaste non-nucleated settlements and social networks were prevalent, broader caste groups were surveyed (see Table 2.1).

Chi-square tests in many cases reveal statistically significant differences ($p < 0.05$) between responses from North Kanara and South Kanara, which is more densely populated, more economically "developed," and where the aggregate health status is relatively high.

Question 1: For the health of the baby, is it better for the baby to be relatively large or small at birth?[7] A majority of informants from both regions expressed a preference for a relatively small baby. The preference for a small baby was significantly more common in North Kanara (see Table

Table 2.1

Survey Sample Characteristics

Variable	South Kanara (*n* = 82)	North Kanara (*n* = 200)
Locale		
Town	29 (35%)	58 (29%)
Progressive roadside village	28 (34%)	21 (11%)
Interior village	25 (30%)	121 (60%)
Economic Status		
Very poor, family monthly income Rs. 100–300	52 (63%)	136 (68%)
Intermediate poor, family monthly income Rs. 301–600	30 (37%)	64 (32%)
Education		
Illiterate	65 (79%)	148 (74%)
Literate	17 (21%)	52 (26%)
Caste		
	Brahman 6 (7%)	Karve 5 (2.5%)
	Christian 8 (10%)	Chamagara & Holeya 9 (4.5%)
	Muslim 10 (12%)	Kamapanth 10 (5%)
	Harijan 18 (22%)	Ambiga 13 (6.5%)
	Shudra 40 (49%)	Achari, Kalasi & Madivala 13 (6.5%)
		Sonagar & Vaisha 14 (7%)
		Harikant 20 (10%)
		Nadava 21 (10.5%)
		Ager 25 (12.5%)
		Namdhari 30 (15%)
		Halakki Gowda 40 (20%)

2.2). Chi-square tests revealed that within each region the frequency of people who prefer a relatively small or large baby did not differ significantly according to locale, economic class, literacy, or caste.

Table 2.2

Preferred Baby Size

	Size of baby		
	Small	Large	Total
South Kanara ($n = 82$)	55 (67%)	27 (33%)	82
North Kanara ($n = 200$)	180 (90%)	20 (10%)	200
Total	235	47	282

$\chi^2 = 20.4; p < 0.001$.

Question 2: During pregnancy, is it better for a woman to eat a greater amount of food, the same amount of food, or less food? Considerable ambivalence from women was encountered when we tried to differentiate whether they thought it better to eat less food during pregnancy or to eat a normal staple diet. Response to the question most often contrasted "less food or the same amount of food" with "more food." The amount of work the pregnant woman was doing at any given time, the season, or her general state of health made it difficult to differentiate less from the usual diet in a precise manner.

A majority of informants from both regions thought it advisable to eat less or the same amount of food as opposed to increasing food intake. This was especially true for the first pregnancy and particularly the case in the last trimester of pregnancy. Significantly fewer women in North Kanara believed in restricting the quantity of food eaten (see Table 2.3). Chi-square tests revealed that within each region, the quantity of food regarded as appropriate did not differ significantly with respect to locale, literacy, or caste.

In South Kanara, a greater number of the very poor thought it appropriate to restrict food intake during pregnancy. A significantly greater percentage, but not a majority, of the relatively better off deemed it better to eat more food during pregnancy (see Table 2.4).

Also, in South Kanara a significantly greater proportion of those who preferred a small baby regarded it appropriate to restrict food intake during pregnancy. Of those who wanted a large baby, a significantly greater proportion said they ate more food during pregnancy (see Table 2.5).

Table 2.3

Appropriate Amount of Food Consumed During Pregnancy

	Quantity of food eaten		
Region	Less or the the same	Greater quantity	Total
South Kanara (*n* = 82)	61 (74%)	21 (26%)	82
North Kanara (*n* = 200)	120 (60%)	80 (40%)	200
Total	181 (64%)	101 (36%)	282

$\chi^2 = 4.63; p < 0.05$.

Table 2.4

South Kanara: Appropriate Amount of Food Consumed During Pregnancy

	Quantity of staple foods eaten		
Economic status	Less/same	Greater	Total
Very poor (*n* = 52)	42 (83%)	9 (17%)	52
Intermediate poor (*n* = 30)	18 (60%)	12 (40%)	30
Total	61 (74%)	21 (26%)	82

$\chi^2 = 4.02; p < 0.05$.

In North Kanara, almost all women preferred a small baby. Appropriate food quantity did not differ significantly according to baby size preference (see Table 2.6). Of the total sample population, 33% of the women who stated a preference for a small baby also deemed it appropriate to consume more food. A question arose as to whether the association of more food with

Table 2.5

South Kanara: Preferred Baby Size in Relation to Appropriate Food Consumption

Appropriate amount of food to eat	Preferred baby size		Total
	Small	Large	
Same or less food	50 (82%)	11 (18%)	61
More food	6 (29%)	15 (71%)	21
Total	56 (68%)	26 (32%)	82

$\chi^2 = 17.8$; $p < 0.0001$.

Table 2.6

North Kanara: Preferred Baby Size in Relation to Appropriate Food Consumption

Appropriate amount of food to eat	Preferred baby size		Total
	Small	Large	
Same or less food	108 (90%)	12 (10%)	120
More food	72 (90%)	8 (10%)	80
Total	180 (90%)	20 (10%)	200

$\chi^2 = 0.06$; n.s.

smaller baby size revealed a mode of reasoning or whether chance or error had determined the responses of the 78 women (Tables 2.5 and 2.6).

To query the possibility that women might think that eating more food resulted in a smaller baby, the following question was posed: "If a pregnant woman eats less food while carrying on a normal work routine, will the baby be relatively large or small?"

Table 2.7

Baby Size When Less Food Is Consumed

Region	Small	Large	Total
South Kanara ($n = 82$)	36 (44%)	46 (56%)	82
North Kanara ($n = 200$)	82 (41%)	118 (59%)	200
Total	118 (42%)	164 (58%)	282

$\chi^2 = 0.34$; n.s.

Table 2.8

**South Kanara: Baby Size When Less Food Is Consumed
(Breakdown by Locale)**

| Locale | Baby size when eating less | | Total |
	Small	Large	
Town	8 (28%)	21 (72%)	29
Roadside village	10 (36%)	18 (64%)	28
Interior village	18 (72%)	7 (28%)	25
Total	36 (44%)	46 (56%)	82

$\chi^2 = 11.86$; $p < 0.001$.

Question 3: If less food is consumed during pregnancy, will the baby be large or small? More than 50% of respondents in each region associated eating less with having a large baby. Looking at responses by locale, the percentage of women giving this response was not significantly different (see Table 2.7). In North Kanara, chi-square tests revealed no significant differences according to locale, economic status, literacy, or caste.

Table 2.9

South Kanara: Baby Size When Less Food Is Consumed (Breakdown by Economic Class)

| Economic class | Baby size when eating less | | Total |
	Small	Large	
Very poor	18 (35%)	34 (65%)	52
Intermediate poor	18 (60%)	12 (40%)	30
Total	36 (44%)	46 (56%)	82

$\chi^2 = 4.0; p < 0.05.$

In South Kanara, chi-square tests revealed that baby size thought to result from restricted food intake varies significantly according to locale and economic class. A greater proportion of women from interior villages associate eating less with having a small baby, and a greater proportion of roadside villagers and townspeople associate eating less with having a larger baby (see Table 2.8). A greater proportion of the very poor associate eating less with having a larger baby and the greater proportion of the intermediate poor associate eating less with having a small baby (see Table 2.9).

GENERAL IMPLICATIONS OF THE SURVEY

A majority of rural poor women in both field areas expressed the opinion that for the health of the baby, a relatively small baby at birth was preferable to a large baby. Differences in responses of rural poor women within each region were not significantly related to differences in economic strata (of the poor), locale (in the rural continuum), educational backgrounds (literacy), or caste communities.[8]

In general, more women considered it appropriate to eat less or the same amount of food during pregnancy as opposed to more food. Differences in the distribution of this opinion among rural poor women respondents within each region was not significantly related to locale, educational background, or caste community. Data suggest that relative economic status may influence opinion on this issue. In South Kanara, but not in North Kanara, economic status was significantly related to ideas about appropriate food intake during pregnancy. A greater percentage of the very poor think it advisable to eat less or the same amount of food during pregnancy than the relatively better off. In North Kanara, however, no such association was found.

Mixed ideas exist as to whether eating less will produce a larger or smaller baby. Three questions warranting follow-up investigation were generated by the survey data: (1) What kinds of ideas exist as to how food consumption affects baby size? (2) How is a large baby viewed? (3) What are the conceptual and behavioral factors that influence whether a woman eats more or less or the same during pregnancy?

ETHNOGRAPHIC RESEARCH ON FOLK DIETETICS DURING PREGNANCY IN SOUTH KANARA: FOOD CONSUMPTION AND BABY SIZE

From our perspective, it is understandable why some informants associated the eating of less food with small baby size. But what reasoning underlies an alternative association of less food intake with larger baby size? An understanding of this association requires a consideration of the ethnophysiology of pregnancy, most notably the concept of *baby space*.

While South Kanarese women distinguish between the womb and belly, this distinction is blurred during pregnancy and referred to more generally as the location where a baby "grows." In Tuḷu, the term may be used to refer to the stomach or womb during pregnancy. A pregnant woman is referred to as a *bañjinālu* (Manners 1886).[9] The custom of stomach binding after delivery practiced by some women reflects the association of baby space and stomach space. It is believed that if the stomach is not bound tightly after the delivery, the large space that the baby occupied will remain and will require large quantities of rice to fill it.

The fetus is viewed as growing in a space occupied by food, wind (gas from gaseous foods), and according to some villagers, urine. Many women noted that the *more space* occupied by other substances, the *less space* the baby would have in which to grow. Accordingly, these women deemed the eating of more food to result in a smaller baby. This notion, in conjunction with a general preference for a relatively small baby provides the rationale for a number of folk dietetic patterns. A few dietary restrictions and lay medical practices followed during pregnancy may further illustrate this point.

A notion exists that a baby must have enough space for movement during pregnancy if a baby's proper development is to occur. For this reason, pregnant women avoid the consumption of gaseous (*vāyu*) foods such as sweet potato, jackfruit, bengal gram, and dhal. These foods are believed to cramp the living space of the fetus, making the baby roll in the stomach and causing, in extreme cases, the umbilical cord to get wrapped around the fetus' neck. Pregnant women commonly link breathlessness to cramped body space — the cramping of the body space shared by baby, food, air, and urine.[10] When breathlessness occurs, women may opt to eat less or attempt to urinate more as a means of reducing this symptom. Some women remove liquid from their stomachs by consuming herbal remedies with diuretic properties, such as cumin and aniseed to increase the frequency of urination. These women believe that more frequent urination will increase "baby space." They also think it decreases the risk of a baby consuming urine, a factor linked to the bloated "large" appearance of some stillborn and sickly babies.

How is a Large Baby Viewed?

The previous reference to sickly babies having a bloated appearance introduces an important dimension to the small baby preference issue. A big baby is not necessarily viewed as a healthy baby. A popular distinction drawn by villagers in discussing body image is between a muscular (*puśti*) body associated with vitality and strength (*dhātu*) and a body characterized by "loose watery flesh." One's *dhātu* is often spoken of both in reference to strength and the capacity to maintain positive health (Nichter 1986). Villagers speak of wanting a strong *puśti* baby and not a large "puffy" baby. It is not simply that South Indian women want a small baby for ease in delivery; they want a baby having strength and positive survival characteristics.

A better understanding of attitudes toward size and strength may be gained by considering analogies posed by villagers when discussing this topic. Villagers noted, for example, that despite the small grain size of indigenous rice in comparison to larger hybrid varieties, indigenous rice was rich in *dhātu*, required less fertilizer and nutrients for growth, and was more durable than hybrid grain varieties. In a similar manner, villagers noted that while a large baby of a landlord fed solely on prestigious tinned formula might have a large impressive body (like the fat landlord), such a body had little strength or capacity for hard work. This type of body was compared to a jackfruit, which is large in size but from which one derives little strength or sustenance, or a *chevu* plant, which if manured grows quickly but is of no practical use or benefit to anyone.

Another association between large babies and ill health centers on what villagers describe as a "puffy" baby: a baby who, though large in appearance, is bloated. We did not personally have the opportunity to see the type of puffy baby described by informants as large and unhealthy, nor were we able to collect reliable data on the incidence of such babies. Some of the symptoms of puffy babies suggest the possibility of a child born to a diabetic mother, a child born of a mother subjected to extensive sulfur medication, or some malfunction of a fetus' ability to take in nutrients and expel wastes. The incidence rate of such babies is perhaps not as important as the notoriety resulting from the birth and subsequent death of a bloated baby. Also relevant, infants who exhibit swelling as a sign of protein calorie malnutrition are often described by parents as being "like that from birth" or having a "constitution" predisposed to this body condition. By constitutional rationale, swelling during infancy is associated post facto with actual or attributed puffiness at birth.

FACTORS INFLUENCING THE DIETARY BEHAVIOR OF PREGNANT WOMEN

In addition to baby size, a number of factors influence the dietary behavior of pregnant women, or at least are employed as explanations for their dietary behavior. These factors include physical activity levels, constitution, and morning sickness. With regard to the first factor, some pregnant women eat less food because they believe that the need for food and one's digestive power are related to one's level of physical activity. For example, an infant who has not yet begun to actively crawl about the house is thought to require less food and water than an infant who is very active. With regard to adults, when the work load of a pregnant woman is decreased during a slack work season, her food intake during that trimester of pregnancy may also be reduced. Slack work seasons are also times of economic difficulty so the rationale cited may be a justification for scarce resources not being more favorably allocated to pregnant women. On the other hand, two cases were recorded where women opted to reduce their food consumption due to decreased physical activity, although they had the resources to maintain, if not increase, their food intake.

A second factor used to explain the quantity of food eaten during pregnancy is body constitution. Many informants emphasized that appropriate food consumption for pregnant women varied in accordance with their body constitution (*prakṛti*). Poor appetite and limited digestive capacity associated with malnutrition were sometimes observed to be interpreted as constitutional attributes of a woman. For example, one woman with a long-standing riboflavin deficiency manifested as angular stomatitis was compelled by folk health ideology to eat a rather bland, tasteless diet (i.e., without chillies) for several months. This restrictive diet further exacerbated her existing state of malnutrition. Concordant with her restricted diet came appetite loss, measured by the amount of rice she consumed. Over time, the family spoke of her angular stomatitis (cracking at the corners of the mouth) as constitutional — as indicative of a predisposition toward heat — also revealed by dry skin and brittle hair. The woman's diminished appetite came to be interpreted as a normal proclivity rather than a state of ill health that had developed. During her pregnancy, this woman consumed a meager diet even by local standards. Her food intake did not attract attention, however, because it was seen as "constitutional." An observation cited by informants in support of an association between constitution, appetite, and food need was that some people who are continually hungry eat a lot but remain thin, while others eat less and appear to gain weight.

Morning Sickness: Heat and Toxicity in the Body

A third factor influencing both the quantity of food eaten during pregnancy and the interpretation of pregnancy desires is morning sickness. Morning sickness is an important factor limiting the amount of food a woman will eat regardless of her ideas about the optimum quantity of food to eat for the health of the fetus. A number of explanatory models of morning sickness coexist. Some women view dizziness and nausea during pregnancy as hereditary, others as a toxic reaction, and still others as caused by an increase in *pitta* and bodily heat.

Pitta, an *āyurvedic* term generally translated as bile, is for the layperson a symptom complex associated with dizziness and nausea, yellow excretions from the body, a bitter taste in the mouth, and overheat in the body. Some informants viewed nausea and vomiting as signs that a pregnant woman's desires had not been satiated and postulated a causal relationship between increased desire, heat, and *pitta*. Others linked *pitta* to an increase in bodily heat resulting from the process of pregnancy. According to folk medical tradition (no doubt influenced by *āyurveda*), sour is a taste identified with reducing *pitta* symptoms. For this reason, pregnancy cravings for sour fruits such as unripe mango or lemon were interpreted by some informants as the body seeking to reduce *pitta*.

The discussion of morning sickness introduces two important health concerns that influence the quality of foods eaten during pregnancy: heat and toxicity. Pregnancy is considered by villagers to be a time of increased body heat. An analogy is sometimes drawn between a woman's body being heated in the same way as a fruit is heated during the process of ripening. Most fruits are deemed by villagers to be hot in their unripe state and relatively cool when ripe. As in the process of ripening, pregnancy is a time of rapid transformation and development and a woman's body is naturally hot during this process. Her body becomes cool when the baby is fully ripened and she delivers.

While increased heat is deemed natural during pregnancy, villagers believe that overheat is dangerous. Minor swelling of the hands and feet are seen as ubiquitous signs of increased heat in the body during pregnancy and are not paid much concern.[11] Burning sensation during urination, scanty urine, or white discharge are taken more seriously as signs of significant overheat. These conditions are generally treated by herbal medicines or diet as opposed to cosmopolitan medicines, because the latter are generally ascribed to be heating for the body and thus contraindicated during pregnancy.

Miscarriage is commonly attributed to overheat in the body, as is the delivery of a premature child. The very classification of a premature baby is linked to ideas involving the effect of overheat. One way in which women determine whether a baby is premature is by the absence of head hair. Baldness is attributed to an excess of heat in the body. Premature babies are treated by lay therapy which places emphasis on cooling the baby. One method of cooling the baby included smearing the baby with "cooling" algae from the bottom of a well.

The eating of foods classified as heating are decreased if not restricted during pregnancy in order that a pregnant woman's already heated body not become excessively hot, resulting in miscarriage. For this reason, fruits considered heating, such as papaya and pineapple, heating vegetables such as pumpkin (*Curcurbita maxima*), bitter gourd (*Momordica charantia*) and bamboo shoots, and heating grains such as wheat are avoided. The intake of salt, a heating substance, is likewise reduced. The consumption of foods classified as cooling is advocated, including such items as tender coconut water, greengram, millet, amaranth, and cumin.

A second health concern during pregnancy that illustrates notions of ethnophysiology is toxicity. During pregnancy a woman's body is considered to be prone to toxicity (*nañju*). An excess of toxins accumulates during pregnancy due to the retention of impure blood usually expelled during menstruation. Several informants noted a propensity for pregnant women to develop wound infections and linked this to blood impurity. If a woman becomes pregnant during lactation and has not yet resumed her menstrual cycle, especially high levels of retained toxins are thought to exist in the body. Concern is expressed that the developing fetus will suffer problems, linked to *nañju*, such as skin infections. A man's sperm, a foreign substance retained inside a woman during pregnancy, is also spoken of as *nañju*.[12] In the first trimester of pregnancy, if a woman experiences discomfort or morning sickness, others may describe this as the effect of the husband's *nañji* growing inside her, *nañji buḷenaga seeksankaḍa jāsti*.

During pregnancy the eating of foods classified as *nañju* producing or *nañju* aggravating are contraindicated. These foods include jackfruit and unctuous vegetables such as brinjal, vine spinach, and drumstick. They also include some of the most commonly eaten and valuable sources of protein, including popular varieties of fish (most notably Indian mackerel, prawns, shellfish, and crab) and blackgram. Herbal decoctions prepared from the bark of *benga* (*Pterocarpus marsupium*) and *poṅgāre* (*Erythinia indica*) are consumed, as they are considered to both purify and cool the blood. These decoctions are warranted when signs of *nañju* and overheat, such as swelling in the hands or feet, appear. Aside from the possibility of a baby being harmed by the *nañju* present in a mother's blood, the baby can be affected by gulping *nañju* food (or urine) while in utero. Folk medicines, such as aniseed and cumin decoctions, are consumed by pregnant women to increase urination as a means of purification. In some families, newborn babies are force-fed water to make them vomit out impurities or will be given the juice of *kēpaḷa* (*Ixorea coccina*) flowers to prevent "bad" water from entering the baby's system. In other areas of South India, babies are fed a spoonful of castor oil for similar reasons (Katona-Apte 1973).

The appearance of vernix on newborn babies is taken as a sign that the mother did not follow a proper diet during pregnancy. Foods such as jackfruit and beaten rice are thought to cause this pastiness on the skin of the newborn — a condition concordant with the physical properties of these foods. To avoid the formation of the vernix on the baby, some pregnant women in the second trimester of pregnancy regularly eat a handful of rice chaff followed by a spoonful of hot oil mixed with water as a means of ensuring a "clean" baby at delivery. This mixture is somewhat like the materials a woman uses to cleanse her body while taking an oil bath. Poor women noted that the wealthy who can afford to consume clarified butter (*ghee*) during pregnancy do not have babies with vernix, as the *ghee* cleanses the baby's skin. One popular midwife in South Kanara encouraged her clients to consume a raw egg mixed with hot water once a week as its slippery consistency was thought to reduce vernix formation.

FOLK DIETETICS AND INDIGENOUS HEALTH CONCERNS: RAMIFICATIONS FOR PUBLIC HEALTH

Folk dietary patterns followed during pregnancy by rural South Kanarese women have public health ramifications.[13] As a means of highlighting nutritional aspects of these dietary patterns, we may consider how women qualitatively and quantitatively alter their diet when pregnant in accordance with health ideology. In respect to the quantitative intake of food we may consider the probable caloric and protein intake of rural women who do and do not increase their diet during the second trimester of pregnancy.

Our computations are only estimates based largely on impressionistic self-report data, cross-checked when possible by spot observational visits. Inasmuch as the correspondence between dietary reports and actual behavior is known to vary significantly among some groups, additional observational and food quantification research is indicated.[14] Our interview data from 10 pregnant women who stated they consumed on an average slightly less than their normal diet were cross-checked four times a month (at different meal times) by local interviewers known to informant families and of similar economic status. By and large, periodic spot visits during food consumption substantiated informant accounts. The variety of foods consumed was checked by seven day food recall studies requiring daily self-reports to local interviewers during each trimester of pregnancy.

Ten women were also interviewed who stated they consumed more food during their last pregnancy. Unfortunately, pregnant women who considered increased food intake appropriate and within their means were not identified for observation during the project. Our data on these women are therefore entirely impressionistic and based on self- and family reports.

One of the issues central to our study of the folk dietetics of pregnancy was the well reported relationship between maternal dietary habits, infant birth weight, and child mortality.[15] As a means of emphasizing the practical implications of this study and the need for additional research on food intake, we present as background a brief review of nutritional studies in rural India with special attention directed toward pregnant women as a group at risk.

Based on studies carried out by the National Institute of Nutrition, Gopalan et al. (1971) estimated that women of reproductive age (15–45 years) represented 21.2% of India's population and that at any given time 20 million women were pregnant. More recently, it has been noted that between 24–30% of women of reproductive age in rural India are either pregnant or nursing (Anderson 1989).

It has been estimated that between 50 and 70% of the rural population of South India has protein-calorie malnutrition (Cantor Associates 1973, Dandekar and Rath 1971).[16] If the data on maternal food intake during pregnancy presented in this chapter are at all representative of rural South India, there is good reason to believe that pregnant women are especially at risk to malnutrition.[17] In addition to protein-calorie malnutrition, 30–50% of South Indian pregnant women suffer from anemia (hemoglobin below 10 g per 100 ml).[18] The nutrient stores of those having successive pregnancies are continually depleted.

Malnutrition among pregnant women contributes significantly to high rates of pregnancy wastage, maternal mortality, low birth weight babies, infant mortality, and low nutrient stores in infants as well as mothers during lactation. Pregnancy wastage among those consuming less than 1,850 kcal and 44 g protein daily has been estimated at 30% (Gopalan and Naidu 1972).[19] Anemia has been directly responsible for 10–20% of maternal deaths and in another 20% it has been cited as a contributing factor (Gopalan et al. 1971, Indian Council of Medical Research 1975).[20] The livers of infants born to mothers of low socioeconomic groups contain only 60% of expected iron, folate, and vitamin B_{12} stores (Indian Council of Medical Research 1975). Such children are at greater risk of developing anemia in early infancy. Anemia in women and infants results in a compromised immune system making them more susceptible to disease.

Forty-six percent of all deaths in India occur among children 0 to four years of age. A closer consideration of the age distribution of these deaths reveals that 60% occur between the ages of one day and 12 months. Nineteen percent of infant deaths occur in the first week of life, 14% between eight and 28 days after birth, and 17% occur between one to six months after birth (Prema 1978, USAID 1980). While the infant mortality rate of India is approximately 129/1,000, studies have found that infant mortality rates for babies weighing 2,000 g is approximately 350/1,000, for babies weighing 2,001–2,501 g, 250/1,000, and for babies weighing 2,501 g or greater, 85/1,000 (USAID 1980).[21] It is estimated that a contributing cause of 44% of infant deaths (0 to six months) is low birth weight.[22]

Patterns of Dietary Prescription and Restriction

When a male member of a family is ill, it is not uncommon for the diet of the family to be altered to accord with indigenous dietary prescriptions, or for the man to be offered special foods. Males also receive preferential treatment in the allocation of staple food resources during times of health as well as during times of illness, when special foods perceived to be important for health are secured on their behalf. In contrast, when a woman is ill or pregnant, provisions for securing special foods are rarely made.[23] As in the case of the woman with angular stomatitis discussed earlier, many women avoid eating foodstuffs prepared for the family which are contraindicated during illness or pregnancy. They rarely alter the family diet for their own benefit or purchase special foods. Among the poor, observations of pregnant women revealed that dietary *restrictions* influence dietary behavior far more than the dietary *prescriptions* reported to us.[24] For example, during pregnancy, the commonly eaten nutrient-rich, low-cost foods listed in Table 2.10 are either consumed less or not at all by women — even when available to other family members. The consumption of nutrient-rich prescriptive foods, such as greengram (B complex, protein), millet (protein, calcium), or coriander and cumin (iron), were not observed to increase significantly unless frank symptoms of overheat were prominent.

Returning to the survey data initially presented, we find that 180 of the 282 women (64%) surveyed stated that it was best to consume the same if not less rice when pregnant. Ten South Kanarese women (of intermediate poor families) who reported they were eating less or the same amount of rice (parboiled) during and before pregnancy were periodically observed. A median estimate as to their rice intake during the second trimester was 430 g of rice per day during a season of more plentiful food.[25] This would yield approximately 1,500 kcal and 36.6 g of protein a day. From spot field observations of actual dietary practices we would estimate another 100–300 kcal and 4–8 g of protein intake a day by way of other foodstuffs. Taking 2,500 kcal and 55 g of protein as the nutrient requirement for the second trimester of pregnancy, we would estimate that the aforementioned group of rural women meet, at best, 72% of their caloric requirement during this time frame.[26] While 80% of their crude protein requirements appears to be met, protein is not maximized for growth until basic calorie requirements are fulfilled, so protein is expended for calories.

One hundred and two informants (36%) favored an increase in the consumption of rice during pregnancy. Notably, however, most of these informants stated that they were in no position to satisfy their present needs let alone increase their intake. Only 10 women who believed increased rice consumption was appropriate were in an economic position to consume rice equivalent to felt needs. These women were interviewed regarding the approximate amount of rice they consumed daily during the second trimester of their most recent pregnancy. From an analysis of impressionistic data, an estimated mean of 600 g of rice was consumed per day by these 10 women. This would yield 2,634 kcal and 51 g of protein. Add to this another 300 kcal and 8 g of

Table 2.10

Examples of Nutrient-Rich Foods
Restricted During Pregnancy

Food	Reason for restrictions	Otherwise scarce nutrient found in this food
Vine spinach	consistency (i.e., unctuous)	vitamin A, calcium, iron
Drumstick	toxic, heating	iron, calcium
Bengal gram	gaseous	B complex, protein
Blackgram	gaseous, toxic	B complex, protein
Groundnuts	toxic	B complex, protein
Beaten rice	fear of vernix	calcium, iron
Soy-enriched wheat bulgar	heating	protein
Indian mackerel, prawns, shellfish	toxic	protein, calcium

protein from other foods and both a pregnant woman's calorie and crude (not amino-specific) protein requirements are met.

Economics aside, it would appear that notions of ethnophysiology and preferred baby size result in dietary behavior that significantly affects nutritional status. This is true in a complex of ways, for increased or decreased food consumption may be related to either having a large or small baby. It is assumed by some health planners that changes in attitude toward baby size and dietary behavior will come with increased primary education, contact with health personnel, and contact with the media. Field observation and survey data did not substantiate this view among the continuum of the rural poor. Economic stratum was associated with a greater preference for increased consumption of food (but not a large baby) in South Kanara, but not in North Kanara. Education and locale (access to the media) did not significantly affect baby size preference or notions of appropriate dietary behavior.

We would suggest that one reason education has had little impact on ideas about maternal food consumption and baby size is that indigenous health concerns and notions of ethnophysiology have not been appreciated or addressed. Nonappreciation of indigenous health concerns has led to ethnocentricity such as health messages that emphasize baby size rather than baby strength, a more appropriate indigenous health concern. The ramifications of this oversight are highlighted by a brief consideration of the reactions of some villagers to preventive medicines promoted by Government PHC field staff which reflect the large baby theme.

Health Concerns and Medicine Taking Behavior During Pregnancy

Notions of ethnophysiology affect medicine taking behavior as well as folk dietetics during pregnancy. This has already been noted in a discussion of the health concern "overheat" and women's reluctance to consume medicines perceived as heating (see Chapter 7). We now consider the theme of baby size and the response of the rural population to three important preventive medicines offered to pregnant women free of charge: ferrous sulfate, tetanus toxoid, and multivitamin tablets.

During a survey focusing on the lay population's maximization of existing health resources, we noted a reluctance by pregnant women to receive these preventive medications from PHC staff in both field areas. This was true even among those women who had already been assisted, or were planning on being assisted by a government nurse midwife during delivery. Interviews with pregnant women revealed that these three medications were highly suspect. They were not suspected of being family planning medications, as we first imagined, but were rejected because of their attributed characteristics. Black ferrous sulfate tablets, for example, were perceived by many villagers as weakening the blood or interfering with the digestive process, as opposed to producing blood (see Chapter 7). Pregnant women perceive a tablet as an inappropriate form of medication because a hard pill is believed to be difficult to digest and is thought to share the same body space as the fetus. In a medicine preference survey, 100 informants were nearly unanimous in their opinion that a liquid tonic — and not tablets — constituted an appropriate medication form for use during pregnancy and the postpartum period. This is one reason why liquid *āyurvedic* tonics are so popular during these times. These tonics are perceived as easily digestible, blood producing, and *dhātu* promoting.

Another reason for not taking ferrous sulfate — omitting it entirely or taking only one pill instead of the recommended three — involved the manner in which PHC staff promoted the supplement. Health staff commonly stated that the tablets were "good for health" and a "tonic to produce a big baby."[27] While this explanation might be appropriate in a Western context or for those with a cosmopolitan orientation, it is quite inappropriate for the lay population in rural South India. Our interviews revealed that many village women perceived ferrous sulfate tablets as a powerful and heating medicine capable of producing a large, but not necessarily healthy, baby.

An unfortunate association was drawn between ferrous sulfate and tetanus toxoid. The latter was considered an "injection tonic." Tetanus toxoid was rarely named or explained to villagers in relation to tetanus, a disease for which an indigenous term (*dhanurvāta*) exists. It was rather ambiguously described in the same manner as ferrous sulfate — "good for health, a tonic for a big baby." What is unfortunate about this representation of ferrous sulfate and tetanus toxoid as tonics causing large babies is that folk health concerns could have been employed judiciously to explain these medications more accurately and in a more culturally sensitive manner. Ferrous sulfate could just as easily have been presented as a medicine for increasing blood and strength in the mother and baby. Tetanus toxoid could have been presented as a medicine that decreased a particular toxicity to which pregnant women are prone.

In a related manner, multivitamin tablets provided freely by ANMs (auxiliary nurse midwives) during pregnancy are rejected by village women. For a rice eater, a state of normality and good health is measured against a set of routine body signs: food transit time, routine defecation patterns, urine color, urine frequency, and so forth (Nichter 1986). One normal body sign for South Indian rice eaters is clear urine. Yellow urine is deemed a sign of *pitta* and overheat, a condition for which medication is sought and a condition believed to be particularly dangerous during pregnancy. On three separate occasions, we observed women consulting a traditional practitioner about *pitta* related symptoms (yellow urine, dizziness, nausea, burning sensation) after having been given "pills" by PHC staff for one reason or another. In one case, the pills given by the PHC staff had been taken two weeks previously, resulting in yellow urine. The other symptoms that concerned the women (nausea and vomiting) were post facto linked to the pills and the incidence of yellow urine. The pills had been discontinued after one day of use.

One last case dramatically illustrates how notions of ethnophysiology affect medicine taking behavior during pregnancy. During a PHC deworming campaign a pregnant woman whose feces were tested was found to be infected with common roundworm (*ascaris lumbricoides*). When it was suggested by a young government midwife that she take piperazine citrate to rid herself of worms, the woman, and in fact her entire neighborhood, were shocked at what they considered most harmful advice. Within local conceptualization, any medicine heating enough to rid one of worms was certainly heating enough to place one at risk to an miscarriage. Culturally inappropriate advice such as this served to undermine faith in government health programs, not just individual staff.

CONCLUSION

There are many ways of approaching the study of folk dietary behavior. In the South Kanara study, we found it more advantageous to focus on what a pregnant woman does to enhance her chances of delivering a healthy baby than to dwell on either what she does not do or on her fears of a difficult delivery. One reason for this study was to generate information useful to health educators in their efforts to reduce infant mortality and maternal morbidity by increasing maternal weight gain during pregnancy. Our research suggests that it is doubtful that village women will be easily convinced to eat more (even where resources permit this) by stressing that a large baby is good for health. An alternative approach to education which addresses preexisting health concerns and notions of ethnophysiology may be better received by this population.

Increased awareness of the relationship between ethnophysiology, folk health concerns, and folk dietetics could do much to generate alternative approaches to nutrition education that are culturally appropriate (Nichter and Nichter 1981). For example, data on the folk dietetics of pregnancy suggest culturally appropriate themes for nutrition education efforts, such as baby space, baby strength, blood purity, health as full bloodedness, and *dhātu* as an indigenous concept of promotive health. Lack of sensitivity to such themes may prove detrimental to public health efforts. The poor response of pregnant women in South Kanara to ferrous sulfate and tetanus toxoid is a case in point.[28] Attempting to alter diet without paying credence to folk dietetics is like attempting to fix a roof (nutrition program) without paying attention to the foundations (notions of ethnophysiology) or pillars (health concerns, felt needs) of the house.

NOTES

1. A notable addition to this work is a dissertation by Anderson (1989) in which she documents food consumption practices among pregnant women in Gujarat and Maharastra. Fifty-eight percent of women in Gujarat and 42% of the

women in Maharastra reported eating less during pregnancy. In contrast, only 12% and 15% of women in Gujarat and Maharastra, respectively, said that they consumed more food.

2. For example, numerous studies have discussed dietary restrictions and pre-scriptions during illness, pregnancy, confinement, lactation, and weaning with reference to the hot–cold conceptual framework. Some of these studies have made reference to notions of physiology found within the classical humoral doctrines of great traditions, yet a paucity of data exists on lay concepts of physiology as they relate to notions of hot and cold. It is noteworthy that there is not a single reference to a study of lay notions of physiology in relation to diet in Christine Wilson's annotated bibliographies (1973, 1979) on studies of culture and diet.

3. While some studies have shown that birth weights follow a socioeconomic gradient (Prema 1978), others have pointed out the limitations of economic explanations for dietary behavior (Taylor et al. 1978a).

4. In a survey conducted by Matthews and Benjamin (1979) in Tamil Nadu, few if any women were found to eat anything extra during pregnancy and many did not feel that lack of food would harm the baby. In survey areas not influenced by a health education project, between 38% and 93% of women did not feel less food would harm their baby and between 76% and 88% did not eat more during pregnancy. In a later survey commissioned by the Indian Ministry of Health and Family Welfare (1985), it was found that a significant percentage of private practitioners and indigenous midwives, in addition to mothers, disapproved of increasing food consumption during pregnancy. In Gujarat, for example, 45% of mothers and 78% of private practitioners deemed it unwise to increase food consumption. Preference for a small baby has been noted in several other areas of the world from East Africa to Latin and South America, Malaysia, the Philippines, and Burma (Cruz 1970, Foll 1959, Fuglesang 1982, Gonzales and Behar 1966, Good 1980, Harfouche 1970, Katona-Apte 1977, Kay 1980, Sharma 1955, Todhunter 1973, Trant 1954, Wellin 1955). Brems and Berg (1988) provide an updated list.

5. Mothers in other South Asian contexts (Reissland and Burghart 1989) have expressed more fear of a large baby or a small birth passage than of the positioning of the baby as a problem causing difficulties in delivery.

6. All women informants had at least one living child under seven years of age and two thirds had a child under four years of age. Most had more than one child. A limitation of the study was that we did not interview young women during their first pregnancy. During subsequent periods of ethnographic field work we have observed marked differences in the way women behave during their first and subsequent pregnancies. A recent study in Gujarat (Gittelson et al. 1994) found that all primigravidae who responded to their survey ate less whereas more experienced respondents reported that they ate as much as before. See also Anderson 1989 and footnote 7 of this chapter for conflicting findings on this issue.

7. More rigorous research is required to determine lay perceptions of what constitutes a normal-sized vs. a large baby. The term "large baby" irrespective of weight was often used to describe a baby who appeared bloated.

8. Similarly, Anderson (1989) found no significant differences in food habits during pregnancy in Gujarat and Maharastra by mother's caste, per capita income, or educational status. However, she did find that there was a significant difference between the stated food habits of primigravidae and multigravidae in the second and third trimesters with more multigravidae saying that they ate less (64% versus 42% in the second trimester; 66% versus 46% in the third trimester). In her sample of Gujarati women, Anderson found that women who said that they ate the same amount of food or more food during pregnancy, were 1 kg heavier than women who said they ate less food. Results of another survey in Gujarat reported that the mean energy consumption of those who said they ate less was on average of 250 kcal lower than the mean energy consumption of those who had not decreased their food consumption (Sewa Rural Research Team 1994).

9. Alternatively, a pregnant woman may be called a *garbhiṇi*, a term referring to the *garbha kōsha*, a more general term for womb (Manners 1886). An idea expressed by one midwife was that there were many *garbha kōsha* in the stomach. During each pregnancy, one *garbha kōsha* was utilized to contain the baby within the stomach.

10. Katona-Apte (1973) has noted that among women in Tamil Nadu it is believed that extra food consumed during pregnancy would lead to irregularity of breathing and choking.

11. Anderson found an association in Gujarat between a woman having edema in pregnancy and self-reports that she ate less food, with 81% of the women with edema saying that they ate less food versus 58% of the women without edema. Anderson notes that eating less could have been a response to the edema. This corroborates observations of dietary restrictions during illness noted in South Kanara.

12. Reference to a man's *nañju* growing inside a pregnant woman may also constitute a derogatory comment about a woman's illicit affair.

13. There is some contention with regard to this issue. On the one hand, Brems and Berg (1988) conclude that deliberate restriction of food intake during pregnancy is likely to have a small but significant effect on birth weight, perhaps partially accomplishing the objective of facilitating childbirth. More recently however, Leslie (1991:16) has noted that since difficulty during delivery is mainly related to infant head circumference (which food restrictions have little affect upon), there are unlikely to be important obstetrical benefits and more likely to be costs for both maternal and infant nutritional status.

14. A review of methods useful in the collection of data on food consumption and a discussion of differences between self-reported and observed nutrient intake may be found in Krantzler and Mullen (1980) and Krantzler et al. (1982).

15. It is recognized that several factors other than pregnancy weight influence birth weight. These factors include length of gestation, emotional stress during pregnancy, and the mother's rate of infections during pregnancy. The latter (incidence of diarrhea, respiratory illness, urinary tract infections) may well interfere with placental function and the maternal–fetal transfer of nutrients. On the variety of factors that may influence birth weight see Margen (1982). On the relevance of seasonal infection rates as a factor influencing neonatal mortality see Taylor, Kielman, and LaSweemer (1978).

16. Studies such as the Tamil Nadu Nutrition Study (Cantor Associates 1973) suggest that approximately one half of Tamil Nadu meet less than 80% of caloric needs. Using national sample survey data from 1961, Dandekar and Rath (1971) estimated that about a third of the rural population's diets are inadequate in calories. This estimate is based on conservative international standards of basic caloric requirements (2,250 kcal) and a drop in the mean available calories per capita in the last 20 years. We view these figures as impressionistic and only suggestive of the magnitude of malnutrition in rural India. An important limitation of this kind of data is that nutritional norms for a reference man (65 kg) and woman (55 kg) age 20–39 are misleading when used to examine the nutritional status of a population. The Food and Agricultural Organization (FAO 1978) has pointed out that figures for recommended nutrient intakes should not in themselves be used to justify statements that undernutrition, malnutrition, or overnutrition is present in a community or group, as such conclusions must always be supported by clinical or biochemical evidence. The FAO also notes that the methodological basis for estimating energy and protein requirements are weak inasmuch as they are based on studies of healthy young men. The reference figures do not take into account intra-group variability. Studies such as those by Dandekar and Rath (1971) have used average energy requirements of a population to determine levels of malnutrition and the poverty line. On the issue of measurement of malnutrition, see Srinivasan (1980). On the controversies surrounding the use of local vs. international standards for calculating nutritional standards and the "small but healthy debate" which calls into question adaptation arguments associated with stunting see Messer (1986, 1989a, 1989b) and Pelto and Pelto (1989).

17. Gopalan and Naidu (1972) make note of one survey carried out in cosmopolitan South India which found that 43% of pregnant women had frank signs of malnutrition. Another survey (Rao and Gopalan 1969) revealed that the incidence of nutritional deficiency signs was higher (51%) in pregnant women who had more than three pregnancies than among those who had three or fewer pregnancies (28%). Numerous nutritional surveys conducted in India have found that pregnant and lactating women of low socioeconomic status consume between 1400–1900 kcal and 38–54 g of protein daily (See National Nutrition Monitoring Bureau 1980; Vijayalakshmi and Lakshmi 1982; as well as Anderson 1989 for an extensive review of the literature). Notably, food intake during lactation is greater than during pregnancy and neither differ

significantly from the intakes of non-pregnant women. Weight gain of impoverished Indian women averages about 6.5 kg. (Indian Council of Medical Research 1977) with primigravidae gaining less than multigravidae (Anderson 1989). Birth weight increases with adequate weight gain of the mother, regardless of her pre-pregnancy weight (Eastman and Jackson 1968; Anderson 1989).

18. Gopalan et al. (1971) and a WHO (1976) report on nutrition programs and health in India estimated that 30% of pregnant women have hemoglobin below 10 g per 100 ml. The Tamil Nadu Nutrition Study (Cantor Associates 1973) estimated that anemia affected 50% of pregnant women. The Voluntary Health Association (VHAI 1975b) estimated that 15–20% of Indian women are anemic at the onset of pregnancy and that 60–70% have hemoglobin levels less than 11 g per 100 ml. Research suggests that in mild and moderate degrees of anemia in pregnancy, iron deficiency was the main factor, while in severe forms folate deficiency is clearly evident (VHAI 1975a). The net iron loss during pregnancy in Indian women is around 350 mg. To meet this demand, a woman needs to absorb 2–3 mg of additional iron daily. Iron absorption from food during pregnancy ranges from 10% in the first trimester to 25–30% at term. On this basis, the iron requirement during pregnancy is computed to be around 40 mg per day — or greater for women with poor iron stores and low hemoglobin levels at the onset of pregnancy. According to a VHAI report (1975a), the mean iron intake of low-income groups is around 18 mg of iron per day, 45% of the recommended allowance. Other hemopoietic factors such as vitamin C, folic acid, and vitamin B_{12} are also deficient.

19. Gopalan and Naidu (1972) mention a study by P. S. S. Sunder Rao who systematically followed 2,537 rural and 2,021 urban women belonging to the lower socioeconomic groups subsisting on diets providing less than 1,850 kcal and 44 g protein daily. The pregnancy wastage observed was about 30%.

20. It is estimated that 20% of Indian women are anemic at the onset of pregnancy and 60% by the last trimester (Indian Council of Medical Research 1975). This figure obscures class differences. A study by Vijayalakshmi and Lakshmi (1982) in South India found that 82% of low income women in the third month of pregnancy had hemoglobin levels under 9 g/dl. Indian women have poor iron stores, low dietary intake of iron, and excessive losses of iron from the gastrointestinal tract due to diarrhea and worm infestations (Vijayalakshmi and Lakshmi 1982). Provision of iron and folic acid supplements to pregnant women has proven to be an effective way to prevent nutritional anemia. Increased birth weights of 270–360 g have been reported of women taking these supplements. Weight gain more than doubles if food supplements and iron/folic acid supplements are taken together (Qureshi et al. 1973; Vijayalakshmi and Usha 1981).

21. Low birth weight is the single most important determinant of the chances of the newborn to survive and to experience healthy growth and development. A WHO report (1980) reviewing data from 56 studies carried out in India,

estimated that 30% of children born are low birth weight. This incidence rate is second only to Bangladesh (50%) among 90 countries surveyed. In India, based on a retrospective study of 10,000 perinatal deaths and 20,000 healthy controls, Mehta (1980) reported that 75% of the perinatal deaths weighed less than 2,500 g.

22. Neonatal survival rates of low birth weight babies may differ by social class and the nutritional status of mothers suggesting the possibility of physiological adaptations. Among nutritionally stressed populations, studies in India and elsewhere (see Stini 1979:400) reveal higher rates of survivorship for lower birth weight newborns. For example, Jayant (1964) reports that survivorship of infants weighing 1,600–2,000 grams is higher among individuals of lower socioeconomic strata than their wealthier neighbors despite superior medical care at delivery. As Stini notes, it is difficult to ascertain whether these higher survivorship of smaller infants reflects early loss of less viable embryos and fetuses. Two points may be raised. First the contribution of the fetus' own genes in determining its size at birth is small while the contribution of maternal factors, both environmental and genetic, is overwhelming (Roberts 1986). Second, if the poor have adapted to having low birth weight babies they have done so only with significant nutritional cost to the mother. A reduction in maternal nutrient stores results from poor nutrient intake during pregnancy, which impairs a woman's own health and the care she is able to provide for her children. The cost of such impairment needs to be viewed over a woman's life course both during and beyond her reproductive years. See Katona-Apte (1979) on this point in relation to differentials in Indian male and female life expectancy in the 1960–70s.

23. Among some castes, special foods are offered to a woman who is pregnant, but this is often done on a ritual occasion (*Seemantha pūjā*), not routinely and/or only during her first pregnancy. Foods offered to a woman may also vary by whether she is residing in her own home or her mother's home during the final months of her pregnancy.

24. A study conducted in Gujarat (SEWA Rural Research Team 1994) similarly described food restrictions during pregnancy. A majority of informants mentioned that fish and meat were to be avoided at this time. In addition, Muslim informants believed that pregnant women should avoid meat, eggs and milk.

25. Bear in mind that the data presented only relate to second trimester food intake and that food consumption is often reduced in the third trimester. In a longitudinal study of 48 women in South India, the mean weight gain between 12–40 weeks gestation was 6 kg. In 130 women followed from week 20 onwards, nearly 50% failed to gain weight from week 32 onwards (Venkatachalam 1962, Venkatachalam, Shankar, and Gopalan 1960).

26. We have used FAO/WHO (1973) nutrient requirement guidelines for caloric needs during the later half of pregnancy (2,500 kcal). For protein requirements, we have followed the guidelines suggested by the Voluntary Health Association of India (VHAI 1975b). Protein requirements based on a diet of

cereals and tubers was estimated to be 55 g by VHAI and 63 g by FAO/WHO. The VHAI (1975a) compiled a table of mean nutrient intake levels of pregnant and lactating Indian women in low income groups based on dietary surveys carried out in various regions of India. The average energy intake during pregnancy was 1,400 kcal (to our 1,800 kcal: second trimester) and protein intake was 43 g (to our 44.6 g). Our estimates were made on the basis of a season of more plentiful food. A recent survey conducted among pregnant women in Gujarat found that the estimated mean energy intake was 1200 kcal/day/woman, or about half the recommended allowance. These findings are consistent with three previous studies of the same population, which found the per capita energy consumption to be in the range of 1200–1500 kcal/day (Seshardi 1991, Sewa Rural Research Team 1989, 1990: all three references cited in Gittelsohn et al. 1994: Chapter 6).

27. Kay (1980) notes that among Mexican Americans foods like milk are avoided during pregnancy because mothers are afraid they will make the baby large and difficult to deliver. However, vitamin and iron preparations are popular and taken in preference to herbal remedies as a means of "enriching blood." The importance of explaining dietary supplements such as ferrous sulfate, folic acid, and vitamin A to lay populations in accordance with emic as opposed to etic health concerns is evident. Good notes that in Iran doctor's advice is suspect because it does not agree with culturally constituted common sense: "I pay my doctor twenty tomans for each visit. I didn't buy any of the medicines he said to buy so the baby wouldn't be so large I'd have to have a caesarian.... Some of those doctors want babies to be so large that they will have to perform caesareans to get them out!" (1980:148).

28. Rates of tetanus toxoid vaccination have gone up significantly since this research was conducted in the mid-1970s. The extent to which this increase is related to mother's demand or health workers' command and the location where mothers choose to deliver is discussed in Nichter 1990 and in Chapter 10.

REFERENCES

Anderson, M. 1989. The Relationship Between Maternal Nutrition and Child Growth in Rural India. Doctoral dissertation, Tufts University, Department of Nutrition, April 1989.

Baroda Operations Research Group. 1972. Food Habits Survey Conducted in Southern India, Vols. 1 and 2. Protein Foods Association of India.

Brems, S. and A. Berg. 1988. Eating Down During Pregnancy. Unpublished discussion paper, UN Advisory Group on Nutrition, September. Population and Human Resources Department, The World Bank.

Cantor Associates. 1973. Tamil Nad Nutrition Study: An Operations Oriented Study of Nutrition as an Integrated System in the State of Tamil Nadu. Washington, DC: United States Agency for International Development.

Cruz, P. S. 1970. Maternal and Infant Nutritional Practices in the Rural Areas. Journal of the Philippine Medical Association 46:668–682.

Dandekar, V. M. and R. Rath. 1971. Poverty in India. Bombay: Indian School of Political Economy.

Eastman, N. J., and E. Jackson. 1968. Weight Relationships in Pregnancy — The Bearing of Maternal Weight Gain and Prepregnancy Weight on Birth Weight in Full Term Pregnancies. Obstetrical and Gynecological Survey 23:1003–1025.

Fisher, S. 1974. Body Consciousness. New York: Jason Aronson.

Foll, C. V. 1959. An Account of Some of the Beliefs and Superstitions About Pregnancy, Parturition, and Infant Health in Burma. Journal of Tropical Pediatrics 5:51–59.

Food and Agricultural Organization (FAO). 1973. Energy and Protein Requirements: Report of a Joint FAO/WHO Ad Hoc Expert Committee. Food and Agricultural Organization.

Food and Agricultural Organization (FAO). 1978. Report of the First Joint FAO/WHO Expert Consultation on Energy Intake and Requirements (Danish Fund in Trust, TF/INF 297). Rome: Food and Agricultural Organization.

Fuglesang, A. 1982. About Understanding. Uppsala, Sweden: Dag Hammarskjold Foundation.

Gittelsohn, J., et al. 1994. Listening to Women Talk About their Health: Issues and Evidence from India. New Delhi: Har Anand.

Gonzales, N. S. and M. Behar. 1966. Child Rearing Practices, Nutrition, and Health Status. Milbank Memorial Fund Quarterly 94:77–95.

Good, M. J. D. 1980. Of Blood and Babies: The Relationship of Popular Islamic Physiology to Fertility. Social Science and Medicine 14b:147–156.

Gopalan, C., S. C. Balasubramanian, B. V. Ramasastri, and K. Rao. 1971. Nutrition Atlas of Asia. Hyderabad: National Institute of Nutrition.

Gopalan, C. and N. Naidu. 1972. Nutrition and Fertility. Lancet 18:1077–1079.

Harfouche, J. K. 1970. The Importance of Breastfeeding. Journal of Tropical Pediatrics 16(3) (Monograph No. 10):133–175.

Indian Council of Medical Research. 1975. Report on Nutritional Status and Pregnancy. Cited in Nutrition in Pregnancy and Lactation, Fact Sheet M-3. New Delhi: Voluntary Health Association of India.

Indian Council of Medical Research. 1977. Maternal Malnutrition: Its Effects on Foetal Nutrition. ICMR Bulletin 7(12).

Jayant, K. 1964. Birthweight and Some Other Factors in Relation to Infant Survival: A Study in an Indian Sample. Annals of Human Genetics, London 27:261–267.

Jeffery, P., R. Jeffery, and A. Lyon. 1989. Labour Pains and Labour Power. Women and Childbearing in India. Manohar: New Delhi.

Katona-Apte, J. 1973. Food Behavior in Two Districts. *In* Cultural Anthropology and Nutrition 2B, Tamilnadu Nutrition Study. Report to USAID Mission, New Delhi, India.

Katona-Apte, J. 1977. The Sociocultural Aspects of Food Accordance in a Low Income Population in Tamilnadu, South India. Environmental Child Health (April):83–90.

Katona-Apte, J. 1979. The Relevance of Nourishment to the Reproductive Cycle of the Female in India. *In* Physiological and Morphological Adaptation and Evolution. W. Stini, ed. Pp. 363–368. New York: Mouton.

Kay, M. 1980. Mexican, Mexican American and Chicana Childbirth. *In* Twice a Minority: Mexican American Women. M. Melville, ed. Pp. 52–65. St. Louis: C. V. Mosby.

Krantzler, N. and B. Mullen. 1980. Measuring Food Intake Patterns. Paper presented at the 4th Annual Meeting of the West Coast Nutritional Anthropology Society.

Krantzler, N., B. Mullen, E. Comstock, C. Holden, H. Schutz, L. Grivetti, and H. Meiselman. 1982. An Annotated Indexed Bibliography on Methods of Measuring Food Intake. Journal of Nutrition Education 14(3):108–119.

Leslie, J. 1991. Women's Nutrition: The Key to Improving Family Health in Developing Countries. Health Policy and Planning 6(1):1–19.

Manners, A. 1886. Tuḷu–English Dictionary. Bangalore: Basil Mission Press.

Manning, P. and H. Fabrega. 1973. The Experience of Self and Body: Health and Illness in the Chiapas Highlands. *In* Phenomenological Sociology: Issues and Applications. George Psalkas, ed. Pp. 251–301. New York: J. Witz and Sons.

Margen, S. 1982. Studies of Maternal Nutrition and Infant Outcome: Statistical Versus Biological Significance. Birth 9(3):197–200.

Mathews, C. and V. Benjamin. 1979. Health Education Evaluation of Beliefs and Practices in Rural Tamil Nadu: Family Planning and Antenatal Care. Social Action 29:377–392.

Mehta, A. 1980. Perinatal Mortality Survey in India. Paper presented at the 3rd International Seminar on Maternal and Perinatal Mortality, New Delhi, India.

Messer, E. 1986. The Small but Healthy Hypothesis: Historical, Political, and Ecological Influences on Nutritional Standards. Human Ecology 14(1):57–75.

Messer, E. 1989a. Indian Nutritionists and International Standards: Concepts and Controversies. Social Science and Medicine 29(12):1393–1399.

Messer, E. 1989b. Small but Healthy? Some Cultural Considerations. Human Organization 48(1):39–52.

National Nutrition Monitoring Bureau. 1980. Report for the Year 1979, National Institute of Nutrition, Indian Council of Medical Research.

Nichter, Mark. 1984. Project Community Diagnosis: Participatory Research as a First Step Toward Community Participation in Primary Care. Social Science and Medicine 19(3):237–252.

Nichter, Mark. 1986. Modes of Food Classification and the Diet–Health Contingency: A South Indian Case Study. *In* Modes of Food Classification in South Asia. R. Khare and K. Ishvaran, eds. Pp. 185–221. Durham, NC: Carolina Academic Press.

Nichter, Mark. 1990. Vaccinations in South Asia: False Expectations and Contemporary Metaphors. *In* Anthropology and Primary Health Care. J. Coreil and D. Mull, eds. Pp. 196–221. Boulder: Westview Press.

Nichter, Mark and Mimi Nichter. 1981. An Anthropological Approach to Nutrition Education. Newton, MA: International Nutrition Communication Service Publications, Education Development Center.

Pelto, G. and P. Pelto 1989. Small but Healthy? An Anthropological Perspective. Human Organization 48(1):11–15.

Population Centre. 1978. Classification of Districts in Karnataka State by Health Status. Population Centre Newsletter 4(3). Bangalore.

Prema, K. 1978. Pregnancy and Lactation: Some Nutritional Aspects. Indian Journal of Medical Research 68 (Supplement):70–79.

Qureshi, S. N., P. Rao, V. Madhavi, Y. C. Mathur, and Y. R. Reddi. 1973. Effect of Maternal Nutrition Supplementation on the Birth Weight of the Newborn. Indian Pediatrics 10(9):541–544.

Rao, M. 1985. Food Beliefs of Rural Women During the Reproductive Years in Dharwad, India. Ecology, Food, and Nutrition 16:93–103.

Rao, V. K. and C. Gopalan. 1969. Nutrition and Family Size. Journal of Nutrition and Dietetics 6:248–266.

Reissland, N. and R. Burghart. 1989. Active Patients: The Integration of Modern and Traditional Obstetric Practices in Nepal. Social Science and Medicine 29(1):43–52.

Roberts, D. F. 1986. The Genetics of Human Fetal Growth. *In* Human Growth: A Comprehensive Treatise, Volume 3. (Second edition). F. Falkner and J. M. Tanner, eds. Pp. 113–144. New York: Plenum Press.

SEWA Rural Research Team. 1994. Beliefs and Behaviour Regarding Diet during Pregnancy in a Rural Area in Gujarat, Western India. *In* Listening to Women Talk About their Health: Issues and Evidence from India. J. Gittelsohn et al., eds. New Delhi: Har Anand.

Sharma, D. C. 1955. Mother, Child, and Nutrition. Journal of Tropical Pediatrics 1:47–53.

Srinivasan, T. N. 1980. Malnutrition: Some Measurement and Policy Issues. World Bank Staff Working Paper No. 373. Washington, DC: World Bank Publications.

Stini, W. 1979. Adaptive Strategies of Human Populations Under Nutritional Stress. *In* Physiological and Morphological Adaptation and Evolution. W. Stini, ed. Pp. 387–410. New York: Mouton.

Taylor, A., I. Emanuel, L. Morris, and R. Prosterman. 1978a. Child Nutrition and Mortality in the Rural Philippines: "Is Socioeconomic Status Important?" Tropical Pediatrics and Environmental Child Health (April):80–86.

Taylor, C., A. Kielmann, and C. LeSweemer. 1978b. Nutrition and Infection. *In* Nutrition and the World Food Problem. M. Recheigl, ed. Pp. 218–243. Basel, Switzerland: Kaiger.

Thimmayamma, B. V. S., P. Rau, V. K. Desai, and B. N. Jayaprakash. 1976. A Study of Changes in Socioeconomic Conditions, Dietary Intake and Nutritional Status of Indian Rural Families Over a Decade. Ecology of Food and Nutrition 5:235–243.

Todhunter, N. E. 1973. Food Habits, Food Faddism, and Nutrition. World Review of Nutrition and Dietetics 16:286.

Trant, H. 1954. Food Taboos in East Africa. Lancet 267(2):703–705.

United States Agency for International Development (USAID). 1980. Paper presented by Cathy LeSar at a Title Two Workshop on Malnutrition and Mortality, March 25–27, New Delhi, India.

United States Department of Health, Education, and Welfare. 1979. Background Paper on India's Health Sector. Washington, DC: Office of International Health.

Venkatachalam, P. S. 1962. Maternal Nutritional Status and Its Effect on the Newborn. Bulletin WHO 26:193–201.

Venkatachalam, P. S., K. Shankar, and C. Gopalan. 1960. Changes in Body Weight and Body Composition During Pregnancy. Indian Journal of Medical Research 48(4):511–517.

Vijayalakshmi, P. and R. N. Lakshmi. 1982. Food Consumption and Metabolic Profile of Selected Expectant Mothers. Indian Journal of Nutritional Dietetics 19:297–302.

Vijayalakshmi, P. and V. Usha. 1981. The Impact of Iron and Folic Acid Supplementation on Expectant Mothers Participating in Modified Special Nutrition Programmes. Indian Journal of Nutritional Dietetics 18:45–52.

Voluntary Health Association of India (VHAI). 1975a. Anemia in Pregnancy. Fact Sheet M-7. New Delhi, India.

Voluntary Health Association of India (VHAI). 1975b. Nutrition in Pregnancy and Lactation. Fact Sheet M-3. New Delhi, India.

Wellin, E. 1955. Maternal and Infant Feeding Practices in a Peruvian Village. Journal of the American Dietary Association 31:889–894.

Wilson, C. S. 1973. Food Habits: A Selected Annotated Bibliography. Journal of Nutrition Education 5(1): Supplement 1.

Wilson, C. S. 1979. Food Custom and Nurture: An Annotated Bibliography on Sociocultural and Biocultural Aspects of Nutrition. Journal of Nutrition Education 2(4): Supplement 1.

World Health Organization. 1976. Nutrition Programs and Health Report of the Regional Office for Southeast Asia, November. New Delhi.

World Health Organization. 1980. The Incidence of Low Birth Weight — A Critical Review of Available Information. World Health Statistics Quarterly 33(3):197–224.

CHAPTER 3

Modern Methods of Fertility Regulation: When and for Whom Are They Appropriate?

Mark Nichter and Mimi Nichter

INTRODUCTION

In many less developed countries women who desire family planning are reluctant to use temporary methods of fertility regulation. Moreover, those who do opt to use them often do so at the end of their reproductive careers. Among younger women who experiment with modern contraceptive methods, many discontinue their use after a short period of time. Professionals have tended to explain poor demand for contraceptive methods on rumors involving fear of side effects and problems associated with improper use. Often such explanations embrace a victim blaming mentality. This particularly seems to be the case in areas of South Asia where screening and/or follow-up services are poor, if available, and the primary focus of family planning workers is to meet state mandated targets.

An understanding of consumer demand for contraceptive fixes requires a combination of health service research which examines the availability and quality of family planning services rendered and anthropological research which investigates social and cultural factors influencing contraceptive decision making and how technical fixes are evaluated.[1] This includes consideration of how alternative family planning methods are assessed and at what point various methods are adopted in a woman or man's reproductive career.

71

This entails an examination of perceived costs and benefits of contraceptive method use over time, health concerns associated with such use, and issues related to the social relations of method use inclusive of concerns about trust and gossip as a leveling device. Anthropological inquiry further demands a critical examination of the rhetoric of noncompliance which simplistically links nonadoption of modern contraceptive methods to ignorance and the spread of unscientific rumors.

In this chapter, we investigate both rhetoric about the non-adoption of modern contraceptive methods in Sri Lanka and popular interpretations of how they work and for whom they are appropriate. Tacit cultural knowledge about the ethnophysiology of reproduction, local health concerns, and lay cost/benefit analysis influenced by such contingencies as food availability, work load, and the age as well as number of surviving children are considered. Reasons why the poor find particular contraceptive methods unsuitable for their use, despite the fact that they desire to space or limit their number of children, are also discussed. Drawing upon cross-cultural literature, we document similar concerns about family planning methods in other countries. Rather than judging Sinhalese health concerns from a decontextualized biomedical perspective, we highlight the rationales underlying local perceptions, rationales based upon different sets of premises about health, body physiology, and pathology. Popular perception of how modern methods of contraception work in Sri Lanka is informed by research on the ethnophysiology of reproduction introduced in Chapter 1. An analysis of contraceptive beliefs provides further insights into this body of knowledge and reproductive health practice.

USE OF MODERN METHODS: SURVEY DATA

A brief overview of family planning prevalence in Sri Lanka points out an enigma in the international health literature which has featured Sri Lanka as a "good health at low cost" success story (Halstead, Walsh, and Warren 1985). Although Sri Lanka boasts a highly educated female population, low infant mortality (18 per 1,000: 1991), and one of the lowest birth rates in South Asia (21 per 1,000: 1991), use of modern family planning methods is relatively low.[2] While a majority of women express interest in controlling their family size, many women have opted for traditional birth control practices rather than modern contraceptive methods, despite the fact that the latter are widely available.

According to the 1982 Sri Lanka Contraceptive Prevalence Survey (CPS), 99% of ever-married women interviewed had knowledge of at least one

Table 3.1

Prevalence Rates for Fertility Regulation

Contraceptive method	1975 WFS*	1982 CPS
Modern methods		
Vasectomy	1%	4%
Tubectomy	9%	17%
IUD	5%	3%
Pill	2%	3%
Condom	2%	3%
Total	19%	30%
Traditional methods		
Rhythm	8%	13%
Withdrawal	2%	5%
Others	4%	7%
Total	14%	25%

*Draws on findings of the World Fertility Survey, utilizing only Sri Lanka data.

modern contraceptive method, and 97% knew of a supply source or service point for this method. Over half of the married women interviewed during the survey had engaged in some form of birth control related behavior. This figure represents a significant increase over the findings of the 1975 World Fertility Survey (WFS) which found that one third of married women interviewed had engaged in some birth control practice. Prevalence rates for both traditional and modern methods of birth control are listed in Table 3.1.

Despite aggressive family planning campaigns conducted between the 1975 WFS and the 1982 CPS surveys, pill and condom use increased only slightly and IUD use declined, although adoption of permanent methods increased due to an increase in tubectomy. Notably, the reported increase in temporary birth control methods in the seven year period between the two surveys was largely due to an increase in the use of traditional practices. Two thirds of CPS respondents stated that they did not want more children. Of these women, 38% reported using traditional practices, 23% reported using modern methods, and 39% reported no birth control related behavior. An issue raised by this data is why *temporary* modern methods of family planning have not been more widely adopted by a largely literate population expressing a clear desire to limit their family size.[3] This issue has also been addressed by Kane, Gaminiratne, and Stephen (1988) who found that of those Sri Lankan couples who had begun contraceptive practices by using a traditional method, only 6% switched to a modern temporary method. The researchers were surprised to find that 26% of those who started with a modern temporary method eventually switched to a traditional method. Additionally, Sri Lankan couples exhibited greater loyalty to traditional methods than to modern methods. Forty two percent who had begun by using traditional methods continued to do so while only 23% who had initiated contraceptive use with modern methods continued to use them.[4]

Sri Lanka has one of the highest literacy rates in the developing world (males 90%, females 82%) and family planning services are widely available throughout the country. What is more, those Sri Lankans who use traditional practices rather than modern methods tend to be the most educated and are just as likely to reside in urban as in rural areas.[5] With regard to age, Kane, Gaminiratne and Stephen (1988) report that even among younger women reliance on traditional methods was more common than use of modern temporary methods.

The Sri Lankan data call into question the assumptions maintained by many health planners that literacy, access to modern contraceptive methods, and deployment of an increased number of family planning workers will add up to a steady rise in modern contraceptive method use — given a situation where economic decision making favors birth control.[6] This reasoning assumes that 1) couples will adopt family planning methods because they are available and have been sanctioned by doctors, and 2) users will be satisfied with the effectiveness of the contraceptive services offered. In the Sri Lankan context, these assumptions beg reconsideration in light of both health care service research focusing on the quality of services provided, and medical anthropological research on users' perceptions of method effectiveness and risk to reproductive capacity over time.

THE RHETORIC OF RUMORS AND SIDE EFFECTS: A CRITICAL ASSESSMENT

The international family planning literature is replete with references to rumors with undermine the effectiveness of programs. Typically, such literature (e.g., Bogue 1975, Liskin 1984) identifies rumors about side effects and then proceeds to demonstrate why these claims are unscientific from a biomedical perspective. Family planning workers are asked to develop effective communication strategies to "dispel" these false rumors by providing accurate information in a convincing way. In some countries, workers have been asked to engage in surveillance to "develop rumor registries, trace rumors to their sources and provide persuasive rebuttals" (Liskin 1984). Tracing rumors to their source is no small task if one takes source to mean the source of their appeal and credibility, not just the reported source of their origin. Rumors about contraceptive methods would not appeal to the public if they did not resonate with some already existing tacit knowledge about the body — knowledge embedded in and reproduced through popular health practices and discourse about health.

The term rumor denotes secondhand information and connotes information which is groundless, made up, and secretive. When employed in family planning discourse, rumor is often spoken of "as if" part of a conspiracy against state health authorities who are looking out for the best interests of the community. Rumor constitutes resistance and resistance undermines program success. Attention is deflected from other factors which may influence how methods are evaluated locally. Non-users are blamed for their ignorance and lack of faith in modern medicine. And yet the very people who reject modern contraceptive methods often make wide use of allopathic medicines for both themselves and their families. This is certainly true in Sri Lanka.

Both the production of knowledge about modern contraception and the production of knowledge about rumors, side effects and noncompliance must be examined critically as each is motivated and driven by implicit agenda. What is labelled as "rumors" are often "social facts" backed by cultural common sense. Rumors consist of health knowledge which runs counter to that propagated by biomedicine and the state health authorities. In such contexts, the term "rumor" is not only pejorative. It also indexes power relations between a dominant medical system and popular health culture as well as angst about resistance to the hegemony of the state.

When considering the meanings of "rumor," it is necessary to differentiate between negative discourse about family planning methods which 1) index health concerns well grounded in popular health culture and social concerns indicative of collective anxieties, such as gender relations, 2) constitute metamedical commentary on modernity and the deterioration of traditional values, and 3) entail an attempt to personally or politically discredit an individual (e.g., a particular doctor or health worker) or faction supporting family planning. In this chapter we focus on the first scenario, although we recognize that these three forms of critical discourse may merge (see Chapter

11). Local interpretations of both the physical and social ramifications of using modern birth control methods will be considered.

The term "side effects" also demands scrutiny. In its most general use, the term denotes an effect other than that directly intended. More commonly, the term specifies some negative or undesired effect of a treatment modality. This understanding of the term eclipses an important differentiation which needs to be made between 1) a negative effect which although undesired is deemed to be functionally related to the way in which the method works, and 2) a side effect which occurs and is unrelated to the effectiveness of the method. We refer to the former as a "negative primary effect" of a method and the latter as an "unintended side effect."[7] A point emphasized in this chapter is that symptoms which some health workers flippantly term "side effects" are interpreted by lay populations as signs of bodily transformation primary to the functional effectiveness of a contraceptive method.

METHODOLOGY

Open-ended ethnographic interviews were carried out with 60 married couples aged 25–40 having at least one child. All informants were lower middle class and literate. Most informants had at least a sixth standard education. Twenty couples were selected from each of three districts (Horana, Galle, and Ratnapura Districts) in low country Sri Lanka.[8] Researchers established rapport with informants prior to an investigation of family planning methods through interviews on issues related to maternal and child health. After seeking permission to discuss family life, each informant was asked to describe what they had heard about family planning methods from health professionals, family members, and friends. Informants were next asked what health benefits and concerns were associated with various methods. Health concerns which were expressed were followed up by questions relating to ethnophysiology, pathology, and how various methods functioned in the body. Informants' own experiences with modern methods were directly elicited only after an opportunity had been provided for them to voluntarily discuss personal experiences.

ORAL CONTRACEPTIVES: HOW THEY FUNCTION

As a category, modern English (*ingrīsi*) medicine is spoken of in general discourse as heating and powerful. While *ingrīsi* medicine is praised for fast action, it is commonly referred to as having uncontrolled "side effects." The

English term "side effects" has been incorporated into popular discourse most likely from its widespread use in the media. Informants tended to interpret "side effects" in terms of an inherent toxicity and heatiness of medical fixes, the effects of which are unpredictable and emergent over time.[9] In contrast, traditional herbal medicine (*sinhala behet*) is perceived as rendering control and balance. Indigenous interpretations of oral contraceptives incorporate preexisting ideas about powerful Western medicine. Sri Lankans are leery of any Western medicine which has to be taken for a long period of time for fear of increasing toxicity and heat. While short-term benefits of Western medicine are appreciated, long-term complications are suspect.

A pervasive notion among informants was that the pill works because of its heating effect in the body. Several explanations were offered in this regard. Some informants noted that taking these pills every day raised the level of heat in the body to such an extent that male and female *dhātu*, a substance associated with vitality and strength, was burned up. This was expressed in Sinhala by the phrase "*dhātu pichenava*," literally *dhātu* burns. When *dhātu* is destroyed, conception is prevented but the health promotive qualities of *dhātu*, linked to strength and vitality, are lost. Other informants explained that the extreme heat in the body caused by taking the pill diluted the *dhātu* (*dhātu direvenava*) to the point where it was no longer strong enough to create a fetus. Other anthropologists have also described how oral contraceptives are believed to be heating to the body.[10]

Another health concern noted by rural Sinhalese women informants was that the excess heat in a woman's body caused by taking the pill rendered the womb dry. Over time, a dry womb became incapable of accepting male seed. As one informant explained:

> A dry womb is like a dry field. If you plant seeds in a field which is not moist, the seed will not take to the soil. A womb which has become totally dry through continued use of birth control pills becomes useless.

Long-term dryness leads to decaying and deterioration of the womb. In the words of another informant: "The womb deteriorates just like a piece of wood left in the sun for many months. It becomes brittle and finally turns to powder."

A concern that drying of the uterus renders a woman infertile has been noted elsewhere. Good (1980) has noted that Iranian women believe the pill prevents pregnancy "through some action on the uterus, making conception at a later time unlikely" (Good 1980:152).[11] Specifically, Good notes that Iranian women believed that the pill dries the uterus. For this reason, many of her young, educated informants opted for abortion as a birth control method rather than risk the loss of fertility and the drying of the uterus by taking oral contraceptives. The condom was also viewed as having adverse effects on the uterus by depriving it of moisture. Many Iranian women complained that the pill caused one's entire body to "dry up" and thus hastened the onset of menopause and old age. Premature drying is a serious matter for Iranian women, as it is believed "that the uterus becomes dry and less strong as a woman gets older and thus less receptive to the male seed" (Good 1980:152). The Iranian concern that dryness leads to infertility appears to be quite similar to ideas expressed by some of our Sri Lankan informants.[12]

While birth control pills are promoted as a temporary method by health educators, many Sinhalese believe they cause permanent damage to the body and are, in effect, a permanent method.[13] Many young women wanting to space their children voiced a concern that after taking the pill for some time, their chance of conceiving would be diminished. The fear that temporary family planning methods (such as oral contraceptives) will make women permanently infertile has been reported worldwide: El Salvador (Bertrand et al. 1982), Gambia (Bledsoe et al. 1994), Iran (Good 1980), India (Rogers 1973), and Philippines (Mercado 1973). This concern influenced the timing of pill use among some of our informants. Of 20 informants using the pill (from a separate sample of oral contraceptive users), almost one third spoke of choosing this "temporary" modern method only after a minimal number of children (in most cases two) had been born, yet where a final decision had not been made with respect to having one more child. Their use of the pill appeared to be related to 1) the delaying of a final decision about family size, not child spacing per se and b) fear of the effects of a sterilization procedure on the overall health of a woman.

THE PILL: SIDE EFFECTS AS PRIMARY NEGATIVE EFFECTS

Several symptoms were commonly noted by informants when they described how birth control pills negatively affected a woman's health.[14] In all cases these symptoms were cited by at least one third of our informants to be "primary negative effects" of the pill — symptoms manifest due to the way the method functioned to diminish fertility. The symptoms shown in Table 3.2 were commonly noted.

The most commonly reported negative effect of the pill worldwide is general weakness and leanness: Iran (Good 1980), Botswana (Liskin 1984), Egypt (De Clerque et al. 1986, Krieger 1984, Morsy 1980), and Morocco

Table 3.2

Symptoms of Oral Contraceptives

Symptom	Caused by the pill through
Weight reduction	heatiness
Burning sensation in urinary tract, digestive tract, hands and feet	heatiness
Headaches	heatiness
Nausea and vomiting	heatiness, toxicity
General body pain	heatiness
Stomach pain	heatiness (causes wounds to erupt in the stomach)
Joint pains	heatiness (causes blood to dry up, interfering with body movement
Drying up of breastmilk	heatiness
Rashes, diarrhea in nursing baby, general failure to thrive of nursing baby when mother is taking the pill	heatiness of breastmilk

(Mernissi 1975).[15] In addition to paying credence to physiological effects of the pill (especially high dose versions of the pill) on a population suffering from anemia and protein-calorie malnutrition, it is necessary to consider cultural response to complaints of weakness as somatic expressions of distress.[16] It is important to consider deep seated cultural meanings evoked by body signs and symptoms which marshall emotive response as well as call attention to the status of social relationships and moral identity (Sobo 1993). It is also worth considering what the afflicted might be trying to accomplish (consciously or unconsciously) by communicating to others feelings of weakness and vulnerability. Depending on social response, reports of weakness can prove empowering in the sense that they may provide a woman with a means by which to articulate problems (somatically if not verbally) as well as negotiate sexual relations in relation to health concerns.[17]

In Sri Lanka, birth control pills are not only considered heating and drying but are in other ways deemed harsh (*sarai*) for the body. As discussed elsewhere (see Chapter 7), the heatiness and harshness of modern medicine is commonly linked to concerns about blood quantity, quality and flow, digestive capacity, and general strength and vitality. Concern about *ingrīsi* medicine being heating, toxic, and capable of effecting one's blood and digestive capacity may increase user sensitivity and potentially affect thresholds of discomfort. In a context where psychosocial distress associated with gender relations and sexuality are involved, diffuse symptoms may be interpreted in relation to the pill as an embodied symbol of liminality.

Such a scenario is described by Good (1980) in her research on contraceptive pill discourse in Iran. Good found that the pill is commonly associated with a core set of complaints — heart palpitations, weakened nerves, hand tremors, shortened tempers, and loss of weight. Good notes that such symptoms comprise a language of somatization for feelings of anxiety and ambivalence associated with contraception and sexual intercourse, fertility and infertility, and the stresses of female sexuality — of being a wife and a mother.

As in Iran, discourse about the pill in Sri Lanka is multivocal. The following case study aptly demonstrates this point. One of our neighbors from a village 40 miles west of Colombo complained to us that she was becoming lean (*kettuyi*). She directly associated her reported weight loss with taking birth control pills. What struck us as odd is that she appeared to be somewhat plump. It became apparent to us over the course of a few months that the woman was employing a somatic idiom of distress (Nichter 1981) to indirectly communicate to us (and concerned others) problems which she was having with her husband. These problems entailed a weakening of their marital relationship.

On conferring with other neighbors we learned that the woman's problems preceded her taking oral contraceptives and involved her husband's increased drinking following the loss of his job at a government bus depot. It was her husband who had physically lost weight as a result of his drinking, but his wife who had lost the "weight" of social status in the community. Her husband plunged the family into debt, made sexual advances toward her during states of drunkenness, and in anger tried to convince her to undergo sterilization in order to receive a cash incentive from the government. The woman feared another pregnancy at this time of economic and emotional instability, yet considered a future pregnancy as a possible means of marital reconciliation as she remembered her husband's kindness during her last pregnancy.

In this woman's ongoing personal narrative, reference to weight loss and the pill served as convenient markers for ambivalent feelings she was experiencing about her husband as well as her own identity. Caught between (in)fertility and the (in)stability of marriage, she became increasingly concerned about her body and vocal about the effect of pills she was compelled to take because of her husband's refusal to use condoms. On more than one occasion, she expressed anger toward the same government which took her husband's job away and placed birth control pills in her hands. Both rendered her family weak and nonproductive. When formally interviewed about the effect of pills on the body, she compared the heatiness of *arrack*, a local distilled alcohol, which dries out the body leaving one thin, to the heatiness of birth control pills, which dry the womb and leave one weak.

BIRTH CONTROL PILLS AND BREASTFEEDING

Another problem related to heatiness as a "primary negative effect" of birth control pills is their affect on lactation. Birth control pills are strongly associated with a reduction in a woman's capacity to produce breastmilk. This was one reason several informants cited for the lack of interest in pills among the poor. "How can a poor woman afford to take the chance of using birth control pills while breastfeeding?" one informant noted. She further questioned, "If her breastmilk dries up, how can she manage to purchase milk or formula for her baby?" Another reason for not using pills while lactating entailed the fear of a woman's breastmilk becoming heaty and harming her baby. A child's illness linked to heaty breastmilk was *mandama dośa*, a sickness marked by a failure to thrive, diarrhea, and skin rashes. Although we came across few women during our research who had actually taken birth control pills while breastfeeding, the impression that birth control pills would reduce breastmilk and harm one's infant was widespread.[18]

Among the middle class, birth control pills may be used strategically by women who wish to stop breastfeeding for one reason or another. The example of an informant from Colombo city provided a case in point. The woman began taking the pill after five months of breastfeeding after expressing a desire to return to work. This was against the wishes of her mother-in-law. The informant brought to her husband's attention family planning advice offered to her by a health educator which emphasized the need for contraception six months after delivery as a means of birth spacing. Complaining of her husband's sporadic use of condoms, she began taking oral contraceptives on her own initiative. While her mother-in-law did not approve of her actions, she encouraged her daughter-in-law to give the infant formula. The taking of oral contraceptives — heaty medicine — constituted a valid reason to stop breastfeeding.

The negative relationship between oral contraceptive use and breastfeeding duration has been more widely reported in Africa than Asia (Jain and Bongaarts 1981, Knodel and Debavalya 1980, Lesthaeghe, Page and Adegbola 1981, Oni 1986, Zurayk 1981). It raises an important policy dilemma for developing countries conjointly committed to child survival and family planning especially in contexts where employment opportunities for women are increasing.[19]

LONG-TERM COSTS OF ADAPTING TO ORAL CONTRACEPTIVES

In a study of side effects experienced by users of oral contraceptives in Sri Lanka, Basnayake et al. (1984) reported nausea, vomiting, headaches, and dizziness as widespread. The authors conclude that Sri Lankan women report similar side effects to women of other cultures and that these reduce as the body becomes accustomed to the pill. The study is a good example of the limitations of biomedical studies of "side effects" which rely strictly on surveys, seek to provide biomedical reasons for symptom occurrence, and offer psychosomatic explanations for their commonality without cultural depth.[20] Notably, in the Basnayake et al. survey, no complaint of heatiness was mentioned. This is surprising when one considers that in our interviews the most common health concern associated with the pill was heatiness. Basnayake and his colleagues structured their interviews around a prepared questionnaire utilizing symptoms most commonly noted in the West. Interviewers conducting the survey asked about anticipated side effects, but failed to investigate relationships between symptoms cited and the processes underlying their occurrence. The user's health culture was overlooked.[21]

The Basnayake et al. (1984) report places emphasis on habituation to the pill as a means of reducing the severity of physical symptoms. What Basnayake et al. fail to appreciate are cultural interpretations of the cost of adapting to a medicine over time. Sinhalese informants made it clear that becoming habituated to the harshness of *ingrīsi* medicine and contraceptive methods in the short-term does not guarantee that one will not suffer long-term consequences from continued use. Long-term habituation requires more than just the body adjusting to the "fix" in the sense of not being "shocked" by its presence (shock manifesting as symptoms). It entails provisions for counterbalancing and removing the negative primary effects of fixes.

Self-Regulation of Oral Contraceptives

Many informants noted that taking harsh birth control pills over time would be detrimental not only for a woman's future fertility, but also for her general health. Taking a birth control pill every day was seen as doing something daily to weaken one's health. Several people voiced the concern that since pills were bad for health, they should only be taken when absolutely necessary. For some informants this meant that it was best to take a pill during those days when it was likely they would "mix" (have sexual relations) with their husbands, as well as for a few days following sexual relations. For others, this meant taking the pill during days perceived to be times of peak fertility. As noted in Chapter 1, cultural perceptions of peak fertility do not always coincide with biological fecundity.

Researchers working in other cultures have similarly found that pill use is mediated by ideas about its negative effects. Krieger (1984), for example, found that among Egyptian women, the misuse of the pill was associated with beliefs about the method: the pill was perceived as a potent, toxic substance that should not be ingested daily. Moreover, its potency was regarded to have sustained action, making daily consumption unnecessary to achieve protection.[22] Among our Sri Lankan informants, we found that it was not uncommon for a woman to discontinue taking the pill when she felt ill, not only from symptoms overtly associated with heat — such as diarrhea and fever — but from more general symptoms such as weakness and giddiness. Tucker has noted similar contraceptive behavior in Peru:

> Pills are given with minimal explanation so that most respondents do not understand the proper way to use them. Women often start taking their pills on the wrong date, forgot to take them for a few days or quit in the middle of the cycle because "they do not feel good." (Tucker 1986:312)

A study by Seaton (1985) in Bangladesh notes that noncompliance with oral contraception involves both unexpectedly high levels of under and overconsumption of pills. His findings and those noted above underscore the need for anthropological research on medicine taking behavior in relation to perceptions of health and fertility.[23]

THE USE OF ORAL CONTRACEPTIVES FOR MENSTRUAL REGULATION

A common notion we encountered is that if contraceptive pills were powerful enough to weaken the *dhātu* or in some other way prevent conception from occurring, then taking several pills at once should affect the body sufficiently to heat, dry, or push out the fetus. One of our informants was in the process of obtaining birth control pills from the Government Health Worker for this purpose when we interviewed her, and four other informants told us without prompting that they had taken multiple tablets as a means of menstrual regulation when their period was overdue. In a study of 20 mothers who had used self-treatment for "abortion" in Galle District (Chullawathie 1984), it was found that 25% had utilized birth control pills for this purpose.

Good (1980) has likewise noted the use of the pill in Iran to induce abortion. She found that it was not uncommon for Iranian women to take a month's supply in one day to bring on menstruation when they suspected an undesired pregnancy. In the Philippines we have observed young women combing through the PIMS catalogue of available drugs for medicines described as contraindicated during pregnancy. Abortion attempts are made with massive doses of birth control pills, drugs such as Cytotec (an ulcer medicine) which has achieved legendary abortion status, and whatever contraindicated drug one can lay their hands on (see Chapter 9 and Nichter and Vuckovic 1994).[24]

Women also use birth control pills for purposes unrelated to contraception. We observed one such use in South India which was also reported in Nepal by Campbell and Stone (1984). This case involved the management of menstruation, a source of pollution, at times when ritual purity is required. Women use oral contraceptives strategically for the purpose of delaying their menstruation so they can participate in religious festivals, marriages, etc.

SURVEYS ON PILL USE: A CAUTIONARY NOTE

Bearing in mind that the misuse of birth control pills as an abortive is commonplace in Sri Lanka, we question the meaning and accuracy of CPS findings. According to the CPS, 82% of the woman surveyed "had knowledge" of the pill. The question arises as to what kind of knowledge they have. From discussions with CPS interviewers, we found that misinterpretation of survey questions by laypersons was common. Several researchers have pointed out methodological problems inherent in knowledge, attitude and practice (KAP) studies (Bleek 1987, Campbell and Stone 1984, Marshall

1972, Smith and Radel 1972). Campbell and Stone, in their validation study of family planning survey research in Nepal, highlight language problems which call attention to the connotative meanings of words used referentially on surveys:

> Problems arise when the concepts embedded in a question evoke special meanings and associations for respondents. People respond not to the formal content of a question, but to associations the questions have for them. (Campbell and Stone 1984:31)

Campbell and Stone cite abortion data as a case in point. They note that all villagers interviewed by their research team knew of abortives, but less than half claimed knowledge of abortion on a national KAP survey. Dominant cultural values casting negative associations on abortion led informants to immediately focus on threatening and gossipy associations which the word carried "causing them to reinterpret straightforward questions put to them in personal terms."[25] Similarly, Marshall (1972) found in India that although every man in the village where he worked knew of vasectomy, one half of the 53 respondents on a KAP survey said they did not. Similarly, informants who had practiced contraception (vasectomy, IUD) did not mention it.

In the Sri Lankan context, we found the dynamics of interviewing about oral contraceptives to be complex for a variety of reasons. All of our respondents answered that they had heard of the pill when directly asked. The majority also answered affirmatively when asked if they knew how the pill was used. However, when probed for details, we found that many women had vague ideas as to the use of the pill, and some regarded the pill to be an abortive and not a means of temporary contraception. We would argue that "knowledge of method" as reported in the CPS needs to be interpreted with considerable latitude. Considering the cultural importance placed on literacy in Sinhalese society, we found that informants did not want to appear "uneducated" by not "knowing" about the pill. Knowledge as hearsay needs to be separated from experience and familiarity with the pill or any other method.

STERILIZATION: HOW IT WORKS

Female sterilization is the most popular modern method of family planning in Sri Lanka. According to the CPS (1982), 17 percent of all married women in Sri Lanka had adopted this method and a Department of Census and Statistics study in 1987 found that 25% of women had undergone sterilization, indicating an increase in its popularity. By comparison, vasectomy has remained unpopular with less than 5% of men using this method (CPS 1982). Several different ideas were noted as to how female sterilization worked. One common idea was that the operation was a turning of the womb (bukka harenava), causing the entrance to the womb to be blocked so that male dhātu could not enter and mix with female dhātu.[26] Another idea was that the mouth of the womb is stitched closed to prevent conception. Other informants described the operation as a tying of a woman's tubes (nara) to prevent dhātu from coming into the womb. Informants working on a tea plantation near Kandy interviewed as part of a separate study,[27] perceived that the operation was a cutting and tying off of the nara with a piece of plastic fishing line (tangoose). Practical everyday experience with fishing line led them to question the permanence of the operation. They conceived of possible slippage in the tying between times of tautness and slackness. It was feared, for example, that if a woman climbed steep hills or did considerable bending and lifting work, this line might loosen or break off, rendering the operation ineffective. Some informants expressed the opinion that an operation was not a reliable method, i.e., that one could become pregnant either because the stitches were not tight — allowing dhātu to leak inside — or because the stitches could come out altogether. Informants in two of our field sites related stories about a woman who had become pregnant after having an operation. In each area we were told that the local doctor and family health worker had explained that "the stitches had loosened," providing a prototype for method failure which supported popular imagery of method function. With regard to these data, it is interesting to note that in a study conducted in the United States (Johnson, Snow, and Mayhew 1978: 859), women informants noted that sterilization was reversible and that "the tubes would spontaneously untie in seven years."

A less common idea which emerged during the study was that a woman's body was cooled by the operation, due to significant blood loss. The cooling of the body created an environment in which it was not possible to conceive. This reasoning followed the indigenous notion that a woman must maintain an optimum level of heat in order to conceive. The idea here is the reverse of that articulated about birth control pills in which overheat in the body rendered the method effective.

With respect to vasectomy, the most common explanation for how the method worked was that the tube (nara) which carries the dhātu was cut and tied, so that dhātu could no longer come out. As a result, semen, which is composed of dhātu and other fluids becomes thin and watery. Some men emphasized that when aroused the dhātu continues to want to burst out but is blocked. This creates a pressure comparable to the feeling of hemorrhoids.

Various male informants stated that this blocking effect could either heighten or inhibit sexual capacity, in either case resulting in frustration. Less data were collected on user perceptions of vasectomy, in part because fewer informants had either personal experience with the method or knowledge of others who did. Interestingly, among those who did discuss vasectomy, the Sinhalese phrase *"shakti ena nahara kapala"* was commonly used, literally meaning the vein that brings *shakti* is cut. The use of the word *shakti*, life energy, as opposed to *dhātu* in this phrase is important because it notes how a vasectomy is not just seen as affecting a man's semen but rather as weakening his vigor, vitality, and most critically, his life energy.

Side Effects of Sterilization

The most common negative symptoms noted in discourse about sterilization were weakness and the inability to do heavy work.[28] Women also commonly mentioned a set of symptoms including leanness, decreased digestive capacity, reduced appetite, heavy bleeding during menses, painful menses (blockage of a normal flow of substance), and decreased sexual desire. Males mentioned pain during urination and pain during intercourse due to blockage and pressure. Ethnophysiological understanding of bodily flow no doubt contributed to the linking of somatic sensations with perceptions of blockage. Some concern was expressed by a few informants that blocked blood and *dhātu* might somehow fester inside the body, a perception reported to be extremely common in Jamaica (Sobo 1993).

Individual contraception related illnesses need to be considered in their own right as well as being part of a somatic idiom of distress which may be engaged for strategic purposes. Complaints of imbalance, weakness, blockage and excessive flow can index the social as well as the physical body. This became very clear to us while following a 40-year-old middle class woman complaining of appetite loss, weakness, and pressure one year following a tubectomy. An *āyurvedic* practitioner treating the woman for several years was interviewed. He revealed that the woman's complaints were at once caused by deranged humors and also constituted a means for the women to withdraw from an unsatisfactory sexual relationship with her husband. He had treated the couple for sexual problems for nine years. Following each sexual contact, the woman would complain to her husband of multiple somatic complaints and state that she was unable to engage in strenuous work for some days. The practitioner would then be consulted at significant cost to the family. The side effects of sterilization amplified her symptoms and inspired a new round of health care seeking behavior for which she was treated by both *āyurvedic* medicine and diazepam.

CONDOM USE

According to CPS data, the reported use of condoms in Sri Lanka is limited to less than 3% of the population, representing an increase of just under 1% in the seven year period between the WFS and the CPS surveys. Notably, a significantly lower percentage of women reported knowledge of the condom than all other methods of contraception, with the exception of withdrawal. These data are surprising when one considers that the *Preethi* condom social marketing campaign has been described as a landmark in the fertility reduction efforts of Sri Lanka (Goonasekera 1976).[29]

Why is reported knowledge and use of condoms so low in Sri Lanka? A number of possibilities exist. First, it is possible that women respondents on the WFS and CPS (neither survey had male respondents) were embarrassed to claim knowledge of a method literally in the hands of men. A second possibility is that other stigma mitigated against reporting condom use. It has been widely noted that condoms are associated with illicit sexual activity (Peru: Maynard-Tucker 1986; the Middle East: Sukkary-Stolba and Mossavar-Rahmani 1982; and India: Marshall 1973). This was certainly true when condoms were first introduced by the Sri Lankan Government Family Planning Association and the Government of India. In India, the condom was traditionally used only with prostitutes. Marshall notes that "because of the resulting guilt by association, it would have been especially embarrassing to both men and women for a person to purchase or be known to use a condom" (Marshall 1973:129). In Sri Lanka, there still remains an association between condom use and illicit sex. Moreover, condom use is looked down upon by the middle class who consider condoms to be a low class contraceptive method and associate them with "uncultured" sexual relationships engaged in by the "uneducated."[30] Government dispensary personnel and private pharmacists reported that many men in the rural areas who do use condoms bypass local points of distribution. They prefer to take a bus trip to the next town to purchase condoms to preserve their anonymity, although such a trip costs at least a rupee plus the price of a condom. Condoms may be obtained at a local clinic for the low cost of five paise (1/20 of a rupee) per condom.

All of our informants had knowledge of the condom and claimed to know how it was used. Two health concerns associated with condom use were commonly noted. First, condoms were described as heating and burning (*ushnayi* and *darelayi*) for both the male and female partner. This "side effect" was linked to friction and the heatiness of rubber. Several informants ventured the opinion that this effect could be minimized by drinking cooling tender coconut water the morning following intercourse. We noted a similar belief in India. A second health concern was that condoms interfere with the natural flow and exchange of *dhātu* between men and women. In both Sri Lanka and South India it is believed that women derive a source of vitality and health during intercourse when they receive male *dhātu*. Men, on the other hand, are generally thought to be weakened by sexual intercourse. This notion underlies the popular Sinhalese practice of a newly married wife serving her husband egg coffee on mornings following intercourse as a means of replenishing his *dhātu* supply. According to village lore, a man becomes lean following marriage while his bride becomes fat from the supply of *dhātu* she absorbs from their lovemaking.[31] This notion also underlies a health concern about lovemaking when one is weak or in ill health. Intercourse at this time is thought to increase weakness and render one more vulnerable to debilitating illness. Other informants spoke of both a man and woman losing *dhātu* during sex. This is one reason why complaints of weakness may be an effective means of avoiding unwanted sexual contact.

Condom use interferes with what may be thought of as *dhātu* economics — a concern taken more seriously by the poor who must maximize scarce resources than by those who have abundant food resources and are more capable of replenishing *dhātu* supply. For the poor, *dhātu* represents a distilled form of vitality produced by the body through a chain of transformations from food to blood to *dhātu*. To discard such a valued source of vitality is considered wasteful. There is a reciprocal exchange side to *dhātu* economics as well.[32] Some informants referred to a balancing which occurs from an exchange of substance between partners. Five of our male informants spoke of losing "something" of benefit from a woman when a condom was worn. Three of these informants used the hot–cold idiom to express a sense of imbalance following condom use while two others described themselves as being "unsettled" after intercourse. One informant during a small group discussion over a vintage bottle of *arrack* alcohol aptly summarized his feeling to the approval of his four companions: "When we use the condom it is something like drinking sweet toddy, but not drinking fermented toddy! The fermented toddy gives you a kick, but the sweet toddy doesn't!"

IUD: HOW IT WORKS

The IUD or "loop" is not a popular method of contraception in Sri Lanka. According to CPS data, only 2.5% of married women respondents reported using this method, 1% lower than the findings of the WFS in 1975. In the Sri Lankan Demographic and Health Survey (1987), only 2.1% of informants reported using an IUD for contraception. While most of our informants had heard the term "loop," few could describe this method beyond stating that it was some kind of barrier which prevented male *dhātu* from entering into a woman. Notably, some women discussed the IUD by referring to it as an operation. Indeed, in one case where a woman had told us that she had had an operation, it turned out that she had not had a tubal ligation as we imagined, but an IUD insertion. For this woman, any procedure which involved lying down in a clinic where a doctor used long instruments inside her body constituted an operation.

A very vague sense of ethnoanatomy emerged from discussions about the IUD. Few women, even users, had an understanding of where the IUD was placed inside of them. Lack of a clear idea as to placement was reflected in a popular health concern involving migration of an IUD within the body. Informants spoke of it being gradually pushed up towards the stomach and beyond. Many conceptualized no clear separation between the womb and stomach or imagined one bodily sac opening into the other. A fear was expressed that if the IUD was pushed into the stomach, an operation would be required to remove it. If this was not done the IUD could move up to the lungs and kill the woman. Women at greatest risk were thought to be those who engaged in sex more frequently, for the loop was imagined to "move up" during more vigorous sexual activity.

The idea that an IUD can travel in the body and lodge in the head or lungs has been noted in Botswana (Larson 1983), Kenya (Huston 1979), India (Liskin 1984), Mexico (Shedlin 1979), and Tunisia (Sukkary-Stolba and Mossavar-Rahmani 1982). In Peru, Maynard-Tucker notes that "some women thought that the IUD floats in the body and can perforate the lungs or brain and eventually kill them" (Maynard-Tucker 1986:312). Peruvian respondents reported that the IUD attacks the head and the nerves.

In Sri Lanka, informants also noted that the IUD could fall out after it was inserted. At the time of insertion, women are advised by health personnel to "feel for the string" following urination. When they fail to find it, they suspect it has fallen out or that it has been pushed up. Some Sri Lankan women noted that heavy work could cause an IUD to fall out. Other informants stated that if a woman had sex with more than one partner, her vagina might become larger, causing the IUD to fall out. If a woman's IUD did fall out, or rumor suggested that it had, this created suspicion that the woman had been having extramarital affairs.

In Sri Lanka, one of the main health concerns associated with IUD use is a loss of blood following insertion. Users attributed weakness from the IUD to an increase in menstrual blood loss. A majority of women users interviewed stated that this might occur. Some informants assumed that this loss of blood was in some way involved with the functioning of the method itself constituting a "primary negative effect." In one instance, an informant stated that she had suffered from continuous bleeding for one month following her loop insertion, but had not sought follow-up care. When we asked her why she thought this bleeding had occurred, she remarked:

> The loop is something made of plastic so it creates a lot of heat. It is like wearing rubber slippers — when you wear them, your feet feel hot and you get heating side effects. The bleeding is caused by this heatiness. Heatiness and bleeding are to be expected. This is how the method works.

Another idea reported was that the loop could cause "cancer." In probing the meaning of cancer, we found that the term was taken from the media and incorporated in everyday speech to denote chronic ill health caused by a foreign substance inside the body. Informants associated the presence of a foreign body with heatiness, toxicity, and wounds within the body resulting in rough (scar like) tissue — cancer.

Ideas circulating about the IUD may in large part be due to the lack of explanation offered to women about possible side effects. In India, for example, Cassen has noted, "it was felt that it was sufficiently hard to persuade women to use the IUD at all and would be harder if they had to be told that they might experience pain or bleeding" (Cassen 1978:158). This strategy of withholding information about potential side effects was not successful in India and rumors, in part based on ethnoanatomical knowledge, spread that the IUD could migrate within the body to the heart and lungs, and could cause penile injury or even death to the husband during intercourse. As a result, IUD adoption rates dropped dramatically.[33] Subsequently, side effects of the IUD were explained and taken more seriously by program personnel (Ainsworth 1985).

An ethical problem related to health service may well contribute to the unpopularity of the IUD in Sri Lanka. In rural Ratnapura, the IUD was widely adopted when it was first introduced, but within a few years many women discontinued its use. A number of informants in this region spoke of the IUD being unreliable and falling out. When we interviewed family health workers about this, we were told that there was little if any screening before IUD insertion.[34] Upon investigation we identified an important reason why the reliability of the IUD was questioned. Several women had an IUD inserted after they found out they were pregnant, thinking this would result in an abortion.[35] When their pregnancy became visible, it gave rise to the notion that a woman could get pregnant, even when having an IUD. When confronted with a pregnant woman following an IUD insertion, clinicians commonly acted "kindly" suggesting the possibility that the IUD may not have been positioned correctly. In so doing, they alleviated suspicion that the woman might have engaged in extra marital sexual affairs should her husband have been away prior to IUD insertion. This kindness undermined perception of IUD efficacy.

SOCIAL CLASS AND PERCEPTIONS OF CONTRACEPTIVE METHOD APPROPRIATENESS

Assuming a "positive deviance" stance to research, we interviewed several satisfied users of contraceptive methods. We asked a lower middle class informant, a satisfied user of both IUD and sterilization, why some women complained of bleeding and weakness after these procedures while others, like herself, did not. She replied that each person's body was different so it responds differently to family planning methods. When we asked in what way people's bodies were different, she noted that some were more heaty than others. She further explained that the pill and IUD were very heaty and harsh so they were not good for women with heaty bodies who could not afford to eat cooling foods. She remarked: "If a woman doesn't eat cooling foods while taking the pill, she loses the ability to conceive — she dries up. If she can eat cooling food while taking the pill, she may still be fertile when she stops."

Three important ideas emerged during our interview with this person: 1) people with different bodies respond differently to modern methods; 2) if one uses a method which has a negative primary effect or an unintended side effect, it is possible to counterbalance this effect thereby reducing harm to the body; and 3) a chief means of reducing negative effects — especially blood loss — is by consuming cooling and strength producing foods. Following this interview we spoke to several lower middle class and poor informants. What emerged was a widespread impression that modern methods of contraception were more appropriate for those who could afford to consume cooling foods such as milk and strength giving foods such as eggs, meat, and some varieties of fish.

Important lessons can be learned from considering distinct social class perceptions of contraceptive appropriateness evaluated in relation to the availability of resources and perceptions of risk. According to the poor, the diet of the wealthy which included milk, eggs, and meat products, enabled them to cope more effectively with the primary negative effects of contraceptive methods. While birth control pills might be appropriate for the middle class, they were not an appropriate method for the poor because they could not afford to routinely balance the heating side effects of pills with the consumption of tender coconut water and cow's milk. Of the six lower middle-class women whom we interviewed who were presently using the pill, all went into elaborate detail about the strategies they employed to cool their bodies. Not having enough resources to routinely consume special foods, one woman resorted to bathing frequently with cool well water and drinking large quantities of cold water. Four of these women noted that they restricted the intake of heating foods such as dry fish (thus reducing their dietary resources), in an effort to counterbalance excess heat in their body.

The idea that "nutritious" food can offset harmful effects of fertility regulation methods has been noted cross-culturally. For example, in Morocco it has been reported that although pills can cause heart palpitations, they can be used safely by women rich enough to afford a "balanced" diet (Mernissi 1975). As one informant noted:

> If you eat only starch and you can never afford milk, meat or bananas ... you are already weak and the pill is therefore dangerous for you because it affects the heart. A weak body cannot take the pill. The day I can afford to have a banana and a glass of milk I will start using the pill again. Until then I have to find another method which is less dangerous. (Mernissi 1975:422)

Writing about Egypt, Morsy similarly notes that:

> The ingestion of powerful medications is also believed to require the consumption of large amounts of nourishing foods. This belief illuminates a rationalization by women for their refusal to consume birth control pills. Women who have used these pills complain that they cause weakness.... "Strong medicine like this needs good eating and we are poor peasants." (Morsy 1980:93)

Similar ideas about the need for "good food" while taking the pill were noted by Sukkary-Stolba and Mossavar-Rahmani (1982) in their five country study in the Middle East.

It is not only the negative primary effects of oral contraceptives which are believed to be offset by more optimum food consumption. Many Sri Lankan informants expressed the view that if a woman could afford to eat eggs, milk, meat, and fish, and refrain from hard work for three months following sterilization, weakness and general malaise could be mitigated. By following this regimen, a woman's body would be allowed to replenish its supply of *dhātu* which had been lost.[36]

Two points may be highlighted. First, decisions whether or not to adopt various family planning methods/practices entail consideration of social and economic constraints as well as perceptions of health risk.[37] Second, contraception is associated with increased vulnerability to ill health, a state which may be mitigated by folk dietetic prescriptions and restrictions. Among the poor, dietary restrictions are more likely to be followed because prescriptions are unaffordable. The result is that in the name of contraception, those already in a debilitated state tend to restrict their diet. When recurring health problems are experienced, their cause or exacerbation are often linked to contraceptive methods in use. Medical staff commonly interpret complaints of "side effects" as being psychosomatic. What they fail to comprehend is that family planning methods are thought to impact on bodily processes which result in symptom manifestation. Symptoms may be the direct result of a method or be caused by bodily processes and latent illness indirectly affected by the properties of medical fixes. That is, causality may be perceived as either primary or secondary. Given a context of chronic ill health (Chen 1986) where a local population is trying to balance humoral influences and produce *dhātu*, concern about the impact of medical fixes is quite reasonable.

SECRECY AND THE IDEAL OF CONTROL: THE IMPORTANCE OF RUMOR

Let us finally consider the phenomena of "rumor" as a social leveling tactic within a culture where sexual control is valued as a religious ideal. Although the Sinhalese are more open to discuss modern methods of birth control than traditional practices (see Chapter 1), there is some reticence especially among the low to middle class to publicly admit that one is using a family planning method. Within the dominant Sinhalese Buddhist culture, control is a highly regarded social value associated with doing or wanting nothing in excess. As Amarasingham (1983) has noted, Sinhalese Buddhist ideology prescribes moderation as an ideal. Anything in excess is believed to lead to unhappiness and ultimately to suffering. Applied to birth control, this cultural value manifests as public secrecy about contraceptive method adoption. Control of one's sexuality is a source of respect and social status. As one informant noted, admitting to use of a method amounts to "telling that you are unable to control your sexual urge and that you are uncultured." Our middle class informants commonly spoke of the uneducated having more children because "they cannot control themselves." These same informants were often the first to emphasize secrecy about method use "so neighbors will not come to know and spread rumors about us."

The importance of secrecy varies by ethnic group, social class, and residence pattern. For example, among lower middle class informants in rural Horana and Ratnapura Districts, great effort was expended on bypassing the normal points of condom distribution to maintain secrecy.[38] The desire for secrecy was further found to affect women's willingness to contact family health workers about IUD related problems. Some informants expressed embarrassment and discomfort when family health workers visited their homes, fearing that this would suggest to neighbors that they were using a family planning method. This kind of behavior points out the weakness of the assumption that greater geographic accessibility to family planning resources necessarily leads to greater use.

The cultural value placed on control of one's sexuality has given rise to social seclusion as well as secrecy. A widespread concern among males is that methods of family planning adopted by women afford them license to engage in extramarital sexual relations. A few women in Sri Lanka and many more in South India reported strained social relations with spouses following use of contraceptives, particularly tubectomy. Women reported that husbands act far more protective of them, monitoring their coming and going and questioning their participation in social activities. As a means of reducing a husband's suspicions, some women who had actively participated in community affairs decreased their participation in social activities following sterilization. These informants described a deep sense of loss over their forced withdrawal from social networks. Family planning methods had removed them from being victims of unplanned families, but they were now victims of suspicion — confining them yet once again.

A sensitivity to cultural values and the devastating impact of rumor influences the way in which doctors explain pregnancy to a husband when he has had a vasectomy or when a woman claims she is practicing birth control, but becomes pregnant. In such a situation, health care providers are faced with discrediting either the woman or the method. Given the grave situation which may result from accusing a woman of infidelity in a country with a high suicide rate, health care providers consistently stated that they protected their patient at all costs when forced with such a dilemma. Of eight private doctors interviewed, six stated they had faced such a situation at least once in the past three years. In each case they linked method failure to the pregnancy in question. Although these doctors behaved in a culturally tactful and kind manner, their remarks reduced confidence in the efficacy of family planning methods.

CONCLUSION

One of the biggest problems with most KAP surveys on contraceptives is that "knowledge" and "familiarity" are conflated. "Knowledge" of a family planning method as reported on the CPS, the WFS, and other such surveys can mean anything from recall of the name of a method to direct experience using it, from familiarity with someone who has tried it to knowledge as an objectified construct of how the method might function. Different forms of contraceptive knowledge exist, ranging from explanatory models rooted in folk health culture to (re)interpretations of information gleaned from bio-medical or traditional medical practitioners. A greater appreciation of the range of "knowledge" people maintain about contraceptive methods can help broaden our comprehension of contraceptive use and non-use among particular groups. A better understanding of the production of knowledge about contraception use/nonuse by practitioners, health officials, and laypersons may provide insights into the motivations and agendas of these stake holders in the family planning arena. Given that this arena is becoming increasingly politicized, research is required which looks beyond the rhetoric of promoters and critics alike.

A population must be prepared conceptually in order to make intelligent choices about family planning methods. This requires a two-way flow of information from potential consumers and providers of family planning services. A first step in understanding the mentality of consumers requires an appreciation of the assumptions which local populations maintain about the ethnophysiology of reproduction, the criteria upon which they base their assessment of existing health fixes, and the concerns they express about the long- and short-term effects of such fixes. To dismiss local health perceptions as misinformation and rumor is medicocentric. It discounts the embodied knowledge of local populations and the empirical observations they make of biotechnology. It also overlooks observations about the social relations of method use. It is necessary to consider public response to health fixes both in relation to how they are delivered (physically and conceptually) as well as how they are experienced socially and bioculturally.

Fertility regulation is an emotionally charged area of biotechnology in which there is much contention among practitioners and the public alike. Reproductive health risks are associated with contraceptive use and there is a need to monitor such use among peoples having different physical and cultural characteristics. Called for is research sensitive to the physical body as well as the social body: who is involved in fertility decision making, what constitutes cultural common sense, and reasons why concern is expressed about contraceptive use at different times during the life span. Such research will need to shift attention away from a narrow focus on "barriers to method acceptance" to a finer grained consideration of 1) which population sectors make use of modern methods when they are available and at what point in their reproductive careers, and 2) segments of the population which express the desire to limit family size but retain reservations about the long- and short-term effects of method use.[39]

In Sri Lanka, as in a growing number of developing countries experiencing socioeconomic transformation, there is public interest in fertility regulation. At the same time there is rising concern about health and doubt about technology gone awry. To meet the demands of these populations and to gain their trust, local health concerns will need to be addressed in a meaningful manner.[40] It is naive to imagine that well entrenched conceptual frameworks such as hot/cold (humoral systems, etc.), basic to the health cultures of ancient civilizations, will vanish in the wake of biomedicine. In this regard it is prudent to bear in mind that:

> The consequence of modern science and technology has not been to overwhelm common sense views and render them insignificant, but to modify them somewhat and increase their cultural significance. (Holzner and Marx 1979)

Rather than work on "dispelling rumor" about contraception, perhaps it is time that we learned how to communicate with the "other," working within their conceptual system(s) while introducing new ideas and encouraging keen observation instead of blind belief. What is needed, as Hardon (1992) has aptly noted, is a shift in thinking about contraception from the need to fit people to technology to the need to fit technology to people. Fitting technology to people requires a careful cultural reading of the body and attentive listening to the voices of potential consumers.

NOTES

1. Research on contraceptive use also demands consideration of gender issues related to communication about family planning, family size, preferences, and responsibility for contraception. On gender differences related to contraceptive use, see Browner and Perdue 1986, 1988, Hoodfar 1994, Jejeebhoy and Kulkarni 1989, Mason and Taj 1987, Maynard-Tucker 1986, Mott and Mott 1985.
2. These figures come from the World Development Report 1993 (World Bank 1993).
3. CPS data indicate that the percentage of women using traditional methods was positively associated with education whereas this was not the case for use of modern methods (Sri Lanka 1983:7), cited in Gendell (1985). For example, 21% of women who had completed primary school used traditional methods compared to 29% who had completed secondary school education or above. Utilization of modern methods averaged 30% among both groups.

4. Gajanayake and Caldwell (1990) contend that the use of traditional methods are significantly underreported because people are reluctant to discuss these practices. Another reason for the underreporting is that the survey instruments were not designed to allow for multiple method use, so the data collected only had limited validity.

5. Several government health education officers told us that the group who had the most questions and the most doubts about modern methods of family planning were the educated — particularly teachers. Often these doubts were associated with information printed in local newspapers wherein large headlines announced news such as "Oral Contraceptives Cause Cancer." We found that statistics that often followed these headlines established that cancer was relatively rare. Informants tended to remember headlines, however, and not supporting data.

6. The Matlab Project in Bangladesh indicated that while access to contraceptives is a necessary precondition for the adoption of family planning, contraceptive prevalence rates are not always high when contraceptives are simply physically available (Cain 1980, Phillips et al. 1982 and 1984, Simmons et al. 1990). There is a real need to understand the user's perspective when designing and modifying family planning programs. KAP surveys are an insufficient mode of research. Qualitative information is required not only on how decisions about reproduction and contraception are made, but about the rationale behind these decisions — i.e., the meaning of modern methods. Such an approach has been advocated by Marshall and Polgar (1976), who have called for a phenomenological approach — "one that demands an understanding of existing and potential fertility regulation methods from the perspective of the client population."

7. See Etkin (1994) for a more detailed discussion of side effects which recognizes the distinction drawn between negative primary effects vital to the action of a medication and unintended side effects.

8. A "micro-demographic" study reported by Caldwell et al. (1987) corroborates our findings in other areas of Sri Lanka including the estate sector. Their paper liberally draws upon research we designed and supervised while working as consultants to the Sri Lankan Bureau of Census and Statistics. While the aforementioned paper accurately reflects major findings reported in our consultant report on Sinhalese and Tamil perceptions of modern contraceptive methods, it underplays the amount of intracultural variability we recorded related to lay perceptions of safe and fertile periods during a woman's monthly cycle. This issue is addressed in Chapter 1 where we draw upon data from a restudy carried out with the assistance of health educators assigned to the Sri Lankan Bureau of Health Education.

9. Heatiness is a "Singlish" term denoting an increase in heat in the body.

10. Similar ideas have been reported by Shedlin (1979), who states the following from her fieldwork among Mexican women:

Oral contraceptives or the "pill" seem to have generated the most variations in beliefs about how it works. It is seen as a medicine which affects the blood or liquid of the woman, man, or both, either to make one or both liquids too weak to join together to begin the formation of the baby. It was also said to enter the uterus and force everything out, or to dissolve the joined liquids and cause them to "bajar" (go down). Thus it is seen as functioning before conception to prevent it, or after conception to destroy it and cause everything involved to leave the body. (Shedlin 1979:13)

11. More recent research on contraceptive use in Iran describes a government push to popularize the use of oral contraception. Hoodfar (1994) conducted a survey of 1000 urban and 1000 rural households in Tehran province where access to information about contraception is high. She found that 25% of both rural and urban pill users took the pill either every other night or only before/after intercourse. Their self-regulated use of pills was associated both with fear of side effects and the desire to conserve a supply of the pills.

12. Although Kane et al. (1988) show that some younger women do adopt birth control pills, our study documents a pervasive concern about how pills may reduce one's fecundity. Future research needs to focus on how long a woman uses a method and whether there are breaks in using a method (what may be termed "method holidays") as a way of reducing harm to the body. For example, MacCormack (1985) notes that in Jamaica the pill is thought to work by mechanically (not chemically) blocking sperm from entering the uterus. Fear that pills may build up over time leads some women to periodically stop taking pills or to wash out the internal body through the use of castor oil.

13. Similarly, Kane, Gaminiratne, and Stephen (1988) found that over half of the women in their sample who switched from using the IUD to traditional methods did so because of concerns about bleeding, physical problems, and concerns about the methods's potential impact on their fecundity. These ideas, however, are mentioned only briefly in passing and are clearly deserving of more attention. Their paper presents some rather questionable data (1988:73, see Table 5) suggesting that women who want to have children shift from traditional to modern methods.

14. In Sri Lanka the drying, heating effect of the pill on one's bodily process is generalized to other processes. A drying of the breastmilk is associated with the drying of the womb — an idea also reported in Iran (Good 1980). The drying–reducing effect of the pill is also associated with weight, an overdetermined symbol of well being in South Asia.

15. Several other studies have reported indigenous perceptions of how the pill works which suggest that they harm the body. These range from a weakening of the body to a weakening of the blood (Shedlin, Hollerback and Hollerback 1981, Maynard-Tucker 1989) to a malicious attack on the forming fetus (Ibanez-Novion 1980) to the eating of "cells" (Scrimshaw 1985).

16. DeClerque et al. (1986) suggest that in relation to the ubiquitous complaint of weakness there may be unique side effects generated through the combined use of high dose pills and endemic health problems (such as anemia) among Egyptian women.

17. Ethnographic research relating to the issue of weakness may be found in Morsy (1980), Good (1980), Nichter (1981), and De Clerque et al. (1986).

18. We have come across similar ideas in both India and the Philippines. Projections of the cost of feeding a baby formula in the Philippines made by Mayling Simpson-Herbert in 1986 are sobering. She estimated that among impoverished residents of Metro Manila, 12.5% of their annual yearly income would have to be spent to feed one infant with formula, should a mother not be able to breastfeed. In addition to avoiding birth control pills during lactation many women try to avoid injections and other strong medicines. This is both because they fear that medicine may be transferred through the breastmilk (which in fact does happen in some cases) and cause harm to the baby and because they fear strong medicine will affect their ability to produce milk. This was one reason mothers diagnosed as TB positive abandoned short course TB medications until their babies were weaned (Nichter 1994).

19. The concern raised by Oni is that if mothers are encouraged to use contraceptive methods in the months following childbirth to postpone subsequent pregnancies, they are likely to reduce their breastfeeding practices and introduce breastmilk substitutes earlier. The potential problems this practice may give rise to include reduced immunological protection against infection as well as increased contamination through bottlefeeding. There may also be a tendency of mother's who use oral contraceptives to associate the effects of these pills to children's illnesses and to engage in abrupt weaning practices (Oni 1986).

20. Surveys often reveal as much about the mentality and gaze of their designers as the people to whom they are administered. In many cases, survey data constitute artifacts of the survey instrument itself. Hardon (1992) draws attention to limitations in the design and interpretation of controlled clinical trials and acceptability studies of contraceptives. She points out that data from clinical trials may not be generalizable to populations of consumers because research populations are not representative and because there is a lack of explicit indicators and criteria to determine acceptability to potential users. Hardon comments on researchers' tendency to define such disorders as headache, dizziness and weight fluctuations as "minor" without a consideration of the interpretation of such symptoms in local health cultures.

21. Margarita Kay (1985) has raised a related point in her work with the Mexican-American community. She has noted that Mexican American women do not attribute the same characteristics to birth control pills and other forms of contraception as are found in the scientific educational materials they are given. She suggests that contraceptive providers have a poor understanding of what properties are salient to their users. The Basnayake et al. report exemplifies this point.

22. In another study in Egypt, Khattab (1978) found that among 70 pill users in a rural village, 24 (35%) were using the pill incorrectly. Many were using the same brand of a 28 day pill cycle where vitamin tablets were intended for the seven days of the menstrual flow. She noted that women started with the supplementary pills while others alternated pills with vitamins to counteract side effects.

23. Seaton (1985) has also stressed that "In less developed countries, the problem of ensuring client compliance in family planning programs are aggravated by educational and cultural environments that do little or nothing to promote an understanding of the perceptions and practices of contraception" (Seaton 1985:52).

24. Medicines and manual techniques are employed to "bring back the menses" or at least induce some bleeding. Bleeding constitutes a reason to visit a hospital where a doctor might be more willing to conduct a dilation and curettage procedure.

25. In addition to problems relating to cultural styles of communication and the dynamics of knowledge production is the limited capability of a structured interview to create an environment fostering the articulation of tacit knowledge. While structured surveys may prove reliable for collecting certain types of microdemographic data, they are an insufficient way of researching the meaning of health related behavior, the production of knowledge about health and family planning, and the interpretation of lived experience.

26. In South Kanara District, Karnataka, India, a tubectomy is referred to as turning the pregnancy bag over (*garbha chila madistare*). Matthews and Benjamin (1979) have similarly reported that a tubectomy in Tamil Nadu is described as "twisting the uterus" or "turning it upside down." A vasectomy in both areas is described as cutting a nerve (*nara*) by many people.

27. This study was carried out in conjunction with the Department of Census and Statistics in 1984.

28. Informants noted that since the operation caused weakness it was more economically viable for the wife to be sterilized than the husband. If a wife could no longer do hard work outside of the home after the operation, she could at least continue with the housework which was perceived to be less strenuous in nature than work outside the home.

29. *Preethi*, a term which means happiness in Sinhala and Tamil, was chosen as the name for the condom and a hand signal was designed so it could be obtained from shops by demonstrating a nonverbal cue, thus reducing embarrassment. Although we found that the product was widely known, the hand signal was much less recognized than we had expected given the popularity described in the literature. In fact, the hand signal approximates another commonly used nonverbal cue meaning excellent.

30. Among the middle class, the words "uneducated" and "uncultured" are often used interchangeably as markers of inclusion/noninclusion. They do not refer

so much to one's literacy or formal education but rather to knowledge and public adherence to Buddhist precepts and practice.

31. A variant idea is that the *dhātu* of a young woman is particularly rejuvenating for an old man — one reason why old men like to marry young girls (Harrison 1976).

32. For a more explicit example of the importance of reciprocal exchange, see Taylor (1988, 1992) who describes reciprocity at the site of the body as central to physical and social health in Rwanda.

33. Similar concerns about the IUD have been reported in other regions of the world. Shedlin (1979:14), for example, noted that women in Mexico "were concerned it would fall out, get lost, appear in various orifices of the body, cause them to become stuck together with their husbands, be felt by their husbands, etc." With reference to India, Marshall has noted: "The IUD was believed by the villagers to operate by increasing the heat in a woman's genital region above the threshold at which conception could occur. Under normal circumstances this would not be considered physically dangerous to a woman, but if she were afflicted with certain ailments that were thought to be "hot" — such as smallpox, diarrhea, or venereal disease — then the additional heat from an IUD could kill her. Since a woman could not be assured of escaping such a disease after she had adopted a loop, the method was best avoided" (1973:128). A lack of understanding about the IUD has also been noted by Johnson, Snow, and Mayhew (1978) in a study in the United States. Among their informants, 53% had incorrect information on the IUD's mode of action. The IUD was seem by many women as a plug that kept the sperm and egg from getting together. This notion of something "plugging" the female was reported by 39% of these women to be dangerous to health (Johnson, Snow, and Mayhew 1978:858). In both India and Jamaica (MacCormack 1985) some women feel that the IUD is unclean in as much as the coil (and its "string") are exposed to the impurities of semen and menstrual blood.

34. IUDs were inserted once a month during a special clinic day. All women interested in IUD insertion therefore had to appear at that time, regardless of when they had had their last menses. IUD insertion is ideally performed during menses. Many women, however, had insertions at other times of the month.

35. Some women had IUDs inserted to induce abortion. After IUD insertion, bleeding is heavy leading these women to believe that "everything inside would be pushed out." If the IUD failed to abort pregnancy, some women would return to the clinic the following month and have it removed.

36. The type of food that a person can afford is a factor which also impacts on sexual behavior. As one Tamil informant explained, "With our present food situation, we can afford to have sex only one to three times a month. This is not because we don't enjoy sex but because when we lose *dhātu* and don't take proper foods to replace it, we become weak."

37. Ainsworth (1985) has provided a useful review of the literature on perceived social and health related costs of practicing contraception and strategies developed to reduce the costs and satisfy unmet needs related to quality of service and access to information method and follow-up service.

38. Coastal Muslims preferred birth control pills delivered directly to the home for the same reason. The need for secrecy was not found among Tamils working on tea estates who preferred to go to sterilization camps in a group. Truckloads of women working on the plantations were driven to the Government Hospital for these camps. When we inquired if this did not make women shy (i.e., that everyone could plainly see what they were doing) we were told by several informants that they felt shy to go alone.

39. Contraceptive methods are weighed differentially across the reproductive lifespan in relation to both a woman's reproductive and productive capacity. While this chapter and studies such as Bledsoe et al. (1994) primarily draw attention to concerns about reproductive capacity, other studies such as Schaler and Goldstein (1986) have noted the fear of the poor of jeopardizing their household production of health as a result of contraceptive use. The risk of the impact of a mother's or father's ill health on the survival of other household members leads the poor to believe that modern methods are suitable for the better off, who engage in less strenuous work, eat better quality foods, and have access to health care.

40. It is important to recognize that many couples who switch from modern temporary methods to traditional methods, or who only use traditional methods may fall outside the family planning source network. Kane, Gaminiratne, and Stephen (1988) suggest that special community based outreach programs need be implemented to reach these couples to educate them about the correct use of traditional methods as well as the availability of modern methods.

REFERENCES

Ainsworth, M. 1985. Family Planning Programs: The Clients' Perspective. World Bank Staff Working Papers Number 676, Population and Development Series Number 1. Washington, DC: The World Bank.

Amarasingham, L. 1983. Laughter and Suffering: Sinhalese Interpretations of the Use of Ritual Humor. Social Science and Medicine 17:979–984.

Basnayake, S., J. E. Higgins, P. Miller, S. Rogers, and S. E. Kelley. 1984. Early Symptoms and Discontinuation Among Users of Oral Contraceptives in Sri Lanka. Studies in Family Planning 15(6):285–290.

Bertrand, J. T., J. D. Araya, R. J. Cisneros, and L. Morris. 1982. Evaluation of Family Planning, Communication in El Salvador. International Journal of Health Education 24(3):183–194.

Bledsoe, C., A. Hill, U. D'Alessandro, and P. Langerick. 1994. Constructing Natural Fertility: The Use of Western Contraceptive Technologies in Rural Gambia. Population and Development Review 20(1):81–113.

Bleek, W. 1987. Lying Informants: A Fieldwork Experience from Ghana. Population and Development Review 13(2):314–322.

Bogue, D. J. 1975. Twenty-Five Communication Obstacles to the Success of Family Planning Programs. Media Monograph 2. Communication Laboratory, Community and Family Study Center, University of Chicago, Chicago, Illinois.

Browner, C. and S. Perdue. 1986. The Politics of Reproduction in a Mexican Village: Signs. Journal of Women in Culture and Society 11:710–724.

Browner, C. and S. Perdue. 1988. Women's Secrets: Bases for Reproductive and Social Autonomy in a Mexican Community. American Ethnologist 15(1):84–97.

Cain, M. 1980. Risk, Fertility, and Family Planning in a Bangladesh Village. Studies in Family Planning 11(6):219–223.

Caldwell, J., K. Gominiratne, P. Caldwell, S. de Silva, B. Caldwell, N. Weeraratne, and P. Silva. 1987. The Role of Traditional Fertility Regulation in Sri Lanka. Studies in Family Planning 18(1):1–21.

Campbell, J. and L. Stone. 1984. The Use and Misuse of Surveys in International Development: An Experiment from Nepal. Human Organization 43(1):27–37.

Cassen, R. H. 1978. India: Population, Economy, Society. New York: Holmes and Meier.

Chen, L. 1986. Primary Health Care in Developing Countries: Overcoming Operation, Technical and Social Barriers. Lancet 8518(2):1260–1265.

Chullawathie, M. K. 1984. Lay Ideas on Fecundity During Women's Monthly Cycle and Post-Partum until Twelve Months. M.Sc. Field Project, Post Graduate Institute of Medicine, Colombo, Sri Lanka.

DeClerque, J., A. O. Tsu, M. F. Abul-Ata, and D. Barcelona. 1986. Rumor, Misinformation, and Oral Contraceptive Use in Egypt. Social Science and Medicine 23(1):83–93.

Department of Census and Statistics. 1978. World Fertility Survey, Sri Lanka, 1975: First Report. Ministry of Plan Implementation, Colombo.

Department of Census and Statistics. 1987. Demographic and Health Survey, Sri Lanka, 1987: Preliminary Report. Institute for Resource Development/Westinghouse, Columbia, MD.

Etkin, N. 1994. The Negotiation of "Side" Effects in Hausa (Northern Nigeria) Therapeutics. *In* Medicines, Meanings and Contexts. N. Etkin and M. Tan, eds. Pp. 17–32. Quezon City, Philippines: Health Action Information Network.

Gayanayake, I. and J. Caldwell. 1990. Fertility and its Control: The Puzzle of Sri Lanka. International Family Planning Perspectives 16(3):97–102.

Gendell, M. 1985. Stalls in the Fertility Decline in Costa Rica, Korea, and Sri Lanka. World Bank Staff Working Papers: Number 693, Population and Development Series Number 18, Washington, DC.

Good, M. J. D. 1980. Of Blood and Babies: The Relationship of Popular Islamic Physiology to Fertility. Social Science and Medicine 14b:147–156.

Goonasekera, A. 1976. Commercial Distribution of Contraceptives in Sri Lanka: The Preethi Experience. (mimeo).

Government of Sri Lanka, Department of Census and Statistics, Ministry of Plan Implementation and Westinghouse Health Systems. 1983. Sri Lànka Contraceptive Prevalence Survey Report: 1982. Department of Census and Statistics, Ministry of Plan Implementation, Colombo.

Halstead, S., J. Walsh, and K. Warren 1985. Good Health at Low Cost. New York: Rockefeller Foundation.

Hardon, A. 1992. The Needs of Women Versus the Interests of Family Planning Personnel, Policy Makers and Researchers: Conflicting Views on Safety and Acceptability of Contraceptives. Social Science and Medicine 35:753–766.

Harrison, P. 1976. Marketing Preethi in a Small Package. Human Behavior 5(3):56–61.

Holzner, B. and J. Marx. 1979. Knowledge Application: The Knowledge System in Society. Boston: Allyn and Bacon.

Hoodfar, H. 1994. Devices and Desires: Population Policy and Gender Roles in the Islamic Republic. Middle East Report (September/October):11–17.

Huston, P. 1979. Third World Women Speak Out. New York: Praeger.

Ibanez-Novion, M. 1980. The Pill and the Traditional Knowledge of the Human Body: A Brazilian Case Study. *In* Research Frontiers in Fertility Regulation. G. Zatuchni, M. Labhok, and J. Sciarra, eds. Pp. 4–72. New York: Harper and Row.

Jain, A. K. and J. Bongaarts. 1981. Breastfeeding: Patterns, Correlates, and Fertility Effects. Studies in Family Planning 12(3):79–99.

Jejeebhoy, S. and S. Kulkarni. 1989. Reproductive Motivation: A Comparison of Wives and Husbands in Maharashtra, India. Studies in Family Planning 20(5): 264–272.

Johnson, S. M., L. Snow, and H. Mayhew. 1978. Limited Patient Knowledge as a Reproductive Risk Factor. Journal of Family Practice 6(4):855–862.

Kane, T., K. Gaminiratne, and E. Stephen. 1988. Contraceptive Method-Switching in Sri Lanka: Patterns and Implications. International Family Planning Perspectives 14(2):68–75.

Kay, M. 1985. Mexican American Fertility Regulation. Communicating Nursing Research 10:279–295.

Khattab, M. 1978. Practice and Non-Practice of Family Planning in Egypt. *In* Social Science in Family Planning. A. Molnos, ed. Pp. 22–29. London: International Planned Parenthood Federation.

Knodel, J. and N. Debavalya. 1980. Breastfeeding in Thailand: Trends and Differentials, 1969–1979. Studies in Family Planning 11(2):355–377.

Krieger, L. 1984. Body Notions, Gender Roles, and Fertility Regulating Methods Used in Imbaba, Cairo. Ph.D. Dissertation, University of North Carolina, Chapel Hill, Department of Anthropology.

Larson, M. K. 1983. Botswana: Family Planning Myths and Beliefs. Cited in Population Reports No. 28, 1984.

Lesthaeghe, R., H. J. Page, and O. Adegbola. 1981. Child-Spacing and Fertility in Lagos. *In* Child Spacing in Tropical Africa: Traditions and Change. H. J. Page and R. Lesthaeghe, eds. New York: Academic Press.

Liskin, L. 1984. After Contraception: Dispelling Rumors About Later Childbearing. Population Reports No. 28, Population Information Program, Johns Hopkins University, Baltimore.

MacCormack, C. 1985. Lay Concepts Affecting Utilization of Family Planning Services in Jamaica. Journal of Tropical Medicine and Hygiene 88:281–285.

Marshall, J. F. 1972. Culture and Contraception: Response Determinants to a Family Planning Program in a North Indian Village. Ph.D. Dissertation, University of Hawaii.

Marshall, J. F. 1973. Fertility Regulating Methods: Cultural Acceptability for Potential Adopters. *In* Fertility Control Methods: Strategies for Introduction. G. W. Duncan, E. J. Hilton, P. Kreager, and A. A. Lumsdaine, eds. Pp. 125–133. New York: Academic Press.

Marshall, J. F. and S. Polgar, eds. 1976. Culture, Natality, and Family Planning, Monograph 21. Pp. 204–218. Chapel Hill, North Carolina: Carolina Population Center.

Mason, K. and A. Taj. 1987. Gender Differences in Reproductive Goals in Developing Countries. Population and Development Review 13(4):611–638.

Matthews, C. and V. Benjamin. 1979. Health Education Evaluation and Belief and Practices in Rural Tamil Nadu: Family Planning and Antenatal Care. Social Action 29:377–392.

Maynard-Tucker, G. 1986. Barriers to Modern Contraceptive Use in Rural Peru. Studies in Family Planning 17(6):308–316.

Mercado, C. M. 1973. Application of Social Science Methodologies to Information Education. *In* IPPF-SEAOR. Presented at the Eighth Meeting of the Regional Information and Education Committee, Singapore, May 9–11.

Mernissi, F. 1975. Obstacles to Family Planning Practice in Urban Morocco. Studies in Family Planning 6(12):418–425.

Morsy, S. A. 1980. Body Concepts and Health Care: Illustrations from an Egyptian Village. Human Organization 39(1):92–97.

Mott, F. and S. Mott. 1985. Household Fertility Decisions in West Africa: A Comparison of Male and Female Survey Results. Studies in Family Planning 16(2):88–99.

Nichter, Mark. 1981. Idioms of Distress: Alternatives in the Expression of Psychosocial Distress. Culture, Medicine and Psychiatry 5:379–408.

Nichter, Mark. 1994. Illness Semantics and International Health: The Weak Lungs/TB Complex in the Philippines. Social Science and Medicine 38(5):649–663.

Nichter, M. and N. Vuckovic. 1994. Agenda for an Anthropology of Pharmaceutical Practice. Social Science and Medicine 39(11):1509–1525.

Oni, G. A. 1986. Contraceptive Use and Breastfeeding: The Inverse Relationship and Policy Concern. East African Medical Journal (August):522–530.

Phillips, J. F., R. Simmons, J. Chakraborty, and A. I. Chowdhury. 1984. Integrating Health Services into an MCH-FP Program in Matlab, Bangladesh. Studies in Family Planning 15(4):153–161.

Phillips, J. F., W. S. Stinson, S. Bhatia, M. Rahman, and J. Chakraborty. 1982. Demographic Impact of the Family Planning-Health Services Project in Matlab, Bangladesh. Studies in Family Planning 13(5):131–140.

Rogers, E. M. 1973. Communication Strategies for Family Planning. New York: Free Press.

Schaler, S. and M. Goldstein. 1986. Family Planning in Nepal from the User's and Nonuser's Perspectives. Studies in Family Planning 17(2):66–77.

Scrimshaw, S. C. M. 1985. Bringing the Period Down: Government and Squatter Settlement Confront Induced Abortion in Ecuador. *In* Micro and Macro Levels of Analysis in Anthropology: Issues in Theory and Research. B. R. DeWalt and P. J. Pelto, eds. Pp. 121–146. Boulder: Westview Press.

Seaton, B. 1985. Non-Compliance Among Oral Contraceptive Acceptors in Rural Bangladesh. Studies in Family Planning 16(1):52–58.

Shedlin, M. 1979. Assessment of Body Concepts and Beliefs Regarding Reproductive Physiology. Studies in Family Planning 10:393–397.

Shedlin, M., M. Hollerback, and P. Hollerback. 1981. Modern and Traditional Fertility Regulation in a Mexican Community: The Process of Decision-Making. Studies in Family Planning 2(7):278–296.

Simmons, R., M. A. Koenig, and A. A. Z. Huque. 1990. Maternal-Child Health and Family Planning: User Perspectives and Service Constraints in Rural Bangladesh. Studies in Family Planning 21(4):187–196.

Simpson-Herbert, M. 1986. The Impact of Infant Feeding in Metro-Manila. RMAF Report, Vol. 2, Manila.

Smith, S. E. and D. Radel. 1972. The KAP in Kenya: A Critical Look at KAP Survey Methodology. *In* Culture, Natality and Family Planning. Marshall and Polgar, eds. Pp. 263–287. Chapel Hill, NC: Carolina Population Center.

Snowden, R. and B. Christian, eds. 1983. Patterns and Perceptions of Menstruation. New York: St. Martins Press.

Sobo, E. 1993. Bodies, Kin and Flow: Family Planning in Rural Jamaica. Medical Anthropology Quarterly 7(1):50–73.

Sukkary-Stolba, S. and Y. Mossavar-Rahmani. 1982. The Cultural Context of Fertility in Five Middle Eastern Countries. Unpublished manuscript.

Taylor, C. 1988. The Concept of Flow in Rwandan Popular Medicine. Social Science and Medicine 27:1343–1348.

Taylor, C. 1992. The Harp That Plays Itself. *In* Anthropological Approaches to the Study of Ethnomedicine. Mark Nichter, ed. Pp. 127–147. New York: Gordon and Breach.

Tucker, G. M. 1986. Barriers to Modern Contraceptive Use in Rural Peru. Studies in Family Planning 17(6):308–317.

World Bank. 1993. World Development Report 1993. New York: Oxford University Press.

Zurayk, H. 1981. Breastfeeding and Contraceptive Patterns Postpartum: A Study in South Lebanon. Studies in Family Planning 12:237.

Section Two

Child Survival

In this section, attention is focused on local interpretations of diarrheal illness and respiratory infection, the two biggest threats to child survival in the less developed countries. To gain insight into perceptions of health in South and Southeast Asia, it is necessary to appreciate bodily ways of knowing which are sensation and symptom based, experiential, and responsive to cultural notions of child development as well as issues of qualitative time and space. It is also important to recognize the wide range of factors thought to render one vulnerable to ill health as well as to predispose, cause, or confound particular types of illness. This is a complex subject because an illness may be caused by a number of different factors which influence the body singly or in conjunction with other factors. Few types of illnesses or symptom states are thought to be caused by one and only one factor. Sickness is often interpreted in relation to other life events and as a sign of misfortune and vulnerability within one's lifeworld.

A subjunctive mode of reasoning guides much deliberation about illness within a household or extended therapy management group. Varying opinions about the cause or course of an illness may be expressed, indexing multisensory readings of the body, prototypical illness experiences, knowledge gained from practitioners or health workers, and information conveyed through the media or read off the back of a medicine bottle. Ideas about etiology are not value free and often reflect concern about the moral dimension of sickness and implicit ideas about responsibility. These ideas often change over the course of an illness trajectory and may be subject to revision following an illness event.

An understanding of the ways in which the afflicted and concerned others describe and provisionally classify illness, perceive etiology, and evaluate symptom severity are important to an understanding of lay health behavior. Such understandings are not, however, sufficient to explain why specific households or individuals respond in particular ways to illness episodes. The logic of practice underlying much health behavior is more complicated. It is influenced by past illness experiences, social and economic contingencies, issues of entitlement which influence selective survival among the poor, perceptions of coexisting treatment modalities ("medical systems"), and the healing capacities of individual practitioners.

Ramifications of interpreting illness in various ways are considered in this section. Lessons learned from over a decade of focused illness ethnographies are outlined and methods found useful in such research illustrated. Moving beyond issues related to mothers and their ability to recognize serious illness, the treatment patterns of practitioners are examined in relation to the productive power of pharmaceutical companies. It is suggested, for example, that through product promotions, practitioners are inadvertently misled into thinking that particular types of illness are more common than epidemiological data would suggest.

CHAPTER 4

Health Social Science Research on the Study of Diarrheal Disease: A Focus on Dysentery

Mark Nichter

INTRODUCTION

Over the last two decades, a number of focused ethnographic studies have been conducted on diarrheal disease. To date, the ethnographic record on local classification of diarrheal disease has primarily been assessed in relation to the needs of oral rehydration (ORT) programs[1] (Kendall 1990, Sukkary-Stolba 1988, Weiss 1988). Given the significant number of diarrheal deaths associated with dysentery (Black 1993, Chen et al. 1980, Ronsmans, Bennish, and Wierzoa 1988, Zimicki et al. 1985), it is time that this record be reassessed and formative research be conducted toward two ends: enhancing dysentery surveillance and developing a corrective to existing diarrhea rehydration messages relevant to dysentery. It is conservatively estimated that dysentery accounts for 20% of all diarrheal related deaths (Bhandari, Bhan, and Sazawal 1992).[2] Translated in terms of child survival, this amounts to approximately 5% of all deaths in children less than five years old, the age group at greatest risk to this complex of diseases. An estimated 740,000 deaths due to dysentery occur each year. Virtually all of these deaths occur in less developed countries (Hermann and Black 1987).

There is clearly a need for primary health care workers and community members to differentiate between secretory–watery forms of diarrhea and invasive–inflammatory forms of dysentery. These two broad categories of enteric infection require distinct kinds of monitoring and care. While in most cases the former may be managed with proper administration of ORT, the latter require prompt antimicrobial therapy. Despite this fact, specific primary health care messages have not been developed for bloody diarrhea in less developed countries.

Ethnographic data collected in South Asia and the Philippines suggest that community health workers often do not discriminate between cases of diarrhea which might involve dysentery when offering advice to child caretakers. Cases of dysentery are not rapidly triaged. While health workers may share with other members of their community concern about blood loss of any type, they have been trained to judge the severity of a case of diarrhea in relation to signs of dehydration.

Given this situation, a corrective to ORT messages which calls attention to dysentery needs to be introduced in a manner at once sensitive to local health culture and existing health education messages. Care needs to be taken not to discredit or deflect attention away from oral rehydration efforts. It would clearly be counterproductive to confuse a public and health field staff already exposed to oral rehydration messages. Moreover, while not in itself a sufficient treatment for dysentery, oral rehydration remains an important resource in dysentery management. Clinically significant dehydration is present in 15–20% of hospitalized dysentery cases (V. I. Mathan, personal communication). Required are health messages which encourage rehydration for all forms of diarrhea, while emphasizing that bloody diarrhea requires prompt medical treatment. This treatment is warranted irrespective of adjunct treatment modalities which members of a local population may feel are required for particular categories of local illness (e.g., treatments to cleanse or cool the body).

In order to construct culturally sensitive triage messages and develop community based treatment algorithms, a community diagnosis needs to be conducted which identifies:

1. Cultural conceptualizations of blood and concerns about blood loss.

2. Local categories of illness associated with bloody stools or watery diarrhea as well as times when diarrhea is expected.[3]

3. The language of illness: the manner in which illness is and is not spoken about within a culture.

4. The sensitivity and specificity of local illness terms for bloody diarrhea which correspond to clinical cases of dysentery.[4]

5. Popular use of biomedical terms for diarrhea and dysentery by practitioners.

6.   Home treatment of different types of illness associated with bloody and watery diarrhea. Of central importance are differences in the consumption of foods, liquids, (including SSS and ORS), and medicines (herbal decoctions, patent medicines, antimicrobials, etc.).

7.   Perceived signs of illness severity influencing health care seeking.

8.   Patterns of health care decision making sensitive to the age of the child and the experience and social status of child care takers.

9.   Dispensing and prescription practices of local doctors when encountering bloody diarrhea and factors influencing medicines dispensed (e.g., antibiotics, antiamoebic drugs, etc).

In the remainder of this chapter, these points will be considered in relation to social science issues germane to future data collection on bloody diarrhea. Before turning to cultural aspects of health care, however, it is necessary to highlight clinical signs of dysentery that are identifiable in field conditions.

DYSENTERY: CLINICAL SIGNS AND TREATMENT ISSUES

What signs or set of signs constitute the best field indicators of dysentery? Dysentery is characterized by frequent, small, often painful diarrheal stools accompanied by blood and/or mucus. Sometimes fever is present. In screening for the presence of shigella, which is the most common and important cause of mortality and prolonged morbidity due to dysentery, the sensitivity of fever and the specificity of mucus in the stool is low (Stoll and Glass 1982). This finding has led Ronsmans, Bennish, and Wieroza (1988) to propose that the simplest criterion that yields the greatest diagnostic sensitivity and specificity is observation of blood in the stool. Some cases are marked by blood at onset, while other cases, particularly among infants, are notable for explosive watery diarrhea in which blood becomes apparent one to two days after onset.

In terms of the clinical management of bloody diarrhea, of central importance is how long child caretakers wait before they bring an ill child to a clinic or source of medical care and what factors influence delay. It is important to understand when bloody diarrhea is deemed serious, how long bloody diarrhea is treated at home or by a traditional practitioner before a health worker or "doctor" are consulted, common drugs administered by local practitioners and patterns of drug resistance.[5] Data are needed on both self-medication with antimicrobials and the amount of drugs patients consume when they are dispensed or prescribed by practitioners.

CULTURAL RESPONSE TO BLOOD IN THE STOOL: WHAT IS KNOWN

Local terms for diarrheal illness marked by the presence of blood have been widely reported in ethnomedical studies conducted in South and Southeast Asia (Bangladesh, Cambodia, India, Pakistan, Philippines, Sri Lanka, and Thailand) Central and South America (Brazil, Costa Rica, Guatemala, Mexico, Nicaragua, and Peru), and Africa (Egypt, Ghana, Mali, Nigeria, and Sudan). The level of specificity of these data has been rather low in that a single term for bloody diarrhea has generally been noted. While this may be the case in some cultural contexts, it is likely that indigenous classification systems are more sensitive to differences associated with the onset and course of bloody diarrhea among children and adults, not to speak of differences in perceived causes.[6] For example, among the Yoruba of Nigeria, a recent study of bloody diarrhea has identified six types of bloody diarrhea, distinguished by a range of characteristics. One of these illness categories is associated with a distinctive treatment pattern which entails only the use of traditional medicines. The other five types of bloody diarrhea are treated by a combination of traditional and commercial remedies, as well as consultations to the clinic.[7]

The relative severity of different categories of diarrheal illness has been identified by researchers often on the basis of interviews in which informants are asked to rank order types of local illness. Such data must be assessed carefully. Rank ordering one illness above others in relation to severity does not indicate that lower ranked illnesses are considered less dangerous. Each and every type of diarrhea may be considered dangerous and debilitating in its own right and be associated with "danger signs" indicating severity. In some cases, one form of diarrhea may be perceived to transform into another when it becomes more severe.[8] In other cases, an illness label may remain unchanged, but changes in perception of severity may influence health care response. For example, "milestone" or "teething" diarrhea may be expected and considered routine for a few days, but deemed dangerous when a child exhibits behavioral changes associated with weakness and vulnerability.

Perceptions of diarrhea severity are influenced by experiences with cholera and typhoid as well as messages about ORT. During interviews with villagers in one area of Mindoro, Philippines, some informants voiced the opinion that secretory diarrhea was more serious than bloody diarrhea although dysentery was more painful. This impression appeared to be related to the attention focused on dehydration by the media (ORT messages broadcast on the radio) and Barangay Health Workers. Among patients attending clinics, fever, pain and vomiting, not blood in the stool, were identified as factors triggering urgent health care seeking. Bloody diarrhea was treated for some time at home by a combination of traditional medicines and over-the-counter drugs purchased at *sari sari* provision shops or a chemist shop in the provincial capital some 25 km away. Drugs employed prior to coming to the provincial hospital included Flagyl (a brand name of metronidazole, an antiamoebic drug).[9]

This pattern of self-treating bloody diarrhea with traditional medicines and allopathic drugs secured from chemist shops was also documented in South Kanara, India, and has been reported in Nigeria (Adisa and Sunmola 1994). What has not been systematically studied is the length of time bloody diarrhea is treated prior to consulting a doctor. Unknown is whether delay varies by illness category or is triggered by a change in the classification of an illness for one reason or another inclusive of "diagnosis by treatment." The latter entails a reevaluation of the nature of an illness based on the failure of a previous treatment, or a perception that this treatment has managed one dimension of the illness (such as its cause) leaving other dimensions to be reckoned with subsequently.

ILLNESS CLASSIFICATION: ETHNOGRAPHIC CONSIDERATIONS

In order to assess the potential usefulness of local illness categories for epidemiological surveillance and community triage messages, two sets of issues arise. First, what is the specificity and sensitivity of folk illness terms in denoting whether an ill person actually has a bloody stool? Second, for those individuals who do not have blood in their stools, what additional sets of characteristics influence both the labeling of an illness episode and patterns of treatment response? In order to appreciate these issues and the methods of data collection needed to address them, a brief discussion of denotative and connotative attributes of illness is instructive.

Medical anthropologists distinguish between the denotative features and connotative aspects of an illness. The denotative features of an illness are referential; they point to specific attributes. These include: a) physical signs such as the presence or lack of blood and/or mucus in the stool, stool color or smell; and b) concurrent symptoms such as teething, mouth sores, fever, rash, prolapsed anus, pain, or strain when defecating, etc. These features also include measures of severity linked to illness onset and duration as well as the progression of symptoms. Where they are culturally meaningful, these factors may constitute important inclusion and exclusion criteria for defining an illness category.

Connotative aspects of an illness identity are less clear-cut and multidimensional. They emerge as a cluster of loosely associated image schema and feelings about an illness experience bringing to mind personal experiences and indexing cultural meanings linked to illness. The connotative dimension of an illness is evocative, episodic, and contextual, flowing from what Good (1977) has described as a semantic illness network: a pool of illness related associations embedded in culture, enriched through personal experience and condensed around core cultural concerns. Connotative aspects of a diarrheal episode might involve subtle cues which trigger the memory of a past illness experience, feelings of fear or vulnerability related to a particular season, celestial event, or environmental happenstance, or ideas about causality linked to humors, sexual behavior, the excessive consumption of sweet foods, witchcraft, or the evil eye. They might also index cultural notions of blame or responsibility, issues related to entitlement which influence health seeking behavior; or the need for secrecy associated with stigma. Bibeau (1981) in Africa and Nichter (1989) in South Asia have provided examples of how connotative aspects of illness influence the manner in which an illness identity is framed, reframed, and negotiated in context.

Recent anthropological research suggest that both denotative features and connotative aspects of an illness contribute to its tentative classification. Classification entails more than a checklist of illness attributes (Fillmore 1975). An illness identity is established in relation to a series of scripts or scenarios of what a prototype of a named illness is like. As Rosch (1978) has noted, a prototype is less a fixed cognitive model than an ensemble of judgements about prototypicality. Typicality may be established in several ways through propositions, image schema, metaphor, and metonymy (Lakoff 1987). An actual experience of illness may share only a "family resemblance" to a prototype scenario. That is, a sharing of specific features may be incidental rather than essential (Rosch 1978). In some cases, particular characteristics of an illness will be dwelled upon in illness narratives. In other cases, however, it is the indeterminacy and ambiguity of an illness which leads to speculation and subjunctive thought.

Of central importance to the epidemiologist is whether and to what extent clinical signs of a disease (e.g., dysentery) constitute a general class of locally named illness or are further differentiated on the basis of culturally meaningful criteria. A consideration of whether an important clinical sign of disease such as blood in the stool is the basis of illness differentiation or an adjunct feature of more important cultural concerns is required. Through interviews and participant observation, the anthropologist investigates when diarrhea is described as a general and "not unexpected" condition and when it is classified more explicitly in terms of distinct illnesses.

A first step is to identify people's ideas about how the illness universe is divided up. Types of illness are identified through free listing. The range of culturally recognized signs and symptoms associated with these folk illnesses are investigated through interviews and illness attribute recognition and sorting exercises (see Chapter 6 and Weller and Romney 1988). Denotative features of diarrheal illness which appear to play a role in illness category inclusion and exclusion at various levels of specificity are noted (Frake 1961). An attempt is made to establish whether individual signs or clusters of signs differentiate one folk illness from other illnesses. Cultural consensus analysis (Romney, Weller, and Batchelder 1986) may be employed to estimate cultural competency and the degree to which individual responses to question frames correspond to shared cultural knowledge. Competency may be tested in relation to the distribution of knowledge between groups of people as well as individuals. This constitutes a proxy measure of the likelihood that particular sets of symptoms will be classified in a given way.

Collection of data on diarrhea related signs and symptoms as they are locally recognized and differentiated facilitates the construction of taxonomic models of illness types. An illness taxonomy is a systematic presentation of logical relations between illness categories based on a "rational man" model of cognitive thought. Figure 4.1 illustrates an abstract model of diarrheal illness differentiation derived from data generated during guided interviews in South India designed to map classes of illness based on signs, symptoms, and causes. Figure 4.2 presents a more expansive semantic illness network analysis constructed out of data gathered from illness stories, cases followed, and open-ended interviews designed to elicit both connotative and denotative factors associated with diarrhea. Both types of models are useful conceptual maps facilitating the interpretation of illness behavior and the presentation of research results. However, the "map is not the territory" (Bateson 1972), and these models serve only as heuristic devices. They are far less useful in predicting behavior than explaining it. Ambiguity, coexisting health concerns, and interpretations of illness contingent on past treatment actions (diagnosis by treatment) are not accounted for by these models, nor are the social relations of negotiating an illness identity.

Illness classification is multidimensional and motivated as well as marked by ambiguity (Nichter 1989, Nichter 1994). For these reasons, research on diarrheal disease requires more than the construction of illness taxonomies and simplistic Knowledge, Attitude, and Practice (KAP) type surveys (Green 1986). KAP surveys elicit clear-cut answers to predetermined questions and assume a "rational man" model of knowledge generation and illness response (Young 1981). The study of diarrhea classification and treatment response

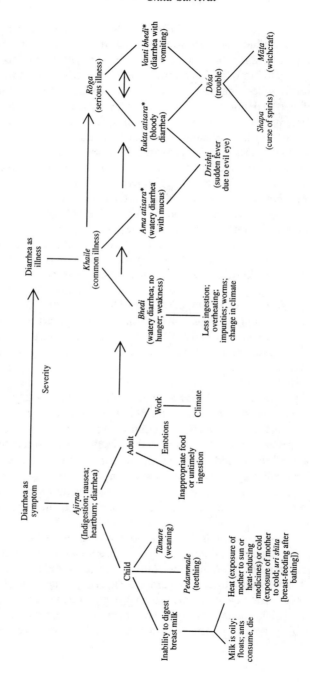

Figure 4.1. Model of diarrheal illness differentiation derived from data generated during guided interviews in South India.

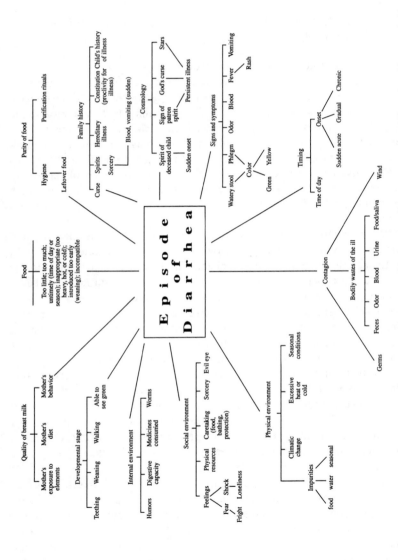

Figure 4.2. Semantic illness network analysis constructed from data gathered from illness stories, cases followed, and open-ended interviews.

requires research strategies which are more dynamic and attend to contingencies.[10]

FROM A TAXONOMY TO A TASKONOMY APPROACH TO ILLNESS LABELING

Consensus in prototypical knowledge of illness categories does not mean illness labels will be used by individuals in a consistent and objective way. In addition to a taxonomy of illness, the field investigator must be responsive to the "taskonomy" of illness labeling.[11] Taskonomy draws attention to the flexibility of illness labeling influenced by social relations, the relative advantages of representing illness in coextensive ways, and emergent knowledge associated with the practical task of caring for the ill. It recognizes performative aspects of discourse which influence the levels of specificity used to describe an illness episode as well as practical dimensions of illness treatment which influence how it is identified in relation to treatment options.

Illness labeling and symptom reporting are invested with meaning and emotion. They are also strategic. A few examples may illustrate this point. In Sri Lanka, bloody diarrhea is associated with excessive heat trapped in the body due to either naturalistic causes (such as the consumption of heaty foods or hard work under the hot sun) or external forces (such as sorcery, evil eye, or spirit contact). When natural causes are suspected, bloody diarrhea is commonly treated by ingesting cooling substances as well as by taking doctor's medicine. Some people, however, are reluctant to consume allopathic medicine for bloody diarrhea as this medicine is considered heating for the body and thought to exacerbate the condition which causes this ailment. Some of the very same people who do not "comply" with doctor's prescriptions for antibiotics when suffering from bloody diarrhea are among those most willing to accept ORS and increase liquid consumption for this condition. Paradoxically, they are among those most likely to reject ORS use for watery diarrhea because "cultural common sense" dictates drying up a watery liquid stool (Nichter 1988).

Among the aforementioned people, antibiotics are viewed as a useful drying agent for watery diarrhea, but are deemed a dangerous heating agent for bloody diarrhea. This perception is precisely the reverse of biomedical wisdom. Yet it does make sense culturally, and as anthropologists have been fond of pointing out, models of reality give rise to models for action. In the present case, explanatory models of diarrhea foster strategic symptom reporting. In 1983, I documented instances where patients afflicted with watery diarrhea reported to practitioners that they had blood in their stool after hearing that the practitioner in question administered antibiotics for such complaints. Practical logic influenced illness presentation. Strategic symptom reporting and illness labeling did not denote lack of faith in biomedicine, but a manipulation of the system toward felt needs. Such behavior is poorly represented by terms such as noncompliance. It is underlain by distinctive perceptions of illness and appropriate treatment modalities.

The study of cultural responses to bloody diarrhea demands a consideration of popular perceptions of physiology (ethnophysiology) and folk epidemiology as it influences the recognition and interpretation of body signs and symptoms. In every culture, certain body signs are attributed particular importance. Blood loss is interpreted differently in cultural contexts where blood quantity is thought to be fixed for life or difficult to replenish, than in other cultures where blood production is perceived to be routine and easily enhanced. Indeed, the importance of blood loss can only be fully appreciated in the context of a consideration of cultural ideas about the purpose, quantity and quality of blood at different times and stages in the life cycle.

Both folk epidemiology and ethnophysiology affect diarrhea management. For example, bloody stools may be perceived either as the focal symptom of illness in need of direct attention or as the effect of a pathological bodily process only secondarily related to the gut. Nations (1987) notes that in Brazil the lung is thought to be connected to the intestinal tract. Mucus tinged with blood in the stool of a young child may therefore be viewed as an overflow from mucus build-up in the lungs. Instead of focusing primary attention on diarrhea, a mother may seek medical attention for an infant's cold.[12]

Bloody diarrhea may also be perceived as the result of the excessive consumption of some type of food or of an internal purification process associated with a primary illness. Among both the Igbo and Yoruba in Nigeria, sugar consumption (especially refined sugar) is associated with diarrhea, bloody diarrhea, and a range of other complaints associated with an inflamed rectum.[13] The association of sugar consumption with bloody diarrhea is multidimensional. Among other things, sugar is believed to make the worms living in a child's gut overactive and bite the stomach. Given such a perception, the administration of SSS is deemed dangerous as the sugar content may worsen the very condition care providers are attempting to manage. While some segments of these populations have come to accept SSS which "tastes like tears and is not too sweet" as a treatment for watery diarrhea, a subset of these "SSS users" fear administering SSS during bloody diarrhea.

In Bangladesh, nearly half of the episodes of diarrhea which accompany measles are dysenteric (Ryder et al. 1976). A majority of these cases involve shigella (Shahid et al. 1983). As in many other parts of South Asia, mothers view diarrhea following measles as evidence that harmful wastes and heat are leaving the body. In Bangladesh (as in India, Pakistan, Sri Lanka, and the Philippines), mothers often delay seeking health care until all signs of a measles rash have subsided. They fear that treatment may retard the "normal progression" of the illness, turn the rash inward, and place their child at increased risk (see Chapter 6). Special dysentery messages may have to be developed for measles in contexts where similar cultural beliefs are prevalent. There is evidence from both India and the Philippines that some, but not all, medicines are thought to impede the healing process during and immediately following measles. Formative research is needed to develop health education messages which encourage mothers of children having measles accompanied by bloody stools to seek prompt medical attention. One avenue such research might take is to examine the perceived properties of medicines presently deemed acceptable by mother for use during measles.[14]

Blood loss can also take on symbolic significance. In both Sri Lanka and South India, blood in the stool or sputum is deemed a sign of malevolence as well as a symptom of illness. Bloody stool accompanied by body pain are symptoms for which a South Asian may well consult an exorcist. These symptoms may not be labeled by an illness term which denotes a condition specified by bloody diarrhea, but rather be considered as a trouble (*dōśa*) associated with sorcery, the evil eye, or spirit contact. In such cases the bloody diarrhea of a child may be perceived as a sign of household vulnerability as much as individual illness. Where such an interpretation of bloody stool (or blood loss) is common, treatment delays may be related to a family's felt need to consult an exorcist prior to seeing a doctor.

Epidemiological research on the prevalence of bloody diarrhea or diarrhea related death in a community may run into problems when investigations index sensitive issues related to troubled social relations. Three examples of such difficulties may be cited. In a study of marasmus and diarrhea associated infant death in Pakistan, Mull (1989) found that following a child's death from the folk illness *sukhi ki bimari*, a mother was considered bad luck and a potential cause of the illness in other children. This led mothers either to deny that their child died of symptoms linked to the illness or to move out of their neighborhood so as to escape being socially ostracized. Both behavior patterns would obviously skew a prevalence study of acute forms of diarrhea in the community.

A second example relates to an Ojitico (Mexican Indian) perception of dysentery among children. It is believed that quarrels between parents result in children's illness which may at first take the form of white dysentery and then transform into bloody dysentery (*jmi yin*) if not cured (Paola Cessa Lewis: personal communication). In this context, a bloody stool can take on moral meaning associated with the actions of one's parents. Another example of such an association involves the perception among the Igbo in Nigeria that a mother's breastmilk spoils if she has intercourse while lactating. Questions about infant diarrhea may index sensitive issues related to traditional post-partum sexual restrictions which are not being adhered to in the present, but which still evoke folk health concerns.

In addition to the moral dimension of an illness identity, danger may be associated with the mere mention of the name of a severe form of diarrheal illness. Informants may feel this calls the illness into one's presence (Nichter 1989, Tambiah 1968). Given such a concern it may be more prudent to investigate the relative utility of posing questions about symptoms rather than employing the names of feared folk illnesses even when they are highly correlated with dysentery.

ILLNESS NARRATIVES

The best but most difficult means of collecting data on how an illness is interpreted and labeled during an illness trajectory is through case following. Less intrusive modes of data collection include conducting interviews about health care seeking response at hospital clinics and verbal autopsy studies in homes (Bentley 1988). Some studies which have used these methods have relied on structured instruments which focus upon clinical signs and practi-tioner consultation patterns. Other studies have paid equal attention to the social relations reflected in illness narratives. Such studies provide insights into how an illness episode has been experienced personally as well as constructed as a communication event. As noted earlier, the negotiation of an illness identity entails judgments about prototypicality which involve illness scenarios as a form of instantiation. Judgments are often tentative and open to revision. As important to the study of "moments of choice" in health care decision making is the flow of communication which informs opinion about illness and those factors influencing this flow of communication.

Primary health care workers need to be receptive not only to illness terms, but also to modes of narration and issues of caretaker identity. The way illness stories structure events make statements to others about the teller of the story. Of crucial importance is responsibility. Health care actions (and delays in action) are often influenced by issues related to the status of a child care taker and fears of being held responsible for inappropriate or overly costly health care seeking behavior. Subtle dimensions of the process of health care decision making are often embedded in illness narratives. For example, when asked directly about health care decision making on surveys, women in many cultures report that it is men who make "the decision." Differences between experienced and less experienced child caretakers are often glossed over. Illness narratives collected from experienced mothers in both South Asia and the Philippines reveal that they are often the ones who recognize the severity of an illness episode and initiate health seeking behavior be it to a doctor or traditional practitioner. Their narratives suggest that when a woman's husband is consulted, it is more to inform him of the gravity of the situation than to seek his permission to act. In many cases, informing a husband constituted a request that resources be mobilized to set in motion a plan of action the mother had already decided upon. In other narratives, however, it was clear that a mother felt compelled to consult her husband or an elder before embarking on a course of action.[15] Response to abstract survey questions about "decision making" may well underestimate a mother's agency in some contexts, while overstating it in others.

Illness stories are the chief means by which health information is transferred in many communities (Early 1982, Jordan 1989, Levin 1979, and Price 1987). In such contexts, teaching stories built around illness narratives may constitute a promising venue for health education. In order for teaching stories to be effective, however, attention will have to be paid to far more than technical points. Health messages need to be designed which are sensitive to perceptions of severity and responsibility as well as to who is involved in health care decision making and at what point in an illness trajectory. As important as an epidemiology of disease is an epidemiology of health communication. We need to consider why some health messages are "contagious" while others are difficult to convey without repeated individual contact by a health worker.

BIOMEDICAL LANGUAGE AND PRACTITIONER TREATMENT PATTERNS

As important to consider as the specificity of folk terms for diarrhea and dysentery are practitioners' use of biomedical terms to describe these conditions. Investigation of the context in which terms are used is necessary, as is study of the consistency of their application. Usage of terms may vary according to the type of patient as well as the setting of treatment, a factor that determines the extent of contact between the practitioner and patients. Also important is the criteria upon which practitioners base diagnosis and the manner in which patterns of rapid diagnosis affect prescription practice. It is important to know how umbrella terms such as "gastroenteritis," "dysentery," and "cholera" are used by all types of practitioners, what signs are associated with these terms, and which forms of treatment are offered for conditions labeled by these terms. Researchers must seek answers to the following questions: What criteria are used by practitioners to differentiate between amoebic and bacillary dysentery? What is the duration of their recommended treatment? Do patients report treatment failure to practitioners or do they tend to seek care from another practitioner when treatment is deemed ineffective?[16]

Additionally, it is important to consider what advice chemist shop attendants give to clients who cite symptoms that are indicative of dysentery. During a small study in a South Indian town (1980), I observed that 15 out of 23 clients complaining of bloody diarrhea were given medication for amoebic dysentery. In most cases the shop attendant did not inquire about the duration of symptoms and in only seven cases was a client advised to visit a doctor.[17] When the ill person was a child under three years of age, the customer was usually told to consult a doctor, but medication was still sold. Studies carried out in the Philippines have reported a similar pattern of treating bloody diarrhea by doctors and pharmacy personnel. A study conducted by the Department of Health (DOH) in collaboration with the World Health Organization (WHO) in 1990–91 found that while blood in the stools was reported in less than 10% of health records, public health workers prescribed antibiotics in percentages ranging from 45–95% (van Staa 1993: 78). Especially relevant here is that metronidazole (an anti-amoebic drug) was prescribed in almost all cases of bloody diarrhea in several study sites around the county. At some sites, anti-amoebic drugs were used in one out of every four diarrhea cases although cases of bloody diarrhea accounted for less than 5% of the patient load.[18] In her study of Filipino pharmacies, van Staa (1993:174) found that anti-amoebic drugs were "top of the mind" treatment in 75% of cases of bloody diarrhea in 45 pharmacies in Quezon city.[19]

What is the pharmaceutical industry's role in educating practitioners and the general public about the signs and treatment of various types of diarrhea? While much has been written about the unethical marketing of antidiarrheals such as Lomotil (G. D. Searle, Chicago), less attention has been directed to the subtle message conveyed by medicine proliferation on the diagnosis of illness. Returning to South Kanara soon after my public health training, I observed what appeared to be gross over-diagnosis of intestinal amoebiasis by doctors as well as chemist shop attendants.[20] Follow-up research revealed that allopathic doctors in the region were more concerned with amoebic dysentery than shigellosis for three reasons. First, they received more information about amoebic dysentery than shigellosis in medical school. Second, the regional medical school was located near the coast where amoebic dysentery is more prevalent than in the interior of the district. Third, doctors were approached by pharmaceutical representatives with new medicines for amoebic dysentery far more frequently than with medicines for shigellosis. Much of doctor's continuing education in India is from product based promotional literature. This literature fostered the impression that amoebic dysentery was quite common throughout the region and not just on the coast.

POPULAR ILLNESS TERMS AND HEALTH PROGRAM EVALUATION

Data about how diarrheal illness is classified are useful not only for health education efforts, but also useful for evaluations of the impact of health programs. A good example is provided by the Bangladesh Rural Advancement Committee (BRAC). By 1986 over seven million of the 16 million households in Bangladesh had been visited by field workers from BRAC who demonstrated the home preparation of ORS. Low rates of ORS utilization were reported in targeted households during an initial evaluation of the program. This led researchers to examine the types of diarrhea perceived by the local population to be treatable, as opposed to routine or untreatable (Chowdhury and Vaughan 1988, Chowdhury et al. 1988). Marked illness specific differences in ORS use were identified. Notably, the rate of ORS use for the folk illness category *daeria* (severe watery diarrhea, including cholera) was very high, but such cases represented only 5% of all diarrhea episodes reported. Cases of *daeria* represented those most likely to lead to dehydration-related death.

CONCLUSION

Bloody diarrhea, a clinical sign of dysentery, is interpreted in many different ways cross-culturally. Knowledge of how bloody diarrhea is described and when it is considered dangerous is relevant for both disease surveillance and health education programs.[21] Caution must be exercised, however, before using folk terms for these purposes. Bloody and other acute forms of diarrhea are not value free conditions in many cultures. Illness terms may be associated with fear, stigma, and moral identity. Case following and illness narratives may provide useful insights into the manner in which acute and invasive diarrhea are both interpreted and talked about during an illness episode and following the event of death.

A consideration of the language used to describe diarrheal disease by doctors and the media is also called for if messages delivered to the community by the private and the public sector are to be coordinated. This is a formidable task which demands attention given to the magnitude of the dysentery problem and the need for a corrective component to ORT messages. An examination of productive knowledge about diarrheal disease and factors influencing how practitioners think about, diagnose, and treat dysentery is required. The pharmaceutical industry's role in knowledge production should not be underestimated, nor should be profit motives encouraging patterns of diarrhea treatment (Nations 1988).

Just as the study of folk terms for diarrhea is important to an evaluation of public health intervention programs (e.g., the example of BRAC), an assessment of how biomedical terms are used in the media to describe invasive diarrhea is likewise important for a critical assessment of how public opinion about health is being managed. Two decades of medical anthropological research on diarrheal illness have elapsed. Many valuable lessons have been learned (see Chapter 5) and new challenges await. These challenges link diarrheal disease to political ecology, the deterioration of environmental conditions, occupational health, and the demand for better hygiene, not just the marketing of simple solutions or the provision of antibiotics appropriate for "this round" of infection.

Let me conclude this chapter with a brief field vignette. In 1990, I visited a long time friend in India who happened to have been suffering from bloody diarrhea for the previous 10 days. Concerned, I encouraged him to see a doctor and have a stool test done in a nearby town where a small lab had recently been set up. "It's not necessary," my friend stated. "I know the cause of the problem." An agriculturalist, he had just spent the past month working with pesticides and chemical fertilizers and was convinced that these were the cause of his ailment. What was needed for this case of "gastritis," he argued, were *āyurvedic* medicines to purify his digestive track and cool his blood. Given the amount of exposure to heating chemicals to which he had been subjected, he reckoned it would take some time for his ailment to be alleviated.

At the same time that my friend's illness was going on, an epidemic of "gastroenteritis" was being reported in the press. Hospital admissions and death rates in neighboring districts and a city only 40 miles away were making daily headlines. Unconcerned, my friend suffered in silence, modified his diet, took *āyurvedic* medicine, and believed his ailment to be the dues he had to pay for engaging in "modern" agriculture. Knowing something about dysentery's high rate of contagion, I washed my hands a lot, drank copious amounts of scalding tea instead of water, and tried not to worry too much. I also wondered whether my friend's empirical observations about occupational health might be right. They were certainly shared by a number of his neighbors.

In the beginning of this chapter, I made a plea for anthropologists to get involved in assisting their public health colleagues to design a dysentery component to ORS messages.[22] The key to such a message would appear to be that anyone having bloody diarrhea should consult a doctor. The story presented above illustrates that such a message will not be introduced into a vacuum. In addition to longstanding folk ideas about the causes of bloody stools are more recent ideas which have varying degrees of scientific merit. These ideas about illness causality are also reflections of larger issues which employ bloody diarrhea as a symbol of defective modernization experienced at the site of the gut and paid for in blood. One can only expect that such social commentary will increase in the future.

NOTES

1. Under the rubric of ORT, I include ORS (oral rehydration salt packets), SSS (home based sugar–salt solutions), and FRS (food based rehydration solutions).

2. For example, in Bangladesh 23% of diarrheal deaths among children under 5 years of age are associated with bloody diarrhea (Fauveau et al. 1992). Bloody diarrhea accounts for 3–11% of all diarrheal episodes of children in this age group (Henry et al. 1992).

3. I refer here to stages of a child's development when "milestone diarrhea" is expected, times of seasonal transition when diarrhea is deemed common, and diarrhea associated with the overeating of seasonal foods by children (e.g., mango).

4. I am using the terms sensitivity and specificity in an epidemiological sense. In this case, sensitivity refers to true positives (those having bloody diarrhea) over all those labeled by an illness term inclusive of bloody diarrhea.

5. Little rigorous research has been conducted on patterns of home care and health care seeking behavior related to folk illnesses associated with dysentery in locales where ORT programs have (and have not) been active. What needs to be assessed are differences in perceptions of severity and management of illness having bloody and watery diarrhea. Such an assessment requires careful attention to adjunct symptoms and factors which influence the ongoing process of folk diagnosis, a process in which initial perceptions of an illness are often revised and reevaluated over time. Also in need of considera-

tion are medicines dispensed, prescribed, and recommended by local practitioners (trained and untrained), pharmacy attendants, and primary health care workers. The correspondence between practitioner treatment and home care with medicines also begs consideration.

6. In some contexts, watery and bloody diarrhea are considered distinct illnesses having differing etiologies, while in other cases these symptoms are considered stages of a common illness or transformation of one form of illness into another.

7. Adisa and Sunmola (1994) have identified six categories of illness associated with blood in the stool. While most of these illnesses are treated by traditional medicines prior to a doctor's consultation, constipation followed by a bloody stool (*edi*) is only thought to be effectively treated only by traditional medicine.

8. See for example, the study of Smith et al. (1993) on diarrhea in rural Nicaragua. These researchers found that bloody diarrhea (*desgaste*) was seen as the end stage of prolonged diarrhea.

9. On the practice of self-medication in the Philippines, see Hardon (1991). For an excellent study of self-medication for diarrhea in the Philippines, see van Staa (1993).

10. For examples of how contingencies related to work load and fears of death can effect illness classification and health care seeking, see Malik et al. (1992).

11. Unreflective empiricism reminiscent of "ethnoscience" has led some medical anthropologists to present decontextualized descriptions of illness categories as if they were mental maps which guided action on the basis of binary reasoning. As noted by Comaroff (1983:9): "Taxonomies are disembodied classifications of terms, whose meanings remain nominal, telling us nothing of pragmatic use, their polysemic quality, their cultural significance." My application of Dougherty and Keller's (1982) concept of taskonomy draws upon Wittgenstein's (1958) theory of "language games" and "words as tools" and Bourdieu's (1990) discussion of "practical logics" brought to bear in context.

12. In such a context, the inclusion of mucus in a dysentery algorithm might reduce the effectiveness of the algorithm rather than increase its specificity.

13. See Brieger (1990) for a detailed description of the Yoruba cultural illness termed *jedi jedi* which is associated with excessive sugar consumption. *Jedi jedi* (literally "eat rear end") is a category of illness which encompasses dysentery, rectal prolapse, hemorrhoids, or constipation. See this chapter and Brieger, Ramakrishna, and Chirwa (1987) for a description of a health education message increasing the acceptability of SSS by comparing its taste to "tears."

Child Survival

14. Given Filipino concerns about the skin, it might be worth exploring a message which draws mother's attention to caring for the internal skin (mucosa) during measles, and dysentery as interfering with the healing process of internal skin.

15. For example, among Mapala Muslims in South Kanara it is against normative behavior for a woman to seek medical help without being accompanied by her husband or some other male relative. In one case of severe toddler diarrhea which almost ended in tragedy, a mother who recognized the severity of her child's illness waited two days for her husband to return so she could consult a doctor. Discovering the case while conducting a round of household interviews near her home, I notified her relative who was able to escort her to a clinic.

16. Studies of pharmaceutical practice engaged in by local practitioners treating diarrhea are called for both to enhance diarrhea management and to reduce drug resistance. For example, Ronsmans et al. (1991) found in a study of 208 allopathic practitioners in Bangladesh (64% who had no formal training), that metronidazole and Furoxyolidone were the two most commonly dispensed/prescribed drugs for bloody diarrhea — although not a form of effective treatment for episodes of bacillary dysentery. Further study revealed that not only were 26% of children suffering from bloody diarrhea treated with these antiamoebic drugs, but 23% of other diarrhea cases as well. A study of drug sensitivity in Ibadan, Nigeria (Lamikanra, Oko-Nai, and Ola 1989), found that in isolates obtained from diarrheal children at an ORT clinic, a high percentage were resistant to a broad spectrum of 11 different antibiotics. The researchers point out that the easy availability and common use of antibiotics for diarrhea in urban Nigeria have contributed to a situation in which children are exposed to multiple antibiotic resistant organisms very early in life. Resistance to drugs commonly used in the treatment of shigellosis (e.g., cotrimoxazole, ampicillin, chloramphenicol) will present a serious challenge for care management in the future.

17. Future studies may make use of research confederates who ask chemist shop personnel about medicines for bloody diarrhea with and without adjunct symptoms for fictitious patients of different ages. Confederate studies carried out in India and the Philippines suggest age specific over-the-counter treatment and referral patterns, as well as variations in medicine recommendations responsive to a clients' educational and economic status. On age related treatment patterns see Oni, Schumann, and Oke (1991).

18. Van Staa (1993) has provided a review of provincial diarrheal disease program (CDD) reports in addition to presenting her own data on treatment of diarrhea in the Philippines. Her study reviews data on prevalence rates of amoebiasis in the Philippines and provides an insightful analysis of the amoebiasis myth which complements data presented from India in this chapter.

19. On the abuse of antiparasitic drugs and the overdiagnosis of amoebiasis see also Munoz et al. (1988) regarding patterns of treating diarrhea in Mexico.

20. I was aware of studies conducted elsewhere in South India on prevalence rates for different types of diarrhea. See Huilan et al. (1991) for more recent data on the prevalence of shigellosis in comparison to amoebic dysentery in India and five other countries.

21. Collection of data on the local classification and language of diarrhea may facilitate better descriptive epidemiological studies. Anthropologists such as Nations (1987), Pfifferling (1975), and Weller, Ruebush, and Klein (1991) have suggested that regional morbidity-surveillance studies may benefit from the incorporation of folk terminology in survey questions that relate to illnesses.

22. This plea was especially for messages aimed at children, although the case study presented involves an adult male. While I have heard several adults link diarrhea/dysentery to pesticide and fertilizer poisoning, I have only heard this explanation applied to children by *āyurvedic* practitioners. In this case, it was the pesticide contamination of vegetables purchased in town which were suspect, not the contamination of local water sources.

REFERENCES

Adisa, J. and G. Sunmola. 1994. Perception of Childhood Bloody Diarrhea and Common Treatment Practices in Rural Yoruba Communities of Nigeria. ADDR Workshop Report, Ibadan Nigeria.

Bateson, G. 1972. Steps to an Ecology of the Mind. Ballantine Books: New York.

Bentley, M. 1988. The Household Management of Child Diarrhea in Rural North India. Social Science and Medicine 27:75–85.

Bhandari, N., M. Bhan, and S. Sazawal. 1992. Mortality Associated with Acute Watery Diarrhea, Dysentery and Persistent Diarrhea in Rural North India. Acta Paediatric Supplement 381:3–6.

Bibeau, G. 1981. The Circular Semantic Network in Nybandi Disease Nosology. Social Science and Medicine 15b:295–307.

Black, R. 1993. Persistent Diarrhea in Children of Developing Countries. Pediatric Infectious Disease Journal 12:751–761.

Bourdieu, P. 1990. The Logic of Practice. Stanford, CA: Stanford University Press.

Brieger, W. 1990. Jedi Jedi, a Yoruba Cultural Disease with Implications for Home Management of Diarrhea. Health Education Research 5(3):337–342.

Brieger, W., J. Ramakrishna, and B. Chirwa. 1987. Education Overcomes a Cultural Obstacle to the Management of Diarrhea. World Health Forum 8:480–482.

Chen, L., M. Rahman, and A. Sander. 1980. Epidemiology and Causes of Death Among Children in Rural Bangladesh. International Journal of Epidemiology 9:25–33.

Chowdhury, A. M. R. and J. P. Vaughan. 1988. Perception of Diarrhoea and the Use of a Home-Made Oral Rehydration Solution in Rural Bangladesh. Journal of Diarrhoeal Disease Research 6(1):6–14.

Chowdhury, A. M. R., J. P. Vaughan, and F. H. Abed. 1988. Use and Safety of Home-Made Oral Rehydration Solutions: An Epidemiological Evaluation from Bangladesh. International Journal of Epidemiology 17(3):655–665.

Comaroff, J. 1983. The Defectiveness of Symbols or the Symbols of Defectiveness? On the Cultural Analysis of Medical Systems. Culture, Medicine and Psychiatry 7:3–20.

Dougherty, J. and C. Keller. 1982. Taskonomy: A Practical Approach to Knowledge Structure. American Ethnologist 9:763–774.

Early, E. 1982. The Logic of Well Being. Therapeutic Narratives in Cairo, Egypt. Social Science and Medicine 16:1491–1497.

Fauveau, V., F. Henry, A. Briend, M. Yunus, and J. Chakroborty. 1992. Persistent Diarrhea as a Cause of Childhood Morbidity in Rural Bangladesh. Acta Paedeatrica 381:12–14.

Fillmore, C. 1975. An Alternative to Checklist Theories of Meaning. Annual Proceedings of the Berkeley Linguistic Society 1:123–131. Berkeley: University of California Press.

Frake, C. 1961. The Diagnosis of Disease Among the Subanum of Mindanao. American Anthropologist 63:113–132.

Good, B. 1977. The Heart of What's the Matter: The Semantics of Illness in Iran. Culture, Medicine and Psychiatry 1:25–58.

Green, E. 1986. Diarrhea and the Social Marketing of Oral Rehydration Salts in Bangladesh. Social Science and Medicine 23:357–366.

Hardon, A. 1991. Confronting Ill Health: Medicines, Self-Care and the Poor in Manila. Quezon City: Health Action Information Network.

Henry, F., A. Uday, A. Wanke, and K. Ayiy. 1992. Epidemiology of Persistent Diarrhea and Etiologic Agents in Mirzapur, Bangladesh. Acta Paediatrica 381:27–31.

Hermann, E. and R. Black. 1987. Strategic and Operational Policy Regarding Dysentery in Diarrheal Disease Control Programs. PRITECH Report.

Huilan, S., et al. 1991. Etiology of Acute Diarrhoea Among Children in Developing Countries: A Multicentre Study in Five Countries. Bulletin of the World Health Organization 69(5):549–555.

Jordan, B. 1989. Cosmopolitical Obstetrics: Some Insights From the Training of Midwives. Social Science and Medicine 28:925–944.

Kendall, C. 1990. Public Health and the Domestic Domain: Lessons From Anthropological Research on Diarrheal Diseases. *In* Anthropology and Primary Health Care. J. Coreil and J. Mull, eds. Pp. 173–195. Boulder: Westview Press.

Lakoff, G. 1987. Women, Fire and Dangerous Things: What Categories Reveal About the Mind. Chicago: University of Chicago Press.

Lamikanra, A., A. Oko-Nai, and O. Ola. 1989. Incidence of Multiple Antibiotic Resistances in Organisms Isolated From Cases of Infantile Diarrhea in a Nigerian Oral Rehydration Therapy Clinic. Annals of Tropical Paediatrics 9:256–260.

Levin, E. 1979. The Nobility of Suffering: Illness and Misfortune Among Latin American Immigrant Women. Anthropology Quarterly 52(3):152–158.

Malik, I., N. Bukhtiari, M. J. Good, S. Azim, M. Nawaz, L. Asraf, R. Bhatty, and A. Ahmed. 1992. Mother's Fear of Child Death Due to Acute Diarrhoea: A Study in Urban and Rural Communities in Northern Punjab, Pakistan. Social Science and Medicine 35(8):1043–1053.

Mull, D. 1989. Health Beliefs and Practices of 150 Mothers in Karachi. USAID Report, Islamabad, Pakistan.

Munoz, O., H. Guiscafre, M. Bronfman, and G. Gutierrey. 1988. Characteristics of the Treatment Prescribed by the Family Physician or the Patient Himself. Arch. Ind. Med. Mex. 19:371–384.

Nations, M. 1987. Epidemiological Research on Infectious Disease: Quantitative Rigor or Rigormotis? Insights From Ethnomedicine. *In* Anthropology and Epidemiology. C. R. Janes, R. Stall, and S. M. Gifford, eds. Pp. 97–124. Dordrecht, The Netherlands: Kluwer Academic Press.

Nations, M. 1988. Mystification of a Simple Solution: Oral Rehydration Therapy in Northeast Brazil. Social Science and Medicine 27(1):25–38.

Nichter, Mark. 1988. From Aralu to ORS: Sinhalese Perceptions of Digestion, Diarrhea, and Dehydration. Social Science and Medicine 27:39–52.

Nichter, Mark. 1989. The Language of Illness, Contagion and Symptom Reporting. Anthropology and International Health: South Asian Case Studies, Chapter 4. (Mark Nichter). Dordrecht, The Netherlands: Kluwer Academic Publishers.

Nichter, Mark. 1994. Illness Semantics and International Health: The Weak Lungs/TB Complex in the Philippines. Social Science and Medicine 38(5):649–663.

Oni, G., D. Schumann, and E. Oke. 1991. Diarrheal Disease Morbidity, Risk Factor and Treatments in a Low-Socioeconomic Area of Ilarin Kwara State, Nigeria. Journal of Diarrheal Disease Research 9:250–257.

Pfifferling, J. 1975. Some Issues in the Consideration of Non-Western and Western Folk Practices as Epidemiological Data. Social Science and Medicine 9:655–658.

Price, L. 1987. Ecuadorian Illness Stories: Cultural Knowledge in Natural Discourse. *In* Cultural Models in Language and Thought. D. Holland and N. Quinn, eds. Pp. 313–342. New York: Cambridge University Press.

Romney, A., S. Weller, and W. Batchelder. 1986. Culture as Consensus: A Theory of Culture and Informant Accuracy. American Anthropologist 88:313–338.

Ronsmans, C., M. Bennish, J. Chakraborty, and V. Fauveau. 1991. Current Practices for the Treatment of Dysentery in Rural Bangladesh. Review of Infectious Diseases 13 (Supplement 4):351–356.

Ronsmans, C., M. Bennish, and T. Wierzoa. 1988. Diagnosis and Management of Dysentery by Community Health Workers. Lancet 1(8585):553–555.

Rosch, E. 1978. Principles of Categorization. *In* Cognition and Categorization. E. Rosch and B. B. Lloyd, eds. Pp. 27–48. Hillsdale, NJ: Lawrence Erlbaum Association.

Ryder, R., D. Scak, A. Kapikian, J. McLaughlin, J. Chakraborty, A. Rahman, M. Merson, and J. Wells. 1976. Enterotoxigenic Escherichia Coli and Reovirul-Like Ageni in Rural Bangladesh. Lancet 1:659–662.

Shahid et al. 1983. Beliefs and Treatment Related to Diarrheal Episodes Reported in Association to Measles. Tropical and Geographical Medicine 35:151–156.

Smith, G., A. Garter, J. Hoppenbrouwer, A. Sweep, R. Perez, C. Gonzalez, P. Morales, J. Pauw, and P. Sandiford. 1993. The Cultural Construction of Childhood Diarrhea in Rural Nicaragua: Relevance for Epidemiology and Health Promotion. Social Science and Medicine 36(12):1613–1624.

Stoll, B. J. and R. I. Glass. 1982. Epidemiologic and Clinical Features of Patients Infected with Shegilla Who Attended a Diarrheal Disease Hospital in Bangladesh. Journal of Infectious Disease 2:177–183.

Sukkary-Stolba, S. 1988. Behavioral Aspects of Child Survival: Oral Rehydration Therapy. *In* Behavioral Issues in Child Survival: A Synthesis of the Literature With Recommendations for Project Design and Implementation. Washington, DC: USAID, Office of Health.

Tambiah, S. 1968. The Magical Power of Words. Man 3(2):195–208.

van Staa, A. 1993. Myth and Metronidazole in Manila. Unpublished Masters Thesis, University of Amsterdam.

Weiss, M. 1988. Cultural Models of Diarrheal Illness: Conceptual Framework and Review. Social Science and Medicine 27:5–16.

Weller, S. and A. Romney. 1988. Systematic Data Collection. Newbury Park, CA: Sage.

Weller, S., T. Ruebush, and R. Klein. 1991. An Epidemiological Description of a Folk Illness: A Study of *Empacho* in Guatemala. Medical Anthropology 13(1–2):19–31.

Wittgenstein, L. 1958. Philosophical Investigations. Translation by G. E. Anscombe. Oxford: Blackwell.

Young, A. 1981. When Rational Men Fall Sick: An Inquiry Into Some Assumptions Made by Anthropologists. Culture, Medicine and Psychiatry 5(4):317–335.

Zimicki, S., L. Nahar, A. M. Sarder, and A. D'Souza. 1985. A Demographic Surveillance System — Matlab. Cause of Death Reporting in Matlab. Scientific Report No. 63(13). Dhaka, Bangladesh: International Centre for Diarrhoeal Disease Research, Bangladesh.

CHAPTER 5

Social Science Lessons from Diarrhea Research and Their Application to ARI

Mark Nichter

Acute respiratory infections are out of control. They represent a largely ignored challenge in the field of communicable diseases. Millions of children die annually, and literally billions suffer acute and chronic morbidity arising from their effects. It is unacceptable that a global scientific community that has developed the micro chip and the capacity to visit the planets should continue to ignore a health problem of these proportions and to accept passively the degree of ignorance and helplessness which presently surrounds this universal problem. (Douglas 1985:1)

In the current worldwide efforts to reduce the heavy load of morbidity and mortality, the least attention has been given to ARI, although it is probably the first or second most important cause of death in developing countries. (Parker 1987:279)

THE MAGNITUDE OF THE PROBLEM

Acute respiratory infections (ARI) are one of the chief causes of mortality and morbidity among infants and children under five in developing countries (Berman and McIntosh 1985, Shann 1985a, WHO 1981, 1983).[1] In much of the developing world, approximately half of all deaths are in children under five years of age. Depending on the region, ARI accounts for between one fifth and one third of these deaths (Leowski 1986, Pio, Leowski, and Dam

1985, Rohde 1983). While surpassed by diarrheal diseases as a cause of death in some developing countries, ARI has been reported as the chief cause of mortality in several other areas (Denny and Loda 1986, Grant 1984), including regions of Africa (Bulla and Hitze 1978, Greenwood et al. 1987), China and Indonesia (Parker 1987, Edmundson and Harris 1989), India (Edmundson and Harris 1989), Guatemala (Mata 1978), Papua New Guinea (Riley and Carrad 1983), Nepal (Adhikari 1985, Pandey, Sharma, and Nuepane 1985), Burma (Aung 1985) and the Philippines (PDH 1986). In the case of Papua New Guinea, 42% of deaths in children under age one and 25% of deaths between ages one and five have been attributed to ARI. In regions of India where rigorous data collection on ARI has been initiated, up to 36% of infant deaths have been associated with ARI (Kumar 1987, Steinhoff and John 1983). Between 500,000 and 750,000 children are estimated to die of ARI in India each year.

Seen in relation to sheer numbers, between two and five million of the world's children died each year from ARI in the 1980s (Lancet 1985, Leowski 1986, Rohde 1983, Stansfeld 1987, WHO 1988a). The latest estimate from the WHO is that of 15 million children's deaths in 1990, four million deaths were attributable to ARI (Pio 1990a, 1990b). This figure amounts to between seven and 13 thousand deaths per day, or 300 to 600 deaths in the past hour. According to WHO (1988a, 1988b) estimates, the following disease complexes are responsible for ARI-related mortality: pneumonia without measles (70%), pertussis (19%), post measles pneumonia (15%), bronchiolitis (5%).

Infants are at greatest risk for respiratory disease-related mortality (Berman, Simoes, and Lomata 1991, Puffer and Serrano 1973, Reddaiah and Kapoor 1988, Riley 1985, Spika, Munshi, and Wojtyniak 1989) while children two to three years of age experience more respiratory infections than other age groups (Stansfeld 1987). Twenty to thirty percent of deaths from total acute respiratory infections that occur in children under five are of infants under two months of age (Berman 1990). The malnourished are also at enhanced risk for ARI mortality (Tupasi, Velmonte, and Sanvictores 1988). Compared to a normal child, a malnourished child is three times as likely to experience bronchitis, and 19 times as likely to experience pneumonia (James 1972, Rochester and Esau 1984, Tupasi et al. 1990a).

Moving to a consideration of morbidity from respiratory disease, studies from several developing countries have reported similar trends in the overall incidence rate of respiratory disease considered as a broad range of upper and lower respiratory infections. Among urban low to middle class children, an incidence rate of four to eight episodes of upper respiratory (non-life threatening) disease per child per year has been widely reported. Among rural children living in areas of less population density, a lower incidence rate of three to five episodes per year has been cited (Pio, Leowski, and Dam 1985). Unlike diarrheal disease, where incidence rates are quite distinct in developing and developed countries, incidence rates of respiratory disease are comparable in the developed and developing worlds. While the incidence of upper respiratory infections is in the same range globally, and mostly of viral origin (WHO 1990), the occurrence of acute episodes of lower respiratory illness (ALRI), particularly pneumonia, is 10 to 50 times greater in developing countries (Mohs 1985, WHO 1984).

Available data suggest that 70–80% of ARI-related deaths are caused by pneumonia which may be due to either viral or bacterial infection (Bulla and Hitze 1978, Puffer and Serrano 1973).[2] Most severe cases of pneumonia are bacterial and treatable by antibiotics (McCord and Kielmann 1978, Shann 1985a, 1985b). Viewing ARI in relation to its burden on the health care system of developing countries, ARI accounts for between 20% to 60% of all pediatric outpatient consultations (Mohs 1985, WHO 1984), 12% to 45% of inpatient admissions (Shann, Hart, and Thomas 1984), and from 8% to 12% of hospital fatalities in countries as diverse as Bangladesh, Brazil, and Thailand (Pio, Leowski, and Dam 1985). A recent study from Burma has documented a startling 31% hospital case fatality rate for ARI (Aung 1985). This is not to infer that treatment for ARI is ineffective. On the contrary, prompt treatment of acute lower respiratory infections with appropriate antimicrobial therapy yields dramatic results (Eigner 1981, McCord and Kielman 1978, Pandey et al. 1991, Smith 1982). For example, when moderate to severe cases of lower acute respiratory disease were assessed in New Guinea, a case fatality rate of 25% was reported among untreated cases. Notably, the case fatality rate fell to only 4% when children were treated with antibiotics at an aid post, health center, or hospital.

DIARRHEA AND ACUTE RESPIRATORY ILLNESS: SIMILARITIES AND DIFFERENCES

Similarities

Diarrhea and ARI are major causes of child mortality in the developing world. Both are caused by a variety of etiological agents of viral, bacterial, and parasitic origin. There is a poor correlation between either syndrome and its possible etiology, making differential diagnosis by signs and symptoms problematic. In their initial stages, lay persons often mistake both ARI and diarrhea for routine bodily responses to environmental or dietary change.

Considerable ambivalence surrounds popular perceptions of causality and contagion. While both conditions are often linked to changes in food or climate, severe illness may be perceived as contagious vis à vis relationships of contiguity. Popular health care often involves either forcing out a waste product (mucus, feces) through purges, or drying out the body.

With respect to the management of both sets of conditions, home care is recommended in early stages. For both sets of conditions a variety of ineffective and expensive, if not outright harmful, over-the-counter medicines exist (HAI, undated). They may mask symptoms, prolong illness, and delay health care seeking. In contexts where antibiotics are available, misuse of these drugs to treat both conditions is common and contributes to drug resistance.[3] An emphasis of primary health care programs has been to teach child caretakers the appropriate use of medicines and recognition of the signs and symptoms of severe illnesses requiring clinical intervention. Acute cases of diarrhea and ARI both require rapid intervention. The use of antimicrobials is indicated in the case of dysentery (shigella) as well as pneumonia.

Similarities also exist with respect to how both sets of conditions have been approached by health programs. In each case, vertical programs have been developed by international health agencies concordant with their own bureaucratic structures and disease control divisions. Diarrhea and ARI are often the focus of separate programs, although the conditions themselves may overlap and be concurrent (e.g., as in the case of measles).

Differences

Important differences between diarrheal diseases and ARI also need to be noted. Effective behavioral interventions exist for interrupting the fecal–oral transmission of etiological agents responsible for most diarrheal diseases. The scope of such interventions in the case of ARI is more limited given the airborne route of transmission of most ARI-related pathogens and risk factors such as combustion of biomass and smoking (inclusive of passive smoking).[4]

The home management of watery diarrhea is accomplished by a relatively simple oral rehydration fix (ORT) which may be prepared at home as a sugar/salt solution or cereal-based fluids, or supplied by a community health worker in the form of an electrolyte salt packet (ORS). While problems in implementing ORT programs exist, simple messages have been developed for caretakers instructing them how to monitor a child's stool output and signs of dehydration in cases of mild to moderate illness. In cases of ARI, it is more difficult to monitor moderate illness. Antimicrobials necessary for the management of ARI of moderate severity cannot be released to the community with the ease of ORS. Moreover, in many countries, political issues surround the use of antibiotics by those other than doctors. Clinical signs of ARI (e.g., the breathing rate, indrawn chest) are more difficult to observe than stool output or a sunken fontanelle, especially among infants. Rates of breathing differ by age, and children with ARI are kept covered in many cultures, making the observation of clinical signs of acute illness, such as chest retractions, difficult. In the presence of health workers respiration rates may rise significantly (Edmundson and Harris 1989). Further, the signs of acute ARI may be confused with conditions causing wheeze.

RESPONSE TO ARI BY THE INTERNATIONAL HEALTH COMMUNITY

While the burden of respiratory disease in developing countries is significant, efforts to engage the community in care management have been relatively recent.[5] It was not until 1976 that the WHO recognized ARI as a high priority health problem meriting a special program. In 1983 a global technical advisory report was submitted to the Secretary General of WHO, and in 1984 an algorithm for classifying and treating ARI was proposed (Douglas 1985, Shann, Hart, and Thomas 1984, WHO 1984). Since that time, ARI has been increasingly acknowledged as a priority area for program funding in the international health community. Reasons for this change extend beyond an increase in knowledge and awareness of the problem. Given the recent advances in diarrheal disease control programs, attention has been shifted to new frontiers of child survival where biotechnology can make a measurable difference in reducing mortality rates linked to specific disease interventions.

ARI has become more attractive to international health agencies as reasonably priced medical fixes for bacterial pneumonia have been identified. While these fixes cannot be made available to the community as readily as ORS, pilot projects have documented that relatively inexpensive antibiotics can be placed in the hands of trained health auxiliaries with impressive results (McCord and Kielmann 1978, Mtango and Neuvians 1986, Pandey et al. 1991, Pio, Leowski, and Dam 1985, Steinhoff 1990, WHO 1988a).[6] This development has led the WHO to advocate active community health worker involvement in the antimicrobial treatment of forms of moderate ALRI (pneumonia), defined in relation to a set of clinical signs and symptoms including subcostal retractions, respiratory rate thresholds, and cyanosis.[7]

Primary Health Center (PHC) staff constitute a second line of care management involved in the treatment and appropriate triage of more advanced cases (WHO 1984).

ARI technical advisory committees associated with the WHO, the International Network of Clinical Epidemiology, and USAID have recognized several issues that need to be considered if community-based ARI programs are to be initiated.[8] A number of these issues require anthropological investigation and entail research questions such as:

1. What is the ability of child caretakers and peripheral health workers to discriminate among mild, moderate, and severe ARI as defined by WHO guidelines?[9]

2. Upon what criteria (signs and symptoms) are ARI-related illnesses judged to be serious by child caretakers?

3. How much do clinically derived ARI algorithms have to be adapted in different cultural contexts to be concordant with local health concerns to prompt appropriate health care seeking responses?

4. Who are the target populations that need to be reached with ARI-related messages? Who is involved in health care decision making for moderate and acute illness? How much are decision makers influenced by predisposing, enabling, and service related factors?

5. What forms of self-care are engaged during cases of mild to severe ARI? How are forms of self-care changing in areas exposed to a proliferation of commercial medicines?

6. What is the role of traditional practitioners and chemist shops in ARI management?

7. To what extent are ARI risk factors such as household ventilation, smoking, and unmodified sleeping arrangements during illness related to ARI?

8. What are the most prudent and trustworthy research method(s) that may be employed to evaluate caretaker, practitioner, and pharmacist related ARI treatment practices?

9. How can practitioners be educated and encouraged to use more efficacious and cost effective therapies? What incentives may be offered to foster more prudent treatment practices?

10. How can the impact of the pharmaceutical industry on both self care (through the use of over-the-counter — OTC — medicines) and practitioner prescription patterns best be evaluated?

MEDICAL ANTHROPOLOGY AND ARI

Where does medical anthropology fit into ARI research, program development, and evaluation? Given the research questions highlighted above, anthropological research is called for at the site of the household, the clinic, the pharmacy, and the provision shop where medicines are stocked. It is also required at the macro level where the production, marketing, and sale of pharmaceutical products impacts on and is affected by health policy. Additional research agenda entail a broader assessment of the household production of health given different patterns of childcare associated with women's work, differential expectations from practitioners within the public and private health sectors, and the political economy of health care provision as it affects the distribution of antibiotics to community health workers.

What has medical anthropology contributed thus far to ARI research? Until 1990 when the WHO began sponsoring exploratory focused ethnographic studies (FES) of ARI, (WHO 1990), little ethnographic research had been conducted (van Ginneken 1990). Data that did exist were largely generated by medical studies of ARI symptom recognition focusing on clinical signs and practitioner utilization.[10] It would appear that social science research on ARI is presently at a stage where social science research on diarrheal disease was a decade ago.

Those of us who participated in diarrheal disease research during the last decade can recall the stages through which medical anthropological research progressed. Initial ethnomedical research pointed out the complexity of illness classification and those predisposing factors influencing illness behavior. This research yielded information that was ethnographically rich, and proposals for program development were suggested (Bentley 1988, Green 1986, Kendall, Foote and Martorell 1984, Mull and Mull 1988, Nichter 1988, Scrimshaw and Hurtado 1988). With the advent of a social marketing approach to popularizing oral rehydration, a generation of program-driven research projects was sponsored which often incorporated an ethnographic component. Marketing themes were assessed in relation to cultural health concerns and the language of illness. Regional product (oral rehydration salt) development demanded a consideration of local weights, measures, taste preferences, and color symbolism. Social networks were evaluated as possible distribution systems, and community leaders were identified as role models to endorse new forms of health care. While ethnographic research was insightful given program objectives, its focus was often narrow and centered on compliance reflecting a "management bias" (Roth 1962).[11]

A next generation of diarrhea research evaluated community response to ORS, indigenous alternatives to commercial ORS (e.g., cereal-based fluids), the political economics of ORS use and non-use by practitioners, practitioner and pharmacist prescription patterns, and the marketing of drugs for diarrhea by the pharmaceutical industry (Chowdhury 1988, Coreil and Genece 1988, Kendall 1989, MacCormick and Draper 1988, Nations and Rebhun 1988, Yoder and Hornick 1992). More recently, attention has turned to invasive and chronic diarrhea. Modification of existing health care messages has been called for in order to convey to mothers the urgency of seeking care for dysentery (Kunstadter 1991, Nichter 1991). These developments mark a correction/reassessment phase in diarrheal management programs.

Many valuable lessons have been learned by social scientists in the course of conducting research on diarrheal disease.[12] These lessons apply to many health care problems in less developed countries and need to be considered in relation to ARI. In the remainder of this chapter, I highlight 15 of these lessons and suggest how they apply to ARI research, using examples from existing ARI studies and research carried out in South India during 1979 and the Philippines in 1989 (Nichter and Nichter 1990, 1994). My intention is not to provide a detailed description of ARI-related behavior in particular cultural settings, which would be beyond the scope of this chapter. Rather, data are presented to illustrate and identify issues that need to be explored cross-culturally. My objective is to pose questions and highlight generic research issues related to ARI inspired by a critical review of diarrheal disease research.

Lessons from Social Science Research on Diarrhea Applied to ARI

1. *Before assessing what is considered abnormal and/or unexpected, consider what is deemed "routine" or "anticipated." Consider "at riskness" to illness from the perspective of the afflicted.* A lesson clearly learned during diarrhea research was that among some people and at some times, diarrhea is expected and treated without the attention it is given in other contexts. Diarrhea at the time of teething, weaning, walking, and other transition times has been found throughout Asia to be linked to child development or adaptation to the environment, and not necessarily deemed an illness.[13] Likewise, dietary and climatic changes are commonly perceived as a cause of diarrhea. Such expectations influence health care seeking. The same is true for ARI-related illness.

My observations in India concur with those of Barriga and Martinez (1987) in Honduras and Aksit (1989) in Turkey. Children are expected to have mucus as part of the developmental process, especially in winter, a time of higher incidence of viral respiratory disease in any case. Respiratory complaints do not evoke much concern among caretakers as long as signs of acute illness such as fever are not present. Questions that remain to be investigated include: Are children with acute respiratory illness treated differently depending on the season? What signs and symptoms distinguish a routine respiratory ailment from a more serious illness warranting treatment? Are children who suffer more frequent or longer existing respiratory illnesses considered at special risk? Are special provisions made for them (e.g., preventive medicines given, diet altered)? If such children are deemed constitutionally predisposed to respiratory illness, do caretakers take such children to practitioners faster or slower (and more or less) than other children? Are expectations for treatment different? Do differences in perceived prognosis influence household investments of scarce resources in medicines or practitioner visits? Are children who have been identified as having a wheeze (asthma or a local correlate) when they are young given more or less care (faster or delayed care) when signs of ARI appear? Are the signs of pneumonia confused with the signs of an illness deemed chronic or constitutional and therefore an expected condition?[14]

2. *Community-based treatment algorithms and triage messages must be responsive to what is already known by caretakers of children.* Attention needs to be paid to common sense as it is culturally constituted and exercised. Doing so entails the study of explanatory models of prototypical illness, the embodied knowledge of caretakers, and treatment practices. Caretakers already have knowledge about children's illness. Much of this knowledge is not amenable to discovery by KAP (knowledge, attitude and practice) type surveys. A good deal of it is embodied, not objectified. Where explanatory models of prototypical illness do exist, they are often embedded in narrative. What caretakers know is often contextualized, practice-based, and emergent at the time of illness. This knowledge needs to be captured by a variety of research methods including observations of actual illness, short video presentations of ill children that trigger recall of experiences, and responses to culturally relevant illness scenarios modeled after illness stories (Nichter and Nichter 1990).

The WHO ARI diagnosis and treatment guidelines, like the diarrheal disease algorithms that preceded them, are built on prevailing clinical wisdom. While they have proven useful in the training of health professionals at the primary health center, they may prove less useful as health education guides in the community unless adapted to address preexisting knowledge and practice. There may well be a need to adapt ARI message content to accord with those signs and symptoms of ARI that caretakers already recognize, take seriously and act upon promptly. The WHO ARI algorithm reflects a clinical gaze that privileges particular body signs in its classification of illness severity. These signs (e.g., rapid breathing, chest indrawing) have been subjected to tests of sensitivity and specificity in the epidemiological sense of these terms.[15] Community recognition and interpretation of these as well as other signs/symptoms associated with ARI-related illness need to be investigated just as rigorously. Required are studies that test for the sensitivity and specificity of emic illness terms matched against etic clinical criteria (e.g., how often a local term correlates with rapid breathing or indrawn chest).[16]

Symptoms included in the WHO algorithm for ALRI will need to be considered from a cultural vantage point. Research on the cultural interpretation of clinical signs of shigella (bloody diarrhea, fever, mucus) by age group and season has been called for prior to the development of community-based treatment algorithms for diarrhea (Nichter 1991); the same type of research is warranted for ARI. How often are clinical signs reported? Does unprompted symptom reporting or lack of reporting correlate with sign recognition or perceived severity? Do more generalized local terms (e.g., difficult breathing) index implicit recognition of unreported body signs?

The recognition of signs is influenced by popular health practices. How likely are caretakers to notice clinical signs of ALRI given the way children are clothed or examined? Are there retractions other than those of the chest (subcostal retractions) that are recognized by mothers or is the stomach rather than the chest observed? In the Philippines, caretakers are careful to clothe the upper body of children with ARI and pay more attention to the superclavicular regions of the body (at the base of the neck) and a bulging stomach or rising shoulders than to indrawn chest. Likewise in both Karnataka State and Maharastra State (India), movement of the stomach is a major focus of a mother's attention during ARI-related illness. Some traditional cures for ARI-related illness entail purging mucus from the stomach.[17] In the Gambia, on the other hand, "open chest" (subcostal retractions) are reported to be commonly recognized (Campbell, Byass, and Greenwood 1990).

Are the symptoms identified by the WHO algorithm recognized in culturally distinct ways? For example, is rapid breathing interpreted positively as a sign of strong lungs, and not a symptom of ill health, while slow breathing is associated with a lethargic, ill child? Saenz de Tejada (1990) has reported that in Guatemala, the quality of breathing of a child experiencing ALRI is often referred to as tiredness (*fatiga*) and more commonly as slow than fast. In both India and the Philippines I have encountered mothers who have observed a child ill with pneumonia and reported slow breathing when the breathing rate was over 50 breaths a minute. Their attention was drawn to the inactivity of the child. Other informants recognized rapid breathing as dangerous in children, but considered this sign less out of the ordinary if the ill child was an infant. Still others associated rapid breathing or pulse with fever present to the touch or "inside fever." Attention was focused on heat, not the lungs. The distribution of knowledge about ARI-related illness among different segments of a population is a research priority as is intracultural variability in symptom discrimination and interpretation.

Signs and symptoms recognized by caretakers as indicators of serious illness and local illness terms used to label serious illness need to be examined in terms of their ability to identify acute lower respiratory tract infection (ALRI).[18] It is, however, not sufficient to "select out" as important only those clinical signs that correlate well with ALRI for inclusion in ARI health education programs, treating other signs and symptoms as "noise." The cultural significance of locally recognized signs need to be considered. Are these signs causes of concern because they are based on popular perceptions of ethnophysiology? In both South India and the Philippines, the color of mucus is regarded as an important sign of illness related to a humoral aggravation (India) or the stage of illness progression (Philippines). While cloudy-yellow mucus is more of a cause of concern in India, clear mucus is the greater concern in the Philippines; yellow mucus is deemed a sign that the illness has "ripened," i.e,, come to fruition.[19] The color of mucus in both locations significantly impacts on health behavior.

Notions of ethnophysiology affect treatment practices. For example, if a congested chest is linked to mucus in the belly cavity of infants, it may be forced out of the body through the use of purgatives. Purgatives are a traditional remedy for diarrhea associated with phlegm in the feces and/or a productive cough in South India. Like diarrhea, ARI-related illness may also be associated with a physical mishap, such as a fall.[20] In the Philippines, a common reason for delaying treatment for ARI is suspicion that the child suffers an internal dislocation (*pilay hangin*) requiring massage. A similar idea exists in Indonesia related to dislocated muscles (*kecetit*). It is also necessary to study what signs of ARI are associated with the supernatural. If an illness is precipitated by sudden fever or accompanied by the presence of convulsions or rolled back eyes in South India, these symptoms are deemed signs of supernatural intervention. This is particularly the case if the child received a sudden shock. Given these signs, a child may be taken to a traditional practitioner prior to a doctor, especially if the child's illness is linked to other signs of supernatural presence in the household.

The bodily feelings and immediate experience of mothers tending to ill children also need to be considered.[21] Just as experienced clinicians "sense" that a child has pneumonia even before they count the respiratory rate, mothers "sense" that a child is seriously ill on the basis of subtle cues in their own, as well as their child's body. These cues include touch, smell, the child's eating behavior, and activity level. Such cues may be valuable to acknowledge in community-based messages, especially as related to children under two months of age. For example, poor feeding has been identified as a sign of moderate ARI. For the breastfeeding mother, attention might be drawn to the pain of an engorged breast as a sign of poor feeding or interrupted feeding.

It is important to consider communication about the nature of an illness beyond a name as a form of classification. In South India, I recorded several sounds used by mothers to index and communicate to concerned others problems their children were experiencing in breathing.[22] These sounds were more commonly used to identify an ARI-related problem than were the names of local illnesses. Instead of merely denoting difficult breathing in an ARI triage message, a message might be constructed around sounds commonly associated with different types of troubled breathing. Before suggesting that such sounds should be used in health messages, however, research needs to be conducted on the sensitivity, specificity, and ambiguity of sound glosses. In the Philippines, some people used distinct glosses to refer to a wheeze associated with asthma (*hapo, hika*) and a grunt (*halak*) associated with pneumonia. Others used one of these two glosses (*halak*) to refer to any type of labored breathing.[23] A similar pattern of generalized term use was discovered in South Kanara (India) with the gloss *dammu*.[24] Distinct terms for labored inbreathing and outbreathing (*ubbasa, nevasa*) exist in the *āyur-vedic* medical system, but are undifferentiated by most of the lay population.

3. Recognize diversity and ambiguity in illness labeling as well as strategic symptom reporting. While cognitive approaches to identifying local illness taxonomies have proven useful in disease-focused behavioral research, they identify schemata subject to negotiation and underestimate ambiguity. Studies of diarrhea/ARI labeling that pay attention to diagnosis by treatment and strategic symptom reporting need to complement taxonomic studies (Nichter 1989, 1991). In my studies of diarrheal disease in South Asia, I have found considerable ambiguity and latitude in the way indigenous as well as biomedical terms for diarrhea (e.g., gastroenteritis, cholera) were used by the lay population and practitioners alike. The same applies to ARI-related illness. In India, the term "typhoid" is used quite generally by local practitioners and the lay population for illness with fever inclusive of pneumonia. In the Philippines, the gloss "weak lungs" is used to denote TB by practitioners wishing to minimize the social stigma of the disease (Nichter 1994). Among the lay population the term is used more ambiguously to denote a wide range of chest/lung breathing complaints ranging from wheeze to recurring cough and TB. Tables 5.1 and 5.2 present data on the wide range of disease states denoted by a set of local illness names in North Kanara District, Karnataka State, India, in 1979.[25]

Intracultural variability in illness labeling needs to be documented as well as those factors which affect the process (taskonomy) of illness labeling including of levels of specificity in the language of illness (Nichter 1989). For example, in South Kanara (India), asthma carries with it a set of negative connotations. Parents of an unmarried girl are likely to refer to her condition using the more generalized terms *shīta* (a cold above the neck) or *usuru kaṭṭuvudu* (breathing trouble), rather than *ubbasa* asthmatic condition).

Age thresholds associated with illness forms are also in need of consideration. In the Philippines, age-specific ideas influence illness categorization in cases of ARI and TB. On the island of Mindoro, many informants perceived TB to be an illness of adults, while "weak lungs" an illness of both adults and children. Separate terms for pneumonia like symptoms were also used. Such distinctions are important because health education employing local terminology needs to consider the generalizability as well as the specificity of messages constructed. This has been a valuable lesson learned in diarrhea research (Nichter 1989).

4. *It is important to know how symptom states are perceived by caretakers. It is just as important to know how rapidly symptom states trigger health care seeking. How much time do caretakers reckon they have to seek treatment before a condition results in death?* Among children, and infants in particular, death from dehydration, dysentery, and pneumonia is rapid. Pneumonia studies from Bagamoya, Tanzania (Mtango and Neuvians 1986), and Jumla, Nepal (Pandey and Daulaire 1988), have reported that death occurs within three to three and a half days from the onset of acute symptoms. It is crucial that information be collected not only on what signs and symptoms are considered dangerous by caretakers, but on perceptions about how rapidly health care actions must be taken. This issue has been identified as crucial in studies of dysentery. There has been a call to study index symptoms such as bloody diarrhea in relation to the rapidity of treatment actions. Likewise, index symptoms of pneumonia such as rapid or noisy breathing, indrawn chest, flaring nostrils, failure to feed, and fever need to be studied in relation to specific health care options (e.g., doctor, hospital, herbalist, exorcist). In the case of ill children being referred to a traditional practitioner, it is imperative to document how long the child is treated before referral and whether referral is triggered by the manifestation of any particular signs or symptoms. In the Philippines, for example, most herbalists I observed who treated *pilay* (dislocations in the chest) referred cases of noisy, rapid breathing in children after a first consultation. Six out of eight called attention to a

Table 5.1

Terms Used When Presenting ARI to a Private Practitioner in a North Kanarese Town (*n* = 65 patients)

Local term	Number of patients citing term	Practitioner's diagnosis	Number of cases
Jwara (fever)	36	Upper respiratory infection	12
		Pneumonia	7
		Influenza	17
Jwara kemmu (fever, cough)	9	Upper respiratory infection	4
		Influenza	3
		Pneumonia	3
		Bronchitis	3
Thandi jwara (cold, fever)	2	Upper respiratory infection	1
		Bronchitis	1
Kemmu (cough)	8	Upper respiratory infection	4
		Tonsillitis	1
		Bronchitis	2
		Pneumonia	1
Thandi (cold)	1	Bronchitis	1
"Cold"	1	Upper respiratory infection	1
Kove	1	"Allergic" asthma	1
Dammu (labored breathing)	7	Asthma	5
		Allergic asthma	1
		TB	1
Total	65		

grunting sound, differentiating it from a wheeze. Children with a grunt were referred rapidly.

5. *In the real world, illnesses are often concurrent, not discrete. Consider treatment actions accordingly when conducting illness ethnographies. Also consider local notions of illness transformation.* In Ghana (Saenz de Tejada

Table 5.2

Local Terms Used When Presenting ARI at a Government Clinic in North Kanara (*n* = 25 patients)

Local term	Number of patients citing term	Practitioner's diagnosis	Number of cases
Dammu (labored breathing)	7	Bronchial asthma	5
		TB	1
		Low blood pressure	1
Kemmu (cough)	14	Bronchitis	6
		Acute bronchitis	5
		TB	1
		Upper respiratory infection	2
Jwara kemmu (fever, cough)	3	Acute bronchitis	2
Rakta kemmu (blood, cough)	1	TB	1
Total	25		

1990), diarrhea and respiratory problems in infants are viewed as interrelated. It is widely believed that infants do not know how to cough and swallow mucus which causes diarrhea. Coughing is thought by some to cause diarrhea and others perceive cough as a symptom of a folk illness (*fisinorego*) primarily thought to be gastrointestinal. As this example clearly illustrates, ARI education programs need to carefully consider the interrelationship between symptom complexes having local relevance. It is also necessary to consider how local populations view diarrhea and ARI when concurrent with other illnesses. Rash illnesses including of measles provide a case in point.

One of the biggest killers of young children in developing countries is measles. Death due to measles is associated with both diarrhea and pneumonia. In India, an estimated 16 million preschool children a year suffer from measles, of whom 200,000 die. Thirty to fifty percent of them die from pneumonia (Singhi and Singhi 1987). Research on diarrhea has revealed that in many regions of Asia and Africa there is a reluctance to treat measles. A pervasive belief is that the body is emitting heat and toxins from within as part of the illness process. Obstructing this process is thought to lead to death. Fear of such obstruction causes people to delay treating diarrhea until the "spots come out." A similar type of reasoning influences the treatment of ARI following "measles" in the Philippines.[26] Fear of *"sikal"* (measles like rashes) affects not only children who appear to have measles, but children who, it is feared, might have it because the disease is reported in the area. Special messages may have to be designed for measles that take into account local health concerns while teaching mothers about the danger signs of pneumonia.[27]

Also in need of investigation are local ideas about illnesses that transform into other illnesses if not treated correctly or if sustained in a latent state. In South India, I encountered villagers who believed that cholera is caused by less acute forms of diarrhea if not treated effectively. I have also encountered the idea that TB and whooping cough can be caused by a transformation of other respiratory illnesses sustained over time.[28] Ideas about illness transformation may affect patterns of health care seeking and/or treatment expectations. They may prove valuable to address in health education messages including those designed for vaccination programs.

6. *Do not focus exclusively on predisposing factors influencing health care behavior; give equal consideration to enabling and service-related factors.* Until recently, anthropologists studying diarrhea focussed most of their attention on cultural factors influencing the labeling of illness episodes, notions of causality, home treatment, and patterns of curative resort. Less attention has been paid to such enabling factors as the economics of care seeking (direct and indirect costs) assessed in relation to time constraints, disposable income, loan availability, or credit offered by practitioners. It is necessary to consider how care-seeking behavior is influenced by household composition, female employment, education, and similar factors. Research by Coreil (1991) has pointed out the importance of considering the success of ORS and immunization programs in relation to a mothers' time demands. Also under-appreciated are service related factors inclusive of the social relations of treatment administration and mother's fears of being scolded for inappropriate health care behavior.

Daulaire (1988) conducted a community utilization study of field staff trained in ARI management in Jumla, Nepal. He found that of those cases of clinical pneumonia identified in the study area, 80% were located during biweekly home visits and not through active consultation of field staff. Reasons why villagers did not actively contact an ARI field worker who could provide medication were investigated each time a child died of pneumonia. In a significant number of cases, enabling and service-related factors impacted negatively on health care seeking.[29] Tupasi (1987), in a study of

Filipino mothers' response to ARI, specifically noted that treatment costs were a primary source of concern influencing health care seeking behavior. Issues of cost determined efforts at self-medication and consultation of traditional healers. In my own study of health economic behavior in India, I documented seasonal patterns of health care utilization directly related to both disposable income and time availability. Health care seeking was delayed during the monsoon season.

7. *Consider differential patterns of health care decision making. Next, consider differential responses to children by parity as well as gender for illnesses considered minor as well as severe.* A research issue meriting increased attention is health care decision making within the household, an arena where competition as well as cooperation coexists. While in some cultures mothers are primary decision makers, in others, such as Turkey, parents are "auxiliary caretakers" of children with fathers-in-law and mothers-in-law being key decision makers (Aksit 1989). In South India, decision making was found to vary widely across caste and class. Among some groups, mothers would make decisions and directly pay practitioner fees from their own cash reserves. When illness was severe and required larger expenditures of pooled household capital, decision making patterns changed and responsibility shifted. In other castes (among Muslims) males made all decisions regarding consultation of any practitioner. In need of investigation are traditional as well as changing patterns of decision making in households where elders are/are not present and where mothers have different levels of education and social mobility (Caldwell 1989, Douglas 1990).

Also in need of study are varying patterns of decision making involving children of different ages, gender and parity. Research from North India suggests that these factors broadly influence practitioner utilization (Miller 1987, Shukla, Bhambal, and Bhandari 1979). Bentley (1988) has provided supporting case material involving diarrheal disease. Aksit (1989) suggests from her study of ARI in Turkey that firstborn children of either gender are favored, possibly influencing patterns of health care seeking.

A further research question emerging out of studies of diarrhea is whether past experience with a serious illness influences future health care/care seeking positively or negatively (Bentley 1988). In need of study are matched groups of households that have/have not experienced the recent loss or near loss of a child with pneumonia. To what extent do "child loss" households now view severe ARI treatable given past experience? Investigation of this subject raises the issue of lay treatment expectations as well as the poor's perception of cost benefit of treating serious illness among infants. In both the Philippines and India I have recorded strong shifts in health care seeking responses on the part of "infant loss parents." Some had altered their present health care seeking behavior in the direction of faster consultations of practitioners. Others delayed consultations under the impression that large investments in medicine delayed, but did not change the inevitable. The latter tended to speak more commonly of "strong" and "weak" infants.

8. *The unit of analysis is not just mothers (caretakers), but practitioners and pharmacists.* Research on ORS has revealed that while one set of health education messages is presented to mothers through the primary health care system, another set of messages is subtly communicated to mothers by practitioners through treatment actions and the media through advertisements.[30] In India, not only has practitioner treatment of diarrhea and dysentery been found to be significantly influenced by medication marketing (Nichter 1991), but dietary and liquid consumption advice is often contrary to the guidelines of health education programs (Viswanathan and Rohde 1990). The commercial health sector must be examined, not just folk beliefs about illness. Use of over-the-counter patent medicines (such as gripe water, barley water, and cough medicine) mask symptom presentation and lead to possible delays in health care seeking. The popularity and consumer demand for such products needs to be investigated in relation to both an appeal to traditional health concerns and the production of new health concerns and imagery.

Pharmacists and their assistants often distribute medications directly. Some mimic the prescription practices of doctors and are influenced by the promotional literature as well as the economic incentives of pharmaceutical companies (see Chapters 8 and 9). Studies of over-the-counter drug sales and prescription patterns need to go beyond a "rational drug use" critique characterized by pharmaco-epidemiology and consider the logic (cultural, economic) of seemingly irrational pharmaceutical behavior (Nichter 1989, Nichter and Vuckovic 1994). Pharmaceutical behavior must be studied in relation to both supply and demand side dynamics. Practitioner response to consumer demand needs to be considered (Kunin et al. 1987, Viswanathan and Rohde 1990).

In addition to studying the spectrum of sensitivity of pathogens to commonly prescribed drugs, it is necessary to evaluate the criteria upon which treatment decisions are made, sets of symptoms (or other indicators) that trigger practitioner treatment responses, and factors such as economics (of the patient, for the practitioner) that influence the administration of particular regimes. Traditional remedies for the treatment of ARI should be studied, but there must also be research on when and how long cough expectorants, suppressants, antihistamines, and bronchodilators are used in the home, prescribed by practitioners, and recommended by chemists as well as primary health care workers (Hardon 1987, 1991). It will be necessary to consider to what extent the use of these products mask symptoms (e.g., antihistamines inducing a sedative effect) and deter health care seeking as well as contribute to infection (e.g., suppressants leading to the retention of sputum and infected secretions).

9. *Use of over-the-counter medication, prescription reuse, and medicine sharing must be taken seriously.* Over-the-counter treatment of illness must be studied both at the site of the pharmacy and through household studies which are sensitive to patterns of medicine sharing and self-treatment modeled after past professional treatment. Household studies of diarrhea treatment in Indonesia in a region subjected to intensive ORT promotion found that in three quarters of diarrhea cases one or more antibiotics were self-administered (Lerman et al. 1988). Research in the Philippines by Tupasi (1987) and Hardon (1987, 1991) further underscore the need for studies of self-treatment. Fifty-five percent of Tupasi's urban sample were found to self-administer medicines during cases of ARI. Twenty-three percent of this sample employed antibiotics. Hardon's study of doctors' prescriptions in the Philippines for diarrhea and ARI suggests that much OTC behavior mimics prescription behavior. During my own research in the Philippines I found that self-use of antibiotics is common once a child had been effectively treated by a prescribed medication that demonstrated that the child was compatible with it. Once deemed compatible (*hiyang*), the medicine was used for "similar" complaints.

Rises in the use of OTC medication needs to be studied in relation to practitioner consultation patterns. Aksit (1989) has reported widespread OTC drug use for ARI treatment in Turkey and a tendency for caretakers to consult pharmacies about doctors' prescriptions before purchasing medicines as well as about use of traditional remedies. In South India, I have observed a rising use of commercial cough mixtures among households who used homemade herbal preparations 10 years ago. In many of these households, however, increased use of OTC medications did not translate into a general pattern of decreased practitioner utilization. These households had become greater consumers of medicines and health services. Also in need of study is whether OTC use delays practitioner seeking in cases of pneumonia among children of different age groups. In the Philippines the impact of OTC use on ARI was more pronounced among children over 18 months of age than among infants. Older children were given OTC medication for longer duration than infants.

10. *Before introducing a medicine to be used by community health workers, study existing patterns of medicine preference and purchase.* For different illnesses and age groups, various forms, colors, and tastes of medicines are preferred (Nichter 1989). Considerable market research has been con-

ducted on consumer demand in the private sector. Social scientists began paying increased attention to demand during ORS social marketing campaigns. A UNICEF-sponsored study of ARI in India (MBA 1989) has recently directed attention to this issue. One of the most interesting findings reported was that significant regional differences existed in medicine preference. In one region of Northeast India (West Bengal), use of injections for ARI was not popular, while use of syrup was popular. In South India, injections and colored pills were preferred and syrup use was low, while in both regions capsules were unpopular. The MBA study also found that blister packs of pills were not popular, perhaps because people wished to purchase pills loosely so that they could judge the demonstration effect of the medication before purchasing a series.

An important issue for further study is the interface between medicine packaging and pharmaceutical behavior. In the Philippines, antibiotic suspension prescribed to mothers of children having ARI is available in two sizes of bottle. Small bottles of suspension are commonly purchased although the dosage prescribed exceeds the amount purchased. Large suspension bottles are not purchased by the poor because they are too expensive; moreover, the medicine's compatibility and demonstration effect have not yet been proven. After consuming a three-day bottle of antibiotic, a child's acute symptoms often subside enough so that purchase of another bottle is not deemed necessary or is delayed. Practitioners have linked this behavior pattern to illness relapse.

11. *When conducting research on practitioner treatment behavior recognize eclectic treatment patterns and differences between the behavior of practitioners in government and private practice.* When conducting illness ethnographies, it is important to pay attention to the appropriation of resources by multiple therapy systems. When and to what extent do "traditional" practitioners use popular allopathic medications in addition to or in lieu of herbal medications? To what extent do they rely on commercial patent products reproducing traditional health concerns or propagating new ones? How does this pattern relate to their willingness to accept ORS as a resource? To what extent is the treatment of cosmopolitan practitioners subtly, if not directly, influenced by popular health culture? In India, hot–cold conceptualization profoundly influences medicine consumer demand and expectations influencing prescription practice and dietary advice for conditions of diarrhea and ARI. Medications prescribed by cosmopolitan practitioners often accommodate biomedical and traditional health care concerns. This pattern is reflected in the common practice of cosmopolitan professionals adding on the *āyurvedic* patent drug Liv 52 to prescriptions of antibiotics.

Doing so implicitly recognizes concerns about the effect of medicine on the digestive process.

Most research on practitioner prescription and diagnosis in less developed countries has been focused on the activities of government health care providers. Only recently in diarrhea research has attention been directed toward private practitioners and pharmacists. Household data on practitioner use in India indicate that the majority of "doctor" contacts are to private practitioners (Duggal and Amin 1989, Nichter 1990). This is true in general as well as with respect to diarrhea and ARI (Basu 1990). It is important to ascertain the extent to which the treatment practices of government and private practitioners are similar or distinct. For example, an ARI study in India conducted by Kumar et al. (1984) found that institution-based doctors tended to misuse antimicrobial medicines far less than general practitioners for reasons that were left unspecified. It would be important to investigate the extent to which differences in treatment patterns were related to the microeconomics of collecting a fee for services as well as to expectations of private practitioners in a competitive market. In the case of diarrhea, it is not profitable for private practitioners to recommend only ORS. This "clinically rational" advice is "economically irrational" and does not meet the expectations of patients who want reduced stool output or a hard stool, not less dehydration. In the case of ARI, practitioner-specific differences in cough syrup and antibiotic prescriptions may be related to profit motives as well as to the need to maintain popularity. Here it may be important to compare the medicine practices of private and government employed practitioners as well as the different practice patterns of government doctors who also have private practices.

While the community's overwhelming preference for treatment was allopathic medicine, only 34% of Kumar's sample of 176 mothers utilized the services of a hospital or health center. The health care resource of choice was a registered medical practitioner having no formal training in allopathy. This finding raises an important and politically loaded policy issue. Should non–degree-holding practitioners and pharmacists undergo ARI training? If additional research finds that the pattern of practitioner utilization reported by Kumar is common, a case may be made for extending ARI training beyond the health care system to a mixed bag of practitioner types.

12. *When designing a disease-control program, one must look beyond priority health needs defined in relation to mortality and consider perceived needs of the community.* The international health community artificially divides up illnesses for disease control programs, emphasizes particular diseases, and defers interest in others as a matter of policy. For this reason ARI and TB often constitute separate program initiatives although they are

Child Survival

closely linked in the popular health cultures of Asia. Would it be more prudent to organize public health programs around the range of health problems a population associates with common causes or treatments? Not to do so may give rise to operational problems. At present, the focus of ARI program activity is moderate to severe lower respiratory infections (pneumonia) amenable to antimicrobial treatment. Emphasis is placed on recognizing and treating pneumonia. Wheezing in children above age two is not a focus of attention. Community health workers trained in ARI are often given antibiotics to treat cases of pneumonia, but not drugs to treat wheezing. This practice may not be understandable to the lay population in areas where wheezing and the causes of ALRI related illnesses are linked to common factors such as mucus "coating the lungs." In the Philippines, antibiotics are considered useful for both types of cases as a means of "melting accumulating phlegm."[31] Felt health needs should be respected.

In South India, wheezing/asthma is perceived by the community to be a rising health problem associated with changing environmental conditions. Wheezing is given serious attention as an ailment reducing work potential and therefore household survival. Practitioners are consulted for wheezing by the poor often at considerable expense. Among those identified as "asthmatics," antibiotics are commonly used by private practitioners, presumably as a means of deterring secondary infections that are commonly believed to be triggered by wheezing.[32] This treatment pattern complements the doling out of antibiotics for diarrhea by practitioners who state that they do so just in case the symptom is, or becomes, associated with bacterial infection. Not to pay attention to wheeze may undermine ARI messages involving appropriate antibiotic use. Community members may view wheezing as an important illness amenable to antibiotic treatment, just as they have been led to believe that diarrhea may be treated by antibiotics.

The ramifications of neglecting wheeze in an ARI program may be significant. Community health workers who are given an antibiotic such as cotrimoxazole and an algorithm for its use in cases of pneumonia may find themselves confronted by members of their community. After seeing the efficacy of antibiotics in cases of pneumonia, community members may exert pressure on a health worker to administer the drug for wheezing. This type of response must be considered and investigated. In contexts where such a response is identified, special education efforts may have to be designed and/or health workers might be supplied with a medication like salbutamol, specifically for wheeze.

13. *Carefully consider the implementation of integrated disease management programs in terms of the social relations of teamwork within the context of a hierarchically structured health bureaucracy.* It is prudent to consider

the advantages and disadvantages of disease control programs that are implemented alone or in conjunction with other health programs. Such an evaluation must consider the perspective of the community, the resources and demands on the health care system as a whole, and the identity and power base of different cadres of the primary health care workers.

Successful ORS programs have often been those tied to integrated child survival programs offering a range of services, and not just to distribution of ORS. ARI treatment programs may do better if coordinated with diarrheal disease programs (and vice versa). Doing so will depend on both the staff dynamics of the health care system and the health problems the community identifies as treatable by health auxiliaries. The demonstration effect of antibiotics in treating pneumonia may lend more credibility to health workers who are attempting to popularize ORS (Rai 1988) and vaccinations. On the other hand, offering medications to community health workers may be viewed by health center staff as reducing their status, defined in relation to medicines as signs of power (see Chapter 11). In such a case, problems created by an ARI program may compound those of a diarrhea management program. Jealousies could lead to interferences in the flow of antibiotics downward and in the supply of ORS. Problems may be anticipated and steps taken to resolve them if staff teamwork is investigated as a central issue in anthropologically informed health service research.

14. *Use local illness categories when evaluating the impact of health interventions.* Assessments of ORS outreach programs in Bangladesh have demonstrated that use rates vary significantly by illness category. Intervention success could only be meaningfully assessed in terms of local treatment expectations by illness category. This analysis made a difference to program planning and evaluation (Chowdhury, Vaughan, and Abed 1988). Applied to ARI, it might be important to gather baseline data sensitive to local illness classification in order to evaluate interventions (e.g., changes in illness classification, consultation patterns, or triage subsequent to educational messages).

15. *Health social science requires transdisciplinary teamwork.* An important lesson learned from diarrheal disease research is the need for collaboration between various types of health and social scientists committed both to their own disciplines and a process of problem-solving that supersedes disciplinary boundaries. Teamwork requires a broad appreciation for the biological, epidemiological, and social aspects of disease and health-related behavior. At stake is not just disease management, but the development of approaches to health care which reflect an ecology of ideas, not just pathogens.

CONCLUSION

Acute respiratory illness looms as one of the greatest threats to child survival. Social scientists can contribute to ARI program development and evaluation in a number of ways. It is hoped that lessons learned during a decade of social science research on diarrheal disease may be applied to ARI problem solving. At present, several ethnographic reconnaissance studies of ARI are under way supported by a variety of international health agencies. For the most part, these studies focus on predisposing factors influencing ARI-related behavior. Longer term and broader-based household production of health studies need to complement such studies and investigate enabling factors influencing household decision making. Also required is health service research focusing on community and practitioner response to health messages (algorithms, etc.) and treatment programs. In this chapter, I have highlighted a number of research issues germane to the study of ARI. These issues have obvious relevance beyond ARI.

NOTES

1. Acute respiratory infections (ARI) include both upper and lower respiratory infections. As the WHO uses the term, acute upper respiratory infection(s) include the common cold, pharyngitis, and otitis media. Acute lower respiratory illnesses include pneumonia, bronchiolitis, croup, epiglottitis, and bronchitis. Pertussis, measles, and TB are not generally incorporated in the WHO definition of ARI. Deaths due to pertussis are often counted in respiratory disease mortality figures. For the purposes of this chapter, I have chosen to use the 1988 WHO classification of ARI and focus on pneumonia as the chief killer of young children.

2. In developing countries bacteria (*S. pneumoniae* and *H. influenzae*) are more often involved in pneumonia than in developed countries. Pneumonia often is compounded by both viral and bacterial infection in developing countries. This pattern suggests the possibility of an antecedent viral infection (Narain 1987, Riley 1985). Influenza virus increases secretions, damages bronchial epithelium preventing the clearance of bacteria, and may well depress T-cell function. Children in developing countries often have high carriage rates of bacterial pathogens (Riley and Carrad 1983). Undernourished, immunologically weak children may be more susceptible to the descent of bacteria from the upper to the lower respiratory tract. It has been estimated that at least 50% of pneumonia cases in developing countries will be responsive to antibiotics (Parker 1987, Pio, Leowski, and Dam 1985).

3. Antibiotic use has little clinical effect on upper respiratory track infections (Sutrisna et al. 1991) or managing most diarrheal diseases (Harris and Black 1991), although widely prescribed by doctors and taken over-the-counter. Little research presently exists on the impact of inappropriate antibiotic use during ARI and drug resistance. What is known is that such use is under reported (Catalono et al. 1990). Nichter has reported widespread OTC cotrimoxazole use in India (Nichter and Vuckovic 1994). It is worth speculating whether this could be associated with alarming levels of cotrimoxazole resistance in neighboring Pakistan (Mostro, Ghafoor, and Nomani 1991). On the OTC use of anti-TB drugs and drug resistance in the Philippines, see Nichter (1994).

4. Common risk factors for ARI and diarrhea morbidity and mortality overlap and are summarized by Stansfeld (1987). They include poor sanitation, overcrowding, low birth weight (Datta 1987, Victora, Smith, and Vaughan 1988), early weaning, poor nutrition, low socioeconomic status, and vitamin A deficiency (Sommer, Katz, and Tarwotjo 1984). Additional factors associated with ARI include the number of children in the household under five years of age (Tupasi et al. 1990a and 1990b, Vathanophas et al. 1990, Victora, Smith, and Vaughan 1988) and air pollution (Armstrong and Campbell 1991, Chen et al. 1990, Pandey et al. 1989).

5. Monto (1989) notes two reasons ARI was not the focus of aggressive intervention programs earlier. First, a paucity of data on etiology was associated with a lack of strategies for prevention and treatment. Testing for the etiology of pneumonia is complicated. Blood cultures, for example, are positive in only 20–30% of bacterial pneumonia cases. Second, ARI was not perceived to be a tropical disease commanding special attention in developing countries.

6. Steinhoff (1990) has provided a critical review of the six trial communitybased ARI intervention projects sponsored by the WHO in Pakistan, Tanzania, Philippines, Nepal, and Indonesia. He points out methodological reasons for differences in the rates of success reported, and cautions against unrealistically high estimates of intervention effect. On another note, the possibility has been raised that community-based interventions may be eclipsed by overuse of antibiotics, leading to resistance. See, for example, Applebaum (1977) and Weinstein (1955). On the other hand, over-the-counter use of antibiotics may reduce rates of mortality in the short-term before resistance becomes a problem.

7. The respiratory rate used to recognize moderate to severe ARI was established by the work of Shann, Hart and Thomas (1984) in Papua New Guinea. It has been subjected to tests of sensitivity and specificity and modified (Campbell and Byass 1988, Campbell, Byass and Greenwood 1988, Cherian et al. 1988). An issue of contention at present is the threshold rate for babies under six months of age, who contribute significantly to ARI mortality (Berman and Simoes 1991, Morley, Thornton, and Fowler 1990).

8. The issues listed are taken from personal conversations with technical advisory group members and notes taken during my own attendance at various ARI meetings in 1989–90.

9. For the purpose of this chapter I have retained the original WHO classification scheme for ARI. In 1989 this scheme was altered from severe, moderate, and mild ARI to severe pneumonia, pneumonia, and cough/cold. Revised guidelines are more sensitive to the different respiratory rates of children of different ages.

10. While little detailed medical anthropological research on ARI had been carried out prior to 1989, culturally sensitive medical research has been conducted in the Philippines (Tupasi 1987), Gambia (Campbell, Byass, and Greenwood 1990), Turkey (Aksit 1989), Nepal (Daulaire 1988) and India (Kumar et al. 1984). This chapter reviews data published prior to the WHO FES studies. See the special issue of *Medical Anthropology* (Nichter, Pelto, and Steinhoff, eds. 1994) which reviews recent studies of ARI-related behavior including those associated with the WHO FES initiative.

11. I am not suggesting that all ethnographic research associated with the social marketing of ORS was narrowly focused and directed toward compliance. Some anthropologists have supported a more adherence-based approach (Barofsky 1978) to health education entailing the marketing of health concepts, not just products, and a negotiation of popular and professional health concerns. See Nichter and Vuckovic (1992) for a distinction between the two approaches as they relate to the practice of social marketing.

12. For overviews of public health lessons learned through the ethnographic study of diarrheal disease and oral rehydration programs see Kendall (1990) and Sukkaray-Stolba (1989).

13. When diarrhea or ARI is an expected state it may be perceived as a disorder concordant with environmental change and not contagion. In South India and the Philippines many forms of diarrhea and ARI (encompassing pneumonia) are not deemed contagious. ARI is associated with temperature changes and types of wind that account for widespread ill health. On the other hand, contagion by contiguity reasoning is employed in cases of dysentery and TB by some people in both places.

14. Saenz de Tejada (1990) reports that in Ghana a notion exists that a child may inherit a "weak chest" because a mother did heavy work while pregnant.

15. Classification of ARI in various contexts has been determined on the basis of the anatomical site of infection, etiological agent and/or route of transmission, and signs and symptoms. The WHO algorithm (up to May 1989) classifies ARI in relation to mild, moderate, and severe ARI on the basis of illness severity and therapy management structured around the recognition of clinical signs and symptoms. Clinical signs of pneumonia are age dependent (Cherian et al. 1988) and a tradeoff has to be made between increased sensitivity in the recognition of moderate ARI and ease in implementing a community-based

treatment algorithm (Campbell and Byass 1988). The Cherian study reports a high sensitivity and specificity for rapid breathing in distinguishing acute lower respiratory tract infections requiring antibiotic treatment from upper respiratory tract infections among children under 35 months of age. Above that age, the sensitivity of rapid breathing, chest refractions, and respiratory rates is not statistically significant but the specificity is high.

16. For an excellent study of the sensitivity and specificity of a local illness term associated with fast breathing in Egypt, see Gadomski et al. (1993).

17. The term *potat ala* is often used to refer to pneumonia among young children in rural Maharastra (Chand and Bhattacharyya 1994). The term literally means "something in the stomach." The chief sign noted by their informants is the stomach going up and down. In South Kanara, mothers of children having pneumonia often identified stomach going in and out (*hōṭṭe woḷage horage hōguvudu*) as well as chest going in and out (*yede woḷage hōguvudu*), tight chest (*yede hiḍidu koḷḷuvudu, yede hiḍi koṅḍu*), and shoulders rising (*egalū mēle keḷage hōguvudu*). The term *guḷḷe* was used for a depression in the stomach or chest. After noting *guḷḷe*, mothers of ill children were asked to point to it. More often they pointed to the stomach. In Guatemala (Saenz de Tejada 1990), chest indrawing is often described as throbbing abdomen (*le brincaba la pancita*) or ribs sticking out (*esgueleto/costillas salidas*). In Ghana (Saenz de Tejada 1990) chest indrawing is not widely recognized and when it is, it is just as often referred to as "stomach breathing" as "sunken chest."

18. Important cultural differences may well exist with respect to how mothers interpret the signs of severe ARI identified by clinicians. Cherian et al. (1988) reported high sensitivity and specificity among Indian mothers with regard to their recognition of fast breathing among children as a sign of ill health. Campbell, Byass, and Greenwood (1990) have likewise documented that Gambian mothers are likely to note one or more of three index signs of ARI when reporting acute illness diagnosed as moderate to severe ARI. By contrast, I found considerable ambiguity in the way South Indian mothers interpreted and described clinical signs of ARI. In South Kanara, the term *dammu* was applied to breathlessness, rapid breathing, and slow difficult breathing. Wheezing and rapid breathing associated with pneumonia were often confused. In some cases, breathing difficulty (*śvāsa yeḷuvudu*) was considered a problem, but not necessarily a disease if not accompanied by fever. Likewise, Aksit (1989), has reported poor recognition of the index signs of severe ARI. Differences between what is reported to researchers in the clinic and recognized in the home need to be considered. Is recognition of rapid breathing in a very ill child the same as recognition of rapid breathing as a sign of illness severity in and of itself? What if other signs such as fever or poor feeding are not recognized? Researchers also need to examine what illness terms connote as well as denote. Does a term for "difficult breathing" index noisy breathing, fast breathing, etc.?

19. In both oriental Mindoro and Bicol (Philippines), many mothers view clear mucus as more dangerous than cloudy mucus due to its capacity to dry on the lungs causing difficult breathing and weak lungs. This perception has also been reported in Guatemala (Saenz de Tejada 1990). Other mothers in the Philippines viewed yellow sticky mucus as more dangerous, having the capacity to stick to the lungs.

20. Diarrhea has also been associated with a child falling, muscle strain, and sudden movements. See for example studies of children's diarrhea in Ethiopia (Olango and Aboud 1990), Indonesia (Ismail et al. 1991) and Mexico among the Ojitico (Cessa, personal communication).

21. In need of consideration are mothers' bodily ways of knowing which are multisensorial, embodied, and experiential. This calls for anthropology "coming to its senses" and practicing what Howes (1991) has termed sensorial anthropology. See Classen (1993) for additional cross cultural and historical examples of how different cultures privilege different sensual faculties. Studies are needed on the relationship between the social organization of the sensorium, sensual competency, and the recognition of signs and symptoms of illness.

22. For example, in South Kanara the sound *kuñyi-kuñyi* denotes a dry cough, *gur-gur* a productive cough, *busa busa* heavy breathing.

23. While *halak* was sometimes used to describe a wheeze, it was almost always used to describe labored breathing and grunting in pneumonia cases observed. This would suggest that *halak* may have high sensitivity in terms of pneumonia recognition, a proposition requiring further research.

24. In South Kanara District, Karnataka (India), distinct terms in the Kannaḍa language exist for fast breathing and wheeze (*selle, usula kaṭṭuvudu*), but the term *dammu* is often used as a general gloss for difficulties in breathing. At other times *dammu* is used to denote gasping (*dammu kaṭṭuvudu*) breathlessness, or slow breathing (*dammu haṭṭuvudu*).

25. In terms of the data presented, the accuracy of the doctor's diagnosis is open to question. The point I wish to make is that illness terms are used in a variety of ways and at different levels of specificity to denote a range of disease states.

26. In Mindoro, fear of "spots going within" is associated with a complex of local illnesses (*tigdas, tuko, buluting tubig, sarampiyon*) having spots and pustulates, and not just measles per se. The term "measles" is used by many people to refer to this complex, a pattern which reduces perceptions of the efficacy of measles vaccinations.

27. The importance of studying measles in relation to ARI mortality is clearly demonstrated by Tupasi et al. (1990a). In a longitudinal study of ARI infection among children in impoverished Manila households ($n = 709$), 18 children died of ARI during the study. Eleven of the 18 (61%) died following measles.

28. The MBA (1989) study of ARI in India found that in Tamil Nadu the terms pneumonia and TB were commonly confused for each other. One reason may be because pneumonia is recognized to predispose one to TB. This was a perception reported in Karnataka and also is common in the Philippines.

29. Other factors included perceptions of medication efficacy and nonrecognition of symptoms as indicative of respiratory illness.

30. Physician and health staff compliance with public health protocols are important to investigate. For example, significant discrepancies have been reported in physician knowledge about appropriate treatment for diarrhoea and treatment practice. Studies from Indonesia (Muniyaya et al. 1991, Gani et al. 1991) and Mexico (Gutierrez et al. 1994), for example, have reported continued overprescription of antibiotics even when ORS use was adopted.

31. On the other hand, antiasthmatics are frequently given to children with ARI in the Philippines (Hardon 1987, 1991).

32. Moreover, among infants (under 18 months) bronchiolitis is often misdiagnosed either as asthma (due to the presence of an expiratory wheeze) or pneumonia (due to the sound of rales).

REFERENCES

Adkikari, N. 1985. Acute Respiratory Infections in Nepal and Problems Faced in Their Management. *In* Acute Respiratory Infection in Children. R. Douglas and E. Kerby-Eaton, eds. Pp. 136–137. Adelaide, Australia: University of Adelaide.

Aksit, B. 1989. Acute Respiratory Infections: Focus Group Interviews Conducted in the Provinces of Srivas and Van. Presented to Workshop on ARI, Hacettepe University, Ankara, Turkey.

Applebaum, P. C. 1977. Streptococcus Pneumoniae Resistant to Penicillin and Chloramphenicol. Lancet 2:955–957.

Armstrong, J. R. M. and H. Campbell. 1991. Indoor Air Pollution and Lower Respiratory Infections in Young Gambian Children. International Journal of Epidemiology 20:424–429.

Aung, T. 1985. ARI in Childhood in Burma: What Happens Now? *In* Acute Respiratory Infections in Childhood. R. M. Douglas and E. K. Eaton, eds. Pp. 93–95. Adelaide, Australia: University of Adelaide.

Barofsky, I. 1978. Compliance, Adherence and the Therapeutic Alliance: Steps in the Development of Self-Care. Social Science and Medicine 12:369–376.

Barriga, P. and B. Martinez. 1987. The Contribution of Ethnographic Research to the ARI Community Plan. Unpublished report, Academy for Educational Development, Honduras.

Basu, A. 1990. Cultural Influences on Health Care Use: Two Regional Groups in India. Studies in Family Planning 21:275–286.

Bentley, M. E. 1988. The Household Management of Childhood Diarrhea in Rural North India. Social Science and Medicine 27:75–85.

Berman, S. 1990. Overview of Pneumonia in Early Infancy. *In* ALRI and Child Survival in Developing Countries: Understanding the Current Status and Directions for the 1990s. Anne Gadomski, ed. Pp. 39–52. Baltimore, MD: The Johns Hopkins Institute for International Programs.

Berman, S. and K. McIntosh. 1985. Acute Respiratory Infections. Reviews of Infectious Diseases 7:29–46.

Berman, S. and E. F. Simoes. 1991. Annotations: Respiratory Rate and Pneumonia in Infancy. Archives of Disease in Childhood 66:81–84.

Berman, S., E. F. Simoes, and C. Lomata. 1991. Respiratory Rate and Pneumonia in Infancy. Archives of Disease in Childhood 66:81–84.

Bulla, A. and K. Hitze. 1978. Acute Respiratory Infections: A Review. Bulletin of the World Health Organization 56:481–498.

Caldwell, J. C. 1989. Routes to Low Mortality in Poor Countries. *In* Selected Readings in the Cultural, Social and Behavioral Determinants of Health. J. C. Caldwell and G. Stantow, eds. Pp. 1–46. Canberra: Health Transition Centre, The Australian National University.

Campbell, H. and P. G. Byass 1988. Simple Clinical Signs for Diagnosis of Acute Lower Respiratory Infections. Lancet 2:742–743.

Campbell, H., P. G. Byass, and B. M. Greenwood. 1988. Simple Clinical Signs for Diagnosis of Acute Respiratory Infections. Lancet 2:742–743.

Campbell, H., P. G. Byass, and B. M. Greenwood. 1990. Acute Lower Respiratory Infections in Gambian Children: Maternal Perception of Illness. Annals of Tropical Paediatrics 10:45–51.

Catalano, M., M. A. Almiron, A. M. Romeo, E. Caruso, P. Murtagh, and J. Harisiadi. 1990. Role of Bacterial Pathogens in Acute Respiratory Tract Infections. Reviews of Infectious Diseases 12:S998–S1000.

Chand, A. and K. Bhattacharyya. 1994. The Marathi "Taskonomy" of Respiratory Illness in Children. Medical Anthropology 15:395–408.

Chen, B. H., C. J. Honey, M. R. Pandley, and K. R. Smith. 1990. Indoor Air Pollution in Developing Countries. World Health Statistics Quarterly 43:127–138.

Cherian, T., John T. Jacob, E. Simoes, M. C. Steinhoff, and M. John. 1988. Evaluation of Simple Clinical Signs for the Diagnosis of Acute Lower Respiratory Tract Infection. Lancet 2:125–128.

Chowdhury, A. M. R. 1988. The Brac ORT Programme in Bangladesh: Description, Evaluation Methods and Results. Community Epidemiology/Health Management Network Research Paper Number Two. Bangkok: Ford Foundation.

Chowdhury, A. M. R., J. P. Vaughan, and F. H. Abed. 1988. Use and Safety of Homemade Oral Rehydration Solutions: An Epidemiological Evaluation from Bangladesh. International Journal of Epidemiology 17:655–665.

Classen, C. 1993. Worlds of Sense. London: Routledge.

Coreil, J. 1991. Maternal Time Allocation in Relation to Kind and Domain of Primary Health Care. Medical Anthropology Quarterly 5:221–235.

Coreil, J. and E. Genece. 1988. Adoption of Oral Rehydration Therapy Among Haitian Mothers. Social Science and Medicine 27:87–96.

Datta, N. 1987. Acute Respiratory Infection in Low Birth Weight Infants. Indian Journal of Pediatrics 54:171–176.

Daulaire, N. 1988. An Ethnographic Study of ARI in Jumla. Unpublished manuscript.

Denny, F. and F. A. Loda. 1986. Acute Respiratory Infections are the Leading Cause of Death in Children in Developing Countries. American Journal of Tropical Medicine and Hygiene 35:1–2.

Douglas, R. M. 1985. ARI — The Cinderella of Communicable Diseases. *In* Acute Respiratory Infections in Childhood. R. M. Douglas and E. K. Eaton, eds. Pp. 1–2. Adelaide, Australia: University of Adelaide.

Douglas, R. M. 1990. The Impact of Socioeconomic Factors on Respiratory Infections in Children. Bulletin of the International Union Against Tuberculosis and Lung Disease 65:8–11.

Duggal, R. and R. Amin. 1989. Cost of Health Care: A Household Survey in an Indian District. Bombay: Foundation for Research in Community Health.

Edmundson, W. and S. Harris. 1989. Management of Pneumonia in India and Indonesia. Social Science and Medicine 29(8):975–982.

Eigner, F. D. 1981. Cough and Fever in Children. Tropical Doctor 11:1–10.

Gadomski, A., G. Aref, F. Hassanien, S. Ghandour, M. El-Mougi, L. Harrison, N. Khallaf, and R. Black. 1993. Caretaker Recognition of Respiratory Signs in Children: Correlation with Physical Examination Findings, X-Ray Diagnosis and Pulse Oximetry. International Journal of Epidemiology 22(6):1166–1173.

Gani, L., H. Arif, S. Widjaja, R. Adi, et al. 1991. Physicians' Prescribing Practice for Treatment of Acute Diarrhoea in Young Children in Jakarta. Journal of Diarrhoeal Disease Research 9:194–199.

Grant, J. 1984. The State of the World's Children. New York: Oxford University Press.

Green, E. 1986. Diarrhea and the Social Marketing of Oral Rehydration Salts in Bangladesh. Social Science and Medicine 23:357–366.

Greenwood, B. M., A. M. Greenwood, A. K. Bradley, S. Tulloch, R. Hayes, and F. S. J. Oldfield. 1987. Deaths in Infancy and Early Childhood in a Well-Vaccinated, Rural West African Population. Annals of Tropical Paediatrics 2:91–99.

Gutierrez, G., et al. 1994. Changing Physician Prescribing Patterns: Evaluation of an Educational Strategy for Acute Diarrhoea in Mexico City. Medical Care 32:436–446.

Hardon, A. 1987. The Use of Modern Pharmaceuticals in a Filipino Village: Doctor's Prescription and Self-Medication. Social Science and Medicine 25:277–292.

Hardon, A. 1991. Confronting Ill Health: Medicines, Self-Care and the Poor in Manila. Quezon City, Philippines: Health Action Information Network.

Harris, S. and R. E. Black. 1991. How Useful are Pharmaceuticals in Managing Diarrhoeal Diseases in Developing Countries? Health Policy and Planning 6:141–147.

Howes, D., ed. 1991. The Varieties of Sensory Experience: A Sourcebook in the Anthropology of the Senses. Toronto: University of Toronto Press.

Ismail, R., H. Aulia, A. Susanto, A. Roisuddin, and M. Hamzah. 1991. Community Perceptions on Diarrheal Diseases. A Case Study in Swampy Lowland Areas of South Sumatra, Indonesia. Paediatric Indonesia 31:18–25.

James, J. W. 1972. Longitudinal Study of the Morbidity of Diarrheal and Respiratory Infections in Malnourished Children. American Journal of Clinical Nutrition 25:690–694.

Kendall, C. 1989. The Use and Non-Use of Anthropology: The Diarrheal Disease Control Program in Honduras. *In* Making Our Research Useful. J. Van Willigen, B. Rylko-Bauer, and A. McElroy, eds. Pp. 283–303. Boulder: Westview Press.

Kendall, C. 1990. Public Health and the Domestic Domain: Lessons from Anthropological Research on Diarrheal Diseases. *In* Anthropology and Primary Health Care. Jeannine Coreil and J. Dennis Mull, eds. Pp. 173–195. Boulder: Westview Press.

Kendall, C., D. Foote, and R. Martorell. 1984. Ethnomedicine and Oral Rehydration Therapy: A Case Study of Ethnomedical Investigation and Program Planning. Social Science and Medicine 19:253–260.

Kresno, S., G. Harrison, B. Sutrisna, and A. Reingold. 1994. Acute Respiratory Illness in Children Under Five Years in Indramayu, West Java, Indonesia: A Rapid Ethnographic Assessment. Medical Anthropology 15:425–434.

Kumar, V. 1987. Epidemiological Methods in Acute Respiratory Infections. Indian Journal of Pediatrics 54:205–211.

Kumar, V., L. Kumar, M. Mand, M. Mittal, and N. Datta. 1984. Child Care Practices in the Management of Acute Respiratory Infections. Indian Pediatrics 21:15–20.

Kunin, C. M., H. L. Lipton, T. Tupasi, T. Sacks, W. E. Scheckler, A. Jivani, A. Goic, R. R. Martin, R. L. Guerrant, and V. Thamlikitkul. 1987. Social, Behavioral, and Practical Factors Affecting Antibiotic Use Worldwide: Report of Task Force 4. Review of Infectious Diseases 9(Supplement 3):S270–S285.

Kunstadter, P. 1991. Social and Behavioral Factors in Transmission and Response to Shigellosis. Reviews of Infectious Diseases 13(Supplement 4):S272–S278.

Lancet. 1985. Acute Respiratory Infections in Under-Fives: 5 Million Deaths a Year. 2:699–701.

Leowski, J. 1986. Mortality from Acute Respiratory Infections in Children Under 5 Years of Age: Global Estimates. World Health Statistics Quarterly 39:138–44.

Lerman, S. L., D. S. Shepard, and R. A. Cash. 1988. Treatment of Diarrhoea in Indonesian Children: What It Costs and Who Pays for It. Lancet 21(2):651–654.

MacCormick, C. and A. Draper. 1988. Cultural Meanings of Oral Rehydration Salts in Jamaica. *In* The Context of Medicines in Developing Countries. S. Van der

Geest and S. R. Whyte, eds. Pp. 277–287. Dordrecht, The Netherlands: Kluwer Academic Publishers.

Marketing and Business Associates (MBA). 1989. KAP Study of Acute Respiratory Infections in Children Below 3 Years of Age in India. UNICEF Report, New Delhi, India.

Mata, L. J. 1978. The Children of Santa Maria Cauque: A Prospective Study of Health and Growth. Cambridge: MIT Press.

McCord, C. and A. A. Kielmann. 1978. A Successful Programme for Medical Auxiliaries Treating Childhood Diarrhea and Pneumonia. Tropical Doctor 8:220–225.

Miller, B. 1987. The Endangered Sex: Neglect of Female Children in North India. Ithaca, NY: Cornell University Press.

Mohs, E. 1985. Acute Respiratory Infections in Children: Possible Control Measures. Bulletin of the Pan American Health Organization 19:82–87.

Monto, A. 1989. Acute Respiratory Infection in Children of Developing Countries: Challenge of the 1990s. Review of Infectious Diseases 2:498–505.

Morley, C. J., A. J. Thornton, and M. A. Fowler. 1990. Respiratory Rate and Severity of Illness in Babies Under 6 Months Old. Archives of Disease in Childhood 65:834–837.

Mostro, T., A. Ghafoor, and N. Nomani. 1991. Antimicrobial Resistance of Pneumococci in Children with Acute Lower Respiratory Tract Infection in Pakistan. Lancet 337:156–159.

Mtango, F. and D. Neuvians. 1986. Acute Respiratory Infections in Children Under 5 Years: Control Project in Bagamoyo. Transactions of the Royal Society of Tropical Medicine and Hygiene 80:851–858.

Mull, J. D. and D. S. Mull. 1988. Mothers' Concepts of Childhood Diarrhea in Rural Pakistan: What ORT Program Planners Should Know. Social Science and Medicine 27:53–67.

Muniyaya, A. and T. Widarsa. 1991. Home Treatment of Acute Diarrhoea in Bali, Indonesia. Journal of Diarrhoeal Disease Research 9:200–203.

Narain, J. P. 1987. Epidemiology of Acute Respiratory Infections. Indian Pediatrics 54:153–160.

Nations, M. and L. Rebhun. 1988. Mystification of a Simple Solution: Oral Rehydration Therapy in Northeast Brazil. Social Science and Medicine 21(1):25–38.

Nichter, Mark. 1988. From Aralu to ORS: Sinhalese Perceptions of Digestion, Diarrhea and Dehydration. Social Science and Medicine 27:39–52.

Nichter, Mark. 1989. Anthropology and International Health: South Asian Case Studies. Dordrecht, The Netherlands: Kluwer Academic Publishers.

Nichter, Mark. 1990. Household Production of Health: Documenting the Relative Contribution of Pluralistic Therapy Systems. Paper presented at the Third International Association for the Study of Traditional Asian Medicine, Bombay, India.

Nichter, Mark. 1991. Use of Social Science Research to Improve Epidemiological Studies of and Interventions for Diarrhea and Dysentery. Reviews of Infectious Disease 13:265–271.

Nichter, Mark. 1994. Illness Semantics and International Health: The Weak Lungs/ TB Complex in the Philippines. Social Science and Medicine 38(5):649–663.

Nichter, Mark and Mimi Nichter. 1990. Navigating Poorly Charted Waters: The Oriental Mindoro Acute Respiratory Disease Study. Geneva: World Health Organization.

Nichter, Mark and Mimi Nichter. 1994. Acute Respiratory Illness: Popular Health Culture and Mother's Knowledge in the Philippines. Medical Anthropology 15(4):353–375.

Nichter, M., G. Pelto, and M. Steinhoff, eds. 1994. Acute Respiratory Infection. Medical Anthropology (Special Issue) 15:4.

Nichter, Mark and N. Vuckovic. 1994. Agenda for an Anthropology of Pharmaceutical Practice. Social Science and Medicine 39(11):1509–1525.

Nichter, Mimi and N. Vuckovic. 1992. Social Marketing and Anthropology: A Critical Perspective. Unpublished manuscript, Department of Anthropology, University of Arizona.

Olango, P. and F. Aboud. 1990. Determinants of Mothers' Treatment of Diarrhea in Rural Ethiopia. Social Science and Medicine 31:1245–1249.

Pandey, M. and N. Daulaire. 1988. The Jumla ARI Intervention Trial. Geneva: World Health Organization.

Pandey, M., N. Daulaire, E. Starbuck, R. Houston, and K. McPherson. 1991. Reduction in Total Under-Five Mortality in Western Nepal Through Community-Based Antimicrobial Treatment of Pneumonia. Lancet 338:993–997.

Pandey, M., P. Sharma and R. Nuepane. 1985. Preliminary Report of a Community Study of Childhood ARI in Nepal. In Acute Respiratory Infection in Children. R. Douglas and E. Kerby-Eaton, eds. Pp. 136–137. Adelaide, Australia: University of Adelaide.

Pandey, M., et al. 1989. Indoor Air Pollution in Developing Countries and Acute Respiratory Infection in Children. Lancet 1:427–429.

Parker, R. L. 1987. Acute Respiratory Illness in Children: PHC Responses. Health Policy and Planning 2:279–288.

Philippine Department of Health (PDH). 1986. Philippine Health Statistics, Health Intelligence Science Report. Manila: Department of Health.

Pio, A. 1990a. Public Health Implications of the Results of Intervention Studies. Bulletin of the International Union Against Tuberculosis and Lung Disease 65:31–32.

Pio, A. 1990b. Respiratory Infections in Children: Overview of the Problem. Bulletin of the International Union Against Tuberculosis and Lung Disease 65:7. World Conference on Lung Health, May 20–24, 1990, Boston, Mass.

Pio, A., J. T. Leowski, and H. G. Dam. 1985. The Magnitude of the Problem of Acute Respiratory Infections. *In* Acute Respiratory Infections in Childhood, Proceedings of an International Workshop. R. Douglas and E. K. Easton, eds. Pp. 3–16. Adelaide, Australia: University of Adelaide.

Puffer, R. R. and C. V. Serrano. 1973. Patterns of Mortality in Childhood. Washington, DC: Pan-American Health Organization.

Rai, K. N. 1988. Treatment of Pneumonia in Children — A Question of Credibility. World Health Forum 9:225–227.

Reddaiah, V. P. and S. K. Kapoor. 1988. Acute Respiratory Infections in Rural Underfives. Indian Journal of Pediatrics 55:424–426.

Riley, I. 1985. The Aetiology of Acute Respiratory Infections in Children in Developing Countries. *In* Acute Respiratory Infections in Childhood. R. M. Douglas and E. K. Eaton, eds. Pp. 33–41. Adelaide, Australia: University of Adelaide.

Riley, I. and E. G. H. Carrad. 1983. The Status of Research on Acute Respiratory Infections in Children in Papua New Guinea. Pediatrics Research 17:1041–1043.

Rochester, D. F. and S. A. Esau. 1984. Malnutrition and Respiratory System. Chest 85: 411–415.

Rohde, J. E. 1983. Why the Other Half Dies — The Science and Politics of Child Mortality in the Third World. Assignment Children 61/62:36–67.

Roth, J. S. 1962. "Management Bias" in Social Science Study of Medical Treatment. Human Organization 21:47–50.

Saenz de Tejada, S. 1990. Popular Notions of ARI in Guatemala and Ghana. Unpublished manuscript, Department of Anthropology, University of Arizona.

Scrimshaw, S. and E. Hurtado. 1988. Anthropological Involvement in the Central American Diarrheal Disease Control Project. Social Science and Medicine 27:97–105.

Shann, F. 1985a. The Case Management of Acute Respiratory Infections in Children in Developing Countries. *In* Acute Respiratory Infections in Childhood. R. M. Douglas and E. K. Eaton, eds. Pp. 78–85. Adelaide, Australia: University of Adelaide.

Shann, F. 1985b. Pneumonia in Children: A Neglected Cause of Death. World Health Forum 6:143–145.

Shann, F., K. Hart, and D. Thomas. 1984. Acute Lower Respiratory Tract Infections in Children: Possible Criteria for Selection of Patients for Antibiotic Therapy and for Hospital Admission. Bulletin of the World Health Organization 62:749–753.

Shukla, R., S. Bhambal, and N. Bhandari. 1979. A Study of Superstitions and Practices on Under-Fives. Indian Pediatrics 15:403–408.

Singhi, S. and P. Singhi. 1987. Prevention of Acute Respiratory Infections. Indian Journal of Pediatrics 54:161–170.

Smith, D. 1982. Patterns of ARI Morbidity, Mortality and Health Service Utilization in the Asaro Valley, Papua New Guinea. Geneva: World Health Organization.

Sommer, A., J. Katz, and I. Tarwotjo. 1984. Increased Risk of Respiratory Disease and Diarrhea in Children with Preexisting Mild Vitamin A Deficiency. American Journal of Clinical Nutrition 40:1090–1095.

Spika, J. S., M. H. Munshi, and B. Wojtyniak. 1989. Acute Lower Respiratory Infections: A Major Cause of Death in Children in Bangladesh. Annals of Tropical Paediatrics 9:33–39.

Stansfeld, S. K. 1987. Acute Respiratory Infections in the Developing World: Strategies for Prevention, Treatment and Control. Pediatric Infectious Disease Journal 6:622–629.

Steinhoff, M. C. 1990. Acute Respiratory Infections: Intervention Studies in Children in Developing Countries. Planning and Analysis of Evaluations of Health Case Interventions in Developing Countries 65:19–22.

Steinhoff, M. C. and T. John. 1983. Acute Respiratory Infections of Children in India. Pediatrics Research 17:1032–1035.

Sukkaray-Stolba, S. 1989. Oral Rehydration Therapy: Behavioral Issues. Behavioral Issues in Child Survival Programs, Monograph No. 1. Washington, DC: USAID.

Tupasi, T. 1987. Health-Seeking Practices of Mothers: Implications for ARI Intervention. Geneva: World Health Organization.

Tupasi, T. E., L. E. de Leon, S. Lupisan, C. U. Torres, Z. A. Leonor, M. E. S. Sunico, N. V. Mangubat, C. A. Miguel, F. Medalla, S. T. Tan, and M. Dayrit. 1990a. Patterns of Acute Respiratory Tract Infection in Children: A Longitudinal Study in a Depressed Community in Metro Manila. Reviews of Infectious Diseases 12 (Supplement 8):S940–S949.

Tupasi, T. E., N. V. Mangubat, M. E. S. Sunico, D. M. Magdangal, E. E. Navarro, Z. A. Leonor, S. Lupisan, F. Medalla, and M. G. Lucero. 1990b. Malnutrition and Acute Respiratory Tract Infections in Filipino Children. Review of Infectious Diseases 12 (Supplement 1):S1047–S1054.

Tupasi, T. E., M. A. Velmonte, and M. Sanvictores. 1988. Determinants of Morbidity and Mortality Due to Acute Respiratory Infections: Implications for Intervention. Journal of Infectious Disease 157:615–623.

van Ginneken, J. 1990. Behavioral Factors Affecting Transmission and Treatment of Acute Respiratory Infections. In Health Transition, Vol. II. J. Caldwell, S. Findley, P. Caldwell, G. Santow, W. Cosford, J. Braid, and D. Broers-Freeman, eds. Pp. 843–864. Canberra: Australian National University.

Vathanophas, K., et al. 1990. A Community-Based Study of Acute Respiratory Tract Infection in Thai Children. Review of Infectious Disease 12:S958–S965.

Victora, C. G., P. G. Smith, J. P. Vaughan. 1988. Influence of Birth Weight on Mortality from Infectious Diseases: A Case Control Study. Pediatrics 81:807–811.

Viswanathan, H. and J. Rohde. 1990. Diarrhea in Rural India. New Delhi: Vision Books.

Weinstein, L. 1955. Failure of Chemotherapy to Prevent the Bacterial Complications of Measles. New England Journal of Medicine 253:679–683.

World Health Organization (WHO). 1981. Clinical Management of Acute Respiratory Infections in Children. WHO Bulletin 59:707–716.

World Health Organization (WHO). 1983. Clinical Management of Acute Respiratory Infections in Children. Geneva: World Health Organization.

World Health Organization (WHO). 1984. Case Management of Acute Respiratory Infections in Children in Developing Countries: Report of a Working Group Meeting. Geneva: World Health Organization.

World Health Organization (WHO). 1988a. Can Community Health Workers Deal with Pneumonia? World Health Forum 9:221–224.

World Health Organization (WHO). 1988b. Case Management of Acute Respiratory Infections in Children. Geneva: World Health Organization.

World Health Organization (WHO). 1990. Programme for the Control of Acute Respiratory Infections: Behavioral Research Priorities. Geneva: WHO/ARI/RES.

Yoder, S. and R. Hornik. 1992. Perceptions of Seriousness of Diarrhea and Treatment Choice: A Comparative Study of Healthcom Sites. Unpublished paper, Center for International Health and Development Communication, Annenberg School of Communication, Philadelphia.

CHAPTER 6

Acute Respiratory Illness: Popular Health Culture and Mother's Knowledge in the Philippines

Mark Nichter and Mimi Nichter

Although Acute Lower Respiratory Infection (ALRI), especially pneumonia, is one of the two chief causes of infant and child mortality in the Third World (Leowski 1986; Monto 1989; Stansfield 1987), it has only become the focus of international health activity recently. Prior to the late 1980s, little health social science research was directed toward cultural and behavioral aspects of Acute Respiratory Infection (ARI), which encompasses both upper and lower respiratory infections.[1] Initial attempts to study behavior related to ARI often took the form of KAP (Knowledge, Attitude, and Practice) surveys. For example, in the late 1980s the UNICEF office in New Delhi requested that we assist an indigenous social marketing firm in developing a multi-state KAP survey of ARI in India. Based on prior research in South India, we expressed reservations about the utility of a KAP survey for generating trustworthy data on ARI identification and care management. The diffuse nature of ARI, the pervasiveness of cough, and its link to many illnesses make interviewing about respiratory-related illness problematic. What was needed, we argued, was research on the utility of various methods for generating data on ARI knowledge, sign/symptoms recognition, perception of severity, home management, and health care seeking.

In 1989, we were approached by members of the World Health Organization ARI Program, who expressed interest in research contributing to the development of a training manual for focused ethnographic studies of ARI. Along with funding for a methodology project, we were given the freedom to select a field site. We chose to conduct research in the Philippines for three reasons. First, pneumonia is recognized as the major cause of death among young children (Tan 1991); of the total number of reported deaths, pneumonia accounts for over three times as many as diarrheal disease in the Philippines (IPHO 1988).[2] Second, the Philippine health ministry was committed to developing a community-based ARI program. Toward that end, the former director of the Regional Institute of Tropical Medicine had already carried out a peri-urban survey of behavior related to ARI (Tupasi et al. 1988; Tupasi, Miguel, and Tallo 1989), and the new director was willing to sponsor an anthropological study. Third, one of the first community ARI intervention trials in the world was being conducted on the island of Bohol. Mindoro, the island of the Philippines selected for study, is distant from Bohol yet shares similar physical and demographic characteristics.

The methodology of the project consisted of three stages. During the first stage, open-ended interviews were conducted with local doctors, pharmacists, herbalists, untrained and government-trained midwives, nurses, Barangay health workers (trained community health workers), and teachers of grade school children. During the second stage, the focus of this chapter, we looked at mothers' recognition of and experience with ARI, explanatory models of ARI, care management practices, and health care seeking behavior.[3] The third stage entailed a confederate study of over-the-counter medicine purchases for ARI at local drug and provision shops, household medicine inventories, and folk medicine.

FIELDSITE AND SAMPLE

Oriental Mindoro (population 560,215, 1988) is located 160 kilometers south of Manila and is separated from Luzon by the Sulu Sea. It is the seventh largest island in the Philippines. Christian Filipinos, mostly Tagalogs, inhabit the area selected for study. This area lies on the coastal plain, 30 kilometers from the region's capital, Calapan. The population of this rural area primarily engages in fishing and rice agriculture. No special health care intervention project had ever been conducted at the fieldsite, a small village of roughly 3,000 inhabitants.

An opportunistic sample of 35 lower-class rural mothers from both fishing and agricultural households was selected to participate in open-ended in-depth interviews as well as a mix of structured research exercises. An additional 20 mothers participated in an illness attribute recognition exercise, ten mothers in a projective illness story exercise, and five mothers in focus groups. All of these informants were current caretakers (mothers, grand-mothers) of at least one child under five years of age.[4] The sample of mothers selected for each data collection task was segmented in order to investigate possible differences in health knowledge between women of different ages and education levels. Roughly one-third of the pool of 70 mothers was below age 30; the remaining ones were in their forties or fifties. All informants were literate; all had attended elementary school; one third had attended high school.[5] Informants reported a median of five living children per family.

Focus groups were used to assess differences in ARI recognition between mothers and health-development workers. Four Barangay (village) health workers, four elementary teachers, four trained government nurse midwives, and four male opinion leaders participated in focus groups structured around an illness video (described below).

METHODS

Guiding the project design is the concept of triangulation, which, following the navigation metaphor, uses multiple points to locate a position.[6] In the present case, multiple methods were employed to study both cognitive and embodied knowledge related to ARI. In addition to open-ended interviews broadly focusing on ARI, we experimented with several other methods in order to generate cognitive data related to illness classification. These meth-ods include: a) free listing of children's illness categories, b) pile sort exercises, c) structured interviews about the signs and symptoms of specific illness categories, and d) attribute recognition exercises using illness names and attributes identified from a content analysis of interview data. Subsam-ples of informants participated in interviews using one or more of the above methods.

To investigate embodied knowledge, as distinct from cognitive knowl-edge, mothers of children ill with ARI were interviewed about physical changes they observed in their children (e.g., touch, smell, sound and rate of breathing, appetite, activity level). Because the number of children observed with ALRI was small, this data set needed to be enlarged. Accordingly, focus groups were structured around a series of short video presentations illustrat-ing the sight and sound of children with pneumonia, wheeze, pertussis, or stridor. Groups of four to six informants were asked to respond to what they saw and any other signs and symptoms they imagined the children might be experiencing. The focus groups were composed of both informants, who had participated in the open-ended interviews and new informants chosen on the basis of specific criteria (see below). Finally, in order to study health care decision making, we both followed cases and elicited responses to a set of projective illness stories that introduced a health care seeking dilemma and conflicting opinions within a mother's therapy management group (Janzen 1978). Interviews with the parents of children ill with pneumonia were also conducted at the nearest government hospital.

FINDINGS

The findings of the study will be discussed in two sections, each reviewing a data set generated by different methods. In the first section, we highlight data about ARI collected from open-ended interviews, case following and volunteered illness narratives. After reviewing ideas about ARI commonly held by our informants, we present data on the emic categories of ARI and the recognition of clinical signs of severe disease. Data collected during structured interviews employing card attribute exercises are then juxtaposed to data collected during open-ended interviews. Eight local illness constructs associated with ARI will be focused on: *bronkitis, bronkomonia, pulmonya, hapo, tuspurina, trankaso, pilay hangin,* and "weak lungs" (*mahina ang baga*).[7]

In the second section, we present data generated during interviews with the parents of severely ill children, with focus groups who were shown illness videos, and with informants about the projective illness stories.

Popular Health Culture and ARI: Data Set One

Filipino mothers recognize that respiratory illnesses (including measles and tuberculosis) are the chief causes of morbidity and mortality in the community.[8] Hot–cold reasoning underlies several perceptions of illness causality as well as preventive health practices related to ARI.[9] Mothers link climate to a majority of respiratory conditions in children, and commonly associate ARI with sudden changes in climate that cause the body to be heated and then cooled by rain or wind. The southwesterly wind, *habagat*, which blows during typhoon season is linked to ill health in general and respiratory conditions in particular. Respiratory illness is also associated with untimely bathing; when a child is hot from the sun, he is not bathed until his body cools down. A woman who has been exposed to cold rain will not breastfeed her child until her body temperature returns to normal for fear of causing her child to develop a cold. Similarly, when a child is wet from the rain she is given a lukewarm bath to regulate body temperature. Daily bathing is directed as much toward maintaining a child's body temperature as it is toward cleanliness.

Coughs and colds are an expected part of everyday life. When they occur, home care begins by keeping a shirt on the child to protect against the wind. Mothers observe that ill children tend to sweat more, and commonly believe that when children sweat their pores are open, placing them at risk of being chilled by cold air and rain.[10] Accordingly, mothers take special care to prevent perspiration from drying on the back of a child (*natutuyong pawis sa liked*). Changing a child's shirt to prevent perspiration drying on the back is a central health care practice. After climatic change, this is the most frequently cited cause of all ARI in the illness narratives.

Mothers rely as much on touch, sound, and smell as they do on sight when determining the health status of their children. Chief health concerns are changes in body temperature (felt on the neck, ears, arms, and stomach), perspiration (amount, smell), the sound of a child's breathing, appetite, and the color of mucus. Symptoms which appear on the surface of the body and have the capacity to disappear within the body are treated with considerable concern. It is thought that they complicate the immediate illness as well as place the child at risk of subsequent illness. The term *lulubog* (disappearing or going within) is a term used for mucus, fever, and rashes. This concern significantly influences ARI-related care management behavior.

Mucus drying inside the chest, associated with difficulty in breathing and with noisy breathing, occurs in conjunction with several respiratory illnesses: *bronkitis, bronkomonia, tuspirina, hapo*, and *mahina ang baga*. All mothers pay attention to the consistency and color of mucus, yet, two patterns of reasoning were discovered — the second pattern is more common than the first. The first pattern is demonstrated by caretakers who deem yellow mucus dangerous because of its sticky consistency and capacity to harden in the lungs. The second is displayed by caretakers who are more concerned with the presence of clear mucus as a sign of developing illness. When clear mucus is observed, mothers do not bathe their children for fear that the cold water may cause the mucus to be absorbed (disappear) inside the body. A common progression of symptoms cited in illness narratives as well as in case reports is as follows: "The mother did not take proper notice and she bathed the child even though he was having clear mucus (*malinaw ang sipon*)."

This second group considers clear mucus more serious than yellow mucus. To these mothers, yellow mucus (*malapot na sipon*) indicates that the illness is coming to an end and mucus dried in the chest is being expelled. Mothers in this group interpret yellow mucus as a sign that it is now safe to bathe the child; bathing serves as a marker of the severity and progress of an illness. Both groups, however, fear that mucus may dry in the chest if it is not expelled and may cause *mahina ang baga* (weak lungs). "Weak lungs" is a common explanation for why a child is susceptible to respiratory illness.[11] In popular health culture, weak lungs is associated with mucus having dried in the chest during previous illnesses, and is also believed a precursor to tuberculosis — an illness many mothers think only manifests in adulthood. Antibiotics are widely believed "to melt" mucus coating the lungs.[12] The use of over-the-counter antibiotics and patient demand for antibiotics from practitioners are both associated with the desire to melt mucus drying inside the chest.

"Inside fever" (*nangingilalim ang lagnat*), a symptom which connotes heat inside the body, not necessarily clinical fever, is associated with rapid breathing, longstanding illness and fatigue, coldness at the extremities, and mucus drying in the lungs. Concern about inside fever leads mothers to treat fever, even low-grade fever, early. Rashes (*sikal*) are also a cause of considerable concern among mothers. Illnesses associated with skin eruptions and pustules (e.g., *tigdas*, *tuko*, "measles") are treated in order to facilitate the rash coming out of the body.[13] Caretakers are afraid of giving children medicines which might interfere with this process. This concern significantly affects ARI-related health seeking behavior. When *sikal* is reported in the area, mothers are reluctant to take an ill child to the doctor even if a rash has · not yet manifested. Instead, they may give home care to encourage the rash to come out.

Another common ARI-related health concern associated with local perceptions of ethnophysiology is *pilay hangin*, a condition caused by fractures or dislocations within the body that block natural "flows."[14] Ailments linked to *pilay* are retrospectively associated with a child falling down, being held too tightly, or being carried improperly by an elder or sibling caretaker. Common symptoms of *pilay hangin* are fever, frequent cough and colds, rapid breathing, and breathing difficulty. It is widely believed that if a child with *pilay* is treated by home care or doctor's medicine, the recovery will be delayed. Mothers commonly suspect *pilay* when a child has a recurring or persistent respiratory illness.

Children suspected of suffering from *pilay hangin* are treated by traditional practitioners, *arbularyos*, who locate the *pilay* within the body through various kinesthetic techniques that display its location. Treatment involves soft massage to the afflicted area. Two patterns of health care seeking exist with relation to *pilay hangin*. In the first pattern an *arbularyo* is consulted after one or two days of home care as a form of first aid before the advice of a doctor is sought. In the second, an *arbularyo* is consulted after a child has been treated by a doctor, but has failed to recover within the expected number of days.

One theme that emerged in several illness narratives involved mothers who had expended considerable money on doctor's medicine with no cure for the child. In desperation they sought the advice of an *arbularyo* only to find that the problem was *pilay hangin*. The *arbularyo* massaged the child who soon recovered, either on his own or after resuming a few days of doctor's medication. The mothers who relate such stories state that this experience influenced their subsequent health care seeking behavior. Among these women, *arbularyos* are now consulted before going to the doctor so one "does not waste money on expensive medicines."[15] Belief in *pilay* is widespread among child caretakers of all age groups and education levels.

Cough and cold as well as folk illnesses associated with ALRI (*bronkitis* and *bronkomonia*) are not deemed contagious, though there is awareness that *tuspirina* (a folk illness associated with pertussis), *trankaso*, and tuberculosis are contagious. Little idea exists that ARIs are caused by germs, except for tuberculosis, which is associated with several other possible causes (Nichter 1994). Knowledge of which illnesses are protected against by immunizations is low although general familiarity with immunizations is high. Although pertussis was present in the community at the time of the study, none of the 35 informants knew that an immunization protected against tuspirina.[16] When asked if *tuspirina* is preventable, all informants responded "Yes, take your child to the seashore in the early morning as the sun is rising."

The purchase of over-the-counter cough syrup and antibiotics (as well as antibiotic sharing) for ARI is commonly reported. Notably, the use of such medicines without a prescription is more common for children over 18 months of age than for children below this age. Mothers are cautious when using antibiotics for young children until a medicine has proven to be compatible, *kasundo* or *hiyang*.[17] A doctor's prescription is initially sought for a child to test its compatibility. Once this is demonstrated, patients often retain the prescription and refill it (or borrow the medicine) when similar symptoms appear.

What signs and symptoms do mothers recall when they think of local illness terms associated with ARI? A content analysis of open-ended interview data was undertaken to identify signs, symptoms, and etiological factors associated with ARI beyond the ubiquitous complaints of cold (*sipon*) and cough (*ubo*). During these interviews, mothers were asked about illnesses that might cause a child to experience cough or difficulties in breathing. Unprompted data (on specific signs) are presented in Table 6.1. Also presented are data generated by a complementary exercise. A deck of 108 illness attribute cards was assembled pooling the attributes gleaned from the

Table 6.1

Signs of ARI-Related Illnesses (Data Set One)

Signs and symptoms	Tuspurina	Trankaso	Bronkitis	Hikal hapo	Weak lungs	Pilay
Breathing						
Difficult/labored		+	+++***	+++***	++**	
Noisy/halak			+++**	+*		++*
Hard			**	++**		*
Gasping for air	+++***					
Fast			+*	++*		++*
Slow			+		*	+*
Like dog	+++***					
Like cat			++***			
Sound of mucus unable to come out	+++***		+++***	++**	++*	
Cough						
Dry and continuous >1 month	+++***					
Dry		++*	+++*	++*		
Productive		+*	+*			
Hard			+++***			*
Chest/Belly/Shoulders						
Indrawn chest			+*	**		
Bulging chest			++**	++*		+
Bulging belly				+*		*
Shoulders raised				+*	++**	
Mucus						
Clear			+++***			++**
Cloudy			+**			
Lungs covered			+++***	+*	++**	*
Fever						
High fever/lagnat	++***	+++**	+++***	+*		+++**
Low grade/sinat		**		+*	**	*
Low grade/recurring		**		*	++**	*
Inside fever	*		++*	+*	++**	++**
Other						
No appetite	+++***	++***	+***	*	+++***	+++***
Perspiring		*	**		++**	**
Poor sleep	***		*	*	**	++**
Flaring nostrils			+**	++*		
Red eyes	+++***	*				
Chills		+**				
Body pain		+++***				*
Long-term weakness	+++***	**			+++***	*

Data type: + = open-ended interview (*n* = 35); * = cards identified (*n* = 20).
Frequency of response: +++ (***) = >50%; ++ (**) = 30–49%; + (*) = 10–29%.

Table 6.2

Causes of ARI

Causes	Tuspurina	Trankaso	Bronkitis	Hika/ hapo	Weak lungs	Pilay
Hereditary	*			+++**	++**	
Perspiration drying on back	+++**	+++***	+++***	+++**	++**	
Climate change/wind	+++***	+++***	++***	++**	++*	
Improper bathing	*	*	+++***	++**	++**	
Exposure to night air/dew	*	++**	+**	**	*	
Child falls/blocked flow in the body						+++***
Contagion	+++***	++**			+*	
Other characteristics						
Doctor's medicine does not cure	*			*		+++***
Not preventable by immunization	+++***	not asked				
Causes weak lungs	++	+	++	+	−	+++
Transforms from other illness	++		+++		+++	

Data type: + = open-ended interview (*n* = 35); * = cards identified (*n* = 20). Frequency of response: +++ (***) = >50%; ++ (**) = 30–49%; + (*) = 10–29%.

open-ended interviews. In the deck were placed terms for clinical signs, locally recognized symptoms, contrasting attributes (e.g., fast/slow breathing, dry/productive cough, clear/cloudy mucus, chest indrawing/chest rising), causes of illness and contagion, and techniques for prevention.[18] Informants were invited to go through the deck and choose appropriate attribute cards for each of several locally named illness complexes. They were then asked to review the pile of attribute cards they selected and to note which symptoms indicated a serious case. Table 6.1 presents data on selected sets of body signs and symptoms associated with five ARIs. Both interview (+) and card attribute (*) data are displayed.[19] Table 6.2 provides data on informant recognition of potential causes of illness.

It is important to recognize illness categories which emerge as distinct and those which overlap. *Tuspurina* and *trankaso* are illnesses with fairly distinct characteristics, the former have a distinctive cough (dog sound, long duration) and blood-red eyes; the latter, body pain and fever. Mothers claim both illnesses are contagious and easily recognized. By contrast, the signs and symptoms of *mahina ang baga* and *pilay* are not very distinctive; rather they are perceived to be hidden conditions. A majority of informants state that if a mother suspects that a child might have either of these two illnesses, she needs to consult a specialist (doctor, herbalist) for a diagnosis. *Hapo* is often used with the English gloss "asthma" to denote noisy breathing (*hika*) that we initially identified as wheeze. Mothers spoke of *hapo* as an easily recognized illness. The illnesses *bronkitis* and *bronkomonia* are lumped together because informants tend to look at these two illnesses as similar except for severity. While both illnesses were deemed to be severe, informants were evenly split on which one they regard as more severe. This illness complex emerged as the most likely to be referred to in a case of ALRI.

Before considering how these illness categories match the clinical signs of ALRI, it is worth contrasting data produced by open-ended interviews and card attribute structured interviews. Except for some shifts in the order of magnitude from middle to high attribute association, the findings of the two types of interviews correspond. In no case did an attribute having middle magnitude association in open-ended interviews have low attribute association in card prompt interviews. The latter data collection exercise served as a quick validation technique. Card prompt interviews enhanced informant recall. Not surprisingly, informants drew attention to a greater number of attributes for each illness, up to double the total number reported in open-ended interviews. However, attributes connoting serious illness remained fairly constant across the two methods.

Ideas regarding illness transformation emerged during open-ended and illness attribute interviews. Cultural models of prodromal relationships between the illnesses described above are presented in Figure 6.1. This figure summarizes the dominant views presented during interviews and was deemed plausible by a panel of five key informants including three mothers, a lay midwife, and an herbal practitioner. It is offered as a heuristic device and does not reflect intracultural variability or ambiguity. *Mahina ang baga* is perceived to result from any of the aforementioned illnesses (including persistent cough and cold) if left untreated.[20]

Recognition of clinical signs and symptoms of ALRI, including the key clinical signs incorporated in the WHO algorithm for pneumonia — rapid breathing, indrawn chest, and cyanosis (Cherian et al. 1988) — as well as fever, noisy breathing, anorexia, flaring nostrils, and convulsions, was ascertained during interviews when informants were asked to note the signs of respiratory folk illnesses. Each sign is discussed separately:

1. Fast breathing (*mabilis ang paghi-nga*): This is recognized by some (less than one-third of informants) as a sign of *bronkitis* or *bronkomonia*.

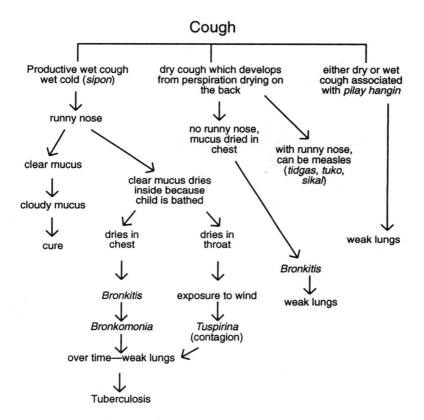

Figure 6.1. Progression of common cough to more serious forms of ARI among children.

Most of the informants who report this sign have had experience with this illness complex within the preceding three years. Notably, almost as many informants associate **slow** breathing with this illness complex as rapid breathing. They link weakness or sleepiness with slow breathing.[21] Fast breathing is more commonly associated with *hapo* than with *bronkitis* or *bronkomonia*, but fewer than 50% of the informants associate this sign with any illness.

2. Noisy breathing: Mothers often comment on the sound of a child's breathing when describing illness. The term *halak*, which is used by local

clinicians to refer to rales, is commonly used to refer to congestion and difficult breathing as well as noisy breathing emerging from the throat or chest. *Halak* is often cited as a sign of *bronkitis* or *bronkomonia*. The terms *hapo* and *hika* are commonly employed to refer to a wheeze described as a cat-like sound. Other informants use the term *hapo* more generally to refer to noisy breathing and a few cite *hapo* as a symptom of *bronkitis*. Some informants indicate a child's breathing as being like that of a cat or pig (for *hapo*) or a dog (for *tuspirina*). All informants who note fast breathing also draw attention to noisy breathing; however, noisy breathing is not always associated with fast breathing.

3. Indrawn chest (*lumalalim ang dibdib sa bawat paghinga*): Relatively few informants report this sign when asked to describe the attributes of any illness. When asked about movement of the chest during respiratory illnesses, informants tend to draw attention to a bulging out or a throbbing of the chest. In cases of *hapo*, more informants draw attention to wave-like motion of the stomach or rising of the shoulders than indrawn chest. One reason indrawn chest may not be recognized is the cultural practice of covering an ill child to protect her from the wind.

4. Flaring nostrils (*bumubuka ang ilong*): Several mothers recognize this as a sign of serious illness and associate it with fast and noisy breathing as well as gasping for air. Several also associate it with *bronkitis*, *bronkomonia*, and *hapo*.

5. Cyanosis: This sign is not reported. When informants are specifically asked to describe the tongue or lips during illness they tend to focus on the presence or absence of a white paste-like coating on the tongue.

6. Fever: All informants include high fever (*lagnat*) when describing the attributes of *bronkitis* or *bronkomonia*. When asked about the duration of an illness, informants often mark days of illness in terms of *lagnat* (manifest fever), as distinct from *sinat* (low grade fever). High fever is cited as one of the chief reasons mothers consult a practitioner. Mothers become concerned if after trying to control a child's fever by a sponge bath, herbal preparation, or over-the-counter medication the fever "rises for three days."

7. Loss of appetite: A major health concern, this symptom is emphasized in every illness narrative. The number three often designates concern in reports of poor appetite as well as fever — e.g., "the child has not eaten for three days." Further, a child's inability to suck is noticed by breastfeeding mothers who suffer discomfort as a result of engorged breasts.

8. Convulsions (*konbulsyon*): This body sign is greatly feared and commonly cited as a marker of serious illness. While convulsions are also believed to signify spirit attack, all mothers state that convulsions will be followed rapidly by consultation with a doctor. Convulsions are associated

Table 6.3

Clinical Signs of ARI Associated with Five Local Illness Categories Card Attribute Data (*n* = 20 rural informants)

	Signs					
	Rapid breathing		Indrawn chest		Cyanosis	Flaring nostrils
Illness	1	2	3	4		5
Bronkitis	–	35%	–	25%	–	25%
Bronkomonia	–	25%	–	–	–	35%
Pulmonya	–	–	–	–	–	–
Weak lungs (*mahina ang baga*)	–	–	–	–	–	–
Hapo/Hika	35%	30%	50%	–	–	–

Rural Oriental Mindoro, Philippines. Signs listed were identified by over 20% of sample: 1. *mabilis ang paghi-nga* — fast breathing; 2. *mabilis ang tibok-nga dibdib* — rapid throbbing of chest; 3. *lumalalim ang dibdib sa bawat paginga* — indrawn chest; 4. *malulug-ok na dibdib* — deep shallow breathing, sometimes indrawn chest; 5. *bamubuka ang ilang* — flaring nostrils.

with inside fever and commonly spoken of with reference to the "eyes rolling to the back of the head."

Data on the association between three clinical signs of ALRI and five folk illnesses generated by illness attribute interviews are presented in Table 6.3. To test whether the use of attribute cards increases recall of clinical signs of ALRI, seven informants who participated in open-ended interviews and did not identify rapid breathing or indrawn chest for any illness other than *hapo* were invited to participate in this exercise. While the total number of attributes they identified for named illnesses increased, in only one case did an informant later identify rapid breathing or indrawn chest as a sign of *bronkitis* or *bronkomonia*.

Data Set Two: Response to Cases of ARI

Seventeen cases of ALRI (pneumonia) were observed, four in the community during home visits, ten at the government hospital, and three during consultations with private practitioners. Twelve of the seventeen cases of ALRI observed are described by child caretakers as either *bronkitis* or *bronkomonia*. In one case the child's illness is labeled *trankaso* by one parent and *bronkitis* by the other, in two cases reference is made to *pilay*, and in four cases the child is described as suffering from weak lungs. Three of the remaining five cases involve pneumonia following measles, while in the other two cases cough (*ubo*) was the only term volunteered. As for illness signs noted by caretakers, difficult or noisy breathing (*halak*) is reported by about 50% while rapid breathing is noted by only three people, and indrawn chest by only one person.

Does mothers' use of the illness terms *bronkitis*, *bronkomonia*, or *halak* correlate well with the presence of pneumonia? Given our small sample size, we may only offer some general impressions. While the use of the terms *bronkitis* or *bronkomonia* often signifies serious illness, the terms correlate with observed rapid breathing or indrawn chest in only about half the cases of ARI we encountered. Likewise, mothers used the term *halak* in association with rapid breathing in only about half the cases of ARI. Mothers often use the term *halak* when a child is congested and has noisy, but not rapid breathing. The term is employed more liberally when we directly prompted mothers to comment on the sound of their child's breathing during cases of ARI. Unprompted use of Tagalog terms for rapid breathing are rare except in relation to *hapo*. We came across no case of observed pneumonia being mislabeled as *hapo*, but did encounter two cases of wheeze accompanied by fever labeled *bronkitis*.

Video presentation of clinical cases of ARI offered us opportunities to gather data about mothers' responses to pneumonia outside of a treatment context. Would community members recognize pneumonia when presented with clinical signs of the illness on video? Would informants be able to distinguish between the sound of a wheeze and the characteristic grunt of pneumonia? Would an illness video provide a useful prop for ARI focus groups? We attempted to answer these questions by abstracting segments of an ARI training film (Shann 1986) which illustrates various ARIs.[22] These segments were transferred to a video cassette for presentation to informants.[23] The scenes include the following: a child experiencing fast breathing, a child grunting, a child with chest indrawing attempting to breastfeed, and a child with pneumonia lying face up clearly exposing his chest. Other segments present wheezing, stridor, and pertussis. This video was shown to seven focus groups (a total of 35 informants) selected according to specific characteristics (mothers, grandmothers, fathers, teachers, barangay health workers, government midwives). Five mothers and two grandmothers who had previously participated in open-ended interviews participated in focus group interviews. These women were placed in groups with women who had not been previously interviewed.

Illness videos proved to be a popular research tool and a useful means of assessing informant recognition of signs and symptoms as well as the seriousness of a case. They also proved to be an effective cross-check on informant differentiation of signs and symptoms as specified in open-ended interviews. Presented first are group responses to video footage in which a child with pneumonia was viewed while trying to breastfeed. Content analysis of group discussions revealed the following signs in five out of the seven groups: weakness, poor sucking by the child, strained and noisy breathing, and mucus sticking inside the lungs. Members of four groups noted deep breathing, fast breathing, rising chest, raising shoulders, and flaring nostrils. Indrawn chest was commented on in only one group.

Table 6.4 summarizes individual informant diagnoses of two video presentations of pneumonia by focus group. Notably, agreement about diagnosis was lacking within as well as across focus groups. An important area of confusion entails whether a child displaying the signs of pneumonia has *hapo* or *bronkitis/bronkomonia*. Two of the five mothers who had identified rapid breathing as a sign of *bronkitis* during open-ended interviews diagnosed the child suffering from pneumonia in the video as having *hapo*.[24] Their misdiagnoses suggest an inability to differentiate sounds of a wheeze from that of a grunt. Confusion is once again documented when groups are shown video footage of a child experiencing a wheeze. Data presented in Table 6.5 illustrate that among child caretakers (not teachers or health workers), as many associate wheeze with *bronkitis/bronkomonia* as with *hapo*. Three of four trained midwives labeled what they observed as "asthma bronkitis," combining the two categories. Also important to note in Tables 6.4 and 6.5 is that both a wheeze and a grunt accompanied by indrawn chest are diagnosed as *pilay* by several informants. All informants who viewed the video footage of pertussis immediately recognized the illness as *tuspirina*, while a wide range of folk diagnoses are offered for the video presentation of stridor. Most informants link this sign to dried mucus in the lungs, but several relate it to *pilay* or weak lungs.

Projective illness stories allowed us to expand our scope beyond the small number of cases of ALRI that we were able to follow in the field. We deemed it useful to experiment with illness dilemma stories to assess probable reasoning guiding health care management. Ten mothers were presented with four illness stories involving treatment dilemmas and competing advice from various members of their families or neighbors. The stories incorporate details from nine real-life narratives presented to us during open-ended interviews. The ten mothers were asked to talk about the illness scenario

Table 6.4

Focus Group Response to Two Video Clips of Children Exhibiting the Clinical Signs of ALRI*

Focus group	Video segment	Hapo	Pilay hangin	Sikal tigdas	Bronkitis	Bronko-monia	Tuspirina	Weak lungs	Other
Men's group (n = 4)	1**	2			1	1	1		
	1***	1				1	1		
Grandmothers' group (n = 4)	1	2			2				Malaria =1
	2		4	3					
Mothers' group >5 children (n = 3)	1	4			1				
	2	4	2						
Mothers of 1–2 children (n = 3)	1		1			2			
	2				3	3			TB = 1
Teachers' group (n = 4)	1					3			
	2				3	3			
Barangay health workers' group (n = 4)	1	3	3		3	1			
	2				3	1			
Trained midwives' group (n = 4)	1				3	1			
	2					4			
Total		16	10	3	21	19	1	0	2

*Multiple responses are recorded. **Scene of breastfeeding child with pneumonia: rapid breath prominent. ***Scenes of child with pneumonia: indrawn chest prominent. In both scenes grunting is audible.

Table 6.5

Focus Group Response to Video Clip of Wheezing*

Focus group	Hapo	Bron- kitis	Bronko- monia	Pilay hangin	Ubo	Other
Men (*n* = 4)	2					gas, heart complaint
Grandmothers (*n* = 4)	1		1	3		
Mothers >5 children (*n* = 5)	1	3	3			
Mothers 1–2 children (*n* = 3)	3			2		worms: 1 weak lungs: 2
Teachers (*n* = 4)		3		3		
Barangay health workers (*n* = 4)	3					
Midwives (*n* = 4)	1	3 "asthma bronkitis"				
Total	12	9	4	8		

*Multiple responses are recorded

presented and indicate what they would do if they were the mother in question. Requests for further information constituted a source of data as important as the provisional diagnoses or the choices of action plans.

Presented below is a translation of one of the four illness stories involving a child likely to have ALRI and a summary of the ten informant responses to the story:

> The wife of a fisherman having 5 children lives in Lag. The weather has not been good with *habagat* wind. It is August and the number of fish caught by the husband has not been good. The youngest child, aged 6 months, has had cough and cold with clear mucus for a week. Last night the child had fever and fast breathing with the sound of *halak* coming from the chest. All day the child has acted very sleepy and she does not suck breastmilk well. The mother is a fish vendor. Her neighbor suggests that the child may have *pilay*

hangin because her 8-year-old daughter who sometimes cares for the baby may have been careless in picking her up and carrying her. The mother is not sure. Her neighbor also offers her some antibiotic medicine given to her by a doctor for her two year old daughter who was ill with a cough last month. Another neighbor suggests she should give *calamansi* (citrus) and honey to the child. The mother is thinking what to do. What advice would you offer?

Diagnosis by informants:
Bronkitis: 3
Bronkomonia: 1
Hapo: 2
Pilay: 1
Not sure: 3

Treatment they would/would not follow:
Not use antibiotic offered by neighbor: 9
See health center doctor for prescription: 10
Use herbal medicine: 10
Go to *arbularyo* to check for *pilay*: 6
Watch child for a few more days to see if there is high fever: 3

Comments made by informants:
Has child been treated for this illness before? 4
Has any medication proven useful? Does the child
    already have *hiyang* (compatibility) for the medicine
    offered by the neighbor? 2
The child is too young to self-medicate: 3
Fast breathing is common among young children and
    not a point of concern, but not eating is serious! 1
Does the family have any money or can they borrow: 6

The differences between the way people respond to illness episodes and the way they classify illnesses struck us as particularly significant. In response to the story presented above, six informants suggest that the mother see an *arbularyo* to check for *pilay*, although only one person specifically classified the illness as *pilay*. Two of the remaining five informants who suggest seeing an *arbularyo* classify the illness as either *bronkitis* or *bronkomonia*. Their decision to check and see if *pilay* might be a hidden factor affecting illness suggests that delays in consulting a doctor may persist even after community members learn more about the signs of pneumonia.

CONCLUSION

In this study we used a combination of methods to enhance our understanding of ARI in the Philippines. We found that focus groups using video presentations of illness and clinic-based interviews were a useful complement to open-ended and structured interviews about respiratory illnesses in the community. The latter helped us understand prototypical ideas about ARI and the cultural meaning of symptoms, document illness categories, and construct illness taxonomies as well as models of illness transformation. The former helped us identify which signs and symptoms people recognize when a child is ill with an ARI, ambiguity in the language used to describe these illness attributes, and the extent to which they are differentiated. Differences between cognitive and embodied knowledge were also documented. Embodied knowledge is evocative and practice-based. Presented with an ill child or video footage of an ill child, mothers make observations about subtle facets of illness not discussed during other types of interviews. The use of body language by informants to illustrate what is going on in the body of the afflicted increased during these interviews. Also, sense-based impressions about the feel and look of a child are discussed in greater detail.

Illness narratives give us an appreciation for the process of health care management that is not immediately apparent from the data produced during structured interviews. For example, during the interviews mothers typically state that they used home treatment for three days at the onset of an illness; however, analysis of illness narratives reveals that mothers often wait five to seven days after signs of marked illness have been observed.[25] Data from illness narratives and projective illness dilemma stories (as well as case following) lead us to appreciate ways in which health care seeking is influenced by factors which do not emerge during the interviews focused on illness-specific behavior. A more "taskonomic" view of health seeking pathways is provided (Nichter 1989). An important finding is that mothers consult traditional practitioners for a broad range of respiratory illnesses based on a form of cost/benefit reasoning. They deem it better to check with traditional practitioners for *pilay* even when this condition is only a remote possibility and other illness terms have been employed to describe the illness episode. The poor do not have the resources to invest in medicines or doctor visits for cases of *bronkitis/bronkomonia*, *hapo*, weak lungs, etc., if the efficacy of these health care options may be impeded by *pilay*.

What does this study have to tell health educators and those involved in health policy? We highlight twelve findings which suggest opportunities for future research and policy consideration:

1. A set of local illness terms overlaps with biomedical classifications of ARI; however, this overlap does not constitute direct correspondence. *Tuspirina* often, but not always, denotes pertussis, and *trankaso* generally refers to upper respiratory tract infections complicated by fever and general malaise. The terms *"bronkitis/bronkomonia"* among children and *"pulmonya"* among adults often denote serious illness, potentially pneumonia. However, these terms also refer to cases of upper respiratory infection accompanied by fever. *Hapo*, while commonly described as "asthma" by community members and doctors alike, loosely describes difficult breathing.[26] Weak lungs is an ambiguous condition applied to ARI as well as tuberculosis.

The local names of illnesses need to be addressed in health education programs, but care needs to be exercised in how they are used given cultural heterogeneity. Communication between health staff and mothers that makes use of emic categories needs to be carefully constructed to increase specificity.

2. *Hapo* or *halak* does not mean the same thing to all people. Most mothers recognize noisy difficult breathing as a significant sign of respiratory illness. Many mothers distinguish a wheeze (*hapo*) from grunting in the chest (*halak sa dibdib*) and noisy breathing emanating from the throat (*halak sa lalamunan*). Other mothers, however, do not differentiate a wheeze from noisy breathing associated with ALRI and use *"hapo"* and *"halak"* as general, sometimes interchangeable, terms for noisy breathing. Could a community-based ARI education program help villagers differentiate between a wheeze and a grunt and link these signs to other signs having clinical relevance?

3. The folk epidemiology of respiratory illness is far removed from models of biomedical epidemiology. While the former focuses on factors rendering one vulnerable to many types of illness, the latter investigates illness-specific pathogen–host–environment relationships. Despite this difference in thinking about causality, Filipinos are predisposed to use biomedicine when ill. At issue is how rapidly they consult health care providers after signs of illness severity manifest or are recognized, and how perceptions of causality influence patterns of self-help and demand for medicines such as antibiotics. This constitutes an important research agenda.

4. Fast breathing is rarely reported as a symptom of ARI and does not correlate well with descriptions of noisy breathing. Among the cases of ARI observed, mothers commonly reported *halak*. Only in cases of very serious illness is this associated with rapid breathing. Rapid breathing is more often recognized as a sign of acute illness when people observe illness videos than when asked to name the signs of *bronkitis* or *bronkomonia*. Notably, this sign is more commonly associated with severe illness by mothers who have had

experience with a child suffering from ALRI in the preceding three years. Would an illness video complemented by the testimonial of such people constitute an effective health education strategy? The popularity of the video-centered focus groups we organized suggests that this intervention might be worth a trial.

5. Mothers' awareness of rapid breathing as well as retractions may be enhanced by calling attention to the intercostal region (chest), not just to the supraclavicular region (lower neck), which is typically covered up. The neck carries cultural significance as a body zone which mothers typically touch when feeling for a temperature. When educating mothers about rapid breathing, educators also need to address a counter-perception linking illness to slow breathing associated with a sleepy, lethargic baby.

6. Few mothers recognize indrawn chest as a sign of acute illness. Even when the chest movement of an ill child is focused upon in video footage of ALRI, a mother's attention is often drawn to the chest rising up, not indrawing. In cases of wheeze, attention to indrawn chest is often eclipsed by a rising up of the shoulders or the wave-like movement of the chest and stomach. Local education programs may find it useful to address these alternative body signs rather than dwelling on one sign and ignoring others. When calling attention to the chest, mothers may be directed to check for chest retractions in the course of changing a child's shirt. Instructions to examine a child in a manner which exposes the child to the wind may prove less popular than encouraging a mother to check for rapid breathing and retractions while checking for perspiration, an established health concern.

7. Given that mothers often measure the severity of illness by fever, this symptom needs to be addressed in ARI education programs for its cultural, if not its clinical, importance. It might prove prudent to draw upon the cultural concept of *inside fever* associated with rapid breathing. Health educators might use this concept to point out that rapid breathing and chest indrawing are dangerous even without manifest fever (noticeable by touch).

8. Flaring nostrils is widely recognized as a sign of serious illness by mothers. Flaring nostrils can occur with a wheeze, as well as constitute a sign of ALRI, so caution needs to be exercised before including this body sign in an ARI education program. On the other hand, as a cultural health concern, it might prove useful if incorporated in a locally constructed algorithm (e.g., when a child's nose flares, check for ...).

9. *Tuspirina*, a folk illness closely related to pertussis, concerns mothers more than most other diseases protected against by immunization. Most mothers recognize the signs and symptoms of *tuspirina*, but very few know that a vaccination protects against this illness. *Tuspirina* needs to be the focus of a special immunization education program.

10. A special education program also needs to focus on the treatment of ARI concurrent with or subsequent to rashes and measles. Children are dying from pneumonia because caretakers delay treatment until a rash manifests or is felt to have run its course.

11. Traditional medical practitioners need to be incorporated into the national ARI program because they see cases of respiratory illness associated with the indigenous illness *pilay*. It is likely that, even with ARI education, mothers will continue to consult these practitioners.

12. Filipino mothers are highly motivated to learn more about ARI.[27] A perception already exists that severe illnesses may transform from more ordinary illness if allowed to progress untreated. This indigenous health concern may be used as a platform for future health education programs.

Focused ethnographic studies of disease complexes are currently gaining favor in international health (Manderson and Aaby 1992; Scrimshaw and Gleason 1992). At a time when it appears to many in the international health community that a standard set of methods and generic questions may be used to frame the cross-cultural study of most illnesses, it is important to highlight the research process in which medical anthropologists engage when identifying methods and research issues appropriate for the study of specific illnesses and populations. Differences and similarities among illness-focused ethnographic studies need to be documented, as does sensitivity to intra-cultural heterogeneity and the production of knowledge. Studies using multiple methods are a significant improvement over KAP surveys as they employ triangulation to improve the trustworthiness of data. They produce useful data for programmatic purposes which reflect some degree of "management bias," but at the same time permit a fair degree of flexibility and capacity to respond to the local context.

Focused illness ethnographies also have their limitations and it is important to recognize the need for complementary broader-based health ethnographies. A few limitations may be noted. First, by their very nature, studies of specific types of illness eclipse perceptions of those factors which render inhabitants of a culture vulnerable to sickness in general. A study of ARI may find that parents delay taking infants to a practitioner out of fear that exposing the child to the elements which may exacerbate the child's cough and cold. In question is whether this behavior is specific to illnesses associated with ARI or to all illnesses? While focused studies provide better data than many methods on that which is freely spoken of, for instance on the symptoms and types of illness recognized, they do not offer much data on what, for culturally significant reasons, is not spoken about. Difficult to assess during focused studies is the social relational dimension of illness negotiation and health care seeking. This dimension is responsive to gender and generation relations, social status, and moral-identity issues.[28]

A population's cognitive response to illness is privileged by focused studies. Broader-based, longer duration ethnographies are needed which pay greater attention to resource availability, entitlement, and distribution within households; the availability and quality of alternative sources of care; and the manner in which sources of care are evaluated. Also in need of consideration are differences in how illness episodes of particular children are responded to concordant with evaluations of the child's chance of survival given its health history and past illness experiences. To be explored are dimensions of semantic illness networks (Good 1977) and health care seeking behavior which entail social, economic, and emotional response to illness in the context of poverty.

Given time constraints and ARI program needs, use of the mix of research methods described herein enabled us to generate important data on Filipino popular health culture and ARI. Medical anthropologists can assist local researchers in conducting such studies in addition to engaging in research which attempts to more fully contextualize ARI-related behavior. The latter will require studies of the household production of health as well as ethnographic study of the behavior of health care providers and the political-economic environment into which an ARI program will be introduced.

NOTES

1. Early ARI studies are discussed in Nichter (1993) and include Campbell (1990), Tupasi (1987), and Wilson and colleagues (1992).

2. The five-year (1983–87) pneumonia mortality rate per 1,000,000 population is 75.6, while in 1988 it was 93. The five-year bronchitis mortality rate is 26 and the diarrhea mortality rate 22.3. Among infants, pneumonia is the leading cause of death, with 11 deaths per 1,000 live births, while bronchitis is responsible for 5.4 deaths and diarrhea 5.5 deaths per 1,000 births (IPHO 1988). During the first half of 1989 at Calapan Provincial General Hospital, approximately two-thirds of all pediatric admissions involved some form of ARI. Almost a third of these admissions involved measles.

3. The following research objectives and research questions guided stage two of the study: A) How are illnesses related to ARI classified locally; named and identified in relation to emic signs, symptoms, perceived causes and responses to treatment options? B) To what extent do the local (emic) terms correspond to biomedical classifications such as pneumonia, asthma, and pertussis? C) How important are the clinical signs and symptoms of pneumonia (as speci-

fied in the WHO algorithm) perceived to be? D) What symptoms related to ALRI prompt individuals to seek immediate health care? E) What cultural perceptions and practices cause delays in seeking health care (from doctors) when symptoms related to ARI manifest?

4. It was not the objective of the sampling strategy to generate data about the distribution of knowledge or practice among women in the community. That would have required random sampling among clusters of households and a more accurate census. Rather, we intended to select a sample of informants representing a broad range of women.

5. Few differences in health beliefs between informants of various age and education groups are documented during this study. However, older women tend to be more concerned about "inside fever" and *pilay hangin* than others.

6. For more information on the concept of triangulation as applied to the use of multiple methods in the social sciences see Denzin (1970), Duffy (1987), Jick (1979), and Lincoln and Guba (1985).

7. The illness terms presented are in the Tagalog language. Many of the terms appear to be derived from Spanish, although we do not suggest that these terms have equivalent meanings: e.g., *bronkitis = bronquitis*; *bronkomonia = broncoeumonia*; *pulmonya = pulmonia*; *tuspurina = tosferina*; *trankaso = trancazo (grippe)*; *mikrobyo = microbios*; *bakuna = vacuna*.

8. This is clearly demonstrated by a participatory rural appraisal technique (Rapid Rural Appraisal 1991) adapted to create histograms of illness magnitude, prevalence, and severity in the community. In each of seven community groups, *bronkitis*, weak lungs, and *tigdas* are identified among the top six illnesses affecting the young.

9. Juxtaposed to observations made in other Asian countries in which we have worked, diet during illness is not altered much in response to hot/cold reasoning. The major dietary concern during a respiratory illness is appetite.

10. Some of the more educated informants link the opening of pores to a child being "open to *mikrobyo*."

11. "Weak lungs" is a term commonly used by doctors to refer to primary complex — the first stage of tuberculosis. It conveys to mothers that their child might have tuberculosis without casting stigma upon the child. For a detailed discussion of the weak lungs–tuberculosis complex, see Nichter (1994).

12. The impression that antibiotics melt mucus emerged in a few open-ended interviews and was validated during pile sort exercises using medication cards. Medications grouped as melting mucus included antibiotics in most cases. The popularity of antibiotics is linked to the health concern of mucus drying on the lungs.

13. "Measles" as used by caretakers refers to illnesses manifesting rash and fever. The term does not always coincide with clinical measles.

14. See Leiban (1976) for a discussion of *pilay hangin* in Cebu.

15. If a mother takes a child to a doctor and the medicine prescribed does not prove effective, either the medicine may not be compatible (*hiyang*) or the child may be effected by *pilay*. It is considered cost-effective to check for the latter before going to the doctor.

16. This finding is validated by card attribute exercises and focus groups following the showing of illness videos. After being shown clinical presentations of ARI including pertussis, respondents were asked what illnesses are protected against by immunizations. Data confirmed that the population recognizes pertussis as the folk illness *tuspirina*, but does not think it is preventable by vaccination.

17. For further information on the concept of *hiyang* as it is applied to medicine, see Hardon (1991) and Tan (1989).

18. The illness attribute recognition technique employs card recognition tasks, but does not constitute a card sort procedure (Bernard 1988, Spradley 1979, Weller and Romney 1988). Card sort exercises were attempted, but found unpopular and somewhat tedious given the range of attributes associated with ARI. Card sorts were found more useful for investigating conceptualizations of medicines.

19. Space precludes a full presentation of card attribute interview data. Presented is matching data for significant illness characteristics and clinical signs of ARI which emerged in open-ended interviews.

20. Weak lungs is also considered by many informants to be hereditary (Nichter 1994).

21. When informants associating slow breathing with *bronkitis* are asked specifically about fast breathing, they tend to link fast breathing with *hapo*.

22. The limitations of the video footage were: 1) the children presented were not Filipino, and 2) the camera angle was such that the clinical signs of ALRI were the main focus. Viewers were set up to see clinical signs and yet their gaze was often directed elsewhere.

23. The method employed is as follows: The group is shown the video two times. On the third showing, segments are presented to individuals. Following each segment, informants are asked to free-associate what they have seen; identify prominent signs and symptoms; indicate other symptoms likely to be present; cite possible causes; name the illness; comment upon its severity; and state whether or not they have seen such a case in the last three years. After a period of free association, questions are posed to group members regarding issues which have not yet emerged in the course of discussion. Additional instructions direct informants to compare illness segments on the basis of severity, voice their opinion about the usefulness of antibiotics and herbal medicines, and comment on the prevention or contagion of the illness.

24. This is not to say that these two mothers would not have known the difference between *hapo* and *bronkitis* in real life. Both have much to say about body signs not present in the video clip which would influence their judgement

(e.g., touch, perspiration, smell, the eyes, sleeping and eating behavior — all forms of embodied knowledge).

25. The illness narrative data coincides with data generated by case following. Days of marked illness are ascertained by a report of fever or noisy, difficult breathing which initiated some treatment action inclusive of the child not being bathed.

26. For a similar finding in India see Nichter (1993) on the use of the term *ubbasa*.

27. Many informants keep newspaper clippings about illness. They have little access to health literature although literacy is high and interest in the subject keen. The Barangay health worker's manual passes through many hands, but contains little information about respiratory illness, particularly about ALRI.

28. During the focused ethnographic study we were not able to examine why particular mothers act on the possibility that their children may have been harmed by spirits or other external agents of sickness. These instances were rarely discussed during project interviews, although encountered during a later period of ethnographic fieldwork. To what extent does this ascription mitigate blame or guilt associated with a child becoming ill due to "mother's carelessness," a common explanation for child ill health in the Philippines?

REFERENCES

Bernard, R. 1988. Research Methods in Cultural Anthropology. Beverly Hills: Sage Publications.

Campbell H., P. Byass, and B. M. Greenwood. 1990. Acute Respiratory Illness in Gambian Children: Maternal Perceptions of Illness. Annals of Tropical Pediatrics 10:45–51.

Cherian, T., J. T. Jacob, E. Simoes, M. C. Steinhoff, and M. John. 1988. An Evaluation of Simple Signs for the Diagnosis of Acute Lower Respiratory Tract Infection. Lancet 2:125–128.

Duffy, M. 1987. Methodological Triangulation: A Vehicle for Merging Quantitative and Qualitative Research Methods. Image 19(3):130–133.

Denzin, N. K. 1970. The Research Act: A Theoretical Introduction to Sociological Methods. Chicago: Aldine Publishers.

Good, B. 1977. The Heart of What's the Matter: The Semantics of Illness in Iran. Culture, Medicine and Psychiatry 1:25–58.

Hardon, A. 1991. Confronting Ill Health: Medicines, Self-Care and the Poor in Manila. Manila: Health Action Information Network.

IPHO. 1988. Annual Report of the Integrated Provincial Health Office for Oriental Mindoro. Philippines: Calapan Provincial Hospital.

Janzen, J. 1978. The Comparative Study of Medical Systems as Changing Social Systems. Social Science and Medicine 12(2b):121–130.

Jick, T. D. 1979. Mixing Qualitative and Quantitative Methods: Triangulation in Action. Administrative Science Quarterly 24:602–611.

Leiban, R. W. 1976. Traditional Medical Beliefs and the Choice of Practitioners in a Philippine City Social Science and Medicine 10:289–286.

Leowski, J. 1986. Mortality from Acute Respiratory Infections in Children Under Five Years of Age: Global Estimates. World Health Statistical Quarterly 39:138–144.

Lincoln, Y. S. and E. G. Guba. 1985. Naturalistic Inquiry. Beverly Hills: Sage Publications.

Manderson, L. and P. Aaby. 1992. An Epidemic in the Field? Rapid Assessment and Procedures and Health Research. Social Science and Medicine 35(7):839–850.

Monte, A. 1989. Acute Respiratory Infection in Children in Developing Countries: Challenge of the 1990s. Reviews of Infectious Disease 11(3):489–505.

Nichter, M. 1989. Anthropology and International Health: South Asian Case Studies. Dordrecht, The Netherlands: Kluwer Academic Publishers.

Nichter, M. 1993. Social Science Lessons from Diarrhea Research and Their Application to ARI. Human Organization 52(1):53–67.

Nichter, M. 1994. Illness Semantics and International Health: The Weak Lungs/TB Complex in the Philippines. Social Science and Medicine 38(5):649–663.

Rapid Rural Appraisal (RRA). 1991. Participatory Rural Appraisal: Proceedings of the February 1991, Bangalore PRA Trainers Workshop. RRA Notes No. 13. Sustainable Agriculture Program. London: International Institute for Environment and Development.

Scrimshaw, N., and G. Gleason, eds. 1992. RAP: Rapid Assessment Procedures. Boston: International Nutrition Foundation for Developing Countries.

Shann, F. 1986. ARI Training Film. Geneva: World Health Organization.

Spradley, J. 1979. The Ethnographic Interview. New York: Holt, Rinehard, and Winston.

Stansfield, S. 1987. Acute Respiratory Infections in the Developing World: Strategies of Prevention, Treatment and Control. Pediatric Infectious Disease Journal 6:622–629.

Tan, M. 1989. Traditional or Transitional Medicine Systems? Pharmacotherapy as a Case for Analysis. Social Science and Medicine 29(3):301–307.

Tan, M. 1991. Philippine Health Matters. Health Alert 7:116–117.

Tupasi, T. 1987. Health-Seeking Practices of Mothers: Implications for ARI Intervention. Geneva: World Health Organization.

Tupasi, T., M. A. Velmonte, M. E. G. Sanvictores, L. Abraham, L. E. De Leon, S. A. Tan, C. A. Miguel, and M. C. Saniel. 1988. Determinants of Morbidity and

Mortality Due to Acute Respiratory Infections: Implications for Intervention. Journal of Infectious Disease 157(4):615–623.

Tupasi, T., C. Miguel, V. Tallo, T. M. Bagasao, J. N. Natividad, L. B. Valencia, M. E. Dejesus, S. Lupisan, and E. Medalla. 1989. Child Care Practices of Mothers: Implications for Intervention in Acute Respiratory Infections. Annals Tropical Pediatrics 9:82–88.

Weller, S. and A. Romney. 1988. Systematic Data Collection, Vol. 10. Beverly Hills: Sage Publications.

Wilson, R. P, M. M. Shale, and K. A. Parker. 1992. Rapid Anthropological Procedures in the Early Planning for Control of Paediatric Acute Respiratory Infections: Lesotho, 1989. *In* RAP: Rapid Assessment Procedures, N. S. Scrimshaw and G. R. Gleason, eds. Pp. 185–202. Boston: International Nutrition Foundation for Developing Countries.

Section Three

Pharmaceutical Practice

In most of South and Southeast Asia, multiple therapy systems coexist and the ad hoc use of a growing variety of commercial medicine fixes is commonplace. Numerous social scientists have studied the status and relative popularity of coexisting therapy systems. Studies placing emphasis on therapy system popularity have provided anthropologists with insights into health care behavior as well as social change and cultural identity. They have also obscured our understanding of everyday health practice in contexts where it is the qualities of medications or the healing attributes of particular practitioners which are of greater relevance to local populations than systems of medicine. When illness strikes, thoughts about and experiences with medications often guide health care behavior, not choices between divergent medical systems and the ideologies upon which they are based. This is especially the case in contexts where medical practice is eclectic, diagnosis is often by treatment, and commercial forms of indigenous medicines are marketed in ways indistinguishable from allopathic medicines.

Pharmaceutical use, medicine popularity and demand, prescription practice and medicine production require investigation in their own right. In this section, a number of issues including the user's perspective of medicine, modes of paying for treatment, and the manner in which collecting a fee for service and lay cost reckoning influence the dispensing and prescription of medicine are discussed. In addition, the cultural evaluation of medications and how this, in turn, influences patterns of pharmaceutical use is reviewed. Micro and macro economic forces affecting pharmaceutical practice are examined as rationales for what has been described within international health circles as "irrational drug use."

The commodification of health is examined in relation to increasing reliance on commercial medicine fixes for health problems, lowered thresholds of tolerance to symptoms, environmental and occupational health concerns, and collective anxieties associated with social transformation and cosmopolitan lifestyle. It is argued that models of primary health care need to extend beyond the public sector to the private sector and address health consumerism.

CHAPTER 7

Popular Perceptions of Medicine: A South Indian Case Study

Mark Nichter

INTRODUCTION

In this chapter, I explore popular perceptions of medicine in South Kanara District, Karnataka State, India.[1] My initial vantage point will be that of a rural semi-literate villager who has access to the rapidly expanding pool of practitioners and medicines available in crossroads towns.[2] These resources have become increasingly accessible since the mid-1970s due to improved transportation facilities and rising wages for agricultural labor and the *beedi* (cigarette) home industry. I focus attention on the most common ways medicines are thought of and spoken about within rural South Kanara.

Before considering local perceptions of medicine, it is important to correct a misleading stereotype of popular health culture in rural India commonly found in the anthropological literature of the 1960–70s.[3] Specifically, the portrayal of the rural villager as thinking within an *āyurvedic* cognitive framework will be questioned. A brief description of a town health care arena, as seen through the eyes of our representative villager, will be presented as a means of highlighting the eclectic practice of medicine in India and the mix (*masala*) of medicines produced and available to the public. My description is meant to complement observations made by Charles Leslie (1975).

Leslie astutely described the widespread eclectic use of indigenous and allopathic (biomedical) medicine by cosmopolitan practitioners in India. He aptly characterized the villager seeking medical assistance as more concerned with questions of cost, time, and empathy than type of therapy system.[4] While my observations largely concur with those of Leslie, his description of therapy choice requires some elaboration. I argue in the next chapter that two different patterns of health care seeking associated with market and pre-capitalist values coexist in India. One is aimed at securing good medicines at a reasonable cost; the other is characterized by the seeking of a practitioner who has the "power of the hand" to heal a particular patient.[5] In the present chapter, I argue that the type of therapy system to which a practitioner is affiliated often matters less to patients than the form and qualities of medicines he dispenses. I document how medicine appropriateness is evaluated both in terms of illness and patient characteristics. The afflicted's relative strength, age, previous experience with medicine, and special disposition (e.g., pregnancy) all influence perceptions of medicine suitability.

ĀYURVEDA AND POPULAR HEALTH CULTURE

In many ways a discussion of the relationship between the *āyurvedic* system of medicine and South Kanarese popular health culture is similar to the discussion about the Brahmanization of the South Kanarese pantheon (Nichter 1977). I will exploit this comparison while noting that *āyurvedic* and Brahmanic world views are closely aligned philosophically (Zimmerman 1987). The South Kanarese pantheon is composed of numerous indigenous Tuluva deities (*bhūta*), as well as pan-Indian gods, just as the popular health sector is composed of numerous folk healers and a few influential *āyurvedic* pundits (a majority of whom are Brahmans or Keralites steeped in Brahmanic tradition). Just as Brahman priests have over the years encompassed Tuluva deities within a distinctly Brahmanic cosmology and organizational structure, so *āyurvedic* pundits have encompassed folk health notions and practices within a highly elaborate and accommodative *āyurvedic* conceptual system.

It is important to note that while Brahmanic tenets about hierarchy and order in the cosmos and *āyurvedic* statements about humors and illness are accepted as authoritative, the actual impact of both Brahmanization and *āyurveda* on local Tuluva culture has been limited. The principles of *āyurveda* are publicly acknowledged as eternal truths, yet the lay person's comprehension of *āyurveda* is limited to a few names of illnesses and medicines.[6] *Āyurvedic* terms have taken on local significance. For the typical villager, an understanding of *āyurveda*'s centralmost principle of body humors (*tridhātu/tridōśa*) is limited to a notion of *dōśa* as troubles.

Within *āyurveda*, humors (e.g., *vāta, pitta,* and *kapha*) index essential bodily processes associated with universal principles manifest in myriad forms.[7] Like the terms "liver" and "pressure" introduced by cosmopolitan physicians, the names of humors have become objectified and synonymous with symptom complexes. In other words, the names of bodily processes in *āyurveda* and bodily organs and measures of body function in biomedicine have been reduced to illnesses.

In some cases, *āyurvedic* and biomedical terms are used interchangeably to mark conditions perceived in folk terms. For example, an excess of *pitta* (often translated into English as bile) is used to describe someone who is high strung and easy to anger. Over the last decade the term BP (blood pressure) has been used in a similar fashion, especially when the person in question is an older man who shouts when angered.[8] *Pitta* is not perceived as a humor which serves a valuable function within the body and BP is not associated with the heart. Both constitute disorders associated with overheat in the body and a hydraulic model of ethnophysiology.

Three points may be made about *āyurveda* which have widespread generalizability in rural India. First, the response to illness by the non-Brahman lay population does not reflect an *āyurvedic* approach to health care despite the fact that *āyurveda* and folk medicine share points of commonality, e.g., a concern about hot–cold, a hydraulic model of the body, concern about the blood and digestion, etc. I do not mean to belittle the impact of *āyurveda* on popular health culture by this statement anymore than I would want to disregard Brahmanic elements of local Tuluva ritual. What I wish to emphasize is that discrete *āyurvedic* practices and medicines, and not a systematic *āyurvedic* model of health and pathology, influence popular health care behavior.

A second point is that the practice of orthodox *āyurveda* represented in classical texts is not presently, nor has it been in recent history, a popular form of therapy available to the masses. Systematic *āyurvedic* treatment is not affordable for most people, is often time consuming, and requires lifestyle changes few people are in a position to make.[9] The notion that systematic *āyurvedic* therapy, based upon *āyurvedic* diagnostic principles, is readily available and inexpensive in village India is unfounded. This myth is propagated by surveys which classify all herbal practitioners as practitioners of *āyurvedic* medicine, confounding herbal medicines with *āyurveda*. This is misleading.

A third and related point is that the system of *āyurveda* as presented in texts and espoused by authoritative pundits is not understood by most folk herbal practitioners. An increasing number of practitioners administering *āyurvedic* medicines gain their knowledge about these medicines from commercial medicine catalogues provided to them by *āyurvedic* medicine companies. Many of these catalogues intermix *āyurvedic* and biomedical terminology in an attempt to "scientize" *āyurveda* while simultaneously emphasizing *āyurveda*'s long, glorious, and sacred tradition. To accomplish this, biomedical disease syndromes are encompassed within a humoral conceptual framework. A mixing of metaphors occurs. Popular health culture in India is a bricolage, an assemblage of eclectic conceptual and material resources.

MASALA MEDICINE IN THE HEALTH BAZAAR

Let us imagine that our representative villager — who we will call Rama — travels to a nearby town to obtain health care for fever and weakness after exploiting more accessible sources of aid from a local herbalist and shop-keeper who stocks a few patent medicines. Numerous small clinics and medical shops are found in most fair sized towns in South Kanara. Rama strolls past a few. As he looks into each shop, he pays little attention to the qualifications boldly written or scribbled under the names of each practitio-ner. This is hardly surprising given the proliferation of abbreviations dis-played on signboards. Abbreviations for licenses from regional and foreign medical schools as well as integrated medicine courses of allopathy and *āyurveda* (from different states at different points in time) are intermixed with initials designating homeopathic correspondence courses, the posses-sion of university certificates (in some cases, certificates of attendance not completion!), foreign training or residence, and membership in little known and often bogus professional societies.[10]

Rather than look at qualifications, Rama focuses his attention on the types of medicines and paraphernalia exhibited in medical shops. It is not possible for him to distinguish the type of therapy system to which a practitioner is affiliated by looking at the medicines and paraphernalia displayed in these shops, however. Many institutionally trained, as well as non-institutionally trained, registered medical practitioners (RMP) engage in an eclectic form of therapy which draws from all existing therapy systems. Their shops display hypodermic sets and stethoscopes as well as hand labelled bottles of *āyur-vedic* tonics, tins of metallic oxides, and a few vials of homeopathic pills. The offices of recent graduates of *āyurvedic* and homeopathic colleges commonly display stethoscopes as well as a carefully laid out stock of commercial *āyurvedic*/homeopathic medicines bottled and packaged in much the same way as allopathic medicine. In most of their clinics, a syringe and a collection of allopathic and *āyurvedic* injectables (indistinguishable to the villager) are also conspicuous. Some clinics are manned by both practitioners of allopathic and *āyurvedic* medicine. As Leslie (1975) has noted, many of these joint clinics are managed by two generation practitioner families adapting to the competitive medical market.

Let us imagine that while passing by the office of an MBBS (biomedically qualified) doctor, Rama sees a stock of allopathic medicines displayed alongside several patent *āyurvedic* medicines having English names. If Rama could read English, he would find the labels of these patent medicines replete with the language of biomedical science. The same medicines are on display in the chemist shops located in the town. Passing by the most popular chemist shop, Rama remembers a request made to him by his postpartum wife. He inquires about the availability of a popular *āyurvedic* tonic (*aristha*) his wife once took, but which he does not see on the shop shelves. Three other commercial brands of the *aristha* are available from a Kerala based company, a company from South Kanara, and another from Bombay. He is asked a brand preference. While thinking about which bottle to purchase, Rama observes other customers. Some present chits to the attendant of the shop and appear to be selecting only a few of the medicines prescribed once they find out costs. Other customers do not have chits and directly ask for medicines by name, while a few customers present symptoms to the attendant and ask for his recommendations.

Rama chooses a familiar brand and continues on his way, anxious to consult a doctor before he misses the last bus home. He passes by the busy Primary Health Center (PHC) with its long line of patients and proceeds to the small clinic of a practitioner he has heard is inexpensive. The medicines and paraphernalia in this practitioner's clinic are eclectic (*masala*) — mixed to both taste and pocket. Rama presents his symptoms: headache and weakness; lack of appetite and a bitter taste in his mouth; burning sensation, cracked lips and feet (indicating too much heat in the body); and intermittent fever. The symptoms are noted by the doctor but he does not ask follow-up questions or physically examine Rama. Rama asks for an injection and receives a B complex injection in addition to two types of pills — one white and one yellow. He pays 8 rupees, a day's wages in 1978, about what he expected to pay.

How might Rama have obtained the name of this practitioner and why did he consult him when there are seven other private practitioners located in the same town? Let us suppose that before his trip to the town, he asked friends and relatives about the type of treatment given by various practitioners. What types of description might he receive? When listening to numerous such descriptions, I found that comments were commonly made about both the general cost of a practitioner's treatment and his healing capacity, described as "power of the hand." "Power of the hand" attributions were generally noted in the context of an illness story involving a serious illness which at least one practitioner had been unable to cure. In some cases, a practitioner was spoken of as having a special ability to heal particular illnesses or age groups while in other cases "power of the hand" attributions were of a more general nature.

The most frequent comments made about a practitioner involve the kind of medicine he dispenses. Occasionally the kind of medical paraphernalia he owns is also noted. Practitioners are described in relation to the forms of medicine they tend to give for particular ailments, e.g., single injection, "double" injection (distilled water and a vial of medicine), injection-powered pills (capsules), or tonics for a particular type of ailment. In the mid-1970s villagers also spoke of practitioners in terms of the type of stethoscope (*dekree*) which they possessed. German, English, and Indian stethoscopes were credited with having varying capacities to locate illness.[11] By the mid-1980s such descriptions were waning. On the increase were descriptions of the medical tests practitioners administered or ordered from small local labs recently established in the town.

Other descriptions of practitioners which Rama might hear from friends portray practitioners as agents of pharmaceutical firms, distributing particular brands of medicine. In the 1970s some villagers described going to a practitioner in the town as going to the "company."[12] This term reflected the impression that it was the brand of medicine which a practitioner stocked which cured, not the practitioner himself. When the medicine administered by a practitioner was not deemed efficacious, the strength and compatibility of the medicine for the patient was questioned more often than the skill of the practitioner. A prevalent idea was that given a set of symptoms, medicine found to be useful for one person might not be effective for another because of differences in body constitution, life style, or previous medicine-taking history.[13]

Perceptions of medicine compatibility depend in part on what patients expect to happen after consuming a medicine and when they expect symptoms to abate. For example, investigations of 150 children experiencing acute episodes of diarrhea, respiratory infections and fever revealed that the average length of time a child was administered medication was three days. Commonly, two to three days of medicine were given to the child following a consultation to a doctor. If symptoms persisted, a new medicine was sought and if symptoms abated, parents often did not return to the doctor to acquire additional medicine even though they were asked to do so. If symptoms persisted, it was more likely that the child's caretaker would consult another practitioner than report back to the first practitioner.

To summarize, rural South Indian villagers explore their options within expanding health care arenas. When searching for treatment of acute complaints, they are attentive to the cost of therapy, practitioner availability (waiting time as well as times available), and practitioner reputation irrespective of the type of therapy system or training course to which they are formally affiliated.[14] A trial and error approach to the seeking of treatment is common. Given this environment, many practitioners feel compelled to adapt their practice of medicine to client demands. Client demands often take the form of illness and age specific preferences for forms of medicine associated with ideas about medicine habituation, compatibility, and power.

HABITUATION (*ABHYĀSA, AUCITYA*)

That plant is a good medicine for fever; it was used by my father. I do not use it. I have taken many injections. Herbal medicine does not "take to" my body. (excerpt from field notes)

The concept of habituation (*abhyāsa*) is a counterpart to the concept of body constitution (*prakṛti*). One is born with a *prakṛti* subject to the characteristics of age and humoral predominance. One achieves *abhyāsa*. In the words of one villager:

Some people are born with the capacity to gain weight easily, others eat but gain little. This is due to their *prakṛti*. One's health, their age, or the seasons may influence their digestive power, but they always have this capacity to gain weight easily. It is their *prakṛti*. *Abhyāsa* requires adjusting, the way a rice eater may adjust to be able to digest wheat after some time. As a parboiled rice eater, I cannot eat wheat, it is heating to my body and I become constipated. Even polished rice causes me to have digestive problems. But to one with *abhyāsa* to these grains they are not heating, but the best of foods.

An analogy was drawn by another informant between the concepts of constitution:habituation, and fate:karma.

Nontransformable		Transformable

hanne baraha
    unqualified fate,
    what one is
	:	*karma*
		    the fruit of one's actions,
		    obligations, responsibilities,
		    what one has

prakṛti	:	*abhyāsa*
one's constitution		what one becomes through experience and habituation

An appreciation of *abhyāsa* is important for an understanding of medicine-taking behavior. It is common to hear villagers describing that a medicine has not been effective because they have no *abhyāsa* for that kind of medicine. This comment is made of both cosmopolitan and traditional herbal medicine. During a health behavior survey in 1974, I asked 100 adults stratified by caste and class whether they thought herbal medicine (folk as well as *āyurvedic*) was as effective as it had been 20 years ago. Over 90% of informants answered that herbal medicine was less effective. Several reasons were given for this phenomena including changes in diet, the decreased potency of medicinal plants due to chemical fertilizers, and increased tea drinking. The most frequently mentioned reason, however, was the increased use of "English" (allopathic) medicine.

According to local reasoning, in order for the body to "take to" a new food or type of medicine, it must first adjust to its properties.[15] For this reason, mothers feed young children minute quantities of food prior to weaning so that the child will become accustomed to the food. In the case of medicine, a young child regularly receives herbal medicines to promote health and prevent a number of culturally defined illnesses. Cosmopolitan medicine is generally not administered to a child until an illness crisis occurs.[16] Cosmopolitan medicines are thought to be too powerful for a young child's body to be able to accommodate. Moreover, it is thought that they interfere with a child's capacity to "take to" the herbal medicines used in the home for preventive as well as curative purposes. Children are gradually introduced to cosmopolitan medicine during an illness crisis wherein it is deemed prudent to manage serious symptoms by English medicine. Over time, it is thought that frequent consumption of English medicine causes the user to lose their habituation to herbal medicine and gain habituation to cosmopolitan medicine. When this happens, herbal medicine is thought to be less effective.

Using allopathic medicine is not without a cost. Many villagers think that English medicine offers a quick cure, but harms one's body and undermines one's health over time. This concern is expressed in different ways. Some people speak of English medicine as heating while others say its continued use leads to bloodlessness and weakness. One literate informant drew the following analogy between chemical urea fertilizer and English medicine:[17]

English medicine and urea are both powerful, heating, and harmful after some years of use.... But, they are popular. Urea makes crops green overnight and increases yield until one day you find that the earth is hot, acidic, and useless. Injections are like that too. You take them and feel better quickly, but later your body turns weak.... The agricultural extension officer tells us to balance urea with potash and other chemicals and that this will prevent the soil from becoming hot. The doctor tells us to eat good food, drink milk, and take tonic and we will not have side effects from the injections he gives us. But this is not how we live.... We don't drink milk or take tonic daily, nor do we use fertilizer the way they tell us.... Such things are costly and we have other needs.

There is a second meaning conveyed by the comment that the use of English medicine leads to weakness. Developing an *abhyāsa* to English medicine, entails entering into a dependency (*dasya*) relationship. The words of one *āyurvedic* practitioner (*vaidya*) capture the sentiment of many villagers:

Allopathic medicines are like eyeglasses. They allow you to see but once you put them on your eyes they do not improve. Your eyes become dim with continual use of glasses and you come to depend on glasses more and more. Eyeglasses are not bad. They are a good crutch, but if one does not need a crutch this may be a bad thing. One leans on the crutch and does not strengthen the leg, one wears the glasses and does not strengthen the eyes, one takes medicines and does not strengthen the body. To become dependent on the medicine bottle makes the company strong, but the body remains weak.

An increasing number of villagers have come to question the long-term utility of English medicines, especially fixes which appear to require continual or repeated use. In some cases this is because only symptomatic treatment is being offered to them, not a cure. A rural doctor with an MBBS degree, the son of an *āyurvedic vaidya*, presented the following illustrative case to me during one of my visits to his clinic.

People are losing faith in English medicines even though they are using them more. See that patient who just visited my clinic? She came in with a painful skin eruption on her hands. She showed me an ointment she has been using given to her by a doctor in town. She used it for two weeks and got relief, but then the problems returned just as they were before. She used it again with the same results. Here is the chit she left behind. It is for a steroid cream. The doctor in town did not inquire as to the cause of her problem. It is because she washes vessels (pots and pans) daily with tamarind which irritates her skin especially in the cold season. Would a town doctor ask such things about a patient's life? No, he sells instant relief and collects a fee and spoils the good name of biomedicine. The woman requested me to give her *āyurvedic* treatment knowing that my father was a *vaidya*.

People may return to using herbal medicine for several reasons. Patients who have an ailment which cosmopolitan medicine has failed to cure may consume blood purifiers, purgatives and diuretics to cleanse the body and prepare themselves for herbal treatment. Other people seek herbal medicine which will enhance their body's ability to respond to English medicine after they have noticed a decline in the response of the allopathic medicines they have been taking for a chronic illness. Some people think it is harmful to take English medicine every day and so suspend treatment temporarily until symptoms flare up, while others approach *vaidya* for medicines to improve the body's ability to "digest" English medicines. During the course of an interview in 1990, a popular rural *vaidya* made a comment which extended the analogical reasoning of the informant cited earlier who drew a comparison between chemical fertilizer and modern medicines:

> You have been coming here for 20 years. Have you not seen that over the last few years people are becoming more interested in natural fertilizers such as *neem* cakes? They have learned a lesson from using chemical fertilizers every year. For a few years the crop yield improves with chemical fertilizers, then after some time it declines. Why? Because the soil has become *uṣṇa* (hot). People notice that there are no worms in the field. They can also taste the difference in the rice they grow. With chemical fertilizers the crop is more, but taste is less. Just as people talk of the land becoming *uṣṇa* from fertilizers, they talk of the body becoming *uṣṇa* from English medicines. Just as the soil becomes weak, digestion becomes weak. Just as the soil becomes unsuitable for worms, the stomach becomes so *uṣṇa* that it is unsuitable for the worms that aid in digestion. Some people are switching back to natural fertilizers and some are switching back to *āyurvedic* medicines. Many people, however, use fertilizers and English medicines for a time and then switch to using natural fertilizers and *āyurvedic* medicines for a while — the way agricultural officers tell us to shift between crops. But in my opinion this is harmful for the body. Some people want to use both medicines at the same time. Did you observe my last patient? She came to me and said, "I have taken so much English medicine that my body can digest nothing, not even the medicine the doctor at the hospital says I must take. The effect of this medicines becomes less and less. Please give me herbal medicines to help my body digest food and the doctor's medicine."

Metamedical reasons also underlie the use of *āyurvedic* medicines. Some people seek realignment with *āyurvedic* medicine as a means of an identity reconstruction which entails the embodiment of "Hindu" values (Nichter 1981). Among this group are the elderly preparing for a good death, as well as those in Hindu revivalist groups who champion *āyurveda* for political as well as personal purposes. The taking of *āyurvedic* medicines constitutes a means of affirming a moral identity. Others consume traditional medicine for reasons described by Farquhar (1994a) with reference to the Chinese. Consumption of such medicine provides a satisfying, empowering remedy for the pressures of modernization (see Chapter 9) as well as an evocative, sensuous experience analogous to the eating of culturally marked foods which trigger a cascade of memories and associations.

POWER

Comments about a medicine's power are common whenever therapy is discussed. Villagers consider medicine in relation to both its inherent power and their ability to accommodate to this power. Powerful medicine is desired by those whose body can stand the "shock" associated with it. A medicine's shock effect is considered carefully when the afflicted is weak, when a chronic illness demands long-term treatment, or if a person is experiencing a heightened state of vulnerability such as during pregnancy or postpartum. Shock is also an important health concern influencing health care decisions involving infants and children rendered weak by multiple or long-term illness. This concern is also heightened during monsoon season, a time associated with blood impurity and poor digestive capacity.

As a category, English medicines are spoken of as powerful yet dangerous. Let us consider what the concept "powerful" means to the villager. Conceptually, power is regarded as unstable, vacillating, and requiring control, a factor evident in ritual healing as well as in the worship of deities (Nichter 1977). While English medicine is praised for its fast action, it is commonly spoken about as having "uncontrolled" side effects. *Āyurvedic* medicine, on the other hand, is referred to as safe, and as establishing control and balance in the body. *Āyurveda* is typically spoken of as "causing no side effects." This statement needs to be understood in relation to what it connotes as well as denotes.

Gleaning my notes on these two general categories of medicines, a set of oppositions emerged which was complementary to oppositions drawn between classes of local and Brahmanic deities particularly by Brahman informants. Rash, blood demanding deities of local *bhūta* possession cults and "cool" Brahmanic gods receiving vegetarian offerings are contrasted. The set of oppositions which emerged during a discussion with one of my key *vaidya* informants are presented below:[18]

Local *bhūta* deities	:	Brahmanic deities
Uncontrolled power/desire	:	Controlled power/balance
Immediate action, often rash	:	Ultimate justice over time
Requires blood sacrifices	:	Vegetarian offerings
English/cosmopolitan medicine	:	*Āyurveda*/herbal medicine
Heating of the body	:	Balances body humors
Reduces blood	:	Produces/enhances blood

English medicine is commonly referred to as heating and *āyurvedic* medicine as neutral (*sama*), although individual medicines within each system are recognized as having heating and cooling properties.[19] The term "heating" is multivocal. Its meaning varies by context and indexes concepts related to strength, control, speed, and affect on the blood. Saying that English medicines are heating is, in one sense, a statement about the speed at which they act. It also indexes associations with uncontrolled activity and heightened danger. The term *sama* when applied as a general descriptor of *āyurvedic* medicine expresses balanced action and the concept of control. Stating that English medicine is heating also infers something about its perceived affect on the blood. The notion exists that heating the blood causes it to evaporate. In Tuḷu, the expression used to explain this process is *netter ajune. Ajune* is a verb used to describe water evaporating from a boiling rice pot. Since digestive capacity is related to the quantity of blood and to one's general strength, the statement that English medicine is heating conveys a sense that one is at risk to general symptoms of malaise as well as symptoms such as burning skin, rashes, and burning urine. All of these symptoms are associated with excess heat in the body.

Some villagers frequent *āyurvedic vaidya* or folk herbalists weeks or even months after taking English medicine for decoctions to cool the body and replenish blood which has been evaporated by excess heat in the body. Herbal medicine is taken as a complement to English medicine to restore the integrity of body processes which powerful medicines have disrupted. The notion that powerful medicine disrupts body processes and causes weakness is one reason why English medicine is not favored for the very young or old. It is not necessarily neglect or inexperience which leads villagers to use English medicine sparingly for infants or the elderly. Hesitation to use powerful medicines may index concern.[20]

Perceptions of a medicine's properties and power influences the "innovative" ways people use it. Medicines administered for one purpose are sometimes used for other purposes on the basis of assumptions about how they affect the body.[21] For example, menses is thought to be a state of overheat in the body — "like a rice pot boiling over." When a woman suffers from amenorrhea (lack of menses) a cosmopolitan practitioner or chemist shop attendant may offer her a hormone booster such as E. P. Forte to induce her period. The popular interpretation of the drug's action is that it causes the blood to heat up such that the wind inside the body pushes the blood outward. Accordingly, a popular belief is that if two tablets are powerful enough to induce menses, then a double or triple dose will heat the body enough to induce an abortion.[22] In the mid-1970–80s a flourishing trade existed in hormone boosters in town chemist shops.[23] Chloroquine tablets, also perceived to be very heating, were reportedly used as an abortive as well.

Perceptions of the power of a medicine are related to both dose and medicine form. Tablets are generally perceived to be weaker doses of medication than injections or capsules ("injection-powered pills"). Capsules are stronger than pills but weaker than injections. A notion exists that a single injection is a weaker dose of medication than a double injection — a term referring to a test dose and an injection, or an injection where the villager observes a vial of distilled water being mixed with a vial of medicine powder.

Perceptions of the power of medicine affect medicine self-regulation and supplementation. Some people try to enhance the power of recommended doses of medication. If one tablet does not yield satisfactory results, two or three tablets are taken simultaneously. If a single injection is given for an ailment for which a friend has received a double injection, another practitioner may be seen for an additional injection without mention being made of prior treatment.[24]

Going to a practitioner is a learning experience for the villager. The villager listens, watches, and interprets what transpires at the clinic in terms of preexisting knowledge as well as subjective reasoning. For example, acts associated with the administration of English medicine may be interpreted as increasing the power of the medicine. In 1976 I questioned informants about the heating (e.g., boiling) of needles before an injection. Some villagers perceived this act not as a sterilization procedure, but a method to increase the power of the medicine and the speed at which it traveled through the body.

Conventional knowledge is reproduced at times of illness, but new impressions are also formed. The perceived action of medicines causes villagers to extend and in some cases reinterpret notions of how bodily processes work. For example, according to notions of ethnophysiology in South Kanara, many channels (*narambu*) run throughout the body. When talking to villagers about *narambu*, I found explanations about the structure of *narambu* networks directly related to experiences with medicine. Some informants told me that *narambu* were all connected. When I asked how they knew this I was told that an injection might be given in the left arm despite the location of the illness in the body. It was reasoned that the medicine must travel through all the *narambu* to get to the location where it was required. Unlike herbal medicine, an injection did not go to the stomach first. Experiences with medicine expand explanatory models of physiology and health.

DIET AND MEDICINE

Disease is a hunger, food a medicine for that hunger. (Kannaḍa proverb)

Since South Indian culture has an elaborate food classification system (Nichter 1986), dietary advice is an expected part of a consultation with a practitioner. One of the few questions asked of a doctor during a consultation is what types of food should and should not be consumed. Responses to this question are interpreted both in relation to the qualities of the illness and the type of medication administered or prescribed. A villager (such as person discussed at the beginning of this chapter) enters a consultation having a number of ideas about which foods should be generally restricted during illness. He expects the practitioner to offer more specific advice related to special attributes of this illness, the patient's body constitution, and the medicine administered.

Foods are thought to enhance and facilitate the action of medicines as well as to provide a means of balancing the extreme qualities of medicines. For example, most impoverished villagers in South Kanara drink milk only during times of illness and when taking medicines. Traditionally, *āyurveda* has placed great importance on milk, buttermilk and ghee both in the preparation of medicines and as a vehicle (*malpuḍi*) to assist a medicine "take to" the body. Milk is thought of as enhancing the medicine's action. When recommended by a cosmopolitan practitioner, however, milk is perceived to play a different role. Milk is thought to reduce and control the heating side effects of English medicine, particularly when injections are received. Villagers interpret the nutritional advice of doctors to mean that the medicine they are taking is so very heating that they require milk as a counterbalancing agent.

Milk is not only thought of as necessary to consume after an injection or capsule, but also as a substance which may be used to limit the action of medicine.[25] For example, piperazine citrate, a deworming medicine is considered to be very heating for the body. According to indigenous notions of physiology, there are an optimum number of worms which exist in symbiotic relationship with the body which are necessary for efficient digestion. When villagers are told that piperazine citrate will remove all worms, they become concerned. Some villagers drink milk a few hours after taking the medicine to reduce its heating action, in an effort to retain at least a few worms.

The importance given to milk also affects medicine compliance more broadly. I documented several instances where villagers were reluctant to take English medicine for long periods of time if a supply of milk was not available to them (see Chapter 3). Others reduced the quantity of medicine they were advised to take because milk was unavailable. Local practitioners who were sensitive to villagers' concerns about the heating qualities of medicines and the cost of milk frequently recommended the ingestion of other cooling substances, such as tender coconut water or lime juice.

While some practitioners are sensitive to folk dietetics other are not. The lack of attention paid to diet by many cosmopolitan practitioners has led some villagers to think that English medicine controls the body in such a way that the effect of food is eclipsed. For example, village women who deliver babies at PHCs are commonly offered food which runs counter to traditional postpartum dietary restrictions. Blackgram, a food classified as toxic (*nañju*) and traditionally avoided during illness (Nichter 1986), exemplifies this situation. In the hospital, protein rich blackgram preparations (*idli*) are served to postpartum women. Women will often eat such foods while in the hospital, but abstain from eating them once they have returned home to convalesce. Several women explained this behavior by stating that when they were taking hospital medicine, diet did not matter because English medicine "controlled" their bodies. In two cases where women suffered infection following hospital discharge, family members blamed inappropriate (*nañju*) foods consumed at the hospital for their illness. One woman explicitly stated that the effects of *nañju* food had only been suppressed, not eliminated, by English medicine. As soon as English medicine was discontinued, the effects of *nañju* had become manifest.

PHC doctors who exercise a lack of sensitivity to folk dietetics undermine public trust in preventive health programs. Villagers perceive that PHC doctors know about medicines which reduce symptoms, but not much about health or dietary needs. While this impression may not decrease doctors' popularity as a treatment resource for illness, it has affected the villagers' evaluation of their preventive and promotive health advice. This is unfortunate since most villagers think it is the doctor's duty to know about local foods and offer advice about diet for health (Nichter 1984).

PHYSICAL CHARACTERISTICS OF MEDICINE

As mentioned earlier, the form in which a medicine is administered is highly significant to the villager. It is not uncommon to hear a patient request a liquid mixture, pills, or an injection during a consultation. Patients express interest in the color and taste of medicines prescribed. There are several reasons for their preferences associated with perceptions of power and efficacy. Injections, as noted above, are considered powerful and heating. In the 1970s, South Kanarese villagers classified injections on the basis of their power by referring to them as Indian, English, or German injections. German injections were the most powerful, based on a burning sensation experienced directly after administration. Injections are very popular, commonly requested and preferred by those who want quick symptomatic relief.[26] For patients who fear that they may be too weak to withstand the shock of an injection, injection-powered pills (capsules) are sometimes requested.[27] For infants and those experiencing chronic debility and weakness, liquid mixtures are requested not only for ease in administration, but also because they are considered to be less powerful and "shocking" to the body.

Preferences for medicine forms influence but do not determine health care seeking. In instances where dramatic curative action is required, health concerns may be temporarily suspended. Such cases do not necessarily have to be life threatening. For example, injections are not generally popular for toddlers. However, they are deemed especially effective for the treatment of infected wounds and rashes where pus is manifest and fear about swelling is expressed. The heating action of injections is thought to dry up infected, weeping rashes and wounds.

During a study of skin ailments, I interviewed several mothers of children with infected scabies (*kajji*). Most mothers expressed the opinion that injections were warranted should their child's condition not improve with home treatment. Five cases of children aged 3–7 years suffering from scabies were followed over a three month period of time. In all five cases, doctors were consulted and antibiotic injections administered to the children. In three cases, the children frequented doctors six or more times for injections during the three month time period. In no instance did a doctor issue instructions to mothers to boil clothes, cleanse the skin routinely, or have the child sleep alone.[28]

In local health culture, *kajji* is associated with both heat in the body and impurities in the blood. Pus is thought to originate from within, therefore the illness is not linked to hygiene. Dietary restrictions are followed against foods thought to increase pus (*nañju* foods) or heat in the body. Regardless of this concern about heat, injections remain a popular treatment modality due to their demonstration effect and ability to dry weeping rashes rapidly. To reduce heat in the body associated with injection use, mothers administered cooling foods and herbal medicine to their children. As in the case of the postpartum woman who expressed the opinion that English medicine only suppressed but did not remove *nañju* from the body, one of the children's mothers administered *āyurvedic* medicine to her child following injections to clean the blood.

Among adults, a health concern associated with medicine taking is that medicine interferes with digestion, resulting in debility. Weakness experienced by a patient during an illness in which pills have been administered is often attributed to the pill's disruption of the patient's digestive process and not to the illness. If tablets cause thirst or a practitioner tells the patient to drink plenty of water with the tablet, the medication is suspected to be not only difficult to digest, but heating as well.

Liquids are preferred for bloodlessness (anemia) and weakness because they readily join with the blood. Medicine in liquid form is especially preferred by pregnant women who feel that injections are too powerful and heating (capable of inducing abortion), but fear that pills might sit in their stomachs. According to indigenous notions of reproductive physiology, (see Chapter 2), the fetus grows in the "stomach pot" and shares the stomach space with food. Some women perceive pills as not only being difficult to digest but also causing ill effects for the fetus.

Among lactating women there is a concern that medicine consumed by the mother is transferred to the baby through breastmilk. This concern influences two behavior patterns, both of which have public health significance. First, when taking "strong" medication, some women cease breastfeeding temporarily if not permanently (see Chapter 3). In two cases where this was observed, a concern about medicine led to sudden weaning and subsequent histories of infant diarrhea. On a breastfeeding survey conducted in 1979, more than a quarter of 80 rural women surveyed cited illness and medicine taking as the reason they stopped breastfeeding.[29] The second pattern, observed in neighboring North Kanara District, involved women who consumed medicines intended for their baby as a means of transferring the medicine's qualities to their children.[30] Both medicines for respiratory infections and diarrhea were consumed by mothers. Three out of five local doctors interviewed about local medicine-taking behavior were unaware of this practice. The other two stated they were aware that some "backward" mothers did such things, but did as a matter of routine they not advise against the practice.

Table 7.1 presents survey data on preferred forms of medications for specific types of illnesses. It may be noted that different forms of medication

Table 7.1

Preferred Form of Treatment, South Kanara District

| | Adults | | | | | | Children | | | |
| | Injec-tions (I) | | Pills and capsules (P) H = herbal | | Liquid mixture (M) | | 0–3 years | | 3–7 years | |
Illness	V	T	V	T	V	T	V	T	V	T
I. Fevers										
Sita jwara									¤(I)	
A cold with fever	¤		¤		¤	+	+(M)	+(M)	¤(M)	¤(M)
chaḷi jwara	+	+			¤	¤	¤(I)		+(I)	¤(I)(P)
High fever with chills					¤	¤	¤(M)	+(M)	¤(P)(M)	¤(M)
Sanni	+	+					¤(I)		+(I)	¤(I)
Prolonged high fever					¤	¤	¤(M)	¤(M)	+(M)	¤(M)
II. Respiratory										
Kemmu			+	+	¤	¤			¤(I)	¤(I)
Wet cough							¤(P)(M)	+(M)	¤(P)	¤(P)
Ubbasa									¤(I)	¤(I)
Wheezing			¤	¤	¤	¤	¤(P)(M)	+(M)	¤(P)	¤(P)
TB	+	+							+(I)	¤(I)(P)(M)
III. Digestive/urinary										
Loss of appetite					+	+	+(M)	+(M)	¤(M)	+(M)
Ajima			¤	¤	+	+	+(M)	+(M)	+(M)	+(M)
Poor digestion			(H)	(H)						
Nitrāna			¤	¤	+	+				
Bloodlessness							+(M)	+(M)	¤(M)	+(M)
Puri					+	+				
Worms							+(M)	+(M)	+(M)	+(M)
Pipaḍike bundapune			¤	¤	+	+				
Constipation							¤(M)	+(M)	+(M)	+(M)
Julab			¤	¤	+	+				
Water diarrhea							+(M)	¤(M)	+(M)	¤(M)
Urchune kakkune	+	¤	¤	+			¤(I)(M)	¤(I)	+(I)	¤(P)(I)
Diarrhea & vomiting								+(M)		
Uri padike			¤	¤	+	+	¤(M)	+(M)	¤(M)	+(M)
IV. Skin										
Kajji	+	+					+(I)(P)	¤(I)(P)	+(I)(P)	¤(I)(P)
Weeping rash										
Nañju	+	+	¤	¤			¤(I)	¤(I)	¤(I)	
Infected wound							+(P)	¤(P)	+(P)	¤(I)(P)
Udarpu	¤	¤			¤		¤(I)(P)	¤(I)(P)	¤(I)(P)	+(I)

+ = Very strongly felt (>70% sample); ¤ = strongly felt (40–70% sample); (I) = injections; (P) = pills and capsules; (M) = liquid mixture; (H) = herbal; V = village (*n* = 30); T = town (*n* = 20).

are preferred for adults, children under three, and school aged children. For example, injections are preferred for fever with chills (*chaḷi jwara*) for adults, but mixtures are preferred for young children with differences of opinion as to appropriate treatment for school-aged children. Town and village differences in medicine preference are noted as well. Notably, injections were just as popular in villages as towns among both the poor and the lower-middle class. Differences in medicine preference between the illiterate and semi-literate were not found to be statistically significant, and are therefore not reported.[31]

Private doctors are responsive to what they perceive to be patients' medicine preferences because they practice in a competitive health care arena. By being so, they reproduce impressions of what constitutes suitable medicines for particular illnesses and age groups. Pharmaceutical companies in turn are alert to the forms of medicines which doctors prescribe and purchase. Medicine supply and demand reinforce one another. An illustration of the extent to which doctors attempt to meet patient preferences is provided by data on how doctors dispense injections to adults. In 1986, I monitored five MBBS (biomedically qualified) doctors and five popular practitioners not formally trained in biomedicine (RMP), who nonetheless administered allopathic medicines. The percentage of adult patients receiving injections from both MBBS and RMP doctors ($n = 100$ patients per doctor) ranged from 30% to 60% of patients seen, regardless of their complaint. A study conducted by Duggal and Amin (1989) in Jalgaon District, Maharastra State, also reported widespread "irrational" use of injections by doctors. For example, these authors report that in this region 73% of cases of cold, 88% of cases of malaria, and 88% of cases of measles received injections.

In the next chapter, I discuss microeconomic factors which foster injection dispensing by doctors. For the moment, I wish to point out that patterns of medicine dispensing both respond to and foster popular demand.

Color and Taste

Medicine are scrutinized in terms of colors since colors are thought to signify a medicine's inherent properties.[32] For example, black medicines are thought to be powerful as well as good at reducing *pitta*, an *āyurvedic* term used in local parlance to denote nausea, dizziness, or yellow bodily excretions (e.g., urine, mucus). While black pills are considered appropriate for vomiting, fever, and fits, they are not appropriate for digestive disorders, weakness, or bloodlessness. This is one reason why black ferrous sulfate (iron) tablets are not popular among pregnant women and those experiencing weakness due to anemia.[33] Both the form and color of this iron supplement are not culturally appropriate for groups at risk to anemia.[34]

White medicines, particularly liquids, are generally attributed neutral or cooling qualities. They are thought to be more easily digested by the body than medicines of other colors and are trusted more when consumed for the first time. Because white pills are often interpreted as cooling, they are considered appropriate for fever, burning sensation, body pain, headache, and a loss of vitality — complaints all linked to a excess of heat in the body.

Red medicines have multiple connotations. For example, red pills are perceived to be heating and good for wet cough and cold. Liquid red medicines are thought to be blood producing, irrespective of whether they are classified as hot or cold. Yellow medicines are generally thought to be heating and to aggravate *pitta* when consumed internally. As a topical medicine, however, yellow ointments are viewed as purification agents. An association is made between yellow and turmeric, a traditional blood and skin purifier used both in the home and for ritual purposes. Burnol, an ointment purchased over-the-counter, is used for a wide range of skin infections and cuts. Its popularity is in large part derived from its yellow color, which villagers associate with turmeric. Here we have an instructive case where the attributes of a traditional medicine have been successfully applied to a commercial medicine with a similar physical characteristic.

Taste, like the form and color of medicine, is also regarded as a sign of a medicine's inherent characteristics (see Table 7.2). Astringent and bitter tasting medicines are generally regarded as cooling for the body and are thought to have a positive promotive/medicinal value. Herbs having a bit-ter/astringent taste (like black tea) are labeled bitter (*kanir*) and are commonly used as folk medicines. For example, a number of *kanir* herbs and shoots of budding trees are used as preventive medicines (*koḍi ośaḍi*) for young children, as well as being used as general medicine for stomach aches, fever, and blood impurities. Salty medicines, on the other hand, are viewed suspiciously by villagers and thought harmful for the bones (causing brittle-ness) if taken for any length of time. Pungent medicines are considered appropriate for cough (as they melt mucus) and as digestive aides, but they are considered inappropriate for skin diseases, urinary tract disorders, or rheumatic complaints.

Lightness and Heaviness

Perceptions of the inherent lightness and heaviness of substances affect the way in which they are evaluated as curative resources. Medicines as well as

Table 7.2

Associations Between the Color, Taste, and Effect of Medicines

Color or taste	Associations/ property (*guṇa*)	Good for	Negative effect
Yellow	*pitta* *uśṇa*	as a topical medicine for *nañju* (septic wounds, skin diseases)	turns feces and urine yellow, phlegm turns yellow, yellow, *pitta* heating
Black	powerful, reduces *pitta*, may be very cooling or heating	vomiting, fever, fits	dangerous, causes digestive disorders, black feces
White	safe, *sama*, i.e., not heating or cooling	bloodlessness, semen loss, septic wounds, fever; cleans the blood; breastmilk	none
Red	powerful, heating, blood producing	cold, wet cough; blood producing	fever, diarrhea, *dhātu* loss (especially tablets)
Bitter	cool, health promoting	cough, stomach pain; preventive medicine	none
Sweet	cooling	fever, children's illnesses	not useful for skin illnesses, worms
Salty	heating, dangerous for bones	none	vomiting, joint pain

foods are considered to be inherently heavy or light. Light is a concept which connotes relative digestibility and low "shock" impact on bodily processes. Those who are young, pregnant, weak, or convalescing are thought to require restorative medicines and supplements which are light and easy to digest. Healthy persons who wish to enhance their present state of health or improve their weight are attracted to medicines which are associated with heavy and strength producing substances.[35] An important distinction is made between: 1) substances which are appropriate for the ill as resources promoting convalescence when one's digestive capacity is weak, and 2) medicines and foods promoting positive health when one's digestive capacity is strong (Nichter 1986).

An analogy provided by one informant was that digestion is like an internal fire. A weak fire must be protected and fed small twigs (light foods) until it catches, while a burning fire may be fed branches (heavy foods) causing it to blaze. This distinction impacts on medicine-taking behavior. Tonics and supplements are taken during illness and convalescence to protect digestive capacity as well as to provide nutrient resources. Products like glucose powder have become immensely popular in India as health supplements marketed as "light" sources of energy which are easy to digest as opposed to sugar or *jaggery* which are considered to be heavy. This central concern in popular health culture — the digestibility of a product — is often highlighted in medicine advertisements.

LOCAL INTERPRETATION OF POLYPHARMACY

Combinations of medicines with different physical characteristics are sometimes interpreted in relation to folk beliefs about the balancing of hot/cold and reducing body humors. Villagers perceive practitioners to counterbalance the adverse effects of one medicine with another medicine. For example, white tablets issued along with red tablets may be interpreted as cooling tablets issued to counterbalance heating tablets. White pills prescribed with a red colored mixture, on the other hand, may be interpreted as a medicine dispensed to dry up one bodily secretion accompanied by a liquid medicine to promote blood production.

Such reasoning influences the medicine purchasing behavior of impoverished clients. I have observed clients come into a chemist shop with a medicine chit from a PHC doctor containing a list of several medicines. If clients cannot afford all the medicines prescribed, they may select medicines on the basis of cost as well as folk evaluation of the overt qualities of the medicines prescribed. In some cases, clients will ask the shop attendant the purpose of prescribed medicines (see Chapter 7). In other cases, it is the form and color of various medications which influences the combination and amount of medicines purchased. I have also observed patients presented with a mix of medicines which they feel are not an appropriate combination.[36] Clients prescribed only pills, capsules or an injection may ask an attendant at the chemist shop for a suitable tonic or mixture to complement or counter-balance the medicines prescribed. In such cases, medicines marketed as increasing digestion, blood, and strength may be recommended by counter staff.

One reason why villagers are generally more willing to take a longer course of medicines from *āyurvedic* practitioners than from doctors of cosmopolitan medicine is that they are provided fuller explanations about the medicines they are dispensed from *āyurvedic* practitioners.[37] Patients often discontinue English medicine when symptoms have abated although they may continue herbal treatments which they perceive as aiding in convales-cence and assisting in normalizing body processes. An illustration of this pattern and its clinical consequences has been provided in a detailed ethno-graphic study of Kyasanur forest disease (Nichter 1987). In this case, doctors attributed a relapse of the illness to patient noncompliance after returning home from hospitals. Patients, particularly the elderly, discontinued medica-tion after symptoms abated because they were afraid that the number of tablets they had been consuming would interfere with their digestive process and recovery. Anorexia, a significant feature of the disease, supported this impression. I have observed a similar pattern among TB patients who seek treatment only during acute episodes of illness. Many private doctors treat such patients with streptomycin injections in an ad hoc manner for a week or two. When symptoms abate, patients purchase tonics and medicines to increase their appetite in lieu of completing a course of medicine.[38]

During acute illness, health concerns related to the effects of medicines are eclipsed by immediate needs. Medicines are evaluated on the basis of their ability to dramatically reduce symptom states. In the case of chronic illnesses, where the demonstration effect of medicines is less dramatic and side effects more notable, concern about the impact of medicine on the body takes on greater importance. The effect of medicines on "healthy" bodily processes is weighed differently. Medicines are evaluated on the basis of how they affect health, defined in relation to bodily processes (e.g., digestion, defecation, sleep) as well as social and work related activities. In situations where culturally valued bodily processes (e.g., menstruation) are compro-mised, medications may be suspended except when acute symptoms flare up and demand symptomatic relief.

CONCLUSION

In this chapter, I have focused on popular perceptions of medicine and illustrated how such perceptions underlie consumer demand and medicine-taking practices. A greater appreciation of how medications are viewed by the lay population provides valuable insights into why illness, age, gender, and class specific patterns of medicine-taking behavior exist. Such insights are clearly different from data generated by studies which focus on patterns of curative resort to "therapy systems." The latter place too much emphasis on "system choice" and not enough on contingencies which lead people to use different types of medication, at different times, for different purposes. Moreover, studies of therapy systems have limited value in contexts where eclectic treatment is common and commercial forms of patent indigenous medicines are undistinguishable from allopathic medicine.

The ways in which popular ideas about medicine influence health care seeking, medicine compliance, and self-regulation are underappreciated by many in the international health field. In the field of medical anthropology, there has been a tendency to privilege explanatory models (EM) of illness when conducting ethnographic research. Explanatory models of medicines are just as important to consider as explanatory models of illness when studying health care behavior. The two often influence one another in contexts where diagnosis by treatment is common and the type(s) of medicine prescribed and consumed mark illness severity as well as patient identity. At issue is not only what types of medicine are deemed appropriate for different illnesses, but which medicines are appropriate for different types of people.[39]

It is prudent to consider what it is about specific types of medication, or combination of medications, which make them popular or unpopular for the treatment or prevention of a particular illness (or a range of illnesses). This is no simple task. It requires a broad based investigation of issues ranging from indigenous notions of ethnophysiology to color symbolism, from cultural conceptualizations of power to health concerns related to medicines gleaned from the observation of other domains of life.[40] Such study demands not only a consideration of medicines in and of themselves, but also of contingencies set up by medicine taking. As we have seen, advice given to patients by practitioners about medicines is often interpreted in relation to preexisting conceptual frameworks which lend themselves to particular types of action. Foods and supplementary medicines recommended along with a medication may mark its identity. These substances may be perceived to enhance the effect of the medicine, reduce its immediate side effects, restore bodily processes once medications have managed symptoms, or may serve to control the power of the medicine.

What can contextualized studies of medication contribute to international health? Such studies are obviously relevant to social marketing approaches to popularizing public health fixes. They are also important for health service research. If the types of medicine being distributed to high risk segments of the population are not being utilized, it is worth considering whether the characteristics of the medicines employed are deemed inappropriate, or whether it is the system of therapy which is unpopular for the task at hand.

In South Kanara, an ethnographic study of medication use led to an understanding of why so many South Kanarese women did not find black ferrous sulfate tablets an appropriate form of therapy for bloodlessness (anemia) during pregnancy. Since black ferrous sulfate tablets were not popular among pregnant or postpartum women, it is worth investigating whether an appropriately colored liquid tonic might be more acceptable and cost effective.[41]

Studies of medicine-taking behavior are also warranted if they help identify dangerous practices associated with popular misconceptions (and unrealistic expectations) about medications. This includes innovative ways drugs are used in keeping with perceptions about their inherent properties. The taking of E. P. Forte and chloroquine as abortifacients is a case in point.[42] Another example is self-treatment with antibiotics for curative as well as prophylactic purposes. Antibiotics are used prophylactically by some Indian males to prevent sexually transmitted disease prior (or subsequent) to frequenting a prostitute. Others self-treat the first symptoms of illness which they associate with risky sexual activity. Given the spread of AIDS, ramifications of this practice in lieu of condom use are obvious.[43]

Public health practitioners can also benefit from studies of medicine-taking behavior which focus on perceptions of when medicines should and should not be taken. The timing of promotive and preventive health fixes impacts on their popularity beyond the issues of access, economics, and convenience.[44] For example, in South Kanara, it is deemed culturally inappropriate (especially for children) to take piperazine citrate during monsoons. The heating properties ascribed to piperazine citrate are considered particularly dangerous at this time of general poor health, humoral imbalance, and overall vulnerability (Nichter 1986). Elsewhere (Nichter 1990), I have described how the timing of vaccination programs also have an impact on their acceptance.

While anthropologists can be an immense help in tailoring health intervention programs to local contexts, they must take care not to become party to simplistic or short sighted approaches to primary health care. This demands a fair degree of reflexivity and the viewing of problems and alternative solutions from a number of different vantage points. The focus of applied medical anthropological research on pharmaceutical practice must extend beyond the purview of compliance to a critical examination of social and economic factors driving both the distribution of medicines and information about these and other biotechnical fixes. In order to hold themselves accountable, anthropologists must look beyond solving immediate health service problems to the conditions which foster ill health and social resources available to alter these conditions. Only then can anthropologists gain perspective on the relative utility of biotechnical fixes and their social consequences. In need of consideration is not only how a community can be encouraged to accept a particular medical fix but also questions such as the following: To what extent does the use of a medical fix which promises protective health reduce concern for community hygiene and undermine a sense of social responsibility?[45]

In this chapter, attention has been focused on cultural perceptions of medicine quality which impact on patterns of consumption. Studies of medicine demand need to be complemented by studies of medicine practice, production, and marketing so we may better understand how each influences the other. In the next two chapters, these issues are considered.

NOTES

1. South Kanara (*Dakshina Kannaḍa*) is a bilingual region. Reference will be made in this chapter to both Kannaḍa and Tuḷu languages.

2. My characterization of this villager is used as a heuristic device and is not meant to gloss over differences in local perceptions of medicine. Through my discussion of this villager, I introduce common impressions about medicines which I recorded between 1974 and 1990. During periodic visits to South Kanara I interviewed several hundred patients seeking medical aid, recorded numerous conversations between members of therapy management groups, and observed interactions in the shops and clinics of a cross-section of practitioners.

3. Assumptions that folk health culture was closely related to *āyurveda* were common in the pre-1970 anthropological literature. See, for example, Opler 1963 and Gould 1965.

4. See Durkin-Langley (1984) for a discussion of multiple therapy system use. It is pointed out that data on treatment preferences is often quite distinct from actual therapeutic choices. Illness-specific patterns of treatment are the exception more than the rule. See Lane and Millar (1987) for a critique of cognitive

models of therapeutic choice which neglect structural variables such as class, gender, and relative status associated with resource entitlement.

5. On this theme, see Nichter and Nordstorm 1989.

6. See Linde's (1987) more general discussion of popular explanatory models which entail the appropriation of parts of expert systems of knowledge held by elite groups modified by cultural common sense. In this case, *āyurveda* has both influenced and been influenced by popular aesthetics as they are lived in the everyday world. Aesthetics influences health related practice as well as reasoning based on relations of correspondence.

7. The body in *āyurveda*, like in Chinese medicine, is fluid and nonanatomical, composed of an "ensemble of processes" (Sivin 1987:91). Of late, these processes have come to be described in relation to an anatomical body which Farquhar (1994b:92) describes (in the Chinese case) as a form of appropriation characteristic of historical materialism.

8. Blood pressure (BP) is commonly perceived as a blood disorder associated with too much heat in the body, an excess of *pitta*, and the need to attend to bodily urges such as urination and defecation. Giddiness is spoken of with reference to *pitta*.

9. *Āyurvedic* therapy is often more expensive than allopathic therapy. Stereotypes about the lower costs of *āyurvedic* treatment require scrutiny in terms of the type of practitioner consulted, the goal of therapy (e.g., cure or palliative treatment), and the range of medicines taken and foods consumed as part of the treatment process.

10. During my first visit to the port city of Mangalore, I counted nineteen different abbreviations under the names of practitioners, nine of which I was never able to identify. During a recent "crackdown on quacks" in New Bombay City (Ramesh 1994), 386 private practitioners were visited during a sting operation in Navi Mumbai municipality. Ninety (23%) of these "doctors" were unable to furnish either a degree or registration certificate although many displayed bogus or little known degree signs.

11. In one sense, the villager's faith in the reading of the pulse by *āyurvedic* professionals was transferred to the stethoscope. The achievements of medical technology were given similar status to the ascribed ability of the practitioner to uncover traces of the truth. The villager's requests for a practitioner to touch the body near the location of illness with a stethoscope also involved the perception that this technology was included in healing.

12. Some practitioners were identified with the brand of medicine they commonly dispensed or prescribed. Pharmaceutical representatives and chemist shop attendants also referred to some doctors in this manner.

13. In 1979 I conducted a health care seeking survey in 50 rural households situated within 5 km of a town having eight cosmopolitan practitioners. The survey revealed that in 37 households, an established relationship with a particular "family" practitioner did not exist. A resurvey conducted 10 years

later revealed that long-term relationships with practitioners were on the increase. Reasons for this change is the subject of continuing research.

14. See, for example, Vinay Kamat's (1995) paper on a popular PHC doctor having an *āyurvedic* degree. The practitioner is renowned for his knowledge of which allopathic medicines are effective for local illnesses. As I have noted elsewhere (Nichter 1981), RMPs with *āyurvedic* training are often some of the most popular practitioners in health care arenas populated by more qualified MBBS doctors. As far as patients are concerned, both utilize similar types of medicine.

15. Some foods and medicines "take to" an individual's body more readily than others. In this sense, compatibility is a combination of disposition and adaptation. I have used the gloss "take to" to broadly describe medicine suitability. In Kannaḍa the term *hidiyudu* is used to express suitability while in Tuḷu the term *pattunu* is used. *Pattunu* is also used to describe food which makes one fat as well as friends with whom one does not quarrel (*yeḍḍe pattunu*). The concept of suitability when applied to medicine, soap, or cigarettes connotes a sense of compatibility which is brand specific, not company specific. This concept is used to describe why the same medicine given by the same doctor to two different people for the same symptoms has a different response. The concept of medicine suitability directs attention to the role of medicine in curing in contrast to the role played by a practitioner's power of the hand (*kayi guṇa*) in healing (on this issue see Nichter and Nordstorm 1989).

16. Breastfeeding mothers may avoid the use of "strong" cosmopolitan medicines for their own health problems, so that the qualities of the medicine will not be transferred to their infant through breastmilk. As noted in Chapter 3, it is feared that strong medicines such as oral contraceptives will be transferred through the breastmilk, harming the infant. On the other hand, a mother may consume a child's medicine to pass the medicine on to the child through breastmilk.

17. See Chapter 13 for an example of how this type of reasoning may be employed in a health education message.

18. Similar oppositions arose during interviews with other informants.

19. *Sama* is a shortened version of the Sanskrit term *samadhātu*. In the regional language, Tuḷu, informants prefaced the use of this term by *wow yeḍḍe* (that's good) or *dāla toñdare ijji* (without causing trouble).

20. In a similar way, delays in taking a sick infant to a Primary Health Center or doctor may be related to concern rather than neglect. If caretakers feel the risks of subjecting a child to the "elements" or "strong medicines" outweigh the benefits, they may opt to keep the child at home or treat the child with local medicines.

21. For other studies on the cultural reinterpretation of medications and the cultural logic influencing the use of modern pharmaceutical see Bledsoe and

Goubaud 1988, Logan 1973, Mitchell 1983, and Cosminsky and Scrimshaw 1980.

22. Women who I interviewed consumed four to eight tablets to induce an abortion. I also encountered a few cases where these tablets were used as a morning after pill.

23. Hormone boosters are also taken by some Hindu women to regulate the menstrual cycle so that they do not menstruate at the time of an important ritual function such as a marriage or trip to a temple. Menstruation would bar a Hindu woman from fully participating in such rituals as she would be ritually impure. Taking a medicine to regulate one's cycle constitutes an expression of agency afforded by technology. For further discussion of menstrual regulation, see Chapter 3.

24. This strategy is not applied to herbal therapy. One reason is because it is not the overt power of herbal drugs which is valued, but the drugs' subtle capacity to engender balance, facilitate purification, and enhance digestion.

25. It may be noted that the ingestion of milk soon after taking tetracycline reduces the positive activity of the drug. In as much as tetracycline was commonly used in India during the 1970s, a study was undertaken to investigate the extent of milk drinking soon after tetracycline medication. Twenty patients prescribed tetracycline were followed and it was found that 16 (80%) had consumed milk soon after taking the medication in an effort to cool the body.

26. Given projections of growing rates of HIV infection in India, it will be important to monitor whether there are changes in popular demand for injections and/or more careful attention paid to how injections are administered and by whom. In 1993, injections still enjoyed tremendous popularity in South India despite newspaper reports on AIDS which linked this disease to the use of injectable drugs as well as prostitutes. Several young men whom I spoke to in Mangalore and Bangalore mentioned needles as a route of HIV transmission, but did not associate injections of medicines with such transmission. One informant overtly told me that HIV infection was not possible through an injection because of the power of the medicine. In 1994 I came across similar reasoning in areas of North and Northeast Thailand where injection doctors are still popular. Longitudinal research on needle use is called for which attends to the pharmaceutical practice of different segments of the population. See Reeler (1990) as well as Whyte and van der Geest (1994) on issues related to injection popularity and use in less developed countries in the AIDS era.

27. Capsules (injection pills) are growing in popularity in South India and an increasing number of medicines are being marketed in capsule form by companies of cosmopolitan medicine (allopathy, ayurpathy, patent medicines, etc.). There has been a concerted effort on the part of capsule manufacturers to popularize this form of medication in medical and pharmacy journals as well as to the general public. One of the most overt advertising campaigns

presented the image of a capsule with the caption "the best way to a patient's body is through his mind." The subtext led doctors to consider how prescribing capsules would lead to greater patient satisfaction as well as compliance. One doctor viewing the ad commented to me that the placebo effect of capsules was increasing and that he now offered capsules in place of "placebo injections" to some of his patients whom he diagnosed as having psychological complaints. He made the astute observation that while injections have been important for these patients to receive in the past as a means of legitimating their sick role, capsules served the same purpose. Capsules were considered legitimate markers (and symbols) of illness especially by a patient complaining of weakness as a primary symptom.

28. In one of the other two cases the child was taken for follow-up treatment to a chemist who sold the mother blood purification medicine and an appropriate topical treatment [benzol benzoate] which he instructed her how to use.

29. See O'Gara and Kendall (1985) for a similar discussion of illness, medicine taking, and breastfeeding.

30. I first observed mothers consuming their infant's medicine while conducting a first-aid clinic in the village in which I lived.

31. Krishnaswamy, Radhaiah, and Raghuram (1983) have discussed gender preferences in medicine form as well as age preferences. Women prefer tablets more than men (especially men under 30 years of age), who tend to prefer injections. Unfortunately, the authors did not probe medicine preferences in relation to types of illness or severity of illness.

32. The colors of foods are likewise thought to signify inherent qualities. The dynamics of color symbolism discussed in anthropological analysis of ritual underlie popular perceptions of foods and medicines. See for example, Beck (1969) and Nichter (1986). Polgar and Marshall (1976) have discussed the importance of colors in a consideration of the marketing of culturally appropriate fertility related medications.

33. For a discussion of how the color and form of iron supplements affects their popularity in other regions, see Morrow (1990).

34. Iron deficiency anemia is an important risk factor for pregnant women in less developed countries (Flemming 1989). A recent international review of iron supplement programs sponsored by the World Bank (Galloway and McGuire 1994) dismisses side effects as the chief reason for noncompliance and shifts attention from issues related to poor demand for iron tablets to poor supply. Our ethnographic research in South Asia would certainly call into question survey data cited in this review. Studies of the demand for iron supplements need to consider both the form and characteristics of iron supplements as well as the way they are presented in antenatal programs.

35. Leela Visaria (personal communication) has noted that in Gujarat the term heavy is used for more powerful medicines. When the medicine of one doctor

achieves no visible demonstration effect a patient will ask for heavier medicines.

36. Polypharmacy, while popular, is not always viewed as beneficial. When a combination of medicines is taken, but not deemed efficacious, the colors or tastes of these medicine may be scrutinized by the villager.

37. I am not suggesting that compliance to *vaidya* is necessarily better than compliance to doctors per se. To make such a claim, one would need to study differences in compliance/adherence by illness as well as by practitioner type and reputation. My remarks about general trends of medicine taking emerge from interview data in which informants stated they would be more willing to follow a longer course of *āyurvedic* than allopathic medicine.

38. Private doctors often did not follow up on suspected cases of TB and provided little advice other than to eat well and come back for another injection. (See also Banerji 1981, van der Veen 1982, 1987, Mankodi and van der Veen 1985, Rangan 1993, and Uplekar and Schepard 1991.)

39. Also in need of study is the role played by the pharmaceutical industry in reinforcing as well as changing longstanding ideas about medicine use. Data on popular perceptions of medicine may provide valuable clues as to why specific forms of medicine are produced for regional pharmaceutical markets, an issue taken up in Chapter 9.

40. Many of the perceptions of medicines presented in this chapter are based upon lessons rural Indians have learned through the use of chemical fertilizers and insecticides. Analogical reasoning is extended from one domain of experience to another such that one type of technical fix is understood in relation to another. The application of analogical reasoning in the service of health education is discussed in Chapter 13.

41. Nutritional anemia due to deficiencies in iron and folic acid are major public health problems in India, particularly among pregnant women. It has been estimated 10–30% of the general population and 30% of pregnant women are iron deficient (hemoglobin levels below 10%). Prophylactic studies have indicated that if pregnant women ingest 30 mg of ferrous sulfate per day during the last trimester of pregnancy not only is their hemoglobin level stabilized, but the birth weight of their infants rise (Gopalan, Raghavan, and Vijayan 1971). If ferrous sulfate tablets can not be made more attractive for consumers, alternative ways of providing such supplements need to be explored. Popular *āyurvedic* medicinal wines (*aristha*), which are rich in iron, are available. It would be worthwhile studying patterns of *aristha* consumption during the pregnancy and postpartum period, and the feasibility of producing such medicines locally at a low cost.

42. See Nichter and Vuckovic (1994) for a discussion of how exposure to a growing amount of information about medicines leads a population to reinterpret this information and apply it toward their own purposes. In the Philip-

pines, for example, literate women reinterpret the warning "counterindicated during pregnancy" as meaning this medicine is an abortive.

43. I have documented such use of antibiotics by men in India, Thailand, and the Philippines and am currently conducting research on the magnitude of this behavior in Cebu City, Philippines. On the issue of how medicines may be reinterpreted and used in unintended ways which foster drug resistance, see my study of TB medications in the Philippines (Nichter 1994). In South India, Isocaldyn, a brand of INH, is popular for many children's diseases from ARI to failure to thrive.

44. Timing needs to be considered in relation to season and climate as well as time of the day. In many cultures, different times of the day are ascribed specific qualities which may affect the perceived action of medicines.

45. Medical solutions to individual cases of illness and preventive fixes against particular diseases may divert collective attention from the need to clean up unhygienic environmental conditions (e.g., water sources, garbage dumps, breeding sites) which set up "communities" for emergent diseases.

REFERENCES

Banerji, D. 1981. The Place of Indigenous and Western Systems of Medicine in the Health Services of India. Social Science and Medicine 15a:109–114.

Banerji, D. 1982. Poverty, Class and Health Culture in India, Volume 1. New Delhi: Prachi Prakastan.

Beck, B. 1969. Colour and Heat in South Indian Ritual. Man (N.S.) 4(4):553–572.

Bledsoe, C. and M. Goubaud. 1988. The Reinterpretation of Western Pharmaceuticals Among the Mende of Sierra Leone (Revised Version). *In* The Context of Medicines in Developing Countries. S. van der Geest and S. R. Whyte, eds. Pp. 253–276. Dordrecht, The Netherlands: Kluwer Academic Publishers.

Cosminsky, S. and M. Scrimshaw. 1980. Medical Pluralism on a Guatemalan Plantation. Social Science and Medicine 14b:267–278.

Duggal, R. and S. Amin. 1989. Cost of Health Care. Survey of an Indian District. Foundation for Research in Community Health, Bombay.

Durkin-Langley, M. 1984. Multiple Therapeutic Use in Urban Nepal. Social Science and Medicine 19(8):867–872.

Farquhar, J. 1994a. Eating Chinese Medicine. Cultural Anthropology 9(4):471–497.

Farquhar, J. 1994b. Multiplicity, Point of View, and Responsibility in Traditional Chinese Healing. *In* Body, Subject and Power in China. A. Zoto and T. Barlow, eds. Pp. 78–99. Chicago: University of Chicago Press.

Flemming, A. 1989. Anaemia in Pregnancy in Tropical Countries. Transactions of the Royal Society of Tropical Medicine and Hygiene 83:441–448.

Galloway, R. and J. McGuire. 1994. Determinants of Compliance with Iron Supplementation: Supplies, Side Effects or Psychology. Social Science and Medicine 39(3):381–390.

Gopalan, C., K. Raghavan, and S. Vijayan. 1971. Nutritional Atlas of India. Hyderabad: National Institute of Nutrition.

Gould, H. 1965. Modern Medicine and Folk Cognition in Rural India. Human Organization 24:201–208.

Kamat, V. 1995. Reconsidering the Popularity of Primary Health Centers in India: A Case Study from Rural Maharashtra. Social Science and Medicine 41(1):87–98.

Krishnaswamy, K. Radhaiah, and T. C. Raghuram. 1983. Drug Usage Survey in a Selected Population. Indian Journal of Pharmacology 15(3):175–183.

Lane, S. and M. Millar. 1987. The "Hierarchy of Resort" Re-Examined: Status and Class Differentials as Determinants of Therapy for Eye Disease in the Egyptian Delta. Urban Anthropology 16(2):151–183.

Leslie, C. 1975. Pluralism and Integration in the Indian and Chinese Medical Systems. *In* Medicine in Chinese Cultures: Comparative Studies of Health Care in Chinese and Other Societies. Arthur Kleinman et al., eds. Pp. 401–418. Washington, DC: John Fogarty International Center, U.S. Government Press.

Linde, C. 1987. Explanatory Systems in Oral Life Stories. *In* Cultural Models in Language and Thought. Dorothy Holland and Naomi Quinn, eds. Pp. 343–368. Cambridge: Cambridge University Press.

Logan, M. 1973. Humoral Medicine in Guatemala and Peasant Acceptance of Modern Medicine. Human Organization 32:385–395.

Mankodi, K. and K. W. van der Veen. 1985. Treatment Failure in National TB Programme. Economic and Political Weekly Vol 20(21):917–926.

Mitchell, F. 1983. Popular Medical Concepts in Jamaica and Their Impact on Drug Use. Western Journal of Medicine 139(6):841–847.

Morrow, O. 1990. Iron Supplementation During Pregnancy: Why Aren't Women Complying? A Review of Available Literature. Geneva: World Health Organization.

Nichter, Mark. 1977. The Joga and Maya of the Tuluva Buta. Eastern Anthropologist 30(2):139–155.

Nichter, Mark. 1981. Negotiations of the Illness Experience: Ayurvedic Therapy and the Psychosocial Dimensions of Illness. Culture, Medicine and Psychiatry 5:1–27.

Nichter, Mark. 1984. Project Community Diagnosis: Participatory Research as a First Step Toward Community Participation in Primary Care. Social Science and Medicine 19(3):237–252.

Nichter, Mark. 1986. Modes of Food Classification and the Diet–Health Contingency: A South Indian Case Study. *In* Food, Society and Culture. R. S. Khare and M. S. A. Rao, eds. Pp. 185–221. Durham, N.C.: Carolina Academic Press.

Nichter, Mark. 1987. Kyasanur Forest Disease: An Ethnography of a Disease of Development. Medical Anthropology Quarterly 1(4):406–423.

Nichter, Mark. 1990. Vaccinations in South Asia: False Expectations and Commanding Metaphors. *In* Anthropology and Primary Health Care. J. Coreil and D. Mull, eds. Pp. 196–221. Boulder: Westview Press.

Nichter, Mark. 1994. Illness Semantics and International Health: The Weak Lungs/T.B. Complex in the Philippines. Social Science and Medicine 38(5):649–663.

Nichter, Mark and C. Nordstorm. 1989. A Question of Medicine Answering: Health Commodification and the Social Relations in Healing in Sri Lanka. Culture, Medicine and Psychiatry 13:367–390.

Nichter, Mark and N. Vuckovic. 1994. Agenda for an Anthropology of Pharmaceutical Practice. Social Science and Medicine 39(11):1509–1525.

O'Gara, C. and C. Kendall. 1985. Fluids and Powders: Options for Infant Feeding. Medical Anthropology 9(2):107–122.

Opler, M. E. 1963. The Cultural Definition of Illness in Village India. Human Organization 21:32–35.

Polgar, S. and J. Marshall. 1976. The Search for Culturally Acceptable Fertility Regulating Methods. *In* Culture, Natality and Family Planning. Carolina Population Center Monograph No. 21. J. Marshall and S. Polgar, eds. Pp. 204–218. Chapel Hill, NC: Carolina Population Center, University of North Carolina.

Ramesh, R. 1994. Crackdown on Quacks in New Bombay. Times of India, August 9, p. 3.

Rangan, S. 1993. Social and Operational Constraints in Tuberculosis Control. FRCH Newsletter 7(6).

Reeler, A. 1990. Injections: A Fatal Attraction? Social Science and Medicine 31(10):1119–1125.

Sivin, N. 1987. Traditional Medicine in Contemporary China. Science, Medicine and Technology in East Asia Series, Volume 2. Ann Arbor, MI: Center for Chinese Studies.

Uplekar, M. W. and Shepard, D. S. 1991. Treatment of Tuberculosis by Private Practitioners in India. Tubercule 72:284–290.

van der Veen, K. W. 1982. Socio-Cultural Factors in TB-Care. A Case Study in Valsad District, Gujarat, India, Working Paper No. 8. Universiteit van Amsterdam. Anthropologisch-Sociologisch Centrum. Vakgroep Zuid-en Suidoost Azie.

van der Veen, K. W. 1987. Private Practitioners and the National Tuberculosis Programme in India. Journal of Research and Education in Indian Medicine 6(3–4) (Special Issue):59–67.

Whyte, S. and S. van der Geest. 1994. Injections: Issues and Methods for Anthropological Research. *In* Medicines, Meaning and Context. Nina Etkin and Michael Tan, eds. Pp. 137–161. Quezon City, Philippines: HAINS Press.

Zimmerman, F. 1987. The Jungle and the Aroma of Meats. Berkeley: University of California Press.

CHAPTER 8

Paying for What Ails You: Sociocultural Issues Influencing the Ways and Means of Therapy Payment in South India

Mark Nichter

INTRODUCTION

Economic considerations are commonly cited as important determinants of health care decision making in less developed countries, yet few ethnographic studies have documented the microeconomic details of health service transactions. In countries having pluralistic health care, we know little about how economic deliberations affect the consultation of different types of practitioners at particular points in an illness trajectory. Little is known about lay cost-reckoning for services rendered, patterns of payment for these services, and sociocultural factors which influence the way in which fees are offered and received. In this chapter, I consider the microeconomics as well as the social relations and cultural meanings of "paying" for therapy in rural South India. Examined will be both market and non-market factors influencing what Bourdieu has termed the "economy of practices" (Bourdieu 1986, 1990) — the practical logics which predispose and guide behavior.[1]

Existing studies of paying for therapy are quantitative, and generally focus on service costs in relation to illness, patient, and practitioner characteristics.[2] Data are collected on amounts of time and money expended to obtain services, medicines, etc. The details of payment, however, are largely left undescribed. This is unfortunate because a contextual understanding of the dynamics of payment sheds light on 1) health seeking and care-giving behavior, 2) treatment expectations and the way they influence practitioner–patient relationships and prescription practice, and 3) perceptions of efficacy. In the course of describing modes of payment to traditional and cosmopolitan practitioners in South Kanara, I discuss the practical logics underscoring transactions involving money exchange. Direct and adjunct payments which define care giving relationships will be focused upon. The meaning given to payments associated with contractual relationships and a market economy will be contrasted to payments which evoke a precapitalist religico-medical ideology and set of exchange relationships. Bearing in mind Kunstadter's (1978) caution against overemphasizing ideal "rational man" ("economic man") explanations of health care behavior, I approach the subject of paying for therapy without a fixed economic gaze limited to market exchange.

Let me begin with a consideration of offerings made to ritual specialists engaged in healing and then juxtapose these to patterns of payment made to *āyurvedic* practitioners and allopathic doctors. A consideration of the latter will lead into an examination of the role chemist shops play in dispensing medicine and distributing charges.

OFFERINGS FOR CONSULTATION SERVICES IN THE TRADITIONAL HEALTH SECTOR

Non-Prescribed Offerings

When first visiting a rural astrologer, diviner, or spirit medium, a client will typically initiate the consultation by presenting an offering in cash or kind. The size of an offering varies in accordance with the status of the client and the specialist, as well as the severity of the case. The manner in which an offering is made as well as the amount given indicates to the ritual specialist something about the case. The example of Subramanya, a local astrologer and exorcist, will illustrate this point. Sitting on the porch of his mud and tiled roof house, crouched before a pile of cowry shells used for divination and a chalk grid depicting the day's stellar coordinates, Subramanya tends to the problems of a steady stream of clients. These clients come from a 50 mile radius to seek divination for a variety of problems relating to health, finances, and family welfare. Before each consultation, a client places money — usually 2–5 rupees — before the stellar grid. Subramanya observes the nonverbal communication of the client, including the manner in which the offering is placed before him and the amount. These observations assist him in ascertaining the probable status of the patient, the urgency of the case, and the client's attitude toward the consultation.[3] For example, an offering of 10 rupees (about 2 days wages for a coolie in 1978) thrown down in great haste by a low income client often suggests to Subramanya one of the following possibilities: 1) the case is urgent, 2) the consultation comes at a time when other modes of therapy have failed, 3) debate exists in the family as to the cause of the problem, and therefore frustration is high, or 4) the client wants more than diagnosis, they want protection. A haphazardly placed smaller sum, on the other hand, might indicate that 1) the client is curious, but not anxious about the cause and nature of the problem, 2) the consultation is more a matter of routine diagnosis/divination than a special event, 3) the client is very poor and is looking for a temporary reprieve from a longstanding problem or 4) faith in the ritual specialist's power is not great.

Once an offering is presented to a specialist such as Subramanya, it is not increased as the consultation proceeds. The amount of the offering proves important, if ritual protection is required in addition to divination. Following divination, a client usually receives blessings and temporary ritual protection from Subramanya. The duration of this protection is time bound and may vary from days to weeks or months.

Two points may be highlighted. First, the size of the initial offering is not thought to affect the quality of diagnosis or divination. The specialist is believed to speak the truth and to entertain questions addressed to him regardless of the amount offered. Second, the size of an offering influences treatment options. The size and manner of presenting an offering figures in an exorcist's decision to either 1) issue a protective device (*rakśanna*) as a temporary preventive measure against malevolent forces, or 2) advise a client to resolve the problem permanently by way of a curative ritual. As described by Subramanya, payment capacity and inclination significantly determine whether a "protective fence" (*bund*) is placed around an individual's "life field" requiring continual mending or whether that which is trying to destroy the field is itself "destroyed, pacified, or controlled." As a ritual specialist, Subramanya collects small periodic offerings for providing short term protection and large offerings for elaborate rituals required to dispel malevolent forces permanently. Offerings for such rituals take the form of both cash and materials necessary for their performance.

Prescribed Offerings

In some healing contexts, offerings are prescribed for specific ritual services or as an adjunct to the fees a client pays a traditional practitioner. Prescribed offerings are required for many healing rituals. These constitute both direct and indirect forms of payment. One type of indirect payment involves the procurement of ritual materials by a specialist on behalf of a client. After completion of the ritual, the specialist retains some of these items for personal use or reuse in future rituals. Direct payments may be in kind, most commonly grain and coconuts, or in cash.

For some illnesses, offerings of "service" must be made as an adjunct to the fees a client pays an *āyurvedic* practitioner. An understanding of the meaning of these offerings requires a consideration of the concept of *karma* and the notion of "partaking" in exchange relationships.

As Mauss has observed (citing India as an example), an exchange of goods or services may constitute not merely a mechanical but a moral transaction.

> The recipient depends upon the temper of the donor, in fact each depends upon the other.... Nothing is causal here. Contracts, alliances, transmissions of goods, bonds created by these transfers — each stage in the process is regulated morally and economically. The nature and intention of the contracting parties and the nature of the thing given are indivisible. (Mauss 1954:58)

In Brahmanic custom, an offering involves the receiver in "partaking" of the giver. For example, Parry (1980) has observed that when Brahman funeral priests accept gift offerings (*dāna*) they absorb the sins (*pāpa*) of their patrons. Ideally, the Brahman who performs the recitation of sacred verses (*japa*), can "digest" or "burn" *pāpa* obtained through *dāna* and by *japa* burn the *pāpa* of the deceased. If, however, the Brahman priest who receives *dāna* is unworthy because he has not performed *japa* or because he uses the *dāna* unwisely, the sins of the receiver are compounded by the sins of the giver and both may suffer.

The theme of "partaking" underscores other relationships between ritual specialists and clients. I briefly examine this theme as it affects the practice of a traditional *āyurvedic vaidya* whom I have described in depth elsewhere (Nichter 1981).[4] According to *āyurveda*, an individual's ills are ultimately related to *karma*, the results of one's past and present actions. The question arises: If suffering from an ailment is a result of one's *karma*, how then can the *vaidya* justify the alleviation of such suffering? The *vaidya* whom I consulted about this issue asserted that *karma* differs from fate (*haṇne baraha*, the writing on one's forehead) in that *karma* may be transformed through good deeds such as the performance of service (*sēva*). *Sēva* engenders merit (*puṇya*) which counterbalances sin (*pāpa*). As a *vaidya*, it was the practitioner's duty to treat a patient's illness and to promote health. In order for his treatment to be effective, it was necessary for patients to perform good deeds to mitigate negative *karma*.

For major culturally marked illnesses (*mahā rōga*), as defined by *āyurvedic* texts, this *vaidya* prescribed *sēva* as an essential part of a treatment program. If a prescribed *sēva* such as the feeding of Brahmans or the poor was not carried out by a patient, then the *vaidya* considered himself likely to be affected by the patient's *karma*. Numerous stories were related by the *vaidya* about patients with *mahā rōga* who failed to carry out prescribed *sēva* and placed *vaidya* in jeopardy. The theme of most stories centered upon how a *vaidya* contracted a similar illness or set of symptoms as the patient. One of the *vaidya*'s favorite stories described how his father experienced partial paralysis, discovered which of his patients was to blame, encouraged the patient to perform *sēva*, and was cured of his ailment.

The treatment of *mahā rōga* requires prescribed offerings, (*karma vipāka*), which are fixed by tradition.[5] Such offerings may be considered an adjunct to payment for a *vaidya*'s services. For the *vaidya*, these offerings and good deeds mitigate the patient's *pāpa* and thus the *karma* which the *vaidya* partakes of as part of the therapeutic relationship. The therapeutic alliance is influenced by mutual obligation concordant with the theme of gift giving. Moreover, healing is performed in the name of *Dhanvañtari*, the patron deity of *āyurveda* and not directly in the *vaidya*'s name. The point to be noted here is that the ultimate responsibility for cure is placed in the hands of the gods. Healing remains a socio-moral activity.

But what of the many minor ailments the *vaidya* treats which are not *mahā rōga*, ailments for which the *vaidya* does not request a client to perform *sēva* or give *karma vipāka* as part of the course of therapy? The *vaidya* noted that the *karma* of such patients was also transferred to the *vaidya*, and that many *vaidya* failed to recognize this. He cited the case of his deceased elder brother who had practiced *āyurvedic* medicine without payment as a *sēva* and means of gaining merit, (*puṇya*). His brother had not directly administered medicine, but only offered diagnoses to patients. His logic had been that diagnosis was a *sēva* while the giving of medication and the collecting of fees involved a *karmic* relationship with the patient. Once diagnosed, patients were referred to an *āyurvedic* compounder with a chit describing the type of medication they needed. The *vaidya* noted that his brother had deluded himself. His brother's patients did involve him in their *karma* regardless of whether he directly gave them medication or received a fee. A failure to realize this and take necessary ritual precautions had shortened his life.

To mitigate the *karma* transferred to *vaidya* from routine complaints, a ritual known as a *Dhanvañtari pūjā* may be conducted.[6] This ritual also gains for a *vaidya* the blessings of the deity *Dhanvañtari* which is thought to increase the *vaidya*'s healing "power of hand" (*kayi guṇa*). Prior to the ritual, a *vaidya* recites *japa* and observes strict purity rules for a stipulated number of days. The number of units of *japa* recited is thought to correspond to the amount of blessings he will receive.

The ritual also serves to recycle the payment a *vaidya* receives for services rendered and thereby shared *karma* accrued for patients. The ritual contains three important events. First, a ritual offering to the nine planets vis-à-vis a sacred fire (*nāva graha hōma*) is conducted to mollify any bad effects associated with these sources of celestial power. Second, a ritual bath is conducted in which any impurities associated with accumulated *pāpa* is removed by a priest. Third, a group of Brahmans who practice *japa* are invited to partake of a meal in the name of the *vaidya*. By partaking of the ritual meal, the *pāpa* which the *vaidya* has accrued from patients is "shared" through an exchange of food.

My informant, a fourth generation descendent of a line of *āyurvedic* practitioners, was the only *vaidya* I encountered who faithfully carried out this ritual on a yearly basis. He described the ritual as an occasion during which he invested part of the payment he received from clients in *sēva* — the feeding of Brahmans. Capital gain (fees for services) associated with a market economy was reinvested in a medico-religious institution based on the practical logic of precapitalist Brahmanic values. This institution enabled the exchange of *karma pāpa* from patient to *vaidya* to priest.

A different sort of relationship exists between patients and practitioners who do and do not share mutual responsibilities to each other in the healing process. In the present case, not only is the patient partially responsible for the outcome of his treatment by mitigating *karma* through an offering of service, but in addition, the patient has a moral responsibility to the *vaidya*. One *vaidya* described this dual responsibility to me by way of an analogy. He stated that just as landlords and tenants traditionally had mutual obligations to each other and to the gods if a good crop was to be received, so the *vaidya* and patient had a mutual responsibility to mitigate *karma* if a cure was to be realized. In contrast, going to a practitioner whom you simply paid for medicine was described as like paying for "contract labor." This image captures two distinct logics of practice. Comparing the relationships between *vaidya*:patient and landlord:tenant evokes an ideal of mutual responsibility and interdependence. The moral investment of a *vaidya* in a patient is complementary to that of parties who share moral responsibility to a piece of land and to the deity of that land. The case of contract labor, where capital is exchanged for work, is likened to an exchange of medicines for fees. In both cases, no longstanding responsibilities or moral obligations exist.

Marriott (1976) has pointed out that in Hindu India, transactions involve a flowing together of essences between persons who are not bounded individual units, but rather permeable human lives constantly involved in an "elaborate transactional and transformational culture". In contexts where Brahmanic values are prominent, such as in interactions with *āyurvedic* practitioners and astrologers, sensitivity to the moral implications of "partaking" influences the logic of practice and the dynamics of exchange relations.

FEES FOR SERVICES

Vaidya

Let us now consider fees for services as a mode of payment. We may take up the case of *āyurveda* first. While the services of some traditional specialists are solely compensated for by offerings of one type or another, other practitioners are paid directly in the form of fees. Consultations to *vaidya* are usually not paid for separately, but are included in the cost of medications.[7] What is *explicitly* sold is medication. Inclusion of fees within medication charges is influenced by two variables: 1) lay reckoning of a reasonable cost range for the forms of medication provided; and 2) the number of days of medicine offered to a patient. The lay population entertains a set of ideas as to how much certain forms of medicine should cost. If a *vaidya*'s charges exceed these anticipated costs, chances are that a patient with limited means will not return to the *vaidya*. Anticipated costs for medicinal oils (*taila*), fermented wines (*aristha*) and herbal decoctions (*kaśāya*) are each reckoned differently. For example, in December 1979, the general price ranges for commonly purchased *āyurvedic* preparations by medicine form are found in Table 8.1.[8]

To retain poor patients, local *vaidya* exercise sensitivity when collecting consultation fees. This entails the setting of fees within "reasonable limits" established by lay cost reckoning.[9] Such limits influence the number of days medicine a *vaidya* gives to a patient per consultation as well as the types of medicines they directly dispense and prescribe. If costs go beyond the limits of expectation, the *vaidya* has two options. The *vaidya* can win the patient's trust by explaining that the medicine is composed of rare or expensive herbs. Conversely, the *vaidya* may administer only those medicines which fall within reasonable limits established by lay cost reckoning, i.e., medicines which allow the *vaidya* to collect a fee. Medications which fall outside the limits of lay cost reckoning are prescribed rather than dispensed.

Table 8.1

Price Range of Commonly Purchased
Āyurvedic Preparations

Medication	Cost
Āyurvedic pills	15–40 paise per pill
Herbal decoctions	Rs. 1–1.50 per one day dose
Medicinal wines	Rs. 3–4.50 per 100 ml
Medicinal oil	Rs. 6–7.50 per 100 ml

100 paise = Rs. 1, Rs. 7 = $1.00.

Older, more established *vaidya* perceived to have "power of the hand" or who are famous for their medicinal preparations are better able to convince patients of the worth of more expensive medicines. The higher the status of the *vaidya* and the greater the purchasing capacity of the client the less of an issue expense becomes. Less established *vaidya*, particularly younger *vaidya*, must win the confidence of poorer patients by sticking within the limits of reasonable cost established by lay reckoning. This is particularly the case if the *vaidya* relies on commercially prepared medicines as opposed to medicines which are self-made. Such constraints influence the types of medical regimes administered, prescribed, and purchased in bulk by less established *vaidya*. For example *amritha aristha*, a medicinal wine indicated in cases of debility and fever, is purchased by *vaidya* from commercial *āyurvedic* companies for approx. Rs. 16 per 40 oz (40 paise per oz). In 1979, a daily dose could be sold to patients for Rs. 1.50 per oz, providing Rs. 1 in hidden consultation fees. This was within the reasonable limits set by lay cost reckoning.

Commercial *āyurvedic* medicines are commonly purchased in bulk by *vaidya* from companies which offer discounts and incentive schemes. In some cases, the brand of medication dispensed by these practitioners is disguised or the label removed. This leads the patients to believe that the medicine is self prepared and of higher quality than commercial products available at *āyurvedic* chemist shops in towns. Costly medicines, such as those containing minerals (e.g., gold, mercuric oxide) or musk (*kastūri*), are generally prescribed but not dispensed to patients by *vaidya*. It is difficult to tag a consultation fee onto a medicine that is already deemed costly. When such expensive medicines are called for, the *vaidya* collects his fees through charges for purification medicines required as a precursor or adjunct to expensive medicines prescribed.

Cosmopolitan Doctors

In a somewhat stereotypic fashion, villagers perceive differences in the quality of service they receive from *āyurvedic* versus cosmopolitan practitioners. Whereas *āyurvedic* practitioners are thought to diagnose illness to the best of their ability, regardless of the amount of payment they receive, doctors are commonly thought to diagnose in accord with the paying capacity of the patient.[10] A doctor's efforts at diagnosis are judged both in terms of time expended with a patient and the doctor's use of artifacts which take on symbolic importance for the patient, such as the stethoscope, blood pressure apparatus, etc. One patient drew a parallel between doctors and lawyers on this point. He related a popular South Kanarese story of the client who upon asking the fees of a lawyer was directed to a shelf of books of varying sizes. A case argued from larger books, the client was told, would cost more than a case argued from books of smaller size. The lawyer was compared to a doctor who, depending on a patient's capacity to pay, either touched them with a stethoscope, placed the stethoscope carefully, or performed other diagnostic tests. A general feeling was that more careful diagnosis was performed on patients who could purchase more expensive medicines.

As in the case of *vaidya*, consultation fees are not charged by most rural based cosmopolitan doctors. They are factored into medication costs.[11] Appropriate fees for rural cosmopolitan doctors are crudely reckoned by laypersons on the basis of the medicine form and the number of days it is administered. In 1980, a medicine cost survey ($n = 50$ low to lower middle class informants) found that one day's supply of pills was commonly reckoned to cost between Rs. 1–1.50, capsules between Rs. 1.50–2.50 and injections at the rate of Rs. 2–5. Differences in the actual charges for medicine were in large part understood by the layperson as being a reflection of the quality and strength of the medication. For example, "single" injections were thought to cost less than "double" injections. Double injections are drawn from two vials (suspension in one and distilled water in the other) and deemed more expensive because they are more powerful.

One of the ramifications of lay cost reckoning in an increasingly competitive cosmopolitan medical market is a pattern of medicine dispensing characterized by the offering of medicines which: a) meet patient's felt needs and expectations; b) fall within the layperson's anticipated price range; and c) facilitate the collection of hidden consultation fees. A similar set of factors guides the behavior of local doctors and *vaidya*. For example, a "dispensing doctor" will dole out three days' tablets to a patient if the actual cost of the medication does not exceed Rs. 2–3. The most the practitioner can charge the patient for these tablets within the range of anticipated fees is Rs. 5. By supplying medication worth Rs. 2–3 he is able to recover Rs. 2 in hidden consultation fees.

In 1980, if medicine charges exceeded Rs. 10, practitioners realized that most poor clients would not return. When required, such medications were prescribed rather than dispensed directly. This served to disassociate the practitioner from high treatment costs. For example, a Rs. 10 injection of an expensive antibiotic would be prescribed while the practitioner personally supplied aspirin or vitamin tablets for three days, yielding a profit as a consultation fee. Since such simple drugs could be purchased over-the-counter, allopathic doctors were observed to disguise the identity of these medications, thereby increasing secrecy and dependency on the practitioner.[12]

When medication is prescribed, a patient is generally asked to return to see the practitioner with the medicine one to three days later. In the case of injections, a practitioner may use the service of "injection administration" as a means of collecting a fee for consultation. The usual cost for this service in 1980 was Rs. 1–2, but by the mid-1980s it had risen to Rs. 3–5. Collection of this fee inhibits private practitioners from referring patients to Primary Health Center (PHC) staff for follow up injections, even when patients live at a distance and are unable to return to the practitioner because of indirect and opportunity costs. When villagers do approach PHC staff living in close proximity to them for injections, they routinely offer them payment even when not directly asked for compensation. Aware of this pattern, many local practitioners have argued against letting "less qualified" health personnel give injections, lest their own status be undermined and a source of fee collection be lost to others.

HOW ARE FEES OFFERED?

In some cases, lay cost reckoning sets in motion payment behavior even before payment is specified by a practitioner. In clinical transactions in the offices of small town practitioners or PHC doctors having a private practice on the side, a charge is often not immediately requested. Rather, an uncomfortable silence follows treatment during which time the patient has the opportunity to offer payment. The patient offers a fee on the basis of the cost reckoning guidelines noted above. After the fee has been offered, the practitioner may accept the fee and act as if money matters of this magnitude are beneath their status. On the other hand, the practitioner may inform the patient that the cost of the medicines given exceed the fee offered. This causes the patient to either offer more money or promise to give more at the next visit. I have observed many occasions when a fee voluntarily offered by a patient exceeded the fee a practitioner routinely demanded from other patients with similar problems.

A contrasting pattern of paying fees involves patients who offer money to practitioners at the beginning of a consultation. In some cases, this is a presentation of all of a patient's funds. In other cases, a patient may make a cash offering to a cosmopolitan practitioner as a sign of respect or to establish a bond, in much the same way as one would make an offering to a ritual specialist when seeking advice. This behavior is commonplace at the Government PHC.[13] Discussion with patients as to why they offered money to doctors whose services are supposed to be free revealed that the money is given either as: a) a bribe (*lāncha*) which may enhance one's chances of getting medicines, rather than a prescription which would require additional expense of both time and money; or b) as kindness (*kuśi*) so the doctor will take interest in them.[14] Giving a PHC doctor a bribe to secure medicine appears no more unusual than offering a ticket attendant a few extra rupees for a seat on a crowded train. "Kindness payments" index another logic of practice as well. Just as offerings serve to establish a moral bond between patient and traditional practitioner, so payments of kindness to PHC doctors constitute attempts, albeit weak attempts, to establish social bonds having moral implications beyond market relations.[15] As one informant noted, in India customary bribes, kindness payments, and offerings to deities and politicians merge.

It is important to note that some villagers who frequent a PHC doctor give small offerings not so much for good medicine as for good diagnosis. A patient offers a few rupees to a doctor in much the same way he would make a token offering to an exorcist or astrologer. In both cases, patients use the specialist as a consultant to find out the severity of their sickness. Once the nature of the illness is diagnosed as serious, these patients consult a private practitioner (possible the PHC doctor at home) for medication and follow-up.

Some private doctors directly tell patients what their charges are at the beginning of a consultation. Others negotiate terms with patients who cannot afford the "best treatment," but want treatment within a given cost frame. In some cases, practitioners extend credit, particularly during slack work seasons.[16] A majority of practitioners interviewed deemed credit extension a necessary evil with two major drawbacks. While a patient initially praises a practitioner for extending credit, it is common for the patient to forget the amount of medication received and the number of visits to the practitioner responsible for the debt. The debt then appears large because it is not seen in respect to lay cost reckoning. The practitioner appears like the merchant who advances rice during times of scarcity for high interest rates. The other drawback is that as debt increases so do the chances of practitioner-hopping, as many rural patients prefer several small debts to one large one. A sample of 15 rural practitioners estimated average losses to extended credit to be one third their outlay for medicines. To cover such fee losses, some practitioners developed a Robin Hood mentality. Patients with greater funds were charged more to offset losses incurred by treating the poor.

Charging higher fees for medical services has its own set of social dynamics. Being charged more, when greater respect is shown to a patient, can constitute a sign of social status as well as legitimate the seriousness of an illness to household member. It is not uncommon for wealthier patients to exploit a discussion of medical charges as a means of marking status in the context of illness stories. In the 1980s, I documented an increasing number of middle class patients who requested better (i.e., more expensive) medicines and diagnostic texts as markers of care, concern, and affection for ill household members. Medicine expenditures constitutes an idiom of concern as well as entitlement, leading those with resources on medical pilgrimages for metamedical as well as curative purposes. Just as there are scripts for culturally appropriate ways of being ill, there are scripts for treatment searches which reflect the moral identity of caretakers.

LAY COST RECKONING, FEE FOR SERVICE PAYMENT AND THE ROLE OF THE CHEMIST

It has been noted that both *āyurvedic* and cosmopolitan practitioners tend to dispense medications which fall within lay cost reckoning parameters. Medications which fall outside these parameters are prescribed. Given this pattern, let us examine the position of the chemist. This will entail brief consideration of the pharmaceutical representatives and their impact on chemist–practitioner relationships in the rural health arena.

Rural practitioners who earn fees through dispensing medicines tend to stock medicines such as vitamins, tonics, digestants, flatulence tablets, and inexpensive antibiotics. These medicines are popular and cost effective from both a therapeutic and fee collection vantage point. Bulk purchase of these medicines cuts their cost appreciably and administration of such medications to clients affords a reasonable vehicle for collecting consultation fees. Pharmaceutical representatives of major pharmaceutical companies regularly visit popular rural practitioners as long as they hold some form of license or degree.[17] Pharmaceutical representatives aggressively seek direct purchase orders from rural practitioners as well as promises to prescribe their products.[18] In return, pharmaceutical representatives offer these practitioners information about drugs, free samples, "buy some get some free" schemes, and significant discounts on medicines purchased. Similar discounts are offered to chemist shops. Profit margins and incentive schemes affect the recommendations which chemist shop attendants give to clients, both lay clients looking for over-the-counter medicines and practitioners who are not visited by pharmaceutical representatives.

Chemist shops derive profit from filling prescriptions written by private and PHC doctors, over-the-counter sales to the informed and uninformed public, and sales to registered medical practitioners who are not directly serviced by pharmaceutical agents.[19] As noted, many prescriptions received from private doctors are for medications which are deemed expensive by lay cost reckoning. Attendants at chemist shops often face rural patients who come in with a prescription chit and have little idea of the cost of medicines. In many cases, these patients selectively purchase medications. Some attendants have become adept at negotiating with clients who ask the prices of the medications prescribed and then proceed to purchase what seems affordable and/or reasonable on the basis of lay cost reckoning. Typically, prescribed medications are brands from a major pharmaceutical firm which has "won over" the practitioner. If a patient has sufficient money for two or three days of prescribed medicines, chemist shop attendants do not generally suggest substitutes, even if sale of substitute products might net them greater profit.[20] However, in cases where a brand medication is far more expensive than a generic drug, a chemist shop attendant may suggest to an impoverished patient that they take a three day supply of a generic drug in lieu of a one day supply of a name-brand medication.[21]

A point to be emphasized is that in rural areas, it is often the chemist shop attendant who informs patients as to the purpose of multiple medicines and the importance of following a course of medication beyond a one or two dose trial.[22] It is the chemist shop attendant who must reason with the patient within a set of economic constraints. For this reason, the potential health education role of the chemist shop attendant is worth careful consideration.[23]

Two other points may be raised regarding the influence of chemist shop attendants on medication use. Chemist shops stock well-known drugs as well as take a chance with the products of less renowned companies who offer lower cost medicine, attractive incentive schemes, and bigger profit margins, but provide less quality control. In addition to being sold as over-the-counter (OTC) medicines and occasionally being offered to poor patients as substitutes for prescribed brand-name drugs, these drugs are in demand among rural registered practitioners not directly visited by pharmaceutical representatives. Chemist shop attendants play a role in passing on information about new and low-cost medicines to these practitioners. Research is needed on the flow of information from pharmaceutical representatives to chemists to practitioners who practice ad hoc medicine. A second point concerns the role of chemist shop attendants in fostering over-the-counter medicine sales and medicine experimentation. Chemist shops engage in pushing products which fetch them higher profits as well as liquidate accumulated stocks of medicines. Little is known about "counter pushing" behavior, to whom medicines are pushed, public recognition of this activity, and clients' critical assessment of recommendations made by chemist shop attendants.[24]

PUBLIC HEALTH RAMIFICATIONS OF PAYING FOR THERAPY

A number of public health issues arise from a scrutiny of modes of paying for therapy and competition in the pluralistic health care arena. Four issues are highlighted for further research. First, because a dispensing practitioner's compensation depends on fees hidden in medicine charges, the practitioner must stock popular medicines and to some extent acquiesce to client demands. Practitioners stock and directly administer medicines which are "fee facilitating" be they essential or nonessential, as long as they provide some relief, meet patients' felt needs, and are judged potent by cultural criteria. The misuse of calcium gluconate illustrates this point. Calcium gluconate injections are administered by a number of practitioners intravenously not to correct calcium deficiencies, but to produce a "heat effect" which is deemed a sign of power by folk health criteria.[25]

India's present pattern of drug production and sales does not accord with an epidemiological profile of India's disease patterns (see Chapter 11). Indeed, attention has been focused on the "irrational" use of drugs by India's medical practitioners. Calling attention to the irrational use of drugs as measured against clinical gold standards begs the questions: rational for whom and rational in what contexts? Given the social and microeconomic environment in which rural practitioners function, clinically irrational practices may make economic sense. More research is needed on the economic factors influencing practitioners' medicine stocking, dispensing and prescription decisions. Credence needs to be paid to their need to collect hidden consultation charges in a competitive medical market influenced by lay cost reckoning.

A second issue raised by the examination of how practitioners collect fees for service entails the reluctance of cosmopolitan practitioners to refer patients to government PHC field staff (e.g., midwives or multipurpose workers) living in close proximity to patients for follow-up services such as the administration of injections. Maximizing the services of these personnel could reduce logistical problems involved in health care delivery.

An understanding of microeconomics leads us to appreciate why private cosmopolitan practitioners are not supportive of activities by PHC staff which reduce their ability to collect fees (see Chapter 11). To acknowledge PHC staff's capacity in a high status domain, such as injection giving, reduces practitioners' own status. It also invites competition from staff who might then be approached by villagers for other medications and services. Practitioner informants cited multiple instances of former PHC staff who had become registered medical practitioners. Fear of competition leads practitioners to undermine the prestige and training of PHC staff through both word of mouth and non-referral.

The practitioner's collection of fees from the sale of medicine raises a third and related issue. As noted, practitioners are reluctant to refer patients to PHC staff for follow-up services because of economic considerations. These considerations are often disguised as moral objections to second-rate treatment of the poor. A similar rationale underlies practitioners' resistance to the idea of villages setting up local medicine cooperatives, an idea explored during a community diagnosis project (Nichter 1984), in which it was found that only four of 15 practitioners supported the concept.[26]

One final issue is identified for future research. Lay cost reckoning is largely determined by medicine form. In the competitive medical marketplace, it would be worth monitoring the way in which medicine production and marketing accords with consumer demand as influenced by popular health culture. For example, to what extent are medicines produced by allopathic and *āyurvedic* medical companies made to fit popular ideas of appropriate medicine form as well as cost? To what extent are marketing campaigns tailored to coincide with lay health concerns and popular explanatory models of how medicines work? The production and advertising of medicines in India warrants investigation as a cultural phenomena at a time when the pharmaceutical market is rapidly expanding.

DISCUSSION

An examination of how villagers pay for therapeutic services and how practitioners collect fees provides a number of insights into health care seeking behavior, practitioner–patient relationships, and medicine distribution patterns. It has been noted that in the traditional health sector the size and manner in which an offering is presented to an exorcist, diviner, or astrologer are interpreted as signs revealing the nature of a client's problem and the relative importance of the consultation. The interpretation of such signs influences diagnosis and therapy management options.

For the traditional *āyurvedic* practitioner, payment involves a notion of moral bonding implicit in the dynamics of exchange relationships. Accepting the services rendered by a traditional *vaidya* involves the patient in moral aspects of healing associated with the meanings of illness in the Hindu cosmology. In order for a patient to be effectively treated by a *vaidya* for a major illness (*mahā rōga*), the patient has to pay off a debt of *karma* in addition to paying a healer. This penance takes the form of a social service which serves to reintegrate the patient into the socio-moral order. Within the Hindu great tradition, the role and identity of the healer is defined in relation to the meanings of illness. The concept of partaking involves the healer not only with the patient, but with society itself. This is exemplified by prescribed rituals performed by the *vaidya*. Priests of the socio-religious order participate in a "healing of the healer" by dissipating the *karma* that a *vaidya* accrues from patients.

The medico-religious ideal of moral bonding between healer and patient found in *āyurveda* may be contrasted to the secular contractual relationship between cosmopolitan practitioner and patient in a market economy.[27] In this context, patient–practitioner relationships are strongly influenced by lay cost reckoning in a competitive health arena which is becoming increasingly client-dependent. Friedson (1970) describes client-dependent practitioners in two ways:

1. They are like businessmen, "neighborhood shopkeepers" whose stock of diagnostic and treatment practices/resources reflect their position between two worlds, the lay health system and that of the professional. The practitioner must on occasion give in to his patients' prejudices if they are to return to him and to refer other patients to him. These practitioners are likely to honor lay demands for popular remedies such as vitamin B_{12} injections, copious use of antibiotics, and prescription of tranquilizers, sedatives, and stimulants.

2. They are dependent upon laypersons for their referrals, which provide them business. Insofar as lay referrals are "inevitably based on lay understandings of illness and its treatment," practitioners' survival depends upon the compatibility of their diagnosis and treatment with that of the layperson. The patient is an "active participant" in the sense that his demands are being met for diagnosis as well as treatment.

Friedson's depiction of client-dependent practitioners may be applied to South Kanara, a context marked by an increase in transportation facilities and a rising number of cosmopolitan and modern *āyurvedic* practitioners who dispense commercial forms of medicine, all of which appear similar to the layperson. In South Kanara, the rural practitioner must win the patronage of the lay population by establishing a reputation for having good medicines and reasonable costs as discerned by lay cost reckoning. In as much as a rural practitioner's compensation depends on fees hidden in medicine charges, the practitioner stocks popular medicines and to some degree acquiesces to clients' demands for particular medicine forms.[28] Practitioners stock medicines which are "fee facilitating," be they clinically essential (rational) or nonessential as long as they provide some symptomatic relief and/or meet patients' felt needs. A practitioner's choice of medications is influenced by his assumptions about what will meet patients' felt needs and what constraints lay cost reckoning imposes on his ability to collect a fee. Adapting treatment to lay cost reckoning imposes a market mentality upon the client–practitioner relationship.

While compelling, Friedson's model is incomplete. Parsons (1976) has argued that describing health care merely in terms of a market model is limited on two counts. First, it undervalues the element of "confidence" that goes with the professional role of the practitioner which is clearly different from that of shopkeeper supplying commercial products. Second, it assumes that practitioners are catering to the consciously formulated and rationally understood wants of sick people — the rational man argument warned against by Kunstadter (1978) and others (e.g., Young 1981a, 1981b).

Parson's critique of Friedson is relevant in the South Kanarese context. Lay referrals and patterns of illness treatment are only partially based on practitioners receptivity to local understandings of illness and their willingness to adapt treatment to local expectations, including cost. Illness identities are often ambiguous and negotiated over time within one's therapy management group (Janzen 1978). Ideas about illness identity are sensitive to perceptions of severity as well as diagnosis by treatment. They are influenced by such contingencies as probable treatment costs and outcome expectations.

They are also responsive to the social relations of health care seeking and the moral implications of illness.

Popular practitioners often, but do not always, display a keen understanding of local health concerns as well as a sensitivity to the ways in which patients do and do not describe illness. These are not the only factors which render practitioners popular. Practitioner popularity is multidimensional and often illness, gender, and age specific. Popularity is influenced by patient expectations as well as practitioner attributions. A key issue is whether a practitioner is being consulted for his medicines or "the power of his hand." In the former case, popularity may be related to practitioner charges, while in the latter case the practitioner's demeanor and the way in which he communicates may be more important.

Lay referral patterns are sensitive to a patient's "power of the purse" and a medicine's "power of the brand" as well as a practitioner's "power of the hand." In some contexts, lay referral is based on market reasoning while in other contexts the search for a healer extends outside the bounds of market relations. In a context where multiple health ideologies coexist, it is prudent to pay heed to Wolf's (1982) observation that in everyday life there is often an interplay between capitalist and precapitalist formations, values, and ideologies. Dominant modes of production and exchange may characterize only part of the total range of interactions in a society.

For routine complaints, a convenient practitioner may be consulted for the medicine commodities he or she possesses. After all, the medicine cures; it is the active agent, and one seeks the best medicine at the lowest price. In other contexts, when multiple attempts at treatment fail, a different kind of health seeking behavior is often initiated. A practitioner is sought with whom one feels confidence and faith. Confidence often entails the sense that the practitioner is diagnosing the person as well as their condition, while faith entails a sense of affiliation, interconnectedness, and interpersonal resonance. While confidence and affiliation are often spoken of in the West in relation to competence, in rural India confidence and faith merge in descriptions of a practitioner's "power of the hand."[29] Ascription of power of the hand places primary importance on the practitioner as active agent, but it is the practitioner's "perceived special relationship" with the afflicted which is of paramount importance.[30] Resort to such a healer is distinct from resort to a practitioner whose relationship with patients is defined in terms of contractual obligations, commodity fixes, and fees for service.

CONCLUSION

In India, health is increasingly being marketed as a commodity obtainable through medicine products which offer the promise of safe passage through a deteriorating physical environment. This ethnographic account of the ways the Indian public pays for therapeutic modalities and the services of healers draws attention to two coexisting health ideologies. It has been emphasized that prevailing market relations characterized by the purchase of curative services has not displaced a precapitalist religico-medical ideology upon which perceptions of healing are based.

Curative efficacy is predicated on universalistic claims, (procedures, measures), while healing is based on particularistic perceptions and relationships of a different order (Young 1983).[31] Either or both may be sought by a patient offering money to a practitioner. The distinction between curing and healing is raised in the conclusion of this chapter not just to emphasize the complexity of health care seeking, but to draw attention to "paying for therapy" as a polysemous cultural performance amenable to what Bourdieu (1986, 1990) has termed the study of an economy of practice. To understand the meaning of paying for therapeutic services in India requires a consideration of the possible relationships framed by an exchange of goods or capital. One must examine yet look beyond what is exchanged to social relations initiated by the exchange. Money offered to one practitioner takes on the meaning of cash capital which defines the bounds of a contractual relationship. Offered to another practitioner, money may constitute symbolic capital. Its exchange marks status and/or initiates a relationship entailing unspoken socio-moral obligations and bonds of affiliation. A different economy of practice guides consultations to such practitioners, irrespective of the system of medicine from which they hail (Nichter and Nordstrom 1989).

An understanding of the social, cultural, and personal meanings of therapeutic transactions requires ethnographic investigation into what the afflicted (and concerned others) is trying to accomplish while engaging in health care seeking. Studies of "paying" for services which are sensitive to different forms of exchange (e.g., offerings, gifts, kindness payments, bribes, and fees for service) provide insights into the agenda(s) of those parties offering and receiving services. A sense of whether transactions are setting into motion short- or long-term, reciprocal or contractual relationships may thus be discerned.

Modes of payment mark such relationships in subtle ways. What may appear in one context to be an exchange which has only instrumental value may in another context index far more. The act of paying for what ails you assumes multiple meanings, ranging from the moral to the mundane.

NOTES

1. While I support Bourdieu's call for the study of an economy of practice, I have not employed his conceptualization of diverse forms of capital (economic, symbolic, social, and cultural capital). Although I find metaphorical extension of "capital" useful in some contexts, I resist such usage in this chapter because it too readily lends itself to economic reductionism. A patient's offering of money to a practitioner may simultaneously involve (and index) economic capital (material assets), symbolic capital (claims to status and prestige on the part of patient and/or practitioner), social capital (obligations and relations of trust), and cultural capital (skills, knowledge, wisdom). The problem with describing practitioner–patient transactions in these terms is that such usage obscures the confluence of implicit and explicit meanings which are negotiated in context. There is considerable ambiguity and overlap between Bourdieu's forms of capital (DiMaggio 1979), just as there is between gifts, offerings, incentive payments and commodities in India (Appadurai 1986). What is important to appreciate are the spoken and unspoken intentions and expectations which frame therapeutic transactions and the potential for rekeying these transactions. The form and quality of therapeutic relations may be transformed during the course of treatment by the attentiveness and sensitivity of a practitioner (or lack thereof) as well as by the performance of the afflicted and concerned others. Making and receiving payments are important dimensions of this performance. Paying constitutes an idiom through which relationships may be framed and reframed, an occasion when the meaning of capital may be transformed by a glance or the manner in which a five rupee note is placed or received.

2. Surprisingly few health expenditure studies have been conducted in developing countries which document expenditure by illness, age and gender, and which take into account the direct, indirect and opportunity costs of illness in terms of both time and income (disposable income as well as loans). This will be the topic of a forthcoming publication.

3. Notes on how Subramanya reads the actions of clients is gleaned from over 100 hours of observation and interviews conducted with him after clients departed. Exit interviews with clients suggest that he was correct in his assessment about three-quarters of the time.

4. The relationship between *āyurveda* and the doctrine of *karma* is multifaceted and has been presented differently by the major formulators of *āyurveda* (Caraka, Vágbhata, and Susruta). For a review, see Weiss (1980).

5. A review of Sanskrit literature on *karma vipāka* is provided by Thrasher (1978). It is interesting to note that Sanskritic texts focusing on *karma vipāka* present abnormality and illness much less as punishments and more as opportunities for prudent persons to mitigate past sins by appropriate countermeasures. Penances prescribed involve a reintegration of the afflicted with society and offerings associated with public utility.

6. Few *vaidya* practice yearly *Dhanvañtari pūjā*. Other *pūjā* are sometimes substituted for *Dhanvañtari pūjā* when a *vaidya* feels he suffers from *karma* accrued from patients. For example, *Satyanārāyaṇa pūjā*, a general all-purpose *pūjā* which has grown in popularity over the last 50 years, is sometimes performed for this purpose.

7. Some renowned *āyurvedic vaidya* and astrologers charge fixed consultant fees, but this was rare in the region studied.

8. Patent medicines included were the following: pills — *Dhanvañtari matre, Bala graha (chine) matre, vāyu matre.* Wines — *Dashamoolaristha, Draksharistha, Amritaristha, Ashoka aristha.* Oils — *Dhañvantari taila, Triphaladi taila, Narayana taila, Brahmi taila.*

9. While not well documented, patient dropout and non-adherence among patients visiting *āyurvedic* practitioners is common. The costs of receiving systematic *āyurvedic* treatment are often higher than what a patient is willing to invest or the rigor of treatment is too demanding.

10. My observation is that divination by traditional practitioners, such as astrologers and exorcists, is often influenced by a patient's paying capacity.

11. In more urban areas of South Kanara and in neighboring Kerala State, doctors charge consultation fees. Fees range from Rs. 5 to Rs. 15. Middle to upper class patients frequent practitioners with high consultation fees as a measure of status as well as to get better therapy. A local joke among rural GPs is that they are the specialists because higher class patients consult specialists first. The trend of visiting specialists prior to local GPs has increased significantly over the last 10 years as has the demand for consultation fees.

12. The local population has become increasingly familiar with common drugs and there has been a marked rise in the purchase of medicines over-the-counter at chemist shops. During initial stages, this entails presenting symptoms to chemist shop attendants. Once names of medicine became familiar, the trend is to ask for medicines by name and consult chemists about less expensive alternatives if known products increase in price.

13. I do not wish to infer that all Government Primary Health Center (PHC) doctors accept money from public patients or maintain private practices. However, the patterns of behavior noted in this chapter are common.

14. In one region of South Kanara investigated, filling a prescription necessitated a day off from work and a bus ride costing half a day's wages. PHC medical supplies are limited. PHC doctors must either be highly selective in allocating free drugs or ration medicine daily in accordance with a supply management plan.

15. See van der Veen's (1979) discussion of the moral bonding aspects of payment for medicine in relation to the issue of "free medicine" and patient mistrust.

16. The offering of credit to patients by doctors and chemist shops appeared to be declining by 1980, but was documented in the 1970s.

17. In the southern region of South Kanara studied, 48% of the practitioners visited by the medical representatives of a major pharmaceutical firm had licenses from *āyurvedic* or integrated medical colleges. Thirty six percent of practitioners ranked as "most popular" had *āyurvedic* degrees.

18. Pharmaceutical representatives do not directly sell medicines to doctors but "pen" orders which are filled by stockists. For details on interactions between pharmaceutical representatives with doctors and chemists, see Kamat and Nichter (1995a).

19. Several studies have been conducted on over-the-counter sales of drugs to individual clients. See, for example, Bledsoe and Goubaud (1985), Ferguson (1981), Greenhalgh (1987), Haak (1988), Krishnaswamy et al. (1983), Logan (1983), Price (1989), van der Geest (1982, 1987, 1988), Wolffers (1987). The information flow between chemist shops and practitioners is little documented.

20. In general, substitute medicines are not suggested to clients with current prescriptions for this might anger doctors, whom chemists depend upon for business. For a discussion of the practice of counter-pushing and medicine substitution, see Kamat and Nichter (1995a).

21. Suggestions about drug substitution are generally made if a customer asks if there is a less expensive alternative. I have, however, observed some rural chemist shop attendants intervene when they encounter an impoverished patient purchasing a partial dose of an expensive brand medicine. Busy town chemists have less time for such interventions and are less inclined to engage in them.

22. Chemist shop attendants do not, as a matter of routine, give clients advice about medications. It is in the context of negotiation of purchases that information about drugs is often exchanged. This is done when attendants have the time, when clients appear to be receptive to advice, and when attendants feel a client has no experience with the drug in question.

23. For a complementary set of studies from Latin America which describe the role of the chemist in educating the lay population and/or practitioners in the use of medications, see Cosminsky and Scrimshaw (1980) on Guatemala, Logan (1983) on Mexico, and Ferguson (1981) on El Salvador. See also Igun (1987), Haak (1988), and Kloos et al. (1986).

24. Important to consider would be differences in client response to products pushed which are associated with popular vs. unknown companies. On the pharmacist's role in fostering self medication see Ferguson (1981), Fabricant and Hirschhorn (1987), Haak (1988), Kamat and Nichter (1995b), Price (1989), and Shiva (1985).

25. This notions stems from personal observation of the use of calcium gluconate and discussion of this practice with Dr. Carl Taylor who has made similar observations in North India.

26. Fifteen rural cosmopolitan practitioners were interviewed about their opinions regarding medicine cooperatives. While all the practitioners recognized that scarce resources were being expended by rural patients on transportation in order to secure common drugs, 11 stated that they would not be in favor of the concept of a local medicine cooperative. All but three cited quackery as an initial reason against the establishment of a cooperative. Eight of the 11 also noted that financial loss associated with the existing pattern of fee collection was a central problem. Only four of the 15 practitioners, all popular practitioners with secure clientele, supported the concept.

27. For further description of allopathic doctors' businesslike manner of practicing medicine in India see Madan (1972). Caroline Nordstrom and I point out that healing relationships may be established with all types of practitioners. It is the quality of the relationship which counts and faith in that practitioner's power of the hand (Nichter and Nordstrom 1989). Like charisma, this power may be ascribed to the personal qualities of the practitioner (or their family, lineage, etc.) or imputed by a patient to a practitioner. In the latter case a patient (or caretaker) has a need to believe in the practitioner's capacities, leading them to interpret the practitioner's actions and words as deeply meaningful. A point to be emphasized is that curative services framed by market relations mitigate against, but do not preclude, healing relationships as perceived by Hindus.

28. Kapil (1988) observes that the collection of consultation fees through medicine sales was also common in 19th century England.

29. Power of the hand is often described by such phrases as: "from this practitioner's hand even water will cure."

30. In some cases, the practitioner serves as a conduit for a special relationship with a higher power or deity, a relationship some practitioners acknowledge through religious icons, pictures of a practitioner's ancestors, etc.

31. Medical anthropologists typically contrast healing and curing in relation to efficacy as seen from the different vantage points of biomedicine and indigenous populations invested in local meaning systems. I view healing in a somewhat different light while acknowledging that healing often entails "impression point" (Stromberg 1985) experiences wherein a new sense of coherence and subjectivity mitigates suffering and establishes a sense of self-efficacy (Bandura 1989). As several anthropologists have pointed out (e.g., Dobkin-de Rios 1981, Finkler 1980), healing does not necessarily require that a patient understand the actions of a practitioner or for that matter that they share world-views. Healing may involve the production, negotiation, or instantiation of social and personal meaning as well as cultural meanings. It is not just the therapeutic event which is important, but the way in which it is interpreted, used, and reused by the afflicted and/or concerned others. The sustained efficacy of a therapeutic transaction entails not only the experience of an initial impression point, but the reproduction of impression points which in Stromberg's words "partake of the power of earlier ones and continually

realign the self" (1985:62). This may be done through the seeing of the world in terms of a religious doctrine (or other ideology) as well as through the telling and retelling of illness and therapy narratives where "truths" are reexperienced.

REFERENCES

Appadurai, A. 1986. Introduction: Commodities and the Politics of Value. *In* The Social Life of Things. Arjun Appadurai, ed. Pp. 3–63. Boston: Cambridge University Press.

Bandura, A. 1989. Human Agency in Social Cognitive Theory. American Psychologist 44(9):1175–1184.

Bledsoe, C. H. and M. F. Goubaud. 1985. The Reinterpretation and Distribution of Western Pharmaceuticals: An Example From the Mende of Sierra Leone. Social Science and Medicine 21(3):275–282.

Bourdieu, P. 1986. The Forms of Capital. *In* Handbook of Theory and Research for the Sociology of Education. J. Richardson, ed. Pp. 241–258. New York: Greenwood Press.

Bourdieu, P. 1990. The Logic of Practice. Stanford: Stanford University Press.

Cosminsky, S. and M. Scrimshaw. 1980. Medical Pluralism on a Guatemalan Plantation. Social Science and Medicine 14b:267–278.

DiMaggio, P. 1979. Review Essay: On Pierre Bourdieu. American Journal of Sociology 84:1460–1474.

Dobkin-de Rios, M. 1981. Social-Economic Characteristics of an Amazon Urban Healer's Clientele. Social Science and Medicine 15b:51–63.

Fabricant, S. J. and N. Hirschhorn. 1987. Deranged Distribution, Perverse Prescription, Unprotected Use: The Irrationality of Pharmaceuticals in the Developing World. Health Policy and Planning 2(3):204–213.

Ferguson, A. 1981. Commercial Pharmaceutical Medicine and Medicalization: A Case Study from El Salvador. Culture, Medicine and Psychiatry 5:105–134.

Finkler, K. 1980. Non-Medical Treatments and Their Outcomes. Culture, Medicine and Psychiatry 4:271–310.

Friedson, E. 1970. Profession of Medicine: A Study of the Sociology of Applied Knowledge. Pp. 305–308. New York: Dodd & Mead.

Greenhalgh, T. 1987. Drug Prescription and Self Medication in India: An Exploratory Study. Social Science and Medicine 25(3):307–318.

Haak, H. 1988. Pharmaceuticals in Two Brazilian Villages: Lay Practices and Perceptions. Social Science and Medicine 27(12):1415–1427.

Igun, U. 1987. Why We Seek Treatment Here: Retail Pharmacy and Clinical Practice in Maidugiri, Nigeria. Social Science and Medicine 24(8):689–695.

Janzen, J. 1978. The Quest for Therapy in Lower Zaire. Berkeley: University of California Press.

Kamat, V. and M. Nichter. 1995a. Monitoring Product Movement: An Ethnographic Study of Pharmaceutical Sales Representatives in Bombay, India. Manuscript submitted for publication.

Kamat, V. and M. Nichter. 1995b. Pharmacies, Self-Medication, and Pharmaceutical Marketing in India. Manuscript submitted for publication.

Kapil, I. 1988. Doctors Dispensing Medications: Contemporary India and 19th Century England. Social Science and Medicine 26(7):691–699.

Kloos, H., T. Chama, K. Abemo, K. Tasdick, and S. Belay. 1986. Utilization of Pharmacies and Pharmaceutical Drugs in Addis Ababa Ethiopia. Social Science and Medicine 22:6653–6672.

Krishnaswamy, K., D. Kumar, and G. Radhaiah. 1983. Drug Sales: Precepts and Practices (Unpublished report). Food and Drug Toxicology Research Centre, National Institute of Nutrition, Hyderabad, India.

Kunstadter, P. 1978. Do Cultural Differences Make Any Differences? Choice Points in Medical Systems Available in Northwestern Thailand. *In* Culture and Healing in Asian Systems. Arthur Kleinman, Peter Kunstadter, E. Russell Alexander, and James Gale, eds. Pp. 185–218. Cambridge, MA: Schenkman.

Logan, K. 1983. The Role of Pharmacists and Over the Counter Medications in the Health Care System of a Mexican City. Medical Anthropology 7:68–89.

Madan, T. 1972. Doctors in a North Indian City: Recruitment, Role Perception and Role Performance. *In* Beyond the Village: Sociological Explorations. S. Saberwal, ed. Pp. 79–105. Simla: Indian Institute of Advanced Study.

Marriott, M. 1976. Hindu Transactions: Diversity Without Dualism. *In* Transaction and Meaning: Directions in the Anthropology of Exchange and Symbolic Behavior. B. Kapferer, ed. Pp. 109–142. Philadelphia: Institute for the Study of Human Issues.

Mauss, M. 1954. The Gift: Forms and Functions of Exchange in Archaic Societies. Pp. 58–59. London: Cohn & West.

Nichter, Mark. 1981. Negotiations of the Illness Experience: Ayurvedic Therapy and the Psychosocial Dimensions of Illness. Culture, Medicine and Psychiatry 5:1–27.

Nichter, Mark. 1984. Project Community Diagnosis: Participatory Research as a First Step Toward Community Investment in Primary Health Care. Social Science and Medicine 19(3):237–252.

Nichter, Mark and C. Nordstrom. 1989. A Question of Medicine Answering: Health Commodification and the Social Relations in Healing in Sri Lanka. Culture, Medicine and Psychiatry 13:367–390.

Parry, J. 1980. Ghosts, Greed and Sin: The Occupational Identity of the Benares Funeral Priests. Man (N.S.) 15:88–111.

Parsons, T. 1976. Epilogue to the Doctor–Patient Relationship in the Changing Health Scene. *In* Proceedings of an International Conference. E. B. Gallagher, ed. Pp. 78–183. Washington, DC: John E. Fogarty International Center for Advanced Study in the Health Sciences.

Price, L. 1989. In the Shadow of Biomedicine: Self-Medication in Two Ecuadorian Pharmacies. Social Science and Medicine 28(9):905–915.

Shiva, M. 1985. Towards a Healthy Use of Pharmaceuticals. Development Dialogue 2:67–93.

Stromberg, P. 1985. The Impression Point: Synthesis of Symbol and Self. Ethos 13(1):56–74.

Thrasher, A. 1978. Some Sanskrit Works on Karma and Their Results. Unpublished paper presented at the Second Karma Conference, Pasadena, CA.

van der Geest, S. 1982. The Efficiency of Inefficiency: Medicine Distribution in South Cameroon. Social Science and Medicine 16(24):2145–2153.

van der Geest, S. 1987. Self-Care and the Informal Sale of Drugs in South Cameroon. Social Science and Medicine 25(3):293–306.

van der Geest, S. 1988. The Articulation of Formal and Informal Medicine in Distribution in South Cameroon. *In* The Context of Medicines in Developing Countries. S. van der Geest and S. R. Whyte, eds. Pp. 131–148. Dordrecht, The Netherlands: Kluwer Academic Press.

van der Veen, K. 1979. Western Medical Care in an Indian Setting: The Valsad District in Gujarat. *In* In Search of Health. S. van der Geest and K. van der Veen, eds. Pp. 145–158. Vakgroep Culturele Anthropologie, Universiteit Von Amsterdam.

Weiss, M. 1980. Caraka Samhita on the Doctrine of Karma. *In* Karma and Rebirth in Classical Indian Traditions. W. D. O'Flayerty, ed. Pp. 90–115. Berkeley: University of California Press.

Wolf, E. 1982. Europe and the People Without History. Berkeley: University of California Press.

Wolffers, I. 1987. Drug Information and Sale Practice in Some Pharmacies in Colombo, Sri Lanka. Social Science and Medicine 25(3):319–321.

Young, A. 1981a. The Creation of Medical Knowledge: Some Problems in Interpretation. Social Science and Medicine 15b:379–386.

Young, A. 1981b. When Rational Men Fall Sick: An Inquiry Into Some Assumptions Made by Medical Anthropologists. Culture, Medicine and Psychiatry 5:317–335.

Young, A. 1983. The Relevance of Traditional Medical Cultures to Modern Primary Health Care. Social Science and Medicine 17(16):1205–1211.

CHAPTER 9

Pharmaceuticals, the Commodification of Health, and the Health Care-Medicine Use Transition

Mark Nichter

The most important myth is the myth of progress or in other words, the business of "onward ever onward." And the first problem that arises from this myth for advertising is that "newer," "bigger," "better," "stronger," "richer" products are put forward in the market and a "still better tomorrow" is envisaged. Nobody has bothered to ask "better than what?" I am still doubtful whether Mexaform or Entero-vioform is more effective than the indigenous herbal medicines dished out by our grandmothers 40 or 50 years ago. But we take so easily to Mexaform because we live in a "pill" age and wish to have recourse to convenience rather than consult a physician or the village healer which involves loss of time. (D'Penha 1971:3)

The country's drug policy is in utter chaos. It has been promoting a "drug culture," the culture of reaching out for a drug on the slightest pretext. This pharmaceuticalisation of health opens up the country for loot by drug companies. (Ghosh 1986:1)

One cannot ignore the long-term effects of encouraging a poorly educated population to develop blind faith in the infallibility of modern medicine and the magical properties of prescribed pills. In India, people who are too poor to buy rice are being led to believe that they need a cough mixture for every cough, an antibiotic for every sore throat, and a tranquilizer to solve the problems of everyday life. (Greenhalgh 1987:316)

INTRODUCTION

In this chapter, I discuss the growing trend toward the commodification of health through pharmaceuticals in India today. Considered is the manner in which pharmaceutical policy, production and marketing, polypharmacy prescription patterns and self-help practices, cultural values, and collective anxieties affect consumer demand for particular medicine products. A point emphasized is that what is being sold to the Indian public today is the notion that health in the short-term can be derived through the consumption of medicines. At a time of increasing environmental deterioration (deforestation, erosion, pollution). rapid unplanned urbanization and industrialization, and related public health problems (Malhotra 1985), the capitalist promise of progress offsets health concerns. The premise that one can buy back health and well being with rising wages and greater access to medicines is popularized. In other words, health has increasingly taken on an "exchange value." The working class tacitly accepts capitalist ideology through their efforts of private appropriation of commodified health. This ideology is being swallowed along with the pills that embody it. Health practices involving medicine taking and giving constitute an agency of socialization where relations of power, dominance, and dependency take concrete form.

Three sets of interactive factors need to be considered if we are to understand the relationship between changing patterns of medicine consumption, sales, and production in India. First we need to appreciate the metamedical meanings associated with health products and the manner in which cultural values shape the succession of medical commodities developed to meet life exigencies. Second, we must contend with India's coexisting medical systems as they have been affected by the market economy and contribute to the commodification of health. Finally, we need to examine health policy as it affects the profitability and therefore production (marketing, etc.) of particular kinds of medicine.

A growing number of studies inspired by a world system approach to political economy have provided evidence of the strategies employed by multinational pharmaceutical companies seeking to secure new markets in developing countries for health products of questionable cost, relevance, and safety.[1] A conspiracy of interests is portrayed with the health and growth needs of the global capitalist industrial body pitted against the health of Third World bodies. These firms, through affiliates and subsidiaries, promote medications with exaggerated claims while downplaying or omitting information about side effects and hazards (Osifo 1983, Poh-ai 1985, Silverman, Lee, and Lydecker 1986, Silverman, Lydecker, and Lee 1992, Zawad 1985).[2] The indigenous "lumpen bourgeoisie" are characterized in some accounts as agents of medical colonization and underdevelopment who exploit and subject the interests of other classes in peripheral countries for the ultimate profit of capitalist in developed "center" countries.

While there is much truth to these claims, the world systems perspective is limited. As Worsley (1984) has noted, we need to look beyond studies of political economy to the agendas of real individuals and how they are influenced by economics and the social relations they entail. To understand pharmaceutical behavior in India, we need to explore the motivations underlying both the demand for and supply of medicines, a dynamic aptly referred to by Fabricant and Hirschhorn (1987) as "push–pull." Better comprehension of this dynamic is of crucial importance to those in international health as it affects both the public and private health sectors (Hercheimer and Stimson 1981).

Toward this end, I focus both on health products designed to meet culturally constituted health problems, and on the local marketing initiatives of indigenous and transnational pharmaceutical companies. Both operate in a context of intensive competition and changing government regulation. In the last ten years allopathic medicines have been the subject of regulation attempts responsive to both national and international health lobbying efforts.[3] Within this environment, there has been a proliferation of both allopathic and patent *āyurvedic* medicines, a range of medicines which I refer to as "ayurpathic medicines" (following John Laping [1984]). Reasons why these drugs are growing in popularity among both practitioners and consumers are considered.

In addition to drawing attention to the forces influencing medicine propagation, the social and environmental impact of health commodification needs to be explored. It is necessary to look beyond the economics of medical practice to the compartmentalization and decontextualization of health problems. In need of consideration are the ramifications of a growing illusion of false security rendered by the inflated claims of medicine fixes. A concern raised in this chapter is that the false consciousness generated by health commodification serves to undermine the impetus to participate in ecological/environmental-based popular health movements in a context where they are of crucial importance.[4]

AN OVERVIEW OF THE PHARMACEUTICAL INDUSTRY

Medicalization is not as dependent on the monopolization of the health sector by any one type of medical practitioner or medical tradition so much as on the microeconomic and political structure that facilitates the penetra-

tion of modern prepackaged pharmaceutical products, their use by a variety
of medical practitioners and by townspeople in curative and preventive regimes. (Ferguson 1981:127)

Let us first gain an overview of the magnitude of the pharmaceutical industry
in India. In India, pharmaceutical policy at once attempts to limit domination
by multinational pharmaceutical firms, yet fosters the proliferation of medicines in the medical market place in the name of free enterprise.

Estimates of the number of pharmaceutical companies in India jumped
from 3,600–4,000 in 1980 to 9,000 in 1986 (VHAI 1986, Jayaraman 1986a,
1986b), and 16,000 in 1988 (Rohde 1988).[5] While 15 companies dominate
the pharmaceutical market, the Government of India has supported scores of
small scale production units through fiscal incentives (Gothoskar 1983). This
policy has been implemented in part to break the monopolies of transnational
corporations and has resulted in a market where the production of medicine
products has escalated.[6] In comparison to Western countries where between
15,000 (UK) and 45,000 (USA) medicine formulations were available for
sale in 1986, approximately 60,000 commercial medicine products were
estimated to be available in India in 1986 (Jayaraman 1986a, 1986b, VHAI
1986), with current estimates exceeding 80,000 brand name products.[7] These
include standard allopathic medicines, "illogical" combinations of medications, and over-the-counter patent medicines marketed, if not developed, to
appeal to popular health concerns.[8]

Competition between pharmaceutical companies is keen. Promotional
expenses are comparable to those found in the West and exceed 5% of total
drug turnover revenues.[9] This figure is well in excess of government alloca-
tions for medications to Primary Health Centers (PHCs) designed to serve
the population at large. Rather than quote national figures to highlight this
point, let me cite local data from South Kanara District on expenditures by
pharmaceutical companies on the activities of their pharmaceutical representatives in the field. Bear in mind that my estimates are conservative and
do not include advertising costs and promotional gifts.

In South Kanara in 1976, approximately 70 pharmaceutical representatives (pharmaceutical reps) routinely visited doctors as well as a dozen
urban and 30 town based chemist shops. By 1986 the number of doctors and
chemist shops in the district had grown dramatically. Three hundred pharmaceutical reps routinely canvased South Kanara District with an additional
200 pharmaceutical reps occasionally visiting an estimated 1,000 doctors
and 109 chemist shops now found in the district.[10] Data were collected on the
activities of pharmaceutical reps from in-depth interviews and observations
of their visits to chemist and doctors in one town (pop. 15,000–20,000) in
1976, 1980, and 1986.

Let us consider data from 1980. During this year, most pharmaceutical reps spent between half to one full day meeting popular doctors and chemist shop owners in and around our sample town. On average, each chemist shop was visited by 10 pharmaceutical reps per day. Given 25 work days per month, at least 100 working days per month were invested in this town by pharmaceutical reps of various pharmaceutical companies. The starting salary for pharmaceutical reps was approximately Rs. 40 per day in 1980 (plus bonuses and Rs. 35 for travel and per diem expenses). Based on these figures, I estimated that Rs. 7,500 a month (Rs. 90,000 a year) was expended on the interpersonal sales activities of pharmaceutical reps to each mid-sized crossroads town in the district. As a point of comparison, the local hospital in this town was allocated a drug allotment worth one third this amount (Rs. 30,000) for the year 1980 to treat an outpatient load exceeding 150 patients per day.

THE COMMODIFICATION OF HEALTH

The term "commodification" has been used in a variety of different ways in the social science literature.[11] Let me therefore be specific about what I mean by the commodification of health. What I am referring to is the tendency to treat health as a state which one can obtain through the consumption of commodities, namely, medicine. This entails an objectification of the body, the decontextualization of sickness as disease (Young 1982), and an economy primarily based on "exchange (labor) value" in contrast to "use value." In its extreme form, health becomes dependent on medicine.

It is broadly recognized in India that an individual's health is contingent upon his/her constitutional endowment and circumstance. The latter is determined by one's physical environment, work, diet, lifestyle, etc., as well as the status of a perpetually changing cosmos spoken about in relation to stars and planets, spirits, and winds. While one's constitution can not be altered beyond changes which occur as part of the human life cycle, it may be managed through regimes (dietary and medical as well as ritual) which counterbalance excess, correct for deficiency, calm, and facilitate the processes of flow within. Circumstance can likewise be mediated. Where one's external environment is unhealthy, those able to purchase health-giving medicine products are able to obtain short-term health as a form of wealth.[12]

To some degree, this characterization oversimplifies the South Indians' association of health with prosperity and sickness with trouble. Health and illness are often deemed to be signs of more general socio-moral states. For the moment, however, let us focus on more immediate "functional" perceptions of health (Kelman 1975). This will enable me to highlight how particular health concerns are elaborated by marketing strategies which play upon collective anxieties and index cultural values.

In present day India, health commodification has been fostered by a rising concern about adulteration and environmental deterioration especially prominent among members of the low-middle to upper classes drawn toward a more cosmopolitan style of life. The upper classes in India, as everywhere, have the capacity to insulate themselves from an increasingly noxious environment. They have the means to create a separate personal environment, acquire imported foods from far off places where the rivers run pure, and purchase tonics and supplements to fill deficiencies and cleanse the blood. Among the less well-to-do, a concern about adulteration is well founded. This concern also serves as an expression of latent anxiety about alienation from cultural perceptions (and embodied habitus) of a "normal body" defined in terms of routine body signs (physical body) and social relations (social body).[13] Body signs (e.g., food transit time) and social relations (e.g., patterns of reciprocal exchange, respect, or entitlement) constitute parameters of well being often unobtainable in contexts of rapid change and modernization. This loss of a multidimensional sense of well being is articulated in many ways. For example, a loss of well being is often communicated through discourse about food, the substance from which health is derived and social relations constituted.

The act of eating and the institution of "taking meals" are events over which one exerts some sense of control in a universe where humans are subject to myriad influences ranging from gods and planets to sorcery and the economic fluctuations of the international market place. While control is realized through the routine of meal taking as a symbolic as well as a physical act, alienation and concern about one's internal milieu and external environment (see Chapter 4) are articulated through complaints about digestion. Digestive problems also serve as a metaphorical expression of social problems such as troubled family relations, feelings of passive aggression, powerlessness, etc. Improper digestion displayed through breaks in one's habitual diet raise a concern about shared identity and impurity in a culture maintaining what Mariott (1978) and Daniels (1984) have described as a fluid sense of self, instantiated through subtle exchange relations at the site of the body. Concern about digestion, weakness, and impurity articulated through poor appetite and medicine use index breaches in social relations as well as states of physical imbalance.

I point this out to argue that the commodification of health has not simply come about as a result of pharmaceutical agents peddling products of dependency or doctors trained to dispense expensive, rarified medicines. The situation is far more complex. A broader cultural context must be taken into account. As Ohnuki-Tierney (1986:77) has noted of Japan, commercialization does not occur in a vacuum: it plays upon deep seated cultural concepts and practices. The pharmaceutical industry has responded to, built upon, and perpetuated cultural concerns as well as capitalized on social insecurities and catered to novelty associated with changing values and appetites for new goods and services (Campbell 1989).[14]

Pharmaceuticalization

A context where functional health (the ability to perform work roles in the short-term) increasingly takes precedence over long-term concerns about well being is fertile ground for a flourishing trade in medical fixes. The proliferation of commercially prepared pharmaceuticals and a concurrent rise in medicine consumption as a response to everyday problems is a concrete expression of health commodification. Health commodities do not have to be pushed, they are demanded. The appeal of medicine is not simply the product of pharmaceutical marketing campaigns.[15] It is part of a much larger phenomenon represented by other fixes and fantasy escapes such as alcohol, movies, romance magazines and television. Just as movie stars in India are prone to fetishization by the masses and are even worshipped as gods, so medicines have likewise been attributed "powers" beyond their active ingredients. I refer here to their ability to render health and protect against sickness in general. In the words of one patron of a Bangalore city chemist shop:

> Whenever I feel an illness has come, I take antibiotics and Liv 52 for one or two days and I am protected. Whenever I feel weakness, I take tonic and when I cannot sleep I take Calmpose and Gastrogin. I have done this for five years and have no need for any doctor. It is the cheap and best way to stay healthy. I am satisfied.

The need for magic in an uncertain world is fodder for pharmaceutical companies who sell medicines to both consumers off the street (through chemist shops) and to practitioners who require some amount of mystification to survive in a competitive medical marketplace. In a context where medicine is freely available over-the-counter, there is continual need for doctors to offer something new to patients. One marketing specialist of a large multinational drug company explained the situation to me as follows:

> You see it is all a case of *brand vitality* and *brand fatigue*. We introduce a medicine and it is popular for some time among practitioners who are our good customers. In many cases, sales peak, level off and then decline. Brand

fatigue has set in. The public purchases the drug, but doctors purchase less because it is a known thing. We monitor sales continually. When brand fatigue occurs a new product will be marketed. Sometimes this drug will be constituted out of a combination of popular products. Brand fatigue drives a market where a limited number of pharmaceutical compounds are differentiated largely by claims, names, and images of potency.[16]

The pharmaceutical industry happily supplies practitioners with a steady stream of new medicines complete with inflated promises, research testimonials, and statistics. The development of new products provides the illusion of progress and breakthroughs. The industry is in turn supported by a state apparatus attempting to nurture a "healthy economy" and create an image of improved health through the increased availability of medical resources. Medicines constitute visible and tangible proof of increasing well being. Commodified health plays an important role as a fetish of modernization. On this note it is worth mentioning that the regulation of pharmaceuticals in India does not fall under the direct authority of the Ministry of Health (dealing with physical bodies), but the Ministry of Petroleum, Chemicals, and Fertilizer, which has a vested interest in the health of the country's industrial body and the exchange of goods in a world system (Sadasivam 1993).

The Appeal of Medicine Advertisements

Medicine advertising in India exploits popular imagery associated with modernization, grass roots nationalization and the fetishization of cultural tradition, and group fantasy as well as anxiety. Its success lies largely in presenting products in such a manner as to interpellate existing health concerns, perceived needs, and tacit desires (Goldman 1992). Medicines are associated with metamedical values through key symbols and images evoking networks of semantic meaning. As Good (1977) has clearly demonstrated in Iran, illnesses are imbued with cultural meanings. Advertising over-determines the capacities of drugs with exaggerated claims which address symptoms, popular health concerns, and associated cultural meanings. This fosters the process of pharmaceuticalization, a term designating the appropriation of human problems to medicines. The latter may be distinguished from medicalization where appropriation by the medical profession gains monopoly power and increased social control in territories of human experience.

In India, the monopoly power of the medical profession is weak. Doctors are administrators of medicine and subject to a client dominant competitive health care arena (Friedson 1970) where catering to patients' wishes and expectations keeps one in business (see Chapter 8). Peer review is weak. As such, doctors are closely tied to the pharmaceutical industry which offers them the resources to remain competitive. The range of products made available is significantly influenced, if not largely determined, by the profit needs of doctors and the pharmaceutical industry, not by the health needs of the country as defined by epidemiological or nutritional data.[17]

The advertising industry has the task of creating an illusion of progress for both the medical profession and consumers of health care. The illusion is that there are products available which are capable of treating each and every symptom and health problem. The appeal of medicine promises was noted by one town doctor having limited means of diagnosis, yet the pressure of competition and rising patient expectations:

> We are not fools, but we want to be fooled. We need to believe that we can do wonders in an impossible situation. I know better than to believe in these broad spectrum antibiotics and tonics, the wide use of steroids, and other such things. But the nature of my practice, the demands on my time, the limited understanding of my patients leads me to give what I am told is best by the companies with the biggest names. Then I can say I am recommending the most prestigious medicines to a patient. And the patient is happy. As a doctor I must diagnose not only the disease but the prestige and the pocketbook of my patients. Definitely, I am influenced by the advertising. That last patient, the Muslim woman who attended with the baby and a two year old child, has been either nursing a child or pregnant for the last five years. Her husband is a timber contractor. She is anemic and weak but tonight her husband will come to her. I could give her iron tablets and offer her advice about diet, and if I did she would never be back and I will have lost a client. So, I recommend a new forte tonic called "Mother's Milk" and I give her a B_{12} injection and I think 'yes, she needs these things' and the tonic may have some trace minerals she needs. We all feel better. The tonic costs Rs. 20 but her husband can afford it. In fact, that beautiful bottle with the picture of a blossoming mother will be shown to all in his house and they will think her husband is a wonderful chap for purchasing it and they will praise me.

The symbolic importance of medicine, especially tonic, will be addressed shortly. For the moment, let me raise concern about the fetishization of medicine by way of a case vignette. In 1984 while visiting a friend in rural South Kanara, I observed a young man, aged 20, diligently reading a medicine advertisement in a newly arrived Kannaḍa weekly magazine. He marveled at this advertisement for an analgesic which promised to relieve pain in minutes. This advertisement showed the transformation of a somewhat cranky mother-in-law into a kind, doting woman inquiring into the welfare of her daughter-in-law after using the product. My inquiries into the young man's interpretation of this advertisement led him to discuss other medicines he had read about and dreamed of purchasing.[18] These included a tonic to give him increased strength through better digestion, a blood purification medicine, a glucose solution named Electrose which he described as "electronic solution" for tiredness (advertised as a glucose solution supplemented by electrolytes), flatulence tablets to take when travelling, liver tablets for giddiness, and other assorted products.[19] From my conversation with this young man and several other literate rural youths, I came to realize that claims of medicine efficacy were often accepted quite literally by this population.[20] Medicines promised magic. As with magic, some medicines were deemed to be authentic sources of power while others were considered to be the bogus product of some imposter trying to dupe the public. In principal, the claims of popular commercial companies were believed, especially if they were foreign. Foreign medicine was held in high esteem, for after all, as this young man noted, "had not Western peoples even travelled to the moon, a fact known to every schoolboy!"

A curious request during my stay led me to consider the fetishism of medicine more personally. One day I was asked by the young man's uncle if I would administer a "foreign" medicine and prepare a talisman for this young man against his fear of the dark. His fear was so severe that it prevented him from leaving the house to urinate at night. My friend's request had to do with the young man's deep seated belief in medicine advertisements and foreign products. Visits to local exorcists had already failed and the family did not wish the stigma attached to bringing the boy to a psychiatrist. My friend had told the boy that as part of my research I had studied exorcism from a renowned exorcist prior to his death. This was partially true in that I had observed this exorcist's practice for several months as part of my Ph.D fieldwork in the mid-1970s. To make a long story short, I prepared a talisman according to a procedure documented in my field notes and offered it to the young man along with a 5 mg tablet of Valium removed from my "overnight bus ride survival kit."[21] The treatment proved to be temporarily effective. The young man felt secure to walk within a radius of 20 feet from the house at night, just far enough to reach a suitable tree behind which to urinate.

I introduce this story to emphasize three points. First, although I had been studying medicine consumption behavior for several years, I had not appreciated how concretely advertisements were interpreted by some members of the population who are less exposed to media hype and critical assessment of exaggerated claims. A notable absence of social science research has been conducted on cultural interpretations and constructions of medicine advertisements and how they change over time as a population becomes more inundated by ads and marketing promotions.[22] A second point is that the request for me to give the young man medicine as well as a talisman was in itself indicative of local recognition that the two work well together. An increasing number of exorcists in South Kanara employ medicines with sacred verse (*mantra*) and talismans. In the 1970s most exorcists I observed were covert about their use of medicines. Some secretly ground up raulofia serpentine tablets commercially available in *āyurvedic* chemist shops and mixed them with turmeric and lime paste which they presented to patients as a substance embodying the power/presence of a deity (*prasāda*) associated with their rituals. Although I was only told about this practice once, I discovered its wider prevalence during research at two popular *āyurvedic* medicine shops in Mangalore city which supplied exorcists with these medicines. By the mid-1980s this pattern of medicine use was shifting. Three out of six exorcists whom I had the opportunity to observe during field trips in the mid-1980s used allopathic medicines in their practice. These medicines were acquired from chemists or from doctor friends. In some cases, use of diazepam or other "calming" drugs (e.g., antianxiety drugs, sedatives, antidepressants) were given to the patients secretly (i.e., in *prasāda*), while in other cases pills were directly dispensed.

A third point underscored by the story reconfirms Alland's (1970) observation that it is often Western medicines rather than "Western medicine" which appeals to non-Western populations. The young man's perceptions of the cause of his fear of the dark were strictly humoral and spirit linked. His fears were associated with a scare ("shock") he had experienced in the night during a high fever when he saw spirits hovering outside waiting to devour his flesh. Medicines promising to control fever and pain, reduce anxiety, and increase confidence appealed to him, not a medical system per se. Indeed, among those medicines on his wish list of drugs to purchase were a mixture of ayurpathic, homeopathic and allopathic drugs. As he gazed into my first aid kit one evening, he sighed and told me that with such medicines one could go anywhere without fear.

THE PHARMACEUTICAL INDUSTRY'S RESPONSE TO "DOUBLE THINK" AND CULTURAL ISOLATION

Not all Indian villagers read advertisements as concretely as the young man described above nor do they ascribe special positive powers to all that is distant and modern.[23] The positive and negative aspects of medicines are discussed by an increasing number of people, medicine stories are told and retold, and ideas abound about the virtues and problems of taking various types of medicines. Medicines are tried and evaluated, often upon the basis of cultural criteria. Advertisements guide medicine searches through promises as well as the offsetting of health concerns associated with medicine taking.

In an advanced capitalist economy a constant stream of new products enters the marketplace and challenges the market share of previous products. These products make claims about being unique or associate themselves with the virtues of past products which have been improved. This is certainly true in India where it is estimated a new product enters the pharmaceutical market every other day. To position these drugs, the virtues of both traditional medicine and bioscience are embraced and coopted.

Life is pervaded by paradoxes, by both continuities and discontinuities. Many people long for both the modern and the traditional, a condition which the late J. P. Naik characterized as "double think."[24] The pharmaceutical industry has responded to this paradox in a variety of ways. Modern forms of traditional medicine have been marketed as the wisdom of past ages, and have been reaffirmed as scientific through the use of biochemical terms and Latin nomenclature. Modern medicines, on the other hand, have been marketed to accord with traditional values. In some cases, allopathic medicines have even been credited with being modern forms of ancient medicines (Burghart 1988).[25]

Tradition is embodied through medicine consumption. Each region and cultural group has had its own share of entrepreneurs who have appealed to caste affiliation in their efforts to sell commodified answers to health problems in a changing world. Cultural affiliation has itself been commodified. Just as Evans Pritchard once wrote that the Nuer consume the soil of their place to maintain a metonymical association with the land, so South Kanarese migrants to Bombay, Bangalore, and the Middle East consume locally manufactured traditional medicines as a means of evoking collective remembrances. Medicine become symbolic and affective resources which play a role in identity construction. Collective memories of the ideals of village life are reexperienced by migrants to Bombay, especially the elderly.[26] This is illustrated in the following interview with a South Kanarese informant who had relocated to Bombay.

> **Anthropologist:** You have just told me you use *draksha aristha* (an *āyurvedic* tonic) made by the Shastri family in Mangalore. Is this the only company from whom you purchase this medicine?

> **Informant:** Yes, I use this tonic only. The tonic is sent to me by my elder sister, or sometimes I purchase it here from a chemist who is also from South Kanara. I buy other medicines from Germany, England, Bombay,

and Calcutta. But the *draksha aristha* we use and the *dasamoola aristha* used by my wife after her delivery are always Shastri brand.

Anthropologist: Are there other brands of these medicines which are of good quality?

Informant: There are many good companies and *vaidya* who prepare such medicines.

Friend of informant: He waters his roots with his Kanarese medicine! (Laughter follows …)

Informant: Yes, it is true. It is of my place. My sister also sends me *koḍi maddu* (a traditional herbal home remedy) to give to my children at the time of year when new buds appear on the trees at home. We are protected by these things. They are from our place. Our people have taken them for many long years.

In this interview a relationship between ancestral home (*mūla sthāna*) and present place of residence is established through the consumption of medicines. This constitutes a secular act akin to the sending of blessed substances (*prasāda*) from rituals at local South Kanarese temples to the homes of those living outside by kin within the district. At times of vulnerability, *prasāda* from home deities is consumed for health and protection. The gift of medicine and *prasāda* articulates social relations involving affiliation, care, reciprocity, and social support.

The taking of *āyurvedic* medicine also provides a means of embodying traditional values in a commodified form. For some, the taking of *āyurvedic* medicine constitutes a medicinal rite-de-passage, a return to a life of balance, purity, proper flow, and a transformed sense of self (Nichter 1981a). In this instance, medicine taking serves metamedical purposes. Through the consumption of medicine, a person may engage in the production of a new moral identity.[27]

FACTORS PROMOTING THE COMMODIFICATION OF HEALTH

The competitive marketing and manufacture of commercial medicines in India began in the 19th century, but it was not until post independence that the medicine market experienced rapid growth (Leslie 1989). Market expansion was no doubt fostered by the setting up of a national health service which placed the public in closer contact with doctors and the remarkable demonstration effect of antibiotics. In the last two decades, several factors have increased public acceptance of, if not dependence on, commercial medicines. As noted in Chapter 8, the very fact that rural practitioners are paid through the dispensing of medicines encourages polypharmacy for each and every ailment.[28] This has led people to become accustomed to receiving medicines for all health problems. It has also helped foster a "pill for every ill" mentality with has increased the purchase of over-the-counter medicines from a growing number of chemist shops. Between the early 1970s and late 1980s I observed a marked lowering of the threshold of discomfort among South Kanara's rural population. More and more people turned to commercial medicines when symptoms arose which would have been treated previously with herbal remedies, if at all.[29] Cultural conventions influencing somatic expression of distress (Nichter 1981b) have also influenced the use of medicine fixes to manage negative emotional states. Medicine taking is an "expressive moment." Myriad medicine products are now available in India for the home treatment of problems (*dōśa*) associated with emotional distress. These medicines have come to constitute new symbolic resources available for articulating metamedical messages from the body of one experiencing distress to significant others.[30]

Consistent with the growing popularity of the term "psychosomatic," practitioners have increasingly begun utilizing mild tranquilizers in the treatment of vague body states which they associate with somatization. Between 1974 and 1986, four chemist shops which I regularly monitored during biyearly visits to South Kanara all reported significant rises in the amount of diazepam used for patient care.[31] For example, in one chemist shop observed in a small crossroads town in 1986, diazepam sales averaged 500 tablets a day compared to sales of 150 tablets a day in 1983. The shop did not report a significant rise in mean clients per day and was not identified as a special source for this common medication. Several doctors whom I monitored during the early 1980s routinely administered diazepam and vitamins to patients complaining of general somatic complaints. In the 1970s, they treated such complaints with vitamin tonics alone. By 1980, the brand name Calmpose had become familiar to both urban and rural residents of South Kanara.[32]

A case study may highlight the use of tranquilizers and antidepressants as a fix for patients presenting vague somatic complaints to doctors. In 1987, I visited the household of a former neighbor, a robust woman in her late 40s whose wit and playful scolding I remembered well. Upon entering her house I was struck by her lassitude and awaited a tale of tragedy. Instead, I found that the family's fortune had improved. The woman's two daughters were married and living nearby, a daughter-in-law had given birth to a healthy grandson who busily played in the courtyard, and the family's debts had been paid off. Inquiring about the woman's health she spoke of a set of symptoms she had presented to me seven years before, symptoms characteristic of anemia and folic acid deficiency. She stated:

> Your medicines helped me the most. They cured the cracking (angular stomatitis) at the corners of my mouth and gave me blood. The doctor's medicines I take now give me good sleep and a good appetite, but I am weak and can not work as I did before. I eat rice gruel and sit quietly, but my mouth is always dry and I am constipated.

Upon examining the woman's medication, I found that she had been taking an antidepressant daily for over a year. Yet a long discussion with her family, whom I knew well, revealed little evidence of anxiety, sadness, or physical symptoms associated with depression. I became curious as to why this woman had been prescribed the medication. I interviewed the practitioner who had prescribed the medicine as well as family members who had accompanied the woman to the doctor. The practitioner had last seen the woman two weeks prior to my visit and recalled the woman as continually complaining of weakness, heat sensations, and slowly moving blood. His diagnosis was that she was suffering from psychosomatic problems related to menopause. During a consultation with the doctor, she volunteered the opinion that perhaps her weakness was related to irregular menstruation and impure blood trapped within her body leading to sluggishness and heat manifested as mouth sores. Presented with these complaints, the doctor interpreted them to be indicative of a psychosomatic problem. The woman's notion of a somatic imbalance within her body was taken as a mental imbalance which the doctor wrongly assumed was linked to unhappy social relations at home. He treated her accordingly. Paradoxically, she came to depend on the medication for an altered perception of health. While her weakness and mouth sores remained, her state of health became redefined in relation to good sleep and appetite. Minimal health was now purchased.

The commodification of health is influenced by many factors ranging from the medicine dispensing practices of doctors and the somatization of distress to perceptions that physical ailments are to be expected as the price one pays for working in a deteriorating environment. For example, digestive complaints are reported to be on the increase by almost all of my long-term lay and practitioner informants. Contributing to this increase may well be the frank adulteration of food, insecticide residue poisoning, and increased consumption of hotel food exposing a greater number of people to disease transmission by unhygienic food handling.[33] Irrespective of the biomedical causes of digestive complaints, they are commonly interpreted by the lay population in humoral terms. This has led many people to routinely consume medications to clean their blood, remove gas (*vāyu*), and improve digestive power as a means of obtaining health in an unhealthy environment.

Concerns about occupational health also lead some people to adopt medicine consumption as a preventive health practice. For example, health commodification reasoning fosters the purchase of tonic by *beedie* cigarette rollers. Tonic is consumed as a means of promoting health while engaging in a vocation recognized to be unconducive to health. The allocation of resources for tonic to *beedie* rollers when they display lassitude associated with the monotony of their work to some extent mitigates the concern of household members. Care and concern are articulated through medicine as a symbol as well as a resource.

The practice of consuming medicines as a means of promoting health is not new. In India, what is new is the range of products available and the range of problems targeted by those marketing medicine. In addition to familiar health concerns has been the addition of new concerns associated with changes in lifestyle and consumer behavior. Medicine products have emerged on the market that not only profess to purify the blood following the consumption of adulterated food, but also following the consumption of allopathic medicines. For those who fear that cosmopolitan medicines render the blood impure, products like "Liv Up" and "Triveng" are available to protect against constipation and weakness "resulting from antibiotic use." Many practitioners address popular concerns by dispensing an eclectic mix of medicines designed to reduce the symptoms of disease as well as the side effects of medicines. Charles Leslie's observation made two decades ago seems very apropos today:

> There is a joke in India that says it doesn't matter whether you consult a *hakim* or a doctor, you will get penicillin anyway. But the joke could be turned around to say it doesn't matter whether you consult a doctor or a *hakim*, your penicillin will be supplemented with a regimen and tonics of unani or *āyurvedic* origin. (Leslie 1967]

TONICS: A SPECIAL CASE OF HEALTH COMMODIFICATION

> Dabur Chyawanprash is a tonic for our times. It toughens you up from deep within.... Are your children frequently ill? Your children don't need to be in a vicious cycle of pills and more pills and harsh chemicals and more reduced resistance. (Product ad in *Times of India*, Bombay edition, 1993)

> Thirty Plus for those in the fast lane. Prevent fatigue, look fresh, resist stress, protect your liver and slow down premature aging caused by stress and

environmental pollution. You will wonder how you ever managed to get through your day without it! (Product ad in *Times of India*, Bombay edition 1993)

A majority of the population surveyed have the erroneous view that daily consumption of tonics is essential to health. It is necessary to remember that nutrition can not be built across the pharmacy counter. (Krishnaswamy and Kumar 1983:4)

Tonic consumption constitutes a clear case of health commodification. A pharmaceutical company executive once described India to me as "a nation addicted to tonics." There is a long tradition of liquid tonic use in India associated with *āyurvedic* restorative and rejuvenation medicines (*rasāyana*). Pharmaceutical companies have responded to the popularity of tonics by competing for a market share of this profitable sector. Their marketing strategies have included extensive mass media advertising campaigns as well as intensive interpersonal sales efforts aimed at practitioners and chemists. Interpersonal marketing has been deemed especially important given that tonics are fairly similar and that brand loyalty for tonics among doctors often carries over into self-purchase behavior by satisfied patients.

Arduous attempts to win over practitioners to specific brands of tonic are understandable considering that before regulation changes in 1983, vitamin preparations were allowed a 100% markup over production costs in comparison to a 40% markup for essential drugs. More recent regulations reduced potential profits to 60% over production costs. In 1983, vitamin sales accounted for nearly two thirds of Pfizer's in-country profits and one third of Abbot's total production of medicines. These companies joined with Glaxo, the country's largest producer of nonstandard vitamin combinations, in protest of new regulations which reduced their profits significantly. A spokesperson for the pharmaceutical companies was quoted as stating that:

If profitable areas of operation became unprofitable then present subsidized production of essential drugs would inevitably stop, leading to scarcity and increased imports.[34]

In this context it is worth noting that in the 1980s roughly 10% of drug formulations in India were vitamins, accounting for 15% of total drug production costs. More than 800 micro and macro nutrient supplements were listed in the Indian *Pharmaceutical Guide* in 1986. While in the early 1980s there was a decline in the total percentage of drugs produced in India classified as life saving and essential drugs, there was an increase in the production of tonics and nonessential drugs. Ironically, the content of popular vitamin tonics often does not match the country's nutritional deficiencies and tonics have been criticized as being an enormous economic waste. Jaya

Rao (1977) and more recently Krishnaswamy, Kumar, and Radhaiah (1983) and Greenhalgh (1987) have pointed out that B-complex drugs which are widely prescribed and self-purchased in India are often not warranted:

> Combinations of B complex containing B_1, B_2, B_6, B_{12} and other vitamins rank first among sales, whereas vitamin B_2 and iron deficiency anaemia are most often encountered in the population. Vitamin B-complex in various combinations and forte preparations are being used without any scientific rationale. These preparations are one of the five largest selling drugs in the country. (Krishnaswamy and Kumar 1983:4)

My interviews with consumers engaged in the self-purchase of B-complex preparations leads me to suspect that the action of this medication is a) widely interpreted in terms of popular images of the liver and bile (*pitta*) strongly influenced by humoral medical tradition, and b) associated with an impression that B vitamins are necessary to counteract the weakening effects of antibiotic use. Doctors and chemists are not simply prescribing or suggesting tonics to "humor" patients. There are economic incentives at stake. Company incentives range from promotional gifts to high profit margins when tonics are directly sold.[35]

Let me briefly present data from South Kanara on the rise in tonic use. In 1979–80, two town chemist shops were monitored. Approximately 10% of the total sales of these shops were for liquid tonics involving approximately 20% of their customers. This amounted to the sale of 20–30 bottles of tonic a day. During this time period, approximately three quarters of 82 poor to lower middle class households participating in a community diagnosis project (Nichter 1984a) reported that a tonic had been prescribed to one or more members by a doctor during the previous year. In many cases, informants stated tonics were recommended each time they received a prescription chit from a practitioner. During a short field visit to the district in 1983, I interviewed members of some ($n = 60$) of the same households. The following table summarizes the data collected on bottles of tonic (*āyurvedic* and allopathic) actually purchased by these households (as distinct from bottles prescribed) during 1979 and 1983 (see Table 9.1).

In each of the three sites, tonic use had increased over the four year period of time.[36] Increases were especially significant among town and village households. Additionally, between 1979 and 1983 the mean number of bottles of tonic consumed by user households rose from slightly less than two bottles per year to over three bottles at an average cost of Rs. 45 in 1983 as compared to Rs. 26 in 1979. One week observational studies of two town chemist shops in 1983 revealed that approximately 20% of their total sales and 45% of prescriptions involved nutritional supplements — a doubling

Table 9.1

Percentage of Households Purchasing Tonic

Locale	Sample size	1979	1983
City	20	90%	100%
Town	20	65%	85%
Village	20	25%	55%

over a 4–5 year period of time.[37] In 1986, an estimate of tonic sales was secured from a representative of a large pharmaceutical company who had worked in the district for over a decade. According to his sales figures, there was a 25% rise in district sales of tonics between 1978–86. Between 30 and 40% of his total sales were for tonics. Questioned as to what were his company's three fastest selling sales items, he noted tonics, antacids, and antiamoebics.

During interviews with chemists and physicians between 1980 and 1990 I was routinely told that tonic had "become a fashion" at a time when money was more readily available. One young doctor interviewed just after completion of his rural based social and community medicine rotation stated:

These people do not place importance on changing their diet once a sufficient amount of rice is eaten. When they are ill they consume less for some days which we have learned will interfere with immunity and catch up growth among children. We tell them to eat eggs and to take milk and fruits and they say, "we are poor people, we can not afford these things." But sir, I do not believe this is the truth. These people will buy tonic for Rs. 15 or 20 and feel happy if we prescribe it. They will not change their diet for more than a few days, if that, and then only because they think diet is necessary for the medicine they are taking. I used to scold them and then I returned to my family home and observed the tonic bottle "worshipped" there too! I have been blind to this. My mother has some *aristha* cure-all and my brother's wife her "forte" vitamins and glucose packets, and my younger brother takes *āyurvedic* capsules for strength. Tonics have become a fashion. In the old days there were not many types to choose from, but today there are so many. Just as people have become more interested in different fashion clothes, they are now interested in different fashion tonics.

Discussions in a town and village area with laypersons in the process of purchasing tonics suggested that the increasing popularity of tonic was related to changing perceptions of the quality of food and changes in lifestyle. One town informant noted:

> I buy a bottle of tonic every couple of months and it lasts for two weeks. For health I should drink it daily, but usually I buy a bottle when I need strength or my wife feels weakness or there is some sickness. Five years ago I took tonic only when I was sick and the doctor gave me a chit to bring it. Now it is a common thing among the people. Why? Life has changed. It's like fuel for cooking. Five years ago, we used firewood. Then the price rose and we used kerosene and then there was rationing so we changed to an electric hot plate. At first I did not like the change, the food had less taste, but cooking was easy. Food tastes better when it is cooked in mud pots over firewood, everyone will tell you this in India even if they are a rich person. But now aluminum and stainless steel pots and gas or kerosene are used for cooking because it is easy and quick. It is like that with tonic. Ten years ago, even five years ago, good quality local rice was available here. Now, nobody grows and hand pounds local rice for sale. Today I go to the shop and buy a mixed thing — chinese rice, IR-8 — a hybrid rice, and rice from upghats (other districts in the Deccan plateau). I am not sure of this rice. It does not have the taste of the rice I ate as a boy nor the strength, but it is available and I buy it because it is easy. So I take tonic for strength, it is also easy. After some time of taking it you develop a habit for it and then you feel you need this tonic to be healthy. Now we are a country of tonic drinkers.

A low-middle class villager noted:

> My daughter has complained of weakness and heat since winter season when she was in hospital and was given medicine for fever. That medicine was very powerful. The fever was cured but she became weak. Now she needs tonic every month. English medicine is like the new hybrid rice strains we receive from your country. They mature faster and give bigger yields but when we plant them it is necessary to add other things to the field or troubles come. Like that, after using English medicine for my daughter, she must have tonic for her health.

Revealed in the above quotes from several informants was a sense that tonics were increasingly needed because of a decline in the quality of life. Tonics offer an easy way to compensate for deficiencies resulting from an impoverished diet perceived in terms of the quality of staple foods.[38] Responding to this impression, a high level pharmaceutical marketing executive told me that nutrient supplements like Horlicks and Bournvita sold much better in South India where people perceived the quality of their foodstuffs as questionable and felt some "deficiency." For this reason, his firm advertised a line of products to fill the "food gap." In North India, I was told, blood purifying tonics are more popular because this population is more concerned about the quality of their blood as affected by non-vegetarian foods. Whether this impression is true or not, his firm played up these themes in their regional advertising campaigns.

Another reason for tonic popularity highlighted in the two narrative segments noted above, was the feeling that modern life entailed reliance on allopathic medicines for short-term functional health. This required tonic use to compensate for extra demands on the body. Tonic use became the price one pays for modern living and the use of modern medicine. Several inform-ants spoke of tonics as a "habit" not simply a fashion, a habit in the sense of a dependency. For the capitalist system, the ultimate measure of success is to have a population not only desire a product which sustains a mode of production, but a population which feels that they "need" and "depend" on this product for their well being. Health productivity and happiness are redefined in relation to the commodity fixes.

This is the market message of several *āyurvedic* tonics such as Dabur Chyawanprash and Ajanta Thirty Plus, as well as a host of other products which capture the popular imagination through creative advertising. The woes of modern living are depicted as well as the negative impact of modern medicines on the body. *Āyurveda*'s ancient answer for modern health needs is provided through products such as Pepcaps, Revital, Triveng, and Aswal Plus which claim to be "immunomodulating" as well as "adaptogenic." Such products promise to "reduce stress" and to "increase resistance to adverse stimuli."[39] The collective message of hundreds of these products is that the environment and the demands of a changing lifestyle place one at risk. Products promise to adapt one's internal environment to the stresses of modern living in a context where there is little one can do about his/her external environment. A promise of both protection and control is sold in a rapidly changing world where prosperity is being paid for at the site of the body. Luckily, ancient solutions to modern problems are available at a cost.[40] Solutions are found in 3,000 year old *āyurvedic* texts as well as in the medical tradition of foreign lands — as the successful marketing of Ginseng products (such as Thirty Plus) bears witness.

The use of tonics has altered over the last two decades. During my initial fieldwork in the mid-1970s, I collected data on tonic use during a study of pregnancy and postpartum related behavior. Among the poor to low middle classes, tonic was an important felt health need during these times and following any surgical operation. Aside from these times, tonic was only purchased at the recommendation of a doctor. Today, tonics are as commonly purchased without a prescription as with one, and tonics are as likely to be purchased for health as for illness.

To some degree, tonic use has come to reflect a sense of prosperity as well as an act of health promotion. Tonic sales peak among agricultural laborers just after harvest season, a time when food is more plentiful. A rise in over-the-counter tonic sales also signals a broad change in attitudes toward the use of commercial medicines. A marked increase in the substitution of commercial tonics for home prepared tonics and herbal medicines has also taken place.

For years practitioners have prescribed tonics for general bodily complaints presented by patients in accord with physical sensations, felt health concerns, and perceptions of body processes. Practitioners often reason that these symptoms are linked to some kind of malnutrition and feel that tonics "might help and can't hurt" in a situation where something has to be given as a tangible form of care and a means of collecting payment. Over time, tonics have come to be expected by the public. Today, the Indian population both requests prescriptions for tonics and uses them for self-care for an increasing variety of bodily complaints. Interviews on the action of tonics associated them with: strength, vigor, blood quantity, blood quality, blood circulation and distribution, the liver, digestion, a balancing of humors and hot/cold, and among some educated informants acid and alkaline blood. Given a wide range of tonics from pluralistic medical traditions, a variety of options exist for managing health problems through tonic use. If one tonic does not produce desired results, there is always another one to try. Let me cite an example illustrating how the range of tonics can influence patterns of health care seeking.

On one memorable occasion in 1983 I observed a patient request tonic for bloodlessness from a PHC doctor for a case involving hookworm infestation resulting in acute anemia. "Doctor," the woman implored, "tonic please." The doctor struggled to convince the patient not to rely on tonic as a cure for her weakness. He prescribed medicine to remove the worms and ferrous sulfate tablets for her anemia. An experienced health center peon informed the doctor that local people avoided worm medicine during monsoon season. During this time of climatic extremes it was considered dangerous for deworming especially when a person was ill and weak. The doctor thought for a moment and then told the woman that if she drank tonic the worms would only drink the tonic and grow fat, increasing their hunger and causing them to become even more troublesome. She was told that the worms must be removed and was given the prescription.

I sent my field assistant to find out what in fact the woman would do. Shortly after leaving the health center, she visited an *āyurvedic* compounder asking for a tonic to give her strength, but one which was bitter, one which would not be consumed by worms which preferred sweet things. Her action was creative and reflected an attempt to reconcile local knowledge and doctor's knowledge. A medicine tonic was sought which was concordant with her ideas about health, risk and the nature of worms.

Three last points may be made concerning tonic use. First, offering tonic to a friend or family member is a means of articulating care and concern. On a number of occasions I have witnessed a husband express affection and concern for his wife or mother through the gift of a bottle of tonic. In critiquing tonic as an economic waste, we must not be so hasty as to overlook the psychosocial importance of tonic exchange and the meaning of tonic as a symbol of well being. Beyond a strict biomedical gaze, we need to consider both the way tonic is used to communicate both distress and concern.

A second point considers how gender and generational relations related to powerlessness are depicted in tonic advertisements.[41] Weakness is a polysemous term which indexes social as well as physical strength and is commonly used as an idiom of distress in India. Tonic advertisements commonly play off images of vulnerability. Young adults who are in the process of establishing a sense of personal and social identity are especially susceptible to such messages. In India this population commonly seeks medicines for weakness although they are in the prime of their physical health.

Observations at a popular *āyurvedic* chemist shop in Mangalore revealed that it was this age group who most frequently purchased tonic without a prescription. Tonic sales were a major source of income for the shop. A review of monthly sales records revealed that 15% of all medicines sold were to women for tonic associated with weakness with an additional 5% of medicines sold for leukorrhea associated with weakness. Another 13% of sales were for male rejuvenation tonics for increasing strength and general vitality. In sum, one third of all shop sales were for tonics associated with adults (aged 18–35).[42]

A final point pertains to children. An important sector of India's expanding tonic market is comprised of tonics for children.[43] Glucose powder has long been marketed in India as a tonic for children as well as for those convalescing. Today, glucose is being superseded by products advertised as more modern sources of health and vitality which active children require. Middle class parents who once purchased an occasional packet of glucose or a monthly can of Horlicks or Bournvita food supplement to augment "poor diet and a child's special needs" are a niche targeted by pharmaceutical companies. An increasing number of products have appeared on the market in the last 5–10 years to improve child health and enhance brain power in a competitive world. Among these products are electrolyte solutions promoted not for dehydration, but for energy. Presented with a box of Electrose brand oral rehydration solution, several town informants interviewed in 1986 associated the product with sports and power. As noted earlier, a popular name for this and similar rehydration products was "electronic solution." In a world where the media directs increasing emphasis toward computers and where satellite dishes are appearing in villages, electronic solution represents the embodiment of modernity in contrast to the balancing of humors, and for that matter, electrolytes.

HOME TREATMENT, CHEMIST SHOPS, AND THE COMMODIFICATION OF HEALTH

Let us return to the observation that self-treatment with home remedies is rapidly being replaced by commercial medications in South Kanara. Home treatment has traditionally played an important role in health care in South Kanara for a wide range of ailments.[44] Survey research carried out in 1975 and again in 1979 revealed that among poor to lower middle class non-Brahmans, home care is most prevalent for preschool children, women, and the elderly.[45]

The form of home care is rapidly changing. In the mid-1970s, the use of commercial medicines in the home was fairly limited and primarily observed in nuclear single-generational households where elders were rarely present. During a household survey in 1975, I found that members of such households often remembered the function of local herbal preparations, but were vague about preparation details and dosage. They were twice as likely to have purchased ready made *āyurvedic* and cosmopolitan medicines as those living in multigenerational households. Today, this pattern has diminished. Increased familiarity with commercial medicines has encouraged active experimentation guided by the suggestions of friends and shopkeepers alike.

In the 1980s, commercial medicines have rapidly become popular home care resources for many common illnesses including diarrheal and respiratory conditions. Informants speak of the ease of taking commercially prepared medicines as opposed to the time consuming process of boiling herbs into decoctions. In addition, they note that when a person takes traditional medicines, this requires stringent dietary regulations. The use of commercial products is often rationalized by statements to the effect that raw herbal products no longer have the power they once did due to pesticides, insecticides, and chemical fertilizers. Increased familiarity with a growing number of chemist shops has been facilitated by better transportation and more patent medicines have become available at provision shops. Medicines which have been prescribed time and again are recognized and rising literacy has exposed more people to advertisements. All of these factors have had an influence on self-help patterns.

Increased cash flow and disposable income in the 1980s have also fostered more vigorous health consumerism. Pharmaceutical companies have recognized this change and targeted rural areas for more intensive marketing campaigns. I was informed by one pharmaceutical marketing executive that the rural sector was given only minimal attention by his company prior to the mid-1970s. With agricultural change and new wealth in rural areas, marketing efforts have been stepped up. He estimated that in India as a whole, rural per capita medicine expenditure in 1981 was Rs. 20 while in 1986 it was two to two and a half times this amount. This estimate is remarkably close to my own approximations of expenditure based on extensive household survey data.

We may briefly consider changes that have occurred in medicine purchasing behavior by viewing data collected at three South Kanarese chemist shops. At one rural chemist shop observed in 1984 for three consecutive days in the winter season, approximately 40% of clients purchased medicines without a prescription. Twenty five percent directly presented a symptom, 5% requested a drug by name and another 10% presented a medicine label or name scribbled on a piece of paper.[46] The shopkeeper noted that over-the-counter purchases of medicine had steadily been increasing over the last ten years. In a second shop observed for the same duration, 28% percent of clients purchased medicine over-the-counter. At this shop only 10% presented symptoms to the chemist and 18% directly asked for a drug by name. Clients of this shop considered the counter attendant more a vendor of medicines than a practitioner in contrast to the first shopkeeper. At both shops, a wide range of medicines were requested without a prescription (other than tonics and vitamins). In order of commonality these included: analgesics, antipyretics and antiinflammatory drugs (45% sold without a prescription), drugs for flatulence, upset stomach, and diarrhea; cough mixtures; topical preparations; and antibiotics.

In urban areas, over-the-counter purchase of medications appeared even higher than that reported in rural towns. The third chemist shop observed was a city chemist shop in Mangalore city.[47] In 1984, over 55% of customers over a three day period of time conferred with the shop attendant about their symptoms and/or the medicines they had taken.[48] The chemist offered them advice about medicines, occasionally substituted generic for more expensive brand name drugs when clients were too poor to purchase prescribed products, and pushed products to known customers with means to purchase them. Many clients referred to the chemist as "doctor." Several openly told me that the shopkeeper was the best practitioner to consult for routine problems because he knew more "company medicines" than doctors. Moreover, he was willing to listen to client's past experiences with drugs (not just symptoms) enabling him to suggest new medicines when previously tried medicines were judged ineffective or to have side effects.

Important to highlight is that a number of customers at this shop purchased medicines to maintain health, not just to cure disease. During exit interviews, many spoke of taking medicines as the cost of urban living. Medicines purchased for preventive/promotive health purposes included tonics, digestive aids, liver medicines, vitamins, sleeping tablets, menstrual regulators, and medicines for constipation, diarrhea, and eye inflammation. These problems were accepted as a consequence of rapid urbanization and lifestyle change occurring in Mangalore.

The data from this urban South Kanarese chemist shop take on greater significance when viewed in relation to a large study on medicine purchasing behavior carried out by scientists attached to the National Institute of Nutrition in Hyderabad (Krishnaswamy and Kumar 1983, Krishnaswamy, Kumar and Radhaiah 1983). This important yet little known study (in the West), may be highlighted to illustrate the rising prevalence of over-the-counter self-treatment. In the study, data were collected on drug purchasing behavior in 10% of all retail chemist shops in the twin cities of Hyderabad and Secunderbad (pop. 2.5 million). Six trained investigators observed the activity of druggists at 330 shops for two hour periods for four days over a four month period. Data were collected on over 26,000 sales involving the purchase of nearly 45,000 drugs. Both prescription and over-the-counter drug purchases were monitored. The following medicine purchasing patterns were noted:

1. Nearly half (47%) of all medicines purchased were for self-care. Of these, 58% were scheduled drugs which were supposed to be dispensed only with a doctor's prescription.

2. Ninety two percent of the prescriptions filled were from private doctors. A majority did not contain the patient's name, provisional diagnosis, dosage schedule, or duration of therapy.

3. The profile of drugs purchased by clients with and without prescriptions were similar (See Table 9.2).

4. Nutritional products (tonics) headed the list of medicines prescribed by doctors. Fifty three percent of all prescriptions and 26% of all self-purchases included nutritional supplements, which accounted for 27% of all medicines prescribed and 19% of all medicines self-purchased. B-complex accounted for 42% of nutritional products prescribed.

Table 9.2

**Profile of Drugs Purchased by Clients
With and Without Prescriptions**

Therapeutic class	Doctor's prescription	Self-purchase
Sulfa/antibiotics	31% (16%)	13% (9%)
Analgesics, antipyretics, and antiinflammatories	26% (13%)	32% (24%)
Gastrointestinal	18% (9%)	16% (12%)
Respiratory	17% (8%)	15% (11%)
Others	8% (54%)	24% (44%)
Total	100% (100%)	100% (100%)

This table was computed from Figures II and IV in Krishnaswamy, Kumar, and Radhaiah (1983). Figures in parentheses refer to percentage of total sales.

5. With respect to major categories of drugs, Table 9.2 provides a brief summary of the percentages of prescription and self-purchases containing various types of drugs and the total percentage of sales they represent.

6. Sedatives and tranquilizers, antidiarrheal drugs, and antihistamines were as commonly purchased over-the-counter as they were prescribed.

7. Antibiotics were used indiscriminately within the urban area. More than 30% of doctors' prescriptions contained antibiotics as did some 13% of all self-purchases. The researchers suggested that the "public was adopting an antibiotic mentality similar to that of doctors."

8. Only 18% of self-medicators and 40% of prescription holders purchased a full course of antibiotics. Thirty percent of self-medicators purchased only a one day supply of an antibiotic requested.[49]

Data from the NIN study complement observations made in six South Kanarese chemist shops with two exceptions. First, self-purchase for antibiotics in Hyderabad was more common than self-purchase observed in rural

South Kanara. Second, in the Hyderabad study, less than 2% of drugs were purchased at the recommendation of a chemist once symptoms were presented by a client.[50] In South Kanara, during the mid-1970s to 1980s, consultation with chemists and medicine recommendations were common at some, but not all, chemist shops. Consultation with chemists (or their attendants) were of two varieties: a) consultation where symptoms were presented and medicines requested, and b) consultations where questions about a medicine's purpose and price were asked. Consultations with rural based chemist shop attendants generally exceeded those of town and city attendants, although a notable exception was documented in the case of one city based chemist who was consulted much like a doctor for routine complaints by one out of every five customers ($n = 300$) during non-peak work hours.

Another reason for highlighting the Hyderabad study is that it suggests that the medicine dispensing/prescribing behavior of doctors has influenced popular health behavior. It has not only had an impact on self-treatment of illness, but also on medicine taking associated with health promotion and illness prevention.[51]

COMMERCIAL *ĀYURVEDIC* AND AYURPATHIC MEDICINES

Little research exists on the commercialization of traditional medications despite the growth of an impressive herbal medicine industry in countries such as Japan, Indonesia, and India.[52] In India, Leslie (1989) has pointed out that the history of commercial *āyurvedic* drugs extends from a period of time when revivalistic ideology fostered the manufacture of traditional medicine as an expression of Indian civilization, to the present where pharmaceutical companies foster "double think" as a means of promoting traditional medicines as modern.

> The revivalist rhetoric that appealed to several generations of Indian nationalists grew stale with repetition, and finally began to appear ridiculous. But this does not mean that the ways people experienced their bodies or their humoral understanding of these experiences changed. The commercially sophisticated and well managed companies that produce *Āyurvedic* and Unani medicines appeal to these experiences and understandings, and their stylishly packaged products appeal to the middle class conviction that modern appearing things are valuable on their own account. (Leslie 1989:22)

In India there has been a steady rise in the number of companies marketing both commercial quality "standard *āyurvedic*" preparations and "patent ayurpathic" products.[53] By commercial quality medicines, I refer to mass produced standard *āyurvedic* medications in contrast to those produced by traditional (*shastric*) production techniques which are labor, time, and fuel intensive. Ayurpathic products are newly formulated commercially produced modern herbal drugs described as *āyurvedic* and thought by the general public to balance body humors. Estimates as to the size of the commercial *āyurvedic* drug market are difficult to come by. Leslie (1989) cites Dr. Kurup, a WHO adviser on Indian Systems of Medicine, as estimating that in 1980, 3000 private companies manufactured *āyurvedic* pharmaceuticals worth in excess of Rs. 50 million. These same companies also produced other *āyurvedic* products, including soap and hair tonic, which were a major source of their profit. More recent estimates indicate that in 1993 there were over 5,000 private companies which manufactured *āyurvedic* medicines in India with drug stocks valued in excess of Rs. 600 crore (6 billion dollars) (see Minwalla 1993).[54]

The growth of the commercial *āyurvedic* pharmaceutical industry has had a tremendous impact on the practice of medicine, local production of *āyurvedic* medicines, and home treatment. Let us first consider how large commercial *āyurvedic* medicine companies have affected the local production and availability of *āyurvedic* medicine. Over the last decade I have seen a number of small traditional *āyurvedic* medicine production units go out of business due to significant price hikes in raw herbs and fuel. These units are unable to compete with the discounts and sales incentives offered to shops and practitioners by large commercial *āyurvedic* companies. Just as companies selling allopathic medicines have engaged in intensive marketing campaigns, pharmaceutical representatives of large *āyurvedic* companies have engaged in aggressive marketing programs. In many instances, they offer more attractive incentive schemes than manufacturers of allopathic medicines.

Let me briefly consider the case of one established *āyurvedic* medicine company in South Kanara using traditional production methods. In 1985 the company sold a 400 ml. bottle of *dasamoola aristha*, a standard *āyurvedic* tonic, for Rs. 25. Several companies located outside the district sold commercial *dasamoola aristha* for Rs. 14. The company, which had an excellent reputation, folded in 1986 after three generations of medicine production. The owner, who also manages a medicine shop, decided it was more profitable to sell commercial products than to produce a quality product at a price deemed unreasonable by a growing number of his customers. During an interview he noted the following:

My profit on a bottle of *āyurvedic aristha* last year was Rs. 2–3 when all expenses were accounted for. If I sell commercial brands I make Rs. 4–6 and get one free bottle of medicine as an incentive for each 10 that I sell. Not only that, but most companies will give me 30 days of free credit and a bonus if I become a steady customer. I get more profit; I also get a guilty conscience. I know medicine and the products I now sell have little medicinal value compared to the medicine I produced. But, then they are used incorrectly anyway. People come in and want a peg of *aristha* to make everything better. They are not following the advice that used to go with the medicine. Look, that rickshaw driver came in here to get a peg of *aristha* for his upset stomach. He comes in everyday. There is no cure for his problem because he is being bounced around in the heat all day, he breathes in smoke and fumes, eats hotel food, drinks tea to stay awake and arrack to go to sleep. He doesn't expect a cure, he just wants some relief to get him through the day, or at least something to make him feel he is doing something good for health. It doesn't matter whether he takes a commercial or a shastric prepared *aristha* for his purposes. Chalk powder would be just as good for him. I feel badly that I am selling this inferior quality medicine, but that is what people are interested in. Actually, it is a *pāpa* (sin), but at least I am only selling it and not making it. To do that would be to dishonor my father and the medicine business he built. My son wants me to mass produce medicines, using electric current instead of firewood, and sugar instead of honey. But I will never do it. Now I am like other chemists. I sell the brand which makes me the most profit. So I stock 200 ml. bottles of commercial *Ashoka aristha* which I sell for Rs. 7 and I make Rs. 3 profit. But, if my customer is not an old client, I say "look here, I have a new product called Vanitaplex and I sell it to him for Rs. 9.50 and make even more profit." It's the same ingredients with an English name. That is the future of *āyurvedic* medicine. This is what will spoil *āyurveda*. But business has never been better!

Let me elaborate on this informant's last point, that the proliferation of patent ayurpathic drugs with English names is the direction of contemporary *āyurveda*. To do so I need to briefly consider the plight of new *āyurvedic* medicine production units. Popular demand for *āyurvedic* medicines has been increasing due to a number of factors including a growing concern that powerful allopathic medicines (such as antibiotics and injections) are hard on the body and produce a variety of side effects which can be reduced by *āyurvedic* medicines (see Chapter 7). Local companies have emerged to meet local market demand for familiar products at the same time that national companies have intensified regional sales campaigns. While some established local companies have gone out of business due to their inability to offer competitive prices for standard medicines, new companies have arisen to meet the challenge of large companies on home turf by mimicking their sales strategies and price schedules.

Two strategies are available for making a profit. First, a local company can maintain its operations in a rural area where labor and firewood charges are low and raw herbs, oil, honey, ghee, etc. are locally available, thereby reducing transportation costs. A medicine of equal or superior quality to that of large commercial companies can be produced and associated with the reputation of a patron practitioner. Some profit may be made in this manner, but a proliferation of alternative competitively priced medicines keeps market prices low.[55] The second strategy is to produce a few quality traditional products to maximize the reputation of a patron practitioner and then market a new patent product which fetches a handsome profit and is advertised as being unique.[56]

The latter strategy adds to the proliferation of patent *āyurvedic* products in India, but why English names? In the first place it needs to be noted that the marketing of unique patent medicines is not a local phenomenon, but a national pattern well established since the 1950s and capitalized on by such companies as Himalaya and Charak.[57] English names for *āyurvedic* medicines have increased in popularity because of a general ascription of "quality" attached to a new, modern and foreign sounding name. Two other factors have popularized English names. First, a price ceiling and excise tax has been placed on an increasing number of allopathic medicines which serves to limit and control profit margins. Medicines labelled *āyurvedic* are not as subject to price control as allopathic medicines. This is one reason that a number of allopathic medicine companies (e.g., Franco India, Walter Bushnell, Dattatraya Krishna) have begun producing modern ayurpathic products and perhaps the reason that one finds the words "*āyurvedic* medicine" written in small letters on the bottom of Vicks Vaporub containers. Whereas chemists and doctors purchase most allopathic medicines for 8–15% below retail price, they may purchase *āyurvedic* medicines for 30% or more below retail price. The economic incentive for selling popular ayurpathic products is obvious.[58]

The second factor is that many MBBS doctors are reluctant to prescribe *āyurvedic* medicines with Sanskrit names despite the fact that patients look favorably at the inclusion of *āyurvedic* drugs in their treatment regime. One doctor described his predicament as follows:

> If a patient comes to me and I say here is a chit for a medicine which you can get from the village *vaidya*, the patient will question why he should see me, since I charge more and he gets the same thing he could have obtained in his village. What he doesn't realize is that I have diagnosed his problem correctly and find this *āyurvedic* medicine a good medicine to be used with other medicines. There have been great practitioners in Indian history and some of the *āyurvedic* products developed are useful, but then many are

nonsense also. To prescribe traditional products is to support *āyurveda* as a whole and this I will not do. Also many traditional preparations have not been prepared in a hygienic manner. But what I can do is prescribe an *āyurvedic* product sold with an English name prepared by a standard company in a scientific way. I can prescribe R compound for arthritis which is actually *Mahārogaraja googalu,* Hepril instead of *Kumāri Asawa* or Feedal instead of *Aśwagañda Aristha* as tonics. These medicines are known to me and used by my family also. For dispensing the medicine with the English name I will be respected. Patients are happy because the medicine is modern and *āyurvedic.* I am happy because I am not supporting other quack medicines included in *āyurveda.* Everybody is satisfied.

The sentiments expressed by this practitioner were echoed by several other doctors whom I interviewed. A growing number of allopathic doctors as well as recent graduates of *āyurvedic* schools who wish to be seen as modern are eager to use *āyurvedic* patent medicines which have attractive profit margins and popular appeal established through advertisements. Responsive to their enthusiasm is an *āyurvedic* drug industry which has produced popular medicines with such English names as:

Bonnisan (baby tonic)
Energic (body resistance, debility, stamina)
Famopolin B (menstrual regulator)
Femix (all women's reproductive health needs)
Gasex (flatulence)
Gastogen (gastric disorders)
Geriforte (anti-stress)
Haemocleen (blood purifier for all skin diseases)
Hamdogen (weak memory, early aging, vigor)
Hincolin cream (stimulates blood supply to the penis)
Hormoprin (inflammatory catarrhal conditions)
Kitt's pulmo tone (respiratory diseases)
Lipidsol (weight loss)
Liv up (constipation and disorders due to antibiotic usage
Liv 52 (prevents hepatic damage, promotes hepatocellular
    regeneration, stimulates appetite and growth)[59]
Manix (sex stimulant)
Masturin (women's health needs)
Mustang (male rejuvenator)
Osteon D (tonic for the total development of children)
Pause (abortive, menstrual regulator)
R compound (arthritis)
Septilin (infections and congestions)
Tentex forte (depressed libido)
Tri sex (male rejuvenator)
Vim fix (male rejuvenator)

Two observations may be made with respect to the ayurpathic products listed above. First, an increasing number of these products are marketed to address popular health concerns which index collective anxieties such as male impotence, women's reproductive health needs, mental distress, and physical lassitude. Second, the insert information and packaging of these medicines refer to *āyurvedas'* legacy, but not humoral theory as such. Presented is metascientific language replete with biochemical and biomedical terms, followed up by testimonials from doctors and vague references to research.[60]

Most insert literature instructs users to check with their doctor before consuming the product. In bold black letters the information provided is specified for "registered medical practitioners only." This hardly discourages over-the-counter self-experimentation with the product. While some trepidation exists about using allopathic medicine for self-treatment until one ascertains the medicine's compatibility with the patient (following its initial prescription by a doctor), this does not hold true for ayurpathic medicines. The overwhelming impression among the lay population is that "*āyurvedic* medicines have no side effects."[61] This is an impression fostered by practitioners and the advertising industry alike, yet a statement identified as dangerous by every *āyurvedic* pundit whom I interviewed.[62] In the words of one pundit:

> All plants are medicines and all medicines are poisonous if used incorrectly. Even too much water can kill a thirst stricken man, even honey and ghee (clarified butter) mixed in the wrong proportions can imbalance the humors and lead to death.

Three issues may be raised. First, while many herbal medicines may be harmless in their traditional form, where absorption rates of active drugs are low, little is known about the long-term effects of newly introduced medicines having different concentrations of essential ingredients.[63] Second, the term *āyurvedic* leads the public to trust a new product and exercise less caution when using it. This false sense of security may reduce the recognition of commerciogenic side effects of medicine leading medicine takers to attribute side effects to symptoms of the illness (Price 1989). A third issue involves the manner in which an implicit "fix" ideology has encompassed "traditional" medicine. ayurpathic drugs are as much the vehicle for the ideology of health commodification as allopathic drugs, regardless of their herbal content.

Over the last few years I have observed an increasing number of people consuming commercial *āyurvedic* drugs with impunity both as curative medicines and as promotive health resources. Recall the *āyurvedic* medicine distributor who noted that people today take these medicines without the dietary and behavioral regimes that once accompanied them. An increasing number of people are clearly looking for ayurpathic fixes for health, fixes which are easy, in tablet or capsule form, and which do not require lifestyle change. While it is true that some people still inquire about what kind of diet to follow when purchasing medicines, an increasing number swallow the pill or tonic and return to life as usual. Commercial *āyurvedic* medicine is for these people "cosmopolitan medicine." It is also, "cosmopolitical" medicine. Pfleiderer and Bichman (1985) have used this term to denote the role of Western medicine in establishing and maintaining the interests of former colonial powers and elites in less developed countries. My usage is somewhat different. It indexes subtle dimensions of capitalist ideology associated with the exchange of labor capital for health through medical fixes in a secular cosmopolitan world. Medicines are cosmopolitical in that they are a conduit for the embodiment of capitalism. Knowledge about body processes is increasingly being replaced by knowledge about medicine products, leading to new patterns of health problem solving such as diagnosis by treatment.[64]

The commodification of health has been advanced by a wealth of ayurpathic products which promise health to the consumer with regular use. Product appeals have aroused collective anxieties and deep fears about vital essences, impotency, impure breast milk, poor mental concentration, and one's inner worth as well as outer complexion. Medicines have appeared in new forms and with new names indexing multiple logics of practice responsive to the requirements of practical situations (Bourdieu 1990). The composition and marketing of many of these drugs has been shaped by cultural concerns. One of the reasons these drugs are so popular is because they are positioned to act on a combination of symptoms recognized in popular health culture to coexist in complexes (e.g., headache, weakness, improper bowel function, memory loss, loss of vitality, reduced sexual drive).[65] New concerns about cancer and heart attack are linked to familiar complexes. The product lists of pharmaceutical companies continue to expand as catalogues of concern, hope, and commodified answers to life's problems.

One more point needs to be made with respect to the popularity of commercial *āyurvedic* medicines. To understand the market and consumer demand for *āyurvedic* medicines one must consider market niches established by medicines which have been removed or regulated. Let me cite the example of E. P. Forte. During the 1970s I was struck by the misuse of E. P. Forte, a combination of estrogen and progesterone (see Chapter 7). Designed as a treatment for amenorrhea and as a hormonal test for pregnancy, the drug was commonly employed in Mangalore as an abortive and morning after pill by women who believed that if a low dose could bring on one's period, a high dose could either prevent pregnancy or cause an abortion. Numerous studies in the United States and Germany found the use of these drugs to be dangerous and they were taken off the market in the West. Despite impressive research in India, it was not until 1983 that the drug was banned.[66] Soon after the drug was banned by the Drug Controller of India, two manufacturers of these products obtained a legal stay against the ban arguing that it "denied women their rights to a valuable medicine" (Shiva 1987).[67] Notably, there was a temporary shortage of these products in South Kanarese chemist shops during this time. Important to highlight here, drugs such as E. P. Forte created a market niche meeting a consumer need. When these drugs became scarce in the market, the demand gap was soon filled by a host of ayurpathic patent medicines such as "Pause" and "Famoplin." [68]

COSMOPOLITAN MEDICINES

Health commodification is fostered by a cosmopolitan lifestyle characterized by consumerism. The term cosmopolitan used in this context refers less to place (urban areas) than to an orientation toward time and a dependency on commercial goods made available by a growing industrial complex.[69] In the example noted above, there is little conceptual difference between the allopathic and ayurpathic medicines sold for menstrual regulation. They both constitute "cosmopolitan drugs" to stretch Leslie's original use of the concept beyond allopathic medicine. In Chapter 7, I made the point that the layperson does not simply view medicines in terms of the *āyurvedic* and allopathic medical traditions, but in terms of illness and age specific preferences for medicine forms, tasks, and agenda. Ayurpathic drugs with English names and allopathic drugs are both "cosmopolitan" medicines offering convenient short-term fixes for health problems. Given the mix of allopathic and ayurpathic medicines commonly prescribed together, patients are often unsure which is which and what kind of shops stock the medicines they need. During the monitoring of a commercial *āyurvedic* medicine shop in Mangalore in 1986, I documented that over one quarter of the clients who walked through the door with a prescription were looking for allopathic drugs and did not know they were in the wrong type of shop.[70] One third of the prescriptions presented to the shop attendant which contained *āyurvedic* medicines were written by an allopathic doctor.

Chemist shops are stocking an increasing variety of commercial *āyurvedic* drugs. Twenty years ago a town chemist shop which I monitored stocked a few varieties of *āyurvedic aristha* which accounted for roughly 5%

of sales. Attendants at this and four other town chemist shops interviewed in 1986 reported between 10–20% of their total sales related to commercial *āyurvedic* medicines. Promoting such sales are the pharmaceutical reps of national *āyurvedic* companies who canvas the same practitioners and chemist shops as pharmaceutical reps from allopathic pharmaceutical companies.[71]

RAMIFICATIONS OF HEALTH COMMODIFICATION FOR COMMUNITY HEALTH

> The abuse of antibiotics is not an answer for infections and is not a replacement for sanitation and hygiene. (Krishnaswamy and Kumar 1983)

> Western allopathic medicine has found itself to some extent in a cul-de-sac, striving over-exclusively for the entirely technological "breakthroughs" so beloved of journalists and so usually untrue, misreported or ephemeral. The need is rather to appreciate the high value of Western linear medicine as one part of wider possibilities.... The idea is slowly percolating that most disease is not due to one agent but to many circumstances in combination. (Jeliffe and Jeliffe 1977:331)

A false sense of security has emerged from the exaggerated claims of curative and preventive health fixes.[72] At a time of environmental deterioration, rapid urbanization, and industrialization, the commodification of health has offset anxiety in some sectors. Health has been decontextualized, made available at a cost. In such a context, transactions have increasingly centered around the exchange of drugs. An ideology consistent with a set of values associated with consumerism and the growth of capitalism is embodied through such transaction. In community health terms, the cost of health commodification is high, for the pursuit of individual health through medicines deflects attention away from collective responsibilities.

To appreciate the possible ramifications of health commodification in India and elsewhere in the developing world, it is instructive to briefly review the history of public health in Europe in the early to mid-1800s. If one looks at the history of public health in Europe at the time of the industrial revolution it is apparent that environmental and sanitation reform did not come about for purely humanitarian reasons despite the religious and moralistic rhetoric of the day (Rosen 1958).[73] In frank terms, it was associated with the growth of an urban middle class and their fear of contamination from the poor. This fear was raised to a fever pitch at a time when multiple epidemics were raging and a miasma (malevolent airs) paradigm of disease etiology was prominent. Public health was not politically neutral; it was championed by the middle class at a time when the political power of this group was increasing. Environmental sanitation reform involved extreme measures and the poor were treated like powerless children. A medical police model of public health control was enforced against an impoverished labor force deemed purveyors of filth, and in Calvinist terms, the "damned." Notably, it was at least three decades, from the 1830s to the late 1860s, before the working class played an active part in the public health movement.

In the developing world today, the false security rendered by a proliferation of medicines for health as well as illness reduces the impetus of both the middle class and the poor to actively mobilize for environmental health, sanitation and hygiene. The medical value of such proven public health resources as tetanus toxoid vaccinations merge with the inflated claims of tonics and the misuse of antibiotics. As a composite they offer compartmentalized protection, quick fixes, and a means toward health which does not rock the boat or deal with the muddied water. At a time of cholera there is always the magic, if not the science, of cholera vaccinations to rely on (Nichter 1990) and when a new disease associated with deforestation emerges, such as Kyasanur forest disease (Nichter 1987a), there is always the vaccination just around the corner in which to place one's faith. And yet a look at emergent and resurgent patterns of disease in India and other developing countries leads one to recognize that an increasing number of diseases are associated with the "development process," rapid urbanization, pollution, environmental deterioration, and disruption of micro as well as macro ecosystems.[74]

Medicine-taking behavior contributes to this scenario of emergent and resurgent diseases. The potential danger rendered by the cavalier use of antibiotics can not be overemphasized. Over-prescription and excessive consumption of antibiotics has been described as a form of environmental pollution:

> Indiscriminate prescribing of antibiotics adds needlessly to mounting pressures for resistant organisms. It may seem an overstatement to describe it as environmental pollution, but when the full and ultimate consequences of the manner of use are grasped, it is less of an exaggeration than might at first appear. (Whitehead 1973:225)

Over the last two decades an increasing number of studies have reported the emergence of antibiotic-resistant strains of bacteria.[75] In one sense these resistant strains pollute our environment. In another sense they articulate the principle of "flexible accumulation" at the cellular level in a era characterized by accelerated communication and information flow, adaptability, and specificity (Harvey 1989, Martin 1991). Until recently, drug resistance has been viewed in relation to a single agent. Resistance to an antibiotic was an inconvenience taken care of by a substitute antimicrobial drug of which there seemed to be several alternatives. Recently, however, scientists have found that mutation of one pathogen to a single drug is not the only mechanism of genetic change and drug resistance. The transfer of genetic material between pathogens (even unrelated species) has been found to facilitate resistance to multiple drugs. In short, a new public health crisis is emerging after a fifty year "golden age" during which it appeared that microbial infections were controllable given the potency of antibiotic resources. As Stuart Levy has noted:

> Today, multidrug resistance is the rule, not the exception among resistant bacteria. We are presently witnessing a massive, unprecedented evolutionary change in bacteria. By developing and using antibiotics we have, in a sense, caused these events to spiral. (1993:103)

Patterns of antibiotic use and resistance foster what Levy has termed the antibiotic paradox, a pattern evident in the Indian context. Doctors in India have liberally used antibiotics for years. As they observed that individual antibiotics lost their potency, they resorted to prescribing multiple antibiotics and using newer generations of antimicrobials pushed by medical representatives who informed doctors of "resistance problems." Over time, these antimicrobials have become ineffective and higher level drugs have been used. Observations and impressions about drug resistance have led private doctors to shift from the routine use of cotrimoxazole, penicillin, teramycin, and ampicillin to gentamicin, norfloxin, ciprofloxacin, and pefloxacin.[76] Given a scenario of multidrug resistance, where newer generation antimicrobials are bound to be more expensive, class relations may be reproduced through access to medicines which come to represent power and wealth in a context where nature robustly resists human domination.[77] The pharmaceutical industry has everything to gain from such a scenario. For the pharmaceutical industry, resistant strains mean new business opportunities and markets for new generations of drugs.[78]

I have gone to some length in considering the ways health consumer behavior is influenced by a combination of political, economic, and cultural factors. One of my reasons for doing so is to call attention to a health care/medicine consumption transition occurring in India and much of the rest of the world. Given the scenario presented, primary health care needs to be reconsidered in relation to existing medicine consumption behavior and those factors influencing this behavior. There is a need to take a hard look at medicine consumerism, and the marketing of medical goods, knowledge and services. Changing medicine consumption practices must be viewed in relation to socialization, the embodiment of tacit knowledge, and changing perceptions of health. Implicit meanings are conveyed by medicines explicitly marketed as short-term fixes. These meanings support an individualistic shortsighted approach toward well being which undermines community health mobilization.

Primary health care needs to be reconsidered in the context of existing health care seeking behavior, and health education needs to be interlinked with consumer education. Without appropriate conceptualization (Fuglesang 1977) of what medicines can and can not do, chances of their inappropriate use are increased. Mystification sets the stage for inflated claims and false expectations.[79] What emerges is medicine taking as a habitual response to ill health, weakness, and distress. One learns to reach for the medicine bottle, injection, or vaccination and little more. A critical consumerist posture toward medical fixes needs to be developed which weighs the merits and costs of alternative means of health enhancement and illness management.

Let me be more specific about what I mean here. The commodification of health is already a strong trend in India, and widespread self-treatment with over-the-counter drugs has been documented for well over two decades (Greenhalgh 1987, Krishnaswamy, Kumar and Radhaiah 1983). Provision of knowledge about common medicines is called for in lieu of the fact that government regulation of the plethora of drugs available is unlikely. Information on how much medicines cost, and for whom and when they are appropriate are of interest to the lay population. Discussion of medicines may be used to set the stage for community activism directed toward: 1) proper administration and equitable distribution of public medical resources for identifiable health problems; 2) cooperative purchasing of commonly used generic medicine resources; 3) the consideration of alternative health maintenance and disease control strategies; and 4) education about drug resistance as a community health issue.

It may be argued that providing information to the community about medicine use goes against medical ethics and will increase self-treatment practices. In countries where drugs are freely available over-the-counter, self-purchase of medicines is already high, and prescription practices are often inappropriate, this argument is weak. Indeed, it is more commonly advanced by constituencies having economic rather than humanitarian motives. Inappropriate patterns of self-care and prescription behavior already exist. They need to be identified and addressed. There is no excuse for the poor spending scarce resources on antibiotics for upper respiratory infections and watery diarrhea. Compiling a list of misguided treatment patterns for common ailments is a first step (VHAI 1986). A second step is documentation of patterns of drug use associated with advertising and drug promotion campaigns. Such data are required if a case is to be made for regulating the content of misleading advertisements, the development of counter-advertisements and the review of drug promotion schemes.

Sending health educators out with tired public health slogans to compete with marketing firms is much like sending David to fight Goliath and await a miracle. Social marketing may prove to be a useful strategy for conveying information about appropriate medicine use so long as it is recognized that the end is not just the sale of more appropriate products, but the provision of knowledge making for a more informed and critical consumer. Those involved in international health need to recognize that the problem is not just irrational drug use, but more invasive and less explicit aspects of health commodification.

CONCLUSION

In South Indian Hindu culture, health, and prosperity are bestowed upon the household, family, and kingdom, for conformity to the socio-moral order by ancestors, gods, and patron spirits. The living maintain reciprocal relationships with these agents. Properly worshipped, they protect and reward. When not appropriately respected, their power may turn to wrath manifest as illness, a form of misfortune as well as a sign of breach in the socio-moral order. In modernizing India, the social order is in transition, and unfulfilled obligations to the living as well as the supernatural are rife. These breaches are consonant with changes in social relations fostered by an increase in cash based contractual labor relations.[80] Needed at this juncture has been a form of magic to ease anxiety and provide a source of immediate security at a time when cultural norms are being violated in increasing measure. Cosmopolitan medicine has been marketed as powerful impersonal magic.[81]

As a form of power rendering immediate demonstration effects, allopathic medicine has become a fetish of an emergent capitalist ideology in need of a symbol of progress. While immensely popular, allopathic medicine has been perceived as a source of danger and impurity as well as power. In Chapter 7, I noted a complementarity in rural South Kanara between fast acting allopathic medicines and powerful, but rash *bhūta* spirits. In contrast, *āyurvedic* medicines are more closely associated with the qualities of pan-Indian Brahmanic deities.[82] Recall for a moment the informant who spoke of his daughter suffering from bloodlessness after being treated by allopathic medicines and how she needed to consume tonic both during and subsequent to treatment. Two images may be juxtaposed. The first is that of the girl drinking tonic and the second, devotees feeding patron *bhūta* spirits with blood offerings. Both constitute acts maintaining a positive relationship with a form of power to which one has entered a dependency relationship. Blood offerings are made to *bhūta* as external sources of power and tonic is taken to replenish the blood once allopathic medicine has extracted its "blood toll" for curative actions. I suspect that in part, allopathic medicines are understood culturally in terms of preexisting ideas about power and dependency. While modernization has been accepted, its cost has been comprehended in physical terms through cultural perceptions of blood, digestion, and strength. This has in turn increased the market for tonics and ayurpathic medicines promising to restore a lost sense of health. Paradise lost has been made available for the cost of a modern elixir based on an ancient formula.

Dependency upon medicines and commentary upon relations of dependency which index medicine use need to be considered in the context of broad social and technological changes taking place in India today. An important aspect of this change involves what Ramanujan (1989) has referred to as a shift from a context-sensitive to a context-free way of thinking and acting about the world. Entailed is displacement of an embodied, grounded, contextual sense of appropriateness. For example, in agriculture a shift has occurred from reliance upon knowledge of the qualities of the land and ecological specificity to the mind set of systematic farming.[83] This mind set is propagated by agricultural extension experts promoting the use of modern hybrid seeds, chemical fertilizers, insecticides, irrigation, etc. In both the case of agricultural and pharmaceutical practice, modern solutions allow one to subordinate, control, and transform sites of activity (the land or body) as a means of correcting for deficiencies, increasing productivity, and protecting against external threats. Practice based, context-specific knowledge is overridden by modern knowledge which focuses upon quantity over quality, be this measured in terms of crop yields or life years.

Local commentary on the ramifications of this transformation in South India is captured by Vasavi (1994) who provides an insightful study of how farmers view the impact of hybrid crops on the quality of their lives. This commentary extends the paradigm of substantialism wherein there is a co-constitutive relationship between qualities of the land, crops produced from the land, food, the body, and health status:

> Hybridization means not only the transformation of agrarian practices and substances but also the transformation of people who produce and consume them. The evaluation of hybrid seeds is extended to both the physical and moral effects of consuming them. Noting that hybrid seeds are delicate, susceptible to disease and require expensive inputs, villagers refer to the current period as *hybrid kala* (hybrid period) and to themselves as *hybrid mandi* (hybrid people). Unlike the sturdy organic seeds, they are like the

hybrid seeds that they sow, *sukshme* (delicate), diseased and needing constant attention.... The imagery reflects the change from an outlook of *swantha* (autonomy) and *thakat* (strength) to one oriented toward quantity, dependency and weakness. (Vasavi 1994:296)

The commodification of health and relationships of dependency also need to be understood in terms of relationships of dependency and a process which Bateson (1972) has described as schismogenesis.[84] This process involves an uncorrected positive feedback loop wherein (to use the case of medicines) increased familiarity with a form or category of medicine increases consciousness of a problem and demand for the product. This in turn fosters increased supply of the product which in turn increases surveillance of the problem and concern about it.[85] An accelerated cycle of medicine supply and demand has been set in motion in India, the iatrogenic effects of which remain to be seen. At the level of micro-ecology, another uncorrected feedback loop has been established. The misuse of drugs such as antibiotics fosters resistance which in turn fosters demand for newer generation antimicrobials which in turn are misused. Resistance escalates beyond mutation of one pathogen to one drug to multi-drug resistant strains of bacterial pathogens which transfer genetic information.

Factors contributing to the process of schismogenesis and commodification of health in India include market forces and pharmaceutical policy as well as social and cultural factors which influence consumer demand and medicine use. To account for this range of factors it has been necessary to consider both medicine prescribing and consumer behavior, the push of pharmaceutical companies and the pull of expectations from a public which maintains both traditional and cosmopolitan ideas about health care. It has been necessary to pay credence to changing perceptions of well being consonant with changing modes of production and the social relations they entail, and the Indian population's attempt to retain agency in an unhealthy environment over which they have little immediate control. It has also been important to consider emerging collective anxieties and medicine's role in displacing these anxieties, as well as individuals' attempts to mediate paradox in a world of competing ideologies given expression in coexisting modes of medical treatment. The implications of health commodification for primary health care are considerable. They impact on the health of individuals, the community, and the micro as well as macro environment.

NOTES

1. A few examples of such studies are Evans (1981), Gustafson and Wide (1981), Lilja (1983), Medawar (1979), Medawar and Freese (1982), Pradhan (1983), Phadke (1982), Shiva (1987), Silverman (1976), Silverman, Lee, and Lydecker (1982), Victoria (1982), VHAI (1986), and Yudkin (1980).

2. Drug promotion and medicine insert information in developing countries often do not include or play down side effects. For example, Silverman, Lee, and Lydecker (1986) note that in India, although significant corrections in drug promotional literature have been realized between 1973 and 1984, warnings do not appear on dipyrone products (Analgin) and Imodium products — two commonly used and abused medications.

3. The regulation of pharmaceuticals in India has been called for repeatedly. For example, the Hathi Committee Report of 1975 recommended a change from brand to generic names for drugs to be implemented in a phased manner. In June of 1979, the Government of India published a notice that five drugs including analgin, aspirin, chlorpromazine, ferrous sulfate, and piperazine salts were to be marketed only with generic names. This order was aborted when the Delhi High Court ruled it was against the free enterprise system. Drug labeling rules introduced in 1981 made it mandatory to include the generic name of drugs in a "conspicuous" manner next to their trade name and to use generic names for newly introduced single ingredient drugs. This practice has not been widely implemented.

4. For example, in urban and peri-urban areas the sense that one can protect one's individual body from disease precludes recognition that contiguous households, neighborhoods, and "communities" are interlinked through shared risk factors. These risk factors range from the presence of breeding sites for vectors to sources of food, air, and water contamination. Recognition of shared risks may be one of the chief factors drawing together disparate households and opening up debate about the allocation of responsibility between the state, municipality, household, individual, etc.

5. Rohde (1988) estimated that 16,000 registered pharmaceutical firms exist in India in contrast to 12,000 Primary Health Centers.

6. In 1980, six countries controlled over 70% of world pharmaceutical production. While no single firm controlled more than 20% of any national market, the top 10 pharmaceutical companies controlled 25% of the world's pharmaceutical trade (Faizal 1983). Many of the large multinational companies have extended their power base in India through subsidiaries and joint ventures. A VHAI (1986) report presents a list of these companies, their subsidiaries, the percentage of their trade constituted by essential and nonessential drug formulations, and their market share.

7. The growth of brand name drugs in India is notable. In 1980 it was estimated that there were 15,000 brand name drugs in India (Shepperdson 1988) com-

pared to 80,000 drugs in 1991. On January 16, 1988, India's Minister of Health was quoted in the *Indian Express Cochin*, as stating that India had no list of essential drugs nor did he have an idea as to the number of drug formulations manufactured in the country. The Drug Controller of India, speaking at the all-India Institute of Medical Science, was quoted as stating that in his opinion the number of formulations available was not excessive. By Japanese standards it is not. Ohnuki-Tierney (1986) notes that over 100,000 medicine products are available in the Japanese market in the mid-1980s. In 1983 there were approximately 2,500 pharmaceutical companies in Japan, 90% of which employed less than 50 people (Pradhan 1983). The U.S. pharmaceutical market has also expanded dramatically since 1986. In 1994, it was estimated that half a million pharmaceutical products were available in the United States, of which 300,000 were over-the-counter preparations (Vuckovic and Nichter 1995).

8. In 1980 the Central Drugs Consultative Committee composed of members of central and state drug control organizations examined a group of fixed dose drug combinations and in over two thirds of cases no therapeutic rationale was found for their existence. Half were deemed frankly harmful. These included combinations such as antihistamines with tranquilizers, antihistamines with antidiarrheals, vitamins with analgesics, antiinflammatory agents with tranquilizers, and antibiotic combinations such as chloramphenicol and streptomycin as well as penicillin and streptomycin. (See the feature article "Dangerous Profiteering" in *Sunday Deccan Herald*, Bangalore edition. January 7, 1990, pp. 1, 4). A report by the Drugs Technical Advisory Board appointed by the Consultative Committee flagged 22 combinations of drugs covering 350 products to be removed from the market. Of these as many as 300 were produced by Indian companies. The pharmaceutical industry argued that these combinations enhanced therapeutic efficacy through increased bio-availability and therapeutic synergism, reduced side effects, increased compliance, and the list goes on to the point of increasing absurdity. While 16 drugs were banned by the committee in 1981 the ban never went into effect and the government's legal power to ban ineffective drugs has been directly challenged in court. See the debate between Jayaraman (1986a, 1986b) and Phadke (1986) as well as Greenhalgh (1987) for further details.

9. Of drug company promotional expenses, Pradhan (1983) has estimated that some 40–50% goes to maintaining a sales and intelligence force comprised of "detail" personnel or what I have termed "pharmaceutical reps." Pradhan cites evidence that detailing is the most effective of all promotion strategies.

10. This figure includes only MBBS doctors and the most popular registered medical practitioners (RMP) with licentiate diplomas. I have pointed out elsewhere (Nichter 1981c:232) that the pharmaceutical industry has maintained a significant financial interest in RMPs. In 1976, of 206 practitioners in five rural taluks of South Kanara visited by the representatives of a major pharmaceutical company, 48% were RMPs. Of their best clients, ranked in terms of

medicine sales, 36% were RMPs. In 1987, interviews with company representatives suggested that the market niche represented by RMPs was decreasing, but still substantial. Documentation of the growth and distribution of doctors and chemist shops in the South Kanara will be the focus of a future publication.

11. My use of the term "health commodification" draws upon several sources. Central is Marx's concept of exchange value. Marx's concept of alienation is also relevant, for just as workers lose control of the products they create, so too they come to lose control of their production of health. Functional health comes to replace experiential health (Kelman 1975). Through health practices and acts of medicine taking, people come to embody a state of "normality" discussed by Gramsci (1971), Althusser (1970, 1971) and Foucault (1980a, 1980b, 1986) in terms of hegemony, internal-state-apparatus, micropolitics and biopower exercised at the site of the body. This subtle process is discussed by Bourdieu (1978, 1990) in relation to habitus, the embodiment of ideology through habitual practice. "Commodification," as I use the term is an example of the process by which "health" purchasing habits in the market place subtly reproduces capitalist ideology. I do not view this process as complete and recognize that the mode of consumption (of medicines) can constitute a mode of producing self-identity which is an expression of agency — albeit an expression largely shaped by a system of needs and desires which is determined (Baudrillard 1988). Following Raymond Williams (1977), I acknowledge the presence of coexisting health ideologies given expression through multiple logics of practice (Bourdieu 1990). For example, in Chapter 8, I argue that a precapitalist perception of healing efficacy counterbalances notions of curative efficacy underlying health commodification.

12. Upon discussing this theme with an *āyurvedic* chemist shop owner it was pointed out to me that the idea of transforming wealth into health was very old. This was done by performing rituals as well as ingesting valuable minerals for their health giving attributes. He pointed out that gold and silver coated pills were extremely popular in *āyurveda*. Gold is believed to have special health giving properties as well as to be the purest (in a ritual sense) of metals. A gold ring worn on the right hand while eating is said to convey health giving properties to the food consumed.

13. Douglas and Wildavsky (1982) in their study of the social conditions underlying societal concern about environmental pollution, argue that alienation and failed confidence in the state foster concern about adulteration. Giddens (1991) notes that a feature of modernity is the permeation of doubt into everyday life and that "risk" becomes fundamental to the way both lay actors and experts organize the social world. Productive power (Foucault 1980a, 1980b) in the form of information disseminated by the press plays off sensationalism and fosters collective anxieties about health which are exploited by pharmaceutical companies feeding off such fears.

14. Campbell's (1989) discussion of consumer pleasure in relation to a stimulation of the senses is insightful, although his characterization of "traditional" vs. "modern" forms of hedonism appears to be somewhat naive. Stimulation is achieved not only through novelty, but also by evoking and (re)experiencing memories and reassuring sensations (Farquhar 1991). On sense based memory see Howe (1991).

15. The appeal of products and what they represent often precedes advertising which capitalizes off of existing demand. This has been the theme of several sociological studies of the advertising industry and consumer behavior in the west (Campbell 1989, Ewen 1976, Ewen and Ewen 1982, Fox 1985, Schudson 1984, and Williamson 1978, to note just a few). In each of these studies it is pointed out that advertising is as much a "mirror as a mind bender." Advertising reinforces as much as it imposes. This is not to underestimate the power of advertising to shape demand and desire, but to call for an assessment of culturally constituted forms of desire, their underpinnings, and the manner in which goods are sold as available, substitutable, commodified forms of desire. Also in need of consideration is the use of products as a means of demarcation through which people define themselves and others (Featherstone 1991).

16. On this issue in the United States, see Goldman and Montagne (1986).

17. For example, India has a deficit of medicine for TB and leprosy while having a proliferation of vitamin tonics (Shiva 1987). Only half of India's minimum requirement of anti-TB drugs and one third of anti-leprosy drugs are produced a year. Among vitamin supplements, vitamin A production has gone down in spite of a shortage of supply. For supporting medicine production figures, see VHAI (1986).

18. This young man's reading of medicine ads is in itself a form of vicarious consumption wherein what is consumed is "dream material" (Campbell 1989: 89) enabling him to imagine other worlds.

19. At a time when a concerted effort is being made to popularize oral rehydration for diarrhea management in South Asia, little attention has been directed to the marketing of "rehydrant" products that detract from the dehydration-diarrhea message. A number of such products are marketed with the image of sports and vigor as a central theme. For example, packets of "Staminade " are marketed as a body salt rehydrant for sports and the label on Electrose specifically states it is not to be used for diarrhea management. This is precisely the situation which Green (1986:365) cautioned against in his consideration of ORS marketing in Bangladesh.

20. Krishnaswamy, Kumar, and Radhaiah (1983) conducted a medicine perception and practice survey in Hyderabad and found that 18% of male subjects under the age of 30 were consuming drugs after being influenced by popular advertisements.

21. Fearing being labeled an American exorcist, I swore the young man to secrecy about the entire incident. I reflected on the ethics of my action and never again engaged in such an activity. The young man was unaware of what the tablet contained, but was aware that it was medicine from the United States. Only one tablet was dispensed.

22. While I agree with Smith (1978) that villagers are not brain washed fools bedazzled by full color advertisements, advertising must not be underestimated as a generator of knowledge as well as secondary desire. James (1983) has similarly questioned the extent to which healthy skepticism is applied by laypersons in developing countries when reading advertisements. James presents data on infant formula as a case in point.

23. As Ewen and Ewen (1982) have noted in their study of advertising in the West, consumers do not necessarily or uniformly accept the sales pitch of advertisements, nor uniformly interpret advertisements in the same way.

24. In relation to Naik's use of the term "double think" see Williams' (1977) discussions of the coexistence of persistence and change. See also Clifford's (1988) discussion of the metanarratives of homogenization and emergence, loss, and invention.

25. Such appropriation and indigenization of medicines in India may be seen as part of a broader process of "inventing tradition" (Hobsbawn and Ranger 1983).

26. On the issue of communities of memory which tie people together and "instruct in subtle ways," see Bellah et al. (1985) and Buck-Morss (1991).

27. The mode of consumption may constitute a mode of producing the self.

28. This pattern of over-medication associated with the microeconomics of fee collection is not a strictly Indian phenomena. A complementary pattern is found in countries where doctors are reimbursed for their services in accordance with a system which gives them incentives for ordering medicines. For example, Emiko Ohnuki-Tierney (1986:83) notes that in Japan doctors are given reimbursement points for prescribing medications, a system leading to medicine pollution (*yakugai*).

29. On the issue of lowering threshold of discomfort see Barsky (1988) and Nichter and Vuckovic (1994). Murray and Chen (1992) and Sen (1990) have drawn attention to differences in self-perceived and observed morbidity as a dimension of health transition. Leaving aside problems of definition related to what constitutes an illness episode and cultural conventions influencing the language of illness, these researchers point out the importance of expectations which influence the reporting of symptoms and the seeking of care. Lowered thresholds of discomfort are associated with health commodification, and are an outcome of a health care medicine consumption transition. On other factors contributing to changes in morbidity rates ranging from the diagnostic response of doctors (e.g., earlier disease detection) and the economic capacity

of patients to seek health care earlier, to changes in population composition and related disease patterns, see Kumar (1993) and Riley (1990).

30. I have described the metamedical messages conveyed by states of ill health elsewhere when considering idioms of distress (Nichter 1981a, 1981b). At present my emphasis is on polyvalent symbolic meanings conveyed by medicines. For example, acquisition of *āyurvedic* medicines such as Tripaladi oil (a well known medicine for sleeplessness, anxiety, and mental coolness) conveys a silent but well articulated message to others about one's state of being. Medicine use sets in motion changes in social interactions. Addition of new medications to popular pharmacopeia is also the addition of new expressive symbolic resources.

31. Kapur (1979) has noted the indiscriminate use of minor and major tranquilizers by practitioners in South India, suggesting that practitioners are guided by the representatives of pharmaceutical firms. In addition to following the recommendations of pharmaceutical representatives and promotional literature, practitioners also mimic the example of clinical instructors and colleagues. For example, one doctor known quite well to me noted that he began using diazepam more commonly after seeing doctors use the drug liberally during family planning camps. He was advised to prescribe the drug with analgesics if women complained of general side effects after they attended camps. Women's complaints were set up to be diagnosed as psychosomatic.

32. While still popular in the 1990s, Calmpose use appears to be dropping off. Several other products (both *āyurvedic* and allopathic) are gaining in popularity among practitioners as well as the public. Allopathic drugs include alprazolam products (e.g., Zolax, Alzolam, Zentax), lorazepam and other short-term antianxiety/antidepressant medications. Barbiturates and antipsychotic medicines are dispensed less commonly by local doctors.

33. Adulteration is a serious health concern in India and a subject increasingly being reported by the press (Shepperdson 1988). Farmers in South Kanara use a number of toxic pesticides evaluated by the WHO as "extremely hazardous." A recent all-India ICMR study found high pesticide residues in milk. It also found that most infant formula sold in the open market had a toxic metal content (arsenic, cadmium, lead) well in excess of acceptable standards (Girimaji 1993). Newspaper reports of food and alcohol poisoning are common in India.

34. A study quoted by Singh (1983) as "initiated by the National Council of Economic Research" found that 23 drug companies lose money on the production and marketing of essential drugs. The implication of the study is that they must sell vitamins at a good profit to remain solvent. A similar argument has been raised with respect to the subsidizing of research costs spent in developing new medicines. Companies claim that they must sell OTC drugs to be able to afford research. In fact, research on medicines for tropical diseases has been meager. While developing countries spend between $15–20 billion dollars a year on pharmaceuticals, research on new pharmaceuticals is

primarily directed toward the diseases of developed nations where 75% of world drug consumption takes place (Patel 1983, Taylor 1986).

35. A wide variety of drug promotion incentive schemes exist ranging from cash discounts and "buy some get some free" schemes to promotional gifts and special credit facilities.

36. Data collected in 1990 suggest that purchases of tonic are not increasing in village areas beyond 1983 levels. Consumption of tonics among young adults may actually be decreasing. While tonic use is still common when a person is recovering from a debilitating illness, general use of tonics in village areas seems to be on the decline, although expenditure on other medicines is increasing. Research is needed on who purchases tonics and why, the percentage of sales to pregnant and lactating women, the chronically ill and elderly, young children and adults. Studies are also needed which document tonic use by occupational category and lifestyle.

37. Greenhalgh (1987) found that nutritional supplements accounted for 23% of drugs prescribed by general practitioners in a sample of large Indian towns. Sixty-seven percent of patients were prescribed supplements. She further reported that half of all money spent on over-the-counter preparations were on vitamin, protein, or carbohydrate supplements.

38. Anxiety over the quality of basic food grains in India has created a new market niche in urban areas for "chemical free" foods. For example, the Green World company markets their products with ironic ads such as: "Food is meant to promote growth in children. Sometimes this growth is called cancer."

39. Popular *āyurvedic* "energizers" are also being marketed to appeal to changing ideals of husband–wife relationships which index sexuality. See for example advertisements for the product Nirvana, manufactured by J. K. Chemicals, the same company which produces Kama Sutra brand condoms. The two products are cross-referenced in ad campaigns which sponsor "soulmate second honeymoon" contests.

40. Medicine fixes are also available to protect against the ill effects of such vices as drinking. Products such as Heptoguard are available as a prophylaxis against liver damage associated with alcohol consumption and a local beer (Gold Lager) has been introduced onto the market containing "health-giving *āyurvedic* herbs."

41. This remains a field impression. Research needs to be conducted on both the kinds of tonic purchased by gender, reasons for purchase, and a content analysis of tonic advertising using male and female stereotypes. On the marketing of medicines and the reinforcement of gender stereotypes, see Querubin and Tan (1986).

42. A new market opening up is the middle aged adults who fear premature aging caused by stress and environmental pollution. Popular tonics such as Revital and Thirty Plus are pitched toward this population.

43. The children's tonic market encompasses both tonics for breastfeeding mothers as well as tonics for children. As Reissland and Burghart (1988:466) have noted, when a baby's health status is poor, one of two possibilities may be suspected: a) the mother's milk may be deficient or unsuitable, or b) the infant's digestive power may be weak. Tonics are marketed for both scenarios and concerned mothers may use both types of products simultaneously.

44. Home care is more extensive among some castes than others.

45. Parker et al. (1979) reviewed surveys on home health care in South Asia conducted during and following the Johns Hopkins Functional Analysis Project (1966–77). They have noted that of the field sites surveyed, self-care was higher in South India than North India or Nepal. A Karnataka based survey found that over a two week period, 9% of the sample population and 42% of those reported to be ill engaged in self-care. In general, more higher than lower caste men and children engaged in self-help, while more lower than higher caste women engaged in self-help. Self-help was noted to be particularly common for fever, upper respiratory infections, diarrhea, skin ailments, and muscular problems. Approximately 40% of the self-help efforts reported involved the use of allopathic medicines.

46. A three day study conducted in the same chemist shop in 1991 found that only 14% of customers directly presented symptoms to the same shop attendant. The shopkeeper attributed this to greater familiarity of drugs among his clientele and more frequent consultations to a growing number of practitioners. Another 38% of his customers asked for a medicine by name or presented an old prescription or medicine bottle, box, etc. Of these customers, approximately half were purchasing medicines for people having chronic or recurrent medical problems.

47. The chemist shop selected was small and moderately busy. It was staffed by the popular shopkeeper who had no pharmacy degree but had been in the business of selling medicine for 15 years. He learned the trade from his father. The shop was registered in the name of a qualified "signature Chemist" who visited once a fortnight to sign papers related to the sale of scheduled drugs.

48. Clients wanting to confer with the shopkeeper tended to frequent the shop at odd hours. During peak hours, customers were very brief in their transactions. When symptoms were presented, this was done in a hurried fashion with only one or two symptoms noted in passing or communicated through body language.

49. These data suggest rampant antibiotic misuse, but patterns of use need to be better documented. Although customers may only purchase a one day supply of antibiotics, we do not know if they return to purchase additional doses the following day. Partial doses of antibiotics may be purchased due to low levels of disposable income as well as the afflicted wanting to test the effect or compatibility of the medicine. In other cases, the medicine may be taken as long as symptoms persist or as a preventable health measure. Patterns of antibiotic use require detailed household based studies.

50. NIN researchers note that this finding may be an artifact of the investigator's presence. Additionally, in large cities like Hyderabad, chemists have less time to interact with patients and therefore people may be less likely to ask them for advice.

51. As I have argued elsewhere (Nichter 1984b) illness prevention has local meaning. It often incorporates the notion of preventing an already existent illness from becoming worse. States of illness may be manifest or latent. In South Kanara, illnesses such as *tamare* (Nichter 1989: Chapter 6) and TB are believed to exist in latent form becoming manifest in times of weakness or overheat. This concept overlaps with biomedical literature on subclinical disease and the relationship between nutrition and infection.

52. See van der Geest and Whyte (1988) for existing studies on the commercialization of traditional medicine.

53. According to India's Drug and Cosmetics Act of 1940, there are two types of *āyurvedic* drugs. Traditional formulations include drugs which follow classic formula noted in one of 56 specific *āyurvedic* texts. Patented *āyurvedic* formulations include combinations derived from ingredients mentioned in any formula mentioned in one of the texts. The recipe is the manufacturer's own and drugs do not have to be standardized or tested for efficacy or toxicity (Minwalla 1993). *Āyurvedic* drugs do not require an expiration date and are not charged excise duty.

54. Dabur pharmaceutical company alone had a 1993 turnover of Rs. 261 crore (approximately $83 million), and output 650% higher than their 1983 turnover. Dabur, an indigenous, largely *āyurvedic* company is the seventh largest pharmaceutical producer in the country. (See *Times of India*, Bombay edition, October 1993, p. 11). Following Dabur's lead is Zandu Pharmaceuticals (Rs. 39 crore), Himalaya Drug Co. (Rs. 31 crore), and Ajanta Pharmaceuticals (Rs. 17 crore). 1 crore = 100 lakh rupees; 1 lakh rupees = approximately $3,350 (1993 conversion rate).

55. Not addressed in this chapter is the production of pure (*shastric*) *āyurvedic* preparations by *vaidya* for use in their own practice. A renowned *vaidya* may charge handsomely for a home prepared medication which is imbued with his person as well as the herbs he uses. Patients will spend more on such products and view them in a different manner. Due to their national reputation companies such as Kottakal also fetch higher prices for their products.

56. It may be noted that while there are numerous patent herbal (*āyurvedic*) drugs sold in India, only a few command large regional market shares. It must be remembered, however, that given India's population even a small local market share translates into a significant number of sales.

57. In some instances new herbal preparations with English names were not introduced as *āyurvedic* although assumed to be so by the public. Himalaya Pharmaceuticals, for example, markets its products as composed of ancient medicines manufactured by modern processes to yield high quality.

58. The economics of drug sales are far more complex. In addition to direct profit margins one must factor in incentive schemes which offer cash and product bonuses. *Āyurvedic* and allopathic medicine schemes vary by company. One must also consider how fast particular products move in relation to the shelf space they occupy.

59. In the mid-1980s Himalaya pharmaceuticals sold in excess of 60 million units of Liv 52 per year. The company employed more than 400 pharmaceutical representatives, 24 of whom operated in Karnataka State.

60. My intent here is not to discredit these medicines, for I happen to think *āyurveda* contains many valuable medicinal resources. I rather wish to highlight the manner in which these medicines are marketed, and the messages subtly conveyed by the form of marketing.

61. Both *āyurvedic* and homeopathic medicines are widely deemed safe to try. Homeopathic medicines were commonly described to me as being "only milk sugar" and "harmless medicine."

62. On the dangers of patent *āyurvedic* medicines, see newspaper reports by Bhatt (1994), Hathi (1991), and Minwalla (1993). See also the scandal surrounding the sale of Mritasanjivani Sura, an "*āyurvedic*" product manufactured by Dabur India Ltd. which contains 24 percent alcohol and was hailed by the Central Council for Research in *Āyurveda* and Sidha (CCRAS) as "irrational." This "medicine" has been linked to several deaths due to "rampant misuse." Despite being censored, it is still available in South India (Indian Express 1993).

63. On the dangers of "modern traditional" drugs constituted out of distilled concentrates of essential ingredients see Lock (1984, 1990).

64. I am not suggesting that diagnosis by treatment is a new phenomena, but that it is taking on new dimensions in a world pervaded by an endless array of medicinal products.

65. It would be valuable to analyze some of the seemingly irrational combinations of medicines sold in India to see whether a cultural logic underlies their locus of action.

66. On the hazards of using this drug see an editorial in *The Antiseptic* entitled "Hazards of Hormonal Pregnancy Tests," Volume 80:4, 1983. Research is reviewed including that of Prof. K. Palaniappan, who found an incidence of hormonal drug use of 31% among the mothers of 52 deformed babies.

67. For a brief but detailed history of campaigns against high dosage estrogen–progestogen products and government of India response to these campaigns, see Silverman, Lydecker, and Lee (1992:110–124).

68. More recent entries onto the menstrual regulation–abortifacient market include Primolut-N, MP Forte, Amorex, Dyena Forte, Abromin, Mensoon, and Cyclonorm-E to be taken in concert with Cyclonorm-P. Menstrual regulators are not just used as abortives, but also to regulate a woman's cycle prior to

important rituals and marriage functions. Menstruation precludes women from taking an active role in such functions (see Chapters 3 and 7).

69. I refer here to the colonization of time and alterations in what Melbin (1978) has termed the circadian cycle of human social life subject to temporal ecology. In simpler terms, Melbin is referring to alterations in the way people organize and "fill time" as this relates to changing expectations, opportunities, activities, and gratification time lag.

70. A three-day observation period in the same shop in 1991 revealed the same pattern with 21% of clients asking for allopathic drugs.

71. I interviewed representatives from both a large *āyurvedic* and allopathic company canvasing the same region of South Kanara. The latter visited 320 doctors and 90 chemist shops while the former visited 250 of the same doctors and 80 of the same chemist shops.

72. See Wallack and Montgomery (1992) on the role of marketing in confusing the public and restructuring public knowledge about health issues by substituting distorted and manipulative sales messages for more accurate health information.

73. I am not arguing that moralism failed to contribute to the public health movement. There is little doubt that public health reform acts in England in the 1840s were motivated by images of immorality and promiscuity occurring in the mines where men and women worked naked to the waist and where illegitimacy was deemed to be rampant. On the history of public health see Rosen (1958).

74. On the manner in which human behavior and environmental changes account for emerging diseases see Roizman and Hughes (1994), Levins et al. (1994), and Henig (1993).

75. For earlier reports of antibiotic misuse and resistant strains of bacteria see Altman (1982), Levy (1982), Nature (1981), Phillips (1979), and Simmons and Stolley (1974). On resistant strains in India see EPW (1990), Jajoo (1982), and summaries of reports reviewed in Greenhalgh (1987). For more recent reviews of antibiotic resistance see Cohen (1992), Kunin (1993), Levy (1991, 1992, 1993), and Shears (1993). Drug resistance is not caused solely by improper antimicrobial use which gives a selective ecological advantage to less susceptible strains of bacteria. Even adequate doses of antibiotics are distributed unequally in body tissues (Baguero et al. 1993:5). Any treatment therefore produces a low-level antibiotic concentration potentially selective for resistant bacteria, although improper usage of antibiotics increases the chances for selectivity to take place (Levy 1992:206). Two other points must also be borne in mind. First, antibiotics are often not very specific in what bacteria they affect, i.e., they affect bacteria which are pathogenic as well as flora which are protective giving resistant pathogens further advantage. Second, resistance has been found to transfer across different species of bacteria which affect humans as well as other animals.

76. Self-medication patterns have followed suit with individuals purchasing single doses of third generation antimicrobials in Indian cities (Vinay Kamat, personal communication).

77. The cost of newer generation drugs may be reduced in India by "me too" pharmaceutical firms which reproduce drugs soon after they reach the market.

78. Unfortunately, research on antimicrobials has waned based on the perceptions that the battle against bacteria had been won by 1) the development of new penicillins, cephalosporines, and quinolones; and 2) markets have been saturated with "me too" products which are variations of existing drugs (Shales, Levy and Archer 1991). No new family of antibiotics can be anticipated in the present decade and there is as much as a 50% drop in pharmaceutical company involvement in developing new drugs in the anti-infective field (Levy 1993).

79. For example, elsewhere I discuss the disappointment of Sri Lankan villagers in ORS which they came to perceive as a medicine for diarrhea, not dehydration (Nichter 1987b).

80. I am not suggesting that obligations to deities were always fulfilled in the past, for I doubt this was the case. A review of Tuluva folklore and interviews with informants at the time when land reform was being implemented revealed that outstanding vows and obligatory rituals were more common. According to lay informants, exorcists, and *bhūta* cult specialists, the frequency of unfulfilled vows increased following land reform.

81. My use of the term impersonal is not entirely satisfactory. Modern medicine, while a secular source of power, is not strictly impersonal. It may embody the attributes of the party offering the medicine which in turn affects its capacity to "take" to the afflicted. This subject is discussed at length in a separate paper (Nichter and Nordstorm 1989).

82. This dichotomy is somewhat artificial in that pan-Indian deities are incorporated into the local cosmos and given locale specific attributes. In other words there is not simply Shiva, but Shiva of such and such place, Shiva of that big tree!

83. Vasavi (1994) notes how the mind set of acting *"sistam"* associated with modernity has pervaded village life in a variety of ways affecting attitudes about education and even marriage choices. The rhetoric of being *"sistam"* is offset by commentary on the ramifications of social change, an apt illustration of Naik's concept of "double think."

84. My use of Bateson's concept of schismogenesis interfaces with Foucault's (1980a, 1980b, 1986) concept of biopower. Biopower is a form of subjugation which operates at microlevels of everyday life through productive knowledge which fosters surveillance as well as disciplined practice. Increased knowledge of illnesses, deficiencies, populations at risk, and products to alleviate problems increase doctors' propensity to treat and prescribe. The lay population is affected by biopower through feeling compelled to regulate their body

in particular ways (including the use of medicine and the consulting of doctors). This feeling sometimes results in action and often in a feeling of what one should or should not do. Biopower in the form of "knowledge about medicines" is exercised through a desire to want to purchase and consume medicines whether one actually does so or not.

85. Another dimension of this feedback loop entails a dropping in levels of tolerance for symptoms associated with the availability of medicines which control, if not alleviate them (Barsky 1988, Fabrega and Manning 1979, Sonberg and Krema 1986).

REFERENCES

Alland, A. 1970. Adaptation in Cultural Evolution: An Approach to Medical Anthropology. New York: Columbia University Press.

Althusser, L. 1970. Reading Capital. Ben Brewster, trans. London: New Left Books.

Althusser, L. 1971. Ideology and Ideological State Apparatuses. *In* Lenin and Philosophy and Other Essays. Pp. 129–186. New York: Monthly Review Press.

Altman, L. 1982. New Antibiotic Weapons in the Old Bacteria War. New York Times, January 10.

Baguero, F., et al. 1993. Effect of Selective Antibiotic Concentrations on the Evolution of Antimicrobial Resistance. APUA Newsletter 11(4):4–5.

Barsky, A. S. 1988. The Paradox of Health. New England Journal of Medicine 318(7):414–418.

Bateson, G. 1972. Steps to an Ecology of the Mind. New York: Ballantine Books.

Baudrillard, J. 1988. Jean Baudrillard: Selected Writings. J. Mourrian, trans. Mark Poster, ed. Stanford: Stanford University Press.

Bellah, R., R. Madsen, W. Sullivan, A. Swindler, and S. Tipton. 1985. Habits of the Heart: Individualism and Commitment in American Life. Berkeley: University of California Press.

Bhatt, J. 1994. Doubts Raised Over Ayurvedic Drugs. Times of India, Bombay Edition. January 9, 1994.

Bourdieu, P. 1978. Outline of a Theory of Practice. Cambridge: Cambridge University Press.

Bourdieu, P. 1990. Logic of Practice. Stanford: Stanford University Press.

Buck-Morss, S. 1991. The Dialectics of Seeing: Walter Benjamin and the Arcades Projects. Cambridge: MIT Press.

Burghart, R. 1988. Penicillin: An Ancient Ayurvedic Medicine. *In* The Context of Medicine in Developing Countries. S. van der Geest and S. R. Whyte, eds. Pp. 289–298. Dordrecht, The Netherlands: Kluwer Academic Press.

Campbell, C. 1989. The Romantic Ethic and the Spirit of Modern Consumerism. London: Basil Blackwell.

Clifford, J. 1988. The Predicament of Culture: Twentieth Century Ethnography, Literature, and Art. Cambridge: Harvard University Press.

Cohen, M. L. 1992. Epidemiology of Drug Resistance: Implications for a Post-Antimicrobial Era. Science 257:1050–1055.

Daniels, E. V. 1984. Fluid Signs. Berkeley: University of California Press.

Douglas, M. and A. Wildavsky. 1982. Risk and Culture: An Essay on the Selection of Technological and Environmental Dangers. Berkeley: University of California Press.

D'Penha, H. J. 1971. Promise and Influence of Government Advertising. Promotion 5(1):3.

Economic and Political Weekly (EPW). 1990. Drug Overuse and Disease. Economic and Political Weekly (August 4):1678.

Evans, P. B. 1981. Recent Research on Multinational Corporations. Annual Review of Sociology 7:199–223.

Ewen, S. 1976. Captains of Consciousness: Advertising and the Social Roots of the Consumer Culture. New York: McGraw Hill.

Ewen, S. and E. Ewen. 1982. Channels of Desire. New York: McGraw Hill.

Fabrega, H. and P. Manning. 1979. Illness Episodes, Illness Security and Treatment in a Pluralistic Setting. Social Science and Medicine 13B:41–51.

Fabricant, S. J. and N. Hirschhorn. 1987. Deranged Distribution, Perverse Prescription, Unprotected Use: The Irrationality of Pharmaceuticals in the Developing World. Health Policy and Planning 2(3):204–213.

Faizal, A. 1983. The Right Pharmaceuticals at the Right Prices: Consumer Perspectives. World Development 11(3):265–269.

Farquhar, J. 1991. Eating Chinese Medicine. Cultural Anthropology 9(4):471–497.

Featherstone, M. 1991. Consumer Culture and Postmodernism. London: Sage Press.

Ferguson, A. 1981. Commercial Pharmaceutical Medicine and Medicalization: A Case Study From El Salvador. Culture, Medicine and Psychiatry 5:105–134.

Foucault, M. 1980a. Power and Knowledge: Selected Interviews and Other Writings. Brighton, England: Harvester.

Foucault, M. 1980b. The History of Sexuality, Volume 1: An Introduction. R. Huxley, trans. New York: Random House.

Foucault, M. 1986. The Care of the Self: The History of Sexuality, Volume 3. New York: Pantheon.

Fox, S. 1985. The Mirror Makers. New York: Vintage Books.

Friedson, E. 1970. Profession of Medicine. New York: Harper and Row.

Fuglesang, A. 1977. Doing Things Together: Report on an Experience of Communicating Appropriate Technology. Uppsala, Sweden: Dag Hammersjold Foundation.

Ghosh, S. 1986. Drug Policy Needs: A Sea-Change. Hindustan Times, March 8.

Giddens, A. 1991. Modernity and Self-Identity: Self and Society in the Late Modern Age. Cambridge: Polity Press.

Girimaji, P. 1993. No Act on Adulteration. The Sunday Times of India, August 22:16.

Goldman, R. 1992. Reading Ads Socially. London: Routledge.

Goldman, R. and M. Montagne. 1986. Marketing "Mind Mechanics": Deciding Antidepressant Drug Advertisements. Social Science and Medicine 22(10):1047–1058.

Good, B. 1977. The Heart of What's the Matter: The Semantics of Illness in Iran. Culture, Medicine and Psychiatry 1:25–58.

Gothoskar, S. 1983. Drug Control: India. World Development 11(3):223–228.

Gramsci, A. 1971. The Intellectuals. *In* Selections From the Prison Notebooks. Q. Hoare and G. Smith, eds. London: Lawrence and Wishart.

Green, E. 1986. Diarrhea and the Social Marketing of Oral Rehydration Salts in Bangladesh. Social Science and Medicine 23(4):357–366.

Greenhalgh, T. 1987. Drug Prescription and Self-Medication in India: An Exploratory Study. Social Science and Medicine 25(3):307–318.

Gustafson, L. and K. Wide. 1981. Marketing of Obsolete Antibiotics in Central America. Lancet 8210(1):31–33.

Harvey, D. 1989. The Condition of Postmodernity: An Enquiry Into the Origins of Cultural Change. Oxford: Basel Blackwell.

Hathi, D. 1991. Grandma's Goodies or Hidden Hazards. Deccan Herald, July 7.

Henig, R. 1993. The Dancing Matrix — Voyager Along the Viral Frontier. New York: Alfred Knopf.

Hercheimer, A. and G. Stimson. 1981. The Use of Medicines for Illness. *In* Pharmaceuticals and Health Policy. Richard Blum, ed. Pp. 36–60. London: Crown Helm.

Hobsbawn, E. and R. Ranger, eds. 1983. The Invention of Tradition. Cambridge: Cambridge University Press.

Howe, D., ed. 1991. The Varieties of Sensory Experience: A Sourcebook in the Anthropology of the Senses. Toronto: University of Toronto Press.

Indian Express. 1993. Despite Delhi Holocaust, Sura Being Sold in Kerala. Indian Express, Bombay edition, December 15.

Jajoo, V. 1982. Misuse of Antibiotics. Voluntary Health Association of India, Document No. D10.

James, J. 1983. Consumer Choice in the Third World. New York: St. Martin Press.

Jaya Rao, K. 1977. Tonics: How Much an Economic Waste. *In* In Search of Diagnosis. A. J. Patel, ed. Pp. 105–112. Vadodara, India: Medico Friend Circle.

Jayaraman, K. 1986a. Drug Policy: Playing Down Main Issues. Economic and Political Weekly 21(25–26):1129–1132.

Jayaraman, K. 1986b. Drug Policy: Reinterpreting Issues. Economic and Political Weekly 21(18):798–800.

Jeliffe, D. and P. Jeliffe. 1977. The Cultural Cul-De-Sac of Western Medicine: Transactions of the Royal Society of Tropical Medicine and Hygiene 71(4):331– 334.

Kapur, R. L. 1979. The Role of Traditional Healers in Mental Health Care in Rural India. Social Science and Medicine 13b:27–31.

Kelman, S. 1975. The Social Nature of the Definition of Health. International Journal of Health Services 5(4):625–642.

Krishnaswamy, K. and D. Kumar. 1983. Drug Utilization: Precepts and Practices. Nutrition News 4:5. Hyderabad: National Institute of Nutrition.

Krishnaswamy, K., D. Kumar, and G. Radhaiah. 1983. Drug Sales: Precepts and Practices (Unpublished report). Food and Drug Toxicology Research Centre. National Institute of Nutrition, Hyderabad, India.

Kumar, G. 1993. Low Mortality and High Morbidity in Kerala Reconsidered. Population and Development Review 19(1):103–121.

Kunin, C. M. 1993. Resistance to Antimicrobial Drugs — A Worldwide Calamity. Annals of Internal Medicine 118(7):557–561.

Laping, J. 1984. Ayurvedya: Its Progressive Potential and Its Possible Contribution to Health Care Today. Second International Congress on Traditional Asian Medicine, Sept. 2. Indonesia: Surabaja.

Leslie, C. 1967. Professional and Popular Health Cultures in South Asia. *In* Understanding Sciences and Technology in India and Pakistan. W. Morehouse, ed. Pp. 27–42. New Delhi: Foreign Area Materials Center, University of the State of New York.

Leslie, C. 1989. Indigenous Pharmaceuticals, the Capitalist World System, and Civilization. Kroeber Anthropological Society Papers Numbers 69–70:23–31.

Levins, R., et al. 1994. The Emergence of New Diseases. American Scientist 82(1): 52–60.

Levy, S. B. 1982. Microbial Resistance to Antibiotics. Lancet 2(8289): 83–88.

Levy, S. B. 1991. Antibiotic Availability and Use: Consequences to Man and His Environment. Journal of Clinical Epidemiology 44(Supplement 2):83s–87s.

Levy, S. B. 1992. The Antibiotic Paradox: How Miracle Drugs are Destroying the Miracle. New York: Plenum Press.

Levy, S. B. 1993. Confronting Multidrug Resistance: A Role for Each of Us. JAMA 269(14):1840–1842.

Lilja, J. 1983. Indigenous and Multinational Pharmaceutical Companies. Social Science and Medicine 17(6):1171–1180.

Lock, M. 1984. Licorice in Leviathan: The Medicalization of Care for the Japanese Elderly. Culture, Medicine and Psychiatry 8(2):121–139.

Lock, M. 1990. Rationalization of Japanese Herbal Medications: The Hegemony of Orchestrated Pluralism. Human Organization 49(1):41–47.

Malholtra, K. 1985. Changing Patterns of Disease in India with Special Reference to Childhood Mortality. Paper, Wenner-Gren Symposium on The Health and Disease of Populations in Transition, October 19. New Mexico: Santa Fe.

Mariott, M. 1978. Toward an Ethnosociology of South Asian Caste Systems. *In* The New Wind: Changing Identities in South Asia. Kenneth David, ed. Pp. 227–238. The Hague: Mouton.

Martin, E. 1991. The End of the Body. American Ethnologist 12:121–140.

Medawar, C. 1979. Insult or Injury. Social Audit: London.

Medawar, C. and B. Freese. 1982. Drug Diplomacy. London: Social Audit.

Melbin, M. 1978. The Colonization of Time. *In* Human Activity and Time Geography. T. Carlstein, D. Parkes, and N. Thrift, eds. Pp. 100–113. London: Edward Arnold.

Minwalla, S. 1993. When Potent Drugs Turn Poison. The Sunday Times of India, Bombay edition. December 5:3.

Murray, C. J. and L. C. Chen. 1992. Understanding Morbidity Change. Population and Development Review 18:481–503.

Nature. 1981. Saving Antibiotics from Themselves. August 20:661.

Nichter, Mark. 1981a. Negotiation of the Illness Experience: The Influence of Ayurvedic Therapy on the Psychosocial Dimensions of Illness. Culture, Medicine and Psychiatry 5:5–24.

Nichter, Mark. 1981b. Idioms of Distress: Alternatives in the Expression of Psychosocial Distress: A Case Study from South India. Culture, Medicine and Psychiatry 5:379–408.

Nichter, Mark. 1981c. Toward a Culturally Responsive Rural Health Care Delivery System in India. *In* The Social and Cultural Context of Medicine in India. Giri Raj Gupta, ed. Pp. 223–236. New Delhi: Vikas Publishers.

Nichter, Mark. 1984a. Project Community Diagnosis: Participatory Research as a First Step Toward Community Involvement in Primary Health Care. Social Science and Medicine 19(3):237–252.

Nichter, Mark. 1984b. Toward a "People Near" Promotive Health Within Primary Health Care. *In* Proceedings of the First International Symposium on Public Health in Asia and the Pacific Basin. Thomas Bendy and Jonathan Raymond, eds. Honolulu: University of Hawaii School of Public Health.

Nichter, Mark. 1987a. Kyasanur Forest Disease: Ethnography of a Disease of Development. Medical Anthropology Quarterly 1(4):406–423.

Nichter, Mark. 1987b. Aralu to ORS: Sinhalese Perceptions of Digestion, Diarrhea and Dehydration. Social Science and Medicine 27:39–52.

Nichter, Mark. 1989. Pharmaceuticals, Health Commodification, and Social Relations: Ramifications for Primary Health Care. *In* Anthropology and International Health, Chapter 9 (Mark Nichter) Dordrecht, The Netherlands: Kluwer Academic Press.

Nichter, Mark. 1990. Vaccinations in South Asia: False Expectations and Commanding Metaphors. *In* Anthropology and Primary Health Care. J. Coreil and D. Mull, eds. Pp. 196–221. Connecticut: Westview Press.

Nichter, Mark and C. Nordstrom. 1989. The Question of Medicine Answering: Health Commodification and the Social Relations in Healing in Sri Lanka. Culture, Medicine and Psychiatry 13:367–390.

Nichter, Mark and N. Vuckovic. 1994. Agenda for an Anthropology of Pharmaceutical Practice. Social Science and Medicine 39(11):1509–1525.

Ohnuki-Tierney, E. 1986. Illness and Culture in Contemporary Japan. New York: Cambridge University Press.

Osifo, N. G. 1983. Our Promotion of Drugs in International Product Package Inserts. Tropical Doctor 13:5–8.

Parker, R., S. Shah, C. Alexander, and A. Neuman. 1979. Self-Care and Use of Home Treatment in Rural Areas of India and Nepal. Culture, Medicine and Psychiatry 3(1):3–28.

Patel, M. S. 1983. Drug Costs in Developing Countries and Policies to Reduce Them. World Development 11(3):195–204.

Pfleiderer, B. and W. Bichman. 1985. Krankheit und Kultur: Eine Einfuhrung in die Ethnomedizin. Berlin: Verlag.

Phadke, A. 1982. Multinationals in India's Drug Industry. Medico-Friend Circle Bulletin, January–February. Pune, India.

Phadke, A. 1986. Drug Policy: Industry's Misleading Arguments. Economic and Political Weekly 21(19):842–843.

Phillips, I. 1979. Antibiotic Policies. *In* Recent Advances in Infection, Vol. I. D. Reeves and A. Geddes, eds. Pp. 151–163. Edinburgh: Churchill Livingston.

Poh-ai, T. 1985. Ciba-Geigy's Cover-Up. Multinational Monitor 6(11):1–3.

Pradhan, S. B. 1983. International Pharmaceutical Marketing. Westport, Connecticut: Quorum Books.

Price, L. 1989. In the Shadow of Biomedicine: Self-Medication in Two Ecuadorian Pharmacies. Social Science and Medicine 28(9):905–915.

Querubin, M. and M. Tan. 1986. Old Roles, New Roles: Women, Primary Health Care, and Pharmaceuticals in the Philippines. *In* Adverse Effects: Women and the Pharmaceutical Industry. K. McDonnel, ed. Pp. 175–186. Toronto: Women's Educational Press.

Ramanujan, A. K. 1989. Is There an Indian Way of Thinking? An Informal Essay. Contributions to Indian Sociology 23:41–58.

Reissland, N. and R. Burghart. 1988. The Quality of a Mother's Milk and the Health of Her Child: Beliefs and Practices of the Women of Mithila. Social Science and Medicine 27(5):461–469.

Rohde, J. 1988. Good Health Makes Good Politics. Economic and Political Weekly (March 26):637–638.

Riley, J. 1990. The Risk of Being Sick: Morbidity Trends in Four Countries. Population and Development Review 16:403–432.

Roizman, B. and J. Hughes. 1994. Effects of Changes in Human Ecology and Behavior in Infectious Diseases: An Introduction. Washington, DC: National Academy of Sciences Press.

Rosen, G. 1958. A History of Public Health. New York: M. D. Publications.

Sadasivam, B. 1993. Toward Drug Policy for Better Health. The Times of India, Bombay edition, September 18:12.

Sanberg, P. and R. Krema. 1986. Over the Counter Drugs: Harmless or Hazardous. New York: Chelsea House.

Schudson, M. 1984. Advertising: The Uneasy Persuasion. New York: Basic Books.

Sen, A. 1990. Objectivity and Position: Assessment of Health and Well Being: Working Paper 1. Center for Population and Development Studies, Harvard University.

Shales, D., S. Levy, and G. Archer. 1991. Antimicrobial Resistance: New Directions. American Society of Microbiology News 57:455–458.

Shears, P. 1993. A Review of Bacterial Resistance to Antimicrobial Agents in Tropical Countries. Annals of Tropical Paediatrics 13(3):219–226.

Shepperdson, M. 1988. The Political Economy of Health in India. *In* The Indian National Congress and the Political Economy of India 1885–1985. M. Shepperdson and C. Simmons, eds. Pp. 160–269. Aldershot, England: Avebury.

Shiva, M. 1987. Towards a Healthy Use of Pharmaceuticals. New Delhi: Voluntary Health Association of India.

Silverman, M. 1976. The Drugging of the Americas. Berkeley: University of California Press.

Silverman, M., P. Lee, and M. Lydecker. 1982. Prescriptions for Death: The Drugging of the Third World. Berkeley: University of California Press.

Silverman, M., P. Lee, and M. Lydecker. 1986. Drug Promotion: The Third World Revisited. International Journal of Health Services 16(4):659–667.

Silverman, M., M. Lydecker, and P. Lee. 1992. Bad Medicine: The Prescription Drug Industry in the Third World. Stanford: Stanford University Press.

Simmons, H. and P. Stolley. 1974. This is Medical Progress? Trends and Consequences of Antibiotic Use in the United States. Journal of the American Medical Association 227(9):1023–1028.

Singh, C. V. 1983. Drug Manufacturers: Rising Temperature. India Today, October 31:106.

Smith, R. 1978. Kurusu: The Price of Progress in a Japanese Village, 1951–1975. Stanford: Stanford University Press.

Taylor, D. 1986. The Pharmaceutical Industry and Health in the Third World. Social Science and Medicine 22(11):1141–1149.

van der Geest, S. and S. R. Whyte, eds. 1988. The Context of Medicines in Developing Countries. Dordrecht, The Netherlands: Kluwer Academic Press.

Vasavi, A. 1994. Hybrid Times, Hybrid People: Culture and Agriculture in South India. Man (N.S.) 29:283–300.

Victoria, C. G. 1982. Statistical Malpractice in Drug Promotion: Case-Study from Brazil. Social Science and Medicine 16:707–709.

Voluntary Health Association of India (VHAI). 1986. A Rational Drug Policy. New Delhi: VHAI Press.

Vuckovic, N. and M. Nichter. 1995. Pharmaceutical Practice in the U.S.: Anthropological Perspectives and Research Needs. Unpublished manuscript.

Wallack, L. and K. Montgomery. 1992. Advertising for All by the Year 2000: Public Health Implications for Less Developed Countries. Health Policy 13(2):204–223.

Whitehead, J. 1973. Bacterial Resistance: Changing Patterns of Some Common Pathogens. British Medical Journal 2:224–228.

Williams, R. 1977. Marxism and Literature. London: Oxford University Press.

Williamson, J. 1978. Decoding Advertisements: Ideology and Meaning in Advertising. London: Marian Boyars.

Worsley, P. 1984. The Three Worlds. Chicago: University of Chicago Press.

Young, A. 1982. The Anthropologies of Illness and Sickness. Annual Review of Anthropology 11:257–285.

Yudkin, J. S. 1980. The Economics of Pharmaceutical Supply in Tanzania. International Journal of Health Services 10(3):455–477.

Zawad, K. 1985. The Fight to Bar Bogus Drugs. Multinational Monitor 6(9):1–3.

Section Four

Health Service Research and Health Communication

Medical anthropologists have important contributions to make to health service research and health communication. By grounding investigations of resource supply and demand, service accessibility and acceptability in the lifeworlds of local populations, anthropologists may help their public health colleagues better understand patterns of health care utilization and expenditure. Health service research may also be enhanced by ethnographic studies of health bureaucracies and service providers which are sensitive to issues of cooperation and competition, professional identity, teamwork, and triage. Through formative research responsive to public health priorities, anthropologists can assist health educators in the development of more meaningful messages by: 1) addressing local images of ethnophysiology and acknowledging popular health concerns; 2) paying credence to local illness terms and conventions structuring the language of illness; 3) maximizing cultural resources (both material and conceptual); 4) embracing popular styles of communication appreciated by local populations; 5) identifying constituencies within a population which may be responsive to different types of informational and motivational messages; 6) monitoring the response of these constituencies to health messages over time facilitating mid-course correction in communication programs; and 7) drawing attention to issues of responsibility implicit in health messages which are potentially victim blaming.

Anthropology has a role to play in monitoring health-related communications originating from both the public and private sectors, where vested interests such as the pharmaceutical industry affect public opinion. Far from being the passive handmaiden of biomedical hegemony, the role of medical anthropologists in health service research and health communication can be proactive, critical, and committed to community-based problem solving.

In keeping with the reflexive stance of this volume, the final section is followed by a brief epilogue — a field vignette which invites us to consider how foreign aid is interpreted in other socio-moral worlds. It serves as a reminder that our actions in the name of health and development are always viewed by the "other" as motivated.

CHAPTER 10

Vaccinations in the Third World: A Consideration of Community Demand

Mark Nichter

Those who plan and conduct public health programmes seldom give the same thoughtful consideration to the human relations aspects of their projects as they give to the physical, technical, and organizational aspects.... What is needed is for programme organizers and administrators to recognize that their undertakings operate in social and cultural as well as physical and biological environments.

(Dhillon and Kar 1963:19)

INTRODUCTION

Over the last decade remarkable success in vaccinating pregnant women and children has been reported by international health agencies. In 1991 UNICEF estimated that vaccinations had saved the lives of some three million children, that the number of infants vaccinated had doubled in the past five years, and that 80% of global EPI goals had been established (UNICEF 1991).[1] Just as impressive have been reports that infants who are immunized maintain a better chance of survival in general, beyond protection from specific EPI diseases.[2] Such data have led to statements being made that: "In a world where so much seems to go wrong, the EPI program is one international initiative that is fulfilling its promise" (Hayden et al. 1989).

What has largely been demonstrated is that given "political will," vaccination rates may be dramatically increased as a result of intensive campaigns which mobilize the community. I use the phrase "mobilize the community" in the sense that leaders endorse vaccination programs, social marketing campaigns blitz the community with spot messages about the timings and availability of vaccinations, primary health care workers engage in active community surveillance, and vaccination camps are held. While there is some talk about the cost effectiveness of vaccination programs (e.g., Anderson et al. 1992) and how vaccination rates may be further increased beyond existing plateaus in the mid-1990s, others have questioned the extent to which vaccination rates will be sustainable once expensive campaigns are phased down given economic constraints.[3]

The philosophy behind intensive vaccination campaigns has been that once the public has been introduced to the benefits of medical technology and has experienced lower rates of illness and suffering as a result of vaccination programs, demand for such technology will follow. In this chapter, I question this assumption and consider community demand for "vaccinations in general" as well as demand for specific vaccinations.[4] I will draw a distinction between *active demand for* and *passive acceptance of* vaccinations. Active demand entails adherence to vaccination programs by an informed public which perceives the benefits of and need for specific vaccinations. Passive acceptance denotes compliance: passive acceptance of vaccinations by a public which yields to the recommendations and social pressure, if not prodding, of health workers and community leaders.

A consideration of community demand for vaccinations requires an examination of popular perceptions of vaccinations as well as local interpretations of immunizable diseases and associated local illness categories. Toward this end, I present data from South and Southeast Asia (India, Sri Lanka, Indonesia), the Pacific Basin (Philippines) and West Africa. After a general discussion, I draw special attention to measles, an illness causing considerable mortality in less developed countries.[5]

Before considering local response to vaccination programs, however, it is worth examining the sociopolitical context into which they are being introduced. Positive press which applauds governmental and international efforts to save the children would lead us to believe that vaccination programs are exceedingly popular and appreciated throughout the developing world. Does such an impression mask voices of dissent, if not a sense of ambivalence and mistrust within these countries? Is there uncritical acceptance of all vaccination programs since the smallpox success story?

VOICES OF DISSENT TO VACCINATION PROGRAMS

While vaccination programs are often introduced with a fair amount of fanfare, they are not always greeted with a great amount of trust by all members of the populace or scientific community.[6] Vaccination programs have in fact provided an opportunity for political commentary as well as the articulation of collective anxieties. For example, in India segments of the population have linked vaccination initiatives to coexisting national directives, most notably family planning. Conspiracy theories have emerged among both conservative Muslim and Hindu groups linking the two programs to hidden political agenda (Nichter 1990).[7] Hindus have been vocal in communicating their fear that Muslims are undermining national population policy by attempting to produce as many children as possible in an effort to gain votes.[8] Muslims fear that the Hindu majority may be covertly introducing family planning through the vaccination program. This concern is shared by Hindus who fear that because some sectors do not voluntarily adopt family planning methods, the government feels justified in controlling population growth through clandestine operations.

Rumors reflecting these fears were legion in the 1970s during India's "emergency" exercise of state power in the name of population control. Mistrust has reemerged in the 1990s, a time of Hindu–Muslim unrest, vaccination program intensification, and press accounts and critiques of new anti-fertility vaccine trials in India.[9] In lieu of a growing fear that the vaccinations women and children are asked to receive may somehow be linked to sterilization, there is a questioning of why so many are needed. As a result of distrust, members of one community whom I interviewed in 1992 articulated their desire to receive vaccinations from private practitioners instead of government Primary Health Center (PHC) staff.[10]

This is not the only conspiracy theory involving vaccinations. One leader of a Hindu group located in a South Indian city (the site of considerable Christian missionary and medical activity) recently engaged me in a discussion about the "real purpose of vaccination programs." The man began by pointing out to me the visual similarity between the Christian cross and a hypodermic set, noting that injections and vaccinations came from foreign Christian countries. Just as Christian missionaries had come to India to convert Hindus in the past and had won over the local population by offering aid in the form of hospitals and schools, so vaccinations were an extension of this scheme. After receiving the protection of vaccinations and foreign medicines, the population would no longer feel the need to adhere to traditional values. They would be "civilized" in a Western sense, at the expense of their moral and ethnic identity. He referred to "Brigade Road youth,"

youth that congregate along a fashionable street in Bangalore (the state capital of Karnataka State), as epitomizing this trend. Like the children of Indians living abroad, such youth rejected their heritage in favor of "Christian values, tastes, and desires." Vaccinations, he said, made them feel immune from the wrath of the gods whom they had forsaken.

This political leader's litany against modern youth and the subversive activities of Christian (i.e., capitalist) purveyors of "development" was launched within the context of a discussion of vaccination programs. The metamedical theme which underlay his discussion is worth further scrutiny. Vaccinations were associated with "civilizing the other" and interpreted in terms of a "process of domestification" analogous to missionary work — only in this case the body is saved at the expense of the soul. But saved for what? The gist of his view was that "the other" (i.e., Hindu) is rendered less dangerous by vaccinations in order to become a citizen-consumer in a "global community" driven by Christian (i.e., Western) tastes.[11] The term colonialism was not overtly referred to by the informant, but it was clear that he suspected a subtle process of hegemony taking place in which secular values were embodied through vaccinations and dependency on Western medicine. Medicines were not seen as neutral, but rather as a vehicle of ideology. Reciting a Sanskrit sacred verse (*sloka*), he assured me that in India this strategy would not be effective. For each disease protected against by a vaccination or medicine, a new affliction would arise as a sign of the power of the gods if the sacred was neglected.[12] In defense of his position, he noted that the control of smallpox had brought new afflictions in this region, such as Japanese encephalitis, Kyasanur forest disease (Nichter 1992), and increasing rates of tuberculosis.[13]

Discussion of vaccination programs has also served as a platform from which to address issues related to foreign policy and national identity. For example, in 1987 there was heated controversy in India's national press about an Indo-U.S. vaccine program. The United States was accused of using the Indian population as guinea pigs for vaccine experiments, despite the fact that the vaccines to be introduced had undergone tests in the United States and that the India's Department of Biotechnology had set up a strict ethical review process. Such charges are not uncommon in developing countries and need to be considered metamedically, that is, in terms of what they have to say about issues related to the "body politic" and "social body" as distinct from the physical body (Scheper-Hughes and Lock 1987, Turner 1987, 1992).

Calling attention to the penetration of Indian bodies with foreign vaccines indexes concern about national boundaries and a sense of moral geography. This is reflected in Indian charges that the epidemiology center the United

States proposed to build as part of the joint vaccination venture would violate national security by collecting "computerized data" on the genetic makeup of the Indian population. Fear was expressed in several newspaper editorials that a national profile of immunity would be collected.[14] Biopolitical imagery was engaged wherein the immune system became a potential battlefield much in keeping with Haraway's (1991) description of cell wars in an era of star wars. The body, conceived of as a strategic system, ceases to be a "stable map of normalized functions and instead emerges as a highly mobile field of strategic differences" (Haraway 1991:211).[15]

Embracing the semantics of defense and invasion, concern was expressed in the Indian press about the "strategic importance of immunocompetence," the need to protect against bioterrorism, and the treatment of AIDS.[16] In one discussion I had with a prominent member of the press at this time, a direct link was made between computer viruses and AIDS. Both constituted man-made sources of communication terrorism in the form of a rapidly proliferating foreign code which needed to gain entry to a population's "operating system" in order to render it immobile. The immune system was described as the body's "operating system."[17]

Poignant charges have also been leveled against international health agencies and donor groups by members of the Indian academic community. Some local scholars have questioned the wisdom as well as the motivation of intensive vaccination campaigns given the health infrastructure of several of India's states. Debabar Banerji (1990a, 1990b), an outspoken critic (and anthropologist) has blatantly accused an "unholy alliance of national and international power brokers" of technocentric colonialism.[18] Counter to the Ministry of Health's claims that India's national vaccination program has been a success, Banerji evaluates the program as a dismal failure in reaching less than one fifth of vaccinable children in one half of India's population. Harsher still is his charge that technocentric approaches to health have been attractive to the ruling classes of less developed countries because they "achieve visible and dramatic improvements in health which divert attention away from the lack of basic survival needs."[19]

Banerji has criticized international agencies for their obsession with herd immunity as well as for their exploitation of the plight of helpless young children.[20] Against figures of "lives saved by immunizations," he questions the allocation of resources to vaccination programs, pointing to opportunity costs and the diversion of resources from other programs such as India's national TB program. The balance of resources expended to keep children under five safe from vaccinable diseases is questioned, given the meager resources expended to improve the quality of life for child survivors. Alluded to is the fact that mortality from diseases such as measles and TB were dramatically reduced in the West as a result of social and sanitary reform long before the advent of vaccines and chemotherapy.

Arguing that vaccination programs represent an example of selective primary health care failure (Walsh and Warren 1979), Banerji calls attention to the need for a community based approach to primary health care. What needs to be clarified is that it is not vaccinations per se which are rejected by critics such as Banerji. The imposition of a vaccination campaign complete with targets, plans for community surveillance, and the possibility of coercion are questioned, as are campaigns rendering the community dependent and powerless to decide upon its own health care priorities are also questioned. It is only when vaccinations are recognized as a perceived need and demanded by the "community" that they become community development resources in a "comprehensive primary health care" sense (Rifkin and Walt 1986).[21]

I highlight this point to distinguish between short and long term vaccination goals and the programs designed to meet them. Programs designed to achieve rapid vaccination coverage to meet time bound targets differ from programs designed to educate a community about vaccinations through appropriate conceptualization. For the most part, global vaccination initiatives have focused on short-term goals with the assumption being that once communities were "covered," the demonstration effect of vaccinations would translate into widespread acceptance and popularity.

But has this been the case? I have been struck by the paucity of evaluations of sustained community interest following vaccination campaigns. The results of one such study are sobering. Visaria, Anandjiwala, and Desai (1990) studied a Gujarati community in India which was the target of an intensive mass vaccination campaign conducted between 1987–88. For two years the campaign was evaluated as highly successful. As a result, it was decided to suspend active surveillance and vaccination camps. In lieu of a third year of intensive outreach efforts, PHC and hospital staff were encouraged to ask parents to vaccinate their children. The hope was that after two years of intensive communication about vaccinations, parents would actively seek out services for their children.

The results of a follow-up survey in 1989 were disturbing. Out of 150 eligible children in seven villages only 14 children (less than 10%) received the appropriate vaccinations. In two villages, cases of measles were reported after a two year interval. The researchers concluded in their report that: "The overall situation is quite puzzling. There seems to be a fatalistic and almost unquestioning acceptance of childhood illness" (ibid.:639).

It could be argued that attitudes toward vaccinations in a rural area of Gujarat reflect the poor educational levels of mothers. A study by Kutty

(1989) in Kerala State, India, suggests that other issues may be involved. Kerala has been heralded as one of the world's "good health at low cost" success stories (Halstead, Walsh, and Warren 1985).[22] Kerala maintains India's highest level of literacy and lowest level of infant mortality (Krishnan 1985). Kutty's (1989) study revealed that regardless of educational status, mothers' attitudes toward vaccination remained surprisingly low in Kerala. Both mothers with less than 10 years of school and mothers with over 10 years of schooling maintained positive attitudes about vaccinations in only 31% and 39% of cases, respectively.[23] While vaccination rates in Kerala are reported to be high, data such as these suggest that demand within the community may wane at any time if not accompanied by a proactive vaccination program.[24]

FACTORS INFLUENCING VACCINATION ACCEPTANCE

In the long run, the success of vaccination campaigns will be measured in terms of community demand for vaccination services. Three sets of factors influence vaccination acceptance and demand once the community has been made aware of this resource: supply and service factors, social factors, and cultural factors which influence how vaccinations are interpreted. I will briefly consider the first two sets of factors and focus on the third in keeping with the objective of this chapter: a consideration of community demand.

Supply-Service Factors

When discussing lower than expected rates of vaccination acceptance, health planners typically call attention to either a) the public's low awareness of the availability of vaccinations or, b) operational problems entailed in keeping the health service infrastructure supplied with vaccines. These problems are compounded by structural and organizational barriers to health care utilization.[25] Health service researchers have repeatedly drawn attention to vaccination accessibility (location and the timing of clinics) as real life constraints facing people who may want to change their behavior (Bonair, Rosenfield, and Tengvald 1989). On the basis of such research, some researchers have argued for community participation in deciding when and where vaccinations are to be made available.

Attention has also been called to missed opportunities on the part of health workers who have failed to vaccinate children when mildly ill or when vaccine wastage might result from opening multidose vials of vaccine for one child.[26] Underappreciated in this literature is the vulnerable position of health workers who are subject to community censorship. Their reasons for not wanting to take risks needs to be appreciated more fully. Many work in a context where responsibility for death is avoided at all costs, to the point that PHC doctors refer critical cases to distant hospitals to retain their reputations. Just as doctors do not follow "rational" drug guidelines because they are subject to community demands (and profit motives), health workers cannot be expected to vaccinate ill children if held accountable for their health by a community which deems vaccinating during illness a sign of disregard.[27]

The ways in which the organizational culture of national health infrastructures influence health worker performance are also underappreciated. This includes factors affecting staff motivation, teamwork, and supervision, as well as patient follow-up (Kulkarni 1992, Nichter 1986). As I have noted in my earlier study of vaccination acceptance (Nichter 1990), faith in health staff is decreased by a target system where attention is focused entirely on the quantity and not the quality of service administered. Staff pressured to meet EPI targets are perceived by many community members as willing to compromise their best interests. The vaccination of mildly ill children is taken as evidence of this. In this context, "missed opportunities" on the part of some staff to immunize mildly ill children may constitute a deliberate attempt to secure community confidence over time.

Each of the factors noted above plays an important role in reducing vaccination coverage. Emphasis on health care delivery issues alone, however, eclipses an even more basic issue: does the "public" want the growing range of vaccines being made available to them? This issue demands a consideration of who the public is, that is, a consideration of different segments of local populations.

Social Factors

As Bonair, Rosenfield, and Tengvald (1989) have aptly noted, the compliance perspective which has driven most health diffusion research fails to get at a broader understanding of how and when new innovations are adopted. Understanding factors which facilitate community demand requires a shift in research focus from "predictors of non-use of vaccinations" (noncompliance) to "predictors of demand" (adherence) and "self-regulation" which pay credence to the agency of community members. In keeping with a social marketing approach to studying consumer behavior, much research on predictors of vaccination acceptance have segmented the population. There has been a tendency to focus on the social characteristics of individuals which predispose them to accept (passively) or seek out (actively) vaccinations. Mothers are the most common unit of analysis (considered in terms of their education or work status), although more research has begun to focus on fathers and elders as decision makers. The birth order and gender of children as predictors of vaccination acceptance and timing (when received) have also been considered.[28]

Such research has provided valuable insights into patterns of vaccination use. For example, studies in North India and Nepal have pointed out gender specific differences in vaccination which favor male children over females (Ahluwalia, Helgerson, and Bia 1988, Sharma, Lohari, and Gupta 1977, and Singh, Goel, and Mittal 1986). Studies in Indonesia (e.g., Kasniyah 1993) have likewise pointed out significant differences between women who work inside and outside the home with respect to vaccination behavior and constraints.

One limitation of this type of research has been that it has focused more on discrete, measurable variables than on pathways and processes associated with vaccination acceptance. We do not know, for example, what it is about a mother's education which predisposes her to have her children vaccinated (e.g., the content of education, affiliation with modernity, social mobility) or contexts in which her education does and does not have leverage. Existing research focuses more on barriers which make it difficult for some groups of mothers to use vaccination services, than it does on demand factors which lead other members of these groups to seek out services even in the face of time constraints.[29]

CULTURAL PERCEPTIONS OF VACCINATIONS AND EPI-RELATED ILLNESSES

Less appreciated than the impact of social factors on vaccination acceptance is the influence of cultural factors on vaccination demand.[30] Cultural factors include not only perceptions of vaccinations and EPI-associated illnesses, but also perceptions of vulnerability and protection as well as the role which medicines play in producing and maintaining health. Consideration of the context (past experiences, contingencies) as well as the cosmos into which vaccinations programs are introduced leads to a recognition of why these programs are often greeted with a fair amount of apathy and ambivalence.

Even where the availability of vaccination services are known and accessible, they are often underutilized.[31] Cultural factors need to be taken into consideration when considering demand for vaccinations in general, for a limited number of vaccinations, and for specific vaccinations. In a previous paper (Nichter 1990), drawing upon data collected from South India and Sri Lanka in the early 1980s, I argued that local populations had a poor under-standing of what vaccinations do and what diseases they protect against. This resulted in both misconceived perceptions and unrealistic expectations. I want to extend this argument by offering additional data reported in the literature and collected in Asia during 1991–92.

It has been widely reported that a) mothers often have little idea or an exaggerated idea of what diseases are protected against by vaccinations and b) mothers with knowledge of any illness(es) protected against tend to accept vaccinations more readily than those unable to specify such illnesses (Burk-ina-Faso: Ciardi 1993; Gambia: Hanlon et al. 1988; Ghana: Arthur 1991; Haiti: Coreil et al. 1989; Honduras: Bonilla, Gamarra, and Booth 1985; Indonesia: Streatfield and Singarimbun 1988; Mozambique: Cutts et al. 1989; Philippines: Freide et al. 1985; South India and Sri Lanka: Nichter 1990). Three sets of issues prompted by these data may be explored.

First, it may be asked what local populations perceive the purpose of vaccinations to be if they are not associated with EPI-related diseases. During field work conducted over the past 20 years, I have consistently recorded two sets of impressions about the purpose of vaccinations. The first of these is that "vaccinations are good for a child's health." The second is that "vaccinations prevent serious illness." These impressions are fostered by vague health education messages offered to mothers by primary health care workers and doctors. Typically these messages are offered as rapid explana-tions for why mothers should comply with health worker directives or as "the only messages illiterate mothers can understand."

Vague messages about vaccinations can have dire, unexpected conse-quences. Given the impression that vaccinations are good for health or protect against all serious diseases, some community members get the sense that all vaccinations are alike and enhance a child's health in some form of incremental fashion. In other words, in lieu of knowledge that specific vaccinations protect against particular illnesses and a belief in the specific etiology of illness, the number of vaccinations rather than the type of vaccinations may constitute demand criteria.

I have encountered this type of thinking in both India and Indonesia. Let me cite data from a recent survey I conducted in rural South India and then discuss data from Indonesia. In South Kanara District, Karnataka State, India, rural mothers ($n = 124$) with a child under the age of five were asked a series of open ended questions about their health care behavior, including their use of and impressions about vaccinations. Coded responses to the following two questions are relevant:

Q1: What is the purpose of vaccinations (*dakku*)?

Protects against specific illness (named by informant)	50%
Protects against all big illnesses (*rōga*)	28%
No idea	18%
Other	4%

Q2: Do all vaccinations (*dakku*) protect against the same illnesses or do specific vaccinations protect against particular illnesses?

Have no idea	42%
Different illnesses are protected against	40%
The same illnesses are protected against	18%

Based on responses to the two questions, it would appear that between 40–50% of mothers surveyed thought that vaccinations protect against specific illnesses. When asked to state which illnesses might be protected against, however, few — less than 25% — named a local illness which encompassed an vaccinable disease other than polio or TB. Of local illness terms reported, almost all were non-vaccinable diseases.[32] Not one informant mentioned a local illness term encompassing tetanus.[33] When probed, some women noted that pregnant women received an injection for this illness, but infants need not if the delivery was not cesarian.[34] Moreover, I was told that this illness was no longer a problem in this region and therefore it was unnecessary to receive a vaccination for it. Government midwives' efforts to encourage pregnant women to get vaccinated were interpreted as netting them personal gain by meeting quotas.

Mothers were asked if they would take their next born infant to a PHC for vaccinations if a health worker did not come to their house to encourage them or check records. Notably, 85% said that they would do so. A wide range of opinions were expressed, however, concerning how many vaccinations they thought it was necessary for the child to receive. It would be misleading to express these opinions quantitatively because the number of vaccinations deemed beneficial was often described in relation to a set of contingencies which depended upon the child's reaction to vaccinations and state of health. An indication of how motivated child caretakers might be to seek vaccinations is indicated by reports of how many vaccinations children aged 15–36 months had received. Of 84 children in this age range, 11% had received no vaccinations, 19% had received one to two vaccinations, 37% had received three vaccinations, 19% had received four, and only 19% had received five to six vaccinations. Most informants resided within five miles of a government PHC or *taluk* (county) hospital offering vaccination services.

One of the major findings of two separate studies of vaccinations in Indonesia was that mothers who do not fully vaccinate their children believe that they are healthy and therefore not in need of further vaccinations (Kasniyah 1992, 1993, Raharjo and Corner 1990). Ms. Kasiynah and I conducted a series of interviews in Central Java to explore factors underlying this perception. Mothers interviewed perceived vaccination as necessary for a child's good health. Their criteria of good health was "no serious illness." Once a child was perceived to be healthy and thus protected against a range of serious diseases *by vaccinations having similar purposes*, they were no longer thought to be in need of additional vaccinations. Maintaining a vaccination schedule was less important for these mothers after the first few vaccinations. It was the *quantity*, not the *qualities* of distinct vaccinations which mattered.[35]

Three other ramifications of "general" messages may be highlighted. The first involves expectations. General messages foster expectations that vaccinations protect against illnesses they are not designed to prevent. Such expectations may contribute to perceptions that vaccinations are not very effective. I have encountered this perception throughout South-Southeast Asia where vaccinations are associated with diarrhea and acute respiratory infection, malaria, guinea worm, goiter, filariasis, dengue, and more! In South Kanara, several informants perceived vaccinations to be similar and to protect against all sudden and serious sickness. They were also reported to prevent skin rashes (*kajji*) from becoming serious, help babies gain weight and grow, clean the blood so no disease will come, and clean the intestines of impurities obtained during the birthing process.

A second ramification of general messages involves perceptions of vaccination compatibility. Given impressions that vaccinations are both "good for health" and "similar," there is a propensity for mothers to evaluate "them all" as incompatible if a child experiences a marked side effect (such as high fever) to any one vaccine. I have encountered this reasoning in both India and the Philippines. In the Philippines, the Tagalog concept of *hiyang* is applied to medicine compatibility in general (Hardon 1991, Tan 1989) as well as vaccinations. I documented three separate instances of an infant's *hiyang* for vaccinations being questioned after they suffered fever and/or illness unrelated to vaccination. In each case, perceptions of compatibility led a mother to weigh the ascribed benefits of future vaccinations against the state of ill health experienced by her child.

A third ramification of general messages is that segments of a population may question why it is that only young children and women are receiving vaccinations. In 1990, in an urban Indian slum, I encountered adults who expressed a need for "government injections" given a sense of perceived vulnerability associated with an outbreak of "gastroenteritis" widely reported by the press. They saw vaccination programs directed at infants and women as privileging these segments of the population while males and older children were left to fend for themselves. During a group discussion of their perceptions of "government injections," the idea emerged that vaccinations prevented illness from becoming serious — in this case simple diarrhea from becoming gastroenteritis. Not distinguishing different types of vaccinations from one another, the group's perception was that the government could not afford to vaccinate everyone routinely. Young children were vaccinated because they were weakest and required smaller doses of medication. Cholera vaccinations were conflated with children's vaccinations, and the groups' perception was that vaccinations were only administered to the general public if political pressure was brought to bear on the government. Cholera vaccinations are in fact used in India as a political ploy to offset fears of epidemic diarrheal disease irrespective of the pathogen in question (Nichter 1990).

On the one hand, criticism that vaccination programs privilege particular segments of the population is a reflection of consumer demand. On the other, it points to tensions over entitlement which might escalate and disrupt vaccination programs in the future, particularly in contexts of epidemics. The issue of entitlement has been reported elsewhere. For example, in Burkina-Faso it has been reported that men feel offended that women and children are the focus of vaccination programs which provide them with free white man's medicine (Ciardi 1993). Vaccinations are loosely associated with a wide range of illnesses and men question why they as the bearers of power and authority are not offered this efficacious agent. After all it is they who "move around" more, so are more vulnerable.

Another issue which arises is whether local illness terms exist which correspond to EPI diseases. In an earlier article (Nichter 1990), I pointed out that while direct correspondence between local illness categories and EPI diseases do not exist in South Asia, significant overlap does exist in the cases of tetanus and pertussis, and to a lesser extent measles.[36] What this implies is that it may be possible to communicate to local populations in countries such as India, Sri Lanka, and the Philippines that specific vaccinations protect children (and mothers) against illnesses associated with these diseases. A problem is posed, however, by the imperfect fit between local illnesses and EPI diseases. The fact that the local terms encompassing tetanus in Sri Lanka and the Philippines also encompass unpreventable illness associated with meningitis or pneumonia means that cases of apparent vaccination failure will exist. The same would be true in South India where a local term encompassing pertussis (*nāyi kemmu*) may also be applied to acute respiratory illness marked by bouts of coughing of long duration. In the Philippines the English term "measles" and the Tagalog terms *sikal* and *tigdas* encompass several different disease states sharing common symptoms (see Chapter 6).[37]

Some health planners have drawn attention to such problems of translation as a rationale for communicating only simple, nonspecific messages to mothers which focus on the timings of vaccination and not their purpose. What needs to be evaluated is the impact of programs making appropriate use of local illness terms and concepts of efficacy on community demand. This would require careful monitoring of the perception of vaccination efficacy given that a) cases of non-vaccinable illness associated with the local illness term will occur, and b) cases of vaccinable disease will occur due to vaccine failure.

At issue is whether increased knowledge of illnesses protected against by vaccinations and more realistic expectations of vaccination efficacy will increase community demand. A case study may illustrate why I think it is important to investigate this issue further. During an ARI study on the island of Mindoro in the Philippines not one person out of a sample of 80 literate mothers (ranging in educational status from basic literacy to college attendance) and eight teachers knew that pertussis could be prevented by a vaccination (see Chapter 6). Most could recognize the disease. When shown an illness video containing illustrations of various acute respiratory infections, they were able to identify this illness as *tuspirina* and in only a few cases was this term used to identify other forms of ARI. In other words the sensitivity and specificity of term use appeared to be high.

At the time of the study, three cases of pertussis were present in the local hospital and vaccination posters referring to pertussis, not *tuspirina*, were posted in community (*barangay*) health stations and the local clinic. When asked if *tuspirina* was preventable mothers stated that when there was an outbreak of this illness, it was useful to take children to the beach to expose them to sea air. In a context where a majority of mothers are literate and interested in children's health issues, is information on the timings of clinics enough? Might vaccination demand have been boosted considerably by drawing attention to *tuspirina*, even if the term might occasionally be applied to an illness which was not pertussis?[38]

A final issue pertains to what vaccinations are perceived to do irrespective of whether they are associated with specific illnesses or illness in general. Let me present some initial observations followed by a case study of measles in South India. While those in public health speak of vaccinations as *preventing* illness, local populations in many less developed countries perceive vaccinations to *protect* against serious illness.[39] This distinction involves more than semantics. Protection is perceived as relative and not absolute, time bound, and contingent upon factors over which humans have some, but not total control. Protection of children and pregnant women from malevolent forces is commonplace and vaccination in the minds of many is as much associated with the protection afforded by talismans as medicines.[40] Indeed, it could be argued that talismans constitute technical fixes of an indigenous science which is based upon assumptions about the nature of the cosmos which differ from our own. Given this scenario, vaccinations require a leap of faith and constitute magic from the vantage point of a population unfamiliar with germ theory. As Hsu (1955) observed some time ago, while the common man in America accepts magic if disguised as science, those in other cultures may be more likely to accept science if presented in relation to existing cultural frameworks which have explanatory power.[41]

Vaccinations are comprehended in terms of indigenous knowledge systems. Imperato and Traore (1969) drew attention to this tendency two decades ago in their study of the Bambara of Mali. The Bambara perceived vaccinations to be like amulets which needed to be renewed periodically.[42] Imperato and Traore emphasized that the Bambara's acceptance of vaccinations had little to do with an altered perception of illness causality. It was rather related to an extension of existing ideas about protection applied to biotechnology.[43]

Both magic and medicine figure into cultural models (Quinn and Holland 1987) employed to interpret technical fixes.[44] How does one explain the significance of the raised skin of a TB skin test? Does an Indian doctor's explanation that this is like a divination procedure constitute a contentious spread of superstition, or is it a viable first-step approach to health education? Those who argue against "unscientific explanations" in favor of vague educational messages need to reconsider their position in relation to how vague "health education" messages are interpreted and what expectations they set up. Is leading a mother to believe that BCG will prevent her child from experiencing TB or vaguely telling her BCG is good for health truthful? Is it more or less truthful than telling her that BCG protects her child from suffering a severe case of TB, just as an amulet protects against spirit attack for some time?[45]

This raises the issue of whether people who do not subscribe to the doctrine of specific causality believe that specific illnesses can be prevented by vaccinations. West African researchers (Arthur 1991, Odebiyi and Ekong 1982) have noted that not all mothers who accept vaccinations have faith in their power to prevent illness. Their reason for accepting vaccinations is related to a perception that they can reduce the severity of illness. Given the results of studies carried out by researchers such as Aaby in West Africa

(Aaby 1991, Aaby et al. 1989), the observations of these mothers may be correct. Aaby has reported that children immunized with measles vaccine (even if under nine months) suffer milder cases of measles if the illness occurs, inferring that partial immunity is possible. Aaby notes that recognition that milder forms of illness occurs has led mothers in Guinea Bissau to perceive "vaccine failure" (illness occurrence) as a visible demonstration of the vaccines utility (Aaby et al. 1986).[46] These women did not maintain an "either/or" assumption that vaccines either prevent illness or don't work.

To the best of my knowledge, the notion that vaccines reduce the severity of measles has not been part of any vaccination campaign in Asia, yet I have encountered the notion in India, Indonesia, and the Philippines. Let me consider the potential significance of working with this notion in the context of a more detailed discussion of measles in South Kanara District, Karnataka State, India. The data presented were collected during the spring of 1992 during the health behavior survey referred to above.

MEASLES: CASE STUDY

Kora is a Kannaḍa term encompassing measles as well as other diffuse skin rashes accompanied by fever.[47] As in other parts of India, *kora* is a) linked to female deities (as well as wild *bhūta* spirits such as Guliga), b) thought to especially trouble those whose body is rendered vulnerable by heat, and c) known to be contagious.[48] It is recognized that *kora* can lead to serious sickness among some children. An even larger fear, however, is that if *kora* is not allowed to run its course it can become especially severe. For this reason, *kora* is not treated with strong medicines until the rash has completely come out expelling internal heat and toxins.[49] Informants stated that if this was not allowed to happen, the illness might act like a "half wounded tiger" and attack with greater force. Other informants stated that the illness might remain latent in the body only to return intermittently over one's life course.[50]

Several mothers expressed the idea that it was better for a child to get *kora* when young and be done with it.[51] Some believed that if small *kora* (small spots) were experienced then serious rashes and large pox diseases would not trouble the person later.[52] In 1991 a few cases of adult onset *kora* were reported in the community.[53] The suffering of these adults was referred to by several informants when stating why it was good to have *kora* when young.

How did these ideas influence perceptions of measles vaccinations? As noted, few informants in our survey mentioned measles (or a local name encompassing it) when asked to name illnesses protected against by vaccinations. When they were directly asked if there was a vaccination which protected children against *kora*, forty-nine percent of 124 rural mothers with children under 5 years of age reported that they had heard of such an injection.[54] When asked if they wished their children to receive it, however, only 6% replied yes, while 78% replied no, and 16% were unsure.

Follow-up interviews revealed that two distinct perceptions of measles vaccinations existed, the first more common than the second.[55] The first perception was that the vaccination offered protection to children, but left them vulnerable to *kora* after the age of 12–15. Even among mothers who thought *kora* could be prevented, some ventured the opinion that vaccinations did not work for all children. Several reported cases of children experiencing *kora* although vaccinated. Their observations could be related to any one of five possibilities: the child was immunized too early (under nine months), the vaccine was ineffective, the *kora* experienced was not measles, the vaccination received was not for measles but a different disease, or the child did in fact have a mild case of measles.

The second perception was that the vaccination reduced the severity of *kora*, but did not prevent it.[56] One informant who maintained this view expressed the opinion that measles vaccinations were more important to receive currently as a result of mobility. In times past, she argued, people traveled little but nowadays transportation was readily available and women commonly traveled with their young children to visit relatives, attend religious functions, and visit the town. Her reasoning was appreciated by another community member who commented that:

> The mosquitoes in one's place trouble you less than the mosquitoes of another place. You are accustomed to your mosquitoes. When mosquitoes of other places bite, your skin swells up more than if you are bitten by a local mosquito. Like that, the *kora* one experiences at home can be tolerated, but vaccinations are needed so one can tolerate the *kora* of some other place.

Without knowledge of germs and the immune system, this informant had grasped a principle concordant with biomedical thinking. Through observation and analogical reasoning, she presented a case for vaccinating children deemed credible by her two neighbors who previously expressed ambivalence about vaccinations.

CONCLUSION

> In practice, populations frequently do not know why they are being immunized, what antigens are incorporated and what benefits this confers to them.

The rush to increase coverage rates reduces the time available for communicating with the people about the values of immunization. (Nabarro 1988:5)

The missing ingredient among health workers is the gift of sensitivity and the process of sensitization. A person sensitized on the subject of immunization will say: "I understand the need for them, I want my children to have them, and I will bring them for you to administer the injections." In this way the request comes from the people, cooperation is assured, everyone is satisfied, and coverage is complete. (Lankester 1986:325)

That a population is illiterate does not empower the state to push a vaccination or vasectomy program without ensuring that all information is available to participants. (Das 1990:43)

The focus of this chapter has been vaccination demand. Paying credence to studies which link demand to supply, timing, accessibility, and convenience, I have called attention to two other factors. These factors are a) trust associated with lay perceptions of the agenda of those advocating and administering vaccinations and b) local interpretations of what vaccinations do and don't do.[57] I have argued on the basis of data presented in this and a previous paper (Nichter 1990) that misconceptions about vaccinations are not only common, but have serious consequences. The assumption that mothers who are non-acceptors of vaccinations (or identified as "vaccination dropouts") have lower levels of concern about their children's health has been questioned. To the contrary, I have argued that it is often health concerns which lead child caretakers to selectively use or turn down vaccination services available to them.[58]

General messages about the purpose of vaccinations are interpreted in terms of local conceptual frameworks, when thought about at all. It is my impression that in most contexts vaccinations are not thought about very much. Vaccinations are accepted passively as a result of interactions with health care providers and because compliance is demanded by those in positions of power. Demand is often low, even among populations having impressive immunization rates. These rates often tell us more about the effectiveness of time and resource intensive programs than about the popularity of vaccinations. Given current budgetary constraints, it is unlikely that such expenditures may be sustained — a reality which makes it all the more important to consider community demand. Moreover, it has been pointed out that resentment and fear flourishes in a context of scarce resources where a) vaccination programs are privileged above other health programs and b) compliance is mandated by the state with little perception of need by the local population.

When vaccinations are thought about by child caretakers, it is just as often in relation to the risk of vaccinations doing harm as the potential of vaccinations being beneficial. Concerns related to a child's current state of health commonly underlay missed vaccination opportunities. Moreover, as we have seen, failure to take advantage of some vaccination services may reflect underlying health concerns. In several cultures, for example, measles is perceived to be a developmental milestone or a necessary illness preventing the onset of more serious forms of illness later in life.

Vaccination demand, when it does occur, is triggered by a) a general perception that vaccinations are good for infants' growth and health, and/or b) a marked sense of vulnerability to serious illness — illness which may or may not actually be protected against by the vaccination sought. In the first scenario, mothers may want a few but not necessarily all vaccinations advised by primary health care workers. If a child is healthy and receives a few vaccinations perceived as similar, then this number of vaccinations may be considered sufficient. Some mothers may consciously engage in self-regulation by deciding how many vaccinations their child should receive. In most cases, however, it is likely that conscious decisions are not made. It is the mother's motivation for securing "additional vaccinations" which wanes once the perceived benefit from vaccinations is realized.

In the second scenario, the factor driving demand is perceived vulnerability to serious illness. This may either take the form of concern about specific illnesses or involve a sense of rising vulnerability associated with social or environmental change. With respect to specific illness(es), an important point raised in this chapter is that lay populations have little idea about what illnesses vaccinations protect against. This situation fosters unrealistic and often misguided expectations which in the short-term may increase demand, but in the long run result in the perception that vaccinations are not all that effective.

Vulnerability may be associated with change which renders a population at increased risk to serious illness, or the perception that this will be the case. Mobility, the changing composition of communities, and exposure to others associated with the unknown lead to an increased sense of vulnerability. In this regard, recall the view of the Indian informant who spoke of "other mosquitoes harming one more than those to which one is accustomed." This informant's perception of increased risk at once indexes fear of the "other" as well as recognition that vaccinations are adaptive and protective. In this case, the informant viewed measles vaccination as useful, not as a protection against an illness which was culturally marked, but as a protection against serious illness which did not originate from *her place*. Measles vaccination better enabled her to live in a changing world marked by social transformation by insuring that the *kora* her children experienced would not be very serious.

This Indian woman's comments led me to reflect on attitudes toward vaccinations which I have encountered in Southern Arizona — a region of the United States with very low (50%) vaccination rates for children not yet registered for school/preschool.[59] On more than one occasion I have encountered mothers who have not deemed it essential to fully immunize their child prior to enrolling the child in a program which mandated vaccination. After all, I was told on one occasion, "the child was at home and not really at much risk."[60]

In the United States, school is perceived as a space where children get ill more often because they are exposed to the germs of other children — "others" who may come from far off places and "even from the other side of the border."[61] Public health messages which draw attention to vaccinating children prior to preschool/school may unintentionally reinforce this perception. For example, one mother I spoke to drew an analogy between an adult getting vaccinations before travelling to a foreign country and a child getting shots before going to school. An additional factor which may foster the perception that illnesses from foreign places are more dangerous than the illnesses of one's own place, is the naming of various types of "flu" with exotic names designating foreign origins.[62] Demand for vaccinations against these illnesses is often higher than demand for routine "school shots."

In light of this discussion, it might prove insightful to reexamine data on differential vaccination rates among migrant populations in light of concerns about vulnerability. For example, Raharjo and Corner (1990) found that in Sumatra, Javanese transmigrants were more positively disposed to receiving vaccinations than members of the local population, although they were not sure what illnesses the vaccinations received protected against. Could differential perceptions of risk associated with moving to a new place and health concerns associated with mobility contribute to differences in vaccination demand? Or are such differences explained by other factors such as an immigrant group's desire to fit in and not anger government officials? What impact does an influx of foreign immigrants or foreign trade (such as that envisioned by the North American Free Trade Agreement) have on regional vaccination demand? These questions invite research attentive to social transformation.

Hirschhorn, Dunn, and Claquin (1986) have suggested that it might be more productive to organize vaccination schedules around regional disease patterns than existing biotechnology. This raises several research questions. Would an approach to vaccination education and service provision which builds upon local perceptions of illness vulnerability foster greater demand for vaccinations than programs which rely primarily on political leverage and the prodding of health staff to secure compliance? Could vaccination demand be increased by raising community awareness of the burden of infectious disease through educational programs which begin by calling attention to familiar illnesses which are already a source of concern?[63] Would education about the signs and symptoms, duration and severity, and cure and prevention of locally recognized illnesses increase vaccination demand? What other issues sensitive to the household production of health might increase demand? For example, in contexts where mothers work outside the home, could information on the number of work days generally lost caring for an ill child having measles or pertussis motivate caretakers?

Planners of health programs who are concerned about issues of vaccination demand and sustainability might profit from paying as much attention to the epidemiology of representations (Sperber 1985) as the epidemiology of diseases. Like infectious disease agents, ideas about illness and biotechnology are also contagious and transmitted from person to person at rates influenced by environmental and other "ecological" factors (Bateson 1972). Researchers such as Raharjo and Corner (1990) have suggested that the goal of demand creation for preventive health services is better served by social marketing than health education. The former focuses on the creation of positive attitudes toward health behaviors and products, the latter on better cognitive understanding of these behaviors and products and why they are necessary. Referencing Coca-Cola as a model of marketing success and placing emphasis on product (vaccination campaign) image, they go on to suggest that health education is an inefficient strategy for demand creation. It is time that we critically examine such advice and consider the long as well as short term goals of public health.[64]

NOTES

1. EPI stands for the Expanded Programme on Immunizations. Initiated in 1974, it includes immunizations against diphtheria, pertussis, tetanus, tuberculosis, measles, and poliomyelitis and includes five vaccines (DPT, BCG, measles, polio, and tetanus toxoid). Estimates of EPI coverage vary by method of measurement used — presence of immunization card in the house, or total number of unit doses reported to be administered nationally divided by the population of eligible children. The poorest immunization rates are for measles and tetanus. Measles claims some one and a half million lives a year. It is

estimated that only 30% of mothers are immunized against tetanus globally and some three quarters of a million children die from neonatal tetanus a year.

2. At issue here is the occurrence of replacement mortality, that is, when death of high risk children from one set of illnesses is averted by immunizations only to have the children die from other illnesses in what Lincoln Chen (1986) has referred to as a context of chronic ill health. This possibility was suggested by Mosley (1985) and Kasongo Project data (1981) which generated considerable debate as well as a series of studies focusing on the utility of immunizations. For a discussion of this literature and data which demonstrate that measles immunizations have long-term utility during childhood see Holt et al. (1990), Garenne and Aaby (1990), and Aaby (1991). Aaby has been vocal in criticizing the replacement death position. He points out that few community studies examine the total impact of health interventions. His data suggest that both children who have experienced measles and live, and children who have received measles vaccine, have lower mortality rates over time than those exposed to neither. Exposure to the illness or the vaccine, he speculates, may stimulate the immune system in some way.

3. Promises of one dose time-release super shots (nasal sprays, pills, etc.) which protect against EPI diseases and more loom on the horizon of the foreseeable future. Considerable research will be needed, however, to discover how many antigens a baby's immune system can handle at one time, such that one immune response does not wipe out another (Gibbons 1994). Until the efficacy and long term effect of such technology is evaluated in less developed countries, and research costs are paid for making such technology affordable, inhabitants of less developed countries will continue to be exposed to an increasing number of vaccinations. On the financial blocks impeding the progress of vaccine research see Cohen (1994). Recent reports in the United States of adult onset pertussis, among those immunized as children, also suggest the possibility that revaccination programs for adults may have to be instituted in some contexts.

4. I use the term "community" in this chapter as a heuristic devise and recognize a tendency within international health and development to reify community as an entity which exists in its own right (Schwartz 1981). As distinct from static structures defined by the state, communities are a fluid collectivity mobilized and defined in relation to sets of activities which bring together people having shared stakes and interests. My use of the term community does not suggest consensus or homogeneity beyond shared habitus (Bourdieu 1977).

5. Measles deaths are commonly associated with pneumonia and diarrhoea. The anorexia which occurs during and following measles is a notable cause of malnutrition.

6. The extent to which community trust of vaccination programs has been lowered by press coverage of ineffective vaccines and inappropriate storage is not dealt with in this chapter and constitutes an area for future research. In need of study is not only the extent to which mistrust leads people to suspect that

"normal" side effects are signs of bad medicine, but the extent to which mistrust leads people to seek out vaccinations from the private sector.

7. On the spread of conspiracy stories as a new form of folklore worthy of serious attention see Campion-Vincent (1990).

8. On Muslim culture as pronatalist in ideology and politics, see Mahadevan (1986), Chapter 8.

9. Fears that vaccinations might be related to family planning efforts emerged during ethnographic interviews, but did not surface as responses to survey questions about vaccination demand. Notably, this perception was articulated by men and not women and did not appear to be widespread. My impression is that the fear is presently latent, but capable of capturing the popular imagination given the right set of conditions. One can only wonder what impact an injectable contraceptive might have on the EPI program given the memory of "emergency" family planning excesses in India during the 1970s and present ethnic-religious tensions. On this note, it is worth mentioning that Talwar and associates (Talwar and Raghupathy 1989) have been experimenting with an injectable contraceptive in India. Although this research has been reported in the press and protested by women's health activists (AIDS Weekly 1992), it is not widely known about. Rumors that such a vaccine exists may impact on EPI irrespective of whether the contraceptive vaccine is ever introduced. Vaccinations have been associated with family planning in countries other than India. Bastien (1989), for example, reports that Ammara peasants in Bolivia who have little idea what illnesses vaccinations protect against, fear vaccinations will cause them to be sterile.

   Conspiracy theories involving vaccinations have emerged recently in the Philippines. The Pro-Life Philippines, Archdiocesan Council of the Laity Manila, Catholic Women's Legal League, and Families for Families International Foundation filed a petition to stop the government of the Philippines from administering anti-tetanus vaccinations. These groups alleged that the Department of Health laced the vaccine with a hormone which reportedly can cause an abortion. Although the DOH responded that the dose was less than one millionth of that necessary to negatively affect a pregnancy, these groups received a court order to stop the administration of the vaccine on National Immunization Day in 1995. Health officials in Metro Manila and the provinces have reported an especially low turnout for vaccinations including oral polio which has been the target of an intensive government campaign.

10. Members of this peri-urban community rarely utilized primary health care services and depended on private practitioners for their health care needs. They viewed vaccination surveillance with suspicion. While the government, in principle, supplied vaccines free of charge to private practitioners, the supply was erratic, many private practitioners did not request vaccines routinely, and there was poor follow up on the part of practitioners with respect to reminding mothers about vaccination schedules. Practitioners complained that mothers frequented more than one doctor, making it difficult for them to

know what vaccinations a child had received. On the growing importance of private practitioners as providers of immunizations in India, see Duggal and Amin (1989). They report that 42% of children surveyed in Jalgoan District, Maharastra, received their immunizations exclusively from private practitioners.

11. The "other" would be included in a global "community" defined in relation to mutual desires as well as perceptions of risk and protection. Similarities may be drawn between missionary activities directed at clothing the natives for their own good (and good health) and attempts to penetrate the surface and vaccinate. Germane to this assessment are the deliberations of Comaroff and Comaroff (1992, Chapter 10) on the relationship of domestification and colonialism in Africa.

12. An example of how deities are perceived to show their power through new disease patterns after biomedicine has controlled diseases traditionally associated with their power is provided by Egnor (1984). Egnor considers the fate of the smallpox goddess, once smallpox was controlled in Tamil Nad, India. On the open ended way in which deities show their power in India see Nuckolls (1992).

13. Kyasanur forest disease was linked to the wrath of local deities (*bhūta*) as the result of both forest clearance and the failure to perform yearly rituals to these patron spirits. A vaccine to combat this deadly disease was promised in the press, but was not forthcoming.

14. Such data would in any case be accessible from hundreds of thousands of Indians living abroad.

15. Haraway explores the emergence of the immune system as a semiotic system, "an elaborate icon for principal systems of symbolic and material difference in late capitalism, a map drawn to guide recognition and miscognition of self and other in the dialectics of Western politics" (1991:204). I would add that in the Indian context this imagery draws meaning from Brahmanic ideology about encoded body substance and fluid self-construction which has influenced several healing traditions and codes of conduct having to do with ritual purity, group identity, and boundaries. On this issue see Daniel (1984), Marriott (1976), and Marriott and Inden (1977).

16. AIDS has also been linked to the "ill effects" of too many foreign influences penetrating India's borders as a form of national encroachment (Jayaraman 1988).

17. Haraway points out that the trope of "space invasion" when coupled to the trope of "infection" evokes the important question of directionality: in which direction is the invasion? Is it the colonized who are perceived as the invader, or he who colonizes? Put less abstractly, when one travels across national borders one requires a series of vaccinations. How is this read? Do the vaccinations protect you from the other, or them from you?

18. While it may be argued that some international agencies/ groups have been overzealous in their efforts to promote vaccination programs without considering opportunity costs, it is somewhat misleading to suggest that there is a conspiracy to coerce foreign governments into accepting vaccination programs (Banerji 1990a, 1990b). Incentives have been offered to countries which accept vaccination initiatives and provisions for United States aid have been tied to vaccination goals. At the same time, researchers in less developed countries associated with groups such as the International Network of Clinical Epidemiology (funded by the Rockefeller Foundation) have been encouraged to test the local effectiveness and efficiency of technological fixes including vaccines. Such groups are by no means rubber stamps for the positions of international agencies. They are not hapless victims of technocentric domination as recent local criticism of vitamin A programs attests (Sadjimin, Dabble, and Kjolhede 1993).

19. Kunitz (1990) echoes this concern by drawing attention to the "seductiveness of an apparently democratic science which cures/protects everyone equally" while deflecting attention away from diseases as "signs of social and ecological settings negatively disposed toward human survival."

20. Other Indian scientists I have spoken to have questioned the importance of establishing herd immunity through vaccinations. Herd immunity to an infectious disease refers to the phenomena wherein a majority of the population is rendered immune thereby protecting those who are susceptible from acquiring the infection by making the transfer of infection less likely to occur across the population. These scientists questioned the ability to reach and sustain levels of vaccination sufficient to insure herd immunity given the size of India's population and social mobility. The extent to which immunity established by vaccinations achieved herd effect (compared to that established by natural disease) was also questioned, given that weak organisms are used in vaccines.

21. A distinction may be made here between a disease prevention model which views people in difficulty (at risk) as like children, an advocacy rights model wherein people are treated as citizens who contract the assistance of experts, and an empowerment model based upon decentralized problem solving and community diagnosis. On this distinction see Rappaport (1981) as well as the community participation literature.

22. High literary rates and political will are held accountable for much of Kerala's success. See Franke and Chasin (1992) for a review of articles which address Kerala's more extensive health services and dedicated physicians and health workers who are directly responsible to a militant and informed public, subject to left-wing radicalism. Kerala's public are more proactive in demanding better health facilities than are the public in other Indian states, an observation I have made over a 20-year period working in neighboring Karnataka State. What I would question, however, is the literature which suggests that there is high public demand for public health services. The ratio of doctors to population is higher in Kerala than anywhere else in India and a large majority of the

public consult private rather than government physicians for most routine health complaints. What needs to be examined is whether existing immunization rates are linked to mothers voluntarily attending vaccination clinics, or whether this is the result of encouragement and follow-up by health workers or private doctors.

23. Kutty (1989) determined mothers' attitudes toward vaccinations based upon 10 forced choice questions. While the utility of this method is open to question, the results of the study are suggestive.

24. On the basis of a 12 district all-India KAP survey of vaccination behavior, a team of marketing researchers estimated that roughly 20% of all respondents were positively predisposed to vaccinations and 5% negatively disposed. The large majority 75% were passive in attitude, 50% being indifferent and fatalistic, and 25% aware of benefits, but without conviction (IMRB 1988:90).

25. For example, see Kulkarni's (1992) assessment of issues affecting vaccination program sustainability in India.

26. For example, Basu (1985), reviewing a wide range of health service research in India, concludes that reasons for failure to vaccinate entails a) lack of awareness (20–44%), b) timing inconvenience (9–29%), c) the child not being well (16%), and d) missed opportunities related to a reluctance among health workers to vaccinate mildly ill children (unspecified).

27. At issue is which children's illnesses are perceived as aggravated by vaccinations. While the literature draws attention to fever, cough, and colds, I have encountered reluctance to receive vaccinations in South India associated with skin rashes, earache, and digestive complaints associated with excessive heat in the body.

28. For example, health social scientists at Gaja Madha University, Indonesia, have studied vaccination acceptance in terms of both the characteristics of mothers and children. Mothers who worked outside the home and were subject to more time constraints were found to have lower acceptance rates than those who worked only inside the home. Mothers who were active members of social groups were more likely to vaccinate their children than were mothers who did not belong to such groups (Kasniyah 1993). Differences between acceptance of vaccinations among mothers who share common work-time constraints is not accounted for. Why did some mothers working outside the home seek vaccinations for their children while others did not? Moreover, why did group membership have a positive affect on vaccination acceptance? Was this related to social identity (an affiliation with development mandates or a sense of modernity) or was it the result of increased information on the purpose or timings of vaccinations? A second researcher (Zulaela 1993) studied the influence of children's characteristics (sex and birth order) as well as family size and found no statistically significant differences. Notably, distance to the health center and the number of times a mother received information about vaccination schedules or clinic timings made little difference in terms of vaccination acceptance. What did make a difference was who told a mother

to get her child vaccinated (health staff versus a cadre of community volunteers) and a mother's education, which may well have been a proxy for other variables.

29. Needed are positive deviance studies which attend to why some people seek out vaccinations when a majority of their peers do not deem it worth their inconvenience.

30. I have placed emphasis on the impact of culture on vaccination demand as distinct from an examination of cultural barriers to vaccination programs. The former draws attention to factors which have a positive as well as a negative influence on vaccination acceptance. Examined are factors which lead people to seek out vaccinations, not merely accept them passively. Cultural barrier research typically identifies factors which interfere with program operations.

31. Vaccination acceptance rates near health posts are not necessarily high. For example, Malison et al. (1987) report that in Uganda health workers were surprised to find that only one third of children aged one to four and one fifth of children under one were fully vaccinated despite easy access to vaccines.

32. The all-India, IMRB KAP survey reported that among those who were aware of "preventable injections," 35% did not know that different injections were associated with different types of diseases. Respondents "expected the preventive injections to protect against a wide range of diseases (diarrhoea, dysentery, vomiting, fever, pneumonia, malaria, cough, and cold" (1988:66).

33. However, when these mothers were probed about measles vaccinations, several reported hearing of them. These data are discussed subsequently.

34. The IMRB (1988) study recorded an impression that if a mother has had no trouble during pregnancy, she did not require a tetanus toxoid (TT) vaccination. In South Kanara, the injection was associated with toxins which enter the body with a wound or build up in the body during pregnancy especially if the wrong foodstuffs are consumed. Swelling of the legs and wounds not healing promptly were associated with these toxins (*nañju*). Not all women were perceived to suffer these problems.

35. The prevalence of this perception is unknown and constitutes an area for further research.

36. Before use of local terms may be considered in EPI education programs, the sensitivity and specificity of terms (in an epidemiological sense) needs to be established (Nichter 1990, 1993). This requires taxonomic as well as taskonomic assessment of term use and sensitivity to intracultural variation. The latter does not necessarily preclude local term use in health education. Specificity of term use may be enhanced in an environment where term ambiguity is high (Nichter 1989, Chapter 4).

37. On local terms for pertussis encompassing other forms of ARI of long duration in India, see IMRB (1988).

38. In my earlier article I noted a similar case in North Kanara District, Karnataka State, India. Once the community found out that whooping cough (*nāyi*

kemmu) could be prevented, the local primary health care worker was scolded for not informing the community. In the Philippine case, school teachers and mothers alike showed great interest in a vaccination for *tuspirina*.

39. Prevention and cure are often confused (Adekunle 1978, Nichter 1984). Prevention can mean preventing an illness from occurring (protection) or preventing it from manifesting or becoming worse. See also Ciardi (1993) who cites the work of Jaffre in stating that in Burkina-Faso, prevention is equated with protection.

40. In South Kanara, for example, both talismans and vaccinations are perceived to provide the user a protective fence (*bund*) which limits the entry of malevolent agents. Stronger fences are needed against more powerful agents of destruction, and like fences, talismans need to be periodically repaired — replaced as a result of environmental damage (e.g., exposure to an eclipse or source of impurity). While vaccinations were not presented by primary health workers as requiring renewal, they were perceived by many as having a time limited effect.

41. For an example of how Americans accept science as magic during times of disease anxiety see McCombie's (1986) discussion of the "AIDS Test" which is similar to the account of the use of cholera vaccinations during cholera epidemics in China (Hsu 1955) and India (Nichter 1990).

42. The Bambara perceived a vaccination to be an amulet which works where Koranic charms and diviners incantations have failed. Just as amulets need to be renewed, so vaccinations were perceived as time bound. In the case of measles, it was believed that this illness could affect one several times. For this reason the demand for revaccination could lead to problems of overuse.

43. An example of how vaccinations are interpreted within local conceptual frameworks is provided by Mull, Anderson, and Mull (1990). Virtually all mothers surveyed in the Hindu Kush region of Pakistan reported that vaccinations could prevent or cure *khudakan*, an illness associated with neonatal tetanus. Vaccinations were popular despite the fact that the illness was believed to be caused by spirits. One reason the vaccination was accepted was because it was administered to mothers for the health of children. According to indigenous belief, this spirit linked illness is passed on from mother to child. Vaccinations offered protection in a manner which was an extension of existing health belief and practices.

44. On the similarities between diagnosis and divination and the need for a broader appreciation of magic see Jules-Rosette (1978), and O'Keefe (1982). On the importance of appreciating analogic forms of thought as they are applied in development contexts, see Nichter (Chapter 13 and 1990) and Fuglesang (1984). On local interpretation of biomedical resources and indigenous criteria of efficacy see Etkin, Ross, and Muazzamu (1990).

45. The association between talismans and vaccinations has been exploited in a Sri Lankan health education program. An analogical approach to vaccination education was piloted by a member of the Health Education Bureau of the Ministry of Health (Mr. B. A. Ranaverra). Each type of vaccination offered to children under five was compared to one of five symbolic weapons displayed on a popular amulet. At a recent meeting with my former colleague in 1992, I was informed that this education approach proved to be successful. An image of an amulet had been used on a national vaccination poster.

46. Aaby et al. (1986) notes that 95% of mothers of children who experienced measles after being vaccinated went on to vaccinate their next child, a rate significantly higher than the general population.

47. Some informants spoke of different types of *kora* distinguishable by the size of spots. *Ame kora* is a term used to refer to the rash some infants experience soon after birth. This rash is deemed a good sign that excess heat and poison are leaving the body.

48. Asked why *kora* troubled some people and not others during an epidemic, I was told that many people experienced *kora*, but did not know it. The illness only manifested if the person was weak or their body became hot. Twenty years ago when I first conducted fieldwork in this area of India, fevers which occurred during summer season were not treated for three days to make sure the illness was not *kora*. Nowadays there is a propensity to treat any fever as soon as it is noticed.

49. Medicines are taken to assist the rash come out and to reduce other symptoms. Such medicines are known as *shamana* medicines which assist the body, but do not interfere with (or control) the illness process.

50. The concept of latent illness is not limited to pox diseases in South Kanara. For example, see a discussion of *krāṇi* and *tāmare* (illnesses associated with states of malnutrition) in Nichter 1989 (Chapter 5). Research is needed on how perceptions of latency impact on health care behavior over time as well as in relation to an understanding of lay perceptions of vulnerability. Critics of vaccination programs in the West have also focused attention on the possibility that "artificial immunity" might "drive the disease deeper into the body where it might latter manifest in more dangerous and disabling ways" (James 1988:33).

51. A few mothers spoke of a child getting fat after measles as the illness was thought to purge the body of impurities which would impede the digestive process.

52. In the local language of illness, the names of pox illnesses are not directly referred to for fear of calling them into presence. To convey the idea that experiencing *kora* would prevent other pox illnesses, the Tuḷu phrase *malla borugi* (big not falling) was used.

53. Of three cases of adult onset *kora* seen by a local doctor, only one was measles. One of the other two cases was chickenpox. A popular *āyurvedic* practitioner linked the "outbreak of *kora*" afflicting these adults to *amlapitta*, a condition characterized by excess heat and poor digestion. This was associated with increased use of chemical fertilizer and insecticide. Juxtaposed to the public health idea that failure to maximize biotechnology (vaccinations) resulted in measles was his idea that biotechnology (chemicals) fostered the epidemic.

54. A few mothers believed that *kora* was protected against by "DPT." One mother noted that she gave her child only two doses of DPT as she was afraid that three doses would suppress *kora* to the point that it would remain latent in the body causing intermittent skin rashes (*kajji*). Two doses, she believed, would lessen the severity of the illness, plus the child would get the illness only once. She also believed that DPT protected against "all sudden sicknesses."

55. Two distinct perceptions of the effect of vaccinations were framed around the concepts of *sthambhana* and *upasamana* — denoting total protection and protection which minimizes a problem's severity.

56. The impression that measles vaccinations renders the illness less severe was also encountered in Java. Remaining to be studied is whether acceptance/demand of measles vaccination is greater among those who think it a) prevents measles or b) reduces its severity. Consideration also needs to be given to whether "reduction of severity" is perceived as interfering with the illness process.

57. Trust of the motives of those advocating and administering vaccinations has been addressed in this chapter. Trust of the skills of those administering vaccinations has been addressed in Nichter (1990).

58. I am not saying that selective neglect in the form of non-acceptance or late and incomplete use of vaccinations does not occur. My point is that health concerns based on cultural reasoning and communication underdevelopment lead some people who maximize other preventive health measures to use vaccinations cautiously.

59. Vaccinations of children in the United States is largely achieved by state coercion — children not being allowed to enter school until they are fully vaccinated. The degree to which state coercion translates into citizen demand and perception of need may be ascertained by a more careful look at vaccination statistics. Approximately half of U.S. children are not fully vaccinated before the age of three, the stage of life when they most need the protection. Community surveys in Arizona suggest the public has poor knowledge of what diseases specific vaccinations protect against. While the press plays up clinic accessibility and cost as reducing vaccination rates, demand factors are relatively unexplored.

60. This perception emerged during exploratory interviews directed toward factors which motivate people to get vaccinations. Information generated by this question frame may differ from that produced by interviews which focus on why child caretakers had not sought out vaccinations for their children in a timely manner. The later frame is more commonly reported in the literature and may cause informants to be defensive.

61. In southern Arizona, especially in the Nogales area, the "wash" which runs between Mexico and Arizona is seen as a route of transmission for dangerous environmental pollutants, infectious diseases, and illegal immigrants associated with crime. Mothers speak of immunizing their children to protect them from diseases which come out of the "wash" (personal correspondence: Michael Pensak).

62. History is rife with examples of how such thinking has served the cause of racism, especially when epidemics have emerged. It is diseases of foreign origin which are perceived to be especially dangerous.

63. On the other hand, would such an approach result in a "success is failure scenario," i.e., a scenario where vaccinations reduce visible cases of disease which in turn reduces perceived need for vaccinations? Or is it possible that better understanding of vaccinations and their purposes may have a ripple effect influencing community demand for other public health services?

64. I am not suggesting that social marketing does not have an important role to play in promoting health resources and concepts. Market segmentation, product positioning and placement, attention to imagery, and the creation of a sense of what is normative and valued behavior are important lessons to be learned from marketing. What is questioned is an approach which "short changes" local populations by selling instead of educating. Vaccinations are not Coca-Cola and the goals of business and public health are not identical. There is a difference between citizens and consumers. Social marketing typically attends to one target at a time and measures success by increases in product use or message retention. The impact of marketing campaigns on coexisting health practices and conceptualizations of health and illness is overlooked. Apparent marketing success may deflect attention away from unintended negative outcomes. For example, Wyatt (1992) discusses how the symbol of the syringe commonly used in the promotion of vaccinations has contributed to a false impression that injections enhance health. Wyatt notes that up to 150,000 cases of paralytic polio a year may be associated with unnecessary injections in India alone. Approaches to the marketing of vaccinations need to be more broadly contextualized and responsible. If syringes are utilized as a powerful, well recognized symbol in vaccination messages, Wyatt suggests that the message advanced should index the dangers of injecting young children. Wyatt raises the thorny issue of how appropriate vaccination behavior may be advocated in a context where considerable inappropriate behavior and mixed messages already exist.

REFERENCES

Aaby, P. 1991. Determinants of Measles Mortality: Host or Transmission Factors? Medical Virology 10:83–116.

Aaby, P., J. Bukh, J. Leerhoy, I. M. Lisse, C. H. Mordhorst, and I. R. Pedersen. 1986. Vaccinated Children Get Milder Measles Infection: A Community Study from Guinea-Bissau. Journal of Infectious Disease 154:858–863.

Aaby, P., I. R. Pedersen, K. Knudsen, M. C. da Silva, C. H. Mordhorst, N. C. Helm-Petersen, B. S. Hansen, J. Thårup, A. Poulsen, M. Sodemann, and M. Jakobsen. 1989. Child Mortality Related to Seroconversion or Lack of Seroconversion after Measles Vaccination. Pediatric Infectious Disease Journal 67:443–448.

Adekunle, L. 1978. Child Immunization — What Are the Impediments for Reaching Desired Goals in a Transitional Society? Social Science and Medicine 12:353–357.

Ahluwalia, I. B., S. D. Helgerson, and F. J. Bia. 1988. Immunization Coverage of Children in a Semi-Urban Village Panchayat in Nepal, 1985. Social Science and Medicine 26(2):265–268.

AIDS Weekly. 1992. Activists Protest Proposed AIDS and Contraceptive Vaccines. April 20:8.

Anderson, N., S. Paredes, J. Legorreta, and R. J. Ledogar. 1992. Who Pays for Measles? The Economic Arguments for Sustained Immunization. Health Policy and Planning 7(4):352–363.

Arthur, P. 1991. Evolution of the Expanded Programme of Immunization in Kassena-Nankana District, Upper East Region, Ghana. Unpublished report, London School of Hygiene.

Banerji, D. 1990a. Crash of the Immunization Program: Consequences of a Totalitarian Approach. International Journal of Health Services 20(3):501–510.

Banerji, D. 1990b. Politics of Immunization Programme. Economic and Political Weekly 30(3):501–510.

Bastien, J. 1989. Cultural Perception of Neonatal Tetanus and Program Implications, Bolivia. Applied Anthropology Meetings, Santa Fe, New Mexico.

Basu, R. N. 1985. India's Immunization Programme. World Health Forum 6:35–38.

Bateson, G. 1972. Steps to an Ecology of the Mind. New York: Ballantine Books.

Bonair, A., P. Rosenfield, and K. Tengvald. 1989. Medical Technologies in Developing Countries: Issues of Technology Development, Transfer, Diffusion and Use. Social Science and Medicine 28(8):769–781.

Bonilla, J., J. Gamarra, and E. Booth. 1985. Bridging the Communication Gap: How Mothers in Honduras Perceive Immunization. Assignment Children 69(72):443–454.

Bourdieu, P. 1977. Outline of a Theory of Practice. Cambridge: Cambridge University Press.

Campion-Vincent, V. 1990. The Baby Parts Story: A New Latin American Legend. Western Folklore 49:9–25.

Chen, L. 1986. Primary Health Care in Developing Countries: Overcoming Operational, Technical and Social Barriers. Lancet 8518(2):1260–1265.

Ciardi, P. 1993. Qualitative Survey of Utilization of Health Sciences, Participation and Health Needs in Burkina-Faso's Rural Communities. World Bank Report, Washington, DC.

Cohen, J. 1994. Bumps on the Vaccine Road. Science 265:1371–1373.

Comaroff, J. and J. Comaroff. 1992. Ethnography and the Historical Imagination. Boulder: Westview Press.

Coreil, J., A. Augustin, et al. 1989. Use of Ethnographic Research for Instrument Development in a Case-Control Study of Immunization Use in Haiti. International Journal of Epidemiology 18(40):901–905.

Cutts, F., L. Rodrigues, S. Colombo, and S. Bennett. 1989. Evaluation of Factors Influencing Vaccine Uptake in Mozambique. International Journal of Epidemiology 18(2):427–433.

Daniels, E. V. 1984. Fluid Signs. Berkeley: University of California Press.

Das, V. 1990. What Do We Mean by Health. *In* Health Transition Volume II. John Caldwell, Sally Fendley, et al., eds. Pp. 27–46. Canberra: Australia National University.

Dhillon, H. S. and S. B. Kar. 1963. Behavioural Science and Public Health. Indian Journal of Public Health 7(1).

Duggal, R. and S. Amin. 1989. Cost of Health Care: A Household Survey in an Indian District. Foundation for Research in Community Health, Bombay, India.

Egnor, M. 1984. The Changed Mother or What the Smallpox Goddess Did When There Was No More Smallpox. Contributions to Asian Studies 18:24–45.

Etkin, N., P. Ross, and I. Muazzamu. 1990. The Indigenization of Pharmaceuticals: Therapeutic Transitions in Rural Hausaland. Social Science and Medicine 30(8):919–928.

Franke, R. and B. Chasin. 1992. Kerala State, India: Radical Reform as Development. International Journal of Health Services 22(1):139–156.

Freide, A., C. Waternaux, et al. 1985. An Epidemiological Assessment of Immunization Programme Participation in the Philippines. International Journal of Epidemiology 14(1):135–142.

Fuglesang, A. 1984. The Myth of the People's Ignorance. Development Dialogue 1–2:42–62. Dag Hammarskjold Foundation Uppsala.

Garenne, M., and P. Aaby. 1990. Pattern of Exposure and Measles Mortality in Senegal. Journal of Infectious Disease 132:531–539.

Gibbons, A. 1994. Children's Vaccine Initiative Stumbles. Science 265:1376–1378.

Halstead, S., J. Walsh, and K. Warren. 1985. Good Health at Low Cost. New York: Rockefeller Foundation.

Hanlon, P., P. Byass, M. Yamuah, R. Hayes, S. Bennett, and B. H. M'Boge. 1988. Factors Influencing Vaccination Compliance in Peri-Urban Gambian Children. Journal of Tropical Medicine and Hygiene 91:29–33.

Haraway, D. J. 1991. Simians, Cyborgs and Women: The Reinvention of Nature. New York: Routledge.

Hardon, A. 1991. Confronting Ill Health: Medicines, Self-Care and the Poor in Manila. Quezon City: Health Action Information Network.

Hayden, G. F., P. A. Sato, P. F. Wright, and R. H. Henderson. 1989. Progress in Worldwide Control and Elimination of Disease Through Immunization. Journal of Pediatrics 114(4):520–527.

Hirschhorn, N., C. Dunn, and P. Claquin. 1986. Universal Childhood Immunization: Issues and Obstacles. Unpublished discussion paper, Resources for Child Health, John Snow Inc., Arlington, VA.

Holt, E. A., R. Boulos, N. A. Halsey, L. Boulos, and C. Boulos. 1990. Childhood Survival in Haiti: Effect of Measles Vaccination. Pediatrics 85(2):188–194.

Hsu, F. L. 1955. A Cholera Epidemic in a Chinese Town. In Health, Culture, and Community. B. Paul, ed. Pp. 135–154. New York: Russell Sage Foundation.

Imperato, P. and D. Traore. 1969. Traditional Beliefs About Measles and Its Treatment Among the Bambaro of Mali. Tropical and Geographical Medicine 21:62–67.

Indian Market Research Bureau (IMRB). 1988. Immunization: Knowledge, Attitudes and Practices. Final Report to UNICEF. New Delhi: UNICEF.

James, W. 1988. Immunization: The Reality Behind the Myth. New York: Bergin and Garvey.

Jayaraman, K. 1988. Storm in India. In Blaming Others: Prejudice, Race, and Worldwide AIDS. R. Sabatier, ed. Pp. 109–113. Philadelphia: New Society Publishers.

Jules-Rosette, B. 1978. The Veil of Objectivity: Prophecy, Divination and Social Inquiry. American Anthropologist 80(3):549–570.

Kasniyah, N. 1992. Social Psychological Determinants of Javanese Mothers' Failure to Immunize their Children against Measles. Unpublished Masters thesis, Centre for Clinical Epidemiology and Brostatistus, University of Newcastle, N.S.W. Australia.

Kasniyah, N. 1993. Socio-Demographic Determinants of Non-Use of Measles Immunization Services Among Javanese Mothers. INCLEN Conference Report, Cairo.

Kasongo Project Team. 1981. Influence of Measles Vaccination on Survival Patterns of 7–35 Month Old Children in Kasongo, Zaire. Lancet 1:764–767.

Krishnan, T. N. 1985. Health Statistics in Kerala State India. In Good Health at Low Cost. Scott Halstead, Julia Walsh, and Kenneth Warren, eds. Pp. 39–46. New York: Rockefeller Foundation.

Kulkarni, M. 1992. Universal Immunization Programme in India: Issues of Sustainability. Economic and Political Weekly 17(27):1431–1437.

Kunitz, S. 1990. The Value of Particularism in the Study of the Cultural, Social and Behavioral Determinants of Mortality. *In* Health Transition Volume II. John Caldwell, Sally Finley, et al., eds. Pp. 92–109. Canberra: Australian University Press.

Kutty, V. R. 1989. Women's Education and its Influence on Attitudes to Aspects of Child-Care in a Village Community in Kerala. Social Science and Medicine 29(11):1299–1303.

Lankester, T. E. 1986. Health for the People or Cash for the Clever? British Medical Journal 293:324–325.

Mahadevan, K., ed. 1986. Fertility and Morality: Theory, Methodology and Empirical Issues. Beverly Hills: Sage.

Malison, M. D., P. Sekeito, P. L. Henderson, R. V. Hawkins, S. I. Okware, and T. S. Jones. 1987. Estimating Health Service Utilization, Immunization Coverage, and Childhood Mortality: A New Approach in Uganda. Bulletin of the World Health Organization 65(3):325–330.

Marriott, M. 1976. Interpreting Indian Society: A Monistic Alternative to Dumont's Dualism. Journal of Asian Studies 36(3):189–195.

Marriott, M. and R. Inden. 1977. Toward an Ethnosociology of South Asian Caste Systems: *In* The New Wind: Changing Identities in South Asia. Kennedith David, ed. Pp. 227–238. The Hague: Mouton.

McCombie, S. 1986. The Cultural Impact of the "AIDS Test": The American Experience. Social Science and Medicine 23(5):455–459.

Mosley, W. H. 1985. Will Primary Health Care Reduce Infant and Child Mortality? A Critique of Some Current Strategies With Special Reference to Africa and Asia. *In* Health Policy, Social Policy and Mortality Prospects. J. Vallin and A. D. Lopez, eds. Pp. 103–137. Liege: Ordina.

Mull, D. S., J. W. Anderson, and J. D. Mull. 1990. Cow Dung, Rock Salt, and Medical Innovation in the Hindu Kush of Pakistan: The Cultural Transformation of Neonatal Tetanus and Iodine Deficiency Disease. Social Science and Medicine 30(6):675–691.

Nabarro, D. 1988. After 1990: The Politics of EPI. Paper presented at the 15th NCIH International Health Conference, May 19–22.

Nichter, Mark. 1984. Toward a "People Near" Promotive Health Within Primary Health Care. Proceedings of the First International Symposium on Public Health in Asia and the Pacific Basin. Honolulu: University of Hawaii School of Public Health.

Nichter, Mark. 1986. The Primary Health Center as a Social System: PHC, Social Status, and the Issue of Team-Work in South Asia. Social Science and Medicine 23(4):347–355.

Nichter, Mark. 1989. Anthropology and International Health: South Asian Case Studies. Dordrecht: Kluwer Academic Press.

Nichter, Mark. 1990. Vaccinations in South Asia: False Expectations and Commanding Metaphors. *In* Anthropology and Primary Health Care. J. Coreil and D. Mull, eds. Connecticut: Westwood Press.

Nichter, Mark. 1992. Of Ticks, Kings, Spirits and the Promise of Vaccines. *In* Paths to Asian Medical Systems. Charles Leslie and Allan Young, eds. Pp. 224–556. Berkeley: University of California Press.

Nichter, Mark. 1993. Social Science Lessons from Diarrhea Research and Their Application to ARI. Human Organization 52(1):53–67.

Nuckolls, C. 1992. Divergent Ontologies of Suffering in South Asia. Ethnology 31(1):57–74.

Odebiyi, I. and S. C. Ekong. 1982. Mother's Concept of Measles and Attitudes Towards the Measles Vaccine in Ile-Ife, Nigeria. Journal of Epidemiology and Community Health 36:209–213.

O'Keefe, D. 1982. Stolen Lightening: The Social Theory of Magic. New York: Vintage.

Quinn, N. and D. Holland. 1987. Culture and Cognition. *In* Culture Models in Language and Thought. D. Holland and N. Quinn, eds. Pp. 3–41. New York: Cambridge University Press.

Raharjo, Y. and L. Corner. 1990. Cultural Attitudes to Health and Sickness in Public Health Programs: A Demand-Creation Approach Using Data from West Oceh, Indonesia. Health Transition 2(2):522–533.

Rappaport, J. 1981. In Praise of Paradox: A Social Policy of Empowerment Over Prevention. American Journal of Community Psychology 9(1):1–25.

Rifkin, S. and G. Walt. 1986. Why Health Improves: Defining the Issues Concerning "Comprehensive Primary Health Care." Social Science and Medicine 23(6):559–566.

Sadjimin, T., M. Dabble, and C. Kjolhede. 1993. Impact of High Dose Vitamin A Supplementation on Inudemic and Duration of Episodes of Diarrhea and ARI in Preschool Indonesian Children. INCLEN Conference Report, Cairo, Egypt.

Scheper-Hughes, N. and M. Lock. 1987. The Mindful Body: A Prolegomenon to Future Work in Medical Anthropology. Medical Anthropology Quarterly 1(1):6–41.

Schwartz, N. 1981. Anthropological Views of Community and Community Development. Human Organization 40(4):313–322.

Sharma, D. B., U. C. Lohari, and R. C. Gupta. 1977. Immunization Status of Infants and Pre-School Children Belonging to Urban and Rural Areas of Jammu and Kashmir. Indian Paediatrics 14:443–448.

Singh, S., R. Goel, and S. Mittal. 1986. Immunization Practices among Children in an Urban Area. Indian Journal of Community Medicine 11:94–104.

Sperber, D. 1985. Anthropology and Psychology: Toward an Epidemiology of Representations. MAN 29(1):73–89.

Streatfield, K. and M. Singarimbun. 1988. Social Factors Affecting Use of Immunization in Indonesia. Social Science and Medicine 27(11):1237–1245.

Talwar, G. and R. Raghupathy. 1989. Anti-Fertility Vaccines. Vaccine 7(2):97–101.

Tan, M. 1989. Traditional or Transitional Medical Systems? Pharmacotherapy as a Case for Analysis. Social Science and Medicine 29(3):301–307.

Turner, B. 1987. Medical Power and Social Knowledge. London: Sage.

Turner, B. 1992. Regulating Bodies. London: Routledge.

UNICEF. 1991. The State of the World's Children. New York: UNICEF.

Visaria, L., J. Anandjiwala, and A. Desai. 1990. Socio-Cultural Determinants of Health in Rural Gujarat: Results from a Longitudinal Study. *In* Health Transition Volume II. John Caldwell, Sally Findley, et al., eds. Pp. 628–643. Canberra: Australia National University.

Walsh, J. and K. Warren. 1979. Selective Primary Health Care: An Interim Strategy for Disease Control in Developing Countries. New England Journal of Medicine 301(18):967–974.

Wyatt, H. V. 1992. Mothers, Injections and Poliomyelitis. Social Science and Medicine 35(6):795–798.

Zulaela, D. 1993. Factors Related to Children Aged 12–51 Months Not Being Immunized Against Measles in Purworejo, Central Java, Indonesia. INCLEN Conference Report, Cairo, Egypt.

CHAPTER 11

The Primary Health Center as a Social System: Primary Health Care, Social Status, and the Issue of Team-Work in South Asia

Mark Nichter

INTRODUCTION

Although many national and international agencies claim to be committed to a participatory approach to helping rural poor, little is known about how to translate ambitious plans into effective action. The record of earlier community development and cooperative efforts is largely a history of failures, resulting more often in strengthening the position of traditional elites than in integrating poorer elements into the national development process. Current calls for involvement of the rural poor in the development process often seem little more than wishful thinking, inadequately informed by past experiences as to the investments in institutional innovation required to give reality to an important idea. (Korten 1979)

Just as the first concern of a bureaucracy is to ensure its survival and to protect itself against inroads from competing organizations, so it is the priority of the professional to protect his or her position within the organization.... Professionals jealously guard traditional prerequisites and privileges and do not willingly surrender something except in exchange for something as good or better. (Foster 1977)

A failure to make primary health care socially relevant by taking into account the existing health care system can render even the most logically conceived strategies virtually impotent or even counter-productive. (Mosley 1983)

One of the most fundamental issues challenging the implementation and thus viability of the primary health care concept in less developed countries (LDCs) is whether teamwork, an essentially democratic concept, can be operationalized within countries having complex hierarchical social structures.[1] Collaborative teamwork between doctors, nurses, midwives, auxiliaries, and volunteers is central to primary health care implementation and outreach (Boerma 1987, Flahault 1976, Schaeffer and Pizurki 1984). While the path of primary health care rhetoric is inspirational, the path of primary health care operationalization is commonly that of the least social and political resistance. The distributional and equity aims inherent in primary health care are often paid lip service while programs implemented in the name of primary health care are accommodated to local power structures and health bureaucracies which are socially, administratively, and politically self-sustaining.[2] This results in a glossed continuation of the previous policy in which health service is a commodity delivered by health professionals and their assistants (Segall 1983). The gloss is often a gesture toward greater "community participation" in the form of a community health worker–volunteer program.[3] Active participation of community members in planning, implementing, and evaluating health services rarely occurs, as this would entail decentralizing the governmental bureaucracy and the devolution of power (Chowdhury 1981, Gish 1979, Heggenhougen 1984, Skeet 1984, Stark 1985, Zacher 1984). Community health workers are typically incorporated into a health infrastructure, and ultimately made responsible to the health bureaucracy and not to the communities they are to serve. Community representatives are asked to facilitate compliance to predetermined programs (Foster 1982).

My purpose in this chapter is not to highlight linkages between political and organizational dimensions of primary health care programs.[4] Instead I direct attention to generic difficulties in implementing primary health care ideology at the Primary Health Center level.[5] These difficulties become apparent from an anthropological assessment of the Primary Health Center (PHC) as a social system embedded in a medical culture and responsive to an encompassing regional social structure. I argue that the ideology of primary health care needs to be considered from the vantage point of PHC staff and in relation to issues involving professional status and personal motivation. Health programs which do not pay credence to the professional identity and social status of health staff may well end up promoting conflict in the name of teamwork and community participation.[6]

This social analysis of problems related to primary health care implementation is focused on South Asia, but is no doubt relevant elsewhere.[7] Typically, teamwork related problems reflect inherent conflicts over knowledge, power, status, and turf associated with the process of professionalization and the form it assumes in each region's biomedical/public health culture. In South Asia these problems are complicated by distinctive hierarchical features of regional social structures.[8]

BACKGROUND

Professional and organizational role conflicts occur within PHCs in both rural South India and Sri Lanka. PHCs are rural-based field hospitals serving a population of between 50,000 and 100,000 people as well as being coordination centers for the promotive/preventive health activities of field staff. In both ethnographic contexts, PHCs are staffed by a combination of hospital-based and community-based workers (Figures 11.1 and 11.2 identify staff discussed). Recently, multipurpose training programs and volunteer programs inspired by primary health care ideology have been implemented in both countries. This has resulted in changes in the scope of work of field staff. Observation of health staff in South Kanara District, Karnataka, India, took place prior to, as well as during, the implementation of these new programs (1974–84). In Sri Lanka, participant observation was engaged in while I was attached to the Bureau of Health Education as a visiting professor between 1983 and 1985. Historical data were gathered through interviews with health staff in a variety of PHCs throughout the southern half of the island.

Role Strains as Inherent in Primary Health Care-Inspired Programs

Taylor (1978, 1984) has noted that the roles and values of PHC staff, in general, are antithetical to the egalitarian ideology of the primary health care movement. PHC field staff are more responsive to health bureaucracy protocol and procedure than community medicine rhetoric.[9] As Rueschemeyer (1972) has argued of professionals:

> People act and think only to a very limited extent with respect to ultimate social values. The norms and values that actually guide men are those incorporated in the more immediate institutional arrangements and role expectations.

Figure 11.1. Status diagram of those health center staff discussed in text.

PHC workers are keenly aware of each other's status, which is in part determined by salary, specialized knowledge, and access to sources of power and symbols of authority. A delicate balance of power and status exists between cadres of health staff. Given this context, strains on inter-staff teamwork may be expected when new cadres are introduced, the scope of duties of a cadre are broadened and merged with another group of workers, and laypersons confuse the differences between cadres.[10] In addition to status conflicts, "zones of ambiguity" are created. Robert Merton has referred to these zones as areas of overlap in role performance between professionals with different training and orientation. Zones of ambiguity were fostered by primary health care inspired programs in both India and Sri Lanka.

SRI LANKA

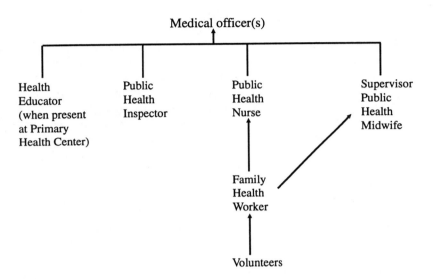

Figure 11.2. Status diagram of those health center field staff discussed in the text.

Examples of how professional status and organizational structure and related role strains affect teamwork within PHCs are discussed. Observations of long-experienced role strains in South India are described, followed by observations of more recent role strains developing within PHCs of both India and Sri Lanka as a result of newly introduced primary health care inspired programs.

I begin with two general observations about PHC staff, the first made by Taylor and the second by Banerji:

> They are often reluctant to delegate tasks which provide social recognition, even when scientific advance has simplified procedures to the point that they can safely become routine.... It is much easier for professionals to delegate preventive procedures which produce only delayed gratification from future benefits. (Taylor 1978)

The ideal of the primary health center exists only in name.... The team leader of the PHC [the doctor] who is the pivot of the institution not only lacks the qualities needed to provide leadership but he is also a most reluctant worker having interests which are often diametrically opposed to the interest of the PHC. (Banerji 1974)

Taylor's observation that tasks conferring social status are not readily delegated applies to professionals' relations with community volunteers and interrelationships between PHC staff. Social status is first and foremost determined by the curative and palliative services a staff member can directly administer. These services and associated medicines/paraphernalia have symbolic as well as operative value and professionals maintain a zero-sum perspective with respect to them. One cadre's gain in terms of access is another cadre's loss. An example of professional role strain exemplifying Banerji's observation may be cited involving medical officers and auxiliary nurse midwives in India.

Medical Officer/Auxiliary Nurse Midwife Relationships in India

In two rural PHCs intermittently studied over a six-year period (1974–80) in South Kanara, two out of three medical officers observed restricted, if not prohibited, their auxiliary nurse midwife field staff from administering even the simplest of curative/palliative medications. Although these midwives had been trained to attend to medical emergencies, they were not even permitted to administer aspirin to villagers during field visits. The rationale of these medical officers was that if field staff were allowed to dispense medicines they would aspire to become "quack practitioners" and would pay less attention to their promotive/preventive health duties. Both of these doctors had thriving private practices and, in fact, wanted to dissuade competition. Moreover, a visible sharing of curative activities and medicines would demystify their role and claims to special knowledge. Such knowledge is presently being challenged by the over-the-counter drug purchases of laypeople in larger villages and towns. Auxiliary nurse midwives recognized that their inability to provide even the most basic of curative/palliative services reduced not only their status, but people's receptivity to their promotive/preventive health advice.[11] Some midwives bought, at their own expense, minor medications to distribute in addition to the limited number of ferrous sulfate and vitamin A tablets they were officially supplied.

Midwives told me that a risk was involved in handing out these simple medicines should their practice become known to the PHC doctor.[12] Even a reputation for having knowledge of medicines could constitute a threat to the medical officer should he come to believe that medicine related advice was being offered to the public by a midwife.[13] This became apparent on one occasion. The case involved one of the aforementioned doctors who severely reprimanded a popular auxiliary nurse midwife because he observed that many villagers stopped by her quarters on the PHC premises after clinic hours. Villagers would stop by to see the midwife, discuss general somatic complaints, and ask questions about a variety of health related subjects. The medical officer became extremely jealous and was threatened by the midwife's popularity. He accused her of quackery because he learned that she had given an elderly woman advice about what tablets to purchase from a local pharmacy to alleviate chronic back pain. Aspirin had been doled out in three day measures for years to the woman by the doctor in his public, as well as private, practice. Inasmuch as the woman was poor and the doctor gained little economically from having her as a patient, we may assume that his outrage toward the midwife was symbolic of a larger issue. The doctor threatened to have the midwife transferred to a distant PHC as a demonstration of his power if "patients" continued to seek her advice first instead of that of the medical officer. The frightened midwife had to mobilize her support network in an effort to get the word out that no one should visit her at her quarters.

What was especially interesting in this case was how members of the community interpreted this interaction. A number of informants suggested that the incident was underscored not only by professional jealousy but also by caste dynamics involving jealousy of a different order. The doctor was a member of a dominant land owning caste, while the midwife hailed from one of many castes of tenants who recently had acquired land through land reform legislation. Just as members of tenant castes had challenged the position of the dominant caste over rights to land, so some villagers reasoned this midwife's actions represented a challenge to the status of this dominant caste doctor over rights to medicines. Medicine constitutes an arena where the caste hierarchy in South Kanara is largely reproduced.[14] While in the case of land, tenants had recourse to the courts and legislation, in the case of medicine the caste network of the doctor within the health bureaucracy and regional political arena was much stronger than that of the midwife. She, therefore, had to back down.

Informants pointed to another auxiliary nurse midwife in an adjoining PHC who was a popular abortionist and who openly flaunted her knowledge of medicine. This woman hailed from a caste having stronger political ties than the midwife previously discussed. It was rumored that through her powerful caste connections, she had been instrumental in having a medical officer transferred. Recently, she had been honored at a special function for her distinguished family planning case record although it was common knowledge that she had motivated most cases after performing illegal abortions in times of dire need. The case of this midwife was cited to me to illustrate how caste factored into PHC power equations. Undeniably, caste served as a factor undercutting or intensifying role strains involving issues of professional status as well as personal economics.

Four years of field experience in rural South India leads me to believe that it is by no means extraordinary for medical officers to underplay the skills of field staff and jealously guard medical supplies for symbolic as well as economic reasons. No doubt, just as some medical officers are more interested in establishing a lucrative private practice than facilitating primary health care, there are other medical officers firmly committed to its implementation. The point to be noted is that the issue of a doctor's "professional status" and the relative caste power of staff within the regional health bureaucracy influences teamwork within local PHCs. The professional status of PHC doctors within the larger health care infrastructure also influences teamwork in the form of referral to county (*taluk*) and district hospitals.

Just as medical officers were reluctant to refer patients for follow up to auxiliary nurse midwives, higher status doctors in larger *taluk* and district government hospitals were reluctant to refer patients to PHC medical officers for follow-up care. Issues of both kindness payments and status underscore this reluctance.[15] Similarly, it was observed that doctors in larger hospitals rarely paid special attention to the referral slips presented to them by patients coming from PHC medical officers. This encouraged the practice of patients going directly to larger hospitals and bypassing the PHC when they perceived their illness as serious. To gain entry into larger hospitals, patients often consulted a hospital doctor in his private practice.

The low rate of referral by some PHC medical officers made it apparent that they perceived the referral of patients to hospital doctors as a loss of private practice as well as prestige. This perceived threat had serious ramifications. For example, the medical officer in one PHC studied was infamous for "taking on any case" and even conducting complicated operations at his local PHC. The PHC was hardly equipped for the procedures he undertook — even by local standards. This medical officer advertised himself as an ex-army surgeon and was given a great deal of respect for his boldness by the local population. He had a thriving private practice and was famous among staff for declaring an operation a success, leaving postoperative care in their hands, and then blaming later complications on poor follow up care or the vague illness category "cancer." While the medical officer's actions were recognized as dangerous by colleagues, his irresponsible behavior was never questioned within the government service largely because of his strong caste-based political connections and local popularity.

The Impact of Targets on Teamwork and Volunteer Programs on Primary Health Care Staff

Another factor that contributes to structural conflicts between health workers is the setting of targets. In India, considerable importance is given to meeting targets, particularly those for family planning. A majority of the time at monthly PHC meetings is devoted to a review of case motivation by individual staff members. Auxiliary nurse midwives and their field supervisors, lady health visitors, are required to generate a prescribed number of family planning cases from a shared geographic region which often remains the same for two to three years. This introduces an organizational conflict which provokes tension and competition between these two cadres as opposed to cooperation, supervision, and continuing education.[16] Fendall (1984) has aptly characterized the ramifications of this situation: "Inspection is often substituted for education, criticism for consultation, and irritation for understanding."

Given the role strains already present within the PHC, what happens when new cadres of health workers are created and changes in the roles of existing cadres are called for? Let us consider the first situation in the Indian context and the second as it exists in Sri Lanka.

A village health guide program in Karnataka, a regional version of the national community health worker scheme, was implemented in the spring of 1984. A young enthusiastic medical officer of one PHC which I observed was presented with the names of "community representatives." This list was prepared by elected officials of the local governing council (panchayat), not the community at large. From these names, the medical officer selected "suitable candidates." Deputed the task of training these volunteers, he focused training activities on first aid, the timings of vaccinations, and family planning methods.[17] Untrained in health education, interpersonal communication, nutrition, or community hygiene, the doctor lectured on those topics with which he was most familiar. Emphasis was placed on the recognition and treatment of the diseases of individuals, not the recognition of broad patterns of social activity enhancing health, engendering disease, and fostering ill health. The doctor took a group of villagers whose own ideas about illness and health were underscored by an ecological view of well being — health as defined in relation to one's physical, social, and spiritual environment — and essentially taught them about technical fixes. Health issues became medicalized and commodified through an emphasis on medicines. The results of such training have been well documented by evaluation teams elsewhere in India:

> It is evident that the community health workers laid emphasis on medical treatment and failed to show an adequate appreciation of the diverse aspects of public health that need attention for improvement in the health status of rural people. If we take their responses to reflect the nature of the training they recently received, it becomes apparent that the training programme was not in tune with the objectives of the scheme.... Community health workers exhibited poor levels of knowledge with respect to referrals, preventive and promotive services and treatment of emergencies. They exhibited a high level of knowledge on the use of medicines. (Bose and Desai 1983)

What has been the response of field staff to the type of training and the scope of a village health guide's activities? The following comment made by one seasoned auxiliary nurse midwife conveys the feelings of many PHC staff:

> Village health guides are being taught about disease and medicine which auxiliary nurse midwives and multipurpose workers were not taught until after much training. The doctor trains the village health guides to give medicines, but we cannot give. We were promised medical kits, but we did not get. Now big people are interested in village health guides. If they are given medicine kits and we are allowed to only walk, talk, and write our names on walls (for supervisor's spot checks), there will be bad feelings between us, isn't it?

According to PHC staff whom I interviewed, the appropriate role for village health workers was that they should act as "motivators" or "assistants" under their, not community, control.[18] The ramifications of this pervasive attitude are described by Maru (1980) who studied a similar community health visitor program implemented five years earlier in a northern state of India:[19]

> Functionaries of the formal health bureaucracy expressed desire to have administrative control over the Community Health Visitor. When asked whether Community Health Visitors should be kept under the formal control of the primary health centers, nearly 90% of the field workers and their supervisors answered in the affirmative.... In relation to the contradiction between community contact and the desire of health staff for administrative control over the Community Health Visitor, it can be hypothesized that in the long run the scheme may be coopted into the formal health organization, first through cultural associations and then through structural absorption.

It is hardly surprising that auxiliary nurse midwives and multipurpose workers feel threatened and wish to control community health guides/workers. Indeed, in their own eyes, issues of status and future pay scale rationalization depend on such control. The situation is aptly summed up by Bose and Desai (1983):[20]

> At the time the community health worker scheme was introduced, no particular care was taken in redefining the activities of the multipurpose workers.... In actual practice the difference in skills and competence required of each is not perceptibly large.... In the initial stages, we did not find much evidence of any conflict between volunteers and staff.... In time there was a feeling on the part of multipurpose workers of having lost credibility in the eyes of the people since they did not carry a personal kit of medicines such as community health workers did. By definition the community health workers were to receive technical guidance and professional advice from the multipurpose workers.... With the passage of time, the community health workers began to realize that their competence was not inferior to multipurpose workers in carrying out activities including the curing of minor ailments. From this realization emerged a feeling of discrimination concerning remuneration although the honorarium they received was for volunteer work.

ROLE CHANGES: THE SRI LANKAN CASE

Sri Lanka provides an insightful case study of how primary health care inspired role change may result in professional and structural role strains reducing health team cooperation.[21] This case also provides insights into the subtle way local politics have influenced professional relationships among PHC staff. We may focus our attention initially on the family health worker, (the equivalent of the auxiliary nurse midwife within India) and the public health nurse, (an equivalent of the lady health visitor in India). We may then turn to consider the role conflict faced by the health educator: whether to assume a role of staff supervisor or staff coordinator.

Among family health workers, a split is presently occurring between the junior and senior members of this cadre. Senior members, originally termed public health midwives, were selected by a competitive examination and assumed clear roles within the health care system as midwives. Their status was fixed and avenues of advancement were open to them including the possibility of becoming a public health nurse. In 1978, the selection procedure for this cadre changed. Selection by a competitive examination was superseded by political appointment from local members of parliament. These officials selected candidates from a general job bank containing the names of applicants desiring a government service job in general. As local power brokers, members of parliament often repaid favors within their personal patronage circles by recommending supporters for jobs from the job bank. This change in the midwife selection procedure coincided with a change in title from public health midwife to family health worker, a change in the dress code, and a change in the scope of work of this cadre.[22]

The current split between junior and senior family health workers is readily apparent at PHC meetings where these two groups tend to segregate themselves. Senior members of the cadre are more conservative than junior members and tend to assert their status by calling attention to their superior midwifery skills. The emphasis of their fieldwork is on maternal and child health activities. Junior members of the cadre note that 79% of deliveries now take place in hospitals, 74% of which are in large central hospitals. In order to deliver in hospitals, women are required to attend a set number of their clinics. Junior family health workers tend to assume that maternity issues are covered at such clinics and view their role more in relation to some of the other 16 tasks allocated to them in their revised multipurpose training.[23] Senior family health workers call attention to the fact that junior members are political appointees who did not originally aspire to become family health workers, but made the best of an opportunity for employment. Junior family health workers in return state that seniors are submissive handmaidens to public health nurses. Senior family health workers retort by stating that it is by their efforts, not that of junior members, that they are now able to wear a white frock "just like public health nurses" instead of a white saree.

Public Health Nurses and Family Health Workers

Issues of status and role integrity created a strained relationship between public health nurses and family health workers, particularly junior members. The change in dress code from white sarees to white frocks was opposed by public health nurses who viewed this loss of visual demarcation as a loss of status for their group. To evoke differentiation at staff meetings or public functions, public health nurses sometimes wear veils, the status of which is little understood by the general public who refer to both family health workers and public health nurses as "nurse *nona*" (nurse woman) or "missy," general terms for nurse. Additionally, public health nurses have made a point to demarcate their status functionally through the provision of medical services associated with symbols of power such as the hypodermic. For example, in many PHCs they do not allow family health workers to administer DPT vaccine! They administer all vaccinations while family health workers are asked to control the crowd and fill out forms.

Issues relating to status and teamwork can dramatically affect the quality of health care management. Junior family health workers interviewed complained that when they gave letters of referral to clients to bring to the PHC, public health nurses paid them little credence. This reflected badly on the family health worker's credibility. Family health workers interpreted this neglect as intentional and a means of reducing their status in the community. Additionally, they complained that when villagers visited a clinic, public health nurses questioned them ("Has the FHW visited you, how often, did she fill out a register, etc.?"), casting the impression that there was little trust in their work as subordinates.

Junior family health workers have begun to question the role of public health nurses to supervise, or perhaps more appropriately, criticize, their fieldwork. They feel that this function may more appropriately be performed by experienced family health workers who have worked up through the ranks to become supervisor public health midwives. At present, family health workers are supervised by both supervisor public health midwives (who have worked up through the ranks) and public health nurses (who have advanced training). Public health nurses blame the new primary health care policy for creating trouble "or at least fanning the smoldering ember" between family health workers and themselves. As one public nurse midwife put it, "It is hardly surprising that junior family health workers have come to think so highly of themselves when they have become the center of attention by ministers and are visited by big people from international agencies who praise them while our work is neglected."

Health Educators

Health educators attached to Sri Lanka's Bureau of Health Education were placed in an awkward position with respect to growing role and status conflicts within the PHC. Health educators have themselves come up through the ranks as former public health inspectors or public health nurses, positions having similar status. Through self-motivation, they chose to apply to the Sri Lankan Bureau of Health Education for a role — not a position. In 1985 approximately 40 health educators made up the Bureau, only seven of whom were formally deputed as health educators while the rest retained their former salary and rank. Eleven of 15 health educators interviewed stated they had been motivated to become health educators as a means of securing higher status. The opportunity to undertake individual projects and the desire to break from their routine were also strong motivating factors.

In the field, health educators maintain a neutral, somewhat ambiguous, status. They are popular among family health workers who use them to boost their own status by arranging special programs. Health inspectors and public health nurses tend to regard health educators as equals drawing a similar salary. In the mid-1980s, however, health inspectors and public health nurses began to question whether perhaps primary health care ideology and programs, which health educators were responsible for propagating, benefitted family health workers and health educators, not themselves.

What made matters structurally more complex was that health educators began to lobby for greater status and pay befitting additional training and role changes. While health educators were once recruited from the ranks on the basis of field seniority and the recommendation of regional health educators, graduation from university now became a prerequisite. This prerequisite was added in an effort to boost the professional status of health educators and to facilitate plans for providing postgraduate training to Bureau staff. Such training was to enhance the Bureau's stature in the Ministry of Health. This act enraged non-graduate public health inspectors, a point vocalized by their union.

To make matters worse, health educators were asked to play a greater "supervisory role" within the PHC.[24] According to government prerequisites for a pay increase, health educators had to assume this role. Some health educators expressed misgivings about assuming this supervisory role recognizing its potential to undermine established working relationships with other professionals at the PHC.

Between 1985 and 1986 I assisted the Sri Lankan Bureau of Health Education in the training of their first batch of M.Sc. health educators in the social and behavioral sciences. One aspect of their training was a systems analysis of the PHC and a structural analysis of their present role and their future role as envisioned by the dictates of the primary health care philosophy. An area of focus was teamwork within the PHC as a prerequisite to implementing primary health care. Health educators recognized that playing a neutral coordinator role within the PHC was the best way that they could accomplish this task, yet they were being compelled to assume a supervisory role resulting in role conflict.

CONCLUSION

Boerma (1987) has noted that while the team approach is considered an essential element of primary health care strategy in developing countries, its impact has not been demonstrated:

> The actual evidence of the effectiveness of the health team approach is limited. Very few case studies exist to demonstrate the effectiveness of the team approach in terms of health outcome or impact. (Boerma 1987:748)

One reason for the poor record of teamwork may well be that what is described as teamwork by health planners is in reality little more than loose compliance to mandated guidelines. Masked by rhetoric about cooperation is competition and passive aggression between cadres of health workers, competition enhanced by the very programs which promote teamwork in word, but not deed.

My reason for highlighting examples of health staff role conflicts related to professional status and organizational structure is to draw attention to the need for an increased understanding of the PHC as a social system. A social systems analysis of PHCs needs to be a prerequisite to planning for change within the health sector in the name of primary health care. Taylor (1978) has noted that health staff "must learn to obtain more gratification from the achievements of the health team than from their personal contributions to individual patient care." This is no small task, particularly if the community is to play a more active role in health care. As Maru (1977:19) has cogently argued:

> If primary health care programmes are to be based on community participation, the policy makers must also plan for simultaneous changes in the structure and culture of the existing health bureaucracy.

Are such changes in the structure and culture of existing health bureaucracies being engendered? The rhetoric for change certainly exists, couched in terms such as "political will." The problem with this rhetoric is twofold. First, it does not confront the reality of the existing sociopolitical context underlying the organizational structure of national health care systems and the international agencies which influence them.[25] Second, this rhetoric serves the altruistic needs of planners more than it does the basic needs and motivations of field staff. Primary health care rhetoric, as it filters down from the state to district to local level, calls upon health staff to perform tasks which, when seen out of the context of total health care and community development, may well be perceived as professionally disadvantageous and threatening to their relative status and security. Furthermore, staff are at once called upon to assume leadership and facilitator roles in the community beyond their social status and without appropriate preparation or support.[26]

Unrealistic expectations from health staff lead to disenchantment, ambivalence, and gamesmanship (Sluzki 1974, Fendall 1984).[27] Even where primary health care rhetoric inspires field staff, it is unlikely that their motivation will be sustained for long unless provisions are made to: 1) address their social needs as professionals, 2) clarify and coordinate the roles of coexisting cadres of health and development workers so as to reduce competition and maximize cooperation, 3) mediate organizational and political factors inhibiting their ability to perform tasks specified by primary health care inspired programs.

On the subject of motivation, a last point may be raised with respect to community volunteer programs. A great deal of care and informed planning must precede any attempt to mobilize a culture's natural potential for volunteerism.[28] Volunteerism is socially transformed when regimented. For example, in Sinhalese culture, volunteerism is accorded a positive cultural value in keeping with the Buddhist ideology of merit (*pin*). Acts of service which require community participation, such as burial preparation, are performed out of a sense of civic and moral duty.[29]

Institutionalization of community participation in the form of myriad community development groups has at once provided frameworks for action and led to the co-option of volunteerism by local power brokers. Co-option has engendered symbolic participation which demeans and diminishes real participation. This, in turn, undermines the potential and reduces the motivation for new forms of community problem solving and interaction. Community groups formed around the rhetoric of participation, with the hidden agenda of power brokerage, have led villagers to become motivated by the spoils of community participation programs, not the process of community participation.

In closing, let me suggest that while the primary health care concept may have been developed in the name of the people, it is beginning to appear to many field staff as top down and better serving the political interests of speech makers than either PHC staff or the community. In order for primary health care to be implemented, far more attention will have to be turned toward fitting the organizational structure of the health system to the new strategy (Pyle 1981) and fostering health staff teamwork in such a way as to engender motivation and insure professional status. In this regard, it needs to be recognized that:

> Institutions not only express their ideologies through explicit statements of principals but also convey them — sometimes in directions quite opposite to

that of their avowed credos — through their organization and program structure. (Sluzki 1974:484)

NOTES

1. The concept of primary health care articulated at the WHO–UNICEF Alma Ata conference in 1978 places emphasis on a broad inspirational definition of health, material as well as nonmaterial factors influencing community health status, community participation, and political will. Following the Alma Ata conference, a heated debated ensued between selective and comprehensive approaches to primary health care. It is beyond the scope of this chapter to review this largely strawman debate. For a review of the issues driving this debate, see Kunitz (1987), Mull (1990), Rifkin and Walt (1986), Taylor and Jolly (1988), Walsh (1988), and Warren (1988). Teamwork is essential to both approaches to PHC.

2. As Mosley (1983:5) notes, primary health care "rather than being a revolutionary force for change, is more often simply added as another appendage to the assortment of vertical programs directed to the masses."

3. Communities are treated as socially discrete, cohesive, monolithic entities and little recognition is paid to local factionalism, hierarchy, or problems of representation. For an excellent critique of the concept of community used in development see Schwartz (1981).

4. For an exemplary analysis of the linkages between the political and organizational dimensions of primary health care programs in Maharastra, India, see Pyle (1981).

5. A consideration of how primary health care programs are situated in local political contexts requires attention to patronage systems. For a consideration of how PHC teamwork is affected by manpower problems and the need for a reorientation of health staff which demands new and different forms of training, see Boerma (1987).

6. Equally important to consider is community factionalism and how newly envisioned health programs will impact on relations of power and social stratification. On the need for community diagnosis which takes into consideration caste politics in India, see Nichter (1984). See Paul and Demarest (1984) for an example of how a community health care initiative can pose a threat to the status quo and galvanize community factionalism.

7. For example, see Bastien (1990) on the breakdown of social relationships between different levels of health personnel in Bolivia due to a lack of appreciation of each others roles. Woelk (1992) addresses structural factors indexing power relations between professionals which inhibit participation in community health worker programs.

8. India and Sri Lanka have distinctive social structures not addressed in this chapter. Caste politics is raised as an issue only in relation to the South Indian case study.

9. Pyle (1981), in a comparative study of nongovernment health projects and government health programs, makes use of a distinction between the former's "results" and the latter's "procedure" orientation. A "results" orientation is characterized by specific objectives and priorities, a problem solving process which encourages teamwork, and accountability. A procedure orientation is largely concerned with inputs, routines, organizational patterns, and the collection of information more for the sake of supervision as control than for facilitating accountability.

10. Smith and Bryant (1988) have noted that one of the major hurdles facing the implementation of comprehensive primary health care is the administrative integration of personnel affected by changing roles and power relationships.

11. In an analysis of 52 USAID-assisted primary health care projects, Parlato and Favin (1982) found that the credibility of the primary health worker is directly linked with drug supply. When an adequate supply of basic drugs exists, the primary health care worker becomes more and more the source of advice on noncurative preventive/promotive health matters.

12. Justice (1986) has written about the paramedical role played by PHC peons (nonformally trained attendants) in the absence of a PHC doctor. The role of the peon and midwife may be contrasted in relation to the present discussion of doctors' response to PHC staff dispensing medicine and/or advice about medicine. In India the status and power of a peon may be quite variable depending on years of service and political affiliation. The job of peon is reserved for members of scheduled castes and this is one position which an employee may keep for several years without being transferred. A peon who has worked at a PHC for a decade or more may wield considerable power although technically their role is at the bottom of the PHC hierarchy. Peons often fill in for other professionals when need be and may gain considerable practical knowledge about the treatment of wounds and routine complaints. The doctor described in the case study felt much less threatened by the PHC peon whom he called upon to assist him in a variety of treatment tasks including that of intermediary in the direction of patients to his private practice. One reason for his lack of concern about the peon's treatment activities in his absence may be the significant status difference between them. On the other hand, another PHC doctor drew attention to a former hospital peon who now "practiced medicine" in his native village. Follow-up of the case revealed that the former peon treated wounds and skin diseases and did not administer injections as the doctor had led me to believe.

13. It is interesting to note that midwives primarily spoke of male doctors being threatened by their distribution of medicine. A far greater percentage of male than female PHC doctors seek an active private practice. Where both a male and a female doctor are assigned to the same PHC, the male doctor usually

sets up a private practice. A number of female doctors who were in this situation felt that male doctors advertised themselves as having superior status and skills to their female counterparts.

14. The caste hierarchy of South Kanara is largely reproduced in the biomedical culture. A majority of doctors hail from Brahman, Bant (dominant caste agriculturalists), and Gowda Saraswat Brahman (merchant) castes. This is hardly surprising for as I have noted elsewhere (Nichter 1978), land owning and merchant caste families faced with land-business partition choices have sought high status occupations for children to reduce partition pressure.

15. For a discussion of kindness payments as incentives given to government doctors by patients, see Chapter 8. Between kindness payments and private practice, a PHC doctor easily doubles his government salary.

16. On the subject of targets, Kinosian and Kinosian (1980:115) note: "the government has tried to improve the performance of its health workers by establishing targets. In theory, the target system is a method of focusing attention on government priorities, and a way of evaluating the workers. In practice, it has distorted the functions of the staff and is partially responsible for the failure to create a multipurpose worker.... The imposition of the individual target system has created conflicts within the PHC. This manifests itself as pressures to falsify records and not cooperate with other staff in order to meet one's own target."

17. In this case, the medical officer took on the village health guide training program as a means to increase his own popularity. He was a native of another district and did not have an active private practice. This medical officer was studied as opposed to medical officers less committed to the scheme as a way of assessing what would be the outcome of the scheme when implemented. No doubt other medical officers with private practices were less eager to implement the scheme. It may be noted that while the training responsibility for health guides was largely allocated to medical officers, the burden for training in other regions often fell to other functionaries such as block extension educators and multipurpose workers.

18. The village health guide program is a Karnataka State counterpart to the national community health worker plan. One of the original ideas underscoring the community health worker program was that the they would not be part of the health bureaucracy. The community health worker was to be responsible to the *panchayat*, providing a check on the work of medical and paramedical staff in health centers and subcenters. See Bose (1978).

19. Maru (1980) found that expressed desire for control of community health workers by PHC staff was inversely related to their level of status in the health bureaucracy. The desire for formal control was the strongest among the lowest level field workers who interact with the community health worker. It decreased as one moved up to the district and state levels.

20. The multipurpose workers referred to were unipurpose workers trained under a new government scheme designed to offer broad skills to all PHC staff. In the PHCs studied, few field staff had been retrained as multipurpose workers as yet. I therefore have refrained from using the multipurpose health worker as an example in my discussions of role strain in this chapter. In relation to this program, Ramasubban (1978) has observed that the conversion from unipurpose to multipurpose workers is mainly on paper and that the scheme is fraught with problems due to issues of status and pay as well as scope of work and overriding targets. Ramasubban cites examples of status conflict introduced by the scheme such as a) family planning health assistants who are only high school graduates are made senior to specialized health workers who are college graduates, and b) block extension health educators, formerly the third senior role in the health center bureaucracy, are reduced to assistants of the medical officer. Ramasubban (1978) notes: "The dissatisfaction which has seized the health worker has come in the way of their commitment to the extra duties arising out of the Community Health Worker scheme as well as their effectiveness in discharging them." Pyle (1981) presents a complementary organizational and political analysis of the multipurpose worker scheme and why it has failed.

21. I do not want to infer that role changes have failed to provide opportunities for enhancing teamwork. School health programs and special training programs such as that for cancer education are occasions when teamwork potential has been realized.

22. Family health workers were originally called *vindamu* in Sinhala, a term denoting a midwife. Linguistically, the term is associated with *vinianu*, one who has felt the pangs of labor. Inasmuch as many female members of this cadre were unmarried, they lobbied to have their title changed to *paol sokya sevika*, family health worker. Family health workers do not object to being referred to as midwife in English.

23. Family health workers who cover a population of 3,000 presently have 16 assigned tasks including: antenatal care, emergency natal care, postnatal care, child care, family planning, immunizations, diarrheal disease, nutrition, school health, family life and adolescent care, control of communicable diseases, treatment of minor ailments, health education, laboratory testing of sugar and albumin, blood filming for malaria, and passive screening of patients, in addition to mental health and cancer detection. Additionally, the family health worker has extensive paperwork to complete. It could well be argued that a blurring of family health workers' service and support functions has occurred, that her scope of field tasks is unrealistic, and that her burden of paperwork is counterproductive.

24. During their 1984 union meeting, health educators submitted a list of demands to the Minister of Health focusing on the issues of salary raise, title, and status. A salary raise was out of the Minister's direct jurisdiction and

supervision duties were spoken of as a means of boosting health educator status and claim for increased salary.

25. See Jobert (1985) and Madan (1987) on the sociopolitical context underlying the organizational structure of the health care system in India. See Morgan (1989) for an insightful discussion of the rhetoric of "political will" as the key to implementing primary health care. Morgan notes that general reference to "political will" depoliticizes national and local power structures making them seem like monolithic entities. It also diverts attention from the role played by international agencies in determining health policies as well as global relations of dependency which perpetuate the conditions of ill health. Kunitz (1987) points out that emphasis on "political and social will" is the functional equivalent at the national level of "responsibility for one's health" at the individual level. In both cases, responsibility for health is shifted away from economic development as a precursor to change, and victim blaming is fostered.

26. A related example which readily comes to mind from India involves *Anganawadi* (kindergarten) workers associated with the Integrated Child Development Scheme. *Anganawadi* workers are generally young women having, on the average, a 7th grade standard education. They are paid less than a PHC attendant (peon), a salary too much to afford them the status of being perceived as a volunteer, and too little to afford them much status within the local government bureaucracy. While *Anganawadi* workers are trained to be village level health workers focusing on child health, most villagers view them as a kind of preschool teacher who organizes a creche program. Yet despite the existing low status of the *Anganawadi* worker and her weak credibility as a health worker, she is asked (in her training, at least) to approach local government leaders, organize community level programs and so on. Needless to say, the track record of the *Anganawadi* worker, in terms of community leadership and organization, is low: "The syllabus emphasizes the role of the *Anganawadi* worker in working with local panchayats. This may be unrealistic, given the fact that most *Anganawadi* workers — young women of the village — will not be seen as influential change agents by older *panchayat* members" (Parlato 1982).

27. Along with unrealistic expectations, one finds top-down decision making and communication flow. A study by Seshachalam (1981) in India found that hierarchical decision making, top-down communication, and use of participative mechanisms mostly to explain decisions already made restrict opportunities for bottom-up communication and contribute to staff ambivalence, shortfalls in program achievement, and even program sabotage.

28. In addition to assessing activities around which members of a population cooperate and "volunteer" time and resources, it is necessary to review a population's history of participation across domains (e.g., health, agriculture, road construction, reforestation) and to consider how the memories of past programs are likely to influence response to future programs. The concept of

"volunteering" requires scrutiny. A useful framework for doing so may be provided by Bourdieu's (1990) notion of cultural, social, and economic capital.

29. The concept of "community" is often reified in public health literature. Communities, like households, are fluid and mobilized around sets of activities (Brownlea 1987, Schwartz 1981, Wilk and Netting 1984). What appears to the outsiders as "community" demarcated by an administrative structure is often a collection of factions which compete as well as cooperate for resources. Volunteerism needs to be approached carefully in relation to both existing patterns of social interaction and opportunities for new forms of interaction given historical changes.

REFERENCES

Banerji, D. 1974. Social and Cultural Foundations of Health Service Systems. Economic and Political Weekly 9:32–34.

Bastien, J. 1990. Community Health Workers in Bolivia: Adapting to Traditional Roles in the Andean Community. Social Science and Medicine 30(3):281–287.

Boerma, T. 1987. The Viability of the Concept of a Primary Health Care Team in Developing Countries. Social Science and Medicine 25(6):747–752.

Bose, A. 1978. An Assessment of the Rural Health Scheme and Suggestions for Improvement. New Delhi: Demographic Research Centre, Institute of Economic Growth.

Bose, A. and P. Desai. 1983. Studies in Social Dynamics of Primary Health Care. Pp. 65–75. Delhi: Institute of Economic Growth, Hindustan Publishing Corporation.

Bourdieu, P. 1990. The Logic of Practice. Stanford, CA: Stanford University Press.

Brownlea, A. 1987. Participation, Myths, Realities and Prognosis. Social Science and Medicine 24:605–614.

Chowdhury, Z. 1981. The Good Health Worker Will Inevitably Become a Political Figure. World Health Forum 2:55–56.

Fendall, R. 1984. Discussion: We Expect Too Much From Community Health Workers. World Health Forum 5:300.

Flahault, D. 1976. An Integrated and Functional Team for Primary Health Care. WHO Chronicle 30:442–446.

Foster, G. 1977. Medical Anthropology and International Health Planning. Social Science and Medicine 11:527–534.

Foster, G. 1982. Community Development and Primary Health Care: Their Conceptual Similarities. Medical Anthropology 6:183–195.

Gish, O. 1979. The Political Economy of Primary Health Care and Health by the People: A Historical Exploration. Social Science and Medicine 13c:209.

Heggenhaugen, H. 1984. Will Primary Health Care Efforts be Allowed to Succeed? Social Science and Medicine 19:217–224.

Jobert, B. 1985. Populism and Health Policy: The Case of Community Health Volunteers in India. Social Science and Medicine 20(1):1–28.

Justice, J. 1986. Policies, Plans and People: Culture and Health Development in Nepal. Berkeley: University of California Press.

Kinosian, B. and M. Kinosian. 1980. Invisible Hand and Iron Fist: The South Indian Health Bazaar. Report submitted to the Professional Studies Program, University of California, Berkeley.

Korten, D. 1979. Community Social Organization in Rural Development. Resource paper for the Ford Foundation, Yogyakarta, Indonesia.

Kunitz, S. 1987. Explanations and Ideologies of Mortality Patterns. Population and Development Review 13(3):379–408.

Madan, T. N. 1987. Community Involvement in Health Policy: Socio-Structural and Dynamic Aspects of Health Beliefs. Social Science and Medicine 25(6):615–620.

Maru, R. 1977. The Community Health Volunteer Scheme in India: An Evaluation. Social Science and Medicine 17:19.

Maru, R. 1980. Community Health Worker: Some Aspects of the Experience at the National Level. Medico Friend Bulletin. Ahmedabad, India, April 1980.

Morgan, L. 1989. Political Will and Community Participation in Costa Rican Primary Health Care. Medical Anthropology Quarterly 3(3):232–245.

Mosley, W. 1983. Will Primary Health Care Reduce Infant and Child Mortality? A Critique of Some Current Strategies with Special Reference to Asia and Africa. Seminar in Social Policy, Health Policy and Mortality. Paris: Institut National D'Études Demographiques. February 28–March 4.

Mull, D. 1990. The Primary Health Care Dialectic: History, Rhetoric and Reality. *In* Anthropology and Primary Health Care. Jeannine Coreil and Dennis Mull, eds. Pp. 28–47. Boulder: Westview Press.

Nichter, Mark. 1978. Patterns of Curative Resort and Their Significance for Health Planning in South Asia. Medical Anthropology 2:29–58.

Nichter, Mark. 1984. Project Community Diagnosis: Participatory Research as a First Step Toward Community Involvement in Primary Health Care. Social Science and Medicine 19(3):237–252.

Parlato, M. B. and M. Favin. 1982. An Analysis of 52 AID-Assisted Primary Health Care Projects. APHA, April 1982.

Parlato, R. 1982. Consultant Report for India, International Nutrition Communication Service. USAID/DSAN-C-0209, Washington, DC.

Paul, B. D. and W. J. Demarest. 1984. Citizen Participation Overplanned: The Case of a Health Project in the Guatemalan Community of San Pedro La Laguna. Social Science and Medicine 19(3):185–192.

Pyle, D. 1981. From Projects to Program: The Scaling Up/Implementation Process of Community-Level, Integrated Health, Nutrition, Population Intervention in

Maharasthra. Unpublished Ph.D thesis, Massachusetts Institute of Technology, Department of Political Science.

Ramasubban, R. 1978. Health Care for the People: The Empirics of the New Health Scheme. Technical Report 16, Giri Institute of Development Studies, Lucknow, India.

Rifkin, S. B. and G. Walt. 1986. Why Health Improves: Defining the Issues Concerning "Comprehensive Primary Health Care" and "Selective Primary Health Care." Social Science and Medicine 23:559–566.

Rueschemeyer, D. 1972. Doctors and Lawyers: A Comment on the Theory of Professions. *In* Medical Men and Their Work. E. Freidson and J. Lorber, eds. Pp. 5–19. Chicago: Aldine Press.

Schaeffer, M. and H. Pizurki. 1984. Human Resources for Health for All. World Health Statistical Quarterly 37:52–83.

Schwartz, N. 1981. Anthropological Views of Community and Community Development. Human Organization 40(4):313–322.

Segall, M. 1983. The Politics of Primary Health Care. Bulletin 14:4. Institute of Development Studies, Sussex, England.

Seshachalam, P. 1981. Decision-Making Behavior in Family Welfare Programme Organization. Social Change 11:49.

Skeet, M. 1984. Community Health Workers: Promoters or Inhibitors of Primary Health Care? World Health Forum 5:291.

Sluzki, C. 1974. On Training to "Think Interactionally." Social Science and Medicine 8(9):483–485.

Smith, D. and J. Bryant. 1988. Building the Infrastructure for Primary Health Care: An Overview of Vertical and Integrated Approaches. Social Science and Medicine 26(9):909–917.

Stark, R. 1985. Lay Workers in Primary Health Care: Victims in the Process of Social Transformation. Social Science and Medicine 20:269–275.

Taylor, C. 1978. Reorientation of Health Personnel to Meet the People's Needs. Assignment Children 42, 67, UNICEF, April 1978.

Taylor, C. 1984. Health Systems Research: How Can it be Used? World Health Forum 4:328.

Taylor, C. and R. Jolly. 1988. The Straw Men of Primary Health Care. Social Science and Medicine 26(9):971–977.

Walsh, J. 1988. Selectivity Within Primary Health Care. Social Science and Medicine 26(9):899–902.

Warren, K. 1988. The Evolution of Selective Primary Health Care. Social Science and Medicine 26(9):891–898.

Wilk, R. and R. McC. Netting. 1984. Households: Changing Forms and Functions. *In* Households: Compararative and Historical Studies of the Domestic Group. R. Netting, R. Wilk, and E. J. Arnould, eds. Pp. 1–28. Berkeley: University of California Press.

Woelk, G. B. 1992. Cultural and Structural Influences in the Creation of and Participation in Community Health Programmes. Social Science and Medicine 35(4):419–424.

Zacher, W. 1984. Discussion: Health Centres Must be Strengthened First. World Health Forum 5:308.

CHAPTER 12

Drink Boiled Cooled Water:
A Cultural Analysis of a
Health Education Message

Mark Nichter

Lack of sensitivity to the health concerns of lay persons, and the introduction of educational messages that fail to take their health culture into consideration result in misinterpretation, the compartmentalization of information, and desensitization to priority issues. The international health literature is riddled with this sermon. Rather than engage in polemic, I will present a brief case study which illustrates why it is important to monitor how public health messages delivered by primary health care workers are interpreted by the populations they serve. The example is taken from Sri Lanka and concerns what might appear to be the most basic of health messages, "drink boiled cooled drinking water."

Four decades ago Wellin (1955) presented an insightful ethnographic account of water boiling education in Peru to demonstrate how this behavior was influenced by culture:[1]

> A trained health worker can perceive "contamination" in water because his perceptions are linked to certain scientific understandings which permit him to view water in a specially conditioned way. A Los Molinos resident also views water in a specially conditioned way. Between him and the water he observes, his culture "filters in" cold, hot or other qualities that are as meaningful to him as they are meaningless to the outsider. (Wellin 1955:100)

The present case complements that presented by Wellin. In contrast to Peru, a large majority of the Sri Lankan population is literate (male 90%, female

393

82%) and have easy access to health facilities (the average person is within three miles of a health center). Over the past two decades, the country has experienced a notable decrease in infant mortality, which is presently 37 per 1,000 births. Diarrheal diseases continue to be a leading cause of morbidity and mortality, accounting for 53% of all infectious disease deaths in 1979. In the same year, these diseases constituted the third leading cause of death for the population at large, yielding 44.9 deaths per 100,000.[2] One study (Pollack 1983) indicated that deaths from water-borne diseases has steadily increased by 49% in the five years between 1971–76. Reviewing existing morbidity/mortality data, Pollack observed:[3]

> The trend of decreasing disease specific mortality in hospitals without parallel decreases in morbidity, suggests that, for specific diagnosis (e.g., gastroenteritis, typhoid fever, and malnutrition), there is an awareness of the availability of curative intervention, but the preventive intervention components have not been emphasized or have been unsuccessful. (Pollack 1983:93)

To learn why preventive intervention has been unsuccessful for water-related diarrheal diseases, forms of behavior identified as main elements in the spread of these diseases were studied: defecation habits, food handling, and water consumption behavior. This chapter is confined to a cultural consideration of the last variable. Public health inspectors and family health workers in Sri Lanka have been encouraging the public to drink boiled cooled water for well over three decades. Despite their efforts, field workers readily admit that the message is largely unheeded.[4] One popular public health inspector with whom I spent considerable time in the field estimated that less than 10% of the rural families he visited regularly prepared and used boiled cooled drinking water. Why should the largely literate Sri Lankan public pay little credence to health messages conveyed by health workers who enjoy some degree of social status in the community?[5] Let us consider two of the more obvious possibilities: fuel scarcity and a lack of time to prepare boiled water. In some areas of Sri Lanka these are undoubtedly important variables affecting water drinking behavior. This was not the case, however, among those informants selected for study in the Horana-Ratnapura region of southwest Sri Lanka. Firewood was available, and if anything, was unnecessarily expended in poorly constructed hearths typically composed of three bricks over which a cooking pot would be placed.

Is the underlying issue one of the local culture not paying much credence to the qualities of water? This certainly is not the case in Sri Lanka. Indeed, one of the few material possessions a Sinhalese Buddhist monk is prescribed to carry is a water filter. Among the lay population, the taste, smell, and inherent qualities of water are important health concerns. Villagers are keen to see the source of their drinking water. This is one reason that closed wells are not popular. Another reason for their unpopularity is that a limited amount of sunlight is believed to be necessary for keeping water fresh. Having to drink water from an unknown source is considered a hardship. In fact, one way a villager expresses to a friend the hardship of having to remain in Colombo city for a period of time is to exclaim "ayyo! pipe *watura* [pipe water] — you have to drink and bathe in it!"

While commuting daily to Colombo from a rural village about one and a half hours away, I observed many passengers on the bus jostling water bottles as well as lunch packets amidst a terrific crowd. Bringing lunch packets from home was easily understood in relation to microeconomics, but water? When questioned, my commuter friends explained that quite frankly they did not trust Colombo "pipe water." They spoke of pipe water as *marana watura* — dead water — or *kivul watura* — water tasting of iron and associated with urinary problems. They disliked the "medicinal" smell of chlorinated water, and felt that boiled cooled water was tasteless.[6] But was it just the tasteless-ness of boiled water which they did not like or were there other reasons for preferring to transport small bottles of their own unboiled well water an hour and a half by crowded bus? Why should they ignore the advice of public health workers?

Before considering why people do not do something, it is often more prudent to consider what it is that they do and why. It is, however, difficult to respond to "why" questions out of context. To ground such questions in context, it is advantageous to engage informants in discussion about practices they easily recognize. In the present case, individual interviews and focus group discussions were initiated around the observation that boiled cooled water was routinely prepared for the ill, but not generally consumed by others. These discussions led me to question a common explanation for lay behavior offered to me by public health colleagues. They reasoned that because the message "drink boiled cooled water" was originally introduced and most adamantly repeated during epidemics of cholera, typhoid, and gastroenteritis, people had come to associate the practice of boiling water with illness.[7]

Three health-related reasons for heating or boiling were identified during interviews and group discussions. The first requires an appreciation of indigenous water management. The qualities of water from different sources vary and affect the purposes for which it is used. When water is plentiful, villagers choose to use different water sources for drinking and bathing in accord with the water's clarity, depth, and exposure to the sun. When water is scarce, an available source is used for many purposes, but efforts are differentially expended to transform the qualities of water used for drinking purposes. For those who are strong and healthy, little concern is expressed about water routinely used except when its color, smell, or taste changes. For those who are ill or in a transitional body state (such as infants and pregnant women), more subtle qualities of water are considered. For example, water from a deep well is believed to have a cooling quality which is harmful for those suffering from or vulnerable to illnesses linked with coolness (body stiffness and pain) or an excess of phlegm (Nichter 1987). On the other hand, water directly exposed (overexposed) to the sun is deemed to be "sun baked" (Karunadasa 1984) and inappropriate for those suffering from or prone to heating illnesses. When these water sources are the only ones available, healthy persons will use them without much restraint. When the same sources are the only ones available to the ill or vulnerable, however, drinking water will be boiled in an attempt to mitigate its excessive properties. For bathing purposes, traditional prescriptions specifying appropriate times for bathing will be more rigorously followed (Nichter 1987).

A second reason water will be heated is to reduce its "shock" effect on those at risk to illness. Shock is an important concept in South Asian health cultures related to vulnerability to illness as well as spirit attack. Shock may be a primary cause of illness or it may compound an existing illness. The body-mind is a continuum in which extreme emotional distress like fear, and extreme physical distress like heat or cold may cause or exacerbate illness. Shock occurs when a person is subjected to an excess of hot or cold, particularly when in a vulnerable state. Out of concern for shocking the body, those predisposed to phlegm problems will not consume cold liquids on hot days. Similarly, the ill will only consume and wash with water which is tepid. The health message "drink boiled cooled water," is interpreted by some villagers in relation to the concept of shock as it pertains to vulnerability as well as illness.[8]

Because many villagers do not associate boiling water with killing bacteria, they place more emphasis on administering tepid, rather than fully boiled water to the ill. It is not uncommon for villagers to boil water for the ill or vulnerable, and then add cool unboiled water to it so as to attain a tepid temperature, thereby recontaminating the water.[9] A point not to be lost sight of however, is that the preparation of tepid water through boiling is an act of caring accorded positive value. This introduces some irony into the context of hospital care. Although the instruction to "drink boiled cooled water" is propagated by health workers, tepid water is not available in government hospitals where patients and their families feel they need it. This fact is cited by lay people as an example of the poor care they receive at public health institutions, as distinct from the poor quality of medicines or doctors.

A third association with boiled water involves the Sinhala concept of lightness (*sehellu*). When ill, a central health concern within Sinhalese popular culture and the learned system of *āyurvedic* medicine is digestion. Dietary regulations vary in accord with the ascribed characteristics of different illnesses. Regardless of the specific characteristics of an illness, however, a general restriction will prevail against the consumption of heavy (*bhara*) foods. Becoming well requires a light diet that will restore normal digestion as a part of the healing process.[10] Indeed, this is fundamental to balancing bodily humors, and the restrictions against heavy foods includes a conception of heavy water.

Well water is considered heavy unless it is boiled. Boiling causes water to lose some quality (*guna*) or residue, which then renders it light. The heaviness of unboiled water is considered good for health when one is in a normal state. Clear, unboiled well water (*hondai watura*) is said to satisfy thirst better than light boiled water. Furthermore, unboiled well water is considered "fresh," "full of life," and "having strength" in contrast to pipe water, which is "dead," and boiled water, which lacks strength. In one informant's words:

> The *guna* of water is like the *guna* of green leafy vegetables. When you eat them fresh, they have life. If you pluck them, transport them and keep them for sale, they lose their life and wilt. When you cook vegetables, they loose their freshness rapidly. It is like that with water. When water is running or in a well exposed to the sunlight, it is fresh. If you collect it and transport it through pipes it is *marana watura*, dead water, and if you boil it, water looses its *guna*, its strength.

The drinking of boiled cooled water is associated with illness — except in the evening — when it may be associated with health promotion. Since heavy food and heavy water are relatively difficult to digest, some people regularly drink "light" tepid water in the evening. Their reasoning reflects a general concern that digestion is weakest during inactivity and sleep. The message "drink boiled cooled water," is interpreted by some villagers in conjunction with the concept of *sehellu* and deemed most relevant for those having weak digestive capacity.[11] This interpretation, like that involving shock, is supported by the advice of *āyurvedic* practitioners to the ill, pregnant women, and mothers of infants.

CONCLUSION

The development of effective health education messages requires formative research which incorporates an ethnographic perspective. In the present case, multiple reasons underlie local interpretations of the "drink boiled cooled water" message.

The message is emphasized at times of epidemics and associated with *āyurvedic* advise to "take a light diet and tepid water" when ill, weak, or vulnerable to illness. Underscoring lay interpretations of these messages are folk health concepts, specifically, ideas about the qualities of water, shock, and digestive capacity. In order for a health message as simple as "drink boiled water" to be communicated effectively, careful observation of habitual behavior and an analysis of popular health concerns is essential. Like water, understanding seeks its own level.

NOTES

1. Wellin's study compared the motives and circumstances of women who boiled water with those who did not. His research illustrates that a combination of culture, ecology, economics, and social status influenced water boiling behavior. Out of a sample of 200 households subjected to a two year period of face-to-face education on the part of a hygiene worker, the number of acceptors rose from 15 at baseline to 26 at the time of evaluation.

2. Statistics on diarrheal diseases were gleaned from the following sources: Pollack (1983) and Gaminiratne (1984:59). It should be noted that district-wise, standardized death rates due to diarrheal diseases differ significantly. These range from 10.1 in Trincomallee and 16.5 in Matara to 127.3 in Batticaloa and 90.8 in Amparai. Percentage deaths due to these diseases range from 1.5% in Kalutara District and 2.9% in Matara to 15.1% in Amparai and 12.6% in Batticaloa. To correct any misconception that urban conditions contrast markedly with rural conditions, it may be noted that the Colombo infant mortality rate due to diarrheal diseases is 158% the national average — although for all age groups it is considerably lower than the national average. Among children one to four years old, 16% of deaths are directly related to diarrheal diseases. During the period 1971–79, of the 10 leading causes of infant mortality, only diarrheal diseases showed no downward trend after 1975.

3. This study conducted by the Sri Lankan Department of Health Services was quoted in the Marga Institute report (Sri Lankan Department of Health Services 1982:93). The report also notes that in the Mahaveli Development region, diarrheal disease accounts for some 40% of all persons seeking medical treatment and that these cases of diarrheal disease are largely related to contaminated water sources.

4. For more recent data which documents the lack of water boiling among the Sinhalese population, see Caldwell et al. (1989:369) who report that only

one-fifth of families in their study sample did so. Also noted is the association of drinking boiled water with illness.

5. Public health inspectors and family health workers enjoy social status in Sri Lanka equivalent to that of a secondary school teacher. As Wellin reported of Peru, advice by health workers to alter health-related behavior carries significantly less weight than the same advice offered by a doctor. This weight was more evident in respect to immunization and family planning — technical fixes — than in respect to water boiling as a long-term enterprise related to preventive health. On this point I must note that in India boiled cooled water is not regularly used even by the educated. In a personal communication, Charles Leslie noted to me that drinking boiled cooled water is uncommon among New Delhi academics. He was told by a Professor of Social Medicine at Benares Hindu University that the highest rate of typhoid in Varanasi in the early 1970s was among faculty and students living in university housing.

6. I do not wish to underplay "tastelessness" as a factor negatively influencing water boiling behavior anymore than time or the cheap availability of fuel. My purpose is rather to identify other cultural factors impacting on water boiling behavior.

7. Routine water supply testing is not performed by Public Health Inspectors and attempts at well purification are only done during epidemics.

8. A subtle but important distinction needs to be drawn between primary and secondary illness prevention related to the concept of vulnerability. Primary prevention denotes the prevention of factors which may either cause illness or "open" one up to the effect of such factors. Secondary prevention entails preventing an illness or state of vulnerability from becoming exacerbated.

9. An opposite case scenario was encountered in Honduras during a cholera epidemic in 1994. A health communication message instructed the population to drink boiled water. Doctors reported that some citizens drank boiling water thinking this was essential to purify the body. While some scalded their mouths, others only sipped small quantities due to this misperception.

10. Generalizing the *sehellu* rationale might prove helpful in getting mothers to administer boiled water to children under three. The concept might also be useful in marketing a weaning food less likely to be shared in the family than the present weaning food *Triposha* to which people ascribe both a strength giving and neutral quality suitable for general consumption. For a short discussion of the CARE weaning food, *Triposha*, see Nichter 1987. A new supplementary weaning food might be marketed as *sehellu* — just what a child needs for its developing or weak digestive system. I am suggesting this idea as an example of how cultural concepts might be used as health resources in social marketing. I do not claim that this particular idea would prove effective, but suggest that it would be worth looking into.

11. Perceptions of vulnerability offset judgements about risk. Some informants who described themselves as having a "strong constitution" did not deem it

necessary to drink boiled water, although they thought this practice was useful for those more prone to illness.

REFERENCES

Caldwell, J., I. Gajanayake, P. Caldwell, and I. Peiris. 1989. Sensitization to Illness and the Risk of Death: An Explanation for Sri Lanka's Approach to Good Health for All. Social Science and Medicine 28(4):365–379.

Gaminiratne, K. H. W. 1984. Causes of Death in Sri Lanka: An Analysis of Levels and Trends in the 1970s. Unpublished report, Department of Census and Statistics, Colombo, Sri Lanka.

Karunadasa, H. I. 1984. Domestic Use of Water and Sanitation: A Behavioral Study. National Water Supply and Drainage Board, Colombo, Sri Lanka.

Nichter, Mark. 1987. Cultural Dimensions of Hot, Cold and Sema in the Sri Lankan Health Culture. Social Science and Medicine 25(4):377–388.

Pollack, M. 1983. Health Problems in Sri Lanka, Part I and II: An Analysis of Morbidity and Mortality Data. USAID, Sri Lanka, June 1983.

Sri Lankan Department of Health Services. 1982. The Marga Institute Report on Intersectoral Actions for Health. p. 93. Colombo, Sri Lanka, September 1982.

Wellin, E. 1955. Water Boiling in a Peruvian Town. In Health, Culture, and Community. B. Paul, ed. Pp. 71–103. New York: Russell Sage Foundation.

CHAPTER 13

Education by Appropriate Analogy

Mark Nichter and Mimi Nichter

INTRODUCTION

> Why should we expect the illiterate villager to adjust to the way of thinking
> of the educated man? Why should he alter his perception of the world to
> understand us?... Is development a one-sided process of duplication?... It is
> perfectly possible for an educated man to adapt to the concepts used by the
> illiterate villager, but he has to study them. (Fuglesang 1977:96)

A South Indian proverb states that "The plant in the courtyard is not a
medicine," meaning that what is familiar and close is often overlooked as a
valuable resource. This proverb is an appropriate beginning for this chapter,
for what we will discuss is not a new method of education but rather a use of
the familiar to explain the new — education by analogy.

In the field of health education far more time, energy, and resources have
been expended identifying what a population does not know or do than in
assessing what a population does know and the way in which it is known.
What is often neglected is a consideration of those concepts of health and
images of body processes which underlie the layperson's health practices.
Due to this lack of appreciation of tacit knowledge and the cultural common
sense (and empirical observations) upon which it is based, cultural resources
are often underutilized by health educators. The use of analogy as a mode of
communication is also overlooked. The value of this mode of communication is that it facilitates contextualized as opposed to decontexualized learning, and conceptual integration as opposed to the compartmentalization of

information. In contrast to introducing new "bits" of health information into a culture irrespective of preexisting knowledge and experience, education by analogy introduces new information within a context of existing associations, experiences and health concerns.[1]

The premise of this essay is that a good analogy is like a plow which can prepare a population's field of associations for the planting of a new idea. If the field of associations is not adequately plowed to accommodate new ideas, it is difficult for such ideas to take root. Indeed, simply introducing ideas irrespective of local culture is much like scattering seeds in the wind. Equal effort needs to be put into preparing the field, improving the plow, and perfecting the spread of seed.

Metaphorical communication and juxtaposition of imagery is a fundamental mode of human communication and a basic form of human understanding.[2] Susan Langer has described this mode of "reasoning" as a primary step in conscious abstraction:

> Every new experience or new idea about things evokes first of all some metaphorical expression.... It is in this elementary presentational mode that our first adventure in conscious abstraction occurs. (Langer 1942:125)

The very process of scientific understanding may be characterized as "starting with metaphor and ending in algebra" (Black 1962).[3] All too often the health educator has attempted to introduce "algebra," nutrition messages based upon nutrient equations, for example, into a villager's world before facilitating an appropriate metaphorical stage of understanding.[4] Health educators need to take stock of the "commonsense rationality" (Schutz 1964) of the villager.[5] Although ideas expressed through analogy, metaphor and proverb may not be logical in a strictly scientific sense, they shape the inchoate by giving it a familiarity which enables actors to adopt a strategy for dealing with a new situation. Analogies may also serve to enhance rapport and problem solving from within the layperson's world.[6]

BANKING VERSUS THE NEGOTIATION MODE OF EDUCATION

During research on the anthropology of health, we observed a range of interactions between laypeople and health professionals including both trained government health staff and indigenous medical specialists. While observing these interactions, we were struck by the general ineffectiveness of health and nutrition education monologues "delivered" to villagers. These attempts to introduce new health ideas were largely ineffective because: 1) they did not address people's health concerns; 2) they were introduced without any reference to local illness categories or ideas about etiology and folk dietetics; and 3) advice was not tailored to the economics of subsistence or the practicalities of village life. Village reality was more often ignored than worked with and villagers were asked to blindly accept new health ideas.[7]

To borrow an analogy from Paolo Friere (1973), information was introduced via a "banking mode of education." That is, information was deposited into a villager's mind verbatim as if the account (i.e., the mind) were empty, the assumption being that interest would accrue over time. The bankruptcy of this type of education in rural South India and Sri Lanka was clearly evident in the dividends it has yielded, namely, the compartmentalization of new information and frank inertia on the part of villagers to integrate new ideas into everyday life.

While living with primary health care field staff, we observed that they themselves did not utilize much of the information they were teaching to others in their own lives on a day to day basis. This is not to say that they did not encourage their own family members to be immunized or to visit a doctor when ill. Their hesitancy to adopt promotive health ideas was evident in their unaltered dietary habits and their inability to express to friends and relatives why nutritional advice should be followed beyond the laconic statement "it is good for health." In discussions with health staff about their training, it was apparent that they had not received advice, let alone instruction, on how to bridge the conceptual gap between the two cognitive universes in which they lived and worked. There seemed to be a tacit assumption on the part of health trainers that once health workers were supplied information, they could then pass it on to villagers in a suitable manner. Training in interpersonal communication skills was largely overlooked as a subject in both primary health worker and community health worker training programs.

In a review of India's community health worker manual, Srivastava (1980) highlights the ramifications of this oversight:

> The work of the CHW (Community Health Worker) requires an extensive facility in self-expression. The manual and the training programme do not consciously generate opportunities in the acquisition or development of such an ability. Simulation exercises recorded by the project team indicate that the CHWs tend to over awe the patient by an excessive use of borrowed terms and associative explanations. The speech interaction is largely one way.... The exposure of the CHWs to terms in the medical sciences creates problems in communicating with the village population.[8] (Srivastava 1980:46)

In contrast to the didactic approach to education utilized by health field staff, we studied the methods employed by popular religious leaders, indigenous medical practitioners, astrologers, and politicians in communicating new information to villagers. What emerged from our observations was a keen appreciation for how analogies were effectively used to include the known while locating and often encompassing the new or unknown. We noted the enthusiastic response which villagers would give religious leaders when they juxtaposed the themes of traditional mythology with a popular movie to emphasize a moral principle; how traditional *āyurvedic* practitioners would convey information about the relationship of body humors by reference to the sun, wind, and rain; and how astrologers discussed social relations with reference to the stars describing in turn the qualities of celestial forces by reference to body humors and kinship relations.[9] Politicians were likewise well received when they referred to India's history, not only in an attempt to recall past glory, but in an effort to present new events in terms of known occurrences or myths which served as timeless charters.[10]

EDUCATION BY APPROPRIATE ANALOGY: A PARTICIPATORY RESEARCH APPROACH

Education by analogy draws upon the popular patterns of effective communication noted above. The fundamental difference between an analogic and banking approach to education is that in the banking approach an educator starts out with an analysis of what a population does not know and then fills in gaps of knowledge as the professional sees them. The educator using an analogical approach begins by studying what a population *does know* conceptually and experientially. The educator–facilitator identifies areas of conceptual overlap between what is known/experienced in daily life and the new information. As opposed to simply depositing bits of information for recall, recall is engendered through cultural associations and through culturally relevant problem solving whenever possible. Participatory research is essential to the generation and testing of appropriate analogies. Through participatory research, lay health concerns and images of health and illness are identified in context through a reflexive process.

Initially, an analogical message is developed which is deemed to be culturally relevant on the basis of preliminary research. It is posed to evoke a response leading to dialogue and feedback. Successful communication is measured through laypeople's response to the initial analogy through elaboration or development of what they consider to be more appropriate or alternative analogies. The latter are often anchored to local sayings, proverbs, or stories. The generation of analogies by villagers either in support or in clarification of the original analogy serves as a check on comprehension. In addition, analogy posing serves as entertainment to villagers by providing an environment in which individuals can share their wit as well as their knowledge.

To provide a more structured sense of the process involved in generating analogical messages, seven ideal steps in framing appropriate analogies for health education may be outlined briefly. This is followed by examples of how teaching analogies were developed in the field in southern India and Sri Lanka.

Steps in Framing Appropriate Analogies for Health Education

1. Deconstructing of health/nutrition messages into underlying assumptions and concepts.

2. Collection of data on indigenous health concerns and lay preventive/promotive health behavior, folk dietetics and folk epidemiology, and indigenous categories of illness. Identification of assumptions underlying health concepts.

3. Cultural free association about health themes in complementary domains of experience. For example, free association about child growth and crop growth among agriculturists, cooking and dehydration among women, night fishing and the collection of night blood for filariasis testing among fishermen.

4. Identification of points of conceptual and experiential convergence between indigenous and biomedical thinking about health. For example, a common concern for blood quantity, digestive capacity, or health as a state of balance.

5. Compilation of a list of familiar referential frameworks within the culture through the collection of popular analogies, metaphors, and proverbs.[11]

6. Selection of analogies for an initial message which either a) point out convergences between indigenous and new health conceptualizations — shared assumptions, health concerns, etc., or b) uses experience in one domain of life to shed light on different domains such as agriculture and health, or cooking and health.

7. Presentation of an analogical lead-in message to a group of community members for their response. Subsequently, the message is rejected, refined, elaborated upon and/or alternative more appropriate analogies are generated. Linkage to proverbs and development of teaching stories may strengthen the point being made.

Described below are the ways in which education by analogy dialogues were developed in South India, Sri Lanka, Kenya and the Philippines. We review analogical approaches to education about nutrition, immunization, and family planning. The examples from India and Sri Lanka which involve nutrition education are detailed in a step-by-step fashion. They are framed around a traditional metaphor for development — the growing rice plant. The thinking which went into the development of a root analogy will be presented first in outline form and will be followed by a compressed rendering of other analogical messages developed through guided dialogue.

THE USE OF TEACHING ANALOGIES IN INDIA

Example One: Nutrition Education in India

"Eat a mixed and balanced diet." Foods recommended by health workers in this message are typically categorized into three or four groups based on nutrient content. The grouping of foods in this manner by health educators is not understood by villagers. Foods which nutritionists group together into one category are often classified by villagers into different categories having distinct properties which accord with folk dietetics (Nichter and Nichter 1981, Nichter 1986). The following aspects of folk dietetics and popular health culture were identified as important to consider when framing nutrition related analogies.

Gather background information

- The process of rice cultivation is well known to the villager. This process requires a proper balancing and regulation of fertilizer and water.
- Rice is not only the staple crop and cultural superfood (Jelliffe 1969); it is a central metaphor for life used in daily conversation. For example, in South India, a growing child is referred to in colloquial speech as a budding or developing rice stalk.
- Digestive capacity and blood quality/quantity are central health concerns.
- Health as balance is an important cultural concept. Balance is expressed through a concern for states of hot/cold and body humors (*tridōśa*).

Identify areas of cultural sensitivity

• The folk dietetic system underlies cultural common sense. Foods are classified in accordance with their qualitative state of hot/cold and lightness/heaviness, and their affect on body humors (Nichter 1986). The soil is also evaluated in terms of its hot and cold properties (Kurin 1983) and analogies are drawn between agricultural and human life cycles.[12]

Introduce root analogy

• The need for a balance of the right kinds of fertilizer in the field is like the need for the right kinds of food in the stomach.

Analogical message developed through dialogue

When cultivating rice, what is necessary? Good soil, a properly plowed field, leaf manure, cow dung, and ash. What happens if there is too little manure, green leaf, or ash? (A discussion typically ensues about crop height, seed head size, weight, rice illnesses and overall yield). Your body is like a field. If the proper mix of nutrients are not given to the field inside, your yield — your health — is poor and your blood weak.

The field needs to be well prepared to cultivate a good rice crop. Preparing the field so the earth can "digest fertilizer" is like enhancing the stomach's digestive capacity so the body can take food and turn it into blood.

Just as enough good soil is needed for rice growth in the field, so enough rice is needed in our bodies for energy and strength. To improve your crop — your health — other things are needed as well. Just as the field needs green leaf manure, so the body requires green leafy vegetables, but as in the case of fertilizer not all leaves are suitable for manure and the best leaves need to be identified in each season. Like dung in the field, the body requires strength giving foods like fish and pulses (e.g., greengram, blackgram). Like ash for the field, the body requires foods which when cooked by the stomach fire provide the body with ash minerals. As in the field, if too much of one item is used and not enough of another, balance is not obtained, and when there is no balance, illness may come by many means.

The above analogical message was developed as an alternative to monologues on food groups presented to villagers by health staff. Once the referential framework of agriculture was introduced it was found that it could be extended to address other nutrition education issues as well. Two examples follow.

Example Two: Tonic Use

Background Information: In the last decade, health has increasingly become commodified and medicalized by medical practitioners and a thriving pharmaceutical industry in both the commercial *āyurvedic* and allopathic sector. A visible outcome is an increased consumption of vitamin tonics, the ingredients of which often do not match deficiencies. Nutrition educators are faced with the task of countering the growing idea that consuming tonic when one is weak is a better investment of scarce resources than investing in a better diet (see Chapter 9). In discussions with agricultural field officers, we found that a complementarity existed between villagers' ideas about tonic and the agricultural fertilizer, urea. Some villagers used urea as a tonic for the soil, failing to heed advice about the importance of balancing urea with other nutrients. As distinct from vitamin tonics, however, villagers were rapidly gaining experience with urea and were beginning to see that if their soil was not balanced, their crop yield would not improve despite the healthy appearance produced by urea when applied to a field. The farmers were learning that using urea without other nutrients left the soil acidic — "hot" — and in a state of imbalance.

Analogic message developed: Health like a good crop cannot be purchased through a bottle of tonic or a bag of urea

When urea is placed on a field the field turns very green but does the crop yield increase? The crop is green and taller but is the grain head any larger? Is there profit or is there just more "show" if urea is used without being balanced by phosphates and calcium? What happens if phosphates are added to the field but not balanced with urea or calcium? The grain head increases in size, but the plant is too weak to support the grain head and it falls to the mud and rots. A balance of fertilizer is needed for a good yield. So it is with the body. Just as urea makes the crop look green quickly, when tonic is taken one feels better quickly. But does one become healthy and strong for long by tonic alone? Urea and tonic can only help the rice field and the body when balanced with other necessary ingredients.

If you wait until you are ill and then run for tonic expecting health, this is like supplying your field with urea at the time of harvest when your crop looks weak. Should one wait until thirsty to start digging the well? (A local proverb)

The indigenous concept of *soku* was used in support of the analogical message introduced above. *Soku* connotes a state of "being all puffed up," of looking big and strong, but actually being bulky and without substance — "like a big vine spinach plant which when cooked reduces to nothing in the pot." A plant which is given too much fertilizer and grows large but has less yield is described as *soku*. In one informant's words "It is as if the plants become intoxicated and forget their function." In dialogues with villagers, the process of a plant becoming *soku* through an excess of urea was compared to the behavior of a person who consumes tonic instead of a balanced diet. Balance was discussed in terms of both the field: stomach analogy introduced above and in terms of folk dietetics (Nichter and Nichter 1981).

Example Three: Diet During Pregnancy

Background Information: Primary Health Center (PHC) staff have been encouraged to instruct rural women to consume more food during pregnancy in an effort to reduce low birth weight babies. Unfortunately, the message of "eat more food to have a bigger, healthier baby" is not well received in rural South Kanara (see Chapter 2). Two reasons for this are fear of a difficult delivery if one has a large baby and a desire not to have a big baby which is *jabala*, a state in humans corresponding to *soku* in plants. The issue became how to educate pregnant women that they needed to eat more (or at least not less) without directly referring to baby size and setting off a chain of negative associations. A plausible alternative was to address the health of the mother and to engage her in a discussion of how her health affected that of her baby after delivery.

Popular health concerns were identified, particularly among women. The first concern identified was "less blood," a condition often corresponding to anemia and general feelings of malaise and weakness. The second concern was the loss of *dhātu* (a body substance) associated with strength and vigor. *Dhātu* is the quintessence of strength giving foods derived from successive processes of transformation and purification. Analogically, blood is refined to become *dhātu* just as milk is churned and boiled to produce *ghee*, clarified butter (Nichter 1986). Healthy breastmilk is thought to contain *dhātu*. When a breastfed baby becomes weak, women suspect that they do not have sufficient *dhātu*. Other features of *dhātu* are that it is stored and it takes time to produce. A wide range of opinions exist however, as to just how long it takes food to become blood and blood to become *dhātu*.[13] We found through dialogue that the two previous nutrition messages could be adapted and conjoined to address the problem of diet during pregnancy.

Analogical message developed: A pregnant woman is like a field, a baby like a rice stalk

When you are thirsty is that any time to start digging a well? At or near the day of harvest if the rice crop looks weak, is that the time to think of adding manure to the field? So it is with a baby growing within its mother. A mother is like a field and her baby like a rice stalk. Just as the field needs fertilizer prior to harvest, so a woman needs to consume foods during pregnancy which will produce blood and *dhātu*. When a woman has enough blood and *dhātu*, her baby will grow strong in the womb just as the rice shoot grows strong in the field which is well fertilized. Like the field where dung, ash, and green leaf take time to be digested by the soil, so food takes time to be digested and become blood and *dhātu*. A pregnant woman needs to produce a stock of *dhātu* and blood. Why? Because a mother looses blood during delivery and because she shares her *dhātu* with her baby through breastfeeding. It is important for a woman to produce a good store of blood and *dhātu* during pregnancy for her health and the health of her baby.

Following this lead-in message, dialogue was generated around the issue of which foods are considered blood and *dhātu* producing within folk dietetics (Nichter 1986). Nutrient-rich foods advised for greater consumption were those foods believed culturally appropriate to consume during pregnancy in addition to being affordable and accessible. Dialogue focused on the quantity as well as the quality of foods consumed, associating these topics with blood and *dhātu* production.

THE USE OF TEACHING ANALOGIES FOR NUTRITION AND IMMUNIZATION EDUCATION IN SRI LANKA

During 1984–85, we assisted the Sri Lankan Bureau of Health Education develop a Masters Degree program in Health Education. As part of field training in anthropology and health communication, students conducted health ethnography research and used these data to develop a health education approach. Some chose to utilize an analogical approach to health message negotiation. The following account illustrates how this approach was applied by one health educator familiar with the South Indian nutrition messages discussed above. A similar theme — comparison of the rice-field to the body — was used by the health educator in Kurenagala, a rice growing area of Sri Lanka. Agricultural practices in this region entail extensive use of chemical fertilizers in contrast to rural South Kanara where agricultural practices are more traditional. The Sri Lankan case presented again illustrates a dialogical approach to working with analogy.

Health Educator's Initial Message: Maternal and Child Health

This morning, I will make a comparison (connection) between the growing paddy field and the growing child. The paddy plant is like a child. The needs of the paddy plant in the field are like a baby's needs in a mother's belly. When planting a paddy field, one needs to do this with good feelings, happiness, and proper preparations if a good crop is to grow. In the same way, during pregnancy a woman needs to have good feelings and a happy home environment. One must care for the field as well as for the developing plant. If the field is not given proper treatment and enough fertilizer, the rice plant does not develop or germinate properly. A mother also must receive care and enough food so she will have sufficient blood so that the baby does not develop *mandama dosa* [an illness associated with protein energy malnutrition].

The health educator asked villagers to draw correlations between the life stages of the growing rice plant and a baby in order to more clearly establish the comparison between the child and the field. Through anthropological research, the health educator had learned that local agricultural terms were used by laypeople to describe and discuss stages in the development of the fetus. For example:

Sinhalese term	Stage of rice development	Stage of human development
bitteravee	seed	egg
vela vee	germinated seed with root	fertilized egg in uterus
gayam phalleh	rice plant	pregnant woman
bandi[14]	flowering plant	pregnant woman in last trimester

Drawing upon the analogical framework described above and villagers' familiarity with rice agriculture, a discussion of vitamin/mineral supplements and immunization was facilitated:

Facilitator: You have learned through experience that a rice field requires fertilizer, weedicide, and insecticide. Like that, a mother and infant require special medicines to protect them and make them strong. What kinds of fertilizer do you give the field and when do you apply them?

Villagers: We give minerals, *mandaposa*, and urea to the rice plant, *gayam palleh*. When the plant flowers, *bandi*, we give TDM fertilizer, *bandiposa*, to ensure a good crop.

Facilitator: In the same way it is necessary to give the field fertilizer, it is necessary to give a pregnant woman these mineral tablets (ferrous sulfate) and vitamins (folic acid, B complex). It is important to take these during the whole time the baby is growing to ensure good health. You also use weedicides in your fields. These are like preventive medicines. There are many types of weeds that grow. Each kind of weedicide is for a specific type of weed. In the same way there are many different kinds of *visabeeja* (local term for germs). What kinds of things do you use to prevent weeds from spoiling a field?

Villagers: We use two kinds of weedicides for the rice plants. At first we use Suropers, and later when the plant is flowering we use Agroxion.

Facilitator: Just the way you use weedicides to protect the crop, so two immunizations (tetanus toxoid) are given to a mother to protect her baby during pregnancy from harmful germs, *visabeeja*.

Facilitator: When do you use insecticides for the field?

Villagers: We mix less powerful insecticides in with fertilizer, like Kaber-furan, to protect the field against insects, *keedēwa*. Powerful insecticides (Andrex 20, Basa) are used only after insects have been seen in the field. These insecticides are dangerous and require careful handling.

Facilitator: Some medicines are similar to insecticides; they are used to control germs, *visabeeja* and prevent sickness. Other medicines are only used when *visabeeja* are seen by doctors the way Basa is used only when insects appear. They are more powerful and need expert handling by a doctor. Although they can be bought at the chemist, they should not be used unless a doctor is consulted. Like insecticides used for difficult insects, there are different medicines for different kinds of *visabeeja*. If you use the wrong kind of powerful medicine or insecticide, it is not only a waste of money, it is harmful for the body, as it is harmful for the field.

We later had an opportunity to engage in a group discussion with eight villagers who had been involved with the analogical method of teaching. The group was composed of six females and two males ranging in age from 20 to 60 years old. The villagers stated that they had all been lectured to in the past by family health workers about nutrition, immunizations, and family planning. When asked the difference between previous talks and their recent experience, all said they found the "education by analogy" approach far more appealing. They explained that with this method, instead of being treated like children who knew nothing, they felt respected for what they knew — agriculture. They were not considered ignorant villagers but acknowledged as astute observers of daily life. They said they felt less afraid to speak their minds in this type of learning environment. Villagers said they gained a sense of dignity from being able to share their knowledge and experience with others. Given the opportunity to articulate their experience in rice agriculture — when and why various agricultural operations were conducted — set them up with a strategy for problem solving about health.

THE USE OF TEACHING ANALOGIES IN KENYA

> Adopting new ideas is easier and more dignified if they relate to existing knowledge systems. There has been a tendency for development work to carry out what one observer sees as "development by destruction" — destroying the very object of the development targets.... Communication needs to be communication aimed at sharing and enhancing self-confidence and a sense of dignity in those whose quality of life is to be improved — that is, if the main objective is the development of the person, the people. (Were 1985:438)

In this depiction of the Kakamega rural health project in Kenya, Were describes a mode of health communication complementary to that developed in South Asia. She notes that priority health problems identified by the community and by health professionals were very similar. In fact, agreement was higher than 90%. Despite the high level of agreement, compliance with health advice was quite low. Investigation into this issue revealed that:

> The tendency was that once a problem was recognized by the people and health staff, the health and other development workers immediately proceeded to expound on their understanding of the cause of the problem and would present their solution without paying attention to how the people explained causation and how they would go about getting to the solution. In spite of the common bricks of perceiving the same problems as problems, the bricks were not used for building further understanding and establishing a rapport. Instead, the next step was that the groups slid back into "those who knew" and "those who didn't know" and needed to be taught. (Were 1985:433)

In an effort to rectify the communication problem between laypeople and health professionals, analogies were developed around a topic identified to be of critical importance — timely immunizations. Immunizations were difficult to explain to villagers because the terms needed to describe them could not easily be translated into the local language. As Were explains, it was not simply a matter of translating the words, but actually finding a way of communicating the concept and rationale behind immunization that presented the problem (see Nichter 1990 and Chapter 10).

An analogical message frame termed the "banana leaf model" was developed as a useful means of explaining the concept of immunization to mothers:

> One of the uses of the banana leaf is to protect against rain. If one is outdoors and notices any sign of rain, one plucks a banana leaf well in advance. If one waits until the raindrops come, one may be drenched in the process of getting the banana leaf, which will render it useless. To keep dry, the banana leaf must be obtained in good time. This is the way it is with immunization. Waiting until a child has signs of infection of the feared disease before having it immunized does not protect the child. It has to be done well ahead of time, just as a banana leaf is obtained before the first drops of rainfall. (Were 1985:440)

The analogy was elaborated to explain to mothers why some children who had been immunized still experienced the disease, if a batch of immunizations had gone bad or if an immune response was incomplete.

> Even if one does get a banana leaf well ahead of the rain, there are occasions on which one may inadvertently pick a leaf with a hole or a tear and the raindrops may still wet one's clothes. This does not mean that "banana leaves are useless in the rain" but simply that they don't always work 100% of the time. (Were 1985:441)

In both the banana leaf analogy and the fertilizer–weedicide–insecticide analogy utilized in Sri Lanka, familiar practices involving prevention in one domain of life experience were identified and extended. This served to legitimate an unseen relationship of cause and effect based on complementarity in another domain.

THE USE OF TEACHING ANALOGIES FOR FAMILY PLANNING IN THE PHILIPPINES

An educational strategy developed by the International Institute of Rural Reconstruction (IIRR) in the Philippines provides an example of how an analogical approach was used with farmers to facilitate understanding of new family planning concepts by reference to existing agricultural practices.[15]

This project is discussed in some detail because it is the only case where an analogical approach has been subjected to formal evaluation. Evaluation of a range of family planning education methods was conducted by the University of the Philippines Institute of Mass Communications (Maglalang 1976). Evaluating different forms of family planning education, it was found that increases in knowledge, comprehension, and retention were highest in an analogical approach group while ambivalence and uncertainty in remembering were greatest among those who were lectured at without visual aids. A unique feature of the IIRR project was that after analogical messages were pretested for comprehension in several field areas, flipcharts and comic books based on analogical themes were generated and widely circulated.

Flavier, a doctor and health educator, describes how this approach was developed after several years of ineffective family planning campaigns among rural villagers:

> I encountered an elderly woman, very respected, more learned than the usual and I confessed my problems.... "I can't seem to put across the messages. How would you do it if you were in my place"? She was unsure and hesitant. She put it this way. "I do not know, but when you were explaining the whole family planning process, what kept coming into my mind were agricultural situations. You mentioned ovary, ovum, uterus, and frankly, they do not sound real to me, but I can understand them in terms of string beans whose seeds are pushed out and grow on fertile fields." (cited in Maglalang 1976:3)

Flavier found the grassroots analogy suggested by the woman attractive from both an illustrative and scientific vantage point. From a biological perspective, just as the ovary is a human organ that has about 300 potential ova capable of replicating the human species, so a string bean is a vegetable with a pod with 12 to 15 ova capable of replicating the species. Assured of the analogy's scientific validity,[16] Flavier decided to return to the village the next week to discuss family planning in terms of string beans. He found that the beans provided relevant demonstration material particularly since they were a common vegetable crop in the area.

> When I talked about the process, I could push the bean and a seed would come out; it was graphic and visual. They could see it externalized and could participate by bringing me string beans from their homes. If I pressed too hard, two seeds would come out and people would joke and say twins. (cited in Maglalang 1976)

As a result of this experience, Flavier came to appreciate the importance of making the abstract — in this case, the workings of a bodily organs — visible and concrete to rural villagers. He was made acutely aware of the importance of providing villagers an "appropriate image" and not merely a concept.

After his initial success with the string beans, Flavier began to search for other referential frameworks from which to generate analogies. He and his staff conducted a systematic study of indigenous farming methods and customs. They simultaneously conducted a survey to determine what villagers wanted to know about family planning. Flavier learned that villagers wanted practical knowledge about family planning — not only what family planning was, but how it worked. The way in which the IIRR, working with Flavier, proceeded to develop an analogical education program highlighting the teaching analogies developed will now be reviewed.

IIRR field workers opened discussions at small group meetings by asking villagers to talk about their agricultural practices in relation to specific topics such as the spacing of plants, what measures they took to induce a barren tree to produce, or what they did to improve the quality of their fruits, etc. Villagers were encouraged to draw pictures of what they were describing in the process of discussions. Some of these pictures became the prototypes for flipcharts which consisted of two images — one of an agricultural operation, and the other a family planning concept to which it was to parallel. The following are examples:

The IUD

An IUD is like a fence which the farmer places around his fields to prevent animals from entering and destroying the garden. Placed inside a woman, an IUD prevents her from getting pregnant by preventing the seed from taking root in the uterus.

The Pill

Horses are a necessity in the villages during the months of May through August to transport agricultural produce to the urban areas. If a horse becomes pregnant at this time, the farmer will suffer many difficulties. To prevent pregnancies, rice bran mixed with glutinous rice is fed to the horses. This mix renders the horse temporarily infertile. A woman, it is pointed out, can likewise be rendered temporarily infertile by taking birth control pills.

The Condom

To collect *tuba*, palm wine from coconut palms, a bamboo tube which resembles a condom is placed at the top of the tree. The juice collects in the tube and when it ferments it becomes a drink. This tube is compared to a condom which collects the male juice. When the juice ferments it becomes a baby.

On the Importance of Practicing Birth Control

If a pomelo tree is laden with many fruits, it will produce fruits which are small and not so sweet. This is also true of the family. If there are too many young children, often they will be small and sickly. In order to avoid the crowding of too many fruits of the pomelo tree, the flowers are reduced and only the better quality flowers are left to grow into fruits. In the case of people, successive pregnancies can be avoided if the methods of birth control are used.

On The Concept of Spacing

Rice seedlings grown in a seed bed grow slowly because the seedlings are near to each other. They need to have ample spacing to grow fast and for the stalks to be healthy. In the same way, a woman who has successive pregnancies may have children who are small and sickly. That is why it is very important to give proper spacing in order to take good care of them as they grow.

DISCUSSION OF THE AGRICULTURAL APPROACH

In the development of agricultural analogies, both we and the IIRR endeavored to find appropriate images complementary to scientific rationales. This is not always possible and pragmatism often dictates practice. For example, the comparison of a fence around a garden is hardly representative of how an IUD works, yet what is ultimately important is not the educator's perception of an analogy, but the villager's perceptions and understanding within their experiential universe. Posing analogies is no easy task and meaning can sometimes be misconstrued by an audience. For this reason we have stressed participatory research and pretesting as important elements in developing analogical teaching messages.

CONCLUSION

In the mid-1970s a good deal of discussion emerged concerning the use of the folk media in development projects.[17] Some communication researchers such as Ranganath (1976) described the folk media in terms of existing institutions (e.g., puppet shows, drama, folk songs) which were popular, non-elitist, and available at low cost. They were presented as a social resource offering great potential for persuasive communication. For these researchers and others (e.g., Eapen 1976), the folk media were ready resources for the propagation of modern health and development messages.[18]

This literature is conservative and suffers from management bias. It solely reflects a modernization approach to development. The folk media are presented as familiar media through which those in the "know" can inject messages to those "who don't know." Rather than being characterized as arenas in which community problem solving may be engendered, folk media are coopted. Notably, cultural performances which challenge development as "underdevelopment" and provide critical commentary are not acknowledged. Examples of such usage of cultural performances abound, ranging from Shivaratri skits in India to community plays in Cuba and Nicaragua, where social problems are enacted and inequities addressed. The potential of cultural performances, both old and new, to engage community members in the act of consciousness-raising in a context which permits critical thinking and the emergence of paradox is little discussed in the folk media and development literature. Instead, a narrow view of the vitality of folk genres is depicted.

Colletta (1975), one of the more sensitive non-formal education researchers, has placed emphasis on looking beyond cultural forms as instruments for development to engaging folk media in the process of problem solving in cultural terms. He joins Fuglesang (1977) in arguing for "appropriate conceptualization" to complement appropriate technology. The process of deconstructing new ideas (products), negotiating knowledge, and fostering critical thinking by posing analogies which clarify instead of mystify constitute one method of facilitating appropriate conceptualization. Analogy posing is a means to initiate problem solving, however, and not an end point. Analogies provide strategies for action which may mask as well as reveal. Their use must be monitored and critically examined. This point follows from Chapter 9 where the marketing of health was considered in relation to the process of commodification.

The potential of analogy as a development resource initiating problem solving is illustrated through a case study in Sri Lanka, where we observed two change facilitators working with groups of women *coir* producers in Galle and Matara Districts. In following the "progress" of this group, we were struck by two observations. The first was the development of a group process which encouraged an airing of alternate views. The 10 to 15 women in each group had to learn to engage in constructive criticism of each other's ideas without being defensive. While this is a difficult enough task to accomplish in any culture, it is particularly challenging in Sinhalese culture, where both indirect verbal and nonverbal communication styles are skillfully employed to minimize overt conflict. An attempt is made in all public occasions to defuse social conflict and mask extreme emotions. This is one reason foreigners stereotype the Sinhalese as always smiling and why joking plays an important role in ritual healing.

The second observation relates to the mode of problem solving employed by one of the groups. Their strategy was based on an analogy between the activities of middlemen and the "vendors" of development schemes. The women in this group had critically assessed the chain of *coir* production and sale from the purchase of coconut husks, leasing of soaking pits, and twisting of fiber to the weighing in, transport, and market sale of the product. By so doing, they had become effectively organized and began to bypass the middlemen (*mudalāli*), who once derived significant profit from their ignorance and powerlessness. These women were now extending their knowledge of *coir* and applying a "*mudalāli* model" to other outsiders who came to their village. Included in their purview were development workers, health care workers, doctors, teachers, etc. Teachers were seen as the *mudalāli* of education, while doctors were considered to be *mudalāli* of medicine and so forth. Even though the women's outlook was limited by their use of the *coir* analogy and an economic gaze, it was also broadened beyond the former narrow "frogs in a well" perspective which had led to their powerlessness. The analogy provided them a strategy, a place to begin, a framework in which to organize their thoughts and center their dialogue.

Our discussion of the coir producers' "*mudalāli* model" of dependency may appear to be somewhat distant from our initial discussion of education by appropriate analogy. Yet it illustrates application of the principles of complementarity and elaboration basic to the analogical thought processes of South Asian villagers which may be maximized in development education. A Kannada proverb states "Telling proverbs is equal to Veda" (holy scriptures). This proverb highlights the importance given to expressions of tacit knowledge often gained through experience, knowledge propagated through teaching stories in the major religions of South Asia.[19] Commenting on our use of analogical messages for health education, one Sinhalese villager remarked, "This way of learning is Buddhist. The Buddha taught this way. It is like the Jataka tales which teach difficult moral lessons about life in a simple way." Perhaps what is lacking in village education today are modern Jataka tales, which in the words of an *āyurvedic* practitioner, "milk, churn, and boil down experience to its simplest clarified form."

NOTES

1. Education by analogy may also be employed to substitute more humane or socially acceptable analogical descriptions of illness for those currently popular at a given time. Sontag (1978) who originally called for a demetaphorization of illness ("laying bare its essential qualities") later came to recognize that illness experience cannot be demetaphorized (1989). Her call for a critical evaluation of metaphor use is in line with the approach we advocated. On the critical assessment of public health and medical metaphor, see Good (1994), Martin (1987), Nichter (1990), and Norton et al (1990).

2. Our deployment of metaphor follows an interactional appreciation of metaphor as a construct used in the understanding and creating of reality as distinct from the describing of reality (Black 1962). Lakoff and Johnson (1980) in their popular book, "Metaphors We Live By," have identified such metaphors as "conceptual metaphors" and have considered metaphor in relation to the production of knowledge. Koveceses (1986) has extended this analysis noting that prototypes of what something is or is about may be constituted by metaphors and analogical frames which structure vague domains of experience in relation to more familiar concrete domains. Accounts of conceptual metaphors often list inventories of interrelated metaphors. Missing is a sense of discourse — how metaphors are used in context. This is of paramount importance to the development of analogical teaching materials meant to contextualize learning. For example, Fernandez (1974), points out that metaphor has at least three functions in discourse: the informative, declarative, and persuasive. The use of metaphor and the introduction of analogy in speech may be associated with different voices and vantages. Use of metaphor may in itself denote a shift in voice or constitute a contrast to a more linear communication form indexing a particular form of social relationship. Choice of alternative metaphorical frames may likewise index social relations through subtle connotations.

3. As Toulmin (1972) has noted, science and to a greater degree the everyday understanding of the world, progresses less as a series of paradigm leaps — scientific revolutions — than as an evolutionary process of reinterpretation and modification of existing knowledge and experience. On the role of metaphor and analogies in science, see Boyd (1979), Hesse (1966), Kuhn (1979), and Leatherdale (1974).

4. We have considered metaphor and analogy as complementary in this chapter. We recognize that the function of these tropes may be distinct. For example, metaphor may be used to reveal complexity or offer poetic surprise while analogy may be used to simplify. Our focus is limited to the general means by which analogical reasoning is infused into the pragmatics of natural language such that correspondences between cognitive domains results in a sense of coherence. The literature on metaphor abounds with conflicting definitions and theories of usage — some semantic and others pragmatic. Our thinking

accords with a correspondence theory of metaphor well summarized by Levinson (1983). Here, emphasis is placed on the incidental and connotational rather than the strictly denotative characteristics of words and the factual properties of referents.

5. Fundamental to an appreciation of commonsense rationality is a recognition of what Bruner (1986) has referred to as narrative thinking and propositional thinking. Each provides a distinct way of ordering experience and relies on different kinds of inference. Propositional arguments are intended to convince someone of universal truths, narratives present sets of connections which make sense in lifelike contexts.

6. Burke has pointed out the strategic use of metaphor in his writing on the meaning of proverbs. See Fernandez (1986) for a discussion of metaphor providing an orientation for action.

7. See also Graham (1979) and Hubley (1988). Graham notes that much of health education offers lengthy do's and don'ts which are often irrelevant to people's lives and the conflicting demands they face. She calls for health education sensitive to social, cultural, and economic dimensions of a populations' lifeworld as well as what Bandura (1986) has referred to as perceptions of self-efficacy.

8. Better manuals are not the answer to better communication skills, although they may be useful tools. Following Jordan's (1989) critique of didactic modes of teaching midwives, we call for apprenticeship training opportunities wherein health communicators can learn to "deliver" messages not just "provide" information. Many of Jordan's insights into apprenticeship learning are applicable to the training of health communicators. Central to this type of learning is a lack of separation between the activities of daily living and the learning of "professional skills." Although we provide a series of steps toward the construction of teaching analogies in this chapter, this list is only a heuristic. As noted by Lave (1987), a learning sequence can not be reduced to a production schedule, and teaching stories can not be replaced by a series of steps or dictums. The evaluation of competence within the apprenticeship mode is "implicit rather than explicit, codeterminus with the work being accomplished rather than subject to a test" (Jordan 1989:934).

9. For an excellent illustration of this process of encompassment vis à vis the use of analogy, see Trawick (1987). Trawick uses Indian data to refute Horton's (1967) depiction of traditional thought as uncritical of existing paradigms. She points out that *ayurvedic* epistemology is open not closed, or to use Levi Strauss' terms, hot not cold, to expansion. For a somewhat related argument which draws attention to systematic experimentation within traditional agricultural communities, see Johnson (1972).

10. The meaning of a message is, of course, only one factor involved in its acceptance. One must also pay credence to the social context in which this message is delivered and aspects of performance which lend it credibility.

11. Proverbs are distillations of knowledge gained through experience. As White (1987) notes, proverbs are "calls to action" which index salient and well known propositions about life. Employing mundane experience to clarify complex situations, proverbs provide "clear paths" for reasoning and action.

12. Kurin (1983:84) cites numerous examples from Pakistan which illustrates analogies drawn between agricultural and human domains. These include seed: sperm, soil: womb, irrigation water: mother's milk, fertilizer: food. He also notes that crops are anthropomorphized and referred to as eating, drinking, and becoming intoxicated. Similar analogies are found in South India.

13. We recorded a wide range of opinions as to how long it took food to become blood and blood to become *dhātu*. Questions as to how many drops of blood it took to make *dhātu* were rarely answered. Some informants believed it took seven days for blood to become *dhātu* and others sixteen days. Both numbers are symbolically associated with completion. Other informants spoke of this process being influenced by age or constitution, and still others perceived some foods as containing *dhātu* properties which immediately entered the blood after digestion.

14. Colloquially, the Sinhalese word *bandiya* means big belly, and is also used in reference to a pregnant woman.

15. Sumantha Banerjee (1979) has similarly argued for the use of analogies, proverbs and teaching stories based on folk knowledge as a means of teaching about family planning in India.

16. In some instances, analogies can be posed which maximize correspondences between local knowledge and what is considered biomedically correct (today). In other instances, an analogy or image may be presented which conveys a theme of public health importance. Examples are the theme of resistance /protection noted by Were in her banana plant analogy and more recently a set of images suggested by Bastien (1987) for introducing ORT in Bolivia. Among Kallaywayas in Bolivia, a complementarity exists between well being in the world and health within the body. Both are dependent on the continual exchange of fluids. This image was used in a set of health education messages addressing a hydraulic image of physiology and an Andean *ayllu* view of the universe.

17. Several development projects co-opted Freirean discourse on education and appropriated local channels of communication. Neglected was the importance of praxis; the process of action-reflection entailing critical evaluation. On the domestication of Freirean pedagogy, see Kidel and Kumar (1981).

18. Others such as Bordenave (1974) have argued quite the opposite "As soon as the people realize that their folk songs, poems and art are being used for subliminal propaganda they will let them die." There is some truth to this fear. Development messages have more often than not been overt as opposed to subliminally inserted into folk media. Audiences in South Kanara were not pleased to find family planning messages pushed at Yakshagana perform-

ances. In the northern part of Karnataka State, Yellamma songs — religious songs to a female deity — were altered to include family planning messages. Villagers rejected performances which incorporated these messages as being both inappropriate and sacrilegious. According to Lent (1982) use of the folk media backfired and villagers were alienated from the family planning program.

19. Health educators need to have on hand a stock of appropriate analogies and teaching stories and learn when and how to introduce them in the course of conversation. Much is to be learned from the study of communication styles of popular religious leaders, medical practitioners, midwives, astrologers, etc.

REFERENCES

Bandura, A. 1986. Social Foundations of Thought and Action: A Social Cognitive Theory. Englewood Cliffs, NJ: Prentice Hall.

Banerjee, S. 1979. Family Planning Communication: A Critique of the Indian Programme. New Delhi, India: Family Planning Foundation, Radiant Press.

Bastien, J. 1987. Cross-Cultural Communication Between Doctors and Peasants in Bolivia. Social Science and Medicine 24(12):1109–1118.

Black, M. 1962. Models and Metaphors. Ithaca, NY: Cornell University Press.

Bordenave, J. 1974. Communication and Adoption of Agricultural Innovations in Latin America. *In* Proceedings of the Cornell–CIAT International Symposium on Communication Strategies for Rural Development, March 17–22. Ithaca, NY: Cornell University.

Boyd, R. 1979. Metaphor and Theory Change: What Is "Metaphor"? *In* Metaphor and Thought. Ed. Anthony Ortony. Pp. 356–408. Cambridge: Cambridge University Press.

Bruner, J. 1986. Actual Minds, Possible Worlds. Cambridge: Harvard University Press.

Colletta, N. 1975. The Use of Indigenous Culture as A Medium for Development: The Indonesian Case. Instructional Technology Report No. 12, September 1975.

Eapen, K. E. 1976. Specific Problems of Research and Research Training in Asian and African Countries. *In* Communication Research in the Third World: The Need for Training. Pp. 18–19. Geneva: Lutheran World Federation.

Fernandez, J. 1974. The Mission of Metaphor in Expressive Culture. Current Anthropology 15:119–145.

Fernandez, J. 1986. Persuasion and Performances: The Play of Tropes in Culture. Bloomington: Indiana University Press.

Freire, P. 1973. Pedagogy of the Oppressed. New York: Seabury Press.

Fuglesang, A. 1977. Doing Things Together: Report on an Experience in Communicating Appropriate Technology. Uppsala, Sweden: Dag Hammersjold Foundation.

Good, B. 1994. Medicine, Rationality and Experience. New York: Cambridge University Press.

Graham, H. 1979. Prevention and Health: Every Mother's Business, A Comment on Child Health Policies in the 1970s. Sociological Review Monographs 28:160–185.

Hesse, M. 1966. Models and Analogies in Science. South Bend, IN: University of Notre Dame Press.

Horton, R. 1967. African Traditional Thought and Western Science. Africa 38:50–71, 155–187.

Hubley, J. 1988. Understanding Behavior: The Key to Successful Health Education. Tropical Doctor 18(3):134–138.

Jelliffe, D. 1969. Child Nutrition in Developing Countries. Washington, DC: U.S. Department of State, AID, Office of the War on Hunger.

Johnson, A. 1972. Individuality and Experimentation in Traditional Agriculture. Human Ecology 1(2):149–159.

Jordan, B. 1989. Cosmopolitical Obstetrics: Some Insights from the Training of Traditional Midwives. Social Science and Medicine 28(9):925–944.

Kidd, R. and K. Kumar. 1981. Co-Opting Freire: A Critical Analysis of Pseudo-Freirean Adult Education. Economic and Political Weekly (January 3):27–36.

Koveceses, Z. 1986. Metaphors of Anger, Pride and Love. Amsterdam: John Benjamin Publishers.

Kuhn, T. 1979. Metaphor in Science. In Metaphor and Thought. Ed. Anthony Ortony. Pp. 409–419. Cambridge: Cambridge University Press.

Kurin, R. 1983. Indigenous Agronomics and Agricultural Development in the Indus Basin. Human Organization 42(4):283–294.

Lakoff, G. and M. Johnson. 1980. Metaphors We Live By. Chicago: University of Chicago Press.

Langer, S. 1942. Philosophy in a New Key. New York: Mentor Books.

Lave, J. 1987. Experiments, Tests, and Chores: How We Know What We Do. In Becoming A Worker. K. Barman and J. Reisman, eds. Pp. 140–155. Norwood, NJ: Ablex.

Leatherdale, W. 1974. The Role of Analogy, Model and Metaphor in Science. Amsterdam: North Holland.

Lent, J. 1982. Grassroots Renaissance: Folk Media in the Third World. Media Asia 9(1):9–16.

Levinson, S. C. 1983. Pragmatics. Cambridge: Cambridge University Press.

Maglalang, D. 1976. Agricultural Approach to Family Planning. Manila: Communication Foundation for Asia.

Martin, E. 1987. The Woman in the Body. Boston: Beacon Press.

Nichter, Mark. 1986. Modes of Food Classification and the Diet–Health Contingency: A South Indian Case Study. *In* Aspects of Food Systems in South Asia. R. Khare and K. Ishvaran, eds. Pp. 185–221. Durham, NC: Carolina Academic Press.

Nichter, Mark. 1990. Vaccinations in South Asia: False Expectations and Commanding Metaphors. *In* Anthropology and Primary Health Care. J. Coreil and D. Mull, eds. Pp. 196–221. Boulder: Westview Press.

Nichter, Mark and Mimi Nichter. 1981. An Anthropological Approach to Nutrition Education. Newton, MA: Education Development Center, International Nutrition Communication Service.

Norton, R., J. Schwartzbaum, and J. Wheat. 1990. Language Discrimination of General Physicians. Communication Research 17:809–826.

Ranganath, H. K. 1976. A Probe Into the Traditional Media: Telling the People Themselves. Media Asia 3(1):25.

Schutz, A. 1964. Collected Papers (Volume 2). The Hague: Martinus Nijhoff.

Sontag, S. 1978. Illness as Metaphor. New York: Farrar, Straus and Giraux.

Sontag, S. 1989. AIDS and its Metaphors. New York: Farrar, Straus and Giraux.

Srivastava, R. N. 1980. Evaluating Communicability in Village Settings. New Delhi, India: UNICEF Publications.

Toulmin, S. 1972. Human Understanding (Volume 1). Oxford: Clarendon Press.

Trawick, M. 1987. The Ayurvedic Physician as Scientist. Social Science and Medicine 24(12):1031–1050.

Were, M. 1985. Communicating on Immunization to Mothers and Community Groups. Assignment Children 69:429–442.

White, G. 1987. Proverbs and Cultural Models. *In* Cultural Models in Language and Thought. D. Holland and N. Quinn, eds. Pp. 151–172. New York: Cambridge University Press.

Epilogue:
A Note on Aid

"Health is not simply a physical or a mental state, it is a moral state, a state of balance and reciprocity." This was one of *vaidya* Ishwara Bhat's favorite messages which we heard time and again while sitting on his veranda reading the newspaper and waiting for the evening meal. One evening remains particularly clear in our memory. The front page of the local paper carried a lead story about U.S. aid to India. An American official was pictured shaking hands with an Indian official in front of what appeared to be a small mountain of wheat. Ishwara gazed over to us and said, "Your country is very lucky because we take the wheat they offer to us as alms, *dana*." We were mildly surprised by his comment and assumed that the local press had at one time run a story on American farm subsidies, a subject which no doubt would have interested Ishwara. It turned out that we had misconstrued Ishwara's interpretation of American aid, for his comment was directed more at moral economy than at market economy. We offer his explanation, as recorded in our fieldnotes, as a concluding note to this volume:

In India, Ishwara remarked, it is believed that when one has committed some *pāpa* (sin), selfishly looked to their own fame and fortune to the detriment of others or forsaken the gods in pursuit of personal gain or desire, the moral order of the universe is such that this action will eventually be counterbalanced. This is recognized by all peoples because a sense of justice is part of being human. Your country is young and reckless, like a teenager whose desires change with each new cinema. Yet you sense this justice and you feel a need to give because you have taken so much. You call this aid, but there

427

is a deeper meaning. A gift is more than the offering of a thing; it involves a relationship, some form of reciprocity.

In India, to minimize the result of negative *karma*, offerings are made to those who may bear this *karma* and through good deeds burn this *karma* or dissolve this *karma*, the way a salty solution may be made less salty by the addition of more and more fresh water. We give gifts of food or cloth to priests or a temple or beggars and feel that the weight of our *karma* has lessened. We are thankful to be able to give these things. It is for our own welfare even more than the welfare of the priest or beggar who accepts things. We stoop to serve.

America sends us aid and expects praise. It is your good fortune to have our people to take this measure of the *karma* you have accumulated. By taking this grain, by eating this food, our people lessen the load of *karma* that is yours. Without us, who would be there to lighten the weight of your *karma*'? And yet your people have not learned one important thing. You have not learned to stoop when giving. Do you see the pride in the face of your politician (in the newspaper) as if he has done a great thing for India? You have not learned that by giving you are helping yourselves. Through helping others, you develop.

AUTHOR INDEX

429

Author Index

SUBJECT INDEX

ABOUT THE AUTHORS

Mark Nichter, PhD, MPH, is Professor of Anthropology at the University of Arizona in Tucson with a joint appointment in the Department of Family and Community Medicine. Dr. Nichter is the coordinator of the graduate program in medical anthropology. He is an active participant in the field of international health, where he is involved in the training and mentorship of health social scientists and epidemiologists in several developing countries. He has served as a consultant for a wide range of international health organizations and ministries of health, universities, and local activist groups.

Mimi Nichter, PhD, is a research associate in the Department of Anthropology at the University of Arizona and Clinical Assistant Professor in the Arizona Prevention Center. She has served as a consultant for many international organizations, including USAID, UNICEF, WHO, and the Ford Foundation, where her work has focused on women and health issues, adolescent health, and the development of culturally appropriate health communication strategies.